CONTENTS

THE 1980s

The 1980s was a time when technology changed the way that people lived and worked. Computers rapidly became an important part of offices, schools and homes, and for those who had the money there were lots of other high-tech luxury goods to buy. But for some these were difficult times and in parts of Britain many jobs were lost.

Some now remember the eighties as a very selfish decade. It was certainly a time for showing off – the way things looked, and sometimes how much they cost, seemed very important. In this book four people tell us what it was like growing up in the 1980s.

REBECCA FORD

Rebecca Ford was born in 1975. She grew up with her two brothers in a town in Carmarthenshire, South Wales.

▶ Rebecca in 1985 aged 10.

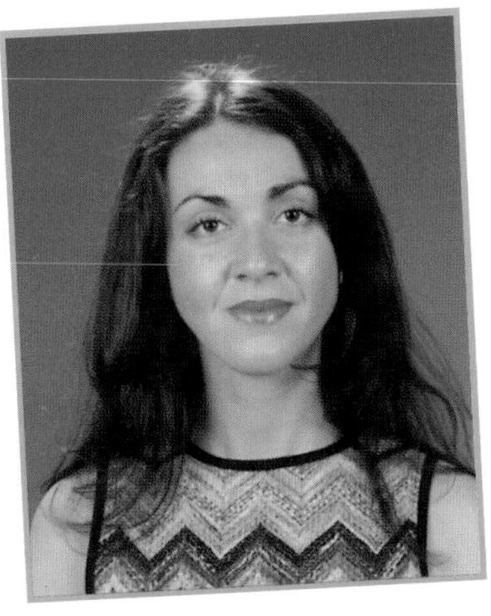

EBRU GARNETT

Ebru Garnett was born in Sheffield in 1972 to parents of Turkish origin. She lived there with her parents and younger brother.

▶ Ebru in 1982 aged 10.

GROWING UP IN THE EIGHTIES

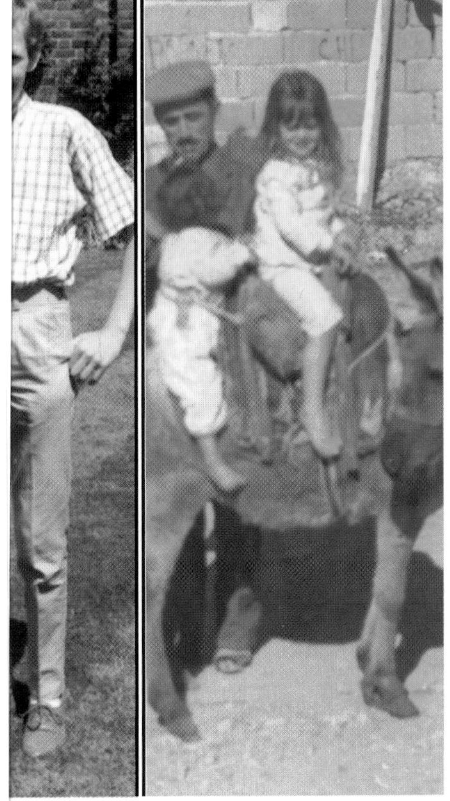

Kathryn Walker

HODDER
Wayland

Produced for Hodder Wayland by
Discovery Books Ltd
Unit 3, 37 Watling Street, Leintwardine, Shropshire SY7 0LW, England

First published in 2002 by Hodder Wayland, an imprint of Hodder Children's Books
This paperback edition published in 2003

British Library Cataloguing in Publication Data
Walker, Kathryn
Growing up in the eighties
1. Children - Great Britain - Social life and customs -
Juvenile literature 2. Nineteen eighties - Juvenile literature
3. Great Britain - Social conditions - 1945- - Juvenile literature
4. Great Britain - Social life and customs - 1945- - Juvenile literature
I. Title II. Eighties
941'. 0858' 0922

ISBN 0 7502 4089 X

Printed and bound by Grafiasa, Porto, Portugal

Designer: Ian Winton
Editor: Kathryn Walker

Hodder Children's Books would like to thank the following for the loan of their material:
Aquarius: cover (centre and right), page 16 © 1989 Grundy TV; **Corbis:** page 6 (bottom), 22 Annie Griffiths, 24 (top); **Discovery Library:** page 7; **Duke of Edinburgh's Award:** page 11 (top left and top right); **Ford:** page 24 (bottom); **Hulton Getty:** page 8 (top) Steve Eason; 25 (bottom); 28 (bottom), 29; **Last Resort Picture Library:** page 13 (bottom); **Motorola Archives:** page 23 (bottom right); **Philips:** page 6 (top right and top left), 20, 23 (bottom left); **Porsche AG:** page 25 (top); **Redferns:** page 18 (top), 21 (bottom); **Robert Opie:** page 10 (top), 12 (top), 13 (top), 14, 15, 17, 19 (bottom), 21 (top), 30; **Vodaphone Group:** page 23 (top right).

Hodder Children's Books
A division of Hodder Headline Limited
338 Euston Road

DARREN HUGGINS

Darren Huggins was born in Birmingham in 1973. He lived there with his grandparents, uncles and aunts throughout the eighties.

▶ **Darren in 1982 aged 9.**

JAMES KESSELL

James Kessell was born in 1971 in Nottingham. In 1979 his family moved to a town in West Sussex, where he lived with his younger brother and sister during the eighties.

▶ **James in 1982 aged 11.**

At Home

The number of electronic gadgets in the home was increasing. Video recorders (VCRs) had been around since the seventies, but in the eighties they became cheaper so more homes had one. New items appeared such as CD players, personal stereos, camcorders for making home videos and home computers.

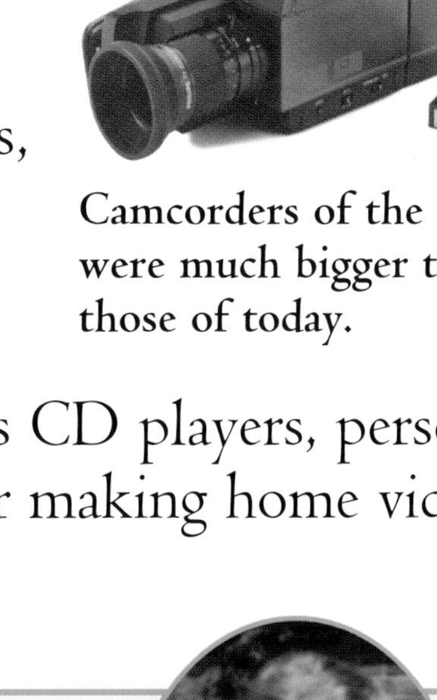

Camcorders of the 1980s were much bigger than those of today.

A 1980s video recorder.

Games consoles that plugged into TV sets became very popular in the eighties.

James

In the early eighties I was given a Spectrum 48k computer for Christmas. I was able to write basic programs with it, but mostly I used it for playing games. It was the latest technology then, but by today's standards it was very, very basic.

Recycling

Throughout the seventies and eighties people looked for ways to reduce pollution and conserve natural resources. Saving certain kinds of household rubbish for recycling was something that everyone could do to help. Many recycling centres opened where people could take their old newspapers, bottles and cans.

HEALTH AND FITNESS

Now that so many families could drive everywhere, there were fears that people were generally not getting enough exercise. Adults and children were encouraged to take more care of their bodies. Exercise classes became very popular and so did fitness videos or audio tapes for exercising along with at home.

Leisure centres began to appear in many towns. People went to gyms and took up aerobics to help them stay healthy as well as look good. Some chose jogging as a way of keeping fit.

Darren

Sport was my life back in the eighties, so I was very fit. I did athletics, long distance running, cricket and played football at district and county levels. I'd also go jogging to keep fit, often listening to music on my personal stereo which seemed to help me set a pace.

At school in the eighties

In the eighties new school exams were introduced. In England and Wales the old GCE 'O' level and CSE exams for 16-year-olds were replaced by the GCSE. 'O' level pupils had been marked only on how well they did on examination day, but the GCSE allowed course-work to count as part of the total mark. This was seen as a fairer way of testing ability.

Primary and secondary schools began to use computers during the 1980s.

James

My 'O' levels were purely exam-based - there was no coursework and therefore no need to put in too much effort at school. It was quite possible to 'cram' between Easter and May. This suited some people (like me) but it didn't always test understanding. 'A' levels were a big step up from 'O' levels. However they were also exam-based and so meant a massive amount of cramming in the final weeks.

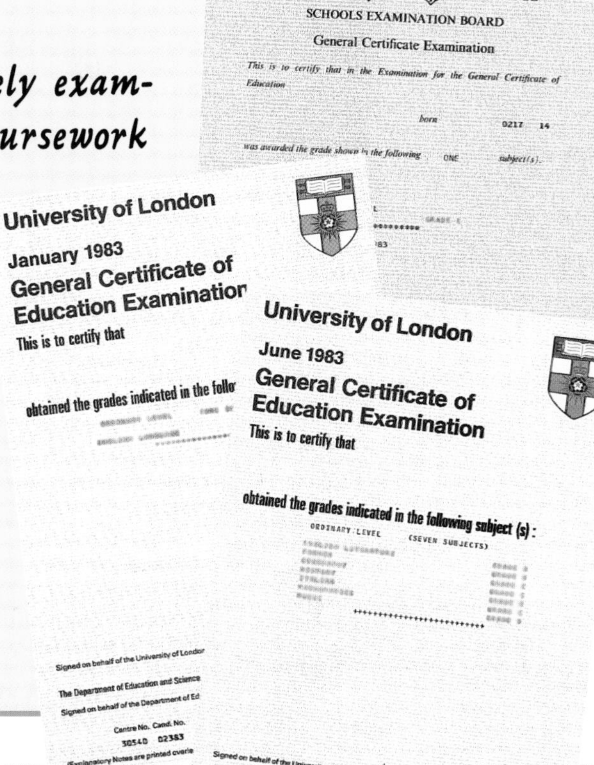

OXFORD & CAMBRIDGE
SCHOOLS EXAMINATION BOARD
General Certificate Examination
This is to certify that in the Examination for the General Certificate of Education
born 0217 14
was awarded the grade shown in the following ONE subject(s).

University of London
January 1983
General Certificate of Education Examinatior
This is to certify that
obtained the grades indicated in the follo
Signed on behalf of the University of London
The Department of Education and Science
Signed on behalf of the Department of Ed
Centre No. Cand. No.
30540 02383
(Explanatory Notes are printed overle

University of London
June 1983
General Certificate of Education Examination
This is to certify that
obtained the grades indicated in the following subject (s):
ORDINARY LEVEL (SEVEN SUBJECTS)
Signed on behalf of the University of London
The Department of Education and Science accepts the examination as reaching the approved standard
Signed on behalf of the Department of Education and Science
Centre No. Cand. No. Date of Birth

National curriculum

Before 1988 schools were free to choose most of the subjects they taught and how to teach them. In 1988 the National Curriculum was introduced, which told schools what to teach and how to test. This meant that throughout state schools in England and Wales children were learning many of the same subjects in the same way and at the same time.

Caning banned

In 1986 corporal punishment, which was physical punishment such as caning, was banned in state schools. Private schools, however, could continue to use it.

Rebecca

My younger brother sometimes got 'slippered' by the PE teacher and that was in a comprehensive school in 1988! The same teacher taught me maths. He was always shouting and I was so scared of him that sometimes I'd pretend to be ill to avoid going to his classes.

Having Fun

Donkey Kong and Zelda were some of the many games programs of the 1980s.

Now so many households had television, video and sophisticated 'hi-fi' systems there was plenty of entertainment to be had at home. The eighties was the decade of video games, and while some were played in arcades, there were many which could be played at home using units that plugged into a TV set. In 1989 Nintendo brought out a small hand-held games unit called Game Boy which allowed people to play games anywhere.

But children still needed to get out of the house to do things and be with other children. The boy scouts and girl guides offered lots of activities and youth clubs gave young people somewhere to meet and organize their own entertainment.

Ebru

I didn't belong to any clubs, but I was one of a group of about 6 or 7 girlfriends and we spent all our spare time together in each other's houses.

Sometimes we'd all watch videos of our favourite programmes and we were always having sleep-overs.

Darren

I took part in the Duke of Edinburgh's Award scheme and got my bronze and silver certificates. One involved going on a canoeing expedition. After a week of training we'd meet once a week to plan our expedition. We had to map it out and work out how much we could carry - the expedition lasted 4-5 days, so we had to take camping equipment. Earning the certificate also involved helping people in the local community and we learnt a lot about dealing with people.

Bronze

Silver

Rebecca

I was with the brownies and girl guides between the ages of 7 and 14. One day someone from school made fun of me in my guides' uniform and after that I stopped going. Instead I started going to youth club once a week where we'd chat, play table tennis and sometimes organize outings.

Other toys and crazes

The BMX, which appeared in the early eighties, was a sophisticated but expensive bike that could be used for stunt riding. A lot of children wanted one, particularly after it featured in the hit film *ET – The Extra-Terrestrial.* Skateboarding was a more affordable craze of the time. Top toys included Transformers, pictured here, which were toy robots that could be made into vehicles, and the Cabbage Patch Kid, which was a bit like an old-fashioned rag doll. But one of the strangest fads of the time that fascinated both adults and children was a puzzle called the Rubik's Cube.

Rebecca

As soon as I got my Cabbage Patch Kid I sent off for its birth certificate. Mine told me I was the mother of Nora, but I didn't like that name so I sent it back and had it changed to Belinda. A year later I received a card on Belinda's first birthday. I had quite a lot of dolls, and here's a picture of me on my birthday with one I got as a present.

Ebru

The Rubik's Cube was made up of coloured squares that could be moved around and the aim was to get it so each side showed squares only of the same colour. I could only ever do one side, so I found out how to pull the Cube to bits and rebuild it when nobody was looking. They were a real craze - in school breaks everybody would start fiddling with their Cubes and hardly a word was spoken.

Eighties Fact

During the eighties over 200 million Rubik's Cubes were sold. A best-selling book on how to solve the Cube was written by a 12-year-old English boy, Patrick Bossert.

BMX bikes were well-suited to riding over rougher ground and BMX racing became a very popular sport in the 1980s.

Darren

My dad bought me my first bike for my birthday. It was a Grister bike that was very fashionable at the time. I was so excited I didn't even say thank you - I just jumped on it and raced off. I hadn't tested the brakes though, so when I tried to stop I braked too hard and flew off over the handlebars.

Films

Many families could now hire films on video to watch at home so it wasn't surprising that fewer people were going to the cinema. But there were some hugely successful films of the time. Some used new computer technology to create thrilling special effects. The popular *Who Framed Roger Rabbit?* (1988) combined film of real actors with computer-generated cartoons.

Fame (1980), was a film about ambitious American teenagers at the New York High School for Performing Arts. It sparked an energetic dance craze, a fashion for dance gear and a TV series. *Flashdance* (1983) was about a working girl trying to get herself a place at ballet school. Like *Fame*, it featured hit songs and spectacular dancing.

James

*I went to see **Jaws III** in 3-D. Everyone was given red and green coloured glasses to wear so that you got the 3-D effect. The film wasn't very good, but the 3-D effects certainly made us scream when severed limbs came floating off the screen.*

Ebru

*Films like **Fame** and **Flashdance** made modern dance very popular. **Flashdance** featured some breakdancing, which is very gymnastic. It really caught on, and groups of teenage boys would often turn up in our town centre, unroll linoleum pads, turn on their ghetto blasters and do some amazing breakdancing. Loads of people stopped to watch and cheer them. I thought they were really cool.*

One of the best-loved films of the decade was *ET – The Extra-Terrestrial* (1982). In it a loveable but rather ugly alien is trapped on Earth and befriends an American boy. Other successes of the time included the adventure film *Indiana Jones and the Temple of Doom*, *Gremlins* which had some cute little monsters and *Ghostbusters* (all 1984).

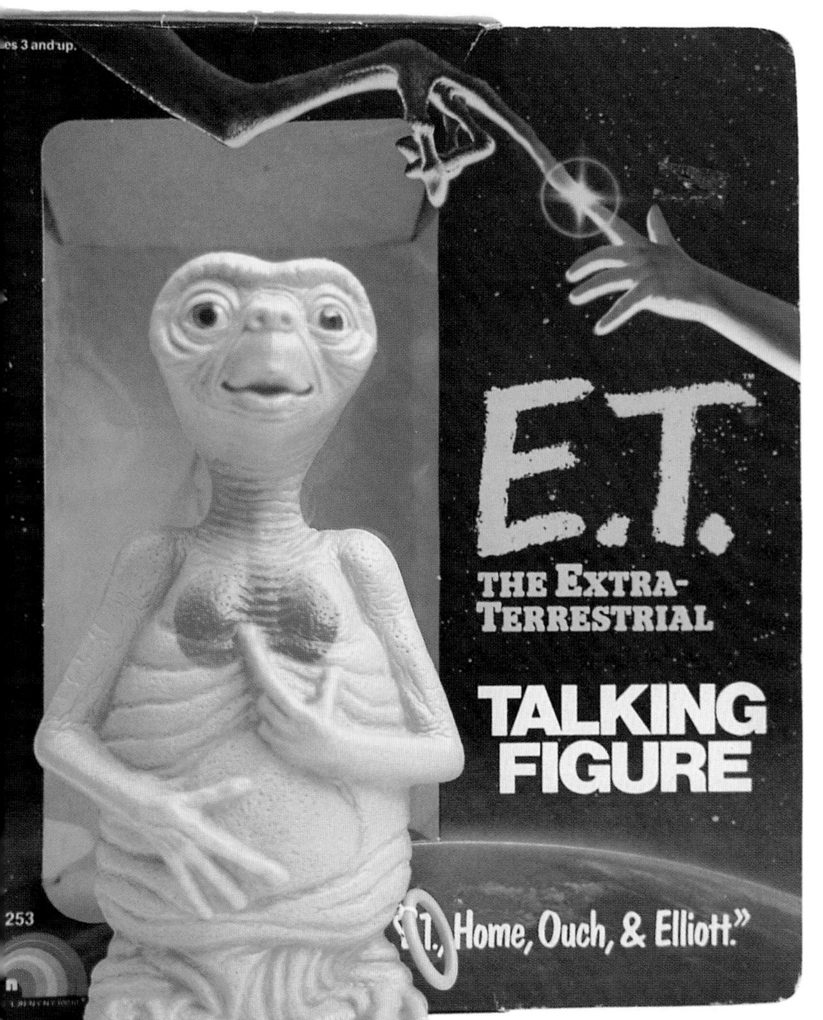

• In 1987-88, 84% of 7-14 year olds reported that they had visited the cinema. In 1998-99 this figure rose to 95%.

TELEVISION

The 1980s brought greater choice of TV viewing. In 1982 Channel 4 went on the air and in 1983 'breakfast TV' started. It meant people had a total of four channels to choose from, unless they had the latest satellite dish or cable TV which allowed them to pick up lots more.

For young children there were animations such as *Fireman Sam, Ivor the Engine* and *Thomas the Tank Engine,* which are still popular today. Realistic drama included *Grange Hill, Byker Grove* and the Australian series *Neighbours,* which although it had been aimed at adults became very popular with children.

Two of the actors in *Neighbours,* Jason Donovan and Kylie Minogue, went on to have careers as pop stars.

Rebecca

*At school we were always talking about **Neighbours**. At first it was shown at lunchtimes, but I think the **BBC** started showing it at tea-time because so many schoolkids liked to watch it. Jason Donovan and Kylie Minogue were having a romance both in the series and in real life. They made a hit single together called **Especially For You** which I bought.*

One of ITV's most successful shows of the time was *Spitting Image*. This was a programme of comic sketches using latex puppets that were caricatures of famous people, often politicians. The series carried on into the nineties.

Spitting Image puppets of leaders of the three main political parties in 1987.

THEN & NOW

• Children seem to be watching slightly less broadcast TV today than they did in the 1980s. In 1986 those aged between 4 and 15 were watching an average of 20 hours of TV per week. In 1999 the average viewing for the same age group was 18 hours per week.

Ebru

*My friends and I loved watching **Blackadder**. This was a comedy set in historical times with Rowan Atkinson playing the main character. We used to video it then go to each other's houses to watch it over and over again. We even used to learn the scripts by heart! **Spitting Image** was another favourite. As the series progressed the puppet of Prime Minister Mrs Thatcher looked more and more like a man, so that in the end she wore a man's pinstripe suit and smoked a cigar.*

Fashion and Music

Sportswear such as tracksuits and trainers were very fashionable and suited the eighties' fitness craze. The film *Fame* started a trend for dancewear such as legwarmers, a kind of long, knitted tube worn over the lower leg. Some dressed up as pirates, dandies and other fantasy characters. They were known as 'new romantics'.

Shorter haircuts with long, floppy fringes, as worn here by pop band Duran Duran, were popular in the 1980s.

People also liked to dress in a way that made them look wealthy. Lots of girls copied the frilly-necked blouses and floral skirts worn by the young Princess Diana. Some young businesswomen wore expensive suits often with big padded shoulders. This became known as 'power dressing' because it made them look successful and businesslike.

James

I generally wore straight 'drainpipe' trousers, shirts and skinny ties. I wasn't particularly into fashion, but I do remember getting my first pair of 501s (jeans). They cost quite a lot at the time - around £30 - but were worth every penny. To have 501s was to be part of the in-crowd and I really wanted to fit in.

Rebecca

I remember having a huge argument with my mother in a shoe shop. She wanted me to have cheap trainers but I wouldn't have them. I told her that if I couldn't have Nike trainers then I wouldn't have any at all. I felt like I'd rather die than be seen wearing the wrong kind.

Clothes with 'designer labels' or displaying well-known logos were in demand. They showed that the wearer had spent a lot of money on them. Children also began to want the 'right' labels or logos on their sportswear. Sometimes people bought cheap copies.

Pop music

Compact discs went on sale for the first time in 1982 and gradually replaced the big vinyl records or 'LPs'. 'Personal stereos' were all the rage. Others preferred to let everyone hear their music and carried around bulky radio/cassette players known as 'ghetto blasters'.

- In 1989 15% of households had a CD player. By 1998 68% of households had one.

A CD player of the 1980s.

Michael Jackson had been a child singer in seventies family band The Jackson Five. In the eighties he was a successful solo musician who combined songs with clever dance routines. His video for his hit *Thriller* was 14 minutes long and sold many millions of copies. Singer Madonna became famous in the 1980s and so did the different 'looks' that she created.

Ebru

Michael Jackson's feature video* Thriller *was advertised days before it was actually shown on TV, and like many others I made a point of staying in to watch it. I was a big fan. I had a picture of him printed onto the back of a pink bomber jacket.

Rebecca

I remember walking around town with my friend, carrying a 'ghetto blaster' blaring out music by Vanilla Ice. We were wearing shellsuits (a shiny kind of tracksuit), enormous trainers, and thought we were very cool.

Dance routines and looks were now an important part of pop music. New romantic band Adam and the Ants dressed like pirates, highwaymen, or whatever suited their songs.

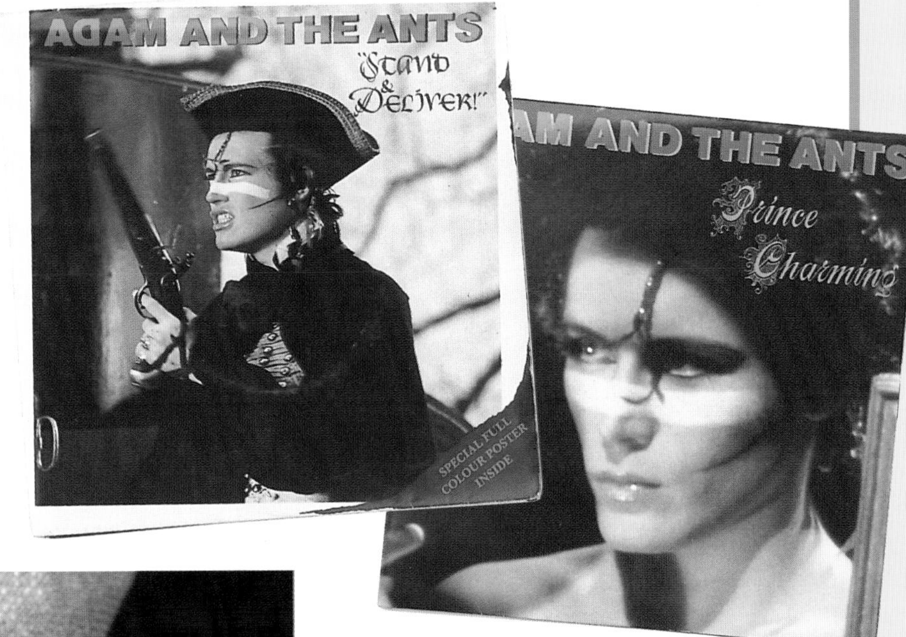

Culture Club were famous for singer Boy George's long braids and heavy make-up (pictured left) as well as for their pop songs.

Videos brought out to promote new singles seemed as important as the music.

Work in the Eighties

In the early eighties people had less money to spend and businesses such as factories had to shut down. In Northern England, Scotland and South Wales many people lost their jobs. In 1981 there were 1 million people out of work and in 1982 this figure rose to 3 million. In 1984 miners went on strike in protest against pit closures and job losses. The strike lasted almost a year, but at the end of it the miners were defeated.

At the other extreme, business boomed in the financial district, where a lot of young professional people were able to 'get rich quick'. They became known as 'yuppies', which stood for 'young urban professionals'. Many of them earned huge amounts of money which they spent on luxury lifestyles.

James

Ours was a typical southeast England middle-class family, and so the recession rather passed us by. I do remember, though, the television pictures of the miners' strike, and visiting my grandparents in Nottingham, where lots of people were collecting money on the streets for the miners' families.

Technology at work

In the 1980s word processors were replacing the office typewriter – correcting or changing documents on a word processor was much easier. Computers also changed the way that many businesses operated. Some people lost their jobs because computers could do their work.

Fax machines were another new piece of office equipment. They could instantly send letters, documents or pictures anywhere in the world using a telephone line. In the mid-eighties mobile phones were available, but they were much bigger than the ones we have today.

Fax machines became popular in the mid-1980s.

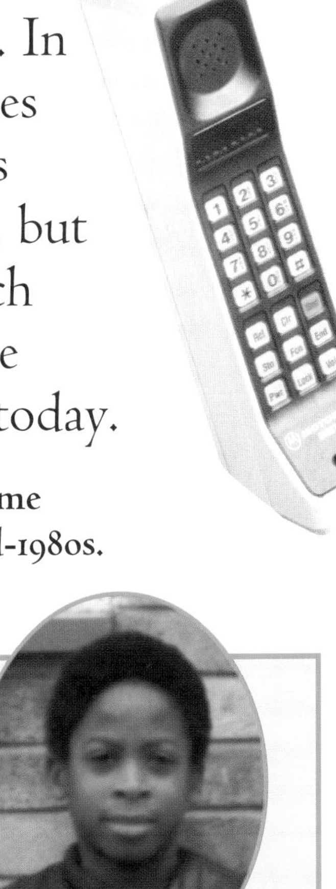

Darren

My dad was always into new hi-tech gadgets. One day he came to the house and produced a mobile phone from his rucksack. It was massive! It had a long aerial and was so heavy that he had to hold it with both hands.

TRAVELLING

The Sinclair C5.

People became very concerned about the air pollution caused by car exhaust fumes. A campaign was launched to encourage people to use unleaded fuel, which was less harmful than the usual '4-star' petrol. Bicycles were a much cleaner way of getting about and more people began using them around towns and cities. Some councils encouraged this by creating bicycle lanes. In 1985 Sir Clive Sinclair invented an electric tricycle called the Sinclair C5. It was environmentally friendly but it never really caught on.

CARS OF THE TIME

Popular cars of the day included the Fiesta, the Escort and also the Mini Metro, which, although it was one of the less expensive cars, Princess Diana was known to drive. Some people became interested in 'classic cars' which were stylish older cars from the fifties and sixties.

THEN & NOW

- In 1985 a Ford Fiesta could be bought for £4,490. Today you can buy one for £7,295.

For those with a great deal of money to spend, the Porsche 911, pictured here, was the car to have. It became a symbol of wealth and success. As a joke, people would put stickers in the windows of their much cheaper cars saying: 'My other car's a Porsche'.

James

The first car we had with electric windows and a sunroof was a Vauxhall Carlton. We used to drive mum and dad mad by constantly whizzing the back windows up and down.

THE CHANNEL TUNNEL

Since the 18th century people had been working on plans and designs for a tunnel beneath the English Channel that would enable people to travel between England and France without the perils of a sea crossing. In the 1970s investigations began into the construction of a tunnel, but were eventually abandoned. Finally, in 1986, an agreement was signed between France and Britain to build a Channel Tunnel that would provide rail links between the two countries. Digging began in 1987 and the tunnel opened in 1994.

HOLIDAYS AT HOME

The British seaside still attracted many holidaymakers but holiday camps were less popular. Many people preferred the freedom of self-catering holidays, when you rented a house or flat and provided your own food. For families it was often cheaper than staying in hotels.

James

We tended to go on self-catering holidays to the seaside, usually in Devon or Norfolk. My parents would rent a farmhouse and we would spend many days on the beach. The summers seemed to be warmer then.

Darren

Every summer the whole family would go off to Blackpool for a holiday. We'd set off together in about six cars and we'd stay in seafront hotels. We had loads of fun there and every year I couldn't wait for holiday time to come round again.

HOLIDAYS ABROAD

By the 1980s air fares had become much cheaper and so lots of people travelled abroad. Holidays in the United States became very popular, particularly in Florida where children could visit Disneyland.

Rebecca

We went to Majorca on a package holiday. The brochure showed a drawing of our hotel instead of a photograph. There were so many stories in the newspapers about people turning up at holiday hotels which were still being built that we were worried about the same thing happening to us. Luckily our hotel did exist!

Ebru

We had lots of family living in Turkey, so I would spend all my summer holidays there. In those days Turkey wasn't really a holiday destination and people here didn't seem to know anything about it. Kids at school would ask me if I was going to be riding a camel or living in a tent there, and if there really were magic carpets.

News and Events

The Royal Wedding

In July 1981 the heir to the throne, Prince Charles, married 19-year-old Lady Diana Spencer in St Paul's Cathedral. The streets of London were crammed with spectators and the wedding was watched by 700 million across the world.

Darren

I watched the royal wedding and thought that it was beautiful. I hoped that one day I'd get married in a big place like they did.

Two royal weddings were celebrated in the 1980s: that of Prince Charles and Lady Diana Spencer in 1981, then that of Prince Andrew and Sarah Ferguson in 1986.

The country celebrated and for many the glamour was a welcome escape from gloomy times. The new princess was very popular and she was always in the news.

Mrs Thatcher

The leader of the Conservative party, Margaret Thatcher, became Britain's first woman prime minister in 1979. She remained prime minister throughout the 1980s, winning three elections in a row. Because of her tough style of leadership she became known as 'the Iron Lady'.

John Lennon shot

In December1980 musician John Lennon was shot dead outside his home in New York by an obsessive fan. Lennon had been a member of the Beatles, the world-famous British pop band of the1960s. The Beatles disbanded in 1970.

The Falklands War

In April 1982 Argentine troops invaded the Falkland Islands, a little group of British-ruled islands in the South Atlantic. Argentina had claimed that they owned the Falklands for many years, but this invasion was unexpected. British troops arrived there in May and by mid-June they had regained control. The war was short but cost Britain about £1.6 billion and over 1,000 people died. In Britain the war aroused feelings of national pride in many people and disgust in some.

Live Aid raised over £40 million for famine relief.

Live aid

In 1984 there was a terrible famine in the East African country of Ethiopia. Pop singer Bob Geldof decided to do something about it, so he persuaded top rock stars to appear in a massive charity concert. In July 1985 the 17-hour-long 'Live Aid' concert was held in London and in Philadelphia, USA, at the same time. 1.5 billion people watched it all around the world. Between performances, heartbreaking film of the dying persuaded millions to give money.

Worst storm for over 250 years

In October 1987 southern England was hit by winds travelling at 115 miles per hour. Nineteen people died in the storm and it caused massive amounts of damage to property. Millions of trees were brought down, many of them blocking roads and railways.

James

The hurricane hit our town very hard. That night was very frightening and we all slept downstairs for safety. Many of our friends' houses were badly damaged and school was shut for several days.

Further Reading

1980s, Nicola Barber, Evans Brothers, 1993.

A Look at Life in the Eighties, Adrian Gilbert, Wayland, 1999

Take Ten Years - *1980s*, Clint Twist, Evans, 1996

20th Century Fashion - *The 80s & 90s*, Clare Lomas, Heinemann, 1999.

20th Century Media: *1980 and 90s Electronic Media*, Steve Parker, Heinemann, 2003

Glossary

aerobics: A form of exercise that helps strengthen the heart and lungs as well as improve muscle tone.

breakdancing: An energetic type of street dancing that involves some gymnastic movements.

classic car: A stylish car of the fifties or sixties.

corporal punishment: A physical form of punishment such as caning.

cramming: Intensive studying during the weeks before an exam.

designer label: A fashion item designed by and carrying the name of a well-known designer.

environmentally friendly: Something that is not harmful to the environment.

logo: A design consisting of a picture or letters that a company uses as its symbol.

National Curriculum: The course of study laid down by the government and followed by schools in England and Wales.

natural resources: Materials that occur naturally in the environment and can be exploited by people, such as wood, oil or coal.

new romantic: An early eighties fashion for dressing in flamboyant and exotic clothes, often in the style of romantic characters such as pirates.

package holiday: A holiday at a set price that includes travel, accommodation and sometimes meals.

power dressing: A fashion amongst eighties businesspeople for dressing in smart, expensive outfits to make themselves look successful and businesslike.

recycling: Treating waste material, such as paper, plastic or glass, so that it can be reused. This helps to protect natural resources and also to prevent damage to the environment caused by waste disposal.

self-catering holiday: A holiday offering accommodation with facilities for preparing your own food.

shellsuit: A kind of lightweight tracksuit, often made of a slightly shiny fabric.

yuppy: A young, ambitious city worker. The word is a shortened form of 'young urban professional' or 'young upwardly-mobile professional'.

INDEX

And I laughed when I saw him, in spite of myself.
A wink of his eye and a twist of his head
Soon gave me to know I had nothing to dread.

He spoke not a word, but went straight to his work,
And filled all the stockings, then turned with a jerk,

And laying his finger aside of his nose,
And giving a nod, up the chimney he rose.

He sprang to his sleigh, to his team gave a whistle,
And away they all flew like the down of a thistle.

But I heard him exclaim ere he drove out of sight,
"HAPPY CHRISTMAS TO ALL,
AND TO ALL A GOOD NIGHT!"

Look out for these other winter classics:

For fun activities, further information and to order, visit www.hodderchildrens.co.uk

By the same Author

BUILDING CONSTRUCTION
Volumes One, Two and Three

CARPENTRY
JOINERY

By J. K. McKay

BUILDING CONSTRUCTION
Volume Four

W. B. McKay
M.Sc.Tech., M.I.Struct.E.

Former registered architect and chartered structural engineer and Head of the Department of Building and Structural Engineering in the Manchester University Institute of Science and Technology.

BUILDING CONSTRUCTION

VOLUME ONE

FIFTH EDITION (METRIC)

By J. K. McKay, B.A., B.Sc.Tech., A.R.I.B.A., C.Eng., M.I.Struct.E.

With drawings by the authors

Longman Scientific & Technical,
Longman Group UK Limited,
Longman House, Burnt Mill, Harlow,
Essex CM20 2JE, England
and Associated Companies throughout the world.

First Published 1938
Second Edition 1943
Third Edition 1953
Fourth Edition 1963
Fifth Edition (metric) 1970
Twelfth impression 1992

ISBN 0-582-42215-9

Produced by Longman Singapore Publishers (Pte)

PREFACE

TO THE FIFTH EDITION

In this edition the various units have been converted to metric terms.

Since the first appearance of this volume in 1938, the materials of construction for simple two-storey structures have hardly changed although techniques have been modified. As the earlier editions were published obsolete methods were given a secondary place and this has been continued once more. They cannot be omitted entirely whilst thirty per cent of building expenditure is still devoted to repair and alteration work.

The chapter contents have been extended and amended. Several of the drawings have been revised or replaced to illustrate up-to-date applications. Eleven new Figures are included as follows: 10, on foundations; 38A, trussed rafter roofs; 39, showing a built-up timber roof truss and interlocking tiles; 55, a storm lipped timber window and cavity walling; 62, metal windows; 65, stairs; 68, portable power tools; 70 and 71, giving larger details of slating; 78, domestic water services and 81, a vocabulary of structural steel components; the associated text has been added and sections on plastering are included.

1970 J. K. McKay.

PREFACE

TO THE FIRST EDITION

DURING the past few years syllabuses in Building Construction have been extensively revised, and to-day those operating in Technical Schools and Colleges approved for National Certificate purposes show general agreement as to what parts of the subject should be treated in the earlier stages.

This also applies to Building Construction as taught in Schools of Architecture, although its treatment and presentation may not be the same.

Accordingly, one of the aims of the author has been to include in this first volume only such matter as is now generally accepted as being suitable for the first stage of the subject. Each chapter is headed with the appropriate section of the syllabus in detail, and this is covered by the text and drawings.

Most of the drawings have been prepared to large size to enable associated details to be grouped conveniently for reference.

In Schools of Architecture, where Building Construction is closely related to Design, the illustrations may prove helpful to the first-year student in preparing his constructional sheets, particularly during the early months of the session, when adequate design subjects are not available and his ability to design is limited.

Attention is drawn to the suggested " Homework Programme." It is recognised that only a relatively small proportion of the details shown in the book can be drawn to scale by the student during a session, and a selection has therefore been made of those which may be regarded as typical; as far as time will permit, additional alternative details should be sketched by students in their notebooks.

Teachers of apprentice-students attending Trade Courses, such as Brickwork and Masonry, Carpentry and Joinery, etc., will find that the subject matter in the chapters concerned more than covers the first-year syllabuses. Whilst the Homework Programme does not apply to such courses, where the subjects need to be developed more gradually and treated in greater detail, it is hoped that the arrangement of Fig. 58, referred to in the programme, will serve as a useful guide to these students in preparing well-balanced sets of homework sheets.

In preparing certain sections of this book the author has had assistance from several sources, and he is especially indebted to Mr D. H. England and Mr W. I. Tarn who gave him many valuable and practical suggestions in connection with the chapter on Plumbing. Thanks are also extended to his colleague Mr E. Spencer for reading the proofs of the chapters on Carpentry and Joinery, and for much useful criticism bearing upon these sections.

W. B. McK.

August 1938

CONTENTS

LIST OF ILLUSTRATIONS

Note: UNLESS INDICATED OTHERWISE ALL DIMENSIONS ON THE FIGURES ARE GIVEN IN MILLIMETRES

CHAPTER ONE

BRICK WALLS, FOUNDATIONS

Syllabus—Brief description of the manufacture of bricks; characteristics. Lime mortar, cement mortar and concrete. Sizes and shapes of bricks; terms; heading, stretching, English and Flemish bonds[1]; 1, 1½ and 2-brick walls with stopped ends; ½ to 1, 1 to 1 and 1 to 1½-brick junctions; right-angled quoins to 1, 1½ and 2-brick walls; piers; rebated jambs with 56 mm and 112 mm recesses to 1 and 1½-brick walls; 275 mm cavity walls. Foundations for ½, 1, 1½ and 2-brick walls; surface concrete; horizontal damp-proof courses. Lintels; axed and gauged flat, segmental and semicircular arches; rough relieving arches; terms. Copings; window sills; steps; corbels and oversailing courses. Jointing and pointing. Plastering to walls.

MATERIALS

Bricks.—Bricks are made chiefly from clay and shale.[2] Clay, a plastic earth, is constituted largely of sand and alumina and may contain various quantities of chalk, iron, manganese dioxide, etc. Shale is a laminated deposit of clay rock which is capable of being reduced to a plastic condition when broken up and ground to a fine state of division. Bricks are approximately 215 mm by 102·5 mm by 65 mm (see p. 3).

Manufacture of Bricks.—The processes of manufacture vary considerably according to the variety of clay used, machinery available, etc., and the following is a brief general description. Bricks are moulded either by machinery or by hand.

Machine-made Bricks.—Most bricks are made by machinery. The various processes are: (1) preparation of the earth, (2) moulding, (3) drying and (4) burning.

(1) *Preparation.*—The clay or shale is excavated, and after large stones or other extraneous matter have been removed, it is conveyed to a pug mill and finely ground by heavy rotating wheels which force it through small perforations in the bottom of the mill.

(2) *Moulding.*—There are two kinds of machine-made bricks, *i.e.*, wire-cuts and pressed.

Wire-cut Bricks are moulded as follows:—The fine clay from the pug mill is forced through a mouthpiece (approximately 215 mm by 102·5 mm) of a machine in a continuous band and conveyed by rollers to a frame which contains several fine vertical wires about 65 mm apart. A portion of this continuous band, equal in length to that of the frame, is pushed forward through the frame by means of a metal plate and the wires divide it into ten or more 215 mm by 102·5 mm by 65 mm slabs of clay.

Pressed Bricks.—Of the many different types of machines for moulding bricks by pressure the simplest is worked by hand and the larger by steam power. The former consists of a metal box the size of a brick, containing a clay slab which has been wire-cut as explained above; a descending metal plate exerts pressure upon the clay to consolidate it; it is then removed. The larger type of machine consists of a rotating table containing twelve or more boxes or dies each being the size of a brick; as the table revolves each die in turn is brought under a hopper containing the prepared clay or shale; a plunger operating in the hopper descends and forces the clay into the die after which the raw brick (or slab of clay) is pushed out as the table rotates.

[1] Flemish bond is sometimes deferred until the second year of the Course.

[2] Sand-lime bricks (consisting of a mixture of lime and sand) and concrete bricks are also manufactured (see Chap. I, Vol. II).

(3) *Drying and* (4) *Burning.*—Both of these operations are carried out in a modern kiln, one type of which contains several chambers, each accommodating 40,000 or more bricks. The wire-cut or pressed raw bricks are carefully stacked with a space between each and in alternate layers at right angles to each other. Heat, produced from gas or coal dust, is gradually applied until a maximum temperature is obtained (which is maintained for approximately two days), when the bricks are then allowed to cool. The loading, drying, burning, cooling and emptying of the kiln may occupy two weeks, and as it is a continuous process, a chamber of finished bricks is emptied daily.

HAND-MADE BRICKS.—Whilst most bricks are machine-made and used for general purposes (on account of their relative cheapness) there is also demand for hand-made bricks for superior facing work. The preparation, drying and burning processes are similar to those already described, but the moulding is done by hand. The mould is of wood or metal and resembles the sides of a rectangular box equal in size to the required bricks.[1] It is either wetted or sanded to prevent the clay from adhering to it. A portion of the prepared clay sufficient to fill the mould is now taken, roughly shaped, and dashed by the moulder into the mould. The clay is pressed with the fingers to fill the mould completely and the slab is levelled off by a wood fillet or a piece of wire drawn across the top; the slab is then removed and finally taken to the kiln, dried and burnt.

Characteristics.—Good bricks should be thoroughly burnt; this makes them hard and durable (the quality of lasting for a long period without perishing) and enables them to withstand pressure. A hard ringing sound emitted when two bricks are struck together indicates that they have been burnt satisfactorily. Generally the bricks should be true to size and shape, with straight edges and even surfaces, so as to facilitate laying them in position.[2] They should be free from cracks, chips and large particles of lime. Unless desired, uniformity of colour is not now specified.[3]

Inferior bricks are generally underburnt and as a consequence are easily broken and are very porous; these are neither hard nor durable and are incapable

[1] Clay shrinks during the drying and burning processes by approximately one-tenth and allowance for this is made by using a mould which is larger than the finished brick.

[2] Bricks having rough surfaces (termed texture) and slightly irregular edges are selected purposely for certain first-class work. Thus the external walls of country houses are frequently faced with such bricks.

[3] Bricks of a variety of colours in tones of red, purple, grey, brown, etc., are now available, and, provided the colours have been carefully selected, brickwork when faced with bricks of mixed shades has a very satisfactory appearance.

of withstanding heavy loads. If they contain coarse grains of uncombined lime, any water absorbed causes the lime to expand, resulting in the partial disintegration of the bricks. They are invariably of poor appearance.

The weight of bricks varies considerably; approximately, wire-cuts are between 2 and 3 kg and pressed bricks from 3 to 7 kg each.

Lime.—Of the several varieties of lime, that used chiefly for brickwork and masonry is known as hydraulic lime.[1] It is produced from limestone or chalk which is burnt in a kiln for three or four days, when it is ready to be made into mortar.

Cement.—That generally used is known as Portland cement because of its resemblance to the colour of the stone of that name. It is manufactured from chalk and clay. The former is crushed and the clay is liquified by the addition of water, when it is called *slip*. These two materials are mixed together in correct proportions and very finely ground; the mixture, known as *slurry*, is conveyed to tanks and then to a kiln where it is gradually subjected to a high temperature and converted into a hard dark-looking clinker; the latter is passed to a mill where it is ground to an exceedingly fine powder to complete the process. The cement is automatically packed into paper or jute sacks, each full sack weighing 50 kg, or it may be delivered " in bulk " (loose).

Sand.—That obtained from pits or quarries is the best for mortar because of its angularity (called " sharp "); failing this, that from river banks or beds is used. Sea sand is unsuitable for mortar as it contains salts which attract and retain moisture, in addition to producing a whitish powder or efflorescence which discolours the brickwork or masonry. Sand should be well graded, *clean*, sharp and free from loam, clay or other impurity. Dirty sand should never be used as it may reduce the adhesive value of the mortar considerably, and in order to ensure a clean sand it is frequently specified that it shall be washed.

Lime Mortar.—This is a mixture of quicklime (burnt limestone—see above) and sand in the proportion of 1 lime : 3 sand, in addition to water. It was once the principal material used for bedding and jointing bricks, stones, etc.; it is used less frequently now as it develops strength very slowly. If mixed by hand, the lime is placed in a heap, sprinkled with water and completely covered with the measured proportion of sand; the lime expands and breaks into small particles owing to the heat which is generated; this is known as *slaking* or *slacking* the lime and the heap should be left undisturbed for at least twenty-four hours so as to ensure thorough disintegration of the lime. As unslaked particles of lime in mortar may cause damage to walling, it is necessary to pass it through a screen to eliminate unslaked lumps; after slaking, the material is turned over with a shovel on a boarded platform, more water is added and the mixing operation continued until the mortar is of the right consistency, neither too stiff nor too plastic. If mixed in a pug mill, the lime and sand are thoroughly incorporated after about twenty minutes' application of the rotating and grinding rollers. The mortar should be used fresh and just sufficient should be mixed for each day's use.

[1] This has the property of setting under water.

Cement Mortar.—This is a mixture of 1 cement : 3 sand. The sand is placed on a platform, the correct amount of cement is added to it, both are thoroughly mixed dry before water is added and the mass gradually worked up into a plastic condition. As cement mortar sets comparatively quickly, it should only be mixed in small amounts and not be used after it has started to set. Cement mortar is used in the construction of piers (see pp. 12 and 13), walling below damp course level (see p. 17), chimney stacks, etc., as brickwork built in cement mortar is much stronger than that built in lime mortar. A mix of 1 : 6 can also be used for general walling; but as this is harsh, then an additive, which forms air bubbles to improve the plasticity, can be included in the mixing water in the proportion of about 3%.

Cement Grout is cement which has been reduced to a thick liquid consistency by the addition of sufficient water.

Cement-Lime Mortar (also known as *compo*).—This is the most usual general purpose mortar comprising 1 cement : 2 lime : 9 sand, or 1 : 1 : 6 if there is a danger of frost as this is quicker setting. The addition of lime improves workability making it easier to place.

Concrete consists of a fine aggregate (or body), a coarse aggregate and a matrix (binding material). The fine aggregate is usually sand, common coarse aggregates are broken brick or stone (or gravel) and the matrix is usually cement. The proportions vary, but a common mix is composed of 1 part cement, 2 parts sand and 4 parts broken brick or stone; the maximum size of the latter depends upon the use to which the concrete is to be put and may be 38 mm (that passed through a 38 mm square mesh sieve) for foundations and 20 mm for reinforced concrete work. The aggregates must be carefully graded from a minimum to a maximum, so that when the materials are mixed the space between the particles is reduced to a minimum and a dense concrete ensured.

The mixing is done either by hand or by machinery. If mixed by hand, the materials in correct proportion are placed on a boarded platform and mixed twice (or thrice) dry and then twice (or thrice) wet. The amount of water added after the materials have been turned over dry (by using shovels) must be carefully regulated, *as an excess of water considerably reduces the strength of the concrete*. The mixing should always be done on a platform otherwise dirt would be shovelled into the mixture and its strength thereby reduced.

If a concrete-mixing machine is used, the materials in proper proportion are charged through a hopper into the mixer, the correct amount of water is then added; the mixer is rotated at a specified speed for a definite period, usually a minute, after which the concrete is discharged from the machine.

The concrete should be carefully deposited where required on the building so as to ensure that the density of the material shall be uniform throughout.

BONDING, SOLID BRICK WALLS

The craft of the bricklayer is concerned with embedding bricks in mortar and suitably arranging them so that the mass, called brickwork, conforms with certain requirements such as strength and appearance. Strength depends a good deal upon the bond. The Building Regulations require external walls to be adequate to prevent undue heat loss from the building; some typical examples of thermally insulated walls for dwellings are given on p. 34.

Bond is the interlacement of bricks produced when they lap (project beyond) those immediately above and below them. An unbonded wall, with its *continuous vertical joints*, has little strength and stability and such joints must be avoided. Fig. 1 illustrates the comparative strength of a bonded wall A and weakness of an unbonded wall B which are shown supporting a load. The portion of the load transmitted to the wall A is distributed over a relatively large area, as indicated within the broken lines C and D, whereas that transmitted to the wall B is practically concentrated on the portion between the continuous vertical joints E and F, with the result that this portion would tend to drop as shown; in addition, the two vertical sections G and H would tend to separate because of the absence of bond. Various bonds are described on pp. 4 and 7.

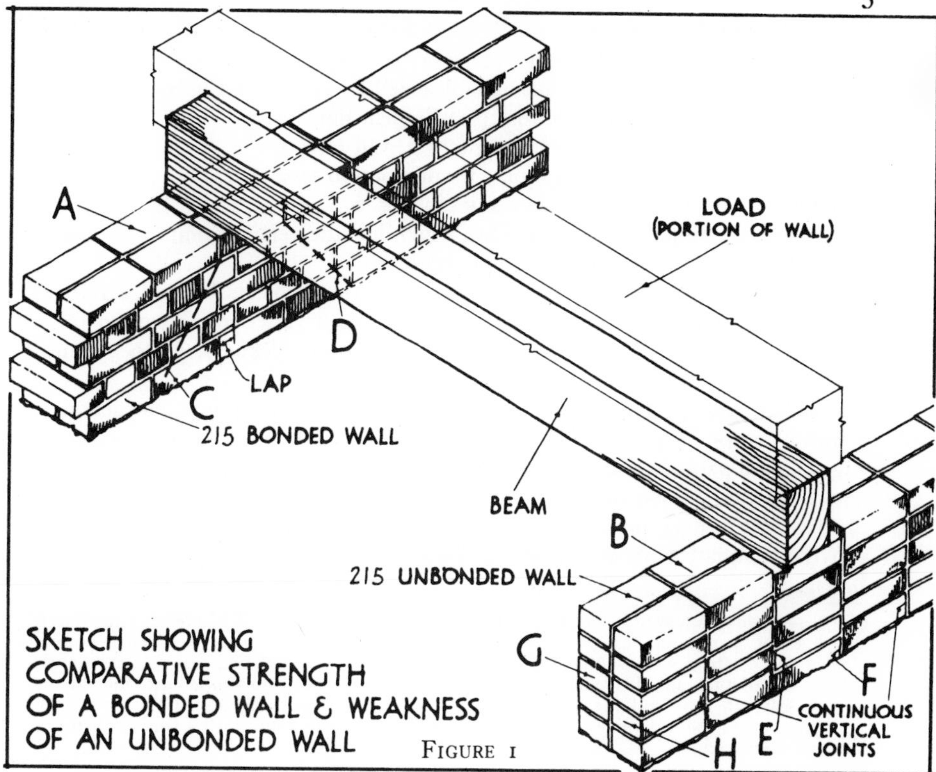

SKETCH SHOWING COMPARATIVE STRENGTH OF A BONDED WALL & WEAKNESS OF AN UNBONDED WALL

FIGURE 1

Size of Bricks.—Uniformity in the size of bricks is essential if the maintenance of the correct bond is to be facilitated during the construction of a wall; time is wasted if a consignment contains bricks of varying sizes as the bricklayer is required to make a selection as the work proceeds.

The length of a brick should be twice its width plus the thickness of one vertical joint in order that a proper bond may be maintained (see A, Fig. 2). Bricks in common use vary in size from 210 to 230 mm long by 100 to 110 mm wide by 38 to 75 mm thick, The following sizes are available: (1) Clay bricks are mostly 215 by 102·5 by 65 mm[1]; using a 10 mm joint this gives a nominal size or format of 225 by 112·5 by 75 mm; this is adopted in most of the Figures in this book. (2) Concrete bricks may be as (1) or 190 by 90 by 65 mm; with a 10 mm joint this makes a format of 200 by 100 by 75 mm.

Terms.—The following defines those which have a general application to brickwork :—

Arris.—An edge of a brick (see A, Fig. 2).

Bed.—The lower 215 mm by 102·5 mm surface of a brick when placed in position (see A, Fig. 2).

Header.—The end or 102·5 mm by 65 mm surface of a brick (see A, Fig. 2).

Stretcher.—The side (usually referred to as the " edge ") or 215 mm by 65 mm surface of a brick (see A, Fig. 2).

Face.—A surface of a brick such as the *header face* (102·5 mm by 65 mm) and *stretcher face* (215 mm by 65 mm) (see A, Fig. 2); is also applied to an exposed surface of a wall.

Frog or Kick.—A shallow sinking or indent (either rectangular, triangular or trapezoidal in section) formed on either one or both of the 215 mm by 102·5 mm faces of a brick (see D and M, Fig. 2); a wire-cut brick has no frogs, a pressed brick has two frogs as a rule and a hand-made brick usually has only one frog; a frog affords a good key for the mortar (see M, Fig. 2) and therefore walls which are required to show thin bed joints should be constructed of bricks with frogs; bricks having only one frog should be laid with the frog uppermost so as to ensure it being completely filled with mortar.

[1] Bricks 50 and 75 mm thick may be obtained.

Bed Joints.—Mortar joints, parallel to the beds of the bricks, and therefore horizontal in general walling; thickness varies from 3 to 12 mm—the most usual thickness is 10 mm shown at U, Fig. 2.

Course.—A complete layer of bricks plus its mortar bedding joint; a *heading course* consists of headers and a *stretching course* comprises stretchers (see U, Fig. 2); a *brick-on-edge course* consists of bricks placed on their 215 mm by 65 mm faces (see J and K, Fig. 17) and a *brick-on-end* or *soldier course* is composed of bricks laid on their 102·5 mm by 65 mm faces (see N and O, Fig. 17).

Brick Gauge.—The height of a number of brick courses, *e.g.*, four courses to 300 mm if 65 mm bricks and 10 mm joints are used. See *Gauge-rod*, pp. 28 and 30.

Continuous Vertical Joints or Straight Joints.—Vertical joints which come immediately over each other in two or more consecutive courses (see B, Fig. 1); although these are sometimes unavoidable (see Flemish bond, Fig. 4) they should not appear on the face of brickwork (see English Bond, p. 7).

Quoin.—A corner or external angle of a wall (see U, Fig. 2 and G, Fig. 6).

Stopped or Closed End.—A square termination to a wall (see Fig. 3) as distinct from a wall which is returned as shown in Fig. 6.

Perpends.—Imaginary vertical lines which include vertical joints (see broken lines at U, Fig. 2); these should be plumb or true.

Lap.—The horizontal distance which one brick projects beyond a vertical joint in the course immediately above or below it; it varies from 46·25 to 102·5 mm, *i.e.*, 46 to 102 mm; or, allowing for the joint thickness, 56 to 112 mm (see U, Fig. 2).

Racking Back.—The stepped arrangement formed during the construction of a wall when one portion is built to a greater height than that adjoining (see U, Fig. 2). No part of a wall during its construction should rise more than 900 mm above another if unequal settlement is to be avoided.

Toothing.—Each alternate course at the end of a wall projects in order to provide adequate bond if the wall is continued horizontally at a later date (see U, Fig. 2).

When a new wall has to be connected to an existing wall and where such provision has not been made, it is necessary to form a sinking or *indent* in each alternate course of the existing wall so that the new work may be properly tied into it; the depth of the indents should be such as to allow the new work to be bonded into the old for at least 56 mm and the width should be equal to the thickness of the new wall. Sometimes the indents are formed three or four courses high with a similar distance between each.

Bat.—A portion of an ordinary brick with the cut made across the *width* of the brick; four different sizes are shown at E, F, G and H, Fig. 2. Applications are illustrated in the following: *Half Bat* (E) at F, Fig. 4; *Three-quarter Bat* (F) at K, Fig. 3; *Bevelled Bats* (G) at N, Fig. 8, and (H) at E, Fig. 8.

Closer.—A portion of an ordinary brick with the cut made *longitudinally* and usually having one uncut stretcher face; seven forms are shown at J, K, L, N, O, P and V, Fig. 2. The *Queen Closer* (J) is usually placed next to the first brick in a header course (see J, Fig. 3); sometimes the abbreviated queen closer V is used (see K, Fig. 3); the queen closer K is obtained by cutting an ordinary brick into two half bats and then splitting one into half; K is more often used than J as it is easier to cut, although (as shown at L, Fig. 3) it generally produces a 56 mm wide continuous vertical joint. The *King Closer* (L), formed by removing a corner and leaving half-header and half-stretcher faces, is shown bonded at D, Fig. 8. The *Bevelled Closer* (N) has one stretcher face bevelled (splayed or slanted) and is shown at E, Fig. 8. *Mitred Closers* (O and P) are only used in exceptional cases as when the ends are required to be mitred (joined at an angle), *i.e.*, quoins of certain bay windows.

The remaining bricks Q, R, S and T shown in Fig. 2 are usually moulded specially to the required shape and are called ***specials*** or ***purpose-mades***, although for common work or where the brickwork is to be covered with plaster, ordinary bricks may be cut by a trowel or chisel to form all but the last of these.

Bullnose (Q).—These are used for copings (see D, Fig. 17) or in such positions where rounded corners are preferred to sharp arrises (see Q, Fig. 7); a brick with only one rounded edge is known as a *Single Bullnose* and one with both edges rounded is termed a *Double Bullnose*; the radius of the quadrant curve varies from 28 to 56 mm.

Splay (R and S).—These are often used to form plinths (see P, Fig. 17); the amount of splay varies.

Dogleg or *Angle* (T).—These bricks are used to ensure a satisfactory bond at quoins which depart from a right angle and are to be preferred to the mitred closers O and P; the angle and lengths of faces forming the dogleg vary.

The above purpose-made bricks are only a few of many which can now be obtained. Most of the larger brick-manufacturing firms make " standard specials " which are kept in stock. Wherever possible, a selection should be made from these, as purpose-mades which differ from the standard are most costly on account of the moulds which have to be made specially and delivery may be delayed.

Types of Bond.—There are many varieties of bond, and in a First Year Course it is usual to confine the instruction to Heading, Stretching, English and Flemish bonds. It is sometimes considered advisable to postpone the study of Flemish bond until the following year. In cavity-wall construction (see p. 13) it is most usual to have stretching bond, but as this is somewhat monotonous, English garden wall bond can be used. This comprises a row of half-bricks to every three rows of stretchers (see A, Fig. 18, Vol. II).

The thickness of a wall is either expressed in millimetres or in terms of the length of the brick, thus: 102·5 mm or ½-brick, 215 mm or 1-brick, 327·5 mm (often specified 328 mm) or 1½-brick, 440 mm or 2-brick, etc.[1]

A bond is usually identified by the appearance of the external face of the wall, and it is this face appearance which is referred to in the following description of bonds. Thus the expression " alternate courses of headers " refers to the arrangement of the bricks on the face, even if the headers in each course are backed by stretchers.

Note that the joints in most of the details are indicated by single lines, the thickness not being shown. Students are not recommended to show the joints by double lines, for, unless they are very accurately drawn, accumulative errors are likely to occur resulting in the bond being shown incorrectly. Drawing is further facilitated if, as shown in the examples, the dimensions of a brick are assumed to be 225 mm by 112·5 mm by 75 mm.

Heading Bond.—*Each* course of a wall consists of headers only. It is used chiefly in the construction of footings (see Fig. 10) and walls which are sharply curved, where the long faces of stretchers would unduly break the line of the curve.

[1] Large modern buildings are usually of steel-framed or reinforced concrete construction which provide for the support of heavy loads by the use of either steelwork or reinforced concrete, and therefore walls which exceed 2 bricks in thickness are rarely required.

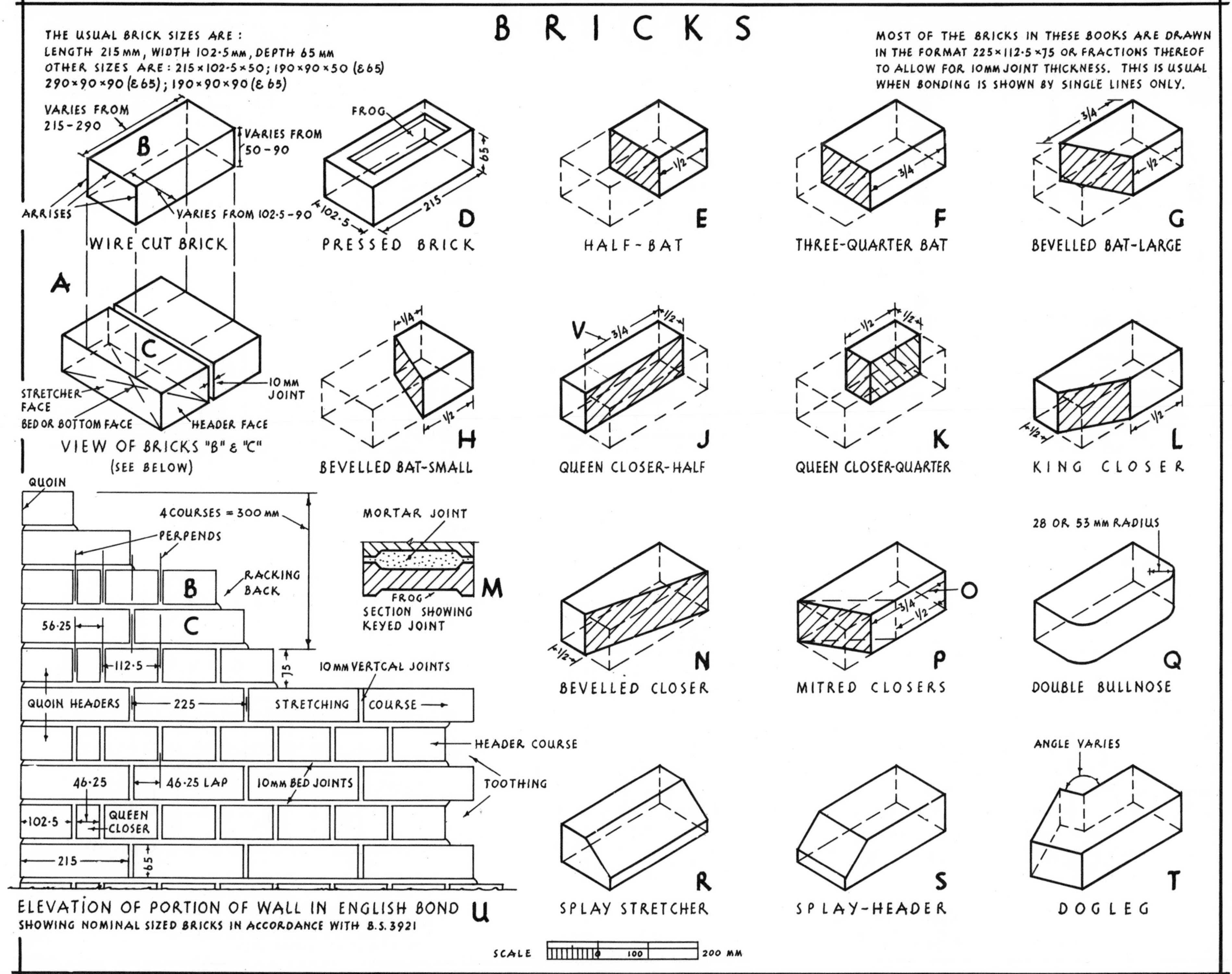

BRICKS
THE USUAL BRICK SIZES ARE :
LENGTH 215 MM, WIDTH 102·5 MM, DEPTH 65 MM
OTHER SIZES ARE : 215×102·5×50; 190×90×50 (& 65)
290×90×90 (& 65); 190×90×90 (& 65)
MOST OF THE BRICKS IN THESE BOOKS ARE DRAWN IN THE FORMAT 225×112·5×75 OR FRACTIONS THEREOF TO ALLOW FOR 10MM JOINT THICKNESS. THIS IS USUAL WHEN BONDING IS SHOWN BY SINGLE LINES ONLY.
VARIES FROM 215-290
VARIES FROM 50-90
ARRISES
VARIES FROM 102·5-90
WIRE CUT BRICK
FROG
PRESSED BRICK
HALF-BAT
THREE-QUARTER BAT
BEVELLED BAT-LARGE
STRETCHER FACE
BED OR BOTTOM FACE
HEADER FACE
10 MM JOINT
VIEW OF BRICKS "B" & "C"
(SEE BELOW)
BEVELLED BAT-SMALL
QUEEN CLOSER-HALF
QUEEN CLOSER-QUARTER
KING CLOSER
QUOIN
4 COURSES = 300 MM
PERPENDS
RACKING BACK
MORTAR JOINT
FROG
SECTION SHOWING KEYED JOINT
28 OR 53 MM RADIUS
BEVELLED CLOSER
MITRED CLOSERS
DOUBLE BULLNOSE
10 MM VERTCAL JOINTS
QUOIN HEADERS
STRETCHING COURSE
HEADER COURSE
TOOTHING
46·25 LAP
10MM BED JOINTS
QUEEN CLOSER
ANGLE VARIES
SPLAY STRETCHER
SPLAY-HEADER
DOGLEG
ELEVATION OF PORTION OF WALL IN ENGLISH BOND
SHOWING NOMINAL SIZED BRICKS IN ACCORDANCE WITH B.S. 3921
SCALE 0 100 200 MM

FIGURE 2

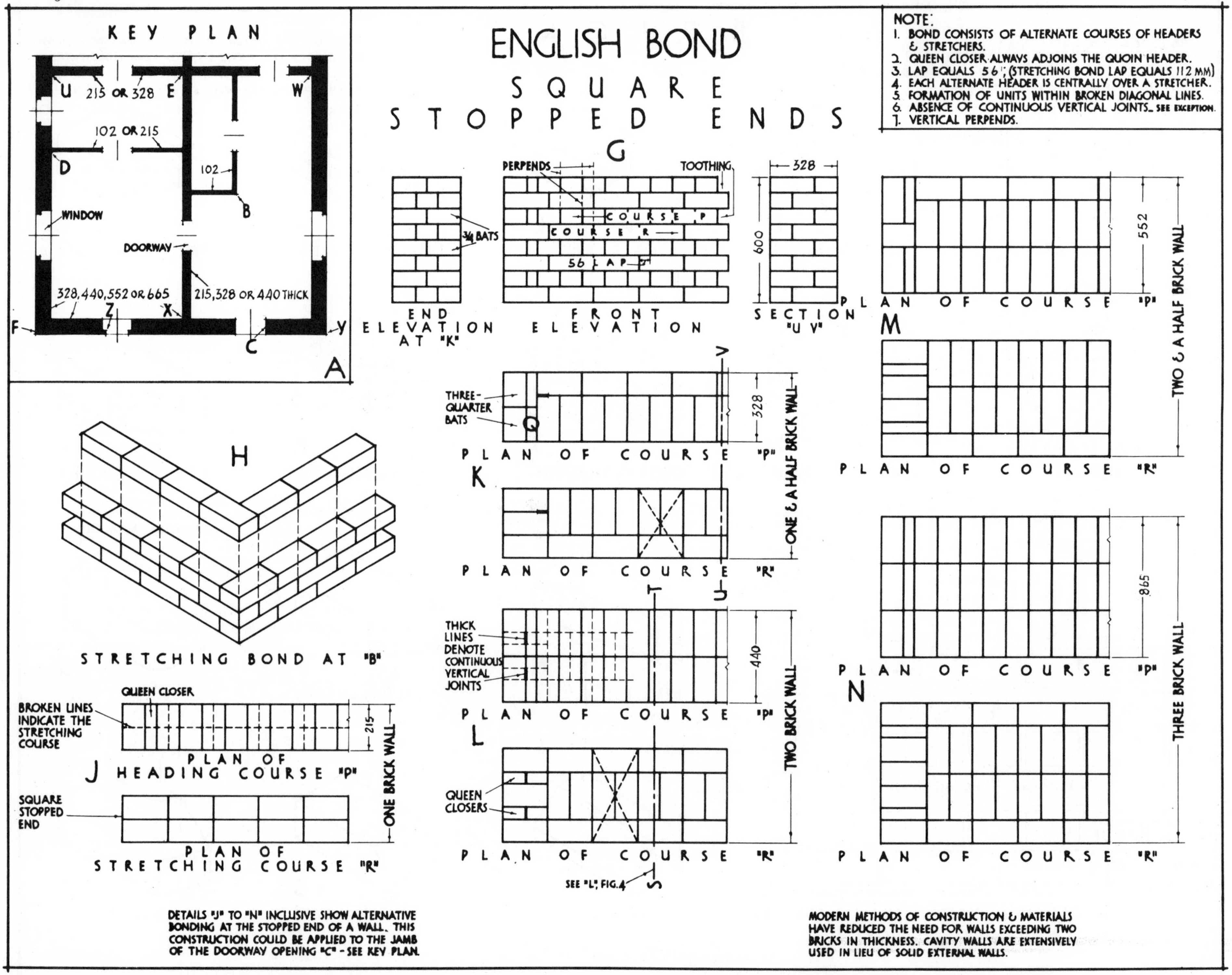

ENGLISH BOND

SQUARE STOPPED ENDS

NOTE:
1. BOND CONSISTS OF ALTERNATE COURSES OF HEADERS & STRETCHERS.
2. QUEEN CLOSER ALWAYS ADJOINS THE QUOIN HEADER.
3. LAP EQUALS 56 (STRETCHING BOND LAP EQUALS 112 MM)
4. EACH ALTERNATE HEADER IS CENTRALLY OVER A STRETCHER.
5. FORMATION OF UNITS WITHIN BROKEN DIAGONAL LINES.
6. ABSENCE OF CONTINUOUS VERTICAL JOINTS_ SEE EXCEPTION.
7. VERTICAL PERPENDS.

KEY PLAN

U 215 OR 328 E W
102 OR 215
D
102
B
WINDOW
DOORWAY
328, 440, 552 OR 665
215, 328 OR 440 THICK
F Z X Y
C
A

G

PERPENDS TOOTHING
3/4 BATS
COURSE P
COURSE R
56 LAP
328
600

END ELEVATION AT "K"

FRONT ELEVATION

SECTION "U V"

THREE-QUARTER BATS
Q
328

PLAN OF COURSE "P"

K

PLAN OF COURSE "R"

ONE & A HALF BRICK WALL

V U T S

THICK LINES DENOTE CONTINUOUS VERTICAL JOINTS
440

PLAN OF COURSE "P"

L

QUEEN CLOSERS

PLAN OF COURSE "R"

TWO BRICK WALL

SEE "L", FIG. 4

552

PLAN OF COURSE "P"

M

PLAN OF COURSE "R"

TWO & A HALF BRICK WALL

865

PLAN OF COURSE "P"

N

PLAN OF COURSE "R"

THREE BRICK WALL

H

STRETCHING BOND AT "B"

QUEEN CLOSER
BROKEN LINES INDICATE THE STRETCHING COURSE
215

PLAN OF HEADING COURSE "P"

J

ONE BRICK WALL

SQUARE STOPPED END

PLAN OF STRETCHING COURSE "R"

DETAILS "J" TO "N" INCLUSIVE SHOW ALTERNATIVE BONDING AT THE STOPPED END OF A WALL. THIS CONSTRUCTION COULD BE APPLIED TO THE JAMB OF THE DOORWAY OPENING "C" - SEE KEY PLAN.

MODERN METHODS OF CONSTRUCTION & MATERIALS HAVE REDUCED THE NEED FOR WALLS EXCEEDING TWO BRICKS IN THICKNESS. CAVITY WALLS ARE EXTENSIVELY USED IN LIEU OF SOLID EXTERNAL WALLS.

FIGURE 3

Stretching Bond.—*Each* course consists of stretchers with exception of a half bat which must be placed at the stopped end of a wall at each alternate course so that the work will break joint. Note that at H, Fig. 3, the break joint is formed by the first or quoin stretcher appearing as a header on the return face.[1] This bond is suitable for 102·5 mm thick walls, such as are required for cavity walls, chimney stacks, sleeper walls and division walls.

English Bond.—This consists of *alternate courses* of headers and stretchers (see Fig. 3). Observe: (1) in each *heading course a queen closer is placed next to the quoin header*[2] and the remaining bricks are headers, (2) every alternate header in a course comes centrally over the joint between two stretchers in the course below, giving a lap of 56 mm, and (3) there are no continuous vertical joints, excepting at certain stopped ends and particularly where queen closers of the form K (Fig. 2) and not J are used. It is this comparative lack of straight joints which gives to English bond its characteristic strength.

Square Stopped Ends.—Fig. 3 shows details of stopped ends to a 1-brick wall (J), a 1½-brick wall (K), a 2-brick wall (L), a 2½-brick wall (M) and a 3-brick wall (N). A key plan of a portion of a building is shown at A, and the treatment of the stopped end of the doorway opening at C (which is called a *square jamb* —see p. 13) would be in accordance with one or other of these details, depending upon the thickness of the wall.

The external walls of a house if built of solid brickwork are usually 328 mm thick, and the division walls are either 102·5 or 215 mm thick; other types of buildings may have thicker walls, but, as already explained, walls exceeding 2 bricks in thickness are now rarely required. *It is now general practice to use cavity external walls.*

Special attention should be taken in the construction of stopped ends of walls as these are often required to take concentrated loads from lintels, etc. (see Fig. 12).

The following should be noted:—

1. At least every alternate transverse joint is continuous from face to face; a 1½-brick wall consists of units comprising a stretcher backed with two headers, or vice versa (see broken lines at K, Fig. 3); a stretcher course of a 2-brick wall is formed of units having a stretcher on each face with two headers in the middle (see L, Fig. 3).

Students at examinations frequently make the mistake of showing non-continuous transverse joints.

2. Walls of an *even* number of *half* bricks in thickness present the same appearance on both faces, *i.e.*, a course consisting of stretchers on the front elevation will show stretchers on the back elevation (see J, L and N, Fig. 3).

3. Walls of an *odd* number of *half* bricks in thickness will show *each* course consisting of headers on one face and stretchers on the other (see K and M, Fig. 3).

[1] Low division walls which are not required to support loads may be built with the bricks placed on edge and in stretching bond; the thickness is thus reduced to 65 mm.

[2] A heading course should never *commence* with a queen closer, for, in this position it would be liable to displacement.

4. The middle portion of each of the thicker walls consists entirely of headers (see L, M and N, Fig. 3).[1]

Flemish Bond.—This comprises *alternate* headers and stretchers in *each* course. There are two kinds of Flemish bond, *i.e.*, (1) Double Flemish and (2) Single Flemish.

(1) *Double Flemish Bond* (see D, E, F and G, Fig. 4) shows the characteristic appearance of Flemish on *both* external and internal faces. As shown at D, each header comes centrally over a stretcher and, unlike English bond, no header comes over a vertical face joint. It is not so strong as English bond because of the large number of short continuous vertical joints (indicated by thick lines) which occur in the longitudinal joints. Some consider that double Flemish bond has a more pleasing appearance and is more economical than English bond.

A difference of opinion exists about the superiority or otherwise of the appearance of Flemish bond, some favour the pattern of units of cross formation which appears on the face—see D, Fig. 4. Where a flush face is required on *both* sides of a 1-brick wall this is more readily obtained in Flemish rather than English bond. This is because the stretcher face of bricks may vary in length due to the unequal shrinkage during the burning process; thus the combined length of two headers plus one joint may exceed the length of a stretcher. Although this defect will not occur in well-made bricks, if it does then a 1-brick English-bonded wall could have one face flush with the other face showing each heading course set back slightly from the stretching course. This irregularity is less pronounced in Flemish bond with its alternate headers and stretchers in each course for the set-back at each short header is more evenly distributed; the resulting appearance is considered to improve the surface texture or character of the work.

Square Stopped Ends.—On reference to the elevation D and the plans E, F and G, Fig. 4, it will be seen that in every alternative course a queen closer is placed next to the quoin header so as to provide a lap of approximately 56 mm. This agrees with the rule for English bond. Attention is drawn to the units of which *every* course in each wall is comprised and which are indicated within the broken diagonal lines. The notes on Fig. 4 should be carefully studied.

(2) *Single Flemish Bond* consists of a *facing of Flemish bond* with a *backing of English bond* in *each* course (see H and J, Fig. 4). It is adopted where expensive facing bricks are required to give the characteristic appearance of Flemish bond and where comparatively cheaper bricks are used as a backing. This bond cannot be applied to walls which are less than 1½-brick thick. It is relatively weak, as can be seen on reference to H and J, which show 225 mm long continuous vertical joints appearing in the longitudinal joints. Note that half bats are used which are known as *snap headers* or *false headers*. An alternative arrangement of bricks in the 2-brick wall at J is shown at K (where the snap-header and full-header backing are substituted by two three-quarter bats);

[1] A scale of 1:10 is generally used when detailing brick bonding; students are recommended to commence with the heading course followed by the stretching course immediately below it; a tracing of the latter course transposed over the heading course will emphasize the fact that there are no continuous vertical joints (see L, Fig. 3).

FLEMISH BOND

SQUARE STOPPED ENDS

DOUBLE FLEMISH

E

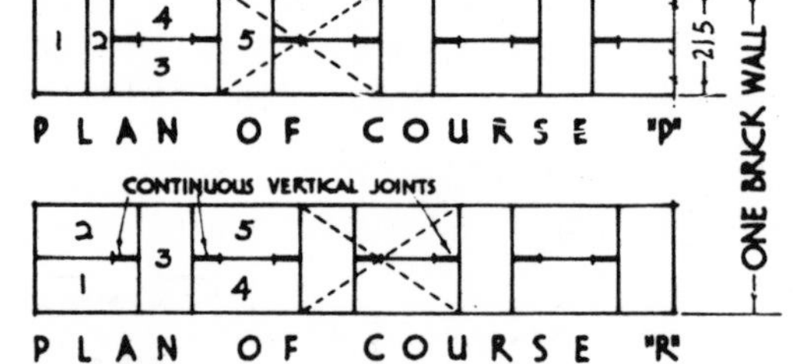

D

COURSE P

COURSE R

900

FRONT ELEVATION

SINGLE FLEMISH

H

PLAN OF COURSE "P"

328

ONE & A HALF BRICK WALL

PLAN OF COURSE "R"

F

½ BAT

328

PLAN OF COURSE "P"

PLAN OF COURSE "R"

ONE & A HALF BRICK WALL

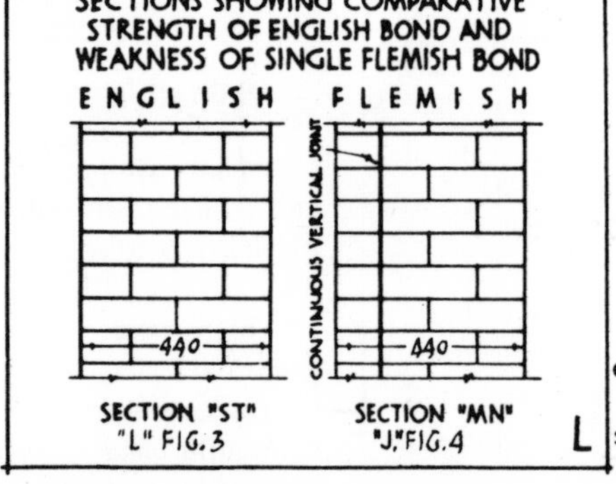

J

N

440

PLAN OF COURSE "P"

TWO BRICK WALL

CONTINUOUS VERTICAL JOINTS SEE NOTE BELOW

PLAN OF COURSE "R"

M

G

440

PLAN OF COURSE "P"

TWO BRICK WALL

PLAN OF COURSE "R"

THE ABOVE ARE ALTERNATIVE DETAILS OF THE STOPPED END OF THE DOORWAY OPENING "C" AT "A" FIG.3.

NOTE:

1. IN DOUBLE FLEMISH BOND, ALTERNATE HEADERS & STRETCHERS IN EACH COURSE ON BOTH FACES.
2. IN SINGLE FLEMISH BOND, ALTERNATE HEADERS & STRETCHERS IN EACH COURSE ON ONE FACE ONLY WITH A BACKING IN ENGLISH BOND.
3. QUEEN CLOSER ALWAYS ADJOINS THE QUOIN HEADER.
4. EACH HEADER IS CENTRALLY OVER A STRETCHER.
5. CONTINUOUS VERTICAL JOINTS SHOWN BY THICK LINES.
6. FORMATION OF UNITS WITHIN BROKEN DIAGONAL LINES.
7. VERTICAL PERPENDS.

ALTERNATIVE BONDING TO COURSE "R" AT "J"

NOTE REDUCTION IN WIDTH OF CONTINUOUS VERTICAL JOINTS

K

¾

440

PLAN OF COURSE "R"

FIGURE 4

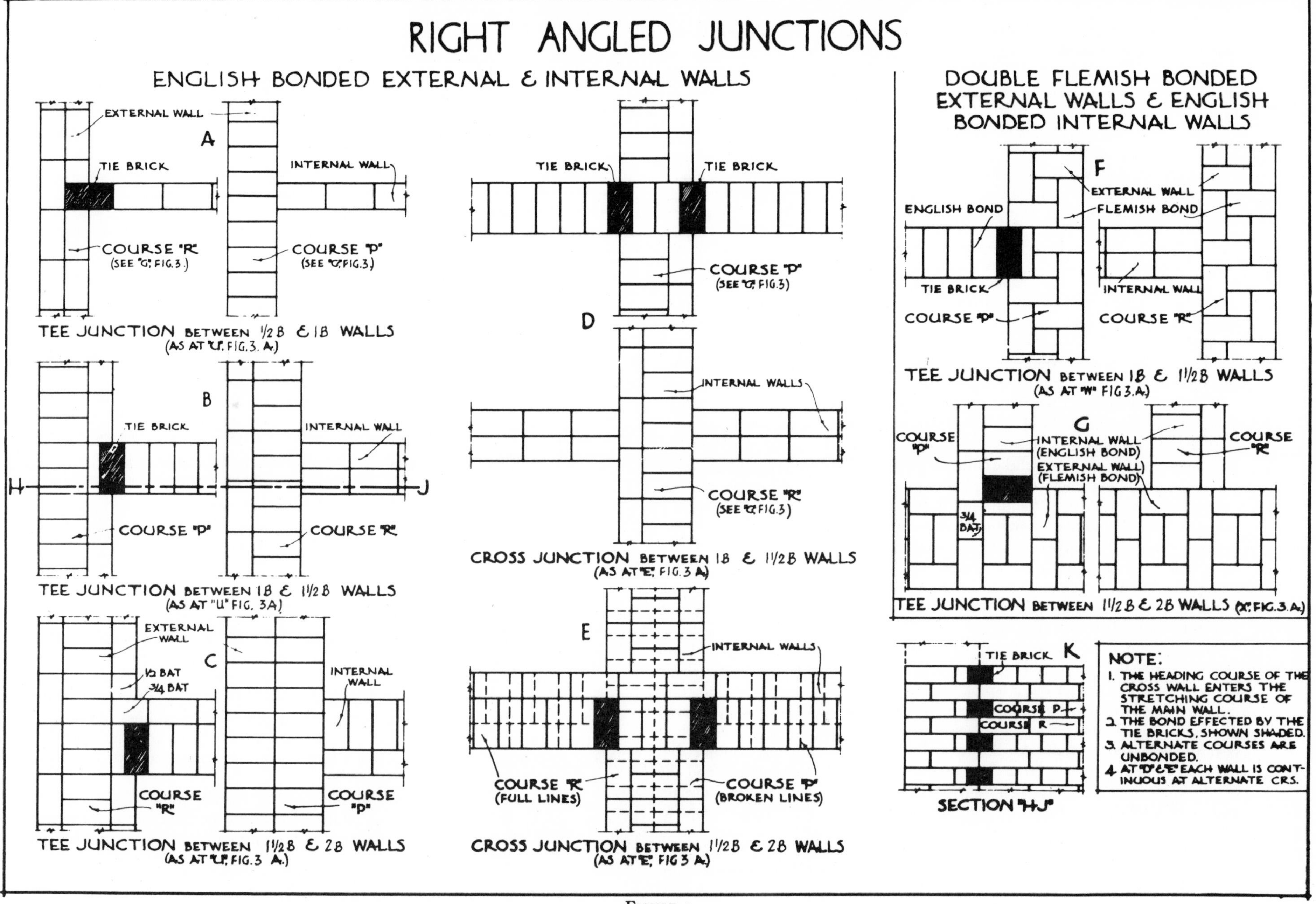
RIGHT ANGLED JUNCTIONS
ENGLISH BONDED EXTERNAL & INTERNAL WALLS
EXTERNAL WALL
A
TIE BRICK
INTERNAL WALL
COURSE "R" (SEE "G" FIG.3.)
COURSE "P" (SEE "G" FIG.3.)
TEE JUNCTION BETWEEN 1/2 B & 1 B WALLS (AS AT "U" FIG.3. A.)
B
TIE BRICK
INTERNAL WALL
H
J
COURSE "P"
COURSE "R"
TEE JUNCTION BETWEEN 1 B & 1 1/2 B WALLS (AS AT "U" FIG. 3A)
EXTERNAL WALL
C
1/2 BAT
3/4 BAT
INTERNAL WALL
COURSE "R"
COURSE "P"
TEE JUNCTION BETWEEN 1 1/2 B & 2 B WALLS (AS AT "U" FIG.3 A.)
TIE BRICK
TIE BRICK
COURSE "P" (SEE "G" FIG.3)
D
INTERNAL WALLS
COURSE "R" (SEE "G" FIG.3)
CROSS JUNCTION BETWEEN 1 B & 1 1/2 B WALLS (AS AT "E" FIG.3 A.)
E
INTERNAL WALLS
COURSE "R" (FULL LINES)
COURSE "P" (BROKEN LINES)
CROSS JUNCTION BETWEEN 1 1/2 B & 2 B WALLS (AS AT "E" FIG 3 A.)
DOUBLE FLEMISH BONDED EXTERNAL WALLS & ENGLISH BONDED INTERNAL WALLS
F
EXTERNAL WALL
ENGLISH BOND
FLEMISH BOND
TIE BRICK
INTERNAL WALL
COURSE "P"
COURSE "R"
TEE JUNCTION BETWEEN 1 B & 1 1/2 B WALLS (AS AT "W" FIG 3.A.)
G
COURSE "P"
INTERNAL WALL (ENGLISH BOND)
EXTERNAL WALL (FLEMISH BOND)
COURSE "R"
3/4 BAT
TEE JUNCTION BETWEEN 1 1/2 B & 2 B WALLS ("X" FIG.3.A.)
TIE BRICK
K
COURSE P
COURSE R
SECTION "H-J"
NOTE:
1. THE HEADING COURSE OF THE CROSS WALL ENTERS THE STRETCHING COURSE OF THE MAIN WALL.
2. THE BOND EFFECTED BY THE TIE BRICKS, SHOWN SHADED.
3. ALTERNATE COURSES ARE UNBONDED.
4. AT "D" & "E" EACH WALL IS CONTINUOUS AT ALTERNATE CRS.

FIGURE 5

this results in a reduction in the length of the continuous vertical joints with a corresponding increase in strength, but an increase in cost due to the labour and wastage of bricks involved in the cutting of the three-quarter bats. This alternative bond may also be substituted for the corresponding course of the 1½-brick wall (H).

The comparative weakness of single Flemish bond is illustrated at L, Fig. 4, which shows a perfectly bonded 440 mm wall built in English bond and an inadequately bonded wall of the same thickness built in single Flemish bond; the continuous vertical joint shown by a thick line in the section through the latter wall is 225 mm wide, as shown in the plan at J, Fig. 4.

JUNCTIONS AND QUOINS

The key plan at A, Fig. 3, shows several connections between walls. One type of connection is termed a *junction* (D, E, U, W and X) and another form is known as a *quoin* (F and Y).

Junctions.—These are classified into right-angled junctions and squint junctions.[1] There are two forms of right-angled junctions, *i.e.*, (*a*) tee-junctions and (*b*) cross-junctions or intersections.

(*a*) *Tee-junctions.*—A tee-junction is a connection between two walls which on plan is in the form of the letter T (see D, U, W and X in the key plan).

Plans of tee-junctions between walls built in English bond are shown at A, B and C, Fig. 5. At A one of the courses of the 102·5 mm internal division wall enters the stretching course of the 215 mm external wall, giving a 112 mm lap, and the alternate course of the division wall butts against the heading course of the main wall. Note the following in connection with details B and C: (1) the heading course of the internal wall is bonded into the stretching course of the main wall, the first header or tie brick (shown shaded) giving a 56 mm lap and being adjacent to a queen closer; (2) the stretching course of the cross wall butts against the heading course of the external wall. The tie bricks are also shown in the section at K, Fig. 5.

Plans of junctions between external walls built in double Flemish bond and English bonded division walls are shown at F and G, Fig. 5. As in the above examples, the key header has a lap of 56 mm.

(*b*) *Cross-junctions or Intersections.*—A cross-junction is an intersection between two continuous walls (see E in the key plan at A, Fig. 3). Details are given at D and E, Fig. 5; the walls are shown in English bond, it being assumed that they are to be plastered. Note: (1) one of the courses is continuous and the course at right angles butts against it; (2) these continuous courses alternate; and (3) a key header forms a 56 mm lap at each side of the non-continuous course.

The above are only a few examples of several methods of bonding at junctions. The arrangement of the bricks depends largely upon the relative position of the walls. Variations of these examples will be necessary when a continuous transverse joint in the main wall does not coincide with a face of the entering course of the adjacent wall. The essential requirements are the avoidance of continuous vertical joints with the employment of the minimum number of cut bricks.

Quoins or External Angles.—There are two forms of quoins, *i.e.*, right-angled or square quoins and squint quoins.[1] As is implied, a right-angled quoin is formed by two walls which meet at 90°. Examples of right-angled quoins are shown at F and Y, Fig. 3.

Square Quoins in English Bond.—Plans of alternate courses of right-angled quoins formed by walls built in English bond are shown detailed at A, B and C, Fig. 6. The following should be noted :—

1. At the same level, the heading course on one face of the angle is returned by a stretching course; thus at A the heading course P is returned by a stretching course similar to R.
2. There are no continuous vertical joints.
3. When the wall is an *even* number of *half*-bricks in thickness the brick figured 3 is a *header* projecting 56 mm (see A and C, Fig. 6).
4. When the wall is an *odd* number of *half*-bricks thick, the brick figured 3 is a *stretcher* projecting 56 mm (see B, Fig. 6).
5. At the 56 mm projection (or quarter bond) of number 3 brick the transverse joint is continuous (see M at B, Fig. 6).
6. In the 1 and 2-brick quoins the heading course of one wall is continuous to the front of the return face and that in the 1½-brick quoin is continuous to the back of the stretching face; the return stretching course in each case butts against the heading course.

When drawing these details (usually to a scale 1:10) the student should set out the outline of the quoin and, commencing with the heading course, fill in the three bricks numbered 1, 2, and 3 followed by the remaining bricks; if number 3 brick is placed in correct position according to either (3) or (4) above and if (5) is complied with, little difficulty will be experienced in completing each course, as the details are in accordance with those of English bond shown in Fig. 3.

Square Quoins in Double Flemish Bond.—Details of these are shown at D, E and F, Fig. 6. Note :

1. In the 1 and 1½-brick quoins the continuous course is that which contains the queen closer; also the butt courses are similar to E and F, Fig. 4, commencing with units which are similar to those shown within the broken lines in Fig. 4.
2. Number 3 brick in the 1 and 1½-brick quoins is a stretcher which projects 168 mm, and in the 2-brick quoin it is a header which projects 56 mm as in the English bonded 2-brick quoin.
3. The half bat at the internal angle of the 2-brick quoin is necessary to avoid a long continuous vertical joint and to form the continuous transverse joint which bounds the characteristic 6-brick unit enclosed within the broken lines.

[1] Squint junctions are detailed in Chap. I., Vol. II.

[1] Squint quoins are usually dealt with in the second year of the Course and they are therefore detailed in Chap. I, Vol. II.

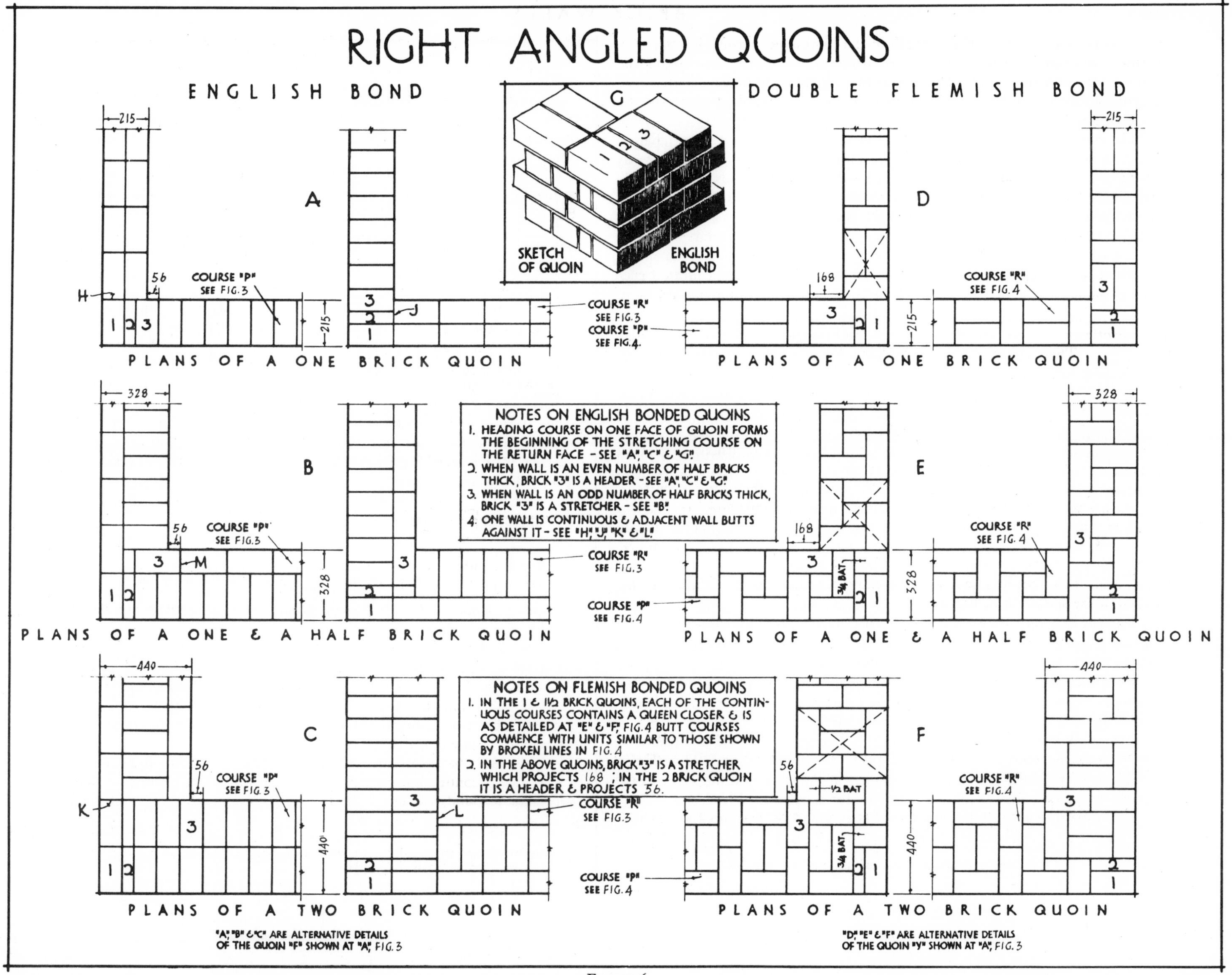
RIGHT ANGLED QUOINS
ENGLISH BOND
DOUBLE FLEMISH BOND
SKETCH OF QUOIN
ENGLISH BOND
G
A
B
C
D
E
F
H
J
K
L
M
215
328
440
56
168
COURSE "P" SEE FIG.3
COURSE "R" SEE FIG.3
COURSE "P" SEE FIG.4
COURSE "R" SEE FIG.4
3/4 BAT
1/2 BAT
PLANS OF A ONE BRICK QUOIN
PLANS OF A ONE & A HALF BRICK QUOIN
PLANS OF A TWO BRICK QUOIN
NOTES ON ENGLISH BONDED QUOINS
1. HEADING COURSE ON ONE FACE OF QUOIN FORMS THE BEGINNING OF THE STRETCHING COURSE ON THE RETURN FACE - SEE "A", "C" & "G".
2. WHEN WALL IS AN EVEN NUMBER OF HALF BRICKS THICK, BRICK "3" IS A HEADER - SEE "A", "C" & "G".
3. WHEN WALL IS AN ODD NUMBER OF HALF BRICKS THICK, BRICK "3" IS A STRETCHER - SEE "B".
4. ONE WALL IS CONTINUOUS & ADJACENT WALL BUTTS AGAINST IT - SEE "H", "J", "K" & "L".
NOTES ON FLEMISH BONDED QUOINS
1. IN THE 1 & 1½ BRICK QUOINS, EACH OF THE CONTINUOUS COURSES CONTAINS A QUEEN CLOSER & IS AS DETAILED AT "E" & "F", FIG. 4 BUTT COURSES COMMENCE WITH UNITS SIMILAR TO THOSE SHOWN BY BROKEN LINES IN FIG. 4
2. IN THE ABOVE QUOINS, BRICK "3" IS A STRETCHER WHICH PROJECTS 168; IN THE 2 BRICK QUOIN IT IS A HEADER & PROJECTS 56.
"A", "B" & "C" ARE ALTERNATIVE DETAILS OF THE QUOIN "F" SHOWN AT "A", FIG. 3
"D", "E" & "F" ARE ALTERNATIVE DETAILS OF THE QUOIN "Y" SHOWN AT "A", FIG. 3

Figure 6

Piers (also known as *pillars* or *columns*) of brickwork are adopted either to support concentrated loads such as are transmitted by arches, floor beams and roofs, or to strengthen walls. Such piers may be isolated (or detached) or they may be attached to walls.

Detached Piers.—Such may be either square, rectangular, circular or polygonal on plan. A plan of a portion of a building in which piers are employed is shown at A, Fig. 7, and a detached pier is shown at C. Such a building may be an arcade or loggia, or it may be considered as a portion of a factory, although modern buildings of the latter type usually have pillars of mild steel or reinforced concrete. Maximum strength is obtained if pillars are constructed with sound dense bricks built in English bond and in cement mortar.

English Bonded Detached Piers (see plans J, K and L and the corresponding elevations D, E and F, Fig. 7).—It is only necessary to show one course of each pier, as in every case the arrangement of the bricks in each course is the same.

Thus the 215 mm pier has every alternate course constructed as shown at J with similar intermediate courses at right angles (see elevation D); the 328 mm pier has alternate courses as shown at K with similar adjacent courses having the stretcher face of two three-quarter bats at the front over the three headers (see E); each course in the 440 mm pier is as shown at L, but every alternate course is turned to the side (see elevation F).

The only continuous vertical joints are those shown by thick lines at K. A stone *pad* or *template* as shown in each elevation is usually provided at the top of a pier to ensure a firm bed for a beam or roof truss and to distribute the load effectively. Detached pillars to which gates are hung are often finished with a coping as illustrated in Fig. 17.

Double Flemish Bonded Detached Piers (see G, H, M and N, Fig. 7).—In the 1½-brick pier (which is the smallest that can be constructed in this bond) continuous vertical joints are produced, as indicated by thick black lines at N; owing to the small size of this pier the true face appearance of Flemish bond is not presented in the elevation at H (as the headers are not centrally over the stretchers), but the pier is nevertheless considered to be in Flemish bond as in each course there is a header adjacent to a stretcher. The short continuous vertical joints shown in the plan M of the 2-brick pier can be avoided if bevelled closers (see broken lines) are used as an alternative.

Piers may be formed with rounded arrises by using bullnose bricks; thus double bullnose bricks (see Q, Fig. 2) may be used in the construction of pier J and single bullnose bricks for the remaining piers.

Attached Piers or Pilasters.—Such are shown at B in the key plan at A, Fig. 7, and some alternative details are given at O to S inclusive. The stability of walls is increased by the use of these piers at intervals, and like those of the detached type they may be used as supports for concentrated loads.

Examples in English bond are shown at O, P and Q. Rounded arrises may be obtained by using bullnose bricks (see Q). The width of a pier is usually a

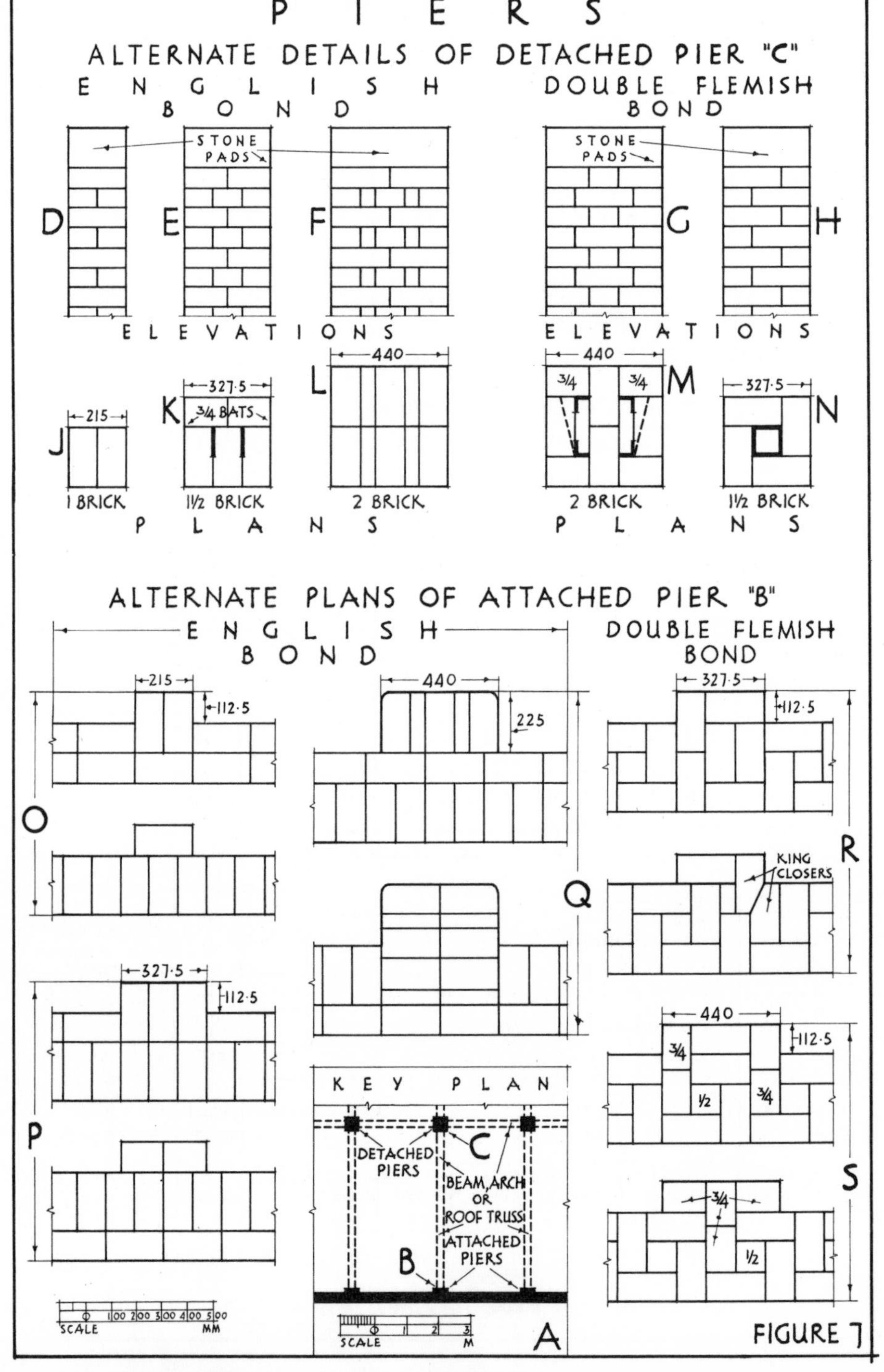

FIGURE 7

multiple of 112 mm and the projection may be either 112 mm (as at O and P), 225 mm (as at Q) or upwards.

The piers and adjacent walling shown at R and S are in double Flemish bond; the 112 mm projection may be increased as required.

A gate pier of the attached type is shown at A, Fig. 17.

Buttresses are piers which are provided to resist thrusts from roof trusses or to strengthen boundary walls, etc. Examples of buttress cappings are illustrated in Fig. 11.

The brick and concrete foundations for piers are referred to on p. 17.

JAMBS

Jambs are the vertical sides of openings which are formed in walls to receive doors, windows, fireplaces, etc. There are three forms of jambs, *i.e.*, (*a*) square or plain, (*b*) rebated or recessed and (*c*) rebated and splayed.[1]

(*a*) *Square Jambs.*—Examples of square jambs are shown in Figs. 42, 44, 49, 50, 52, 54, 56 and 57 in connection with door and window openings. The stopped end details in Figs. 3 and 4 show the construction of the brickwork.

A frequent cause of dampness in buildings is due to door and window frames being fixed in openings with square jambs on account of the pointing becoming defective and allowing wind and rain to enter.

(*b*) *Rebated Jambs* (see Fig. 8).—These details are shown in both English and double Flemish bond. The plans and sketch C show that a rebated jamb consists of (1) an outer *reveal* or face, (2) a recess and (3) an inner reveal.[2] Window and external door openings are best provided with rebated jambs for the reasons stated below, and applications of these are illustrated in Figs. 43, 48, 55 and 60.

As is implied, the outer reveal is that portion of the jamb which is seen from the outside; it may be 102 mm (see D, M, G, etc., Fig. 8), or it may be 215 mm wide (see Q and R). The recess varies in depth from 56 mm or less—suitable for external doors (see Fig. 48) and casement windows (see Fig. 55) to 102 mm—suitable for windows of the boxed frame type illustrated in Fig. 58. A 56 mm recess is shown at D and that at K is 112 mm deep.

The object of the recess will be appreciated on reference to F, Fig. 8, which indicates by broken lines the relative position of a window frame; the protection afforded by the outer "nib" of brickwork assists effectively in preventing the access of rain into a building between the frame and adjoining brickwork; the bedding and pointing of the frame (see p. 84) affords additional protection.

Rebated jambs having 102 mm outer reveals and 56 mm recesses in 1, $1\frac{1}{2}$ and 2-brick walls built in English bond are detailed at D, E and F, Fig. 8; these are plans of the alternate courses T and U shown at A. The corresponding courses in double Flemish bond are shown a tG, H and J. Jambs with 112 mm recesses are shown in English bond at K, L and M, and in double Flemish bond at N, O and P. Examples of rebated jambs in both English and Flemish bonds having 215 mm outer reveals and 56 mm recesses are detailed at Q, and with 112 mm recesses at R. These details may be associated with the window Z shown at A, Fig. 3, and which is shown in the alternative elevations A and B, Fig. 8; the former indicates 65 mm thick bricks built in English bond and B shows 50 mm thick bricks built in Flemish bond.

Excepting at Q and R, the joints of the brickwork above and below the window opening are indicated by broken lines. Consideration should be given to the size of the bricks to be used and the desired thickness of joints when deciding upon the sizes of door and window openings. The width of an opening should be a multiple of 1 brick for English bond and for double Flemish bond the width should be a multiple of 1 brick up to 440 mm thick and a multiple of $1\frac{1}{2}$ brick afterwards, in order to maintain vertical perpends and the normal face appearance of the bond above and below the opening. Thus, for English bond the size of the opening may be 215 mm, 430 mm, 645 mm, 860 mm, etc., plus the combined thickness of the vertical joints; for thick walls built in double Flemish bond the width may be 430 mm, 748 mm 1075 mm, etc., plus vertical joints; it will be noted that in Fig. 8 the width of the window opening is (3×215 mm)+(4×10 mm)=685 mm for English bond and (2×215 mm)+(3×102·5 mm)+(6×10 mm)=798 mm for Flemish bond. The figured dimensions on working drawings should include the thickness of the joints, although the thickness has not been drawn in the given examples in order to facilitate draughtmanship. The height of openings must conform with the brick courses if an unsatisfactory appearance is to be avoided (see p. 20).

A careful study of the details shows that either king, queen or bevelled closers or half, three-quarter or bevelled bats are employed in order to prevent continuous vertical joints and to obtain the correct face appearance; note that any half bats and header queen closers are placed on the inner face at least 102 mm from the sides of the openings in order to prevent their displacement and to provide a strong support for the ends of the lintels (detailed in Fig. 12).

BRICK CAVITY WALLS[1]

The hollow or cavity wall is now the most usual one for domestic buildings. The simplest form is 275 mm thick having two 102·5 mm thick leaves of brickwork separated by a 70 mm cavity but connected at intervals by wall ties. In comparison with a 215 mm thick wall which uses the same amount of bricks as a 275 mm cavity wall, the latter affords better protection to rain penetration to the inside of the building and greater resistance to heat losses from the room. In order to exclude dampness, the minimum thickness of a solid wall is 328 mm,[2] hence the 275 mm cavity wall is more economical. The prevention of dampness, improved insulation and economy of the cavity wall are substantial advantages.

It is not usual to ventilate the cavity as this seriously affects the insulation

[1] Rebated and splayed jambs are detailed in Chap. I, Vol. II.

[2] Sometimes frames are fixed in *reverse* rebated jambs (see D, Fig. 57).

[1] Some teachers prefer to leave this until the second year of the course. The subject is introduced here and is considered in greater detail in Chap. I, Vol. II. See also p. 4.

[2] There have been, of course, many thousands of houses erected in the past with external walls only 215 mm thick. Whilst much depends on the permeability of the bricks and the soundness of the mortar, such walls on exposed sites are invariably damp internally. In sheltered places in towns the 215 mm wall, in many cases, has been satisfactory; probably in an equal number of cases damp patches have developed.

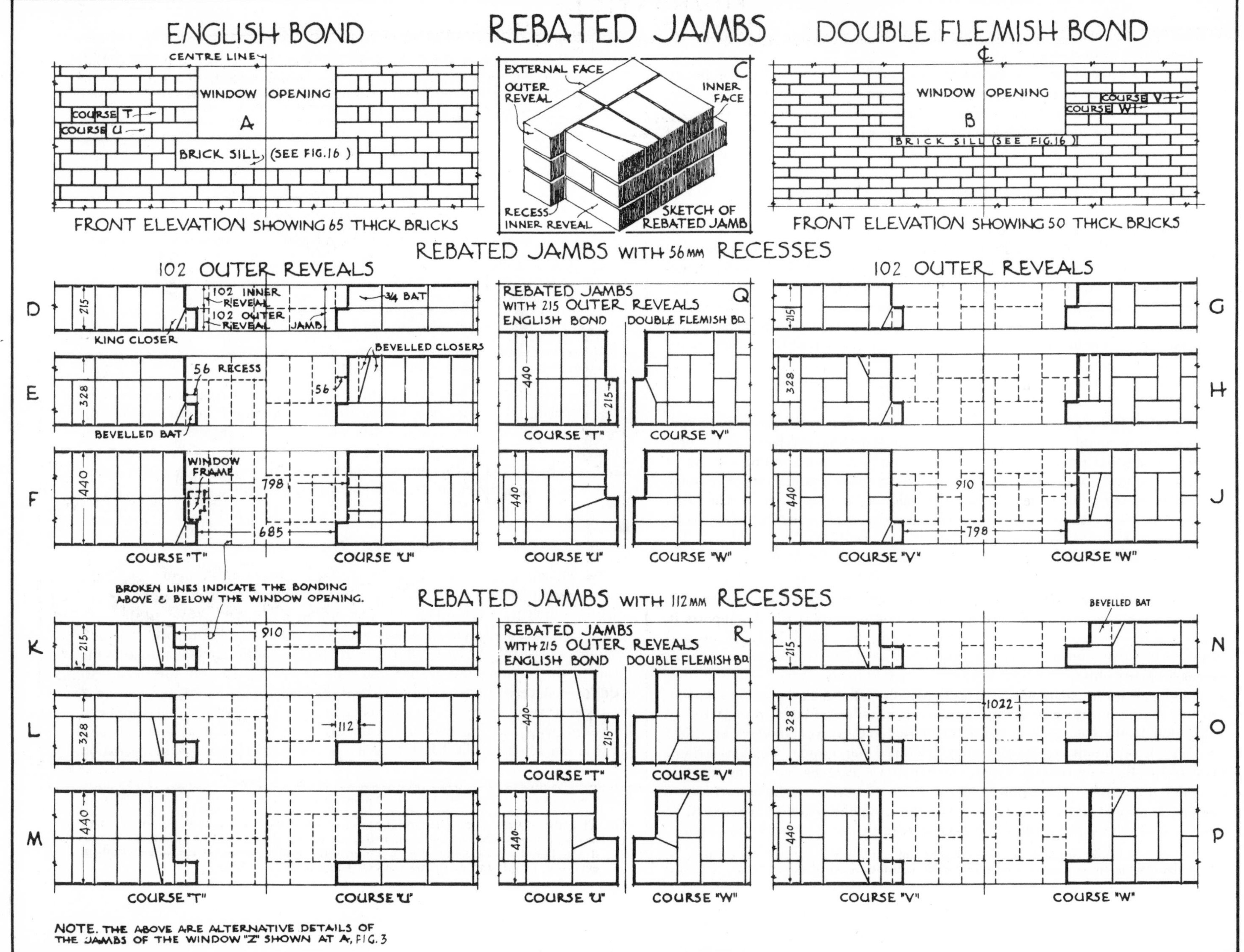

ENGLISH BOND
REBATED JAMBS
DOUBLE FLEMISH BOND
CENTRE LINE
WINDOW OPENING
A
COURSE T
COURSE U
BRICK SILL (SEE FIG.16)
FRONT ELEVATION SHOWING 65 THICK BRICKS
EXTERNAL FACE
OUTER REVEAL
INNER FACE
C
RECESS
INNER REVEAL
SKETCH OF REBATED JAMB
WINDOW OPENING
B
COURSE V
COURSE W
BRICK SILL (SEE FIG.16)
FRONT ELEVATION SHOWING 50 THICK BRICKS
REBATED JAMBS WITH 56MM RECESSES
102 OUTER REVEALS
102 INNER REVEAL
102 OUTER REVEAL
JAMB
3/4 BAT
KING CLOSER
BEVELLED CLOSERS
56 RECESS
BEVELLED BAT
WINDOW FRAME
798
685
COURSE "T"
COURSE "U"
REBATED JAMBS WITH 215 OUTER REVEALS
Q
ENGLISH BOND
DOUBLE FLEMISH BD.
COURSE "T"
COURSE "V"
COURSE "U"
COURSE "W"
102 OUTER REVEALS
910
798
COURSE "V"
COURSE "W"
D
E
F
G
H
J
BROKEN LINES INDICATE THE BONDING ABOVE & BELOW THE WINDOW OPENING.
REBATED JAMBS WITH 112MM RECESSES
910
112
REBATED JAMBS WITH 215 OUTER REVEALS
R
ENGLISH BOND
DOUBLE FLEMISH BD.
BEVELLED BAT
1022
COURSE "T"
COURSE "U"
COURSE "T"
COURSE "V"
COURSE "U"
COURSE "W"
COURSE "V"
COURSE "W"
K
L
M
N
O
P
NOTE. THE ABOVE ARE ALTERNATIVE DETAILS OF THE JAMBS OF THE WINDOW "Z" SHOWN AT A, FIG.3

Figure 8

of the wall, slight ventilation is provided at the drainage gaps left in certain vertical joints as described below.

The ties used to strengthen and aid the stability of the wall are of several kinds, the simplest being made of galvanized wire shaped as a figure of eight. They are put in the bed joints to span the cavity. 450 mm apart vertically, 900 mm apart horizontally and staggered (Fig. 13, Vol. II). At the jambs of openings the vertical spacing of the ties is reduced to 300 mm. It is important to keep the cavity free of mortar droppings which would collect on the ties and make a bridge for dampness to the inner leaf. The bottom of the cavity can be cleaned out if temporary gaps are left at the base of the wall.

Where the cavity is bridged as at lintels, sills and at the jambs of openings, a d.p.c. must be provided. These are shown in Fig. 55. The lintel detail at B shows the felt or lead d.p.c. tucked into the inner leaf and extending downwards to the outside; it is desirable to leave a few of the vertical joints open in the first outer course on the lintel so that water can drain from the cavity. (Similar gaps should also be provided at the base of the wall below the d.p.c.). The detail at E shows the d.p.c. nailed to a groove in the timber sill and passing to the outside of the wall. The rebated jamb plan detail at D also has a d.p.c. which is taken up the full height of the window.

The top of a cavity wall is preferably bridged with one or more courses of 215 mm bricks to increase stability and to enable the roof load to be shared between both leaves (see E, Fig. 39 and G, Fig. 71). The base of the wall is normally constructed as at A, Fig. 10; this has one weakness on damp sites where a timber joisted ground floor is used, water may penetrate the two leaves and spread over the site concrete. This action is eliminated if the cavity at the base of the wall is filled with fine concrete to a distance 150 mm below the d.p.c. (see D, Fig. 10).

FOUNDATIONS

In its widest sense the term foundations may be defined as an expanded base of a wall or pier in addition to the ground or subsoil which supports it. The ground which receives the building is known as a natural foundation, and the extended bases which are constructed of concrete or masonry are called artificial foundations.

An artificial foundation may consist of: (1) a concrete bed only (see A, B and D, Fig. 10), or (2) one or more courses of stone-work (see section DD at B, Fig. 20) which are wider than the wall or pier they support and which are called *footings* or (3) a concrete bed together with footings (see C, Fig. 10). Type (1) is the most common, being known as a *strip foundation.*

The object of a foundation is to distribute the weight to be carried over a sufficient area of bearing surface so as to prevent the subsoil from spreading and to avoid *unequal* settlement of the structure.

Whilst slight settlement or subsidence of a building may, in some cases, be unavoidable, it is essential that any such subsidence shall be uniform. Unequal settlement is the usual cause of cracks and similar defects occurring in walls, floors, etc.

The size and type of foundation depend upon the character of the subsoil and the weight which is transmitted to it. The bearing capacity of a soil means the maximum load per unit of area (usually in terms of kilonewtons/sq. metre) which the ground will support without displacement. As the nature of the soil varies considerably it follows that the capacity of the soil to support loads is also variable.

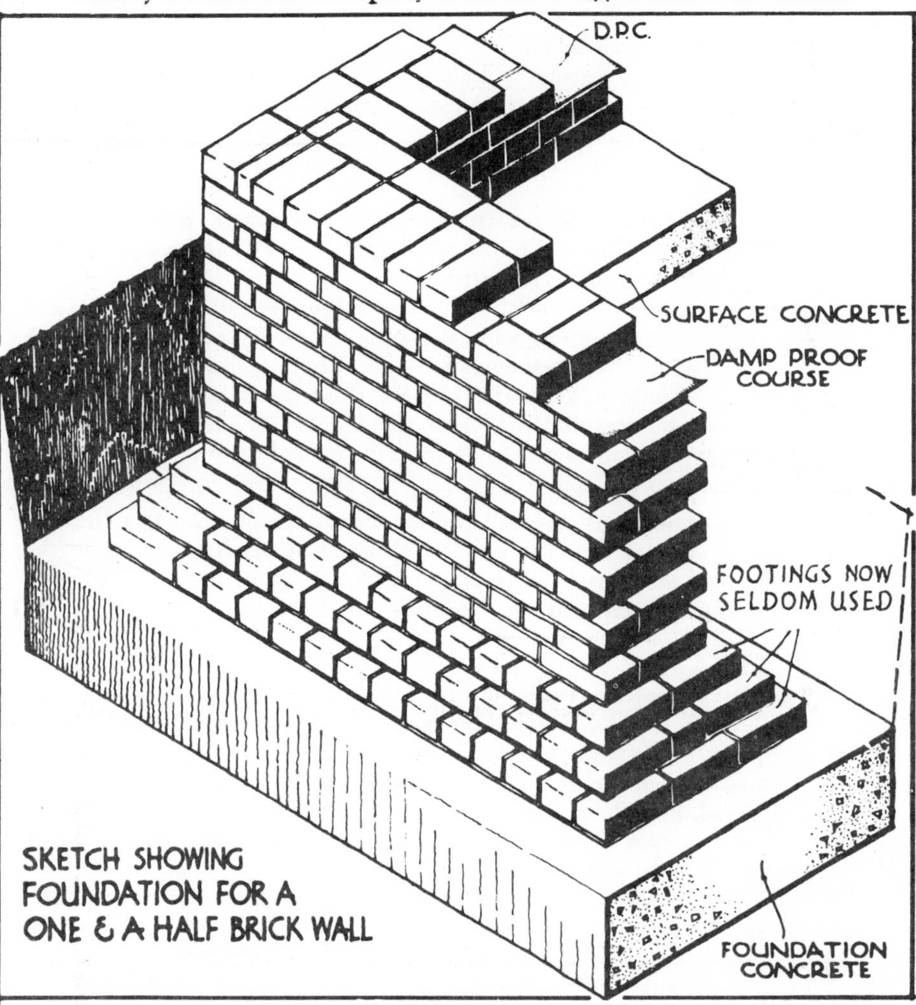

FIGURE 9

This difference in the bearing capacity of soils may be experienced on a single building site, as frequently its character is not exactly the same throughout. Hence it is not always possible to adopt a uniform size of foundation for the whole building, even if the walls and piers may support equal loads.

The design of foundations to support heavy loads is beyond the scope of this volume and the following are typical details only. The requirements of many local authorities in respect to foundations (especially for small buildings which transmit relatively light loads) have been modified considerably within recent years. Briefly, the following are the requirements of the Building Regulations :—

The foundation shall be :—

(1) Constructed to sustain the dead and imposed loads and to transmit these to the ground in such a way that the pressure on it will not cause settlement which would impair the stability of the building or adjoining structures.

(2) Taken sufficiently deep to guard the building against damage by swelling or shrinking of the subsoil.

For domestic buildings where strip foundations are used the concrete shall be composed of 50 kg of cement[1] to 0·1 m³ of fine aggregate and 0·2 m³ of coarse aggregate and the regulations are satisfied if :—
(*a*) There is no wide variation in the type of subsoil beneath the building and there is no weaker type of soil below that on which the foundations rest which would affect stability. (*b*) The foundation width is not less than that summarized below and given fully in Table II, Vol. IV for different subsoils and loadings, and in any case not less than the width of the wall. (*c*) The thickness of the concrete is not less than its projection from the base of the wall or footing and in no case less than 150 mm.

For a two-storey house the wall load is usually not more than 33 kN/m; the foundation width for different subsoils would then be: Rock, equal to the wall width; compact gravel and sand or stiff clay, 300 mm; loose sand, 600 mm (as A, Fig. 10); soft clay, 650 mm; very soft clay, 850 mm.

Examples of foundations are given in Fig. 10; they should be at a minimum depth, in this country, of 450 mm so as to be unaffected by frost.

The one at A shows a typical strip foundation on loose sand where the minimum width is 600 mm for a 275 mm wall; this necessitates a 162·5 mm thick strip to comply with (*c*) above.

450 mm is about the minimum width of shallow trench that can be excavated by hand, but where machine excavation (see Chap. I, Vol. IV) is used, the 305 mm wide type at B is satisfactory in compact sand or stiff clay; the whole of the trench is filled with concrete.

The type at D has to be used on soft clay which is liable to expansion and contraction due to the variation in water content. At a depth of 915 mm this action is normally absent in the U.K.

The one at C illustrates the use of a course of brick footings which were often used in earlier days (when cement was not the reliable product it is today) to give a gradual spread of the load. The rule illustrated is a useful one and

[1] From 1 January 1971 cement is available in 50 kg. bags.

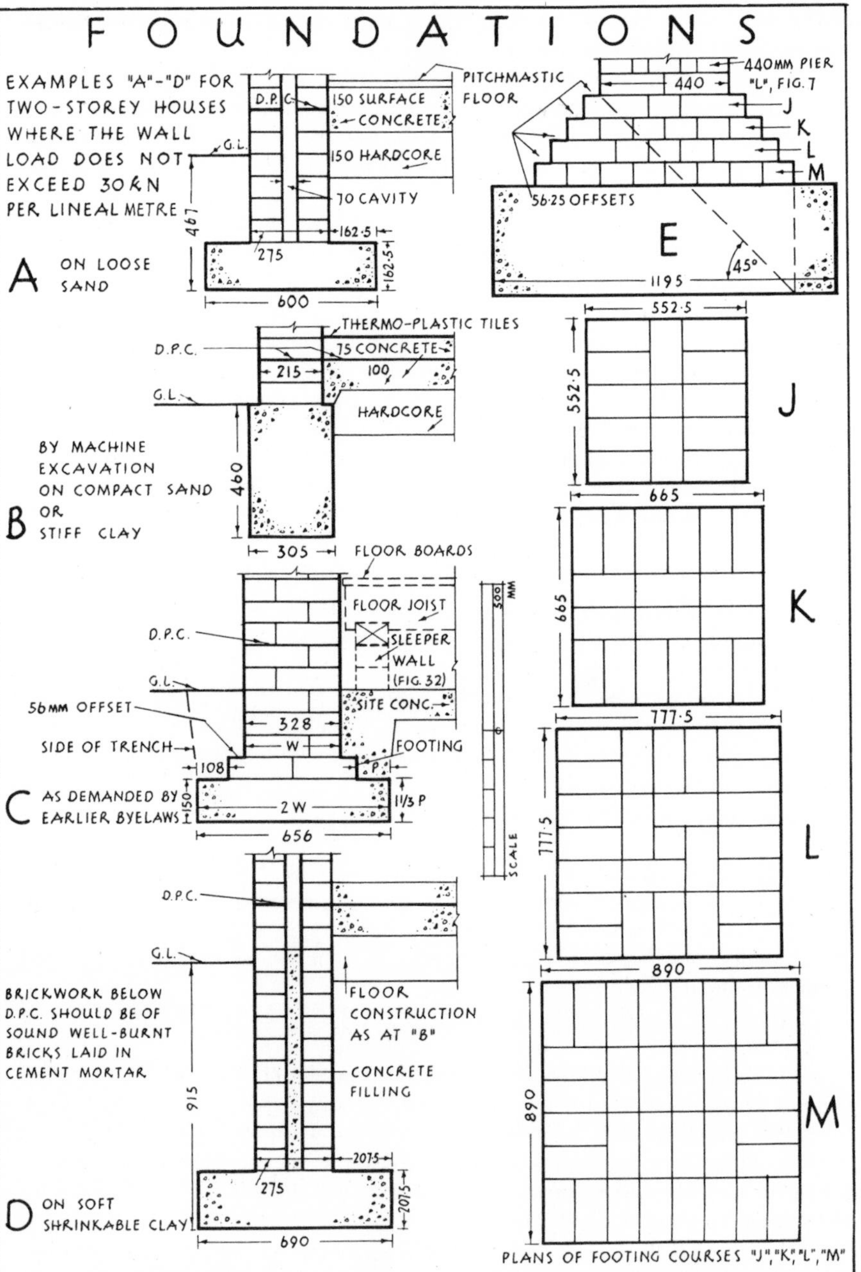

FIGURE 10

consisted of making the concrete foundation twice the wall width and of a thickness equal to one and one-third its projection from the footing.

The depth of the foundations varies with the character of the subsoil and the relative importance of the work. Clay soils are liable to expand and contract, and such movement may cause damage to the foundations unless they are placed at a sufficient depth; if such sites are waterlogged it may be desirable to adopt 900 mm deep foundations. It is not necessary to exceed 450 mm depth in many situations; this is the minimum to prevent damage by frost. All brickwork below the ground level should be built in cement mortar in order to increase its stability, and engineering bricks are preferred.

The construction of the floor shown by broken lines at C is described on pp. 58 to 64.

Pier Foundations.—An example of a foundation suitable for a detached pier (as illustrated in Fig. 7) is shown at E, J, K, L and M, Fig. 10. Whilst footings may be dispensed with and the foundation designed in accordance with the Building Regulations, it should be noted that brick footings serve a useful purpose in gradually transmitting the concentrated load from the pier to the concrete.

Timbering to foundation trenches is described on pp. 79–80.

DAMP PROOF COURSES

One of the chief essentials in building is that the structure shall be dry. A damp building is unhealthy to those who occupy it, it causes damage to the contents of the building, and it gradually impairs the parts of the structure affected. There are various causes of dampness in walls, the chief of which are : (1) moisture rising up the walls from the adjacent ground, (2) rain passing down from the tops of walls, (3) rain beating against the walls which may absorb the water to such an extent as to show dampness on the internal faces and (4) the absorption of water from defective rain-water pipes.

With reference to the first cause, the student of Building Science (a subject which normally forms part of a grouped course in Building) will have probably studied the structure of a porous material such as a brick; he may have carried out tests to determine its *porosity* (the percentage of its pore space), relative *permeability* (its capacity to permit the passage of water through it), and the amount of water that it will absorb. He will appreciate that brickwork below the ground level will draw the moisture from the ground and may impart it from one course to another for a considerable height. The amount of moisture absorbed depends upon the water content of the soil and the quality of the bricks, mortar and workmanship.

To prevent water absorbed from the soil rising and causing dampness in the wall and any adjacent woodwork and plaster, a continuous layer of an impervious material is provided. This layer is known as a horizontal damp proof course (d.p.c.) The position of such a course varies from 150 to 300 mm above the ground level (see sections in Fig. 10). The level should not be less than 150 mm otherwise soil (forming flower beds and the like) may be deposited against the external face of a wall at a greater height than the impervious layer and thus water may be transmitted from it to the wall above the damp proof course.

Some of the materials used to form horizontal damp proof courses are :—

Asphalt.—The raw material is a chocolate-coloured limestone which is impregnated with bitumen or natural pitch. It is quarried and imported from the West Indies (Lake Trinidad), France (Seyssel), Switzerland (Val de Travers) and Germany. Fine grit in varying proportions is added and completely incorporated with the asphalt at a vey high temperature, after which it is cast into blocks (weighing about 25 kg each). These are received on the site, when they are re-heated and applied in the following manner : Wood battens are fixed horizontally along both faces of the wall with their top edges usually 13 mm above the top of the course of the wall which is to receive the asphalt. The heated material is placed on the wall between the battens and finished off by means of hand floats to the top of the battens. The asphalt is kept slightly back from the external face of the wall so that it may be pointed with cement mortar after the wall has been completed; this covers the dark line of the asphalt and assists in preventing the asphalt from being squeezed out and discolouring the brickwork, especially if it is subjected to intense action of the sun. Asphalt forms an excellent damp proof course, it being impervious and indestructible; in addition it does not fracture, if, on account of unequal settlement, cracks are caused in the brickwork.

Fibrous Asphalt Felt.—There are many varieties of this damp proof course, one of which consists of a base of tough hessian (woven jute cloth) or felt which is impregnated with and covered by a layer of hot natural bitumen, and sanded on the surface or covered with talc to prevent the layers from adhering to each other. It is obtained in rolls, 22 m long and in various widths from 102·5 mm to 915 mm. In laying it in position, a thin layer of mortar is spread on the brickwork and the damp proof course is bedded on it. It should be lapped 75 mm where joints occur and lapped full width at all crossings and angles. It should be pointed in cement mortar.

This type of damp proof course is extensively used, it being easily handled and, provided it is adequately impregnated with bitumen and obtained from a reputable manufacturer, it forms a thoroughly reliable damp-resisting material. Some of the cheaper varieties are practically worthless; they are comparatively thin and both the bases and the bitumen are of inferior quality; such should be avoided. It is not suitable for certain classes of stone walling, *i.e.*, Lake District Masonry (described on p. 45), as the weight of the ragged undressed stones cuts it and produces defects through which moisture may pass to cause dampness.

Slates.—Such a damp proof course consists of two layers of sound slates embedded in cement mortar composed of 1 : 3 cement and sand. A layer of mortar is spread over the brickwork, upon which the first layer of slates is bedded with butt joints; more mortar is spread over these slates and the second layer of slates is laid in position so as to form a half lap bond with the first course of slates (when the slates are said to " break joint "); the next course of brickwork is then bedded in cement mortar on the top layer of slates. The slates must extend the full thickness of the wall, be at least 215 mm long, and be neatly pointed in cement mortar. It is a very efficient damp proof course and has been used on important buildings.[1] It is used in connection with Lake District walling and similar construction as it is not damaged by the sharp edges of the rough stones. This damp proof course is liable to be broken if unequal settlement occurs, causing water to be absorbed through the cracks.

Lead.—This is a costly but very effective damp proof course. It consists of a layer of sheet lead (see Chapter VI) which weighs from 3 to 8 lb. per sq. ft.[2] embedded in lime mortar.[3] It is either lapped as described for fibrous asphalt felt or the joints may be welted (see p. 144). The mortar does not adhere to it readily unless the lead is well scored (scratched).

Another variety of this class of damp proof course consists of a continuous core of light lead (weighing only 1·22 kg/m^2) covered both sides with bituminous felt which is surfaced with talc to prevent sticking of the folds. It is made in two or three grades of varying widths and in rolls which are in 8 m lengths. It is an excellent damp proof course, especially for damp sites, and whilst it is more expensive than the above, it is more durable.

Copper.—This is another excellent damp proof course. The copper should be at least 0·022 mm thick, lapped or jointed as described for lead, and embedded in lime or cement mortar.

Blue Staffordshire Bricks.—These provide effective damp proof courses. They are built in two to four courses in cement mortar; the colour of the bricks may render them unacceptable for general application.

Plastic.—This is a relatively new type of d.p.c. material. It is made of black polythene, 0·5 or 1 mm thick in the usual walling widths and roll lengths of 30 m.

The second cause of dampness stated on p. 17 (*i.e.*, rain passing down from the tops of walls) may be prevented by the provision of a horizontal damp proof course either immediately below the top course of brickwork or some little distance below it. Thus, in the case of boundary walls, the damp proof course may be placed immediately under the coping (see Figs. 17 and 27), and parapet walls may be protected by continuing the cover flashing (see p. 143) the full thickness of the wall. Similarly, a horizontal d.p.c. should be placed in a chimney stack at its junction with a roof.

Vertical damp proof courses which are necessary to exclude dampness in basement, etc., walls are described in Chap. I, Vol. II.

[1] Horizontal slate damp proof courses are used in both the Anglican and Roman Catholic cathedrals at Liverpool. In addition, lead and blue Staffordshire bricks are used in connection with the latter building.

[2] *I.e.*, 13·5 to 35 kg/m^2. Despite the change to metric units lead is still made in these Imperial weights but specified as "No. 3 lead, No. 4 lead etc.," according to its Imperial weight (see p. 142).

[3] Certain mortars, especially cement mortars, act upon lead and ultimately destroy it; such should therefore not be used as a bedding material for lead damp proof courses.

SURFACE OR SITE CONCRETE

The area of a building below wood floors must be covered with an impervious material[1] in order to exclude dampness. The material used may be concrete or asphalt. The Building Regulations require a 100 mm layer of concrete consisting of 50 kg of cement to not more than 0·1 m^3 of fine aggregate (sand) and 0·2 m^3 of coarse aggregate (broken brick, stone, etc.), laid on a bed of broken bricks, clinker, etc. The concrete should be well surfaced with the back of the shovel (known as "spade finished"); its top surface must not be below the level of the ground outside the wall of the building. Surface concrete is shown in Fig. 10. Besides excluding dampness, surface concrete prevents the growth of vegetable matter and the admission of ground air.

Dwarf 102·5 mm walls, known as *sleeper* and *fender* walls (see Fig. 32), are sometimes constructed on the surface concrete (see C, Fig 10, and R, Fig. 32) or they may have the usual concrete foundations (see Q, Fig. 32). The site concrete adjoining the walls may be finished as shown at C, Fig. 10 (this is the best method if a separate sleeper wall as shown is to be supported), or at A and B, Fig. 10.

Offsets.—These are narrow horizontal surfaces which have been formed by reducing the thickness of walls. C, Fig. 10 shows 56·25 mm offsets. Wider offsets than these may be required to support floor joists, roof timbers, and the like. Walls of tall buildings are formed with offsets; thus a 15 m high wall may be 440 mm thick at the base, 215 mm thick at the top, with an intermediate thickness of 328 mm, and the 112 mm wide ledges or shelves so formed are termed offsets. A broken vertical section through a portion of such a wall is shown at A, Fig. 11. The 112 mm offsets support horizontal wood members called wall plates which receive the ends of the floor joists (see p. 60).

The plan at B, Fig. 11, shows an alternative and cheaper method of supporting wall plates than at A. In the latter the increased thickness of the wall at the base to form the offset is continuous for the full length of the wall, whereas at B the wall plate rests upon small piers which are usually not more than 790 mm apart. Two methods of forming these piers are shown at C and D, the former being the stronger as it is bonded into the main wall and the latter is not. The foundation for pier D is strengthened if the site concrete is formed to occupy the space at W.

Corbels.—These are similar to offsets except that the ledges are formed by oversailing or projecting courses (see Fig. 11). They are constructed to support floor beams, lintels, etc. As a load carried by a corbel tends to overturn the wall, certain precautions are taken to ensure a stable structure; these are: (1) the maximum projection of the corbel must not exceed the thickness of the wall, (2) each corbel course must not project more than 56·25 mm, (3) headers

[1] Vegetable soil or turf covering a site should be removed as a preliminary building operation; the excavated soil may be spread over that portion of the site set apart for the garden, etc., and the turf may be stacked (rotted turf is a valuable manure). The depth of soil removed varies from 150 to 230 mm and the site concrete is laid on the exposed surface. The omission of the concrete has been a frequent cause of dry rot (see p. 57).

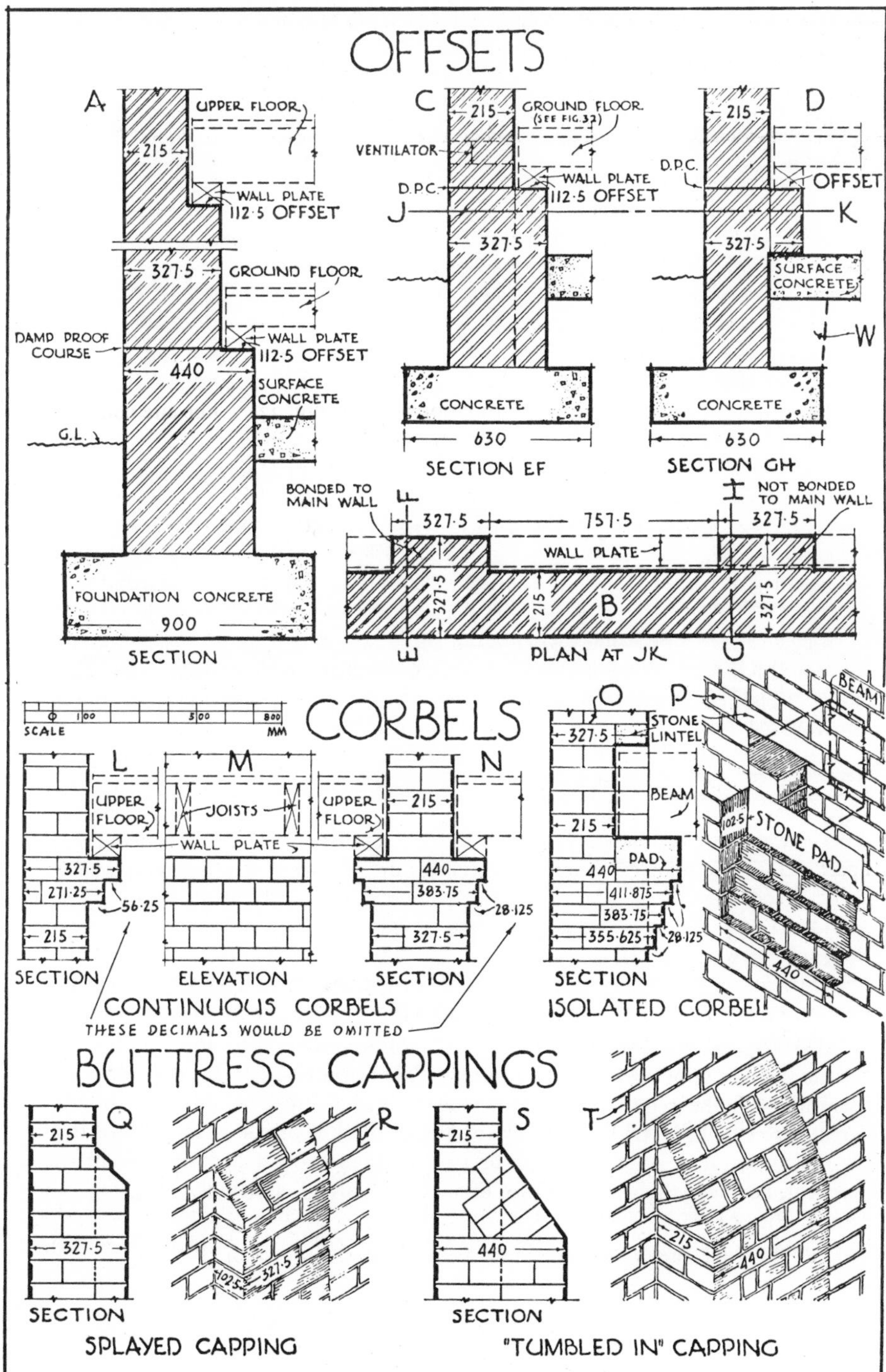

Figure 11

must be used as they are more adequately tailed into the wall than stretchers, and (4) only sound bricks and workmanship should be employed. The corbels shown at L, M and N are continuous and that at O (with the sketch at P) is an example of an isolated or non-continuous corbel. The latter is used to support concentrated loads (as transmitted from large floor beams) and the stone pad is provided to distribute the load more effectively.

Oversailing Courses.—These are frequently employed as decorative features, as for example in the construction of *cornices* (a crowning member of a wall), *string courses* (provided between the base and top of a wall), *eaves* (top of a wall adjacent to a roof) and *chimney stacks* (the upper portion of brickwork which encloses chimney flues—see Figs. 38 and 75). Simple examples of brick oversailing courses are shown at E, Fig. 17, D, Fig. 38, and J, Fig. 70. Stone cornices etc., are detailed in Figs. 24 and 26.

Buttress Cappings.—Buttresses have been referred to on p. 13. These are usually completed with simple cappings (see Fig. 11). The section at Q shows the capping to consist of two courses of splay bricks of the type illustrated at R and S, Fig. 2; a sketch of this capping is shown at R. The sketch at T shows another weathered capping formed of ordinary bricks which are tilted or tumbled into the wall; the section at S shows the cutting of the bricks which is involved.

As mentioned on p. 13, the vertical sides of doorways and window openings are known as jambs. The top or head of such an opening consists of a *lintel* or an *arch*, or both, and the bottom of a window opening is called a *sill* whilst the bottom of a door opening is usually provided with one or more steps or *threshold*.

LINTELS

A lintel is a member of wood, brick or concrete which is fixed horizontally and used to support the structure above the opening. Most lintels now are of reinforced concrete.

In the class in Building Science the student will study the behaviour of lintels or beams when loaded. Experiments will show that if a wood beam is loaded as indicated at T, Fig. 12, it will change its shape as the load increases. The beam will bend, and if it is ultimately broken it will be seen that the fibres of the upper portion are crushed and those of the lower portion are torn apart; the bending action tends to contract or compress the upper fibres and to stretch the lower fibres. Hence the statement that the " upper part is subjected to a stress called *compression* and the lower portion to a stress known as *tension* "; the fibres along the centre of the beam are neither in compression nor tension and this horizontal plane is called the *neutral axis*. In addition, the load tends to produce either vertical, horizontal or diagonal cracks which indicate failure in *shear*. Lintels must of course be sufficiently strong to resist failure by compression, tension, shear and deflection.

Wood Lintels.—These are usually of redwood (see p. 59). The size depends upon the thickness of the wall, the span (distance between opposite jambs) and the weight to be supported. The depth is approximately one-twelfth of the span with a minimum of 75 mm; the width may equal the full thickness of the wall—as is necessary for internal door openings (see B, Fig. 52)—or the width of the inner reveal as shown at B, Fig. 12. A further example of a wood lintel is illustrated in Fig. 44.

Built-up lintels may be used for larger spans; the section at B, Fig. 12, shows such a lintel which comprises three 175 mm by 75 mm pieces bolted together with 13 mm diameter bolts near the ends and at every 380 mm of its length; a part elevation is shown at C and indicates the bolts which are provided with the necessary nuts and washers (see J, Fig. 80). An alternative to this built-up lintel is shown at H; this consists of two 175 mm by 50 mm pieces (which bridge the opening and have a 150 mm bearing or *wall-hold* at each end) and 50 mm thick packing or distance pieces at the ends and at 380 mm centres; holes are bored through the continuous pieces and packing pieces through which bolts are passed to secure them and ensure that the pieces will act as one unit; the elevation of lintel H is similar to that at C except that the packing pieces would be indicated by broken lines at each bolt, as shown at J.

The ends of the lintels have a 175 mm wall-hold and are bedded on mortar so as to ensure a level and firm bearing. Wood lintels afford a ready means of securing the heads of door and window frames (see p. 98).

Brick Lintels.—As is implied, a brick lintel is a horizontal member consisting of bricks which are generally laid on end and occasionally on edge. It is a relatively weak form of construction and is quite unsuited to support heavy loads. They should therefore be used to span small openings only (unless they are to receive additional support as explained later) and the span should not exceed 900 mm.

A section and part elevation of a brick lintel are shown at A and B, Fig. 12. Cement mortar should be used, and pressed bricks having a frog on each bed are better than wire-cuts. The term *joggled brick lintel* is sometimes applied to this type when bricks having frogs are used, the joggle or notch being formed by the widened joint at each frog; the joggle assists in resisting the sliding or shearing action to which the lintel is subjected.

The lintel is constructed on a temporary wood support known as a turning piece (see p. 80); mortar is spread over the lower, back and front edges of each brick before being placed in position; when all of the bricks have been laid, grout (see p. 2) is poured through the holes which have previously been formed at the top until each frog is completely filled with the liquid mortar; M, Fig. 12, shows a section through a brick-on-end lintel with the frog and the hole at the top indicated by broken lines. If grouting is not adopted care must be taken to ensure that the joints are properly filled and flushed with mortar.

The depth of the lintel depends upon the size of the opening and the appearance required; it varies from 102·5 mm to 215 mm. For the sake of appearance it is essential that the top of the lintel shall coincide with a horizontal joint of the general walling (see A and G, Fig. 12), otherwise a partial course of brickwork would be required between the top of the lintel and the bed joint of the wall above it; *such a split course is most unsightly.* A common depth is that which is equal to two courses of the adjoining brickwork (see G); one end of each brick is carefully removed (usually with a hammer and bolster—see 35, Fig. 19) and the bricks are placed in position with the cut ends uppermost; the grouting operation is facilitated as the frogs are exposed at the top.

An alternative method of forming the ends of a brick lintel, which has a somewhat stronger appearance, is shown at F in the elevation A, Fig. 12.

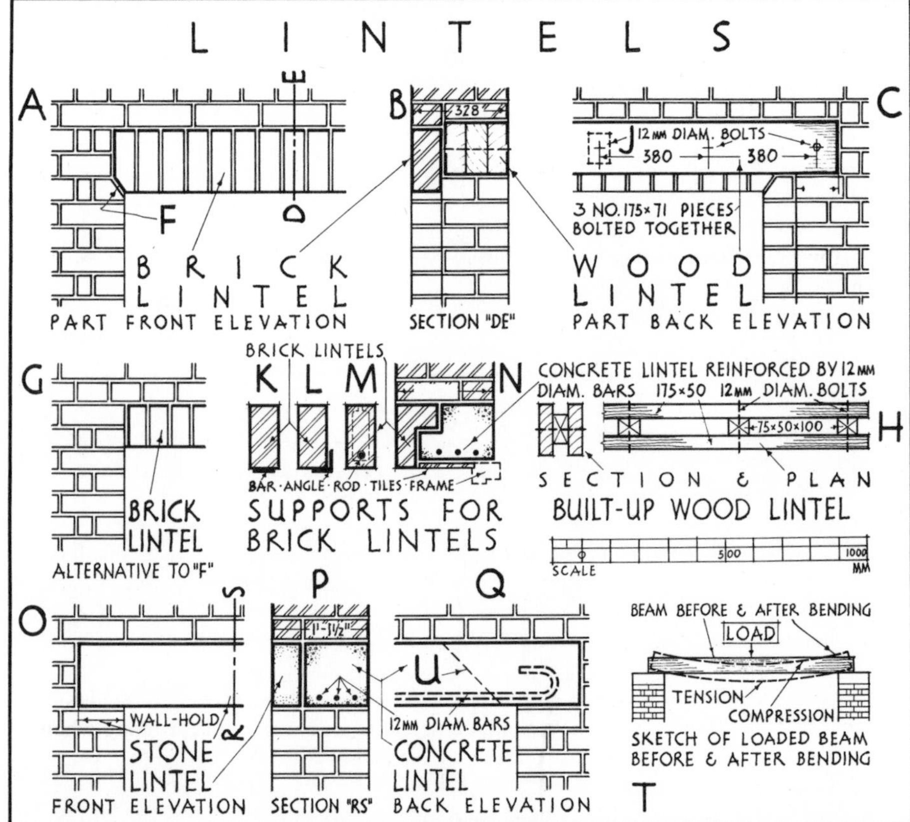

FIGURE 12

Brick lintels are sometimes known as " soldier arches " presumably because of the upright appearance of the bricks. This is a misnomer, for such does not comply with the requirements of a true arch as defined below. Incidentally great care should be taken to ensure that each brick is placed absolutely vertical as the appearance is spoilt if one or two of them show a departure from the vertical, however slight. Examples of such an " arch " are shown at A, Fig. 44, and B, Fig. 54.

Supports for Brick Lintels.—Additional support must be provided if a brick lintel is required for a greater span than 900 mm. Alternative methods of such reinforcement are shown in section at K, L, M and N, Fig. 12. At K a 75 mm by 10 mm steel flat bar (see Fig. 80), having a 150 mm bearing at each end, is used. For spans exceeding 1 800 mm it is recommended that one of the following should be used: (*a*) a steel angle (see Fig. 80) having 150 mm bearings as shown at L and in detail W, Fig. 54, or (*b*) purpose-made bricks supported by a reinforced concrete lintel as indicated at N or (*c*) a reinforced brick lintel which is illustrated at M. The latter consists of a 20 mm diameter steel rod which is threaded through the bricks before they have been grouted; each end of the rod is bedded 150 mm into the wall; the bricks used for this purpose are holed during the moulding process before being burnt, the centre of each hole being approximately 38 mm from the underside of the lintel. The exposed surfaces of the above flat bar and angle may be rendered inconspicuous by painting them to conform with the colours of the bricks; alternatively they may be completely covered by the door and window frames; the soffit or underside of the concrete lintel at N between the brick lintel and the door frame may be covered by bedding 12 mm thick tiles to the concrete as shown.

It is a common practice for small spans to bed brick lintels directly upon the heads of the door and window frames; such frames should be set back for not more than 25 mm from the external face of the wall (see C, Fig. 44).

Stone Lintels or Heads.—These are rectangular blocks of stone of varying thickness and depth; the latter should be at least 215 mm. It should course with the adjacent brickwork as shown at O, Fig. 12. Additional examples are shown in Figs. 22, 24, 58 and 61.

Concrete Lintels.—A suitable mix of concrete consists of 1 part Portland cement, 2 parts sand and 4 parts gravel or broken brick or stone of 20 mm gauge. The lintel may be cast *in situ* (in position) or precast (formed and allowed to set before being fixed); the former is cast in a wood mould (with 32 to 38 mm thick bottom and sides) which is removed when the concrete has set. The precast method is more often employed as the lintels can be formed in the wood moulds well in advance to allow them being sufficiently matured for fixing when required and the construction of the walling above them may be continued immediately after fixing. As concrete is comparatively weak in tension, the use of plain concrete lintels should be limited to spans not exceeding 900 mm and not used to carry point loads, otherwise failures may occur which are usually due to shear and which may produce fractures such as that indicated by the broken line U at Q, Fig. 12. If this span is to be exceeded, the lintel must be strengthened by using mild steel bars or some other form of steel reinforcement. A simple type of ***reinforced concrete lintel*** is shown at P and Q; the number and size of the reinforcement depend upon the span, width and load to be supported; the steel is placed in the moulds and at about 25 mm from the bottom; the concrete is poured in, care being taken in packing it round the reinforcement. The ends of the bars are hooked as shown in order to increase the bond or grip between them and the concrete. If precast, the top of the lintel should be marked so that the fixer will bed it with the reinforcement lowermost. Other examples of a reinforced concrete lintel are shown at A and C, Fig. 25, and B, K and O, Fig. 58.

An example of a boot-shaped lintel is shown at B, Fig. 55.

ARCHES

An arch is a structure comprising a number of relatively small units[1] such as bricks or masonry blocks which are wedge-shaped, joined together with mortar, and spanning an opening to support the weight above. Because of their wedge-like form, the units support each other, the load tends to make them compact and enables them to transmit the pressure downwards to their supports.

Terms.—The technical terms applied to an arch and adjacent structure are shown in the isometric sketch (Fig. 13); the following is a brief description :—

Voussoirs.—The wedge-shaped bricks or blocks of stone which comprise an arch; the last voussoir to be placed in position is usually the central one and is known as the *key brick* or *key stone*; it is sometimes emphasized by making it larger and projecting it above and below the outlines of the arch. The key shown in the sketch consists of several 12 or 20 mm tiles.

Ring, Rim or Ring Course.—The circular course or courses comprising the arch. The arch in Fig. 13 consists of three half-brick rings, the one at D, Fig. 15, has two half-brick rings, and those at E and F, Fig. 15, and F and J, Fig. 41, have each a one-brick ring.

Extrados or Back.—The external curve of the arch.

Intrados.—The inner curve of the arch.

Soffit.—The inner or under *surface* of the arch; in some localities the terms " soffit " and " intrados " are accepted as meaning the same.

Abutments.—The portions of the wall which support the arch.

Skewbacks.—The inclined or splayed surfaces of the abutments prepared to receive the arch and from which the arch springs (see A, Fig. 15).

Springing Points.—The points at the intersection between the skewbacks and the intrados (see A, Fig. 15).

Springing Line.—The horizontal line joining the two springing points.

Springers.—The lowest voussoirs immediately adjacent to the skewbacks.

Crown.—The highest point of the extrados.

Haunch.—The lower half of the arch between the crown and a skewback.

Span.—The horizontal distance between the reveals of the supports.

Rise.—The vertical distance between the springing line and the highest point of the intrados.

Centre (*or Striking Point*) *and Radius* (see Fig. 13).

Depth or Height.—The distance between the extrados and intrados.

Thickness.—The horizontal distance between and at right angles to the front and back faces; it is sometimes referred to as the *width* or *breadth* of the soffit.

[1] Steel and reinforced concrete arches of large span are adopted in bridge construction.

In some districts the term " thickness " is considered to have the same meaning as " depth "; to remove any doubt, the arch at A, Fig. 15, would be specified as being a " flat gauged arch, 290 mm deep with 102·5 mm wide soffit, to a 1135 mm opening."

Bed Joints.—The joints between the voussoirs which radiate from the centre.

Spandril.—The triangular walling enclosed by the extrados, a vertical line from the top of a skewback, and a horizontal line from the crown; when arches adjoin, as in Fig. 13, the spandril is bounded by the two outer curves and the horizontal line between the two crowns.

Impost.—The projecting course or courses at the upper part of a pier or other abutment to stress the springing line; sometimes moulded and known as a *cap* (see Fig. 13, and D, Fig. 15).

Plinth.—The projecting brickwork at the base of a wall or pier which gives the appearance of additional strength; also known as a *base*.

Arcade.—A series of arches, adjoining each other, supporting a wall and being supported by piers.

Classification of Arches.—Arches are classified according to (*a*) their shape, and (*b*) the materials and workmanship employed in their construction.

(*a*) The more familiar forms of arches are either flat, segmental or semicircular, whilst others which are not so generally adopted are of the semi-elliptical and pointed types.[1]

(*b*) The voussoirs may consist of either (1) rubber bricks, (2) purpose-made bricks, (3) ordinary or standard bricks cut to a wedge shape and known as axed bricks or (4) standard uncut bricks. The following is a brief description of these bricks :—

1. *Rubber Bricks, Rubbers, Cutters or Malms.*—These are soft bricks, obtainable in various sizes, and of a warm red or orange colour. They can be readily sawn and rubbed to the desired shape. They are used in the construction of *gauged arches* (see below).

2. *Purpose-made Bricks.*—These are specially hand-moulded to the required shape and are used for good class work in the construction of *purpose-made brick arches* (see below). Owing to the standardized form and size of many arches, stocks of the more commonly used purpose-made voussoirs are carried by the larger manufacturers, and delivery is thereby expedited; such bricks are usually machine-pressed.

3. *Ordinary Bricks Cut to Wedge Shape.*—These are standard bricks which have been roughly cut to the required wedge shape by the use of the bolster and dressed off with a *scutch* or axe (see 34, Fig. 19). They are used in the construction of *axed brick arches* (see p. 24).

4. *Ordinary Standard Uncut Bricks.*—When such bricks are used in the construction of arches, the bed joints are not of uniform thickness, but are wedge-shaped. They are used for *rough brick arches* (see p. 24).

Flat, Straight or Camber Arch.—There are three varieties of this type, *i.e.*,

[1] These are illustrated in Fig. 19, Vol. II.

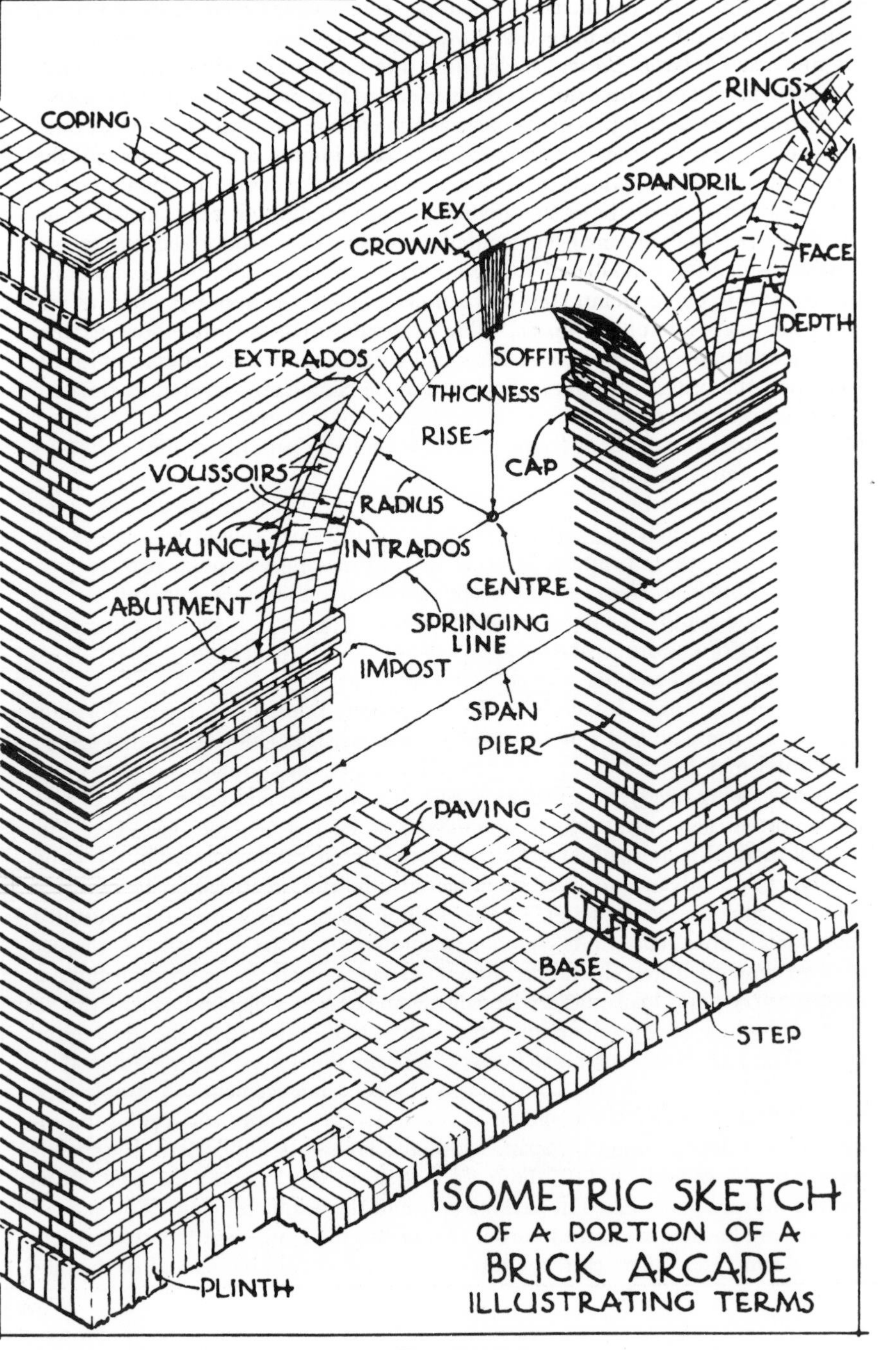

FIGURE 13

(*a*) gauged flat arch, (*b*) purpose-made flat arch and (*c*) axed brick flat arch, depending upon the class of bricks and labours used in their construction.

(a) *Gauged Flat or Camber Arch* (see A and C, Fig. 15).—Rubbers are used. The extrados is horizontal and the intrados is given a slight curvature or *camber* by providing a rise of 1·5 to 3 mm per 300 mm of span; thus the arch at A would have a rise of approximately 12 mm. The reason for the camber is to avoid the appearance of sagging which is produced if the intrados is perfectly horizontal and which defect would be accentuated if the slightest settlement occurred. The angle of the skewbacks may be 60° (as shown at A and C) or the amount of skewback (the horizontal distance between the springing point and the top of the skewback) may equal 38 mm per 300 mm of span per 300 mm depth of arch (as shown at A, Fig. 48, and A, Fig. 54). The adoption of the latter rule gives a more pleasing appearance (compare A and C, Fig. 15, with A, Figs. 48 and 54); if it had been applied to the two arches in Fig. 15, the amount of skewback at A would be $38\times\frac{1135}{300}\times\frac{290}{300} = 139$ mm, and at C it would be $38\times\frac{685}{300}\times\frac{290}{300}=84$ as compared with 167 mm, which is common to both arches when the skewback has a slope of 60°.

This type of arch is not very strong and should be limited to spans of from 1 220 to 1 520 mm unless they are strengthened by means of a steel bar or angle, as described on p. 21. Observe that in each case the extrados coincides with a horizontal joint of the adjacent walling and thus a split course is avoided (see p. 20); the intrados of the arch at A, Fig. 15, also coincides with a bed joint; this is not always desirable, as the brick at T is difficult to cut on account of the sharp edge produced; such is avoided if the intrados comes midway up the course (see S, Fig. 15).

" Gauge " means " measure " and a characteristic of gauged work is its exactness. The bricks are accurately shaped as described below and the bed joints are very thin, being as fine as 0·8 mm, although a thickness of joint varying from 3 to 6 mm is much favoured. Such accurate work is possible by the use of rubbers and a jointing material known as *putty lime* (lime chalk which has been well slaked, worked up to a consistency resembling thick cream and passed through a fine sieve).

When drawing this arch to scale, the student should note that all bed joints of the voussoirs radiate towards the centre and that the 75 mm measurements (or 50 mm if the general walling is constructed of 50 mm bricks) are set off along the *extrados*.

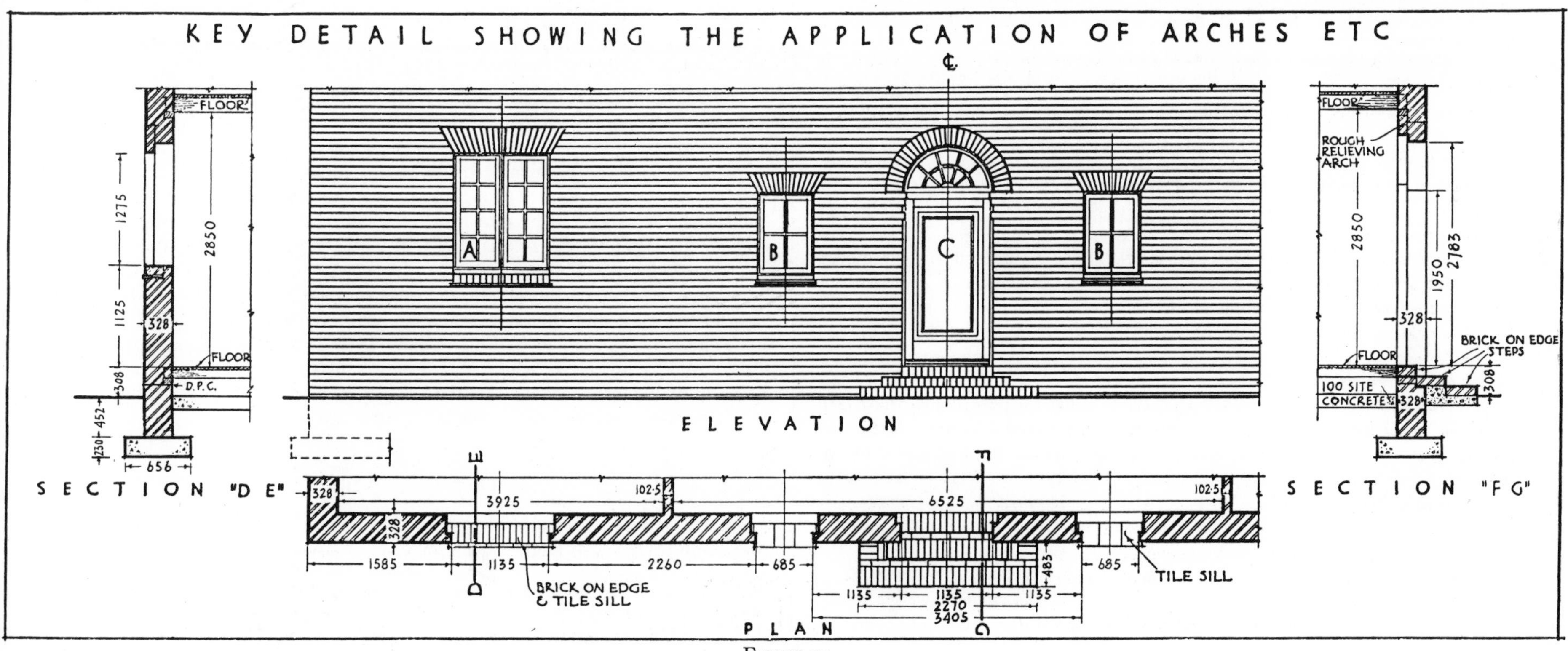

FIGURE 14

Students make a common mistake in measuring off along the intrados. When the bricks are 65 mm thick at the extrados, satisfactory jointing results if the number of voussoirs in the arch when divided by 4 gives a remainder of 1, *i.e.*, 13, 17, 21, etc.

Construction of Arch.—In order that the rubbers shall be correctly shaped, a full-size drawing of the arch (showing the voussoirs and joints) is prepared and thin pieces of zinc, called *templets*, are cut to the shape of the voussoirs shown on the drawing. The *bevels* or inclinations are marked on each voussoir by tranferring them from the templet which is placed on it. The voussoirs are then sawn to shape with each saw-cut parallel and near to the marks. They are finally dressed down to the marks by rubbing each cut surface on a slab of hard stone or by using a rasp (see p. 128). A 150 mm long groove (about 13 mm deep and 25 mm wide) is formed on each bed to form a key for the mortar and each rubber is numbered in accordance with the corresponding number on the drawing for guidance to the bricklayer.

The wall at each side of the opening will have been built and the skewbacks prepared to receive the arch, as indicated by the thick outline N shown at A, Fig. 15. The *turning piece* (see A, D and E, Fig. 41) upon which the arch is to be constructed will have been carefully fixed in correct position. When very fine joints are required, each voussoir is dipped into the putty and its bed covered, any putty in the groove is removed, and the brick is placed in position by pressing the bed coated with putty against the adjacent brick. When all of the voussoirs have been placed in position, cement grout is poured into the joggles formed by the bed grooves. It is usual to work from each skewback towards the centre and complete with the key brick. The voussoirs are kept plumb by using a *straight-edge* (a 75 mm by 22 mm piece of well-seasoned wood about 1 800 mm long) and, as the work proceeds, it is placed horizontally against the faces of the walling at the skewbacks when any voussoir not in true alignment is tapped either backwards or forwards as required.

If thicker joints are desired, the mortar is applied by a *trowel* (see 31, Fig. 19) in the usual way, care being taken that the joints are of uniform thickness and radiate to a common centre. This is ensured by using a cord or " line " as shown at A, Fig. 41; one end of the line is attached to the nail driven into the strut at the centre; the position of each voussoir and its bed joint is marked along the top of the turning piece, and as each voussoir is placed in position the bed is made to coincide with the line which is stretched taut. A piece of wood, called a *trammel* or *radius rod* (see M, Fig. 41), may be used to traverse the face of the arch instead of the line.

A templet or wood *pattern*, shaped as shown at *a*, *b*, *c*, *d* at A, Fig. 15, may be employed to ensure that all of the skewbacks are made to the correct angle. The bricks forming a skewback can be readily and accurately cut if a line parallel to it is marked on the wall, as shown by the broken line X at A, Fig. 15, when the measurements taken along the arrises of the shaded bricks which are intercepted by the mark are transferred to the bricks to be shaped.

(b) *Purpose-made Brick Flat Arch* (see B, Fig. 15, A, Fig. 48, and A, Fig. 54).—This arch differs from the gauged arch type in that purpose-made bricks (see above) are used instead of rubbers; the jointing material and the thickness of the joints are the same as for the general walling; the camber and size of skewback are as described for gauged arches. This type of arch is frequently employed in good-class work.

(c) *Axed Brick Flat Arch.*—This is similar to (*b*) except that its appearance is not so satisfactory as the voussoirs are ordinary bricks cut to a wedge shape as described on p. 22. This type of arch is now used only for common work.

Segmental Arch.—Half elevations of two varieties of this arch are shown at F and G, Fig. 15. The geometrical construction for determining the centre for the curved extrados and intrados and from which the bed joints of the voussoirs radiate is shown. There are four varieties of this type of arch, *i.e.* :

(a) *Gauged Segmental Arch* (see G, Fig. 15).—It is constructed of rubbers upon a temporary wood support called a *centre* (see F, Fig. 41). Cross joints may be omitted if desired.

(b) *Purpose-made Brick Segmental Arch* (see F, Fig. 15).—This is similar to the above, except that purpose-made bricks and not rubbers are employed and the thickness of the joints is the same as that of the adjoining brickwork.

(c) *Axed Brick Segmental Arch.*—Whilst this arch resembles (*b*) its appearance is not so good, as it is constructed of ordinary bricks which have been cut to the required wedge shape.

(d) *Rough Brick Segmental Arch.*—

This consists of one or more half-brick rings constructed of ordinary stock *uncut* bricks; as the bricks are not cut, the joints are wedge-shaped. Such arches were adopted when appearance was secondary (as in plastered walls) because of their relative cheapness. The arch was used to relieve a wood lintel of the weight of superincumbent brickwork. Such are called *Rough Relieving or Discharging Arches*; they are also sometimes referred to as *Jack Arches. Rough relieving arches are now obsolete.* They were formerly employed when openings exceeding 1·2 m spans were provided with comparatively thin wood lintels. Reinforced concrete lintels, designed to support the brickwork, etc. above them, are now preferred to wood lintels, especially for large spans.

Semicircular Arch (see D and E, Fig. 15, which shows half elevations of two varieties).—The impost may be omitted. It is constructed on a centre (see p. 82 and J, Fig. 41). There are four varieties of semicircular arches, *i.e.*, (*a*) gauged semicircular arches, (*b*) purpose-made brick semicircular arches, (*c*) axed brick semicircular arches, and (*d*) rough brick semicircular arches. Excepting for the shape, they are similar to the four classes of segmental arches. An example of a gauged semicircular arch is shown at E; this may have cross joints to give a " bonded face." The purpose-made brick type is shown at D and the axed brick arch is similar; the number of rings may be increased if desired. The rough brick class, like the segmental arch, has V-shaped joints.

The arches illustrated in Fig. 15 have been related to the small building shown in part in Fig. 14 which is an example of a typical working drawing, it being fully dimensioned to enable the bricklayer to set out the work accurately.[1]

Stone heads and arches are described on p. 49.

WINDOW SILLS

A sill provides a suitable finish to the window opening and it affords a protection to the wall below. Sills may be of brick, brick with one or more

[1] Although the thickness of the joints of the brickwork (including those of the arches) has been shown in Fig. 15, it is usual for students when preparing homework sheets to show the joints by single lines only.

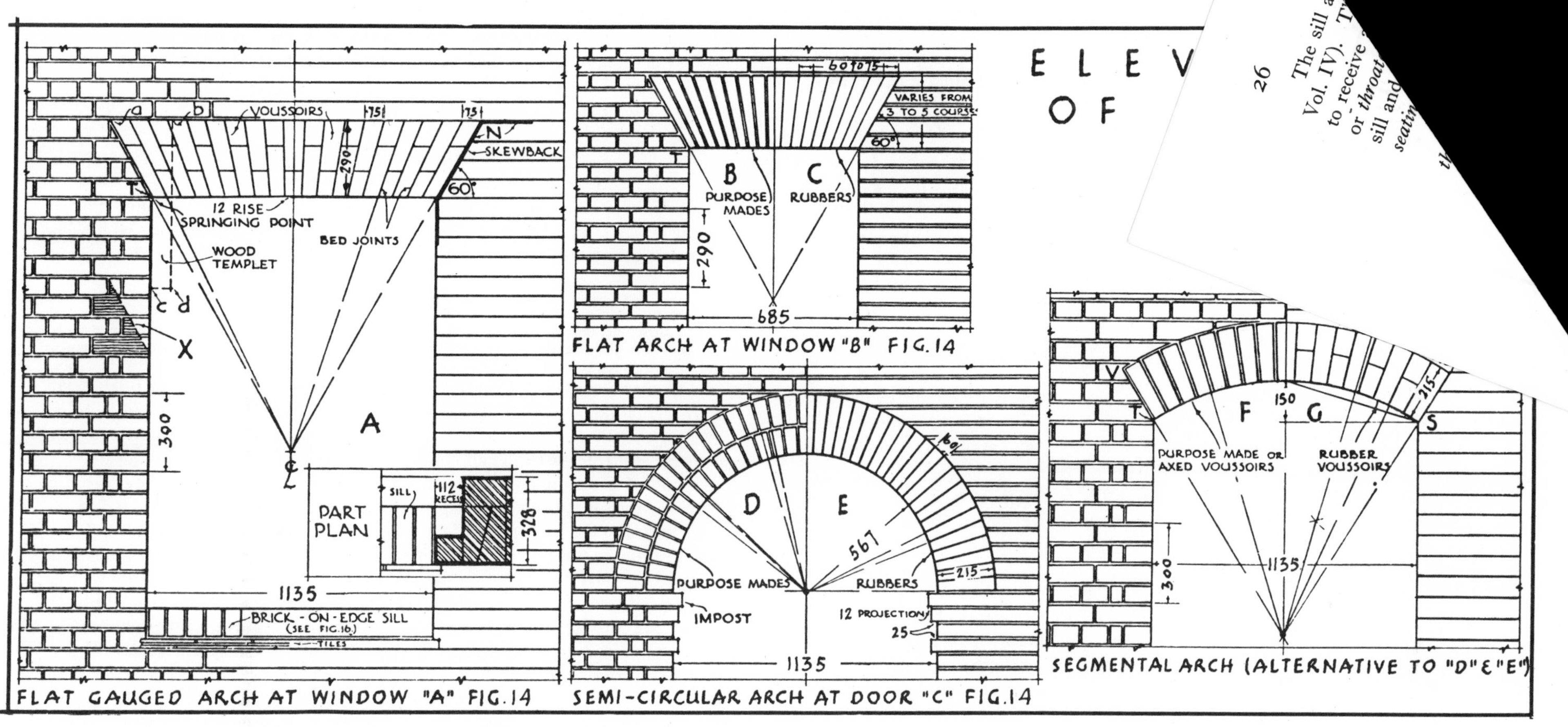

FIGURE 15

courses of tiles, tiles, stone (natural or reconstructed), concrete, terra-cotta and wood. The top of a sill should have a slight fall outwards to prevent the lodgment of water; this slope is called the *weathering* of a sill.

Fig. 16 shows three forms of external sills.

That at A shows a section and part elevation of a brick sill upon two courses of tiles. Standard bricks are placed on edge and are slightly tilted. The tiles vary from 13 to 45 mm thick; those shown are 16 mm thick. Ordinary roof tiles—(known as *plain tiles*, see Fig. 72)—are sometimes used; these are approximately 270 mm by 165 mm by 13 mm. Purpose-made tiles, called *quarry tiles*, are thicker than plain tiles and are usually square of 150 to 300 mm length of side. The tiles are given a 20 mm projection beyond the face of the wall (see section) and a 20 mm projection beyond the jamb (see elevation); they are laid to break joint (see also A, Fig. 41). The tiles must be solidly and uniformly bedded in mortar otherwise they may be easily damaged.

An alternative arrangement is shown at B, Fig. 16, where a double course of tiles is bedded on a brick-on-edge course. An equally satisfactory and inexpensive finish is provided by a double course of tiles bedded on the top course of the general walling (see B, Fig. 14). The tiles may be given a much greater slope if desired (see E, Fig. 55), and the brick-on-edge course may project 20 to 25 mm beyond the face of the wall.

An internal sill of one course of tiles (F) is shown at A, Fig. 16.

Lead-covered brick-on-edge sills are shown in Figs. 56 and 57.

C, Fig. 16, is of moulded concrete, or reconstructed stone (see he top surface is weathered and slightly moulded; it has a groove wrought iron *weather bar* (see p. 104). The underside is grooved *ed* to throw off the water and prevent it from passing underneath the staining the brickwork below. The ends of the sill are called *stools* or *gs* and provide level beds to receive the jambs.

In all cases the sills should course with the adjacent walling in order to avoid e unsightly split courses which have been referred to on p. 20.

Sills should be protected during the construction of the building, otherwise falling bricks, etc., may cause damage. This protection is usually in the form of pieces of wood which rest upon the sills and are tightly fitted between the reveals.

Stone sills are described on p. 49.

THRESHOLDS

The bottom of an external door opening is provided with one or more steps which form a threshold. Such may consist of bricks, stone or concrete.

Fig. 14 shows a threshold consisting of three steps which are formed entirely of bricks laid on edge.

An alternative to this, to a larger scale, is shown at D, Fig. 16. Ordinary standard bricks may be used, but they must be very hard, otherwise the edges or arrises will be readily damaged. The steps must have a satisfactory foundation, hence the concrete bed. The height of each step, called the *riser*, is 130 mm although this varies from 115 to 175 mm. The risers consist of bricks laid on end and the rest of each *tread* (or horizontal portion) comprises bricks laid on edge. Treads should be at least 280 mm wide so as to afford adequate foot space. The top step is given a slight fall (about 3 mm) to discharge water away from the door. The two lower steps have returned ends; this gives a much better appearance than when all steps are of the same length. The bonding of the bricks is shown on the plan and elevation. The whole of the brickwork should be in *cement* mortar.

A single step in bricks on edge is shown in Fig. 13.

The threshold at E, Fig. 16, consists of two steps having brick-on-edge risers and 60 mm thick stone treads. The stone must be extremely hard and fine-grained, and the upper surfaces should not be polished, otherwise they become slippery, especially in wet weather. Unless the stone is hard it will wear badly and the arrises will be readily damaged. The edges may be slightly rounded, or splayed (chamfered) or—providing the stone is particularly hard—square as shown. The treads must be well and uniformly bedded in cement mortar. This form of step is also detailed in Figs. 42 and 48.

Stone steps are shown in Figs. 24, 43 and 65. Similar steps may be formed in concrete, although these do not look so well as those in stone. A concrete step, which is a continuation of the concrete floor, is shown in Fig. 44.

It is advisable to defer the construction of thresholds until the completion of the building, otherwise they may be damaged during the building operations unless adequately protected.

COPINGS

Copings are provided to serve as a protective covering to walls such as boundary walls (yard and garden walls) and parapet walls (those which are carried up above roofs). Their object is to exclude water from the walling below.

Very serious damage may be caused to a wall if water gains access, especially during cold weather when the water may freeze. Under such conditions the resulting expansion may rapidly disintegrate the upper courses of the brickwork. In addition, the water may penetrate sufficiently to cause dampness to bedrooms, etc.

The most effective coping is that which throws the water clear of the wall below. The fewer joints in the coping the better, and the jointing and bedding material should be *cement* mortar. Copings may be of bricks, bricks and tiles or slates, stone, terra-cotta and concrete, and all must be sound and durable.

Some of the simpler brick copings are shown in Fig. 17. They form an effective finish to a brick building.

A portion of a garden wall is shown at A, Fig. 17, and alternative copings which would be suitable for this and similar walls are shown at B to L inclusive.

Brick-on-Edge Coping.—The section at B and part elevation at C shows this type, which consists of ordinary hard and durable bricks laid on edge. It has a simple but satisfactory appearance, is inexpensive and is adopted extensively. Another application is shown at M, Fig. 36, and in Fig. 74. Sometimes the bricks are placed on end, or as shown in Fig. 13, the coping may consist of two courses with the lower set back about 13 mm and comprising bricks-on-end and the upper course set back a similar amount and consisting of bricks-on-edge.

Bullnose Coping.—This is shown in section D and the elevation is similar to that at C. The double bullnose bricks are placed on edge.

Semicircular Coping (see E and F).—The purpose-made semicircular bricks are bedded upon an oversailing stretching course of ordinary bricks. The space between the stretchers (about 60 mm as shown in the section) should be filled solid with pieces of brick and mortar if the dwarf wall is likely to be subjected to side stresses from traffic, etc. The curved surface of the coping and the weathered or *flaunched* bed joint cause water to get away quickly, and the projecting course assists water to drip clear of the wall.

A similar coping, shown at G and H, consists of a top course of double bullnose bricks placed on edge upon a projecting course of bats (or stretchers similar to E with the intervening space filled as above described).

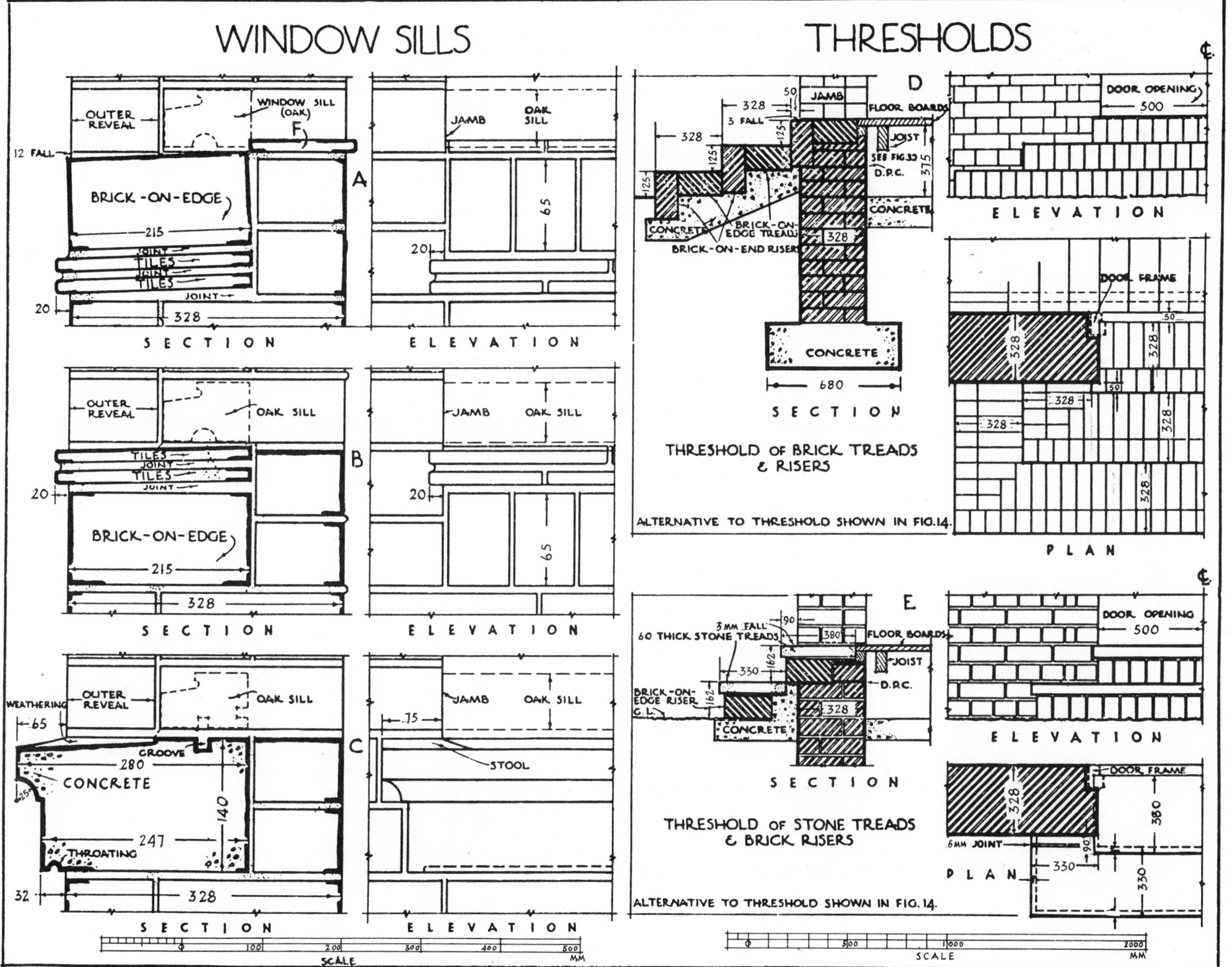

WINDOW SILLS
THRESHOLDS
OUTER REVEAL
WINDOW SILL (OAK)
F
12 FALL
BRICK-ON-EDGE
215
JOINT
TILES
JOINT
TILES
JOINT
20
328
A
JAMB
OAK SILL
65
20
SECTION
ELEVATION
OUTER REVEAL
OAK SILL
TILES
JOINT
TILES
JOINT
20
BRICK-ON-EDGE
215
328
B
JAMB
OAK SILL
20
65
SECTION
ELEVATION
WEATHERING
65
OUTER REVEAL
OAK SILL
GROOVE
280
CONCRETE
25
140
247
THROATING
32
328
C
JAMB
OAK SILL
75
STOOL
SECTION
ELEVATION
SCALE
MM
D
50
JAMB
328
3 FALL
FLOOR BOARDS
328
125
JOIST
SEE FIG.35
D.P.C.
375
CONCRETE
BRICK-ON-EDGE TREAD
BRICK-ON-END RISER
328
CONCRETE
680
SECTION
THRESHOLD OF BRICK TREADS & RISERS
ALTERNATIVE TO THRESHOLD SHOWN IN FIG.14.
DOOR OPENING
500
ELEVATION
DOOR FRAME
50
328
328
328
328
328
PLAN
E
3MM FALL
90
60 THICK STONE TREADS
380
FLOOR BOARDS
JOIST
330
162
D.P.C.
BRICK-ON-EDGE RISER
G.L.
328
CONCRETE
SECTION
THRESHOLD OF STONE TREADS & BRICK RISERS
ALTERNATIVE TO THRESHOLD SHOWN IN FIG. 14.
DOOR OPENING
500
ELEVATION
DOOR FRAME
328
380
6MM JOINT
90
330
PLAN
330
SCALE
MM

FIGURE 16

Brick-on-Edge Coping with Tile Creasing.—One form is shown at J and K. The tile course is known as a *creasing* and serves to throw the water clear of the wall. The creasing may also consist of two or more tile courses, laid in cement to break joint. A creasing consisting of a double course of slates in cement may be used instead of tiles.

Saddle-back Coping (see L and M).—This is effective, it provides a satisfactory finish and may be used in conjunction with either a tile or slate creasing. Brick or terra-cotta saddle-back copings can also be obtained which have throated projections and resemble the stone coping shown at C, Fig. 27.

A vertical joint in a coping is a potential weakness, and therefore one of the demerits of brick copings is the comparatively large number of such joints which have to be made. Hence it is advisable to provide a horizontal damp proof course on the top course of the brickwork before the coping is fixed (see p. 17).

Whilst a simple brick coping can form an attractive feature of a brick structure and is extensively used, copings of stone are often preferred even for brick erections. Stone copings are illustrated in Fig. 27.

PLINTHS

The projecting feature constructed at the base of a wall is known as a plinth. It gives to a building the appearance of additional stability.

Three forms of simple brick plinths are shown in Fig. 17.

Brick-on-End Plinth (see N and O).—As is implied, this plinth consists of a course of bricks laid on end, projecting about 20 mm and backed with ordinary brickwork.

Splayed Plinth (see P and Q).—This comprises two stretching courses of purpose-made splayed or chamfered bricks similar to those shown at R, Fig. 2. If preferred, the top course may consist of headers similar to that at S, Fig. 2.

Moulded Plinth.—One of the many moulded types is shown at R and S, and consists of a simple curve (called a *cavetto* mould) and a narrow flat band known as a *fillet*.

Stone plinths are detailed in Fig. 25.

TOOLS, CONSTRUCTION, JOINTING AND POINTING

Tools.—The tools in general use by a bricklayer are: trowel, plumb-rule, straight-edge, gauge-rod, line and pins, square, spirit-level, two-foot rule, bolster, club hammer, brick hammer and chisels. Other tools used for special purposes include: bevel, scutch, saw, pointing-trowel, frenchman, jointer, pointing-rule and hawk.

Trowel (see 31, Fig. 19).—Consists of a steel blade and shank into which a wood handle is fixed; used for lifting and spreading mortar on to a wall, forming joints and cutting bricks. It is the chief tool of the bricklayer.

Plumb-rule.—A dressed piece of wood, 100 mm by 13 mm by 1 400 mm to 1 800 mm long, having parallel edges, holed near the bottom to permit slight movement of a lead *plumb-bob* which is suspended by a piece of whipcord; similar to that shown at A, Fig. 28, but with parallel long edges; used for plumbing (obtaining or maintaining a vertical face) a wall.

Straight-edge.—A piece of wood, about 75 mm by 13 mm by 900 mm long having parallel edges; used for testing brickwork (especially at quoins) and checking if faces of bricks are in alignment. Longer straight-edges are used for levelling concrete, etc.

Gauge-rod or Storey-rod.—Similar to the straight-edge but 100 mm by 19 mm by 2·7 m long, upon which the courses, including the joints, are marked by horizontal lines; courses which conform with the tops and bottoms of window sills, springing points of arches, etc., are also indicated on the gauge; used at quoins in setting out the work and ensuring that the courses are maintained at correct level and uniform thickness.

Line and Pins (see 33, Fig. 19).—The line (at least 30 m long) is wound round two steel pins: used to maintain the correct alignment of courses.

Square (see 26, Fig. 19).—Consists of a steel blade and wood stock or entirely of steel; used for setting out right angles from the face of a wall (as required for openings), testing perpends and marking bricks preparatory to cutting.

Spirit-level (see 17, Fig. 19).—Used, in conjunction with the straight-edge, for obtaining horizontal surfaces.

One-metre Rule (see 1, Fig. 67).—Used for taking measurements.

Bolster (see 35, Fig. 19).—Made of steel; used for cutting bricks; the edge of the tool is placed on the brick where required when a smart blow with the hammer on the end of the steel handle is usually sufficient to split the brick.

Club Hammer or Lump Hammer.—Similar to that shown at 27, Fig. 19, and with the head weighing from 1 to 2 kg; used in conjunction with the bolster, chisels, etc.

Brick Hammer.—Similar to that at K, Fig. 69, but without the claw and with a chiselled end instead of that shown pointed; used for cutting bricks (especially firebricks), brick paving, striking nails, etc.

Chisels.—Similar to those at 1 and 5, Fig. 19; those shaped as shown at 5 are usually 19 mm wide with 300 to 450 mm long octagonal steel handles; used for cutting away brickwork, etc.

Bevel (see 30, Fig. 19).—Used for setting out angles.

Scutch or Scotch (see 34, Fig. 19).—Used for cutting soft bricks and dressing cut surfaces.

Saw (similar to that shown at 19, Fig. 67).—Used for sawing rubbers (see p. 22).

Pointing Trowel.—Similar to that at 31, Fig. 19, but much smaller; used for placing mortar into joints, etc.

Frenchman.—A discarded table knife the blade of which is cut to a point which is bent 10 mm at right angles to the blade; used for tuck pointing (see p. 31).

Jointer (see 32, Fig. 19).—This has a steel blade (50 to 150 mm long), the edge of which is either flat, grooved, concave or convex rounded; used for jointing and pointing brickwork (see p. 31).

Pointing-rule (see 18, Fig. 19).—A dressed piece of 75 by 22 mm wood having a bevelled edge with 10 mm thick wood or cork distance pieces fixed on the bevelled side; used for jointing (see p. 31).

Hawk or Hand Board.—A 225 mm by 225 mm by 13 mm board having a 20 mm diameter stump handle in the centre; used for holding small quantities of mortar during pointing operations.

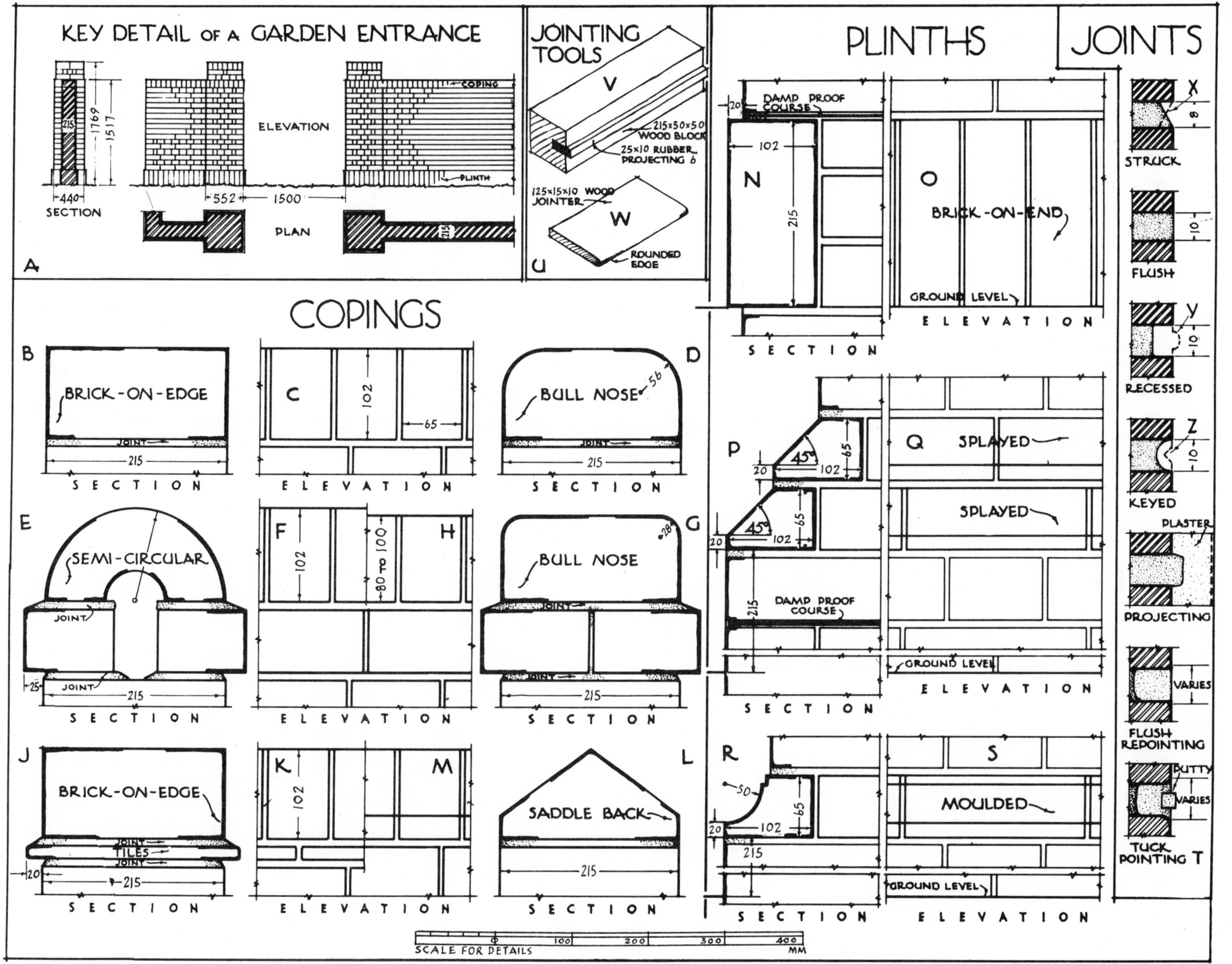
KEY DETAIL OF A GARDEN ENTRANCE
COPING
ELEVATION
PLINTH
SECTION
PLAN
1769
1517
215
440
552
1500
A
JOINTING TOOLS
V
215×50×50 WOOD BLOCK
25×10 RUBBER PROJECTING 6
125×15×10 WOOD JOINTER
W
ROUNDED EDGE
U
PLINTHS
JOINTS
DAMP PROOF COURSE
20
102
N
215
O
BRICK-ON-END
GROUND LEVEL
SECTION
ELEVATION
X
STRUCK
FLUSH
Y
RECESSED
Z
KEYED
PLASTER
PROJECTING
VARIES
FLUSH REPOINTING
PUTTY
TUCK POINTING T
COPINGS
B
BRICK-ON-EDGE
JOINT
C
102
65
D
BULL NOSE
56
P
45°
Q
SPLAYED
E
SEMI-CIRCULAR
F
80 TO 100
H
G
28
DAMP PROOF COURSE
J
TILES
K
M
L
SADDLE BACK
R
50
S
MOULDED
SCALE FOR DETAILS
100
200
300
400
MM

Figure 17

Construction of a Wall.[1]—The corners or *leads* are first built to a height of several courses (see U, Fig. 2) and the walling between the corners is completed course by course. Normally the leads should not exceed 900 mm in height.

Each quoin is set truly vertical by placing an edge of the plumb-rule against one of the faces, any adjustment of the bricks being made until the wall is true; the return face is then plumbed. The gauge-rod is used to ensure that the brick courses are correct. Each course is now constructed, aided by the line and pins; one of the pins is inserted in and near the top of a vertical joint (usually on the return face of the wall) and, after the line has been stretched taut, the second pin is inserted to bring the line level with the top of the course to be built and at a slight distance (about 3 mm) from the face.

Before being laid in position the bricks should have been wetted[2] (particularly in hot weather) to prevent them from absorbing moisture from the mortar.

In constructing a wall, the bricklayer collects sufficient mortar on the trowel and spreads it on the last completed course for several bricks ahead (not less than 900 mm length of bed being recommended). He then presses the point of the trowel into the mortar and draws it in zigzag fashion along the centre of the layer to form a level and uniformly thick bed. A brick is taken, placed in position, and pressed into the mortar against the last laid brick; a smart tap with the edge of the trowel or the end of the handle may be necessary to bring the brick into line. The mortar which has been squeezed out beyond the face of the wall is " cut off " by and collected on to the trowel[3] and returned to the heap of mortar on the board. The cross joint is then formed, a small portion of mortar being taken on the trowel and pressed on the end or side of the brick to form a vertical joint against which the next brick is pressed.[4]

" Plumbing-up " by means of the plumb-rule should be frequently resorted to as new brickwork has a tendency to overhang; the work is corrected and a vertical face obtained by tapping the handle of the trowel (or using the brick hammer) against the bricks concerned.

Perpends must be kept vertical; this is checked as the work proceeds by placing the straight-edge flat on the course and slightly projecting beyond the face. The stock of the square is set against the underside of the straight-edge with the blade coinciding with the last-formed vertical joint and (if the work is satisfactory) with that in the course next but one below.

The plumbing of the reveals of openings and the perpends adjoining them should receive special attention.

In the construction of thick walls, mortar is spread on the bed and the outer bricks on both faces are first laid as described above; the inner bricks are then pressed and rubbed into position to cause some of the mortar to rise between the vertical joints, which are finally filled flush with liquid mortar or grout.

Hand-made bricks, having only one frog, should be laid with the frogs uppermost to ensure that they will be completely filled with mortar. Machine-pressed bricks, having two frogs, should have the " lower " frogs filled with mortar before being laid in position. Care must be taken that certain textured or rustic bricks are laid on their proper beds; it is not uncommon to see these laid " upside-down ".

Jointing and Pointing.—Joints on the face are usually compressed by one or other of the methods referred to below so as to eliminate pore spaces along which water may pass. The nature of this finish depends upon the type of bricks used and the appearance required.

[1] The setting out of buildings is described in Chap. I, Vol. II.

[2] Certain smooth-surfaced machine-pressed bricks should not be watered, otherwise they are difficult to lay.

[3] The mortar may be left slightly projecting if the surface of the wall is to be plastered.

[4] The projecting mortar which has been removed is often trowelled on to the end of the brick to form the vertical joint. When this is the only mortar applied, the joints are inadequately filled and inferior work results.

When this finish is done in sections as the brickwork proceeds the operation is called *jointing*; when it is deferred until afterwards it is known as *pointing*. The following examples are illustrated at T, Fig. 17.

Struck Joint.—This is probably more extensively used than any other. It is a good weather joint as it permits of the ready discharge of water. Its appearance is not entirely satisfactory for every class of work as it exaggerates any inaccuracy of the lower edges of the bricks (owing to the difference in the thickness of the bricks which may exist); its smooth mechanical character detracts from the appearance if adopted for bedding and jointing sand-faced bricks of good texture. It is best used in conjunction with smooth-surfaced machine-pressed bricks of uniform colour.

This joint is formed when the mortar is sufficiently stiff (usually after four stretchers or their equivalent have been laid) by holding the handle of the trowel below the bed joint and smoothing the mortar several times in one direction with the blade to an approximate bevel of 60°. The vertical joints are usually formed by pressing the tip of the trowel down the centre to produce a V-section, or these joints may be flush (see below). The vertical joints are first struck, followed by the bed joint.

Overhand Struck Joint (see broken line at X).—It should not be adopted as water collecting on the ledge may pass through the mortar to cause dampness on the inside, or frost action may destroy the upper edges of the bricks, especially if they are not of good quality.

Flush or Flat Joint.—As shown, the joint is flush with (in the same plane as) the face of the brickwork. When rubbed, it forms an excellent finish for first class faced work.

Mortar is pressed into the joints during the progress of the work, any depressions are filled by the addition of mortar, and when this is " semi-stiff " each joint is carefully rubbed in one direction by a piece of rubber held against the wall. This gives a satisfactory texture which agreeably conforms with that of a sand-faced brick.

Provided the mortar is of good quality, this joint gives a satisfactory finish to rustic brickwork if it is just left as the mortar is cut off with the trowel, no attempt being made to smooth the surface of the joint. The fairly rough texture of such joints gives to rustic brickwork a more satisfactory appearance than smooth struck joints.

The flush joint is also adopted for walls requiring smooth internal faces such as may be required for factories, cellars, coal-houses, garages, etc.

Recessed Joint.—This is very satisfactory for facing work of good textured bricks and good quality mortar. The bricks should be carefully selected of uniform thickness and the bed joints should be at least 10 mm thick.

The joint is made by applying a jointing tool immediately after the projecting mortar has been cut. This tool may be similar to the jointer (see 32, Fig. 19) or the improvised tool shown at V, Fig. 17; the thickness of the rubber should equal that of the joint. The rubber accommodates itself to any irregularities of the brick edges as it is pressed in and worked to and fro until the mortar is removed. That shown at V is suitable for the bed joints, a similar shorter tool being used for the vertical joints. The bricks must be hard and durable, otherwise any water collecting on the ledges may become frozen and cause pieces to flake off.

Keyed Joint.—Such joints give an appearance to the brickwork which is distinctively attractive.

It may be formed with either the convex rounded jointer (see above) or the wood jointer shown at W, Fig. 17, which varies in thickness with that of the joint. The vertical joints are formed first, followed by the bed joints. The latter are formed by using the jointer in conjunction with the pointing rule (see 18, Fig. 19); the rule is usually held by two men against the wall with the bevelled edge uppermost on the same level as and parallel to the lower edge of the joint; the jointer, resting upon it, is pressed into the soft mortar and passed along several times in both directions until the required depth is obtained, the surplus mortar falling between the distance pieces of the rule. The vertical joints should have a slightly less impression than the bed joints.

Vee-joint (see broken lines at Z).—Its effect is to give the appearance of narrow joints, especially if the colour of the mortar resembles closely that of the bricks. It is not recommended. The joint is made as described for the keyed joint and with a steel jointer having its lower edge suitably shaped.

Projecting Joint.—As stated in a footnote on p. 30, the inside faces of walls which are to be plastered (in addition to external surfaces which are to be rough-cast) are left with the mortar projecting. This gives a good key for the first coat of plaster, as shown. Another good key is afforded if the joints are raked out to a depth of about 12 mm before the mortar has set.

In addition to its form, consideration should be given to the colour and texture of the joint. Bricks of various colours and textures are now obtainable, and it is very important that the colour of the mortar should conform with that of the bricks. Thus, mortar composed of lime and *yellow* sand is very suitable for certain sand-faced bricks.

Pointing and Re-Pointing.—It has been stated that pointing is the method of finishing the joints after the whole of the brickwork has been completed. It may be applied to a new building just before completion, or it may be used on existing buildings when the joints have become defective.

The first operation in pointing is the removal of the mortar for a depth of 12 mm to give an adequate key for the fresh mortar, after which the face is brushed down with a bass broom to remove pieces of mortar and dust and finally well drenched with water. The material used for refilling the joints may be either lime mortar or cement mortar and the colour should conform with the brickwork (cement can now be obtained in a variety of colours for this purpose).

Waterproofed lime and Portland cement mixtures are now extensively used for pointing; the former mixture may consist of 1 part lime to 3 parts sand gauged with a solution of 1 part waterproof compound to 15 parts water; alternatively a mortar composed of 1 part waterproofed cement (containing 2 per cent. of the waterproofing compound) to 3 parts sand can be used.

The form of joint to be used for pointing or re-pointing depends a good deal upon the condition of the brickwork. If the edges of the bricks are true and in good condition the joints may be selected from the struck, flush, recessed or keyed varieties described above; if the edges are damaged, the mortar should be finished with the flush form of joint.

Tuck Pointing, as illustrated at T, is occasionally adopted where the jointing material has become defective and the brickwork at the joints has become ragged. Generally it is only used when an alternative flush joint would cause the joints to appear excessively wide; in course of time it becomes defective.

Tuck pointing is done in the following manner: The joints are raked out, brushed and watered as before described. Coloured cement may be used to match the colour of the existing brickwork and this is trowelled with a flush joint and rubbed as described for flush jointing—a small trowel being used together with a hawk (see p. 28) to hold the mortar. A 5 mm or 6 mm wide by 3 mm deep groove is immediately and carefully formed along the centre of each joint. With the aid of the pointing-rule and a flat edged jointer (32, Fig. 19) the groove is filled or " tucked in " (hence the name given to the pointing) with *putty lime* (see p. 23) to which a small amount of silver sand has been added. The putty is given a maximum projection of 3 mm and both top and bottom edges are neatly cut off by means of the frenchman (see p. 28), the bent pointed end of which removes the surplus material as the knife is drawn along the edge of the rule. The bed joints are formed first, in about 2·5 m lengths (when two men are working together), followed by the vertical joints.

Bastard Tuck Pointing.—This is an imitation of tuck pointing and is formed entirely of the infilling mortar. The profile of the joint is similar to that of tuck pointing but the band which projects consists of the pointing material. Whilst this does not look so well as the true tuck pointing, it is more durable, but the projecting mortar is apt to become affected by weather action.

Another form of pointed joint which projects is known as a *beaded joint.* This is indicated by broken lines at Y, Fig. 17. It is formed, in conjunction with the pointing rule, by a jointer having a concave edge. It is liable to be damaged and is not recommended.

PLASTERING TO WALLS

INTERNAL PLASTERING

Plastering is a relatively cheap means of providing a durable hygienic surface to walls and ceilings.

First-class plastering is done in three layers, *i.e.* :—*render* coat (10 mm) (known also as a *pricking* coat), *floating* coat (6 mm), and *setting* coat (3 mm), to give a total thickness of 19 mm. Now, for much general building work, the render coat is omitted, the floating coat is made thicker and the overall thickness is 16 mm; this is sufficient for all but very rough walls.

Formerly, *lime plaster* was the basic material for this purpose, mixed with sand and, more latterly, cement, for certain layers; the constituents are measured by volume. Thus for walls, a typical specification for the first coat[1] used to be (and still is, in some areas) $\frac{1}{3}$ cement : 1 lime putty : 3 sand, incorporating 0·535 kg of clean ox hair per 0·1 m^3 of this *coarse stuff*; for the second coat, 1 lime putty : 2 sand; with neat lime putty for the final coat. The lime used was the *non-hydraulic*[2] or *fat lime* prepared in a pit on the site one month before use by

[1] An alternative undercoat still chosen in some places is *black-pan mortar* obtained by grinding down ashes in a pug-mill and adding lime.

[2] A second type of lime is *magnesian lime* sometimes used for plastering and mortar mixes.

A third is *hydraulic lime* which can set under water (unlike the non-hydraulic type), it was once used for concrete mixes before the introduction of Portland cement; it is still used for mortars.

mixing *quicklime* (CaO), obtained by burning limestone in a kiln, with water to form *lime putty*. The latter process is known as *slaking* or *hydration* and the putty has the formula $Ca(OH)_2$. Such mixes containing lime and cement shrink on drying out, hence each coat was allowed to shrink before further coats were added. This lengthy procedure delayed completion of the work and lime plasters have been replaced almost entirely by *calcium sulphate* or *gypsum plasters*[1] for these have the following comparative advantages: set within a few hours, produce a harder finish, expand slightly on setting and, finally, they enable decoration to proceed at an earlier date.

Lime is still used in two ways because it improves workability, making plastering easier, and in some cases accelerating the set of gypsum plasters (see below), viz.: (1) to *gauge* gypsum mixes [see (*c*) below], and (2) in lime mixes gauged with gypsum plaster [see (*b*) below]. For these purposes, *hydrated lime*, obtainable as a powder requiring mixing with water only 24 hours before use is often a more convenient form of lime putty than that obtained from quicklime on the site. The addition of lime reduces hardness and in final coats decoration by oil paints cannot proceed until the wall has dried out; this may take from 6 to 12 months. Distempered finishes are unaffected.

Calcium Sulphate Plasters.[2]—These are in two groups subdivided into four classes A, B, C and D, in B.S. 1191.

Gypsum ($CaSO_4.2H_2O$) is the raw material for the first group (classes A and B); it is mined in this country and several parts of the world. When gypsum is heated, water is expelled and a white, grey or pink powder is obtained. This is class A plaster and is known as Plaster of Paris ($CaSO_4.\frac{1}{2}H_2O$). When mixed with water it sets within a few minutes, so it is unsuitable for general plasterwork but it may be used for patching. An additive (a retarder) must be incorporated with it to delay the set and so produce class B plasters (*retarded hemi-hydrate gypsum plasters*) which are softer than the two remaining classes.

The second group, classes C and D, are based on chemically produced *anhydrous calcium sulphate* ($CaSO_4$) obtained as a by-product or by heating the gypsum to a higher temperature than for group one. These classes are slow in hardening and so the additive is an accelerator to make them suitable for plastering.

(*a*) *Plaster of Paris—class A.*—A neat mix of this or one gauged with lime (*i.e.* $\frac{1}{4}$ to 1 plaster : 1 lime) can be used for repair work in small patches.

(*b*) *Retarded hemi-hydrate gypsum plaster—class B*,[3] is made in three main types:—undercoat, finishing and dual-purpose; it should be made in small batches.

For undercoat work (known also as *browning*) the normal proportions are 1 plaster : 3 sand for brick walls and 1 : $1\frac{1}{2}$ for concrete surfaces. Hair is sometimes added to the mix on backgrounds such as metal lathing to reinforce it especially whilst it is setting.

This class is also used to gauge traditional 1 lime : 3 sand batch mixes where one part of plaster is added to about nine batches of the coarse stuff. Lime hastens the set.

Class B finishing coats are used neat on strong backing coats of plaster and sand, and on those of cement and sand. An alternative finishing coat is $\frac{1}{4}$ to $\frac{1}{2}$ plaster : 1 lime, but this is a lime mix gauged with plaster and has a softer finish. A special finishing type (without lime) gives the best surface on plasterboards and fibreboards.

The dual-purpose grade can be used for both under and finishing coats except for one coat work on plasterboard or fibreboard.

(*c*) *Anhydrous gypsum plaster—class C.*[1]—This is also made in the same three types as above; due to the slower setting time these can be worked longer.

For undercoats a 2 plaster : 1 lime : 5 sand mix is suitable. Finishing coats can be applied neat or have a small amount of lime added to aid plasticity. The dual-purpose type is used for both coats.

This class is unsuitable for finishes to plasterboards and fibreboards as it has insufficient adhesion.

(*d*) *Keene's or Parian Plaster—class D.*[2]—This is made in the same three types but is generally designed for use as finishing coats. As they provide a hard surface, they are much used for external angles, often on a cement and sand backing (see p. 107).

Like (*c*) above it is not usually suitable for a board finish and *lime should not be added to finishing coats.*

General.—The mixing water must be clean and free from impurities. The sand should be clean and well graded; rounded particles are preferred to the harsher kinds and a clay and silt content, up to a maximum of 5%, aids workability. Plaster should be stored in a dry place. Cement should not be mixed with gypsum plasters. Strong layers of plaster should not be laid over weaker ones. Class B plaster can be allowed to dry out immediately after application, but classes C and D require up to 48 hours for adequate hydration and so should not be permitted to dry out during this period.

All classes should be applied before they start to stiffen and re-tempering after the commencement of the initial set must not be allowed. Tools and the mixing boards (*spot boards*) must be thoroughly cleaned after each batch has been used because portions of old plaster left on the boards will accelerate the set of the

[1] Commonly, but inadvisably, also known as "hardwall plaster."

[2] An addition to this range is *Perlite plaster* (e.g. Murilite) in four grades: (1) as an undercoat on brickwork, (2) on metal lathing, (3) on concrete and plasterboards and (4) as a finishing coat. It does not need the addition of an aggregate such as sand for it is supplied ready for use incorporating expanded *perlite* (a very light mineral of volcanic origin) and gypsum plaster. The product is therefore ready for use on water being added, it is one-third the weight of, and has better insulating qualities than, ordinary sanded mixes.

[3] *E.g.* Carlisle, Gothite, Thistle.

[1] *E.g.* Sirapite, Statite, Xelite.

[2] *E.g.* Keene's, Parian, Supavite. Often termed Keene's *cement*.

next mix. The intermixing of different classes is inadvisable. Gypsum plasters cannot be used in damp situations and lime or preferably cement plasters are better in such places. Plastering with the latter mixes must be given time to dry out and shrink after each coat; this lengthy waiting time is eliminated with gypsum plasters.

Due regard must be paid to the nature of the background and an appropriate mix selected as described above; gypsum mixes are best for concrete walls. For brickwork 1 cement : 2 lime : 9 sand, and 1 class B plaster : $1\frac{1}{2}$ to 3 sand according to the porosity of the bricks are suitable (the denser the bricks, the stronger the mix) for undercoats. Walls lined with fibreboard, plasterboard, metal lathing and wood wool should be treated as for ceilings—see pp. 67–68.

Brick walls must have their joints raked out 10 mm or keyed bricks can be used. Smooth concrete surfaces must be roughened by (1) hacking, or (2) the application of a thin 1 cement : 2 sand splatterdash coating, or more easily (3) by applying a retarder to the formwork which prevents the setting of the outer skin of concrete enabling this to be wire brushed and roughened. These provisions are vital in ensuring adequate adhesion between the background and the undercoat; similarly, render and floating coats must be scratched whilst they are setting to give a good key for later coats.

Excessive draughts must be prevented whilst the set is taking place, the drying out should be allowed to proceed naturally, traffic on floors having a plastered ceiling should not be allowed until the set has been completed. The cracking of plaster frequently occurs where there is a change of background, as for example, between the walls of a house and the ceiling. This can be prevented by having a cornice or by making a horizontal cut with the trowel at the junction.

The plastering of ceilings is described on pp. 67–68.

Plastering Technique.—Door and window frames, skirting plugs and similar joinery work—known as *first fixing*—having been completed, the surfaces to be plastered are prepared as described above and cleaned. Wall surfaces are done first and those that are very porous are dampened if necessary. Assuming that three-coat work is being used, the render coat is mixed and applied evenly by a plasterer's trowel; this is made reasonably true by a two-handed trowel about 1 to 2 m long known as a *Derby float*. If metal or timber angle beads (see pp. 122-123) are used instead of Keene's cement (see pp. 32 and 107) at the angles, they are fixed before the render coat. Before the undercoat has hardened, the surface is well scratched to give a key for the next layer. *Screeds* or 150 mm wide strips of floating coat are then formed vertically at 1·8 to 3 m intervals, they are made plumb and in exact alignment. Intermediate screeds are than made about 1 m apart and the spaces between are filled and levelled as before. The surface is again roughened, the setting coat applied, and this is polished with the steel trowel just before it sets; over-trowelling is deprecated as it can cause *crazing* (fine hair cracks). The technique is similar for two-coat work.

Cement and/or lime undercoats must be allowed to dry before further coats are added and unlike gypsum mixes, the surfaces must first be sprinkled with water.

Skirtings, architraves and other cover moulds should not be fastened—known as *second fixing*—until the plastering has set.

PLASTERING FAILURES.—*Popping*, *pitting* and *blowing* caused by unsound lime and that which has not been slaked properly. The unslaked particles expand to leave small holes in the plaster.

Poor adhesion caused by high suction of the backing, too rapid drying out or by moisture being imprisoned in the wall which subsequently emerges through the plaster in the form of blisters. Due also to inadequate key and incorrect choice of plaster.

Cracking due to shrinkage on drying out, it is associated with cement or lime mixes. Movement of the background is also responsible, as for example the drying out of timber ceiling joists. Caused also by using sands containing more than 5 per cent silt and clay. Failure to provide discontinuity (see preceding column) where the background changes is another reason.

Ceiling Collapse. Wood lath and plaster ceilings are rarely used now, they collapse (as will metal lathed ceilings) if the key is inadequate or if they are vibrated by traffic before they have set. Ceilings on concrete surfaces must be given a good mechanical key (see preceding column).

EXTERNAL PLASTERING OR RENDERING

Rendered walls are an alternative finish to facing bricks, they can be made in different colours and are used in places where clay bricks would be out of harmony with the surrounding landscape or where the only local brick is a concrete one of dull appearance. Rendering is used extensively as a waterproof finish to *no-fines* concrete walls, such walls are made from 300 mm thickness and upwards and consist of 1 part cement : 8 parts of large aggregate (13 mm); sand is not included in the mix and a sound well-insulated wall results because of the air voids.

Gypsum plaster mixes are quite unsuitable for external rendering; much traditional work still exists and this is made of lime mixes protected by paint. Cement : lime : sand mixes are now adopted and the proportions of these three materials is again dependent on the nature of the background and also upon the degree of exposure. A good key must always be provided, the bricks must be well fired and durable and the joints raked out 13 mm; surfaces should be dampened if they are too dry before plastering starts and strong finishing coats must not be applied over weaker undercoats.

Of the many types of rendered finishes, the following are popular: scraped finish, roughcast (wet-dash), pebble dash (dry-dash) and machine finishes. Smooth well-trowelled surfaces should be avoided as they tend to "craze" (see preceeding column), if cracks develop they are very obvious. The range of cement : lime : sand mixes given below varies in strength in order to suit the degree of exposure; two types of background are considered: viz., (*a*) strong, as given by dense bricks and concrete, and (*b*) moderately weak as with lightweight concrete, etc.

Scraped Finish.—1 : 1 : 6 to 1 : 2 : 9 on (*a*) and (*b*) backgrounds for both undercoats and finishing coats, the top 1·5 mm of the latter is scraped off just as it begins to harden. This removes the top fatty skin which tends to develop during the application of the wood trowel which should always be used in preference to the steel trowel.

Roughcast Finish.—1 : 0 : 3 to 1 : 1 : 6 for (*a*), with 1 : 1 : 6 for (*b*) as both undercoats and the second coat. Whilst the latter is still soft, a mix of the same proportions but including 60% of 6 mm gravel in the aggregate is thrown on to the wall to give the wet-dash finish. This is more durable than the next finish described.

Pebble-dash Finish.—The mix and procedure is the same as for rough-casting except that the thrown-on coat consists of dry pebbles or crushed gravel only; the pebbles tend to drop off in time.

Machine-made Finish (Tyrolean).—The undercoat procedure is the same as for the scraped finish. The final coat is thrown on by the blades of a small hand machine, alternatively it can be sprayed on by a hose delivering the mix by air pressure.

THERMAL INSULATION OF WALLS

1. The subject of thermal insulation is described fully in Chap. 12, Vol. 4.

The Building Regulations give approved specifications for the thermal insulation of walls; there are four main types:—

1. Cavity walls with insulation material applied to either side of the inner leaf. For example a two leaf brick wall, each leaf at least 100 mm thick enclosing a 50 mm minimum width cavity with 10 mm thick expanded polystyrene insulating board stuck to the inner face of the inner leaf. The board is in 1800 and 2400 mm lengths, 600 and 1200 mm widths and 10, 25, 38 and 50 mm thicknesses. The joints in the board are covered with scrim cloth (p. 68) and the face of the board plastered.

2. Cavity walls with a brick outer leaf and an inner leaf 150 mm thick made of lightweight concrete blocks of density not exceeding 500 kg/m^3. This type of construction is the most usual being cheaper than type 1 above.

3. Cavity walls with the cavity filled with urea formaldehyde foam. Holes are bored in the wall and the foam injected. This method has been used widely but failures have occurred due to water penetration.

4. Solid walls of lightweight concrete block rendered externally and plastered internally, the block being 240 mm thick made of concrete of density not exceeding 500 kg/m^3.

Thermal insulation of roofs is described on p. 141.

CHAPTER TWO

MASONRY WALLS

Syllabus—Classification of stones and brief description of the quarrying, preparation and characteristics of limestone and sandstones. Surface finishes. Tools. Natural bed. Defects in stone. Classes of walling, including random rubble uncoursed, random rubble built to courses, squared rubble uncoursed, squared rubble built to courses, regular coursed squared rubble, polygonal, flint, Lake District and ashlar. Dressings to door and window openings, including inbands, outbands, lintels, arches, sills, mullions, transomes, and steps. Plinths. Simple string courses, friezes, cornices, parapets and copings. Joints, dowels, cramps and plugs. Mortar jointing. Construction of walls. Lifting appliances.

THE art of construction in stone is called masonry.[1]
BS 5390: Code of Practice for Stone Masonry is relevant.

CLASSIFICATION OF STONES

Rocks are divided into the following groups: (1) igneous, (2) sedimentary and (3) metamorphic.

(1) Igneous rocks have been formed by the agency of heat, the molten material subsequently becoming solidified. The chief building stone in this class is *granite.*

(2) Sedimentary rocks are those that have been formed chiefly through the agency of water. Most of them have been derived from the breaking up of igneous rocks, the particles, conveyed and deposited by streams, accumulated to form thick strata that have been hardened by pressure. The principal building stones in this group are *limestones* and *sandstones.*

(3) Metamorphic rocks form a group which embraces either igneous or sedimentary rocks which have been changed from their original form (metamorphosed) by either pressure, or heat, or both. *Slates* (see Chapter V) and *marbles* come under this class.

Limestones and sandstones are those which are used chiefly for general building purposes.

Limestones.—A limestone consists of particles of carbonate of lime cemented together by a similar material. Portland stone and Bath stone are in this class.

Portland Stone, obtained from the Isle of Portland (Dorset), is one of the best-known limestones, and stone from one of the beds or seams, known as *Whitbed* (see Fig. 18), is one of the best building stones used in this country for high-class work. Whitbed varies in colour from white to light brown, the latter being the best; it is durable, and, on account of its fine grain, is easily carved and moulded. The *Basebed*[1] is not so durable and should only be used for external purposes after careful selection. The *Roach bed* is not suitable for general building purposes on account of the large number of cavities which are present, but because of its great strength and good weathering properties it is used in the construction of sea walls and similar marine work.

[1] More advanced masonry is described in Vols. II and IV.

Bath Stone, obtainable in the vicinity of Bath, is used for general building purposes. It varies in colour from white to light cream or yellow, it has a fine grain and, because of its relative softness, it can be easily worked.

Sandstones.—These are composed of consolidated sand and consist chiefly of grains of quartz (silica) united by a cementing material. The quartz grains are practically indestructible, and the quality of the stone therefore depends essentially upon the cementing material which may be silica (forming siliceous sandstones), oxides of iron (forming ferruginous sandstones), calcium carbonate (forming calcareous sandstones), etc.

Many excellent building sandstones are quarried in Derbyshire, Lancashire and Yorkshire. Stancliffe stone (Darley Dale, Derbyshire) is light brown or honey coloured, is very strong and durable, and, although relatively difficult to work on account of its hardness, it can be moulded to give fine arrises. Woolton (Lancashire) stone is used in the construction of the Liverpool Anglican Cathedral. Some of the Yorkshire stones are exceedingly hard (especially those from the Bradford and Huddersfield districts) and are suitable for steps, landings, flags, as well as for general walling where fine mouldings are not required.

QUARRYING

The methods adopted in quarrying stone vary and depend upon the type and its depth below the surface. Most stone is obtained from open quarries, but where it is very deep (such as Bath stone) underground mining is used.

[1] The basebed is slightly whiter and the texture is somewhat finer than the whitbed; it is easily worked on account of its fine and even grain, and is suitable for internal work as for monuments and for purposes where carving or much fine detail is required.

Fig. 18 shows a section through the face of an open limestone (Portland) quarry. As much as possible of the overburden (which varies from a few feet to 15 m thick) is removed by mechanical excavator,[1] hand picking and cranes. The top and skull caps are loosened by blasting.

After the roach bed has been cleared, the stone is removed from each stratum. This operation is facilitated by the presence of natural vertical joints and horizontal beds of shells which separate the layers of stone. Commencing from one of the right-angled vertical joints, a number of strong metal wedges (see C, Fig. 19) are inserted at intervals along a shell bed and gradually hammered in until the stone is split horizontally and the slab becomes detached; if necessary, it is divided vertically by wedging (see B, Fig. 19). Each block is now lifted clear of the stratum by means of a crane, roughly squared up by the use of a large hammer and loaded into a truck for transit to the works for final dressing.

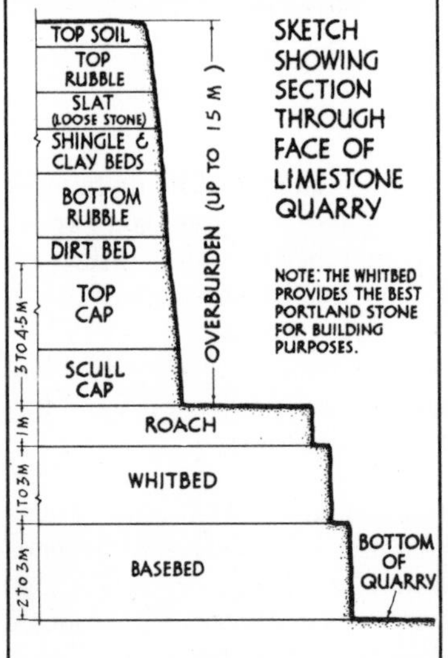

FIGURE 18

Blasting is sometimes needed in sandstone quarries because of the hardness of the stone. Briefly, a series of deep holes (about 25 mm in diameter) is formed by a drilling machine at the required distance from and parallel to the face of the quarry; a small charge of black gunpowder and a fuse are placed in each hole and the hole is partially packed or tamped with sand; the fuses are connected to a battery and the charges fired; this explosion is sufficient to shake the mass of stone; the holes are now cleared of tamping and the second or main charges inserted and again fired simultaneously. This removes a large bulk of stone which is only slightly shattered because of the use of two blasts. The large blocks are then divided by splitting and wedging (see below) and roughly squared up for dispatch to the works for subsequent dressing. They are from 0·7 to 0·8 m³ in size, although much larger blocks are obtainable.

There is very little overburden in many of the sandstone quarries. Thus in the Stancliffe (see p. 35) quarry it does not exceed 2 m in depth; the depth of the present working face is 50 m although some of the best stone is obtained at a depth of from 2 to 3 m.

Blasting is not necessary in those sandstone quarries where the beds are thin and frequently divided by natural fissures. Thus, in quarries from which much of the "walling stone" used for "Rubble Work" (see p. 40) is obtained, the thickness of the beds of good building stone varies from a minimum of 50 mm to a maximum of 1·2 m and comparatively little labour is required for its removal.

PREPARATION

Whereas formerly the whole of the labours involved in dressing building stones after removal from the quarry were done by hand, by the "banker mason," most of this work is now executed by machinery. There are certain *surface finishes* which can only be worked by hand; these are described below.

Machine Dressing.—The machines used include the frame saw, circular saw, rubbing bed, and planing and moulding machines; some of these are shown in Fig. 36, Vol. II.

The rough block of stone from the quarry is first taken to the *frame saw* which converts it into a number of slabs such as are shown at A, Fig. 19, the thickness of the slabs varying in accordance with requirements.

[1] Earth moving machinery is described in Chap. I, Vol. IV.

The frame saw is the best machine for cutting hard stone. The speed of cutting depends upon the number of cuts and the hardness of the stone. Hard sandstone may be cut at the rate of 150 mm (thickness) per hour and Portland stone may be cut at the rate of 300 mm per hour.

The frame saw has a rectangular horizontal frame, suspended by rods, which holds several (sometimes six) plain or corrugated steel blades, each blade being from 75 to 150 mm deep, 5 mm thick, and from 2 to 4·5 m long. These blades are parallel to and at adjustable distances from each other. Electric or other power is supplied to give the frame a short backward and forward motion at a rate of from 150 to 180 strokes per minute.

During this process, water is supplied immediately over the cuts. At the same time an abrasive agent such as sharp sand, chilled shot (small steel balls) or carborundum is applied along the length of the cut to assist the cutting action. Sand should be the abrasive used for the sawing of Portland stone as steel shot tends to discolour the stone on account of rust.

The frame is raised after the sawing operation has been completed, the table is pushed clear of the frame, and the slabs are unloaded and taken to another machine for the next dressing operation.

Assuming that these slabs of stone are required for general walling, each is now conveyed to the *circular saw* for the cutting of the remaining faces. There are two types of this machine, *i.e.*, the *diamond saw* and the *carborundum saw*.

The diamond saw.—This consists of a circular steel blade, one size being 1·5 m in diameter and 6 mm thick. Some 240 diamonds are secured in small U-shaped sockets round the edge of the blade. The slab of stone is clamped on to a moving table which is caused to travel towards the blade at a uniform rate; at the same time the blade rotates at a speed which varies from 500 to 600 revs. per min.

The cutting rate of the machine depends upon its power and the hardness of the stone. Thus a 15 kw machine will cut from 645 to 1 000 cm² of Portland stone per minute. Whilst this rate is considerably faster than that of the frame saw, the circular saw can only deal effectively with stones which are less than 1 m thick. Only limestones or soft sandstones should be cut by means of the diamond saw, hard sandstones cause an excessive wearing action on the sockets and blade.

The carborundum saw.—This has a 50 mm wide continuous rim of carborundum which is dovetailed round the periphery of the steel blade.

Its cutting rate is half that of the diamond saw. It is preferred to the diamond saw on account of the more accurate work which it produces, and it is therefore very suitable for the *jointing* (forming the ends) of cornices and similar stones which have been moulded. Cuts as fine as 6 mm are obtainable.

Water is supplied during the cutting operation in order to cool the blade of each of the above two circular saws. Some circular saws have two blades. Another type consists of a blade which traverses the fixed stone as it rotates, and it is therefore particularly useful for cutting long stones.

The above operations are usually all that are necessary for the cutting and dressing of stones for walling, but it is sometimes required to have the surface of each stone which will be exposed when fixed, *rubbed* so as to remove the machine marks. This is accomplished on a machine called a *rubbing bed*.

This consists of a steel circular table, about 3 m in diameter, which rotates. The stone is placed on the bed, clamped from above, and as the table rotates, the abrasive action of carborundum, sand and water eliminates the machine marks.

Cornices, string courses, plinths, etc., are moulded by means of *planing and moulding machines*. After the moulding operations have been completed as described below, the stone is jointed into the required lengths by the carborundum saw as explained above. Intersections of mouldings are usually worked by hand, the maximum length of mouldings being machined so as to reduce the hand labour to a minimum.

A simple type of planing and moulding machine consists of a cutting tool of cast steel suspended from a box at an angle of about 45°. Cutting tools are of various shapes and sizes and their cutting edges are shaped the reverse of the desired moulds. One end of the stone is first hand-moulded to the required section. The tool traverses the stone backwards and forwards until it conforms with the section cut at the end.

In another type of planer the stone is fixed to a moving table below a fixed tool.

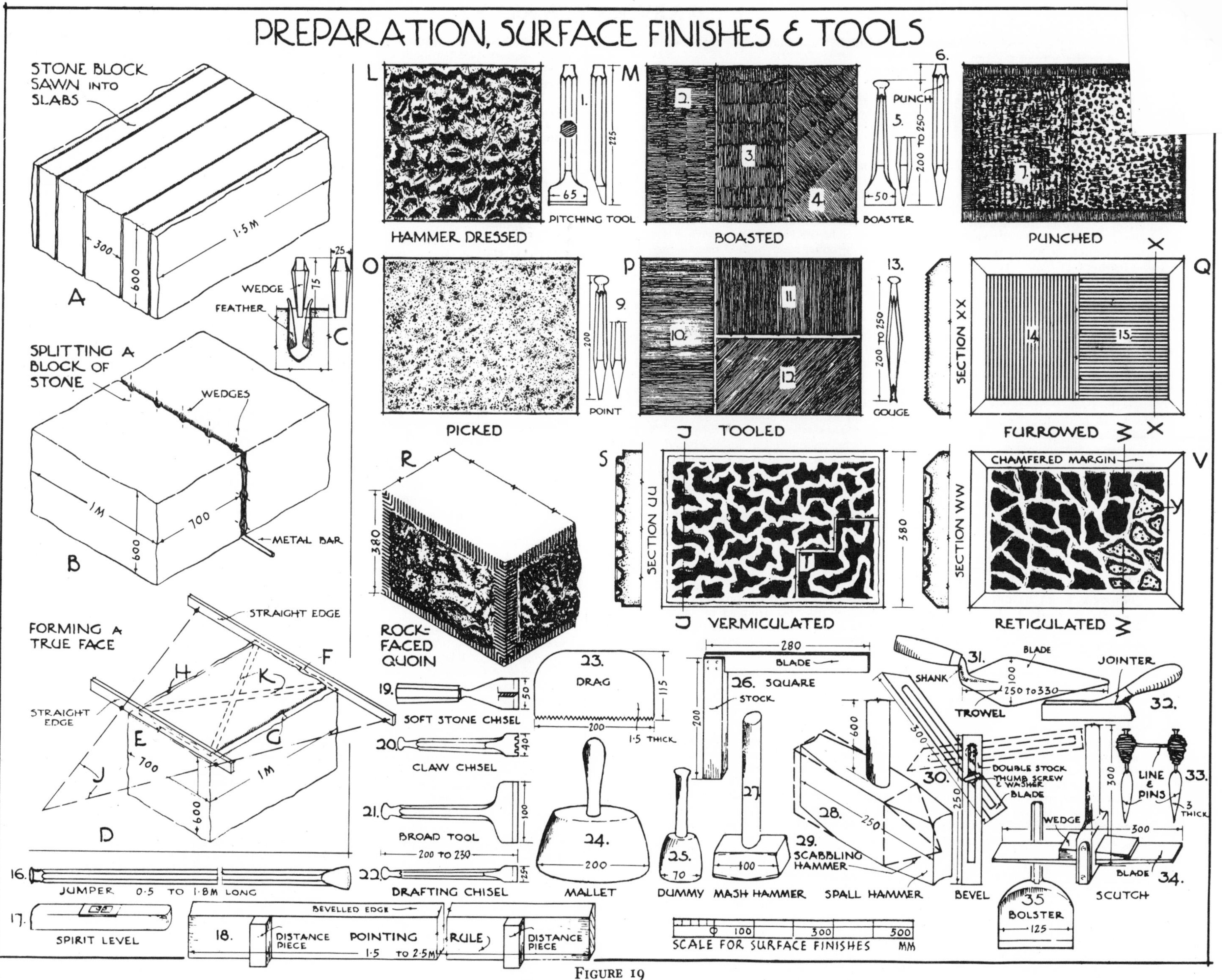

PREPARATION, SURFACE FINISHES & TOOLS
STONE BLOCK SAWN INTO SLABS
1·5 M
300
600
A
WEDGE
FEATHER
25
75
C
SPLITTING A BLOCK OF STONE
WEDGES
1M
700
600
METAL BAR
B
FORMING A TRUE FACE
STRAIGHT EDGE
STRAIGHT EDGE
H
K
F
E
G
J
700
1M
600
D
L
HAMMER DRESSED
1.
65
225
PITCHING TOOL
M
BOASTED
2.
3.
4.
BOASTER
50
5.
PUNCH
200 TO 250
6.
PUNCHED
7.
8.
O
PICKED
9.
200
POINT
P
TOOLED
10.
11.
12.
13.
200 TO 250
GOUGE
SECTION XX
FURROWED
14.
15.
Q
X
X
R
380
ROCK-FACED QUOIN
S
SECTION UU
J
J
VERMICULATED
380
SECTION WW
W
W
RETICULATED
CHAMFERED MARGIN
V
Y
16.
JUMPER 0·5 TO 1·8M LONG
17.
SPIRIT LEVEL
18.
BEVELLED EDGE
DISTANCE PIECE
POINTING RULE
1·5 TO 2·5M
DISTANCE PIECE
19.
50
SOFT STONE CHISEL
20.
40
CLAW CHISEL
21.
100
BROAD TOOL
200 TO 230
22.
25
DRAFTING CHISEL
23.
DRAG
115
200
1·5 THICK
24.
200
MALLET
25.
70
DUMMY
26. SQUARE
280
BLADE
STOCK
200
27.
100
MASH HAMMER
28.
600
250
29.
SCABBLING HAMMER
SPALL HAMMER
30.
300
DOUBLE STOCK
THUMB SCREW & WASHER
BLADE
250
BEVEL
31.
BLADE
SHANK
100
250 TO 330
TROWEL
JOINTER
32.
33.
LINE & PINS
3 THICK
300
300
WEDGE
BLADE
34.
SCUTCH
35
BOLSTER
125
0 100 300 500
SCALE FOR SURFACE FINISHES MM

FIGURE 19

In both of these types, after each traverse, the box automatically swings over to bring the tool in the correct position for the return.

Another type of machine has four cutting tools and is therefore particularly effective for large cornices.

There is also a moulding apparatus known as the *Pneumatic Dressing and Carving Plant*. This consists of an air compressor which operates tools of various shapes and sizes called pneumatic hammers. The finest carving, as well as the heaviest dressing, can be executed by these tools.

Hand Dressing.—In the absence of machinery, the following are certain of the operations which are performed by hand:—

Splitting, Stoping, Wedging or Coping.—A large block of stone is split into smaller units as shown at B, Fig. 19. Straight lines are marked on three of the faces along which a narrow groove is chiselled by means of the punch (6, Fig. 19) or wide chisel called a nicker. Shallow holes at 150 to 225 mm centres are formed along the groove, a steel bar is placed under the stone in the same plane as the groove, steel wedges or gads or wedges and feathers are placed in the holes, and the wedges are gradually and uniformly hammered in until the stone splits.

Large blocks of hard sandstone are divided at the quarry as described but the work is expedited by using a pneumatic drill to form 100 to 150 mm deep holes to receive the wedges.

Snapping.—This is adopted for splitting hard stones which are about 150 mm thick. In splitting a block of stone, a groove is formed on all four sides and in the same plane. The pitching tool (1, Fig. 19) is held vertically and struck smartly as it is moved along the groove on each face. A piece of waste stone is placed under the block and a few blows of a heavy hammer on the latter (which is protected by a piece of wood) will be sufficient to snap the stone. Alternatively, a continuous nick is formed across the top and both sides, the block is turned over on to a small stone and split with a smart blow from a heavy hammer.

Bath or similar stone is best divided into units by sawing immediately after it has been quarried, as it then contains moisture (*quarry sap*) which renders it comparatively soft.

Forming a True Face.—A true face is worked on the stone as follows and as shown at D, Fig. 19. The *marginal draft* E is first formed by the mason using a drafting chisel (22, Fig. 19) and wood mallet (24) or electric hammer and chisel to remove the superfluous stone to a level slightly below that of the deepest hollow on the rough face. The draft must be level as tested by a straight-edge, although an experienced mason can dispense with this. A similar parallel draft is formed at F in the same plane as E in order that the face shall be " out of winding or twist." This is tested by placing straight-edges on the drafts and sighting through as indicated by broken lines at J. Drafts G and H are then formed and the whole of the superfluous stone between them removed by means of the pitching tool (1), punch (6) or point (9). After continuous furrows have been formed across the face with the point or punch, the ridges may be removed by the chisel claw (20) and mallet; the chisel is worked parallel to the furrows, the teeth preventing the formation of holes. Diagonal drafts (K), in addition to the marginal drafts, are necessary for working a true face on a large stone. The adjacent surfaces may be dressed in a similar manner, the square (26) being used to ensure that the adjacent surfaces are square and also for marking any necessary lines.

The terms *plain work* or *plain face* are applied to the labour on a stone to form a true face. *Half plain work* describes a similar but rougher dressing, such as is only necessary for beds and joints.

Surface Finishes.—The finishes which may be given to the *face* (exposed surface) of a stone are many and varied, but those applied to the *beds* (upper and lower surfaces), *joints* (ends) and *back* of the stone are more limited, as the essential requirements are reasonably smooth and square surfaces.

The finish varies with the stone and the class of work for which it is required. Thus for *rubble work* of the *random rubble, uncoursed* class (see Fig. 20), very little labour is expended, whereas certain other finishes are both elaborate and costly. Stone which is roughly shaped and dressed is known as *quarry-dressed.*

Quarry Dressing.—Stone quarried in many districts is walled in its rough state. In certain quarries the stone lies in thin beds and splitting is all that may be necessary to fit the blocks for walling on account of their natural smooth faces and flatness of bed. Such smooth-faced stone is known as *self-faced* and has been used extensively in the construction of houses. Other stone may require a small amount of labour, such as *hammer-dressed* and *straight-cut* finishes.

Hammer-dressed.—Also known as *hammer-faced, quarry-faced, quarry-pitched* and *rustic-faced*, its appearance somewhat resembles that shown at L, Fig. 19. The face is roughly shaped by means of the mash hammer (27, Fig. 19) used to remove the larger raised portions of stone and shape it. The blocks are sometimes squared, the beds and joints being dressed back some 75 or 100 mm from the face (see plan in Fig. 22). This is done by using the square to mark the boundaries and working the pitching tool along them. This enables the stones to be fitted more closely together to give reasonably uniform thick joints.

Straight-cut.—This is applied to the faces of small blocks of stone used for *squared rubble* and *regular coursed rubble* (Fig. 22). The larger blocks are split at right angles to the natural bed (see p. 39) into smaller blocks and it is this split surface which provides the face, the slightly uneven texture being very effective. These small blocks are quickly squared by applying the mash hammer along the edges, followed by the punch.

Elaborate Dressing.—The following are some of the finishes which are worked by hand on squared stones: Boasted, punched, picked, tooled, furrowed, rock-faced, scabbled, combed, vermiculated and reticulated.

Boasted or Droved (see M, Fig. 19).—A true face is first formed as described above. This is then boasted or finished with the hammer and boaster (5) by forming a series of 38 to 50 mm wide bands of more or less parallel tool marks which cover the whole surface. These marks may be either horizontal (see 2), vertical (3) or at an angle of 45° (4) as required, and in making them the boaster is moved in the direction of the band at each stroke. This is a common finish which is applied to relatively inexpensive work, and it is also an intermediate dressing which is subsequently tooled, fluted, etc. (see below).

Punched, Broached or Stugged (see N, Fig. 19).—Depressions are formed on the rough surface with the punch (6). It may take the form of a series of parallel ridges and hollows (7), or the punch may be held almost vertically and driven in to form hollows at about 25 mm apart (8). It is used especially on the lower portions of large buildings.

Picked, Pecked or Dabbed (see O, Fig. 19).—This is similar to but finer than punched work, the small pits being formed by the point (9). Fine dressing is sometimes called *close-picked* or *sparrow-picked.* It is used for quoins and occasionally for general faced work.

Tooled or Batted (see P, Fig. 19).—The face is first boasted to bring it to a regular surface, after which a series of continuous and parallel horizontal (10) or vertical (11) or diagonal (12) fine chisel lines are formed with the batting or broad tool (21) which is caused to move in the direction of its *edge.* It is usual to specify the number of lines per 25 mm the number varying from 8 to 10, depending upon the hardness of the stone and the degree of fineness required. This is a common dressing for ashlar work (see p. 47). Note the difference in the appearance between boasted and tooled work, in the former the marks are flat and not continuous, whereas in tooled work the lines are deeper and are continuous.

Furrowed or Fluted (see Q, Fig. 19).—The surface is first boasted and then rubbed (see p. 36); 6 to 10 mm wide flutes (see section XX) are then carefully formed by a gouge (13) either vertically (14) or horizontally (15). Lines showing the arrises of the flutes are lightly scored and these serve as a guide to the mason as he works the gouge along each. This finish is sometimes applied to the fillets or flat bands of cornices, string courses, door and window architraves, etc.

Rock-faced, Rusticated or Pitch-faced (see R, Fig. 19).—After the marginal drafts have been worked (see above), the pitching tool is used to remove certain of the superfluous stone in the centre which is left raised or rough to imitate a rock-like surface. It is bolder than hammer-dressed work and is sometimes applied to plinths to give a semblance of strength and solidity.

Scabbled or Scappled.—This is similar to the latter, the scabbling or scappling hammer (shown by broken lines at 29) being used to remove some of the irregularities.

Dragged or Combed.—This finish is given to soft limestones, such as Bath stone, by the application of drags (23). These drags are steel plates (about 2·5 mm thick) having serrated edges, and graded into " coarse," " second " and " fine," according to the number of teeth per 25 mm. After the surface of the stone has been brought to the required level by means of the dummy (the head of which is made of zinc or pewter and is shown at 25) and soft stone chisel (19), the coarse drag is dragged backwards and forwards in different directions across the surface until the tool marks have been eliminated; this is followed by the second drag and finally by the fine drag until all scratches have disappeared.

Vermiculated (see S, Fig. 19).—The face is brought to a level and smooth finish. Marginal drafts are sunk at least 10 mm below the surface, when sinkings are then worked to a depth equal to that of the drafts (see section UU) so as to form a winding snake-like (*verminous*) ridge which is often continuous (as shown at T) and which has to be carved by means of gouges (13).

Reticulated (see V, Fig. 19).—This is similar to vermiculated, excepting that the ridges or veins are less winding and are linked up to form a network of irregularly shaped sinkings or *reticules*; the bottom of these hollows is sometimes sparrow-picked (see p. 38) with a fine point (9) as shown at Y.

Neither vermiculated nor reticulated rusticated dressings are applied much to modern work, probably on account of their expense, but they are occasionally adopted for quoins and to decorate and emphasize horizontal courses. They must be done with great care and to a bold scale if they are to be effective.

Chisel Drafted Margins.—Besides marginal drafts which vary from 20 to 50 mm and are necessary in the working of a true face (see p. 38), drafts are also used for the sake of appearance and some of these are shown in Fig. 19. These may be pitched (see L), square (N and S) or chamfered (Q and V). Stones which have been hammer-faced must be pitched or roughly trued up at the edges if close-fitting joints are needed. Drafted margins are usually given a boasted finish (N), or the surfaces may be rubbed (S) or tooled (R). Quarry-pitched walling must have drafts (called *angle drafts*) worked on both sides of the arris of each quoin stone and on jambs of door and window openings (see B, Fig. 20). This is to permit the use of the plumb rule and line to ensure plumb and accurate walling during its construction, the face of the drafts giving the line of the wall.

Tools.—A few of the many tools used by the mason have been referred to on the foregoing pages and illustrated in Fig. 19. Chisels are struck either with the mallet (24)—which is made of hardwood such as beech or hickory—or the hammer. The striking ends of mallet-headed chisels are broader (see 5, 9 and 13) than those which are hammer-headed (*e.g.*, 1 and 6) to prevent damaging the mallet. Cutting tools which have to withstand heavy impacts are usually made entirely of cast steel, others used for the dressing of soft stones may have wood handles (19) and these are struck with the dummy (25) which has a zinc or pewter head. Other tools, such as the trowel, square, line and pins, bevel, etc., have been described on p. 28.

Natural Bed.—Sedimentary rocks, such as limestones and sandstones, are stratified or laminated (due to the deposition of successive layers or laminae during the formation of the stone) and occur in beds of varying thickness. The layers are usually parallel to the bed and the term " natural bed " is applied to the surface of the stone which is parallel to these layers or bedding planes.

The beds are generally more or less horizontal, although in some quarries they are inclined (see A, Fig. 69). Some stones show the laminations very clearly, in other varieties the bed can only be detected with the aid of the microscope. The direction of the natural bed of certain sandstones is indicated by an examination of the small embedded flakes of mica (a silicate of a shining dark hue) which lie flat and parallel to the bed, and that of some limestones by the position of the minute shells which lie flat in the direction of the bedding planes. The trained mason can usually ascertain the lie of the bed on working the stone, it being easier to dress it in the direction of the planes. In order to prevent mistakes, it is the practice in some quarries to mark the direction of the natural bed on each stone before dispatch.

It is important that the stone shall be built in the correct position in relation to the natural bed, otherwise serious defects may occur. Thus for:

(*a*) General walling, the stone should be bedded on the natural bed so that the laminations are horizontal and at right angles to the pressure and thus the stone is better able to support the superimposed weight. This position is indicated by thin parallel lines at 1′, Fig. 24.

A wall should *never* be constructed of stones which are " face-bedded," *i.e.*, with the laminae vertical and *parallel* to the face of the wall, for in this position the action of the weather may cause decay along the edges of the stone, and, in extreme cases the exposed layer may separate and flake off.

(*b*) Cornices, string courses and similar projecting courses should be constructed of stones which are " edge-bedded " or " joint-bedded," *i.e.*, the stones are bedded with the laminations *vertical* and at *right angles* to the face of the wall (see 2′, Fig. 24), otherwise the mouldings may be defaced by weather action.

If the natural bed were vertical and parallel to the face of the wall, portions of the stone may flake off, as at O, Fig. 26, where part of the cornice on the left of the broken line may become detached. Similarly, if the natural bed were horizontal any undercut mouldings and horizontal fillets (flat bands) would tend to disappear, *e.g.*, the lower portion below the broken line at P, Fig. 26.

An exception to this rule applies to quoin cornice, etc., stones which are returned, as the return faces would be face-bedded and would result in rapid loss of shape; therefore such must be carefully selected compact stones, free from obvious laminations, and bedded on the natural bed.

(*c*) Arches should be constructed having the natural bed of the voussoirs normal to the face of the arch and perpendicular to the line of thrust (see 3′, Fig. 24).

DEFECTS

The following are some of the defects in stone :—

Vents.—These are small fissures or hollows in the stone which may cause it to deteriorate rapidly, especially if exposed. Stone with vents should not be used for building purposes.

Shakes or *snailcreep* are minute cracks in the stone containing calcite (a carbonate of lime) and forming hard veins which, in course of time, project beyond the general face on account of their greater durability. It is not advisable to use stone containing them on account of the difference in texture which results.

Sand-holes are cracks which appear in the stone and which are filled with sandy matter. *Clay-holes* are vents which contain matter of a clayey nature. Both are readily decomposed when subjected to the action of weather, and the stone should be rejected.

Mottle is a defect which causes the stone to have a spotted appearance due to the presence of small chalky patches. Such stone is unfit for building purposes.

An inherent defect which occurs in Portland stone is the presence of shells (known as *shelly bars*), fossils, cavities and flints. These are often not detected until the large blocks from the quarry are being converted into smaller units, the saw-cuts revealing their presence. The affected portions must be removed and therefore waste results.

The presence of clay and oxide of iron is apt to cause disfigurement of the stone, producing brown-coloured bands which interfere with the uniformity in colour of the stone and diminish its durability.

Classification.—The various classes of walling may be divided into :

1. *Rubble Work*, which consists of blocks of stone that are either undressed or comparatively roughly dressed and having wide joints, and
2. *Ashlar*, consisting of walls constructed of blocks of carefully dressed or wrought stone with narrow joints.

RUBBLE WORK

1. *Rubble Work* includes :

(*a*) Random Rubble	(i) Uncoursed. (ii) Built to courses.
(*b*) Squared Rubble	(i) Uncoursed. (ii) Built to courses. (iii) Regular coursed.
(*c*) Miscellaneous	(i) Polygonal walling. (ii) Flint walling. (iii) Lake District masonry.

(a) Random Rubble.—The stones are those which have been quarry dressed (see p. 38). The principles of bonding referred to on p. 3 apply equally well to this class of work as they do to brickwork. Unlike bricks, the stones are not of uniform size and shape, and therefore greater care and ingenuity have to be exercised in arranging that they shall adequately distribute the pressure over the maximum area and in the avoidance of long continuous vertical joints.

The bond should be sound both transversely (across the thickness of the wall) and longitudinally. Transverse bond is obtained by the liberal use of *headers* (or *bonders*) and *throughs*. Headers are stones which reach beyond the middle of the wall from each face to overlap in the centre (sometimes called *dog's tooth* bond). Through stones or throughs extend the full thickness of the wall (see Fig. 20). Satisfactory stability may reasonably be assured if one-quarter of the face consists of headers (approximately two per square metre), in addition to one-eighth of the face area of throughs (one per square metre).

Unless the relative impermeability of the stones is satisfactory it is not advisable to use through stones for external walls, as moisture may be conducted through them and cause dampness on the internal faces. This may be prevented by either (*a*) using three-quarter bonders or (*b*) using throughs extending to within 20 mm of the internal face and covering the ends with slate bedded on good mortar. The latter method is only applied if the internal faces of the walls are to be plastered.

The footings should consist of concrete (see section CC at A, Fig. 20) or, in the case of garden walls, large flat-bedded stones twice the thickness of the wall in width (as in elevation at A, Fig. 20).

(a) (i) Random Rubble, Uncoursed (see A, Fig. 20).—This is the roughest and cheapest form of stone walling and consists of stones which are usually quarried near, if not on, the building site. The face appearance varies considerably on account of the great difference in the sizes and shapes of the material used. The " waller " takes the stones, morr or less at random (hence the title), from the heap and builds them in to form the strongest bond, any inconvenient corners or excrescences being knocked off the stones if such will assist in this operation. The larger stones are flat-bedded and packed or wedged up with small pieces of stone or *spalls* (see figure); the intervening spaces are then filled in with the smaller stones, no attempt being made to form vertical joints. The joints are well filled and flushed with mortar; these are sometimes of considerable width on face, being as much as 50 mm or more in places. A reduction in the quantity of mortar results if small pieces of stone are driven into the mortar at the face joints; these splinters may also be used to wedge up the stones; such joints are said to be *galleted* (see A). The larger stones are selected for the quoins and jambs to give increased strength and, incidentally, to improve the appearance.

Boundary walls constructed of this class are usually given a slight batter on both faces, as shown, to give additional stability (see p. 54).

It is common to build dwarf walls, such as garden or field boundary walls or fences, of common rubble *without* mortar. Such is known as *dry rubble* walling. The stability of these walls is entirely dependent upon the careful interlocking and bonding of the stones.

(a) (ii) Random Rubble, Built to Courses (B, Fig. 20).—This walling is similar to the above, excepting that the work is roughly levelled up to form courses varying from 300 to 450 mm thick. These courses usually coincide with the varying heights of the quoin and jamb stones.

In the construction of the wall, the quoins are built first (as for brickwork—see p. 30), the line is stretched level with the tops of the quoin stones, and the intervening walling is brought up to this level. One of the courses is shown numbered in the order in which the stones would be bedded. The stones are set in mortar and at every course the work is well flushed with mortar and pressed into the internal joints.

This forms a stronger wall than the uncoursed type (long continuous vertical joints being more readily avoided), although the somewhat regular horizontal joints at the courses detract from its appearance.

Provided the site and stone are satisfactory, one course of through stones at E (equal to twice the thickness of the wall) is a sufficient foundation for boundary walls, otherwise a double course (E and F) would be required as shown in the section.

Note.—Although the illustrated examples refer to boundary walls, this form of construction has been adopted in the erection of thousands of houses and farmsteads in various parts of the country.

(b) Squared Rubble.—The stone used is generally one which is found in quarries in thin beds, or in thicker beds of laminated stone which can be easily split into smaller units. Little labour is necessary to form comparatively straight bed and side joints; the stones are usually squared and brought to a hammer-dressed or straight-cut finish (see p. 38) although they may be given either tooled (see p. 38) or dragged (see p. 38) surface finishes.

Fig. 21 shows a gable wall (*i.e.*, an end wall which is continued up to and sometimes above the roof line and the upper portion of which conforms with the shape of the roof) of a building which may be constructed in any one of the three types of squared rubble. A portion of the wall is drawn to a larger scale in Fig. 22 and details of three varieties are shown. The stones forming the window may be given a smoother finish than that of the general walling so as to form a contrast. A description of the head, sill, mullions, transome and coping is given on pp. 49–52.

(b) (i) Squared Rubble, Uncoursed (F, Fig. 22).—This is often known as *Square-snecked Rubble*. The stones are available in various sizes and are arranged on face in several irregular patterns. A very effective appearance results if the walling comprises a series of combined units consisting of four stones, *i.e.*, a large stone called a *riser* or *jumper* (generally a bonder or through stone), two thinner stones known as *levellers* and a small stone called a *sneck* or *check*.

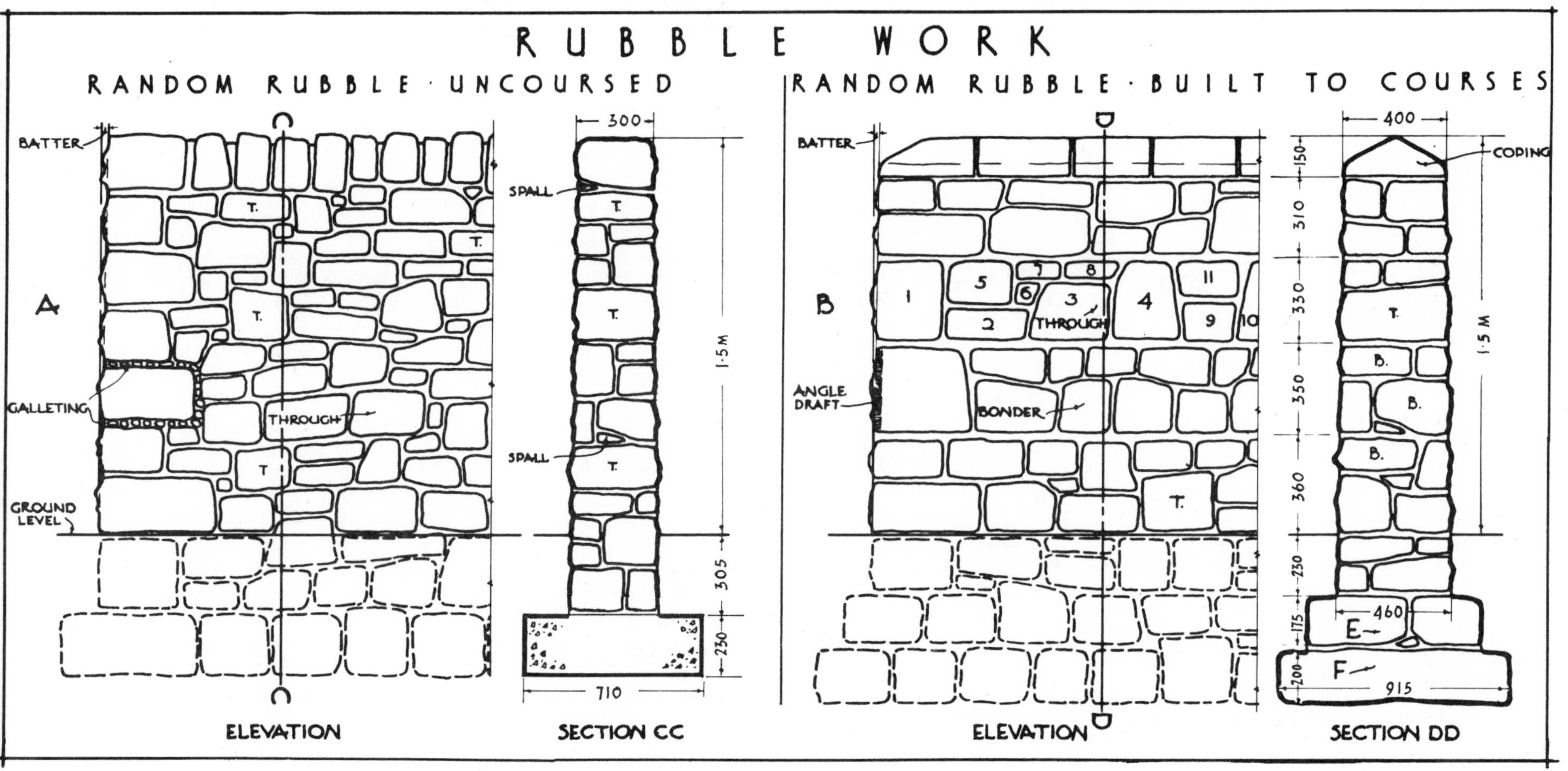

FIGURE 20

Although uniformity is neither essential nor desirable, it is found that an extremely well-bonded wall of pleasing appearance results if the approximate depths of the snecks, levellers and risers are in the proportion of 1 : 2 : 3 respectively; thus, if the depth of the sneck is 75 mm, that of the levellers would be about 150 mm and the depth of the riser would be approximately 225 mm, as shown. The vertical joint between each pair of levellers is more or less centrally over a riser, and the snecks link up with the risers.

The snecks are characteristic of this class of wall (hence the name) and their object is to prevent the occurrence of long continuous vertical joints. As shown

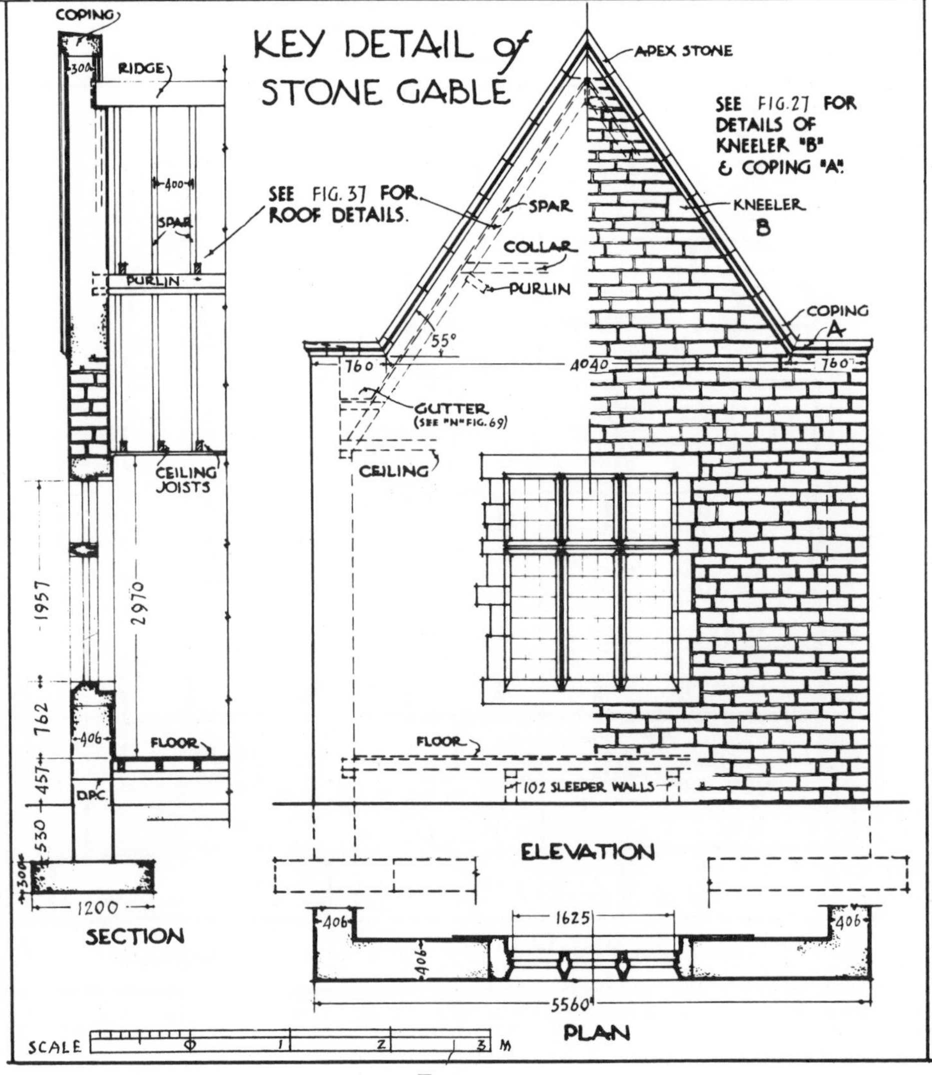

FIGURE 21

on plan, the side joints of the face stones are only dressed square for about 75 mm from the face which is usually only quarry-dressed (see p. 38). Another form of snecked rubble is shown at F, Fig. 23.

(b) (ii) Squared Rubble, Built to Courses.—The stones are similar to those used for snecked rubble, but, like the random rubble built to courses class, the work is levelled up to courses of varying depth. The squared face stones may be arranged as shown at B, Fig. 20, or each course may consist of quoins, jamb stones, bonders and throughs of the same height, with smaller stones built in between them up to the height of these larger stones, to complete the course. This latter arrangement is sometimes known as *Coursed Header Work* and is shown at G, Fig. 22.

(b) (iii) Squared Rubble, Regular Coursed (H, Fig. 22).—This type of walling is built in courses of varying height, but the stones in any one course are *all* of the same depth. The stones vary from 50 to 225 mm thick and are from 150 mm to 225 mm wide on bed. The faces may be pitched to give a rusticated appearance, or they may be dressed to a smoother finish, the straight-cut dressing described on p. 38 being particularly effective.

This work is very popular in certain parts of the country where there is available a plentiful and convenient supply of hard stone of good colour and satisfactory weathering quality. Many buildings in Lancashire and Yorkshire are built of this class of external walling.

Regular coursed rubble walling which consists of large squared blocks that are usually either hammer-faced or pitch-faced is sometimes called *Block-in-Course.* It is usually associated with heavy engineering work, such as in the construction of sea walls, retaining walls, etc., and is not often used in general building work.

(c) Miscellaneous.—There are many variations of walling which may be classed under Rubble Work. These variations are due to the particular characteristic qualities of the local materials available and the traditional forms of construction peculiar to those localities. The three examples mentioned under class (*c*) on p. 40 are all well known, and hence their inclusion. It should be observed that, owing to the comparative cheapness of bricks, these have, to a certain extent, replaced the local material and thus none of the following three examples are adopted for new work to the same extent as formerly.

(c) (i) Polygonal Walling (A and B, Fig. 23).—The stone used for this class of wall, although tough, can be easily split and dressed to any shape. It is hammer-pitched on face to an irregular polygonal shape and is bedded in position to show the face joints running irregularly in all directions.

In one class of this work the stones are only roughly shaped, causing them to fit together only approximately. This is *Rough-picked* and is shown at A. A second class shows more accurate work as the face edges of the stones are more carefully formed to permit of the small blocks to fit more intimately into each other to form what is called *Close-picked* work (see B). Walls faced with this material are generally backed with brickwork. This work is perhaps better known as *Kentish Rag* on account of a limestone found in Kent which has been used fairly extensively for this

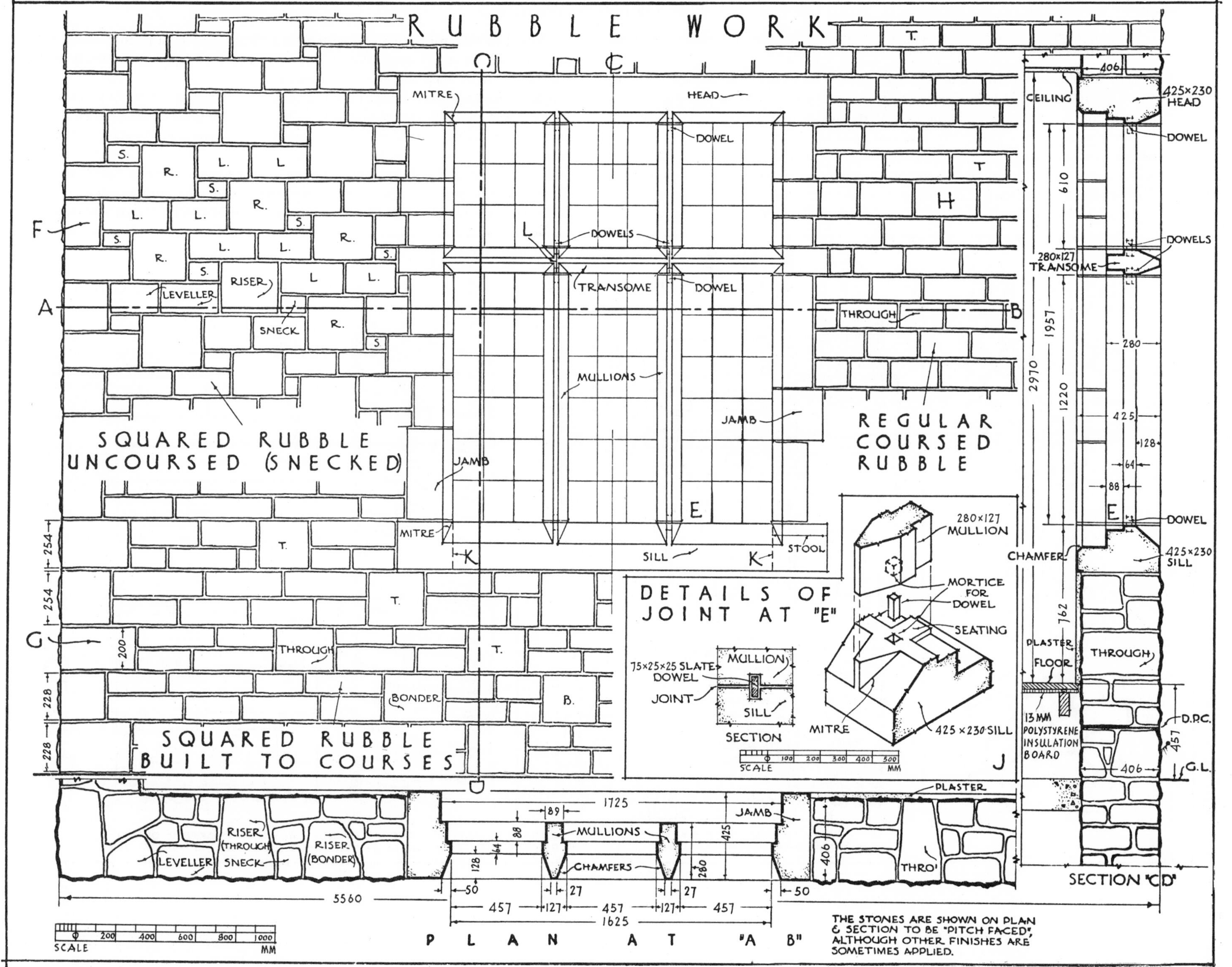
RUBBLE WORK
C
C
MITRE
HEAD
DOWEL
DOWELS
TRANSOME
DOWEL
L
MULLIONS
JAMB
JAMB
MITRE
E
SILL
STOOL
K
K
S.
R.
L.
L
S.
R.
L.
L.
S.
S.
R.
L.
L.
R.
S.
S.
L
L.
RISER
LEVELLER
SNECK
R.
S
F
A
B
THROUGH
T
T
H
SQUARED RUBBLE UNCOURSED (SNECKED)
REGULAR COURSED RUBBLE
T.
T.
T.
THROUGH
BONDER
B.
G
254
254
200
228
228
SQUARED RUBBLE BUILT TO COURSES
DETAILS OF JOINT AT "E"
280×127 MULLION
MORTICE FOR DOWEL
SEATING
MULLION
75×25×25 SLATE DOWEL
JOINT
SILL
SECTION
MITRE
425×230 SILL
SCALE
MM
J
406
425×230 HEAD
CEILING
DOWEL
610
DOWELS
280×127 TRANSOME
1957
2970
280
1220
425
128
64
88
E
DOWEL
CHAMFER
425×230 SILL
762
PLASTER
FLOOR
THROUGH
13 MM POLYSTYRENE INSULATION BOARD
D.P.C.
457
406
G.L.
SECTION "CD"
PLASTER
1725
89
JAMB
MULLIONS
88
64
128
425
RISER (THROUGH)
RISER (BONDER)
LEVELLER
SNECK
CHAMFERS
280
406
THRO'
5560
50
27
27
50
457
127
457
127
457
1625
SCALE
200
400
600
800
1000
MM
PLAN AT "AB"
THE STONES ARE SHOWN ON PLAN & SECTION TO BE "PITCH FACED", ALTHOUGH OTHER FINISHES ARE SOMETIMES APPLIED.

FIGURE 22

purpose. It is common in the southern counties. A soft sandstone has also been adopted to give a similar appearance.

(c) (ii) Flint Walling (C and D, Fig. 23).—The stones used in this class are flints or cobbles. They vary in width and thickness from 75 to 150 mm and in length from 150 to 300 mm, being irregularly shaped nodules of silica. Although extremely hard, they are brittle and can be readily snapped across. They are sometimes employed for the construction of walls in those counties where the flints are readily obtainable from the gravel beds which are often associated with chalk or limestone. Buildings near the coast have been constructed of walls in which the rounded flints from the beach have been used.

The external walls, which are generally from 350 to 450 mm thick, may consist of either (1) a facing of flints which have been snapped transversely across the centre, with a backing of the undressed flints as in section GG, or (2) similar but with the broken surfaces of the facing flints squared at the edges as shown at D or (3) undressed flints throughout. The face arrangement may either be uncoursed, built-to-courses or regular coursed. Uncoursed flint walling especially is deficient in strength on account of the small-sized material. This is partly made good by the introduction of through stones (two to every square metre), or continuous courses—known as *lacing courses*—of long thin stones or bricks or tiles at vertical intervals of 1 to 2 m and stone or brick piers at about 1·5 m

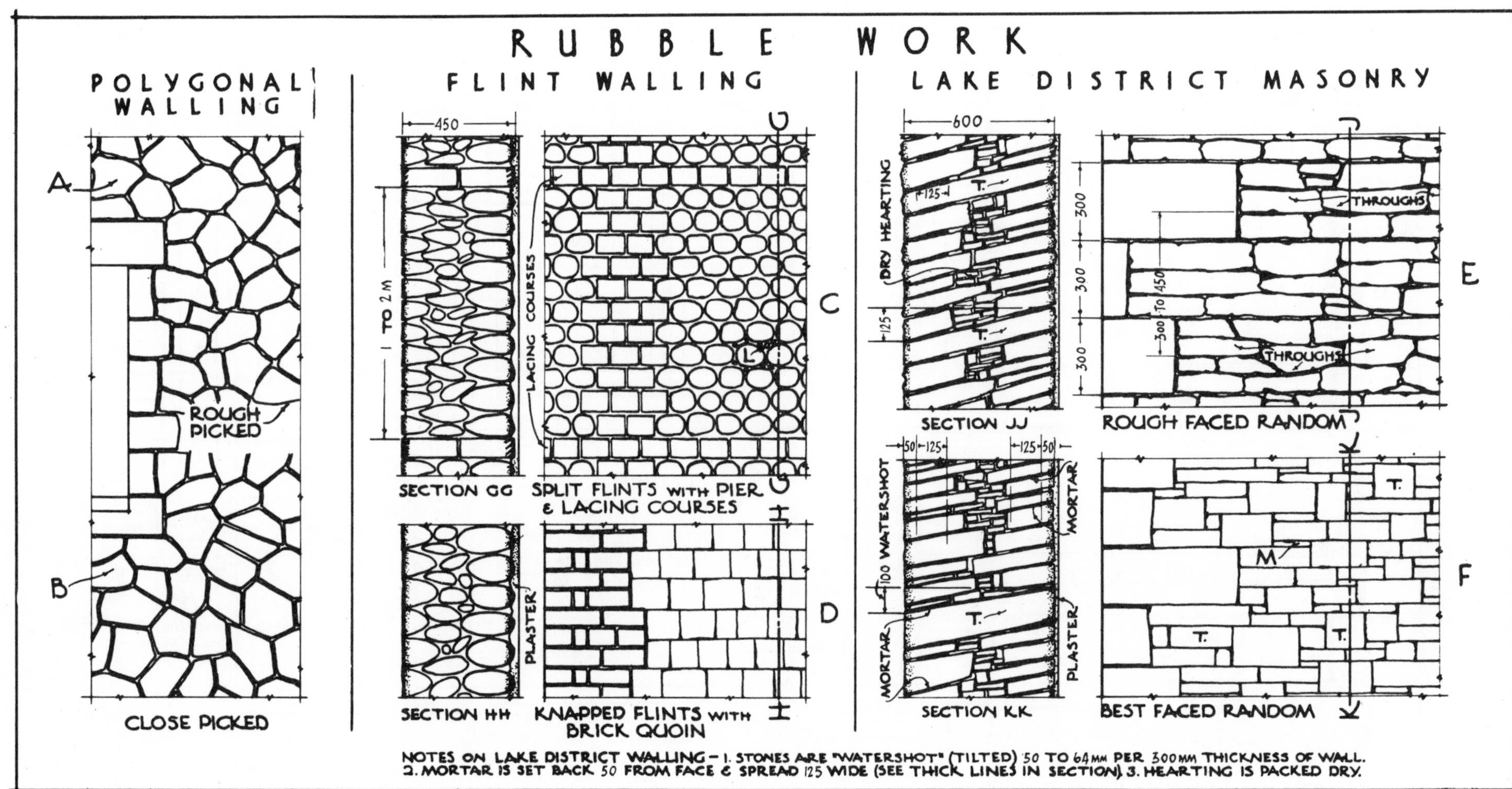

FIGURE 23

intervals; alternatively, brick headers may be inserted in diagonal lines across the face to give a diaper appearance.

An elevation and section of a portion of a wall faced with split flints, backed with undressed flints, and provided with brick lacing courses and piers are shown at C. The snapped flints are laid in courses. This is known as *polled* facing.

The facing flints are placed in position with the black or dark grey split surfaces outwards. This facing may either be built up with the body of the work, or the wall may be constructed by bedding the face flints on both sides to a height of about 225 mm, when a thick layer of soft mortar is spread in between into which the nodules are placed to force the mortar up between them—this is known as *larrying*; alternatively, *grouting* may be adopted, liquid mortar being poured over the nodules packed in the heart of the wall to fill up the interstices. The split or polled flints should be at least 100 mm long from front to back, and the internal facing flints are laid as headers in order that they may be well tailed into the body of the wall. Thin flakes removed from the flints may be used to gallet the joints for the reasons stated on p. 40 and shown at L.

Knapped flint facing, in conjunction with a brick quoin, is shown at D. The larger cobbles are snapped across, and the split surfaces are dressed (knapped) to give faces which are approximately 100 mm square. This is the best type of flint walling and is sometimes known as *gauged* or *squared* flint.

The facing flints are laid very close together so that little, if any, mortar joints are visible. Knapped flint work is sometimes arranged to form panels between stone or brick dressings, when the flints are sometimes unbonded, *i.e.*, the vertical joints are continuous.

When the flints are undressed throughout (as for cottage work) the external and internal face flints are laid as headers and the hearting of headers and stretchers are tightly packed between. The appearance is improved if the mortar joints on the outer face are well raked back with a pointed stick. If the joints are brought up flush with the face of the work, the appearance which results of only small portions of the flints surrounded by broad joints is not good.

The colour of the crust of the flint varies from a white to greyish blue, but, when snapped, the broken surface is almost black (flecked with brown or white) and glassy in appearance. Thus polled and knapped facing is of a shiny black colour, and that of undressed flint work is much lighter.

Cottages in the Norfolk district were sometimes constructed with 328 mm thick external walls with brick foundations, and above ground level they consisted of flint work with 102 mm brick internal linings having continuous heading courses every fifth course. The brick lining provided a good surface for plastering and reduced the amount of plaster required.

(c) (iii) Lake District Masonry (E and F, Fig. 23).—This is peculiar to buildings in certain parts of Cumberland and Westmorland. The stone, which is a slate, is obtained locally. The colour of the two varieties used chiefly for walling is olive (popularly known as " blue ") and green,[1] both are durable and used for the best work. The stone arrives on the job in irregularly shaped flat-bedded blocks varying from small pieces to a maximum size of approximately 600 mm wide by 900 mm long. These blocks are broken and dressed by the wallers to the size and shape required as the work proceeds. The amount of dressing done depends upon the desired face appearance of the wall. There are two types of this masonry, *i.e.*, *rough-faced random walling*, *built to courses*, and *best-faced random walling*.

[1] This stone is often the waste from the slate quarries.

Rough-faced Random Walling, Built to Courses (E, Fig. 23).—The faces of the stones are roughly dressed and the stones are irregular in shape. The blocks are closely fitted together, spalls being used to pack up the larger of them, and at vertical intervals of from 300 to 450 mm they are levelled up to the *watershot* (see below) to form a continuous joint which is more or less horizontal. The through stones form continuous courses at from 600 to 900 mm intervals.

Best-faced Random Walling (F, Fig. 23).—This resembles square snecked rubble (Fig. 22), the stones being squared on face with the hammer. The faces are naturally smooth and the stones are referred to as being *self-faced*. Some of the snecks are very thin (*e.g.*, that at M is only 20 mm thick). Unlike the last mentioned, the throughs are staggered, and on an average two throughs per square metre of face are allowed.

The walling is constructed in a manner which is unique and much skill is demanded of the wallers. As shown in the sections, the wall in effect consists of three portions, *i.e.*, inner and outer faces with an intermediate " hearting." Particular attention is drawn to the through stones which are tilted downwards towards the external face. This is known as " watershot," and the amount of watershot is 50 to 64 mm per 300 mm thickness of wall. Thus if the watershot is 50 mm, the back edge of the bed in a 600 mm thick wall will be about 100 mm above the corresponding front edge. The remaining face stones are given a similar watershot. The top bed of stone window and door heads and the bottom bed of window sills are watershot. As mentioned on p. 18, the damp-proof course consists of two courses of slates in cement mortar. The quoins are of limestone or slate. The characteristic colour and rich texture of the stone give a delightful appearance to this class of work.

Solid walls vary in thickness from 525 to 750 mm.

Alternatively, a 320 mm thick *cavity* wall having a 160 mm slate outer leaf, 70 mm cavity and 90 mm concrete brick inner leaf can be made.

The solid type of wall is constructed in the following manner: The wall is often started with the stones watershot, as the natural face of the stone is not square but canted to the bed.[1] The wallers work in pairs, the more experienced man working on the outside and the other inside to assist in the packing up of the face stones with small pieces of stone or spalls. Both faces are partially bedded in mortar which is set back from each face some 50 or 75 mm, and the width of each layer of mortar after it has been spread and squeezed out by the weight of the stone is about 125 mm. Mortar is not usually applied to the side joints as sufficient is squeezed up when the

[1] This is due to the cleavage planes being inclined to the bedding planes (see A, Fig. 69).

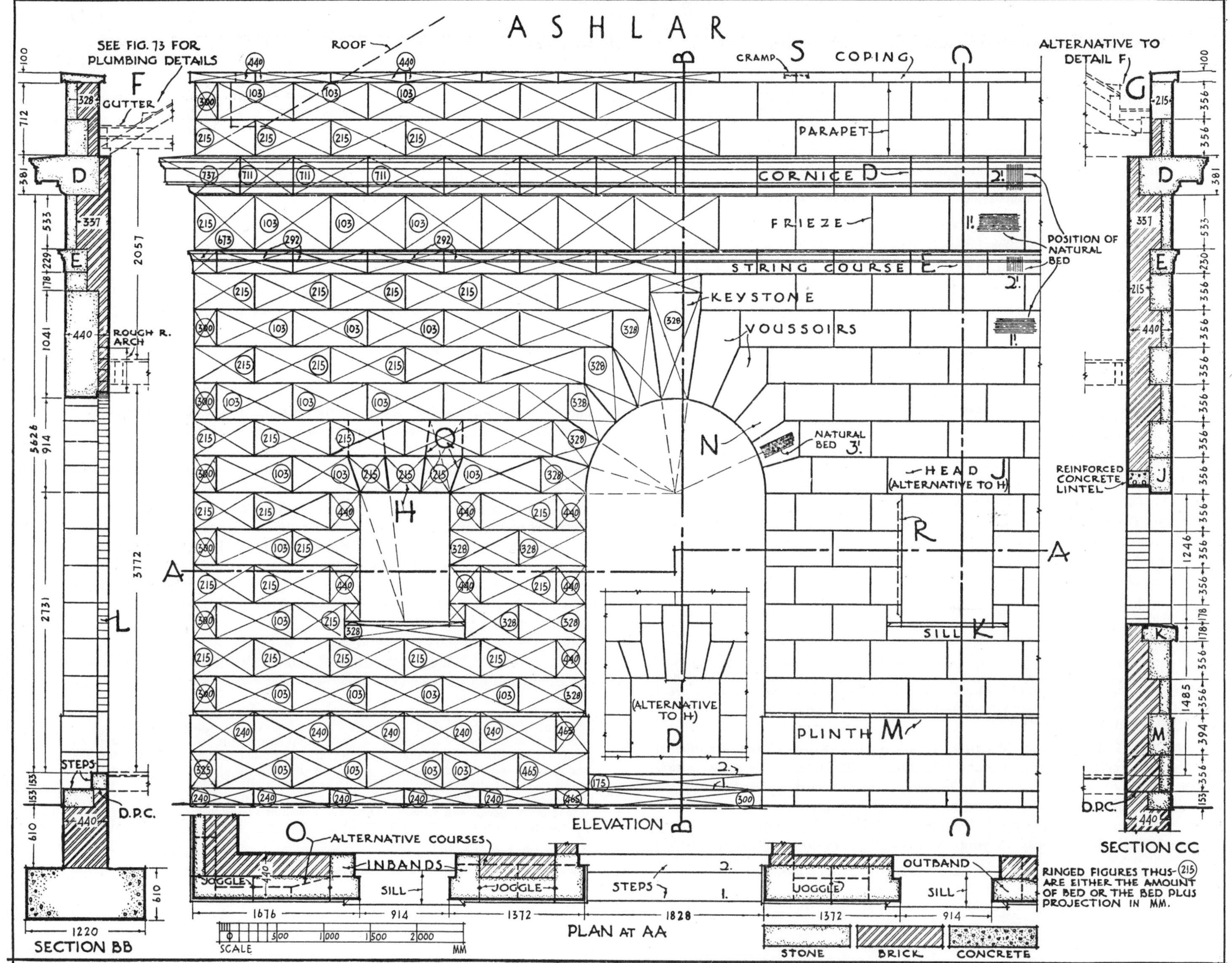
ASHLAR
SEE FIG. 73 FOR PLUMBING DETAILS
ROOF
CRAMP
COPING
ALTERNATIVE TO DETAIL F
GUTTER
PARAPET
CORNICE D
FRIEZE
POSITION OF NATURAL BED
STRING COURSE E
KEYSTONE
VOUSSOIRS
ROUGH R. ARCH
NATURAL BED
HEAD J (ALTERNATIVE TO H)
REINFORCED CONCRETE LINTEL
SILL K
(ALTERNATIVE TO H)
PLINTH M
STEPS
D.P.C.
ELEVATION
ALTERNATIVE COURSES
INBANDS
OUTBAND
JOGGLE
SILL
STEPS
SECTION BB
SECTION CC
PLAN AT AA
SCALE MM
STONE
BRICK
CONCRETE
RINGED FIGURES THUS (215) ARE EITHER THE AMOUNT OF BED OR THE BED PLUS PROJECTION IN MM.

Figure 24

stone is bedded. The maximum overlap in the centre is given to the stones in both faces of the wall. The hearting between the two-faced portions consists of small stones *packed dry*. The object of this is to ensure that any water penetrating the outer face will pass down the dry filling to the throughs below, which on account of the watershot, will not penetrate and cause dampness on the internal face. If any of the mortar joints were continuous from front to back, dampness would be caused by capillary attraction.

This form of construction has been proved to be most effective in resisting dampness in a district with a notoriously high rainfall, and it is for this reason that it is still employed in that area.[1]

ASHLAR

2. *Ashlar*.—This class of masonry consists of blocks of accurately dressed stone with extremely fine bed and end joints. The thickness of these joints is often only 3 mm and rarely exceeds 5 mm.[2] Such accurate work is only possible when the blocks are cut perfectly true to the required shape, and therefore the beds and joints at least are sawn. The backs are usually sawn, except when the ashlar is to be backed with rubble, when they may be given a rougher dressing. The surface finish is usually that left by the carborundum saw or it may be rubbed; several of the more elaborate dressings described on pp. 38–39 may also be applied.

The face arrangement of ashlar may resemble either of the three varieties shown in Fig. 22, the regular coursed being common with the courses of varying height, depending upon the size and character of the building. *Great care must be exercised when determining the sizes and proportion of the blocks of stone to ensure that they will conform with the general scale of the building.* Badly proportioned stones, which may be either too small or too large for the purpose, will completely mar the appearance of the work.

An adequate bond of blocks of uniform size is obtained if the length of each stone is from twice to thrice the height and if the courses break joint as shown in Fig. 24. There is a risk of the stone being fractured if unequal settlement occurs and if the length exceeds three times the height, although this length may be increased to five times the height if the stone is exceptionally strong.

Ashlar is sometimes given a face appearance resembling that of Flemish bond in brickwork. Occasionally it is arranged in courses which diminish in thickness from the base upwards, or alternately the courses are arranged with comparatively thick courses alternating with thinner courses.

Compound Walls.—Ashlar is the best grade of masonry and it is also the most expensive. In order to reduce the cost, it is the practice to construct walls faced with blocks of ashlar having a minimum thickness on bed combined with a backing of a cheaper material. Such are called compound walls. In " stone " districts, the usual backing is rubble (see D, Fig. 25), otherwise the backing is generally of brickwork (see Fig. 24).

It is essential that the facing shall be effectively bonded with the backing, and if the latter is of brickwork, unnecessary cutting of the bricks must be avoided. Effective bonding results and wastage of bricks and labour in cutting avoided when: (*a*) the ashlar courses are alternately 102 and 215 mm thick on bed, (*b*) the thickness of the backing is a multiple of half-bricks and (*c*) the height of each course of ashlar conforms with the combined height of the brick courses and the thickness of the bed joints.

On account of the thin mortar joints of the ashlar and the larger number of bed joints of the backing, it is necessary that the latter joints shall be as thin as possible so as to guard against unequal settlement. Cement mortar is frequently used for the backing; if the facing is of Portland stone, care must be taken to prevent the cement from working through and discolouring the face of the ashlar, and it is for this reason that the back of each ashlar block is covered with lime mortar (consisting of 1 part *grey* lime and 2 parts sand). Black mortar should not be used for the backing as this has been known to stain Portland-stone facing.

So as to ensure the ashlar vertical joints being completely filled with mortar, a vee-shaped notch is usually formed in each vertical joint surface so as to form a square hole between each pair of adjacent blocks. In constructing ashlar, mortar is spread on the front edge of the vertical surface (about 50 mm wide) of the last fixed stone; the adjacent stone is then placed in position, the back of the vertical joint is pointed with the mortar, and liquid mortar (grout) is poured down the hole to form a *joggle* so as to fill completely the space between each pair of stones (see Plan AA, Fig. 24, and N, Fig. 26).

The complete beds of the ashlar blocks shall be square with the face. If a bed is " worked hollow " (*i.e.*, the surface is brought below the outer edge of the stone to form an equivalent to a frog of a brick) there is a danger of the pressure being concentrated on the outer edge, causing the stone to crack and splinter off or spall (see p. 53 and X, Fig. 27).

Fig. 24 shows a portion of a building which is faced with ashlar backed with brickwork. Most of the ashlar courses are of uniform height and (excepting where the work is interrupted by windows) are alternately 215 and 102 mm thick on bed. This permits of a brick backing consisting of alternate sections which are 215 and 328 mm thick respectively. The plan at AA shows the special bonding in alternate courses owing to the presence of the door and window openings. The splaying of the back of the outband (see below) at O is often done to avoid continuous vertical joints.

The bonding of the quoins (sometimes called *scuntions* or *scontions*) should be noted, where the 215 mm thick courses are continued to the return face. An unsatisfactory appearance, indicating weakness, would result if the 102 mm thick courses were to show on the return face.

The diagonal lines and the ringed figures shown in the elevation indicate the extent and amount of bed respectively of each stone. This conforms with the usual practice, the diagonals being especially necessary when cornices, etc., comprise two or more stones in height.

The plan at B and the sketch D, Fig. 25, show the wall faced with ashlar with a backing of rubble.

Door and Window Openings.—As shown in the plan AA, Fig. 24, the jambs are bonded by using alternate headers (called *inbands*) and stretchers (termed

[1] In addition, this style harmonizes best with an exceptionally beautiful landscape.

[2] There are exceptions to fine jointed work, for example, at the Anglican Cathedral, Liverpool, where the large sandstone (Woolton) blocks are constructed in cement mortar and pointed with a mixture of 1 part white cement to 3 parts Leighton Buzzard sand, and the thickness of the joints is about 13 mm.

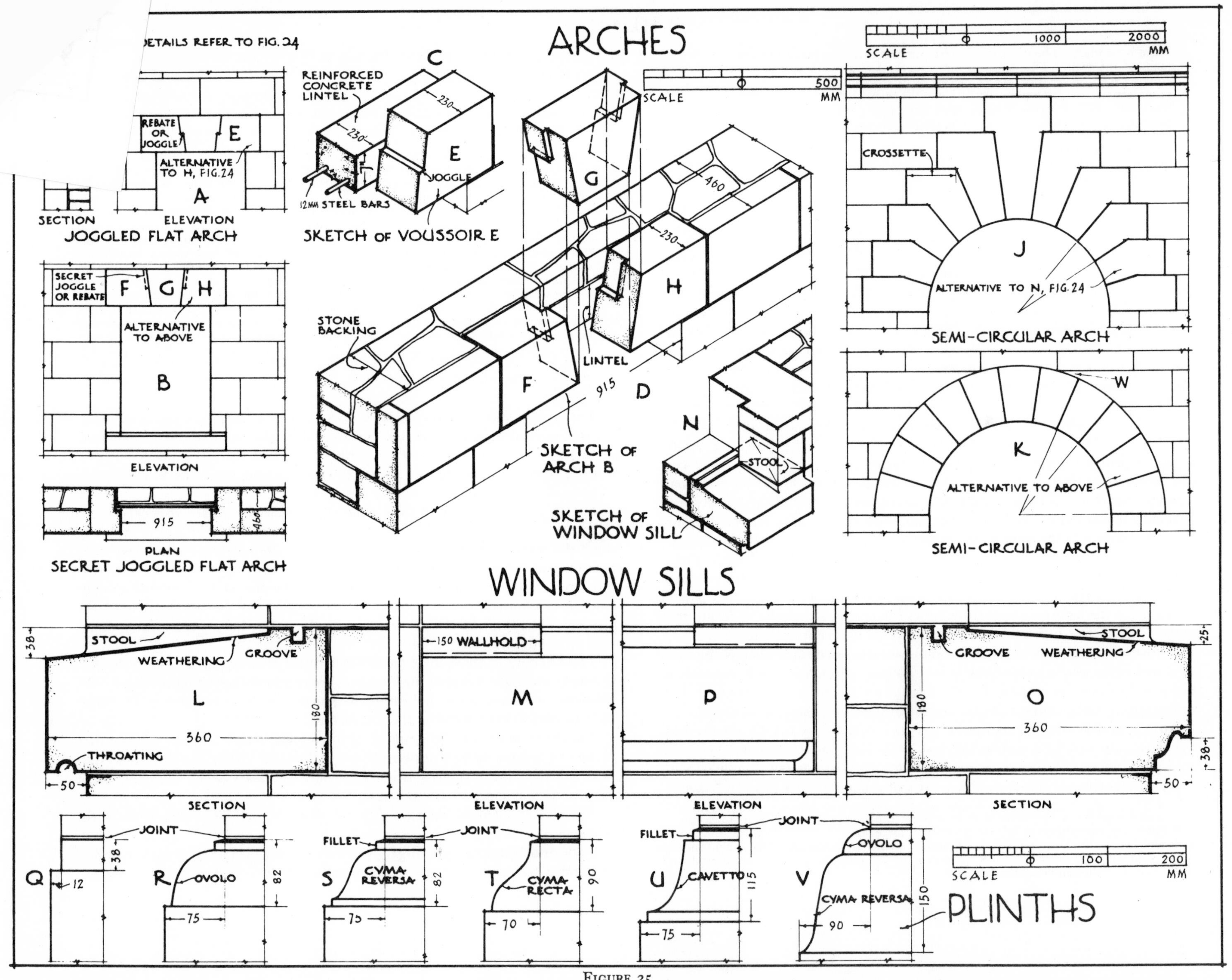
ARCHES
DETAILS REFER TO FIG. 24
REBATE OR JOGGLE
E
ALTERNATIVE TO H, FIG. 24
A
SECTION
ELEVATION
JOGGLED FLAT ARCH
C
REINFORCED CONCRETE LINTEL
230
E
JOGGLE
12MM STEEL BARS
SKETCH OF VOUSSOIR E
SCALE
500
MM
G
460
230
H
STONE BACKING
F
LINTEL
915
D
SKETCH OF ARCH B
N
STOOL
SKETCH OF WINDOW SILL
SECRET JOGGLE OR REBATE
F G H
ALTERNATIVE TO ABOVE
B
ELEVATION
915
460
PLAN
SECRET JOGGLED FLAT ARCH
SCALE
1000
2000
MM
CROSSETTE
J
ALTERNATIVE TO N, FIG. 24
SEMI-CIRCULAR ARCH
W
K
ALTERNATIVE TO ABOVE
SEMI-CIRCULAR ARCH
WINDOW SILLS
38
STOOL
WEATHERING
GROOVE
L
360
180
THROATING
50
150 WALLHOLD
M
P
GROOVE
WEATHERING
STOOL
25
O
180
360
38
50
SECTION
ELEVATION
ELEVATION
SECTION
JOINT
Q
38
12
R
OVOLO
82
75
FILLET
JOINT
S
CYMA REVERSA
82
75
T
CYMA RECTA
90
70
FILLET
JOINT
U
CAVETTO
115
75
OVOLO
V
CYMA REVERSA
90
150
SCALE
100
200
MM
PLINTHS

FIGURE 25

outbands), the former being rebated to receive the door or window frames. Sometimes the outer edges of these stones are splayed or *chamfered* which may be stopped (see broken lines at R) or may be continued round the head to form intersections called *mason's mitres* (see Fig. 22).

The head of an opening is finished with either a lintel or an arch, and the bottom is completed with a sill.

Lintels or Heads.—These have been described on p. 21.

Arches.—Brick arches have been described on pp. 21–24, and the terms geometrical construction, etc., there detailed are also applicable to stone arches. The temporary supports used in the construction of stone arches are shown in Fig. 43.

Flat Arches (see H, Q and P, Fig. 24, and A, B, C and D, Fig. 25).—Alternatives of that at H are shown at Q (partly indicated by broken lines and showing the arch equal to two courses in depth) and P, which shows a *stepped extrados.*

The alternatives at A and B, Fig. 25, are called *joggled* or *rebated* arches. That at A shows the keystone with small (about 25 mm) projections at the joints which fit into corresponding sinkings worked on the adjacent voussoirs; the object of these rebates or joggles is to prevent sliding taking place and dropping of the voussoirs. An isometric sketch of one of the voussoirs, with a portion of a reinforced concrete lintel behind it, is given at C. An alternative to arch A is shown at B; this shows *secret joggles* or rebates as they are not seen on the face; the construction is more clearly shown in the sketch at D.

Semicircular Arches (see N, Fig. 24, and J and K, Fig. 25).—That at N shows a stepped extrados. The best appearance is obtained if an elliptical constructional line is drawn and the top of the vertical portion of each joint made to conform with the ellipse. An alternative arch is shown at J where each voussoir has an elongated horizontal portion (called an ear or crossette) which courses in with the wall.

That at K has a semicircular intrados and extrados. This type usually necessitates the cutting of some of the adjacent walling stones to an awkward shape (see W).

Segmental Arches, having either curved or stepped extradoses, are also built of stone. The geometrical construction of these is similar to that required for brick arches (see Fig. 15).

Window Sills.—Reference should be made to the brick sills described on pp. 24–26 as the terms are applicable to stone sills (see Figs. 22, 24 and 25). The sill shown in Fig. 22 is weathered, twice rebated and chamfered; that shown in section L and part elevation M, Fig. 25, would be specified as a "350 mm by 175 mm sunk weathered[1] and throated sill, grooved for water bar," and that at O and P, Fig. 25, is sunk-weathered, moulded and grooved, the upper portion of the mould forming a throat to prevent water trickling down the face of the masonry below. See p. 104 regarding the bedding of the water bar. The level seatings

[1] Note that *sunk* weathering begins with a vertical sinking.

or stools formed at the ends of the sills to support the jambs may be finished externally as shown in Fig. 25, or they may be weathered as indicated at C, Fig. 16; seatings, as shown at J, Fig. 22 are also formed for the mullions.

The sills are in one length, having a 150 mm wall-hold at each end. They should be solidly bedded *only* under the jambs—and mullions (Fig. 22)—with the intervening portion of each bed left perfectly clear of mortar until the building has completely settled and the mortar in the walling has set. The joint is then neatly pointed.

If this is not done, and the sill is bedded solidly throughout its length as the rest of the work proceeds, the sill may be fractured unless it is very thick and is of very hard stone. This damage is due to the unequal stress produced by the pressure transmitted from the jambs being concentrated only at the ends and not evenly distributed throughout the entire length of the sill; this unequal pressure tends to cause the portions of the wall immediately below the ends of the sill to settle more than the portion under the centre of the sill. To prevent such damage, each sill is sometimes constructed of three stones as shown in Fig. 22, the two vertical joints (indicated by broken lines at K) being in the same vertical plane as that of the jambs. When this is done the central stone of the sill may be bedded solid.

The appearance of the sill shown in Fig. 22 (the face of which is flush with the wall) is sometimes preferred to that of the sills shown in Fig. 25 which project beyond the wall.

The latter type causes water to drip clear of the wall below, whereas when the face of the sill is in line with that of the wall, disfiguration of a building results (especially if it is faced with Portland or similar light coloured stone) by the staining of the walls immediately below the sills. This is due to the water (which collects dirt from the windows and dust from the weathered portions of the sills) passing down the walls. Further, unless the bed joint between each sill and the wall is well pointed, water proceeds through the joint to cause dampness on the internal face of the wall.

Mullions and Transomes.—The window shown in Fig. 22 is divided into six lights.[1] The vertical dividing stones are called mullions and the horizontal dividing stone is known as a transome. The mullions are rebated to receive the window frames and are chamfered to conform with the jambs, etc. They are connected at the bed joints to the head, transome and sill by *dowels* of either slate or gunmetal, which prevent displacement (see J and p. 53). The transomes are rebated for the window frames, they are weathered and the ends are stooled as for window sills. It is customary to divide a transome into units with a joint over each mullion, as a single stone may fracture if the settlement at the jambs exceeds that at the mullions.

Steps.—Two steps are shown at the door opening in Fig. 24. The stone should be a hard wearing sandstone and should be carefully selected. Much of the description on p. 26 is applicable to these steps (see also p. 123 and Fig. 65).

Plinths.—Brick plinths are described on p. 28. An enlarged detail of the upper portion of the plinth at M, Fig. 24, is shown at Q, Fig. 25, and alternative

[1] A window of this type is often provided with steel frames and leaded lights instead of wood frames and sashes. Metal windows are described in Chapter IV.

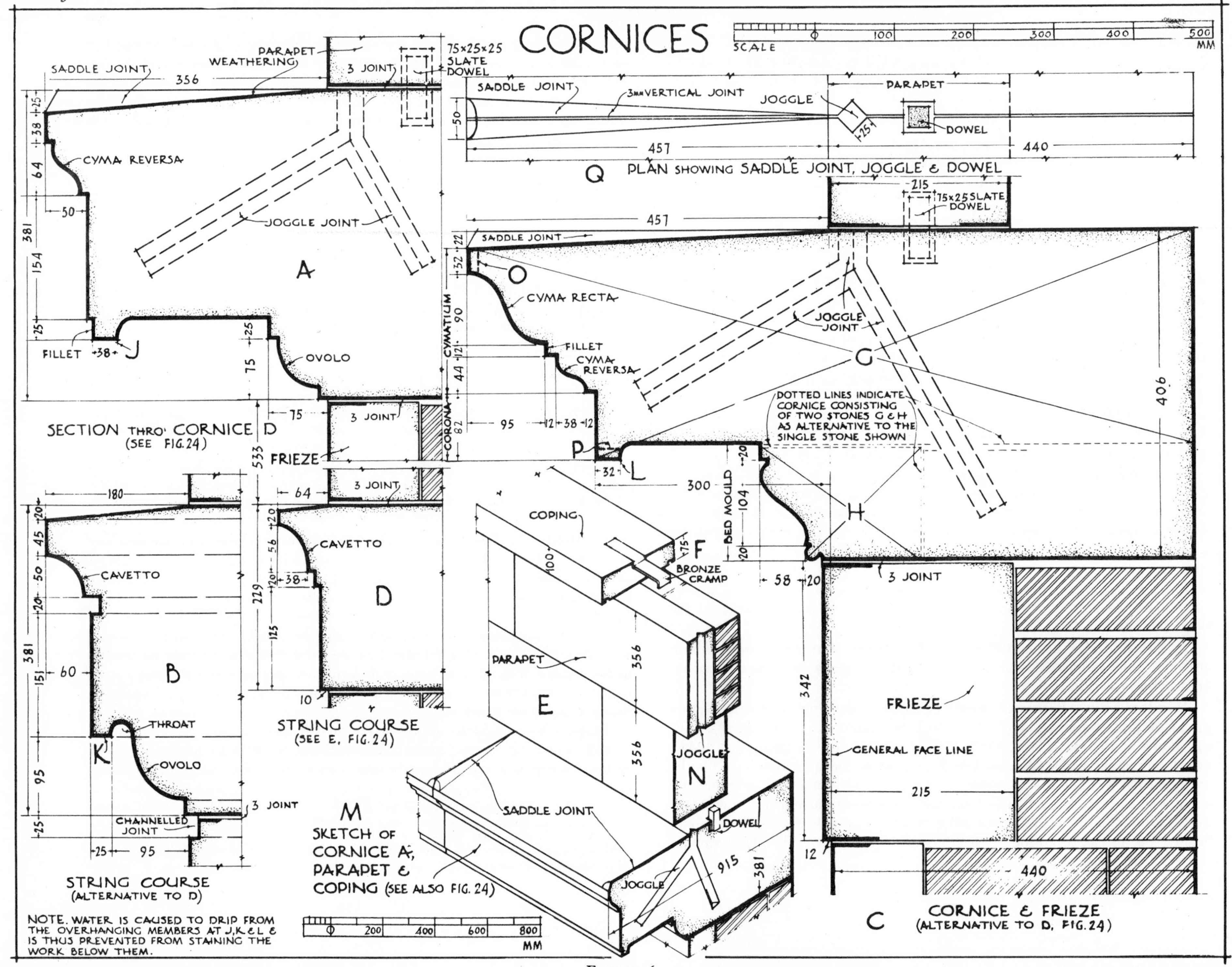
CORNICES
SCALE
100 200 300 400 500
MM
PARAPET
WEATHERING
SADDLE JOINT
356
3 JOINT
75×25×25 SLATE DOWEL
CYMA REVERSA
JOGGLE JOINT
A
FILLET
J
OVOLO
SECTION THRO' CORNICE D
(SEE FIG.24)
SADDLE JOINT
3mm VERTICAL JOINT
JOGGLE
PARAPET
DOWEL
457
440
Q
PLAN SHOWING SADDLE JOINT, JOGGLE & DOWEL
215
75×25 SLATE DOWEL
O
CYMA RECTA
CYMATIUM
FILLET
CYMA REVERSA
CORONA
JOGGLE JOINT
G
DOTTED LINES INDICATE CORNICE CONSISTING OF TWO STONES G & H AS ALTERNATIVE TO THE SINGLE STONE SHOWN
406
FRIEZE
P
L
300
BED MOULD
H
3 JOINT
CAVETTO
D
STRING COURSE
(SEE E, FIG.24)
COPING
F
BRONZE CRAMP
PARAPET
E
JOGGLE
N
FRIEZE
GENERAL FACE LINE
CAVETTO
B
THROAT
K
OVOLO
CHANNELLED JOINT
STRING COURSE
(ALTERNATIVE TO D)
M
SKETCH OF CORNICE A, PARAPET & COPING (SEE ALSO FIG. 24)
SADDLE JOINT
DOWEL
JOGGLE
915
381
200 400 600 800
MM
C
CORNICE & FRIEZE
(ALTERNATIVE TO D, FIG.24)
NOTE. WATER IS CAUSED TO DRIP FROM THE OVERHANGING MEMBERS AT J, K & L & IS THUS PREVENTED FROM STAINING THE WORK BELOW THEM.

FIGURE 26

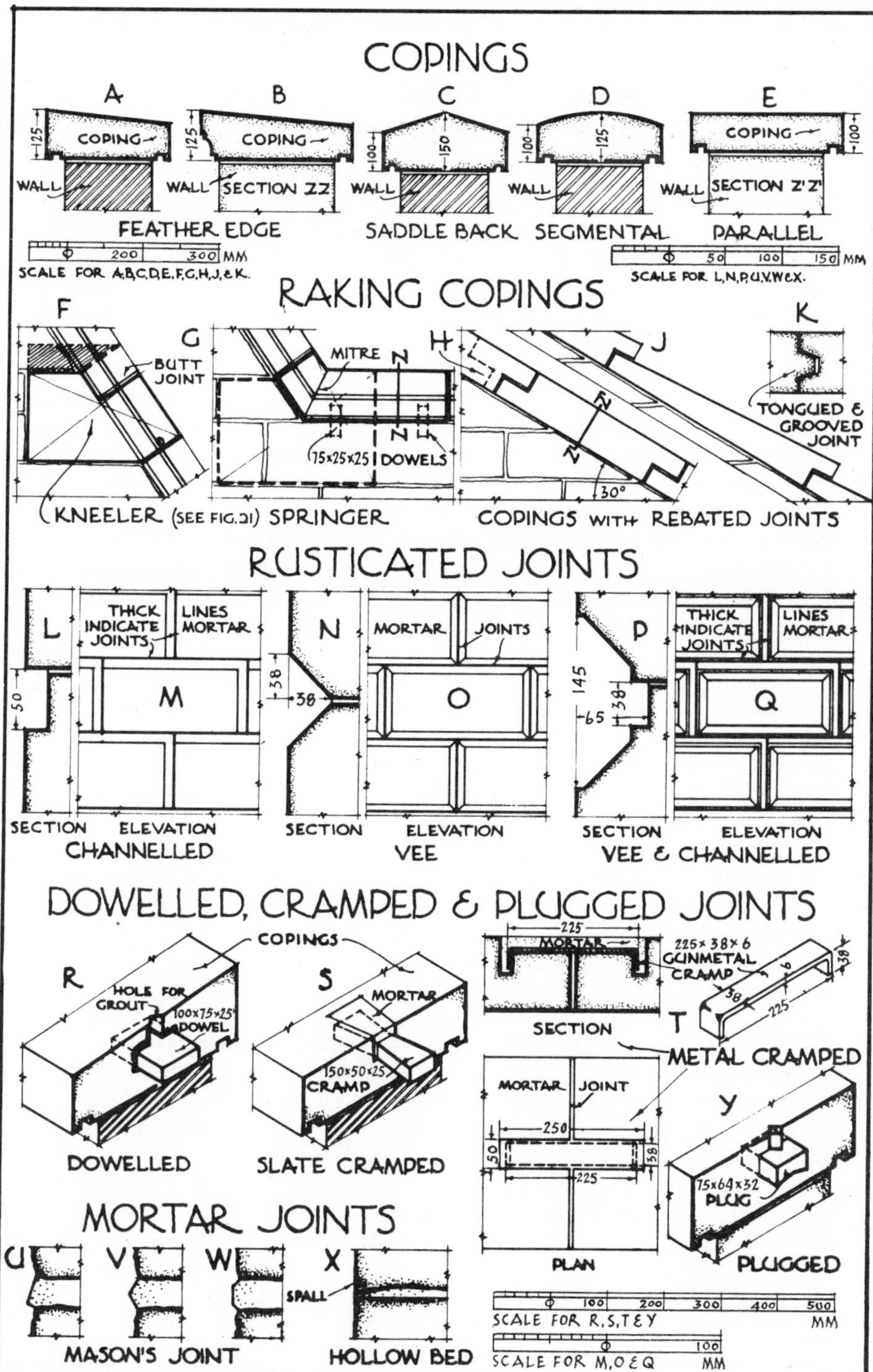

FIGURE 27

plinth mouldings are shown at R, S, T, U and V, Fig. 25. In each case the top of the projection is slightly weathered to prevent water lodging and passing through any defect in the joint. The names of the mouldings are stated in the figure.

String Courses.—A string course is a horizontal course of masonry (or brickwork) which usually projects and is provided as an architectural feature. A simple example is shown at E, Fig. 24, and this is detailed at D, Fig. 26. A larger string course is illustrated at B, Fig. 26; because of the greater projection, it is possible to incorporate a throat with the lower (ovolo) moulding which prevents water trickling down and staining the work below.

The upper portion of the facade (elevation) shown in Fig. 24 consists of a coping, parapet, cornice and frieze. These are described below in the order that they are constructed.

Frieze.—This is a stone course which is surmounted by a cornice. That at D, Fig. 26, is a detail of the frieze shown in Fig. 24. If there is not a projecting member immediately below the frieze (such as a string course or architrave) emphasis may be given to the frieze by projecting it slightly as shown at C, Fig. 26.

Cornices.—A cornice is a comparatively large projecting moulded course which is fixed near to the top of a wall. Its object is to provide an architectural feature which will serve to discharge water clear of the building and thereby protect the *face* of the wall.

Cornices vary considerably in detail.[1] Two designs are shown in the sections A and C, Fig. 26, and A and D, Fig. 76, the two former being alternative details of the cornice shown in Fig. 24.

The projecting portion of a cornice consists of the *cymatium* and the *corona* (see C, Fig. 26). The cymatium is composed of two or more mouldings, that at C consisting of a narrow flat band or fillet and a cyma recta moulding which is separated by a second fillet from a cyma reversa or ogee moulding. The corona has a comparatively broad vertical face with a recessed soffit which stops water from travelling along it to the face of the wall. The lower portion of the cornice is spoken of as a *bed mould*, which at C consists of a fillet, ogee moulding and a bead.

The upper projecting portion of the cornice is weathered and the vertical joints are *saddled* to prevent water from penetrating them.[2] A saddle joint is shown at A, C, Q and M, Fig. 26. It is formed by rounding off the stone from the top bed to the weathering at each end; this prevents rain from lodging on top of the joint. The saddle is rendered inconspicuous by bevelling it backwards from the front edge as shown.

The stones are joggle jointed at the ends to prevent any movement due to unequal settlement which would cause irregularity in the horizontal lines of the cornice. Such joggle joints (down which grouted mortar is poured) are

[1] See p. 93 concerning the importance of well-designed mouldings.

[2] Weathered surfaces of cornices and similar projecting members built of comparatively soft stone should be protected with sheet lead or asphalt (see Fig. 76). Saddle joints are not required when this is done.

shown by broken lines at A and C and by full lines at M. Metal cramps may also be used (especially for securing quoin cornice stones) to resist any movement which tends to separate the joints (see p. 53).

Parapet.—This is the upper portion of a wall which is used as an architectural feature to cover a gutter (as in Fig. 24, when it is sometimes referred to as a *blocking course*, as it blocks from view the gutter behind it) or to protect the edge or *verge* of a roof (see Fig. 21). It is provided with a coping, and its weight assists in tailing down the cornice below it. The stability of the parapet is increased if each block of stone in the lower course is connected to the cornice by means of one of two slate dowels (see Fig. 26 and p. 53).

Copings.—Brick copings are described on p. 26. Sections through stone copings are shown at A to E, Fig. 27. The *feather edge* coping (A) is an enlargement of that at F, Fig. 24; that at B is a detail of the coping shown in Fig. 21. The *saddle back* coping (C) provides a more effective covering than those at L, Fig. 17, and B, Fig. 20, because of the throated overhanging portions, although the latter section is more in keeping with the rough character of the wall which it protects. The *segmental* coping D is occasionally used for dwarf walls where the curved surface can be seen to advantage.

The tops of some walls are inclined or raked and are protected by *raking copings* (see Fig. 21). Such copings need not be weathered as the rain is quickly discharged down the slope in the direction of their length and therefore the *parallel* coping E, Fig. 27, is suitable for such positions. Raking copings, if not supported, would tend to slide. This is prevented by the provision of adequate supports at the bottom and at intermediate points (see A and B, Fig. 21). The intermediate supports are called *kneelers* or *knee-stones* (see F, Fig. 27), which is an enlargement of B, Fig. 21. A kneeler is a block of stone (which should be well tailed into the wall) with the inclined or raking portion worked to the section of the coping stones and finished square to form butt joints with the adjacent coping stones. The butt joint may be formed as indicated by the thick broken line at F, but this requires a larger stone having the portion shown shaded removed. The lower support is provided by a *springer* or *footstone*—see A, Fig. 21 and the enlarged detail at G, Fig. 27. This may be shaped as shown partly by broken lines at G (the thin diagonal lines indicating the extent of the stone) which, like the kneeler, is well tailed into the wall, or it may take the form indicated by the thick full lines at G when two slate dowels (see p. 53) are used to secure it to the stonework below and so provide an adequate resistance to the thrust from the raking coping. The top stone at the intersection of the coping is termed an *apex stone* or *saddle stone*, the raking portions being worked solid to the section of the coping to form a vertical mitre (see Fig. 21).

When the rake or inclination is less than 40°, the joints between coping stones are sometimes *rebated* (indicated by full lines at H, Fig. 27) to prevent water penetrating through them into the wall below. The correct rebate shows the upper portion of the upper stone overlapping the lower portion of the lower stone. The object of the rebate would be defeated if the rebate was reversed, as shown by broken lines at H. An alternative form of raking coping is shown in the side elevation J, Fig. 27.

MASONRY JOINTS

The following are some of the various joints which are used in masonry: butt, rebated, tongued and grooved, rusticated, saddled, joggled, dowelled and plugged. Some of these have been referred to on the previous pages.

Butt or Square Joint.—This is extensively adopted and is formed by placing the square surface of one stone against that of another. Of the many examples of this joint which have been illustrated are the ashlar joints at B, Fig. 25, and those at F and G, Fig. 27.

Rebated or Lapped Joint (see A, B, C and D, Fig. 25, and H, Fig. 27).—In the former figure the check or rebate prevents movement between the arch voussoirs, in the latter example the rebate is adopted to secure a weather-tight joint. Another form, known as a *rebated and broken joint*, is shown at J, Fig. 27.

Tongued and Grooved Joint (see K, Fig. 27).—It is now rarely used. It consists of a tongue or projection worked along one edge of a stone which fits into a corresponding groove in the adjacent stone. It is sometimes adopted as an alternative to the rebated joint in flat arches and between the horizontal slabs forming the landings of stone staircases.[1] It is also known as a joggled joint, which must not be confused with the mortar joggled joint described below.

Rusticated Joints (see Fig. 27).—Plinths, lower storeys of buildings, and quoins are sometimes emphasized by the use of blocks of stone which have their margins or edges sunk below the general face. The term " rusticated " is applied to such masonry. That at L and M shows a *channelled* or *rectangular* joint and is often adopted (see also B, Fig. 26). Note that the sinking is on the *lower* stone; if the bed joint was at the bottom of the channel, water would lodge on the bottom and perhaps penetrate into the mortar joint. The vee-joint at N and O is formed when stones having chamfered edges are placed in position; see also Q and V, Fig. 19. A more elaborate form of vee-joint is shown at P and Q, Fig. 27, and is known as a *vee and channelled* joint.

Saddle Joint.—These are illustrated at A, C, M and Q, Fig. 26, and have been described on p. 51.

Joggles, Dowels and Cramps.—In order to prevent movement and displacement of certain stones the ordinary mortar joints between them have to be supplemented and strengthened by various means. This additional strength is obtained by the employment of joggles, dowels and cramps.

Joggled Joint.—The mortar joggled joint is adopted for the end joints of ashlar, especially when the blocks have a small bed (see p. 47), and for cornice

[1] Stone landings are seldom used nowadays, reinforced concrete construction being preferred.

stones (see p. 51). The grooves down which the grout is poured are roughly formed by means of a hammer and punch (see 6, Fig. 19).

Dowelled Joint.—Stones which are liable to become displaced are prevented from doing so by the introduction of dowels at the joints (see J, Fig. 22 and G, Fig. 27). Dowels are either of slate or gunmetal (an alloy of copper and tin) which are from 25 to 50 mm square in section and two or three times the thickness in length. They are set in cement mortar. A horizontal dowel in an end joint is usually run in with grout (through a vertical hole prepared for the purpose) after it has been inserted and the adjacent stone fixed (see R, Fig. 27).

Cramped Joint.—The joints between stones which are liable to be pulled apart in the direction of their length are reinforced with either metal or slate cramps.

Details of a metal cramped joint are shown at T, Fig. 27, which may be considered to be an enlargement of that shown by dotted lines at S, Fig. 24, and used to connect the coping stones. The cramp is a piece of *non-corrosive* metal,[1] such as gunmetal, which is from 25 to 50 mm wide, 6 to 13 mm thick and 225 to 450 mm long with ends which are turned down from 20 to 40 mm. The cramp must be fitted in tightly, after which it is grouted and covered with either cement or asphalt. A *slate cramped* or *keyed joint*, consisting of a double dovetailed piece of slate set in cement, is shown at S, Fig. 27. It is not so effective as the metal cramped joint.

Plugged Joint (see Y, Fig. 27).—This is an alternative to the cramped joint but is now rarely adopted. It is formed by sinking a hole (dovetailed on plan) below the top surface and a vertical vee-joggle in each end of the adjacent stones. The stones are jointed in the usual way (the hole and joggle being kept free from mortar), after which cement grout is poured down to form a *cement plug.* Formerly, molten lead was poured in to form what was called a *lead plug.*

MORTAR JOINTING

The thickness of the mortar joints varies considerably, thus for ashlar the joints may be as fine as 3 mm whereas those in random rubble work may exceed 50 mm width on face. Certain of the joints used for brickwork illustrated at T, Fig. 17, are also suitable for stonework, *e.g.*, flush joints are used for ashlar and the keyed or vee-joint may be adopted for thicker joints. The *mason's joint* is also used for wide joints. This may be of the three forms shown at U, V and W, Fig. 27. The two former are sometimes used for rubble work, and that at W is frequently adopted for pointing. These projecting joints should be of cement mortar if the character of the stone will permit it.

As mentioned on p. 47, the beds of ashlar blocks should be square with the face. When hand-dressed, there is a tendency for the mason to work *hollow* beds when very fine ashlar joints are required. This may cause the edges to spall off when the stone is fixed owing to the pressure not being distributed over the whole area of the bed but concentrated at the edges. A portion of a hollow bed is shown at X, Fig. 27, where the bed surface of the upper stone only is concave. The shaded triangular portion is likely to be splintered off, especially if the joint is not completely filled with mortar. There is little likelihood of the beds being worked hollow when the stone is sawn by machinery.

[1] Corrodible metal, such as wrought iron, must *never* be used for cramps, bolts, etc., which are fixed in stonework. Extensive damage has been caused to masonry which has been connected by wrought iron fastenings on account of them corroding. During its formation, the rust exerts pressure upon the stone to such an extent as to fracture it.

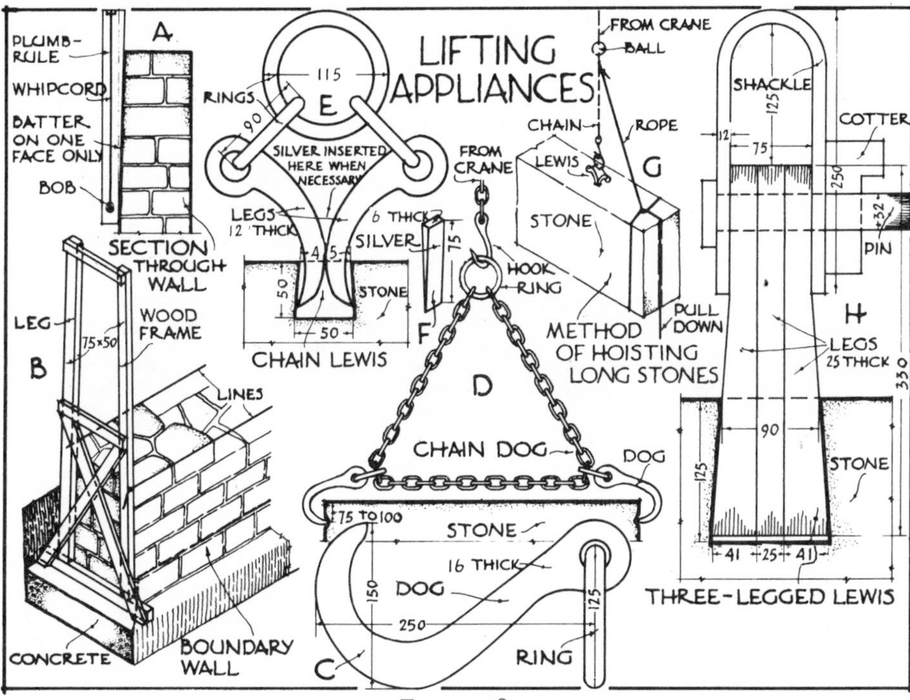

FIGURE 28

The mortar specified for jointing masonry depends a good deal upon the character of the stone. Mortar joints for ashlar should be as inconspicuous as possible, and it is often necessary to experiment with various compositions of mortar until the desired colour (which should conform with that of the stone) is obtained.

That used for walling built of sandstone is sometimes composed of 1 part Portland cement and 4 parts sand, and occasionally a little lime is added.

The mortar recommended for certain limestones, *e.g.*, Portland stone, consists of 1 part Portland cement, $2\frac{1}{2}$ parts *lime putty* (well slaked lime mixed with water to a consistency of a paste) and $3\frac{1}{2}$ parts stone dust (powder obtained by the crushing of waste pieces of the limestone). *Neat* cement should *never* be used for grouting Portland stone blocks, as this may cause staining of the face of the work; only liquid mortar of the above composition should be used for this purpose.

Rubble walling (especially if of sandstone) should be built with cement mortar composed of 1 part cement to 4 parts sand, as the strength of the work depends very largely upon that of the mortar.

Construction of Masonry Walls.—Much of the description on p. 30 referring to the construction of brickwork is applicable to stone walls. The batter which is sometimes given to walls may be maintained by the use of the plumb-rule which has one edge shaped to the required batter (see A, Fig. 28). Where a wall is to receive a batter on both faces (as at B, Fig. 20), the batter is preserved by the use of frames built of wood.

One form of such a frame is shown at B, Fig. 28. The frame is shaped to that of the section of the wall, and the outside edge of each inclined leg coincides with each wall face. During the construction of the wall a frame is fixed temporarily at each end. The correct alignment and the batter of each face are maintained by two lines, the ends of which are wound round nails driven into both legs of each frame at the required height.

LIFTING APPLIANCES

Blocks of dressed stone which are too large to be lifted by hand are raised by means of a crane or other hoisting apparatus and lowered gently into the correct position in the wall. Various appliances, such as Chain Dogs and Lewises, are used for this purpose—see Fig. 28.

Chain Dogs.—Dogs in various sizes are made of steel and shaped as shown at C. The stone to be lifted has a hole (about 20 mm deep) punched in the centre of each end and from 75 to 100 mm down. A steel chain is passed through the ring of each dog and is hooked on to the chain from the crane (as shown at D) and the points of the dog are placed in the holes of the stone. When the chain from the crane is wound up taut, the dogs bite into the stone, which is hoisted and lowered to the required position. Chain dogs grip the stone very securely and are particularly suited for lifting heavy stones and long stones with narrow beds.

Chain Lewis.—This comprises three steel rings and two curved steel legs (see E). The legs vary in size. The hole which is formed in the centre of the top bed of the stone is *slightly* dovetailed. If it is excessively dovetailed there is a tendency for the lewis to be pulled out owing to the legs bursting the stone during the lifting operation. The size of the hole varies from 50 to 75 mm deep; the 50 mm deep hole shown is about 20 mm wide.

The lewis is placed carefully into the hole, one leg at a time. If the hole is found to be too large, a narrow wedge-shaped piece of steel, called a *silver* (see F), is driven down between the legs. When the crane chain or that from a pulley block (which is hooked through the large ring) is wound up, the two smaller rings pull the upper ends of the legs together and thus cause the lower ends to grip the stone. For stones which are more than 1 m long, additional control is obtained if a length of rope is secured to the sling from the crane, as shown at G. The rope is generally secured by two half-hitches just below the " ball," it is then passed round the stone at one end, when a man pulling on the rope can assist in directing the stone as required as it is being lifted.

Lewises are used for lifting stones up to from 800 to 1000 kg in weight, and, as they can be expeditiously fixed, they are used for general purposes probably more frequently than any other form of lifting device.

Another form of lewis, known as a *Three Legged Lewis*, is shown at H. It consists of a parallel piece of steel between two dovetailed steel legs, a shackle, a round steel pin which passes through the shackle and legs, and a cotter. The hole in the stone must be cut accurately to the shape and size of the legs, as shown. The two dovetailed legs are inserted in the hole, the centre leg is driven down, the pin is passed through holes in the shackle and legs, and the cotter is driven down to make all secure. The hook from the sling is passed through the shackle, when the stone is then ready for hoisting. If the hole in the stone has been cut too large, a piece of zinc passed between a pair of legs before they are assembled may be sufficient to enable the lewis to grip the stone securely.

The crane operator must exercise reasonable care during the hoisting operations and the blocks of stone must be hoisted with uniform movement. Any sudden jerk of the crane chain may cause the stone to slip, with disastrous results.

CHAPTER THREE

TIMBER, FLOORS AND ROOFS

Syllabus—Brief description of the structure, growth, seasoning, preservation, sizes, conversion, defects, classification, characteristics and uses of softwoods and hardwoods. Ground floors, sizes and spacing of joists, boarding, joints, ventilation. Single upper floors up to 3·7 m span, strutting, trimming to fireplaces and voids. Ceilings. Pitch, span and evolution of roofs; single roofs including flat, lean-to, double lean-to, couple, close couple and collar types; double roofs, purlins, hips, valleys, trimming to voids, treatment of eaves; trussed rafter roofs; simple principles of framing, framed roofs; built-up roof truss. Timbering to shallow trenches, lintels, turning pieces and centres up to 1·8 m span.

Structure of Timber.—A cut section through a portion of a tree which produces timber used for building purposes is shown at A, Fig. 29. This shows that the structure (or arrangement of the various parts) comprises (*a*) a central core of fibrous (thread-like) woody tissue (woven particles) called the *pith* or *medulla* which disappears in time, (*b*) inner concentric rings of woody tissue called *heartwood* or *duramen* (durability), (*c*) outer and lighter coloured concentric rings of woody tissue called *sapwood*, (*d*) radial narrow bands of tissue called *medullary rays* or *transverse septa* (partitions) which contain cells and radiate from the centre and (*e*) the *bark*.

The irregular concentric rings of tissue, forming the heartwood and sapwood, are called *annual rings* or *growth rings* as in temperate climates one ring is generally formed annually. A diagrammatic view of a portion of an annual ring of a softwood (see p. 58) is shown in cross-section at B, Fig. 29; this is much enlarged, for the number of rings may vary from three to forty per 25 mm. A ring, consisting of rows of cells of variable size which run longitudinally (parallel to the trunk), is divided into an inner portion called the *spring wood* and an outer and darker portion known as the *summer wood*. The cells diminish in size from a maximum forming the spring layer to a minimum at the outer layer; in addition, the cell walls of the summer wood are thicker than those of the spring wood. Hence summer wood is more compact and darker coloured than spring wood. The cells communicate with each other through holes in their sides, and the narrow cells in the medullary rays also communicate with the annual ring cells.

Certain timbers have annual rings which are very distinct and the spring wood and summer wood are easily distinguished; others have rings which are indistinct and there is no contrast between the two. The medullary rays are well defined in certain woods but usually they are only perceptible through the microscope (see p. 56).

Growth.—Moisture, salts, etc., are absorbed from the soil by the roots of the tree, and in the early spring these ascend through the cells (see B) to the branches to develop the leaves which convert the absorbed material, called *sap*, into liquid food suitable for the tree. Meanwhile the *cambium*—a thin covering of cells between the bark and the last-formed annual ring (see A)—produces new cells which form the springwood of the next annual ring. In the late summer and early autumn the food descends between the spring layer and the bark to form the denser summer wood of the annual ring. Thus trees which produce timber used for building purposes grow outwards immediately under the bark and are called *exogens*, as distinct from *endogens* which mainly increase in size by growth at their ends. The cells in the medullary rays act as reservoirs for tree food.

In course of time the layers next the pith become stronger and the cells cease to convey sap; this is the *heartwood*. The outer part of the tree, or *sapwood*, contains much more sap and is softer and lighter in colour than the more mature heartwood. Sapwood is also known as *alburnum* due to its relatively light colour.

Building timbers are divided into softwoods and hardwoods (see p. 59).

Felling.—Trees used for building purposes should be felled as soon as possible after reaching maturity. If felled prematurely, the wood is not so durable and contains an excess of sapwood; if cut after its prime, it produces timber which is brittle and the central portion especially may show evidence of decay. The time taken before trees reach their prime may vary from fifty years (*e.g.*, ash) to a hundred years (*e.g.*, oak). The best time for felling trees is in the autumn just before the fall of the leaf (when the sap is still thin) or during winter after the fall of the leaf (when the trees contain little sap), as during these periods the evaporation of moisture and the resulting shrinkage are comparatively small.

Seasoning.—Timber cannot be used for either carpenters' or joiners' work immediately it has been felled because of the large sap content. Most of this moisture must be removed, otherwise the timber will shrink excessively, causing defects in the work and a tendency to decay. Elimination of the moisture increases the strength, durability and resilience of the timber, the wood is lighter in weight, easier to work with the saw and other tools, it maintains its size and it is not so liable to split, twist or warp. The process of removing the moisture is called *seasoning* or *maturing*. This is accomplished by either (*a*) natural or (*b*) artificial means. In recent years the latter methods have been considerably improved and extensively employed; natural processes are not now so frequently adopted owing to the longer period required.

(a) *Natural Seasoning.*—Immediately after felling the branches are removed, the trees are cross-cut into *logs* and the bark is stripped. If the logs are of softwood, they are shaped by machine sawing to a square in cross-section (called *baulks*) and stacked (as shown at C, Fig. 29) under cover to allow the air circulating round them to remove much of the moisture content. Hardwood trees are usually sawn by machinery along their length into *planks* (pieces from 50 to 150 mm thick at least 250 mm wide) and stacked with cross-lags (pieces of wood about 13 mm thick) between, as shown at D, Fig. 29. Thin pieces of wood (as shown at E) are nailed to the end of each plank to prevent the timber splitting during the drying process. This is known as *Dry Natural Seasoning*, and the time occupied depends upon the size and character of the timber. Thus, *softwood* boards, 25 mm thick, may take two months to season and 50 mm thick planks four months; *hardwood* of the same thickness may take about three times as long to season.

The time occupied in seasoning is much reduced if the timber is subjected to *Water Natural Seasoning*. By this method, the logs may be floated down a river to the sawmill or they may be placed in the river, totally submerged with the butt (thick) ends facing upstream, left for a fortnight to allow the water during its passage through the pores to eliminate much of the sap, when they are removed, sawn and stacked as shown at C.

(b) *Artificial Seasoning.*—The time taken for this varies from approximately one to two weeks. The process is carried out in kilns of which there are several types. One form consists of a long chamber, about 2·5 m wide and 3 m high. The timbers, which should be of the same thickness, are carefully piled and sticked (cross-lagged) on trucks which run on rails extending the full length of the kiln. Hot air (heated by passage over steam pipes) is circulated amongst the timber by means of fans. The temperature of the air and its rate of flow vary with the size and class of wood. The humidity of the kiln during the seasoning is rigidly controlled; if it is too low, it is at once raised by the admission of steam.

It is important to note that the *whole* of the moisture content (" m.c. ") is not removed from the timber when seasoned. A certain amount is allowed to remain. Thus, for internal work (as for floor boards, doors and panelling), the timber is allowed to remain in the kiln until the moisture content is reduced to 12 per cent.; the maximum for good-class carpenters' work is 20 per cent. If timber is used in a position where the humidity of the atmosphere is in excess of that in the timber, the latter will absorb moisture from its surroundings and swelling will result. Conversely, if the timber is insufficiently seasoned (*i.e.*, contains an excess of moisture), it will, if fixed in a very dry position, lose a certain amount of moisture and will shrink. Therefore if movement of the timber is to be kept to a minimum, the moisture content should approximate closely to that of its environment. The extent of shrinkage movement in timber may vary from about 6 to 13 mm per 300 mm of original width if the moisture content is reduced from 20 to 10 per cent.

Preservation.—In order to increase the durability of seasoned timber it is sometimes necessary to apply a preservative. Next to painting the most common preservative process is *creosoting*, which consists of placing the timber in steel cylinders in which hot creosote (an oil distilled from coal tar) is admitted and forced into the pores of the wood. A less effective method is to apply two or more coats of creosote to the surface of the timber. Treatment by metallic salts (copper based) is also adopted.

Conversion.—A log of timber is converted into various pieces to which the following terms are applied. *Basic lengths* rise from 1·8 to 6·3 m in increments of 300 mm.

Deals are sawn pieces of softwood which are from 50 to 100 mm thick by 225 to under 250 mm wide.

Battens are from 50 to 100 mm thick by 125 to 200 mm wide; *slating battens* are from 13 to 32 mm thick by 25 to 63 mm wide.

Boards are under 50 mm thick by 100 mm or more in width.

Scantlings are from 50 to 100 mm thick by 50 to 100 mm wide. The term is often applied to the dimensions of a piece of timber, thus " the joist is of 100 mm by 50 mm scantling."

Quarterings are square sections of from 50 to 150 mm side.

Strips are under 50 mm thick and less than 100 mm wide

There are various ways of converting a log into planks, deals, boards, etc., *i.e.*, (*a* radial sawing, (*b*) tangential sawing and (*c*) slab sawing—see Fig. 30.

(a) *Radial, Rift or Quarter Sawing.*—Four forms are shown at A. That at B is the best if the timber has well defined medullary rays, as in oak. The log is first sawn into four pieces (or is " quartered ") and each quarter is cut into boards which, like the medullary rays, are radial. The rays appear irregularly on the surface to produce the *silver grain* (or *figure* or *flower*) which is so highly valued for high class joinery work. It is an expensive form of conversion, as much waste results. More economical methods are shown at C and D, although the latter especially does not show up the figure to the same advantage. Comparatively thicker boards or planks are obtained by the method shown at E.

(b) *Tangential Sawing* is shown at F, and adopted when the timbers have ill-defined medullary rays and distinct annual rings, as in pitch pine, the boards have their faces tangential to the annual rings and show up to advantage.

(c) *Slab Sawing* (see G).—The inner pieces are rift sawn and the outer slabs approximate to tangential cuts. This gives less waste and it is therefore the cheapest.

As already mentioned, timber shrinks as its moisture evaporates, and the heartwood shrinks less than the sapwood. H shows the distortion which occurs.

The maximum shrinkage occurs in the direction of the lines of the annual rings; it is much less in the radial direction (parallel to the medullary rays) and it is almost negligible in the direction of its length. The thickness of the plank J varies from a maximum at the centre (where there is little moisture in the heartwood) to a minimum at the circumference (owing to the larger amount of moisture in the sapwood and the shrinkage which takes place in the direction of the arrows). The piece of quartering, indicated by broken lines at K, is distorted as shown on account of the shrinkage in the direction of the rings being more extensive than that radially. Similarly the plank at L shows the shrinkage and warping which occurs. In each case the broken lines indicate the shape of each piece of timber before seasoning.

Thin boards, used as floor boards, should be rift sawn to give the best results (see O), but on account of the expense a cheaper method of conversion is often adopted and is

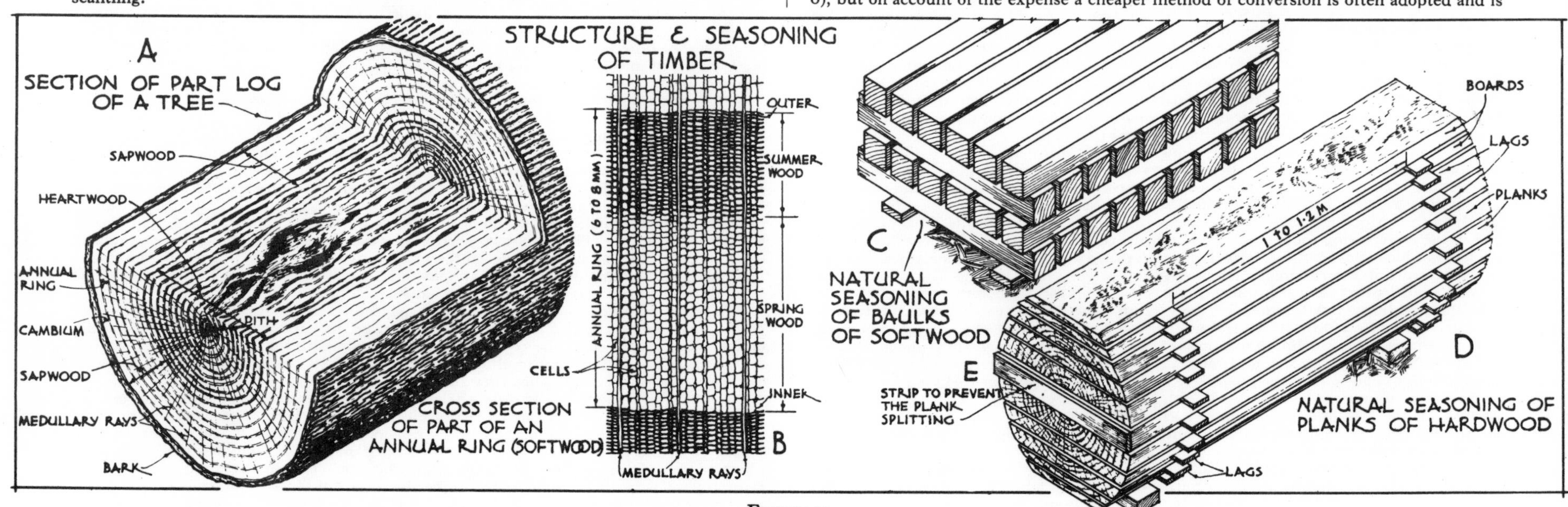

FIGURE 29

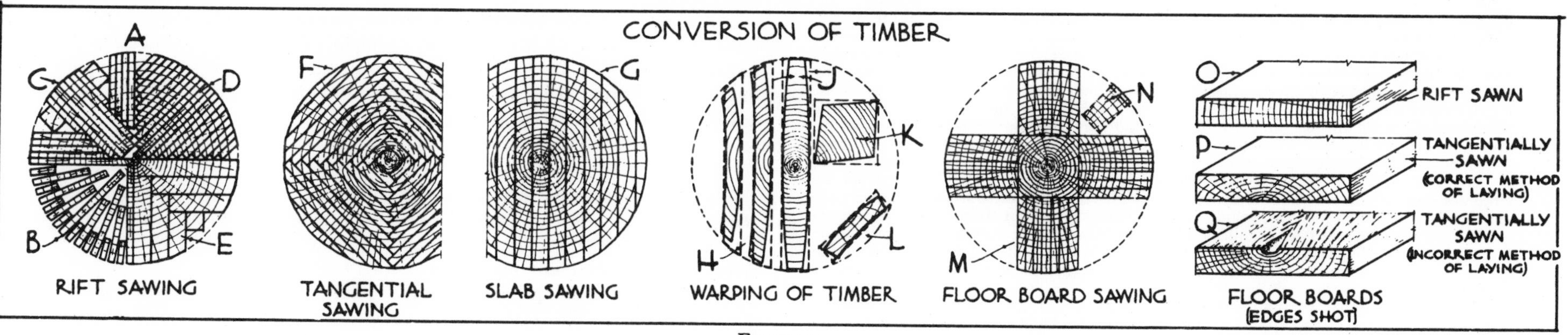

FIGURE 30

shown at M, when the remaining sections, consisting of sapwood, are converted into scantlings as required, as at N. Although rift sawn boards shrink less and have better wearing qualities, such boards are often sawn tangentially for economy. Tangentially sawn floor boards should be fixed with the heart side downwards (as at P); if they are fixed with the heart side upwards, there is a tendency for portions to be kicked out as shown at Q.

Defects.—The defects in timber may be classified according to (*a*) those developed during its growth, and (*b*) those occurring after it has been felled. Class (*a*) includes Deadwood, Druxiness, Foxiness, Coarse Grain, Twisted Grain, Cup Shakes, Heart Shakes, Upsets and Knots. Class (*b*) are Doatiness, Dry Rot, Wet Rot, Shrinking, Swelling, Warp, Wane, Chipped Grain and Chip Mark. Some of them are shown in Fig. 31:—

Deadwood.—Applied to redwood which is deficient in strength and weight and having an abnormal pinkish colour; is the result of trees being felled after they have reached maturity,

Druxiness is an incipient (early) decay which appears as whitish spots or streaks; is due to fungi (a form of plant life) gaining access, probably through a broken branch, and setting up decay.

Foxiness.—Reddish or yellowish brown stains in oak caused by over-maturity or badly ventilated storage during shipment; is an early sign of decay.

Coarse Grain timber has very wide annual rings caused by the tree growing too rapidly; wood is deficient in strength and not durable.

Twisted Grain or Fibre (see D).—Fibres are twisted to such an extent that a relatively large number are cut through when the log is converted into planks, etc.; such planks or boards will twist or wrap; caused by wind action in branches twisting the tree trunk.

Cup Shakes or Ring Shakes (see A).—Cracks or clefts developed between two adjacent annual rings; interfere with conversion of timber, resulting in waste; caused by sap freezing during ascent in spring.

Heart Shakes (see B).—Shakes which begin at the heart or pith of the log; a single cleft is not serious. A *Star Shake* consists of several heart shakes somewhat in the form of a star; render conversion of timber difficult and uneconomical. They are an early sign of decay and are caused by shrinkage in an over mature tree.

Upsets or Rupture (see E.)—Fibres deformed due to injury by crushing during the growth of the tree.

Knots are sections of branches present on the surface of wood in the form of hard dark pieces. It is almost impossible to obtain certain converted timbers entirely " free from knots " (as is sometimes specified). Those known as " tight knots " are sound (being securely joined to the surrounding wood) and are not objectionable unless large. Wood with " large " or " loose " knots should not be used as they are unsightly and readily removed; wood containing many knots is difficult to work. Knots are a source of weakness if present in timber to be used as struts or similar members.

Dote or Doatiness.—From of incipient decay indicated by patches of greyish stains speckled with black which are relatively soft; due to imperfect seasoning or badly ventilated storage and found in American oak, beech and birch.

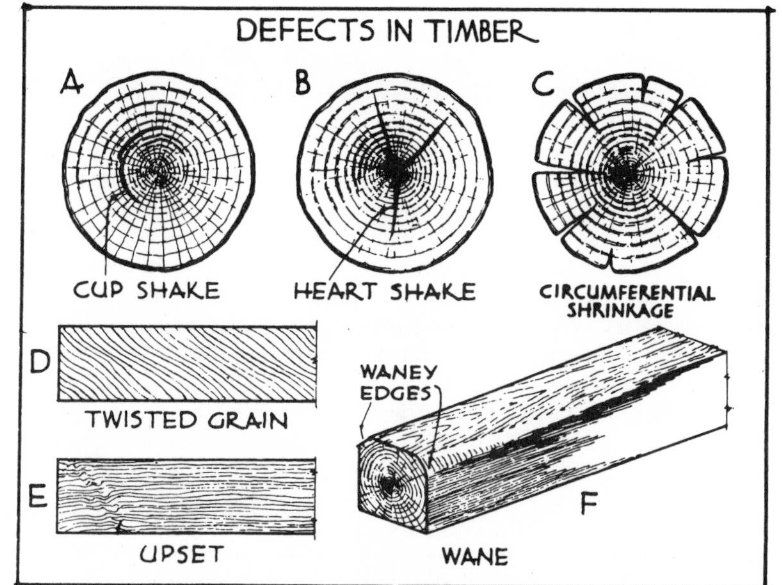

FIGURE 31

Dry Rot.—Decay caused by fungus which feeds upon the wood and reduces it to a dry and powdery condition. It may appear as masses resembling cotton-wool with grey or brown coloured strands which branch out in network formation to adjacent timber. Badly affected timber has little or no strength and readily crumbles by pressure of the fingers. Timber containing an *excess of sap* and in *badly ventilated positions* is readily affected (see pp. 60 and 77). Diseased or suspected timber must be removed at once.[1]

Wet Rot is a chemical and not a fungoid decay of timber; affected portions are reduced to a greyish brown powder and these only need to be removed and replaced; caused by timber being subjected to alternating wet and dry conditions.

Shrinking and Swelling.—When the amount of moisture in timber is reduced during seasoning the wood shrinks, and if it absorbs additional moisture after seasoning an increase in volume results. The extent of this movement is referred to on p. 56 and is influenced by the manner of conversion, moisture content and proportion of heartwood.

Circumferential Shrinkage (see C).—Defect denoted by clefts which radiate from the circumference of the log towards the centre; clefts decrease in width from the outside and are usually limited to the sapwood; result of shrinkage which occurs during seasoning.

Warp is distortion or twisting out of shape which may occur during shrinkage; in one form (when is it called *bow* or *bowing*) the plank or board is slightly curved in the direction of its length and in another form (called *cup* or *cupping*) the timber is curved in cross-section.

Wane is the original splayed or rounded surface of the tree which remains at the edge or edges of a piece of timber after conversion; sometimes known as *waney edges*. A baulk with two waney edges is shown at F. Wane is due to converting too large a baulk from a tree; not considered to be determinal if used for shoring, piling, etc., and in positions where the appearance and large amount of sapwood are unimportant considerations.

Chipped or Torn Grain is a slight defect caused by the planing machine or tool removing a portion below the surface of the wood as it is being dressed.

CLASSIFICATION

Timbers used for building purposes are divided into two groups called (*a*) *softwoods* and (*b*) *hardwoods*. This division has been established by long usage and is not in accordance with the relative hardness of the woods (as certain softwoods are harder than some hardwoods) but is concerned with the specific species of the trees. Thus softwoods are a group which is confined to *conifers* which are evergreen (having leaves throughout the year) trees having needle-like leaves and which bear cones (seeds contained in conical sheaths), whilst hardwoods form a class of *broad leaf* trees which cast their leaves in the autumn.

Softwoods are in general characterised by (1) distinct annual rings, (2) indistinct medullary rays, (3) comparatively light colour and (4) the heartwood and sapwood are not readily distinguished. They are classified as Group I or II according to the species (see p. 59).

Hardwoods have (1) less distinct annual rings, which are closer together than in softwoods, (2) distinct medullary rays, (2) richer colour and (4) darker coloured heartwood which is readily distinguished from the sapwood.

The thickness of the annual rings varies, thus in redwood (see Table I.) the number of rings varies from five to thirty per 25 mm. This variation is due to the difference in the length of the summer. Where the summer is short, as in North Russia, there is comparatively little growth each year, and therefore the number of rings per 25 mm is large. Generally, the annual rings of hardwoods are closer together than in softwoods on account of hardwood trees being slower in growth.

Particulars of certain softwoods and hardwoods are given in Table I.

Carpentry embraces construction in wood which is stressed due to the load it supports. Such construction may be permanent in character, as floors, roofs and partitions, or it may be of a temporary nature, *e.g.*, timbering for trenches or similar excavations, centering for arches and formwork to support reinforced concrete floors, etc., during construction. The following is a description of some of these structures :—

[1] The detection and cure of dry rot are described in Chap. I, Vol. III.

FLOORS

Wood covered floors[1] may be divided into two classes, *i.e.*, (1) suspended floors consisting of bearing timbers, called *joists*, in addition to the *boards* which are used to cover them, and (2) solid floors which consist of either wood boards or blocks upon a concrete foundation.

(1) **Boarded and Joisted Floors.**—Such are usually classified into: (*a*) *Single Floors*.—This class consists of only one set of joists, called *common joists* or *bridging joists*. (*b*) *Double Floors*.—In this class, additional and larger joists, called *binders*, are introduced to support the bridging joists. (*c*) *Triple or Framed Floors*.—Such a floor comprises three sets of joists, *i.e.*, bridging joists which transmit the load to binders, which are in turn framed into and supported at intervals by larger joists called *girders*.

Double and triple floors are required for buildings of large area. Whereas formerly the binders and girders were of wood, this material is now rarely used for this purpose. If wood joists are to be used in conjunction with binders, the latter are now usually of mild steel, when they are called *steel beams* or *girders*—or *rolled steel joists*, abbreviated to "R.S.J.'s" (see H, Fig. 80). Floors of large span are now usually constructed of fire resisting materials, such as (i) reinforced concrete beams and slabs, or (ii) main steel beams to which are fixed secondary steel beams that support floors consisting of either small steel beams encased in concrete, concrete floors with expanded metal or similar reinforcement, or patent fire resisting terra-cotta or concrete blocks. Such floors are detailed in Vols. II, III and IV.

Single Floors.—The floors of domestic buildings, *e.g.*, houses, are generally of this type, and the following description is applicable to the construction of a typical ground floor and an upper floor of such a building.

Floor Insulation.—The Building Regulations require that suspended floors be insulated to a given value if: (1) the floor is not resistant to the passage of air and (2) if the space beneath the floor is not fully enclosed apart from ventilation by air bricks (see p. 63). It cannot be said that the t. & g. floorboard (see p. 63) is completely air-resistant so it is advisable to insulate the floor to the required value by nailing 12·5 mm thick expanded polystyrene slabs on top of the floor joists before the boarding is fixed.

GROUND FLOOR

Fig. 32 shows the plan, sections and various details of a ground floor which is of the single floor class.

Sizes of Joists.—The sizes of joists depend upon (*a*) span, (*b*) distance between each joist, (*c*) load on the floor and (*d*) the timber used.

[1] Cork, rubber, mosaic, fireclay, quarry, thermoplastic, and marble tiles are also used to cover floors, see Chap. I, Vol. III.

TABLE I

GROUP	NAME	SOURCE	WEIGHT (kg per m³)	CHARACTERISTICS	USES
SOFTWOODS	REDWOOD (Northern Pine, Scotch Fir, Red Deal, Yellow Deal)	Russia, Norway, Sweden, Finland	530	Reddish brown heartwood, yellowish brown sapwood; well defined annual rings, medullary rays invisible; works easily; very durable when painted; strong.	Doors, windows, floors, roofs, and general internal and external carpentry and joinery of good quality.
	WHITEWOOD (White Deal, White Pine, European Spruce)	Do.	430	White to whitish yellow; well defined annual rings; slightly difficult to work owing to hard knots; not durable for external work	Internal work, as for floors, roofs, and shelving of cheaper grade than above; shuttering.
	CANADIAN SPRUCE (Quebec Spruce, White Spruce)	Eastern Canada	450	White; well defined annual rings; straight grained, easy to work; liable to wrap; not durable	Roofing, flooring, scaffolding.
	DOUGLAS FIR (British Columbian Pine, Oregon Pine)	British Columbia (Western Canada), Oregon State (U.S.A.)	530	Pink to light reddish brown; well defined annual rings (spring wood and summer wood approximately of equal width); fairly easy to work; fairly durable for external work; should be rift sawn for flooring	Doors, panelling, flooring, interior fittings, sleepers, piling.
	PITCH PINE . . .	Texas and Lousiana (U.S.A.)	650	Light red; well defined annual rings with large proportion of summer wood (dark) which gives good figure; contains much resin, hard to work; very durable and strong	Doors, windows, roofs, floors, panelling, sleepers, piling. Used for good class work.
	WESTERN RED CEDAR .	Canada	380	Reddish brown; distinct annual rings; straight grained, easy to work; very durable under all conditions; brittle	Roofing shingles (boards), panelling joinery.
HARDWOODS	OAK	England, America, Austria, Russia, Japan	690 to 850	Light yellowish brown to deep brown; fairly well defined annual rings, well defined medullary rays; rift sawing gives beautiful figure; hard and durable (excepting American); very strong	Doors, windows, floors, roofs, stairs, panelling, furniture, gates, fences and general carpentry and joinery of high class quality.
	TEAK	Burma and Siam (India), West Coast (Africa)	650	Light golden brown; annual rings defined by belts of porous tissue, fine medullary rays; very good figure; difficult to work; durable, fire resisting and hard wearing	High class general joinery as for doors, windows, stairs, panelling, furniture.
	MAHOGANY . . .	Honduras (Central America), Cuba (West Indies), S. Nigeria (Africa)	480	Rich reddish brown; indistinct annual rings, distinct medullary rays; good figure; not durable for external work. Cuban (Spanish) best, but most expensive and now difficult to obtain	High class internal joinery, especially for decorative work, as for panelling, bank and shop fittings, newels and handrails, furniture.
	ROCK MAPLE . .	North America	740	Light reddish brown; indistinct annual rings, very distinct medullary rays; "Curly" or "Bird's-eye" maple has distinctive and pleasing figure of dark " eyes " with curly dark lines; durable (if used internally) and very hard wearing	High class flooring, panelling, furniture.
	ELM	England	560 to 690	Dull reddish brown; distinct annual rings and medullary rays; durable if kept dry or wet but if not subject to both; tough and elastic	Weather boarding, piling.
	BIRCH	British Isles	670	White to light brown; indistinct annual rings and medullary rays; strong, tough, not durable	Plywood, doors and furniture.

Timber required for first class carpentry and joinery should be sound, bright (*i.e.*, free from discoloration), square-edged, thoroughly seasoned to suit the particular use, free from shakes, large, loose or dead knots, warp, incipient decay and other defects which would render it unserviceable for its purpose. It should be free from stained sapwood and the amount of bright sapwood should not exceed the following (for redwood): 5 per cent. for first class joinery, 7 per cent. for medium class joinery and 10 per cent. for carpentry; this amount is influenced by the normal temperature of the building in which the timber is to be fixed.

Softwoods are classified in three groups. Group S1 comprises Douglas Fir, Pitch Pine and European Larch. Group S2 includes Canadian Spruce, Redwood, Whitewood and Western Hemlock. Group S3 consists of European and Sitka Spruce, and Western Red Cedar.

(*a*) Intermediate supports to ground floors are usually provided in the form of 102 mm thick walls, called *sleeper walls* (see below), which are built at a maximum distance apart of 1800 mm, and therefore only small joists are required for ground floors. As upper floors of this class have not such intermediate supports, the joists span from wall to wall (usually across the shortest span) and therefore they are relatively large.

(*b*) The spacing of joists varies from 300 to 400 mm centres (the distance between the centre of one joist and that next to it). If 25 mm thick boards are used, this distance is generally 400 mm.

(*c*) The minimum safe superimposed load (or live load) allowed on floors varies with the type of building, thus it is 1·5 kN/m^2 for a house and from 2·4 to 9 kN/m^2 for a warehouse.

(*d*) Suitable timbers for floors are referred to in Table I. Redwood is the best softwood for this purpose.

TABLE II, FLOOR JOISTS

Maximum clear span (m)	Size of Joist (mm) (spaced at 400 mm centres)	Maximum clear span (m)	Size of joist (mm) (spaced at 400 mm centres)
0·99	38 by 75	3·75	50 by 175
1·26	50 by 75	3·75	38 by 200
1·63	38 by 100	4·07	63 by 175
2·03	50 by 100	4·27	50 by 200
2·33	38 by 125	4·21	38 by 225
2·83	38 by 150	4·64	63 by 200
3·23	50 by 150	4·79	50 by 225
3·29	38 by 175	5·21	63 by 225

Table II, derived from the Building Regulations, gives the maximum clear span for different floor joists of Group II softwood (see p. 59) spaced at 400 mm centres when the dead load on the floor is not more than 0·25 kN/m^2 (it rarely exceeds this amount in a domestic floor).

Wall Plates.—These are wood members, generally 100 mm by 75 mm or 115 mm by 75 mm which: (*a*) serve as a suitable bearing (100 to 115 mm) for the joists, (*b*) uniformly distribute loads from the joists to the wall below, (*c*) provide suitable means of bringing the upper edges of the joists to a horizontal plane to receive the floor boards and to ensure a level surface and (*d*) afford a fixing for the ends of the joists.[1] They are solidly bedded level on lime mortar by the bricklayer for the full length or width of the floor (see broken lines at F, Fig. 32). Joints in long lengths are formed as shown at G. This is called a *half lapped joint* or *scarf*. The vertical cut extends to half the thickness of each plate and after the cut surfaces have been fitted together, nails are driven in to make the joint secure. Intersections between wall plates are formed as shown at H. Ground floor wall plates are usually placed immediately over the horizontal damp proof course.

It is the usual practice to rest the ends of the joists upon the wall plate and fix them by driving nails through their sides into it (see U). If the joists vary slightly in depth, their upper edges are levelled by removing a portion of the wall plate as required to form a *housed joint* (see K and L).[1] Other forms of joints which may be applied to the ends of deep joists are *notching* and *cogging*. A *single notched joint* is shown at M, the lower edge of the joist being cut to fit over the wall plate (such as may be supported by a sleeper wall). A *double notched joint* is shown at N and is formed by cutting both joist and wall plate. A *single cogged joint*, used at the ends of joists, is shown at O, the joist being cut on its lower edge to correspond to the uncut portion or *cog* on the plate. Where the joist cut coincides with the cog after two sinkings have been formed in the plate, it forms a *double cogged joint* (see P) such as may be adopted when joists are supported by sleeper wall plates. Neither notching nor cogging (sometimes called *caulking*) are much used.

Reference is made on p. 57 to a particularly virulent disease of timber known as dry rot. It is necessary to safeguard against this disease by using only well seasoned timber and to *provide adequate ventilation*. Free circulation of air to all ground floor timbers is therefore essential, and it is for this reason that wall plates should be supported either (*a*) by sleeper walls built parallel to and about 50 mm from the main walls (see this construction shown by broken lines at C, Fig. 10) or (*b*) upon offsets (shown at A, C and D, Fig. 11) or (*c*) upon corbels (see L, M and N, Fig. 11). If, on the score of economy, the wall plates and ends of the joists are built into the wall, it is necessary to form an air space round the sides and tops of the joists (see K, Fig. 32), and it is also advisable to apply two coats of creosote (see p. 56) or other preservative to the wall plates and to the ends of the joists. Attention is drawn to the provision made to ensure an adequate circulation of air under the wood floor shown in Fig. 32 where air bricks (one type being shown at V) are fixed in the external wall, bricks are omitted in the 102 mm division walls to form ventilating openings (abbreviated to "V.O.") and voids are formed in the sleeper wall (when it is said to be "honeycombed").

[1] Wall plates are frequently omitted in cheap work (as shown at L, Fig. 36) and the ends of the joist are packed up with pieces of slate, etc. This is an undesirable practice as repeated vibration tends to disturb such bearings, resulting in unequal settlement of the joists and an uneven floor surface.

[1] A less satisfactory method of levelling up joists is frequently resorted to *i.e.*, the ends of the lower joists are packed up by inserting thin pieces of wood between them and the wall plate.

An enlarged detail of an air brick built into a wall is shown at U. Air bricks are obtainable in various sizes, colours and textures to conform with the brickwork; they must be well perforated; an alternative form of ventilator is a cast iron ventilating grate.

Sleeper wall foundations have been referred to on p. 18. A sleeper wall is honeycombed simply by omitting bricks during its construction. The voids may be arranged haphazard, or as shown by the two alternative forms indicated in section DD. All sleeper walls must be provided with damp proof courses.

It is sometimes necessary to resort to either offsets (for ground floors) or corbels (for upper walls) to provide support for the wall plates, as shown in Fig. 11. Alternatively metal bars, called *corbel brackets* (see T, Fig. 32), may be used. These are of mild steel or wrought iron, from 75 to 100 mm wide by 10 mm thick by about 430 mm long with ends turned 50 mm in opposite directions. They should be painted and built 215 mm into the wall at from 760 mm to 900 mm apart.

An alternative form of wall plate is shown at S, Fig. 32. This is a 50 or 75 mm by 10 mm mild steel or wrought iron plate of any suitable length. It is rarely adopted.

Whilst joists may be placed in any direction, it is usual to fix them across the shortest span. A space about 50 mm should be left between the wall and the first joist which is parallel to it. When joists forming floors of adjacent rooms run in the same direction, the overlapping ends on the division walls are nailed to each other and to the wall-plates (see Y′ at A, Fig. 32).

The plan of the room shown in Fig. 32 includes a fireplace. The construction of fireplaces is described in Vol. II, as it is outside the scope of the syllabus of a First Year Course. In order however to make a description of ground floors complete it is necessary to make a brief reference to certain portions of a fireplace. A wall is built round the fireplace to retain the concrete hearth (and the material supporting it) and to support a portion of the floor. This is called a *fender wall*[1] and its thickness may be 102 or 215 mm, depending upon its height and the load which it has to support. A fireplace may be constructed within a recess as shown in the Figure in which case the Building Regulations require that the hearth:—(1) Projects at least 500 mm in front of the jambs (the sides of the fireplace opening). (2) Extends at least 150 mm beyond the sides of the opening. (3) Is not less than 125 mm thick.

If the heating appliance is not in a recess requirement (3) above applies, but in lieu of (1) and (2) the hearth must be of a size so as to contain a square having sides not less than 840 mm long.

The site concrete should be well brushed, and all debris below the floor removed before the floor boards are fixed. Dry rot may be caused by small pieces of wood, shavings, etc., left below a floor becoming affected (probably on account of dampness) and spreading to the members of the floor. After the joists have been levelled, with their upper edges in the same plane, they are now ready to receive the floor boards.

[1] Ground floor joists are often trimmed as described on p. 65 for upper floors. This is in lieu of the fender wall construction, and is to be preferred as moisture (especially if the site is a damp one) may be transmitted from the filling to the wall plates and ends of the joists and may cause dry rot.

Floor Boards.—Some of the timbers used for floor boards are stated in Table I (p. 59). Redwood is used for ordinary good class work, whitewood and spruce for cheaper work, and pitch pine and the hardwoods (such as oak and maple) are employed for first class floors.

The sizes of floor boards vary from 100 to 25 mm wide and from 25 to 38 mm thick; the narrower the boards the better, for then the shrinkage of each will be reduced to a minimum, the joints will not appreciably open, and there will be less tendency for the boards to cup (see p. 58). Hence 100 mm wide boards (specified as being " in narrow widths ") are used for first class work, 115 mm wide boards for average good work and 175 mm wide boards for commoner work. Boards of 25 mm nominal (see below) thickness are used when the joists do not exceed 400 mm centres. The size is that after the boards have left the saw and is known as the *nominal* or *stuff* sizes, but after the boards have been shaped as required and dressed (or *wrought*) the sizes are reduced and are known as *net* or *finished* sizes. Thus a floor board has one side (which is of course laid uppermost) and both edges planed, and a 175 mm by 25 mm (nominal size) board is reduced to 170 mm by 20 mm net, and a 32 mm (nominal) board has a finished thickness of 27 mm; the net width includes the tongue (see Q, R, V and W, Fig. 34). Boards are obtained in random lengths from 4·8 to 6·3 m (see *Basic lengths*, p. 56); although 7 m long boards are available.

The boards may be converted by sawing from the log, as shown in Fig. 30, or from battens; thus six 100 mm by 25 mm (approximately) boards may be obtained from one 200 mm by 75 mm batten by two saw cuts down its depth (" deep cuts ") and one cut down its thickness (" flat cut ").

The labours such as rebating, tonguing, grooving and planing floor boards (see Fig. 34) are carried out in one operation by a machine called a Planing and Matching Machine. Thus boards which are tongued and grooved (see R and U, Fig. 34) are made as follows : The sawn board as it passes horizontally through the machine is first smooth finished on the lower surface. As it proceeds it is planed and grooved on one edge, tongued on the other as the board is reduced to the correct width, and just before it leaves the machine the board is reduced to the required thickness.

The latest type of this machine, when fed automatically, can produce 180 m of tongued and grooved boarding per minute.

Joints.—Various *edge* or longitudinal joints between floor boards are shown in Fig. 34. These are described below.

Square or Plain Joint (see P).—The edges are cut and planed at right angles to the face or side, when they are said to be either *shot*, *butt jointed* or *straight edged*. This joint is never used for good work unless the boards are to be covered by another layer of boards to form what is called a *double boarded floor* (p. 64).

Rebated Joint (see Q).—A 10 mm wide tongue, one-third the thickness of the board is formed along the lower edge of one board and fits into a slightly wider

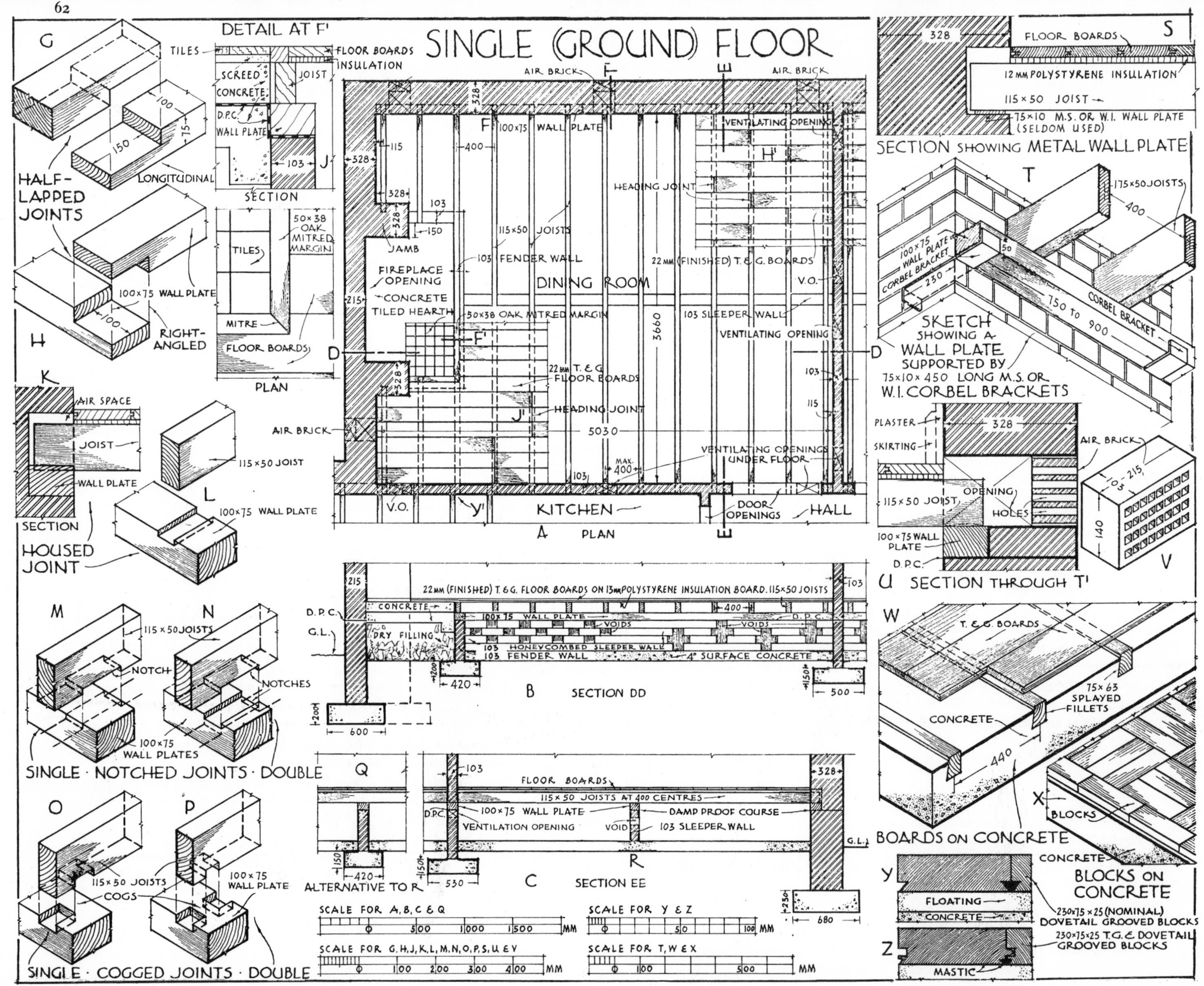
SINGLE (GROUND) FLOOR
DETAIL AT F'
TILES
FLOOR BOARDS
INSULATION
SCREED
JOIST
CONCRETE
D.P.C.
WALL PLATE
SECTION
50×38 OAK MITRED MARGIN
MITRE
FLOOR BOARDS
PLAN
HALF-LAPPED JOINTS
LONGITUDINAL
100×75 WALL PLATE
RIGHT-ANGLED
AIR SPACE
JOIST
WALL PLATE
SECTION
115×50 JOIST
100×75 WALL PLATE
HOUSED JOINT
AIR BRICK
100×75 WALL PLATE
VENTILATING OPENING
HEADING JOINT
JAMB
115×50 JOISTS
103 FENDER WALL
22MM (FINISHED) T. & G. BOARDS
FIREPLACE OPENING
CONCRETE TILED HEARTH
DINING ROOM
50×38 OAK MITRED MARGIN
103 SLEEPER WALL
22MM T. & G. FLOOR BOARDS
VENTILATING OPENINGS UNDER FLOOR
KITCHEN
DOOR OPENINGS
HALL
PLAN
22MM (FINISHED) T. & G. FLOOR BOARDS ON 13MM POLYSTYRENE INSULATION BOARD. 115×50 JOISTS
CONCRETE
100×75 WALL PLATE
D.P.C.
G.L.
DRY FILLING
VOIDS
103 HONEYCOMBED SLEEPER WALL
103 FENDER WALL
4" SURFACE CONCRETE
SECTION DD
115×50 JOISTS
NOTCH
NOTCHES
100×75 WALL PLATES
SINGLE · NOTCHED JOINTS · DOUBLE
115×50 JOISTS
COGS
100×75 WALL PLATE
SINGLE · COGGED JOINTS · DOUBLE
FLOOR BOARDS
115×50 JOISTS AT 400 CENTRES
100×75 WALL PLATE
DAMP PROOF COURSE
VENTILATION OPENING
VOID
103 SLEEPER WALL
ALTERNATIVE TO R
SECTION EE
SCALE FOR A, B, C & Q
SCALE FOR Y & Z
SCALE FOR G, H, J, K, L, M, N, O, P, S, U & V
SCALE FOR T, W & X
FLOOR BOARDS
12MM POLYSTYRENE INSULATION
115×50 JOIST
75×10 M.S. OR W.I. WALL PLATE (SELDOM USED)
SECTION SHOWING METAL WALL PLATE
175×50 JOISTS
100×75 WALL PLATE
CORBEL BRACKET
750 TO 900
SKETCH SHOWING A WALL PLATE SUPPORTED BY 75×10×450 LONG M.S. OR W.I. CORBEL BRACKETS
PLASTER
SKIRTING
AIR BRICK
115×50 JOIST
OPENING
HOLES
100×75 WALL PLATE
D.P.C.
SECTION THROUGH T'
T. & G. BOARDS
75×63 SPLAYED FILLETS
CONCRETE
BLOCKS
BOARDS ON CONCRETE
CONCRETE
BLOCKS ON CONCRETE
FLOATING
CONCRETE
230×75×25 (NOMINAL) DOVETAIL GROOVED BLOCKS
230×75×25 T.G. & DOVETAIL GROOVED BLOCKS
MASTIC

FIGURE 32

rebate formed on that adjacent. This joint is rarely used for edge joints, but is sometimes adopted in good work for heading joints (see below).

Tongued and Grooved or Feathered and Grooved Joint (abbreviated to "t. & g." or "f. & g.") (see R and U).—This is used more frequently than any other for good work. A narrow projecting tongue or feather is formed just below the middle along one edge and a groove along the other. The tongue is slightly smaller than the groove (thus for a 10 mm wide tongue the groove is approximately 12 mm deep) to enable the boards to be fitted closely together at the top and bottom surfaces when the tongues are engaged in the groove. The tongues are sometimes slightly rounded off so as to facilitate the laying of the boards and prevent them being damaged during the process.

Rebated, Tongued and Grooved Joint (see V).—This is a good but expensive joint and is sometimes adopted for hardwood floors where the boards are to be secured by nails which are required to be concealed. As described on p. 64, floor boards are usually fixed to the joists by *top nailing*, *i.e.*, the nails are driven through the entire thickness of the boards. This gives a somewhat unsightly appearance which is avoided if *secret nailing* is adopted, *i.e.*, each board is secured by hammering one or two nails through the tongue into each joint.

Splayed, Rebated, Tongued and Grooved Joint (see W).—This is another joint which is secretly nailed. It is an improvement upon that at V owing to the thicker and stronger tongue.

Ploughed and Tongued Joint (see X).—Grooves are formed or "ploughed" in the square edges of the boards to receive hardwood tongues or "slip feathers." It is rarely employed unless very thick boards are required and where the ordinary tongued and grooved joints would result in an excessive waste of material in forming the tongues.

Heading or End Joints.—Wherever possible, the boards should be sufficiently long to reach from wall to wall of a room in order to avoid end or heading joints. Where such joints are necessary, as for large floors, they usually take the form of the square joint shown at P. Each adjacent board is cut to cover half of the thickness of the joist below, the ends are closely butted together, and four nails are driven in, two on each side of the joint. Another form of end joint is called the *splayed* or *bevelled heading joint* (see Y); the ends are splayed to give a tight fit, and two nails are hammered in at an angle as shown. Rebated heading joints (see Q) are sometimes specified for good work. The appearance of the work is spoilt if the heading joints form one continuous line over the same joist. They should be laid to *break joint* as shown on the plan at H′, Fig. 32; sometimes they are arranged as shown at J′ when not more than three heading joints appear in one line, but the appearance is not so satisfactory.

(*Note.*—The boards used to cover the floor shown at A, Fig. 32, would not require heading joints, as 5·1 m long boards (see p. 61) would be used; the heading joints at H′ and J′ have been shown to illustrate their application.)

Cramping and Nailing Boards.—The joints must be as close as possible before the boards are nailed. The best means of effecting this is to employ an appliance known as a metal *cramp*, the plan of one of which is shown at A, Fig. 33.

Cramping is performed in the following manner: After the top edges of the joists have been levelled, starting from one wall, the first board is laid at right angles to the joists and nailed. Five or six boards are laid loosely upon the joists. Two cramps are placed temporarily over joists which are some 600 or 900 mm from the

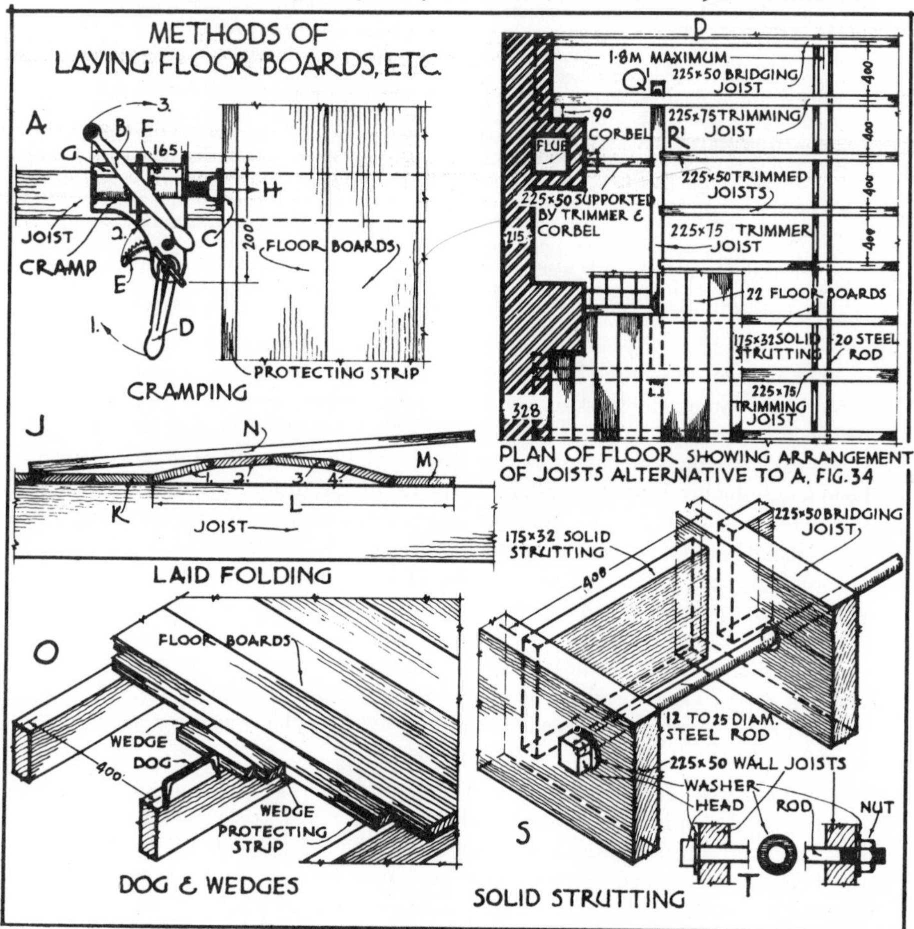

FIGURE 33

ends of the boards. Each cramp is fixed to the joists as shown at A, the arm D is rotated in the direction of the arrow "1"; this causes E to rotate towards the joist in the direction of the arrow "2", when the grooved surface on E and the sharp metal points at F (which project from the side and under the top plate at G) cause the cramp to grip the sides of the joist. A rough strip of wood is now inserted between the floor board and the plate C to protect the edge of the board, the arm B is rotated in the direction of the arrow "3", and this causes the plate C to move forward as shown by the arrow H to exert considerable pressure on the boards until the joints between them are completely closed. The boards are then nailed as described below, the cramps and the strip of wood are removed, and the operation is repeated on the next five or six boards. As the work proceeds towards the opposite wall, the last few lengths of boards cannot be cramped owing to lack of space. These boards may be brought up tight by using a piece of floor board which is inclined with the upper edge against the wall and the lower edge against the protecting strip; a few smart knocks with a heavy hammer on the upper end of the piece of board will close up the joints.

When a cramp is not available the joints between the boards may be closed by "jumping them in" or "laid folding." This method is shown at J, Fig. 33. Assuming that the floor has been laid up to K, a board M is nailed at a distance L which equals the width of the five boards when placed in position tightly by hand less 6 to 13 mm depending upon the width of the boards; the four boards, 1, 2, 3 and 4, are then placed as shown and forced into position by jumping on the board N which is laid across them. The boards are finally nailed and the operation repeated.

Another method is adopted in the absence of a cramp, as shown at O, Fig. 33. A metal *dog* is driven into a joist, and the boards (four or five at a time) are brought close together by tightening the hardwood wedges by means of a hammer.

When the boards are secretly nailed, and each board has therefore to be cramped and nailed separately, it is usual to cramp each board with the aid of a strong chisel which is driven into the top of a joist close to the protecting strip and used as a lever. The blade of the chisel is forced against the strip and the pressure closes the joint.

The boards are secured by oval wire nails (see A, Fig. 66) the length of which should be 2½ times the thickness of the boards. When top-nailed, two nails are driven through each board to every joist which it covers, including two nails at the ends. The nails are about 25 mm from the edges, and after the boards have been fixed, the heads of the nails are driven below the surface by using a hammer and *punch* (see 10, Fig. 67). Tongued and grooved boards (in addition to square and rebated boards) are usually top-nailed as shown by broken lines at S, Fig. 34. Occasionally they are secretly nailed as shown in the two positions at T, the higher position being the better of the two as the tongue is less likely to be damaged. The secret nailing of boards which are jointed as shown at V and W has been mentioned on p. 63. The heads of these are also punched. In order that water and gas pipes, electric cables, etc., which are frequently run below the floor boards, may be readily accessible, the boards over them are not nailed but screwed.

In good work it is customary to fix a *hardwood margin* round all fireplace hearths, as shown in the plan at A and the detail at J, Fig. 32. This ensures a more accurate finish and a neater appearance than is presented if the ends of the boards are stopped against the concrete or tiles. The floor boards, are rebated to receive the 50 mm by 20 mm oak margin which has mitred angles; if 22 mm thick boards are used, the margin is of the same thickness and the ends or edges of the boards are butted against it.

Double Boarded Floors.—Double flooring is sometimes required for buildings of the factory type (where the floors are subjected to excessive wear) and for domestic and other buildings which require good class floors. As is implied, the floors are laid in two thicknesses. The first covering or sub-floor (or counter-floor) usually consists of 20 mm roughly sawn square edged boards laid diagonally across the joists to avoid their joints coinciding with those of the boards above. The upper boards may be of 20 to 25 mm (nominal) hardwood (usually oak or maple) which are fixed at right angles to the joists.

(2) **Wood Covered Concrete Floors (Solid Floors).** Such floors are of concrete, they may be covered with wood boards or blocks (see W and X, Fig. 32). Other finishes suitable for solid floors are given in Chap. I, Vol. III.

Boards on Concrete (see W).—Wood *fillets* are partially embedded in the concrete floor and the boards are fixed to them. Special precautions must be taken to prevent dry rot; the concrete must be dry, the fillets treated with a preservative, and the top of the concrete given two coats of bitumen. Alternatively the concrete is laid in two layers with a d.p.c. between (see B, Fig. 10).

The concrete floor is laid to the level of the underside of the fillets and the top surface must be level throughout. The fillets are placed at 400 mm centres and kept temporarily in position by nailing cross battens to them. More concrete is then placed in position to within 13 mm of the top of the fillets. Both sides of the fillets may be splayed, although it is more economical if only one side is splayed (as shown at W), when one pair of fillets may be obtained from a 115 mm by 75 mm scantling.

Blocks on Concrete (see X).—The concrete floor is covered with wood blocks, a bituminous material or mastic being used as an adhesive. The blocks may be of well-seasoned softwoods (such as redwood, British Columbian Pine and pitch pine) or hardwoods (such as oak, maple and teak). Their nominal sizes vary from 225 to 300 mm long by 75 mm wide by 25 to 38 mm thick. Two of many types are shown at Y and Z, Fig. 32, the former being the simplest and is commonly used. The blocks are fixed by dipping the lower portion into the hot bituminous mastic, and then bedded on the concrete to which the mastic adheres. When they are pressed down, the liquid mastic rises in the grooves, as shown by the blackened portions in the illustrations. The thickness of the mastic is almost negligible. The blocks are laid to various designs, those most common are of the herring-bone and basket (shown at X) patterns. A simple border consisting of one or two rows of blocks is placed next to each wall.

The concrete floor is finished with a *floating* coat (or *screed*), usually 25 mm thick, consisting of 1 cement : 3 sand. It must be finished quite level and must be absolutely dry before the blocks are fixed, otherwise the mastic will not adhere to it. The building must be thoroughly dry before such floors are laid, otherwise the seasoned blocks will absorb moisture and may swell to such an extent as to cause the floors to rise in the centre. A d.p.c. membrane must be included in the concrete floor.

Cleaning Off and Protecting Floors.—On completion, wood floors should be *traversed* or "flogged." This consists of planing the boards to a level and smooth surface either by hand or machine. Hardwood floors are afterwards scraped (see scraper, p. 128), rubbed smooth with glass-paper (see p. 128) and finally oiled or waxed and polished. Floors should be protected against damage during subsequent building operations by liberally covering them with sawdust. This prevents plaster, paint and dirt from soiling and scratching the boards or blocks and the sawdust absorbs moisture.

UPPER FLOOR

The plan, section and various details of an upper floor of a room which is of the same size as the ground floor already described are shown in Fig. 34. The bridging joists are placed across the shortest span, and as there are no intermediate supports (such as sleeper walls), their clear span is 3·67 m. In accordance with Table II (see p. 60) the size of these joists will be 175 mm by 50 mm. An alternative arrangement of joists which would be adopted if the shortest span was in the other direction is shown at P, Fig. 33.

Trimming.—Where fireplaces and openings (such as are required for staircases) occur, the bridging joists cannot be supported at both ends by the walls, and the introduction of additional wood members is necessary to receive the ends of the joists which have to be cut. This operation is known as *trimming*. The trimmed opening at the fireplace shown at A, Fig. 34, has a thick joist, called a *trimming joist*, which is 508 mm from the fireplace and spans the full width of the room. This joist supports at one end two cross joists called *trimmer joists*, and the latter in turn support two pairs of short joists known as *trimmed* or *tail joists*. At the alternative plan P, Fig. 33, the two trimming joists have one trimmer framed to them which supports four trimmed joists. Thus a trimming joist is one which has one or more trimmers connected to it, and a trimmer carries cut bridging joists called trimmed joists. The arrangement of the timbers shown in these two plans is in accordance with the Building Regulations (summarised in Fig. 34) controlling the construction of wood floors adjacent to fireplaces.

Trimming and trimmer joists should be thicker than bridging joists on account of the greater weight which they have to support. It is usual to make the thickness of a trimming joist 25 mm greater than that of the bridging joists and a trimmer joist supporting not more than six bridging joists to be the thickness of the trimming joists. As the bridging joists are 50 mm thick, it will therefore be necessary to use 75 mm thick trimming and trimmer joists.

Joints.—The following joints used at trimmed openings are shown in Fig. 34: Tusk tenon joint, dovetailed housed joint, bevelled housed joint, and square housed joint.

Joints between joists at a trimmed opening should be well designed and constructed. On p. 19 reference is made to the behaviour of a loaded wood beam and to the stresses of compression, tension and shear which are produced. If a portion of a joist above the neutral axis is removed, the joist will be less effective in resisting compression stresses, and if the lower portion is cut and partially removed the joist is weakened to resist tension stresses. This must not be ignored when notches for pipes are made in joists, as a careless workman when fixing water, etc., pipes under floor boards may reduce the strength of joists enormously either by excessively notching them or by indiscriminate notching. The aim therefore should be to make the joints as secure as possible with a minimum removal of wood and reduction in strength of the main members, *i.e.*, the trimmers (to which the trimmed joists are connected) and the trimming joists (to which the trimmers are joined).

Tusk Tenon Joint (see L, Fig. 34, and Q′, Figs. 33 and 34).—This is the strongest form of joint used in floor construction and for this reason it should be adopted for the connection between the trimmer and trimming joists. The tenon which is cut on the end of the trimmer (and passes through the mortice formed in the trimming joist to some 100 to 125 mm beyond it) is in the *centre*[1] of the trimmer. The projecting piece or *tusk* provided below the tenon transmits most of the weight and enters from $\frac{1}{8}$ to $\frac{1}{4}$ into the trimming joist. The bevelled or slanting portion above the tenon, called the *horn* or *haunch*, strengthens the tenon. The trimmer is brought tight up against the trimming joist by driving a wood wedge down through a hole formed in the tenon; the side of the hole (shown by a thick line in section J′J′) should be cut to the same angle as that of the tapered wedge and this hole must be long enough to allow the trimmer to be forced in the direction of the arrow until the joint is tight.

A modified form of tusk tenon, called a *bevelled haunched joint*, is sometimes adopted between a trimmer and each of the trimmed joists (as at P, Fig. 33), where it is not possible to have projecting tenons on account of the hearth. This is similar to the tusk tenon joint, except that the tenon does not project, but is cut flush with the outer side of the trimmer. When the tenon formed on the trimmed joist has been inserted, the sides of the mortice in the trimmer are slightly pared to receive two small wedges which are driven in to tighten the tenon; 150 mm wire nails are then hammered in from the top and sides of the trimmer and through the tenon. A further modification consists of a shorter tenon (with tusk) which enters a corresponding mortice in the trimmer. Long nails driven in from the top of this joist make the joint secure.

Dovetailed Housed or Notched Joint (see M).—This is another good joint which is used to connect trimmed joists to a trimmer joist. The end of the trimmed joist is formed to correspond to the housing (one edge of which is dovetailed as shown) made in the trimmer to receive it and is dropped into the housing. Long nails are then driven in slantwise from the outer face of the trimmer and through the end of the trimmed joist. Applications are shown at R′ in P, Fig. 33, and A, Fig. 34.

Bevelled Housed Joint (see N).—This is a cheaper but an effective alternative to the dovetailed housed joint and is used for the same purpose. It is known as a *half-depth joint*, as the depth of the housing equals half the depth of the joist. The joint must be nailed securely. Note that the amount of timber removed from the trimmer varies from nil at the top fibres (where the compression stress is greatest) to a maximum at the neutral axis.

Square Housed Joint (see O).—This is another half-depth joint which may be adopted for supporting short trimmed joists as at S′ in A, Fig. 34.

[1] Sometimes the *underside* of the tenon is made to coincide with the centre of the joist. Although this forms a somewhat stronger joint, it is more difficult to make tight.

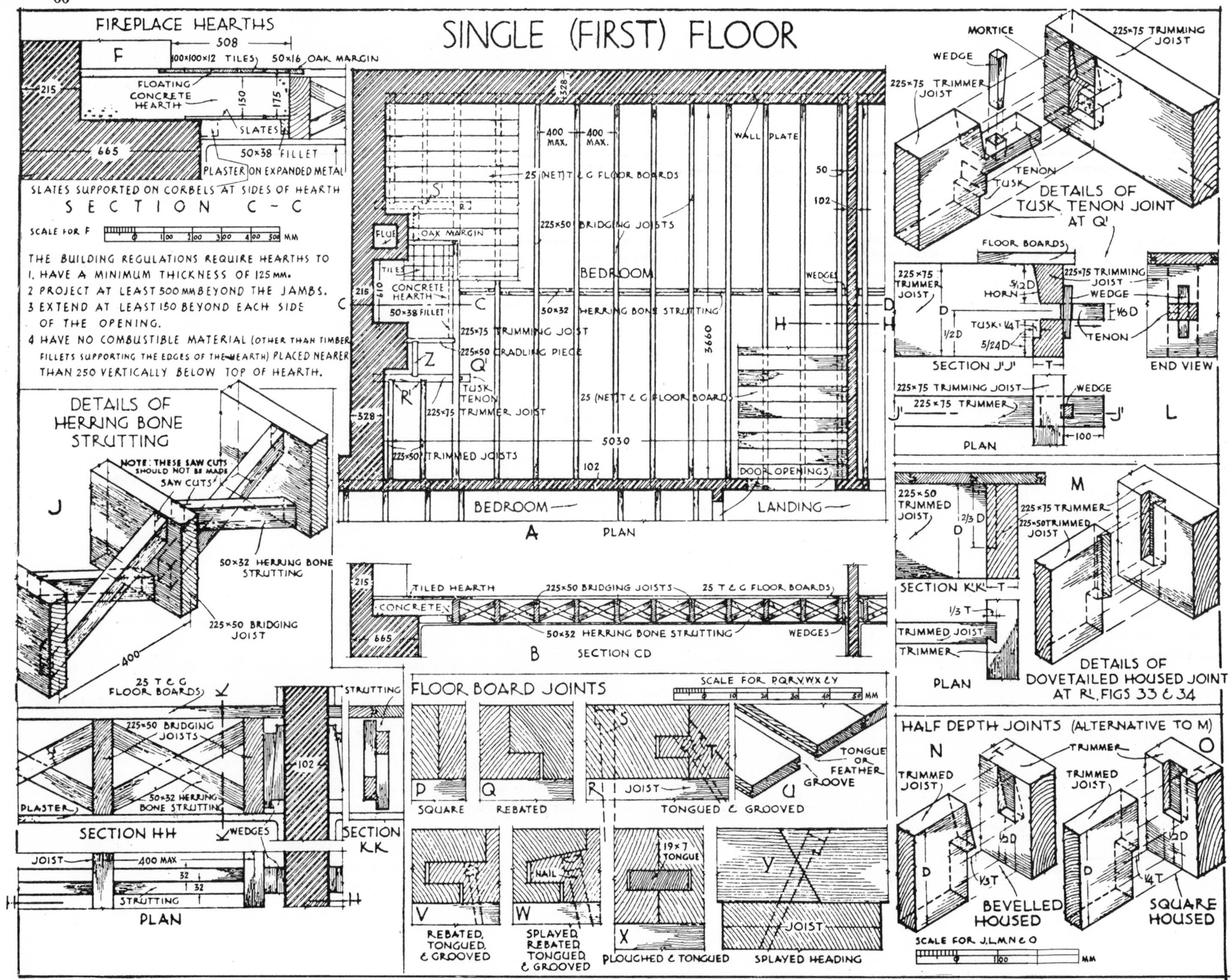
SINGLE (FIRST) FLOOR
FIREPLACE HEARTHS
508
F
100×100×12 TILES
50×16 OAK MARGIN
215
FLOATING
CONCRETE
HEARTH
150
175
SLATES
665
50×38 FILLET
PLASTER ON EXPANDED METAL
SLATES SUPPORTED ON CORBELS AT SIDES OF HEARTH
SECTION C-C
SCALE FOR F
100 200 300 400 500 MM
THE BUILDING REGULATIONS REQUIRE HEARTHS TO
1. HAVE A MINIMUM THICKNESS OF 125 MM.
2 PROJECT AT LEAST 500 MM BEYOND THE JAMBS.
3 EXTEND AT LEAST 150 BEYOND EACH SIDE
OF THE OPENING.
4 HAVE NO COMBUSTIBLE MATERIAL (OTHER THAN TIMBER
FILLETS SUPPORTING THE EDGES OF THE HEARTH) PLACED NEARER
THAN 250 VERTICALLY BELOW TOP OF HEARTH.
328
400 MAX.
400 MAX.
WALL PLATE
25 (NET) T & G FLOOR BOARDS
S'
FLUE
OAK MARGIN
225×50 BRIDGING JOISTS
50
102
TILES
BEDROOM
WEDGES
215
610
CONCRETE HEARTH
C
C
D
50×38 FILLET
50×32 HERRING BONE STRUTTING
H
H
225×75 TRIMMING JOIST
3660
225×50 CRADLING PIECE
Z
Q'
TUSK TENON
R'
225×75 TRIMMER JOIST
25 (NET) T & G FLOOR BOARDS
328
5030
225×50 TRIMMED JOISTS
102
DOOR OPENINGS
BEDROOM
LANDING
A
PLAN
MORTICE
WEDGE
225×75 TRIMMING JOIST
225×75 TRIMMER JOIST
TENON
TUSK
DETAILS OF
TUSK TENON JOINT
AT Q'
FLOOR BOARDS
225×75 TRIMMER JOIST
225×75 TRIMMING JOIST
5/12 D
HORN
WEDGE
D
1/6 D
TUSK=1/4 T
1/2 D
5/24 D
TENON
SECTION J'J'
T
END VIEW
225×75 TRIMMING JOIST
WEDGE
225×75 TRIMMER
J'
J'
L
100
PLAN
DETAILS OF
HERRING BONE
STRUTTING
NOTE: THESE SAW CUTS SHOULD NOT BE MADE
SAW CUTS
J
50×32 HERRING BONE STRUTTING
225×50 BRIDGING JOIST
400
215
TILED HEARTH
225×50 BRIDGING JOISTS
25 T & G FLOOR BOARDS
CONCRETE
665
50×32 HERRING BONE STRUTTING
WEDGES
B
SECTION CD
M
225×50 TRIMMED JOIST
2/3 D
D
225×75 TRIMMER
225×50 TRIMMED JOIST
SECTION K'K'
T
1/3 T
TRIMMED JOIST
TRIMMER
PLAN
DETAILS OF
DOVETAILED HOUSED JOINT
AT R', FIGS 33 & 34
25 T & G
FLOOR BOARDS
K
STRUTTING
225×50 BRIDGING JOISTS
102
50×32 HERRING BONE STRUTTING
PLASTER
SECTION HH
K
WEDGES
SECTION K K
JOIST
400 MAX
32
32
STRUTTING
H
H
PLAN
FLOOR BOARD JOINTS
SCALE FOR P,Q,R,V,W,X & Y
0 10 20 30 40 50 MM
S
T
TONGUE OR FEATHER
GROOVE
P
SQUARE
Q
REBATED
R
JOIST
U
TONGUED & GROOVED
19×7 TONGUE
NAIL
Y
V
REBATED, TONGUED, & GROOVED
W
SPLAYED REBATED TONGUED & GROOVED
X
PLOUGHED & TONGUED
JOIST
SPLAYED HEADING
HALF DEPTH JOINTS (ALTERNATIVE TO M)
N
O
TRIMMER
TRIMMED JOIST
TRIMMED JOIST
1/2 D
1/2 D
D
1/3 T
D
1/4 T
BEVELLED HOUSED
SQUARE HOUSED
SCALE FOR J,L,M,N & O
0 100 MM

FIGURE 34

Strutting.—Floors (excepting ballroom floors) should be as rigid as possible, otherwise undue stress may be transmitted to the supporting walls and plastered ceilings may be rendered defective on account of the vibration produced. Deep joists have a tendency to twist or tilt sideways. It is necessary therefore to stiffen the floor by providing cross *bracing* or *strutting* in continuous rows and at intervals not exceeding 1·8 m apart. There are two forms of strutting, *i.e.*, herring bone and solid.

Herring Bone Strutting (see A, B, and J, Fig. 34).—This is unquestionably the best form, and comprises pairs of inclined pieces of timber which are tightly fitted between the joists. The size of each piece varies from 50 mm by 32 mm to 50 mm by 50 mm, and these are secured to the sides of the joists by one 65 mm nail at each end.[1] Provided the walls are sufficiently strong, folding wedges are driven in between the wall and the adjacent joist, and in line with the strutting, as shown; these are allowed to remain as they increase the efficiency of the strutting. This form of strutting is still effective even if the joists shrink in the direction of their depth and thickness, for the depth shrinkage especially tends to reduce the inclination of the struts, with a corresponding increase in compression.

Solid Strutting (see P and S, Fig. 33).—The simplest form (and one which is frequently adopted for cheap work) merely consists of nailing short lengths of floor board in a continuous row between the joists. *This is quite ineffective*, and it is practically a waste of material and labour forming it on account of the shrinkage which occurs in the thickness of the joists and causes the struts to become loose as their length is then less than the clear distance between the joists.

To make the strutting effective it is necessary to fix a long circular steel or wrought iron rod (varying from 13 to 25 mm in diameter) through the whole of the joists and near to the strutting, as shown. The rod is threaded through the holes which have been augured through the neutral axis of the joists. The nut is tightened after the struts have been fixed and again tightened by means of a spanner before the floor boards are laid. *This form of strutting (with rod) is now seldom adopted.*

Hearths.—Building regulations stipulate that the hearth in front of a fireplace shall project at least 500 mm beyond the front of the jambs, have a minimum thickness of 125 mm and shall extend at least 150 mm beyond each side of the opening. They also require that no combustible material (other than timber fillets supporting the edges of a hearth where it adjoins a floor) is to be placed nearer than 250 mm vertically below the top of a hearth unless such material is separated from the underside of the hearth by an air space of not less than 50 mm.

One method of supporting a first floor hearth is shown at F, Fig. 34.

The section at F includes a 150 mm thick concrete hearth which is finished with tiles to give an overall thickness of 175 mm. The hearth is formed *in situ* (or permanent position) and a temporary support must be provided for the front hearth. This support is shown to consist of slates. At the outer edges of the hearth the slates rest on a 50 mm by 38 mm timber fillet nailed to the trimming joist, at the inner edge they rest on the brickwork below the concrete hearth. On each side of the fireplace recess the slates rest on corbels shown by broken line at F, they also rest on fillets nailed to the cradling pieces (see below). The concrete is then placed in position. Two short joists are provided to afford a support for the floor boards at the ends of the hearth, and between the fireplace jamb and the trimming joist. One of these, called a *cradling piece*, is housed at one end into the trimming joist, and the other end rests upon a short brick corbel (as shown at P, Fig. 33), as it must not enter the wall owing to the proximity of the flue from the ground floor fireplace. The second piece (Z), to which the ends of the floorboards are nailed, is housed into the trimmer and the cradling piece. In the alternative plan at P, Fig. 33, a cradling piece only is required. This may be a 50 mm by 50 mm fillet coinciding with the edge of the hearth and supported by it, or it may be an independent short piece of 225 mm by 50 mm joist supported by the trimmer and corbel as shown.

In districts where stone is readily available, a 75 mm thick stone *flag* is sometimes used instead of concrete to form the front hearth. This flag is supported by a brick corbel course along one edge (or it may be built into the brickwork), and the other edge rests upon a wood fillet which is well nailed to the trimming joist or trimmer as the case may be. Concrete is placed upon this stone to bring the thickness up to that required by the Building Regulations, and this is generally covered with tiles. Concrete is used to form the back hearth which is brought up to the level of the front hearth.

PLASTERED CEILINGS

Plastered ceilings are the usual type of finish to joists in domestic work; students should have read " Plastering to Walls " on pp. 31–33 before proceeding with this section.

For a joisted ceiling, the wood lath and plaster finish was the traditional method. Riven laths 38 mm wide, from 3 to 13 mm thick were nailed to the joists 10 mm apart, the coarse stuff was well laid on to the laths so that the plaster penetrated the gaps and spread out behind them. This gave a good mechanical key and resulted in first-class work free from cracks which are sometimes common with present-day board finishes. Wood lath and plastering and lime based mixes have now been replaced, very largely, by metallic lathing or plasterboard covered with gypsum plaster mixes :—

Expanded Metal Lathing (XPM), which should be protected from corrosion by galvanizing (if condensation is expected) or by stove dried asphaltum paint, is nailed to the joists and given three coats of plaster. XPM is made in sheets

[1] It is a common practice to make short saw-cuts at the ends of the pieces to receive the nails (see J) to avoid (so it is claimed) the nails splitting the timber. This should not be done as the holding power of the nails is thus reduced.

610 to 680 mm wide and 1·8 to 2·75 m long, the thickness varies with the joist spacing, *e.g.* 0·56 mm and 1·2 mm for joists at 350 mm and 450 mm centres respectively; 0·7 mm metal being used for the usual domestic joist centres of 400 mm. The short way size of the mesh is 6 mm and 10 mm, the former for hairless plaster, both being used when hair is added. The sheets are fixed with 32 mm galvanized clout nails or staples at 100 mm centres. The joints must be lapped at least 25 mm and wired together every 100 mm with 1·2 mm galvanized soft iron wire.

For concrete floors, the XPM is fixed to flat bars suspended below the floor. 22 mm by 6 mm flat bars supported at 1·2 m intervals and placed at 450 mm centres are commonly used; a 6 mm dia. suspension rod will support 1·5 m^2 of ceiling.

Render coat and floating coat mixes applied to the lathing can be 1 cement : 2 lime : 9 sand; as well as aiding plasticity during application, the lime also minimises corrosion; 0·5 kg of hair is added to 0·093 m^3 of first coat. Such mixes must be allowed to dry out thoroughly before further coats are added. The same coats using gypsum plaster (class B or C) can be 1 plaster : 2 to 3 lime : 8 to 9 sand. A suitable finishing coat on both these mixes is 1 plaster (class B or C) : 2 to 4 lime putty. Special class B metal lathing plaster is also used for undercoats in the proportion 1 plaster : 1 sand, this can be finished as above, or with neat class B, C or D plaster.

Plasterboard consists of a core of gypsum plaster bonded between two sheets of heavy paper; there are four types from 10 to 13 mm thick: baseboard, lath, plank and insulating baseboard. They are all similar except that the latter has a covering of aluminium foil on one side (that placed next to the air space and which is not plastered), and are obtainable in several sizes; 1·2 m by 1·8 m wallboard being commonly used. The boards are nailed to the joists at 150 mm centres with 32 mm by 2·2 mm galvanized plasterboard nails. They should be fastened so that the joints are staggered. The joints are strengthened by a strip of 100 to 125 mm wide jute *scrim cloth* which is plastered over them as they are being filled. When this has set, the surface is levelled with a coat of plaster between the scrimmed joints and a final coat is applied over the whole area; this is two-coat work (13 mm thick) and used for good quality work. A cheaper finish is one-coat work (5 mm thick) the plaster skimming follows immediately after the joints have been scrimmed, and the mix is neat class B plaster. The same setting coat is used for two-coat work on a floating coat of 1 class B plaster : 1½ sand. Lime must not be used in these mixes on plasterboard.

Insulating fibreboard is used in a similar way, scrimmed and plastered (preferably in one coat) with special low setting expansion quality class B plaster.

Plasterboard can also be used alone without having a plaster finish. In this case the board has chamfered edges in which a strip of linen or paper reinforcement is bedded in a special fine plaster which is also used to flush-point the joints.

The thermal insulation of ceilings is described on p. 14 with reference to roof construction.

ROOFS

Terms.—Most of the following terms used in connection with roof construction are illustrated in Fig. 35 and subsequent drawings.

Covering.—The external material laid or fixed on a roof to protect the building. The materials used are: Slates, interlocking and plain tiles (see Chapter Five), pantiles (burnt slabs of clay, shaped to a flat S in cross-section, 350 mm by 250 mm by 16 mm), asphalt (as described on p. 17, laid on concrete in two or three layers to a finished thickness of 20 mm or 30 mm), asphalt felt (see p. 17 and Q, Fig. 36), lead (see Chapter Six), zinc (thin sheets laid somewhat like lead to form a cheaper and inferior covering), copper (an excellent but costly material laid in sheets), corrugated sheets of asbestos-cement or galvanised wrought iron, stone slabs (similar to slates but from 10 mm to 20 mm thick), shingles (slabs of cedar or oak which are from 300 to 600 mm long, from 60 to 150 mm wide and 6 to 13 mm thick), patent glazing (sheets of glass supported by lead covered wood, steel or reinforced concrete bars) and thatch (bundles of straw or reeds laid to a thickness of about 300 mm).

Spars or Common Rafters.—Similar to joists but inclined. The distance apart depends upon the covering material and is usually 400 mm centres for slates. The *head* of a spar is the upper end, and the *foot* is the lower end.

Span.—Usually taken to be the clear horizontal distance between the internal faces of the walls supporting the roof. The *effective span* is the horizontal

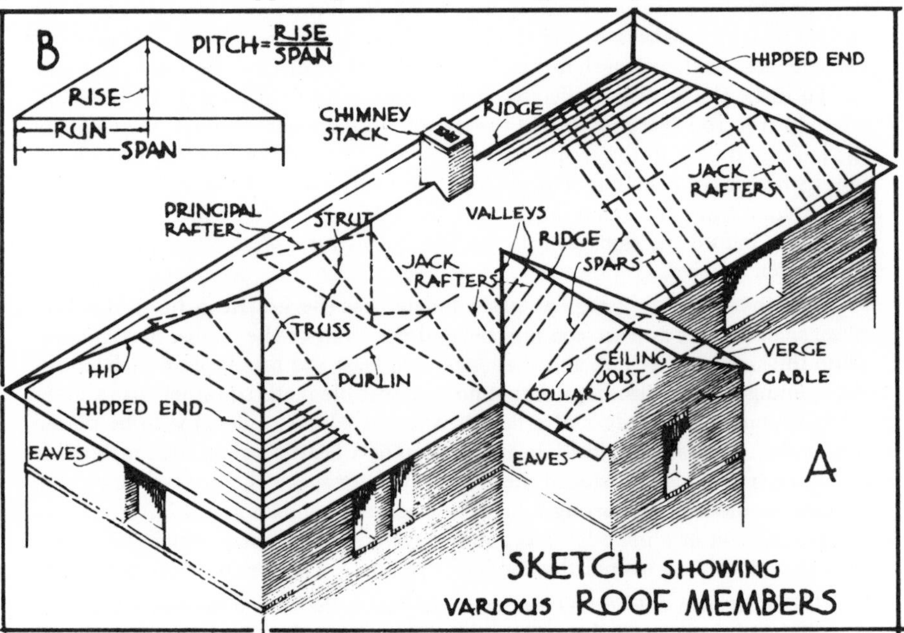

FIGURE 35

distance between the centre of the supports. The span of spars is the inclined distance from support to support, thus in Fig. 37 the span is the distance from ridge to purlin, purlin to purlin, and purlin to wall plate.

Rise.—The vertical height measured from the lowest to the highest points.

Pitch.—The slope or inclination to the horizontal expressed either as $\frac{\text{rise}}{\text{span}}$ (see B, Fig. 35) or in degrees. It varies with the covering material in accordance with Table III which gives the *minimum* pitch :—

TABLE III

Covering material	Rise (mm) (in 100 mm run) (see B, Fig. 35)	Minimum Pitch	Angle
Asphalt and copper . .	1·25	$\frac{1}{160}$	$\frac{3}{4}°$
Lead and zinc (excluding drips every 3 000 mm run)	1·25	$\frac{1}{160}$	$\frac{3}{4}°$
Asphalt felt, corrugated asbestos and iron sheets . . .	10	$\frac{1}{20}$	$5\frac{3}{4}°$
Slates, large	40	$\frac{1}{5}$	$21\frac{3}{4}°$
Slates, ordinary . . .	50	$\frac{1}{4}$	$26\frac{1}{2}°$
Slates, small	66·6	$\frac{1}{3}$	$33\frac{2}{3}°$
Pantiles	45	$\frac{9}{40}$	24°
Shingles, cedar . . .	50	$\frac{1}{4}$	$26\frac{1}{2}°$
Shingles, oak	100	$\frac{1}{2}$	45°
Patent glazing . . .	50	$\frac{1}{4}$	20°
Stone slabs	66·6	$\frac{1}{3}$	$33\frac{2}{3}°$
Plain tiles and thatch . .	100	$\frac{1}{2}$	45°
Interlocking tiles . . .	50·8	$\frac{23}{80}$	30°

These angles are often departed from, thus, although lead is commonly used to cover flat roofs which have a minimum rise of 1·25 cm for a 100 cm run, it is occasionally used to cover steeply pitched roofs. The angle of 45° should not be adopted as roofs with this pitch have not a satisfactory appearance—compare the roof shown at V, Fig. 36 (which has a slope of 45°), with that in Fig. 37 (which has a 55° pitch). The ideal pitch is considered to be 54° 45′ and roofs pitched at any angle between 50° and 60° look well.

Wall Plates.—These receive the feet of the spars. They vary in size up to 115 mm by 75 mm and are bedded and jointed as described on p. 60.

Eaves means " edge," and the eaves of a roof is its lower edge. The eaves may terminate flush with the outer face of the wall, when it is known as a *flush eaves* (see W, Fig. 36), or it may project as shown at X and Y, Fig. 36. When the feet of the spars are exposed as indicated at X they form an *open eaves*, when the feet are covered as shown at Y, a *closed eaves* results. A *fascia board* (or *fascia*) is the thin piece of wood fixed to the feet of the spars (see W and Y, Fig. 36). The under portion of an overhanging eaves is called the *soffit*. *Soffit boards* are shown at Y, Fig. 36, and D, Fig. 38, and the cross-pieces of wood illustrated in the latter figure to which these boards are nailed are called *soffit bearers*. The lower portion of a roof is sometimes tilted so as to improve its appearance; this is accomplished by nailing short pieces of wood, called *sprockets*, to the spars (see Figs. 37 and 38).

Ridge Piece or Ridge.—This is fixed at the highest point to receive the heads of the spars.

Hip is the line produced when two roof surfaces intersect to form an external angle which exceeds 180°. A *hipped end* is a portion of roof between two hips (see A, Fig. 35). The timber at the intersection is called a *hip rafter*, and the foot of this rafter is usually fixed to a horizontal cross-member called a *dragon beam* which is secured at one end to an *angle tie* (see Fig. 37). A hip rafter supports the upper ends of short spars and it may be required to carry the ends of purlins (see below).

Valley is formed by the intersection of two roof surfaces having an external angle which is less than 180° (see Fig. 35) and the wood member at the intersection is called a *valley rafter*. The feet of short spars are nailed to a valley rafter.

Jack Rafters.—These are short spars which run from a hip to the eaves or from a ridge to a valley (see Fig. 35).

Verge is the edge of a roof which runs from eaves to ridge at a gable (see Fig. 35).

Purlins are horizontal timbers providing intermediate supports to spars, and are supported by walls, hip and valley rafters, and roof trusses (see Fig. 35).

Roof Trusses are structures formed of members framed together, they support purlins in the absence of cross-walls. See example in Fig. 39.

Boarding or *Sarking* consists of 25 mm (nominal thickness) boards which are nailed to the *backs* (upper edges) of spars, and to which slates and other roofing materials are secured.

Battens are small pieces of wood to which slates, tiles, etc., are secured. They are generally fixed by the slater or tiler and are referred to in Chapter Five.

Classification of Roofs.—

(*a*) *Single Roofs* consist only of spars which are secured at the ridge and wall plates. The various forms of this type are : (i) flat, (ii) lean-to, (iii) double lean-to, (iv) couple, (v) close couple and (vi) collar roofs.

(*b*) *Double or Purlin Roofs.*—In this type additional members, called purlins, are introduced to support the spars.

(*c*) *Trussed Rafter Roofs.*—These comprise light trusses formed by framing together spars and ceiling joists with intermediate members. They have replaced almost entirely purlin roofs for domestic work.

(*d*) *Triple or Framed Roofs* consist of three sets of members, *i.e.*, spars that are partially supported by purlins, which in turn are carried by trusses.

SINGLE ROOFS

The various forms of this class are illustrated in Fig. 36. The sizes of the

spars specified on the drawings must not be taken to be economical in all cases, for, in addition to the span, these sizes depend upon the weight of the covering material, the distance centre and centre, and the wood employed. Table IV gives the approximate average weight of various covering materials:—

TABLE IV

Material	Weight kg/m²	Material	Weight kg/m²
Zinc and copper	2·4	Lead (including rolls)	33·5
Asphalt felt	3·6	Thatch	33·5
Corrugated iron	12·0	Asphalt, 20 mm thick	43·0
Boarding, 25 mm thick	14·4	Slates	43·0
Shingles, cedar	7·2	Pantiles	47·9
Corrugated asbestos-cement	16·8	Plain tiles	62·2
Patent glazing (steel	28·7	Interlocking tiles	36·0
,, ,, (aluminium)	19·1	Stone slabs	86·2

Tables in the Building Regulations give the size of a spar according to its span, pitch and the load carried; the most usual size is 100 mm by 50 mm.

(i) *Flat Roof*.—This is shown in Fig. 36 by the small-scale plan and section at F and A, and enlarged details at Q, R and S. The upper surface must be inclined sufficiently to throw off the water, and, as felt is the covering material, the minimum inclination is 10 mm in 100 mm run.[1] If the under surface is not required to be level, the inclination is obtained by inclining the joists to the required fall towards the eaves. If a level ceiling is required, the fall may be obtained by either tapering the joists with the top edge of each sloped to the required fall; more usually the joists are fixed level and a small tapered piece of wood nailed on top of each. The tapered pieces are called *firring pieces* or *firrings*. As shown at R, they are the same width as the joists, and the depth varies from a maximum of 50 mm at S (which is a detail of C) to 13 mm at Q (a detail of B). Tongued and grooved boards are nailed on top of the firrings, and this boarding should be dressed smooth in order to remove any sharp edges which may cause damage to the covering material. A fascia board is nailed to the ends of the joists. The herring bone strutting is necessary if the ceiling is to be plastered, otherwise it may be omitted.

Bituminous felt and lead are the most common covering materials employed for this class of roof. Lead flats are detailed in Chapter Six. That shown in Fig. 36 is covered with felt, of which there are many varieties.

In the example, three layers of the felt are used, with a coat of bituminous solution between and on top. The felt (which may be similar to that described on p. 17) is in 900 mm wide rolls. The first layer is laid direct upon the boarding, lapped 75 mm at the joints with solution between and nailed along the joints at 75 mm intervals. Hot solution is now applied over this first layer and a second layer of felt is laid with 75 mm joints (not nailed). This is brushed over with solution and a third layer of felt is laid as described and given a coat of the hot bitumen. Grit (or slate granules) is now rolled into the solution to protect the felt from the action of the sun. The intersection between the flat and the wall is made watertight by continuing the layers of felt over the triangular fillet in the angle. The upturned edges of the felt are covered with a lead cover flashing as described on p. 143. Roofs of temporary buildings are usually covered with one layer of felt.

Lead Covered Flat.—The lead details of the flat shown in Fig. 74 are described in Chapter Six, and reference is there made to the groundwork, *i.e.*, the timber construction. The flat is divided into two by a drip and each half is subdivided by two rolls. The boarding is given a fall towards the gutter and the joists supporting it are laid across the shortest span. The fall is obtained by fixing firrings to the tops of the joists. These firrings increase in depth from a minimum of 13 mm at the lower joist to a maximum at the upper end (see A, P and T, Fig. 74); deep firrings are avoided at the upper half of the flat by using deeper joists as shown. The wood construction of the drips and rolls are detailed in Fig. 74, and will be more readily understood if consideration of this flat is deferred until the subject of leadwork is studied. The gutter is constructed of 50 mm by 38 mm *gutter bearers* at 400 mm centres, fixed at different levels to give the necessary fall to the boarding. These bearers are supported by the wall at one end and by a 38 mm thick longitudinal fillet or bearer nailed to the side of the lower joist (see P, Fig. 74). The construction of the cesspool is similar to that described on p. 148.

(ii) *Lean-to Roof* (see H, Fig. 36).—This is the simplest form of pitched roof and consists of spars inclined at 30°[1] against a wall. An enlarged detail of J is shown at G, where the wall plate is supported by two brick corbel courses. Alternatively metal corbel brackets as shown at T, Fig. 32, may be adopted. A cheaper method consists of nailing the upper ends of the spars to a continuous 75 mm by 50 mm *wall piece* or *pitch plate* which is *plugged* with its 75 mm face next to the wall. Plugging consists of driving wood wedges (see F, Fig. 49) called *plugs* at intervals into the joints of the brickwork. The ends of the plugs are cut flush with the face of the wall and the wall piece is nailed to them. The construction at the eaves is similar to that at X, except that there is no horizontal tie. The spars are V-shaped notched at both ends and fitted to the wall plate; this is one form of a *birdsmouth joint*. Another form is shown at K, Fig. 37. The depth of the notch should not exceed one-third that of the spar. Notching the spars counteracts the tendency for them to slide downwards. The eaves detail is referred to on p. 74. The roof may be boarded as shown at X or battened as shown at Y.

(iii) *Double Lean-to*, *Pent* or *V-Roof* (see M and O, Fig. 36).—Pent means penned or closed in, and this form consists of two lean-to roofs which are enclosed by and sloped from the two outer parapet walls to a party or division wall over which a gutter is formed. Sometimes the lower ends of the spars are

[1] As three layers of felt have been used, the minimum inclination may be reduced to that for lead, *i.e.*, 1·25 mm in 100 mm run.

[1] This slope is suitable if slating is the covering material.

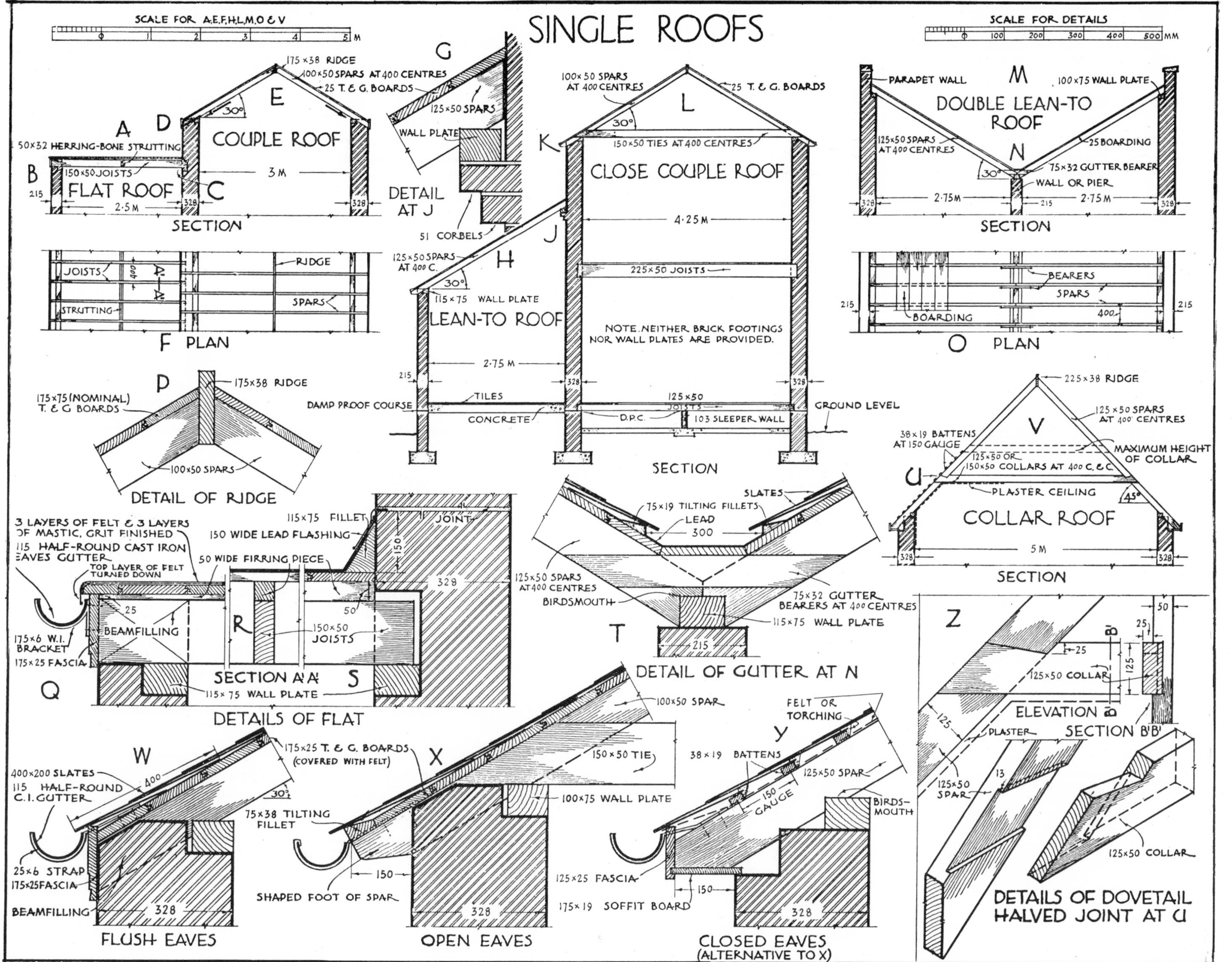
SINGLE ROOFS
SCALE FOR A.E.F.H.L.M.O & V
SCALE FOR DETAILS
COUPLE ROOF
FLAT ROOF
SECTION
F PLAN
DETAIL AT J
LEAN-TO ROOF
CLOSE COUPLE ROOF
NOTE. NEITHER BRICK FOOTINGS NOR WALL PLATES ARE PROVIDED.
DOUBLE LEAN-TO ROOF
O PLAN
DETAIL OF RIDGE
COLLAR ROOF
DETAILS OF FLAT
SECTION A A'
DETAIL OF GUTTER AT N
FLUSH EAVES
OPEN EAVES
CLOSED EAVES (ALTERNATIVE TO X)
DETAILS OF DOVETAIL HALVED JOINT AT U

Figure 36

secured to a beam which runs parallel to the main walls, and, if necessary, is supported at intervals by brick, wood or steel pillars. A detail of the gutter is shown at T and a description of the slating and plumbing work is given in Chapters Five and Six.

This roof is not adopted often as it is expensive on account of the extra walling required and because the gutter is a potential source of weakness.

(iv) *Couple* or *Span Roof* (see E and F, Fig. 36).—It is so called as each pair or couple of rafters is pitched against each other and supported at the upper ends at the ridge, as detailed at P. A detail of the eaves at D is shown at W and described on p. 74. It should not be used for buildings having a greater span than 3·7 m unless the walls are exceptionally thick. The roof is of bad design as it has a tendency to spread at the feet (as shown by the thick arrows) and thrust out the walls. *It is not recommended.*

(v) *Close Couple Roof* (see L, Fig. 36).—This is a vastly better form than the last described, for each couple of rafters is closed by a horizontal tie—hence the name. This tie is connected to the feet of the spars and prevents them spreading outwards. The best form of connection between the ties and the feet of the spars is the *dovetail halved joint* (detailed at Z and described below) but in cheaper work the ties are just spiked to the spars. A plastered ceiling is often formed on the underside of the ties, they are then called *ceiling joists.* Such joists, when they exceed 3·7 m in length, should have 50 mm by 32 mm vertical *hangers* nailed to every third or fourth spar and to a horizontal 75 mm by 50 mm *runner* which is nailed to the joists (see Fig. 38 and p. 74); this prevents the sagging of the ceiling joists and cracking of the plaster. The span of this roof should be restricted to 4·9 m unless the size of the ties is increased or they are supported by hangers, when the span may be increased to 6 m. The sizes of ties (redwood) are given in Table V when the spars are at 400 mm centres in a tiled roof.

If hangers or struts are used for spans of 3·7 m and upwards, the depth of the ties may be halved.

The detail of the open eaves K is shown at X and an alternative closed eaves is illustrated at Y. These are described on p. 74.

This roof conforms with sound principles of construction. For a tiled roof with spars at 400 mm centres the maximum span of 50 mm by 100 mm spars is 2·34 m, for 50 mm by 125 mm spars the maximum span is 2·91 m —see Building Regulations.

TABLE V, TIES (mm)

Maximum Span (m)	Size (mm)	Maximum Span (m)	Size (mm)
2·72	50 by 100	4·7	50 by 175
3·39	50 by 125	5·34	50 by 200
4·04	50 by 150	5·98	50 by 225

(vi) *Collar Roof* (see V, Fig. 36).—This is similar to the close couple roof except that the horizontal ties are now placed higher up the roof, and are called *collars.* The latter may be placed at any height between the wall plates and half-way up the roof, the broken lines indicating the position when at the maximum height. Obviously the lower the collar the more effective it becomes in preventing the rafters from spreading and causing damage to the walls. It follows therefore that the close couple roof is stronger than the collar roof, but the latter is more economical in wall height for, as shown at V, the plastered ceiling may be formed on the underside of the collars and the lower portion of the spars.

The *dovetail halved joint* at U is detailed at Z. A 13 mm[1] sinking is formed on the side of the spar and the upper edge is dovetailed. The end of the collar is checked out 13 mm, and the remainder of the thickness of the collar is dovetailed along the upper edge as shown so that when the collar is fitted to the spar it will be housed to the extent of 13 mm (see section B′B′). The collar is then well spiked or bolted to the spars.

This joint is effective in resisting both tension and compression stresses. Thus any tendency for the spars to spread (when the collar would be in tension) is counteracted by the top shoulder (edge) of the collar bearing on the upper edge of the dovetailed notch formed on the spar, and the spars are prevented from sagging (to produce a compression stress in the collar) by the inclined abutment of the collar which is fitted tightly against the underside of the spar near each end.

The sizes of collars should conform with the sizes of ties given above (the " maximum span " being the length of collar). It is not economical to adopt the collar type of single roof for spans exceeding 4·9 m.

DOUBLE OR PURLIN ROOFS

These are shown in Figs. 37 and 38. Purlins are introduced in this class of roof to provide intermediate supports to the common rafters. Purlins are necessary for roofs with spans of 5·5 m and upwards, otherwise the spars would need to be increased to an uneconomical size. The maximum inclined span of 100 mm by 50 mm spars is 2·4 m and this should be reduced to 1·8 m when the roofs have a low pitch and are covered with heavy material. The introduction of sufficient purlins permits the use of comparatively small spars.

All the single roofs shown in Fig. 36 *may be altered to double roofs by the addition of one or more sets of purlins.*

Fig. 37 shows the plan F of a portion of a double roof of the collar type, together with a section at E. A hipped end has been introduced so as to illustrate the application of hip rafters. The spars are inclined at 55° (see p. 69) and

[1] Alternatively, the depth of the notch in the side of the spar is increased to 25 mm and the end of the collar is checked out by a similar amount so that when assembled both sides of the collar are flush with those of the spar.

two purlins are provided at each side to support the spars which have a clear span of 1·7 m. The spars are nailed to the wallplate, purlins and ridge, and to reduce any tendency for the rafters to slide downwards they are cogged (see p. 60) 25 mm over the purlins,[1] in addition to birdsmouthing their lower ends to the wall plates (see K). At the hipped end the spars are cut short (when they are called jack rafters) and the heads are spiked to the hip rafters.

Purlins are supported by cross division walls of bedrooms, etc. (which are carried up to the underside of the purlins), and at the ends by the hip rafters to which they are shaped and well spiked or bolted. The ends may be fixed to valley rafters in a similar manner. The purlins may be placed normal (right angles) to the spars as shown at E, or they may be fixed vertically as shown at N and O, Fig. 37, and in Fig. 38. A secure bearing on the walls is provided when the purlins are vertical, and in good work stone pads are introduced at the supports to effectively distribute the weight on to the wall (see broken lines at N). Joints in long lengths of purlins are best arranged to coincide with and lap at the wall supports (see N and O).

Jointing known as *scarfing* or *splicing* is resorted to when a purlin is required to be increased in length. The best form for purlins is the *splayed* or *raking scarfed joint* shown at R where the length of joint is from two to two and a half times the depth of the purlin. Right angled cuts are made at the ends of the splayed portion as shown. Three or four 12 mm diameter bolts, tightened by nuts, make the joint rigid. A mild steel or wrought iron strap should be fixed at the underside of the joint (see sketch). This joint is also used for lengthening a ridge where the length need only be one and a half times the depth; a metal strap is not required and long nails are used instead of bolts.

Fishing is an alternative form to scarfing. A fished joint is formed by butting the two squared ends of the timber together and connecting them by means of two metal (or wood) plates (one top and bottom) and bolting them as for a scarfed joint. The length of the plates equals four times the depth of the jointed member, and if wood plates are used their thickness should equal one-quarter the depth. This is a suitable joint for struts which are subjected to compressional stresses.

The collars are usually fixed to the spars immediately below the lower set of purlins, as shown in section AB. These collars are dovetail halved jointed to the spars as shown at Z, Fig. 36. As the span of the collars is approximately 4·25 m, their size is 175 mm by 50 mm (see Table V on p. 72). A plastered ceiling could be formed by nailing plasterboard to the underside of the collars and the lower portions of the spars (see broken lines).

Hip rafters usually support comparatively heavy loads from the purlins. They must be of sufficient strength to prevent sagging and must be fixed securely. The head of each rafter is nailed to the ridge, and in order that the load from the rafters shall be adequately distributed on to the walls, it is necessary to

[1] Cogging is omitted in cheap work.

The following table gives the sizes in mm of purlins for different spans for tiled roofs:—

Table VI, Purlins (mm)

Size of purlin (mm)	Spacing of purlins (m)		
	1·8	2·4	3·0
	Max. purlin span (m) for $22\frac{1}{2}°$–30° roof slopes (figs. in brackets for 30°–$42\frac{1}{2}°$ slopes)		
63 × 150	1·83 (1·92)	1·59 (1·66)	1·42 (1·49)
63 × 225	2·74 (2·87)	2·38 (2·49)	2·13 (2·23)
75 × 175	2·33 (2·42)	2·02 (2·11)	1·81 (1·89)
75 × 200	2·66 (2·77)	2·31 (2·41)	2·07 (2·16)
75 × 225	2·99 (3·11)	2·59 (2·71)	2·32 (2·43)

Purlins exceeding 5 m in length are not economical. In the absence of cross-walls or partitions, trusses are provided to limit the unsupported length of purlins to 5 m.

employ a special form of construction to receive the feet of the rafters and to make the angle of the roof secure. If the feet of the hip rafters were, like the spars, simply birdsmouthed and spiked to the wall plates, the concentrated inclined thrust may be sufficient to push out the quoins of the building. This construction is shown at E and F, Fig. 37, and in the details at G, H and J.[1]

An *angle tie* or *brace*, placed diagonally across the corner, is notched to the wall plates, and to counteract the thrust, these notches should be dovetailed as shown by the broken lines in the plan H. The wall plates are half-lapped for the same reason, and as shown their ends project some 75 mm. This angle tie carries one end of a beam, called a *dragon* (or *dragging*) *beam* which is the chief support for the hip rafter. This beam is tusk tenoned to the angle tie and single cogged over the wall plates. The foot of the hip rafter is connected to the dragon beam by means of an *oblique tenon joint* and bolt as shown. After the hip rafter has been fixed, the whole of the framing is made rigid by tightly driving down the wedge of the tusk tenon. For lowly pitched roofs, and where the eaves is not sprocketed, the foot of the hip rafter is sometimes projected beyond the outer face of the wall to the line of the projecting feet of the spars. In this case the rafter is notched over and is tenoned nearer to the outer end of the dragon beam.

The lower ends of jack rafters are fitted and spiked to the vertical faces of valley rafters (see P and Q, Fig. 75).

The eaves details are described below.

This type of roof in which purlins and collars are employed is often adopted especially for houses) on account of its sound and economical construction. It is particularly suited for spans which do not exceed 7 m.

Fig. 38 shows another type of double roof. It is similar to the close couple type (p. 72) with the addition of purlins. The 100 mm by 50 mm spars are pitched at 30° (depending upon the covering material and required design), birdsmouthed to the wall plates, notched over one pair of purlins and spiked to the ridge. The ceiling joists or ties are secured to the wall plates and the feet of the spars as already described, and as they are supported by two sets of

[1] Consideration of this construction may be deferred to the second year of the Course.

hangers and runners, the size of these joists need only be 100 mm by 50 mm or 125 mm by 50 mm, depending upon the weight of the roof covering. The hangers and runners have been described on p. 72. Sometimes the runners are notched over the ceiling joists to afford additional rigidity to the latter.

It is important that the lower ends of the hangers are not secured to the runners until *after* the slates or other covering material have been fixed, otherwise the weight of this material may cause the spars to sag slightly, which in turn would depress the ceiling joists through the hangers. It is the practice therefore for the carpenter to nail the runners to the ceiling joists and the upper ends of the hangers to the spars or purlins, and to defer nailing the lower ends of the hangers until the slater or tiler has completed his work.

Trimming is required at chimney stacks, dormers, skylights, etc.; and the construction is much about the same as that for floors (see p. 65). The names of the various spars concerned are similar to those applied to floor trimming, *i.e.*, *trimming spars* (or rafters), *trimmer spars* and *trimmed spars* (see A and C, Fig. 38). The joint between the trimmer and trimming spars may be either a tusk tenon (see L, Fig. 34) or a similar joint without the tusk, called a *pinned tenon joint* (see A and C, Fig. 38). That between the trimmed and trimmer spars should be either a dovetailed housed joint (see M, Fig. 34) or a bevelled haunched joint described on p. 65.[1] The trimming of a roof round a chimney stack which penetrates a roof midway between the eaves and ridge is detailed at E, Fig. 75.

Eaves Details.[2]—It is important that the eaves of a roof should be carefully designed. It is a common mistake to use an excessively deep fascia, and the clumsy effect which this produces is shown at M, Fig. 37. An excessive projection of the eaves in proportion to the size of the building is another error. As a general rule overhanging eaves should be of minimum depth. Over-elaboration should be avoided, the simpler the detail the better.

Flush, open projecting and closed projecting eaves are noted on p. 69.

Flush Eaves.—Two examples of this type are shown at Q and W, Fig. 36. The fascia is only sufficiently deep to cover the ends of the joists or spars, to which it is either nailed or screwed. In the latter detail the fascia projects slightly above the boarding in order to tilt the slates (see Chapter Five). The thickness of the fascia need not exceed 25 mm (nominal), and, if preferred, one or more fillets may be formed as shown.

Open Projecting Eaves (see X, Fig. 36).—The feet of the spars project 150 mm and are shaped as shown or as indicated at C and F, Fig. 71. It is not necessary to provide a fascia to an open eaves. A simple open projecting eaves is shown at C, Fig. 72.

Closed Projecting Eaves.—There are two forms of closed eaves, *i.e.*, those with sprockets and those without.

An example of the latter is shown at Y, Fig. 36. The ends of the rafters are sawn to the shape as shown, the soffit board is nailed to the spars, and the fascia is finally fixed with the edge of the soffit board engaging in the groove prepared to receive it. It will be observed that the brickwork is set back 102 mm so that if the soffit board shrinks in width no unsightly gap appears along its length between it and the wall. The fascia projects above the backs of the spars as shown in order to tilt the bottom course of slates. Another example is shown at A, Fig. 71 where a fillet is used to tilt the slates, so the depth of the fascia is reduced to 100 mm; the soffit boarding is fixed to 50 mm by 32 mm bearers nailed to the spars.

A sprocketed eaves may be formed by (*a*) fixing the sprockets on the backs of the spars or (*b*) nailing them to the sides of the rafters.

An example of the former is shown in Fig. 38. The construction is made clear in the enlarged detail at D and the isometric drawing A, the latter showing one end of a spar cut, the next spar is shown with the sprocket fixed, and the next with the sprocket and bearer fixed. The soffit boards are *tongued*, *grooved and V-jointed*, and at hipped ends, etc., the ends of the boards should be carefully mitred (see S, Fig. 37). The bedmould should be *scribed* to the wall (" scribe " means to mark for accurate fitting, and in this case scribing is necessary to ensure that the back of the mould shall fit the more or less irregular surface of the brickwork). A brick-on-end course, projecting 20 mm as shown, provides a simple and effective finish and also forms a flat arch for the window.

The sprockets shown at K and L, Fig. 37 give a graceful sweep to the lower portion of the roof. Here they are fixed to the sides of the spars and the wall plate. They are inclined at an angle which equals the difference between a right angle and the pitch of the roof (*e.g.*, $90° - 55° = 35°$). Sprockets should not be given an inadequate slope such as is shown at M, for, besides detracting from the appearance, it makes it difficult for the slater or tiler to negotiate the angle at the intersection between the sprockets and spars unless a triangular fillet (shown by broken lines) is fixed. A roof with a flat slope is also difficult to make watertight at the eaves. The construction of the eaves is similar to that already described, but attention is drawn to the alternative methods of supporting the soffit bearers. That at K shows one end of each bearer nailed to a fillet which is plugged to the wall, the other end being nailed to the side of the spar. The bearers at L are let into the wall at one end (*pockets* or holes being left by the bricklayer for this purpose) and these ends are tightly wedged. The sprockets are shown in the plan F. Those nailed at each side of the hip rafters are necessary to provide a means of fixing the upper ends of the two short sprockets at each corner and the bearers to which the fascia (mitred at the angle) and the mitred ends of the soffit boards are nailed. One of these bearers is shown at T but has been omitted at S in order to show the mitre between the soffit boards.

A detail of a similar eaves is shown at G, Fig. 71.

Beamfilling or Windfilling.—This is the brickwork which is continued up between and to the back of the spars after the latter have been fixed. This is shown in all the eaves details (sometimes by broken lines), and, for obvious reasons, it is especially necessary when the roofs have open eaves.

[1] In cheap work the trimmed spars are simply butt-jointed and nailed to the trimmers.
[2] Students should defer consideration of the slating details until Chapter Five is reached.

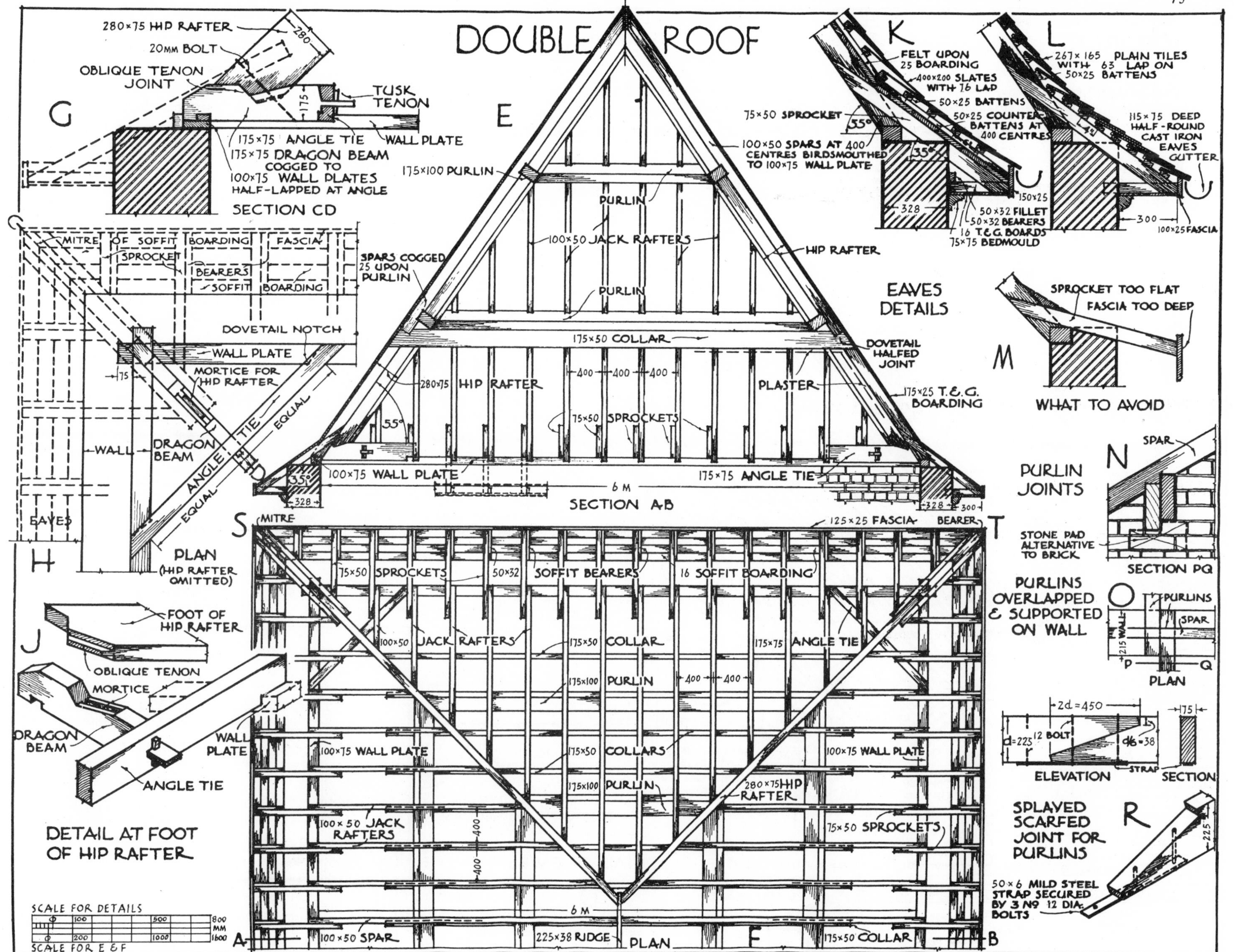
DOUBLE ROOF
280×75 HIP RAFTER
20MM BOLT
OBLIQUE TENON JOINT
TUSK TENON
G
175×75 ANGLE TIE
WALL PLATE
175×75 DRAGON BEAM COGGED TO
100×75 WALL PLATES HALF-LAPPED AT ANGLE
SECTION CD
E
175×100 PURLIN
PURLIN
100×50 JACK RAFTERS
PURLIN
175×50 COLLAR
280×75 HIP RAFTER
75×50 SPROCKETS
100×75 WALL PLATE
175×75 ANGLE TIE
6 M
SECTION AB
100×50 SPARS AT 400 CENTRES BIRDSMOUTHED TO 100×75 WALL PLATE
HIP RAFTER
DOVETAIL HALFED JOINT
PLASTER
175×25 T.&G. BOARDING
SPARS COGGED 25 UPON PURLIN
K
L
FELT UPON 25 BOARDING
400×200 SLATES WITH 76 LAP
50×25 BATTENS
75×50 SPROCKET
50×25 COUNTER BATTENS AT 400 CENTRES
267×165 PLAIN TILES WITH 63 LAP ON 50×25 BATTENS
115×75 DEEP HALF-ROUND CAST IRON EAVES GUTTER
150×25
50×32 FILLET
50×32 BEARERS
16 T.&G. BOARDS
75×75 BEDMOULD
100×25 FASCIA
EAVES DETAILS
SPROCKET TOO FLAT
FASCIA TOO DEEP
M
WHAT TO AVOID
MITRE OF SOFFIT BOARDING
FASCIA
SPROCKET
BEARERS
SOFFIT BOARDING
DOVETAIL NOTCH
WALL PLATE
MORTICE FOR HIP RAFTER
WALL
DRAGON BEAM
ANGLE TIE
EQUAL
EQUAL
EAVES
H
PLAN (HIP RAFTER OMITTED)
J
FOOT OF HIP RAFTER
OBLIQUE TENON
MORTICE
DRAGON BEAM
WALL PLATE
ANGLE TIE
DETAIL AT FOOT OF HIP RAFTER
S
MITRE
125×25 FASCIA
BEARER
T
75×50 SPROCKETS
50×32 SOFFIT BEARERS
16 SOFFIT BOARDING
100×50 JACK RAFTERS
175×50 COLLAR
175×75 ANGLE TIE
175×100 PURLIN
100×75 WALL PLATE
175×50 COLLARS
175×100 PURLIN
280×75 HIP RAFTER
100×50 JACK RAFTERS
75×50 SPROCKETS
6 M
100×50 SPAR
225×38 RIDGE
PLAN
F
175×50 COLLAR
A
B
PURLIN JOINTS
N
SPAR
STONE PAD ALTERNATIVE TO BRICK
SECTION PQ
PURLINS OVERLAPPED & SUPPORTED ON WALL
O
PURLINS
SPAR
215 WALL
PLAN
2d = 450
d = 225
12 BOLT
d/6 = 38
ELEVATION
STRAP
SECTION
SPLAYED SCARFED JOINT FOR PURLINS
R
50×6 MILD STEEL STRAP SECURED BY 3 No 12 DIA. BOLTS
SCALE FOR DETAILS
SCALE FOR E & F

FIGURE 37

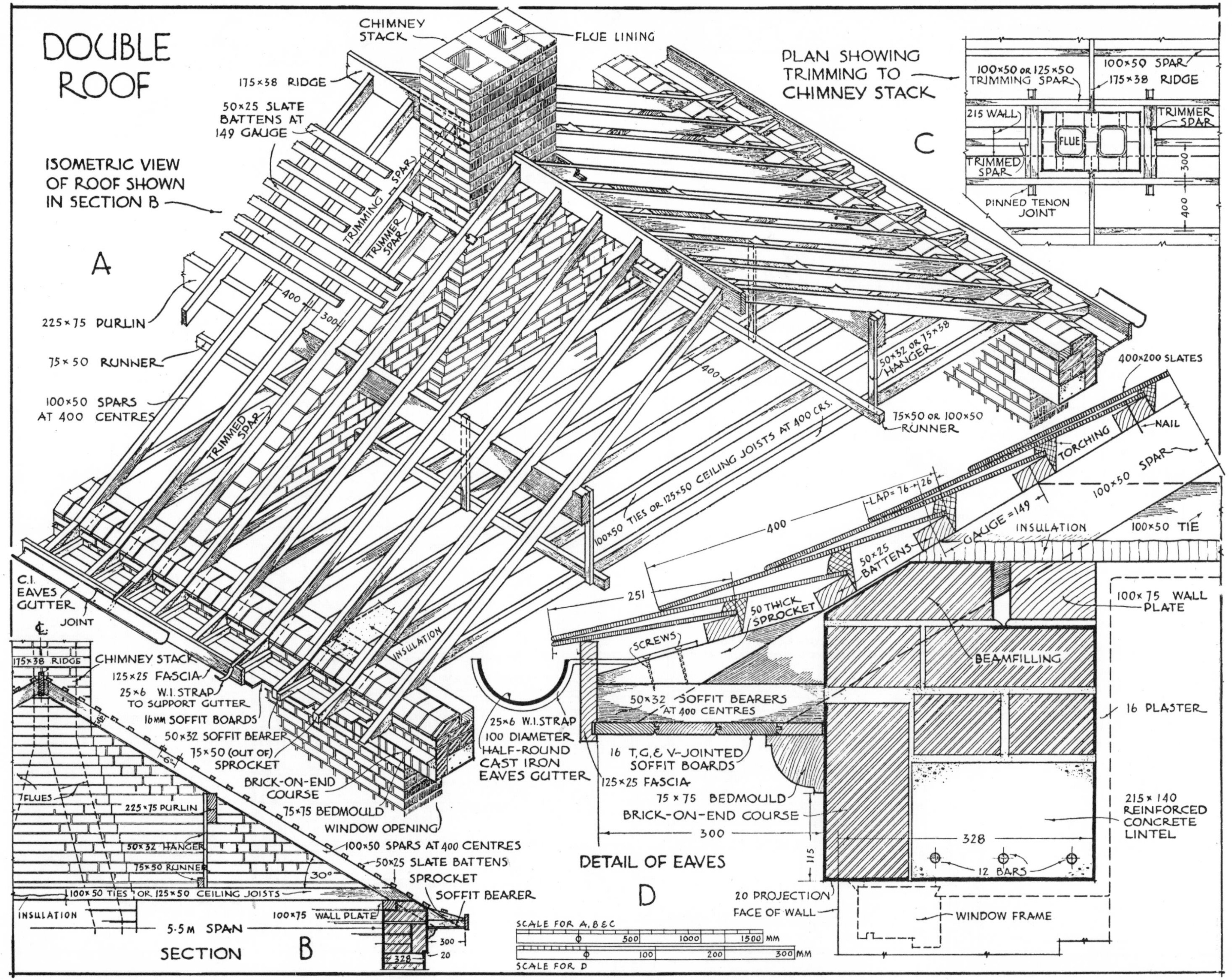
DOUBLE ROOF
CHIMNEY STACK
FLUE LINING
175×38 RIDGE
50×25 SLATE BATTENS AT 149 GAUGE
ISOMETRIC VIEW OF ROOF SHOWN IN SECTION B
TRIMMING SPAR
TRIMMER SPAR
A
225×75 PURLIN
75×50 RUNNER
100×50 SPARS AT 400 CENTRES
TRIMMED SPAR
C.I. EAVES GUTTER
JOINT
INSULATION
100×50 TIES OR 125×50 CEILING JOISTS AT 400 CRS.
50×32 OR 75×38 HANGER
75×50 OR 100×50 RUNNER
PLAN SHOWING TRIMMING TO CHIMNEY STACK
C
100×50 OR 125×50 TRIMMING SPAR
100×50 SPAR
175×38 RIDGE
215 WALL
TRIMMER SPAR
FLUE
TRIMMED SPAR
PINNED TENON JOINT
400×200 SLATES
NAIL
TORCHING
100×50 SPAR
LAP=76
GAUGE=149
INSULATION
100×50 TIE
50×25 BATTENS
50 THICK SPROCKET
100×75 WALL PLATE
SCREWS
BEAMFILLING
50×32 SOFFIT BEARERS AT 400 CENTRES
16 PLASTER
25×6 W.I. STRAP
100 DIAMETER HALF-ROUND CAST IRON EAVES GUTTER
16 T,G,& V-JOINTED SOFFIT BOARDS
125×25 FASCIA
75×75 BEDMOULD
BRICK-ON-END COURSE
215×140 REINFORCED CONCRETE LINTEL
12 BARS
DETAIL OF EAVES
D
20 PROJECTION
FACE OF WALL
WINDOW FRAME
175×38 RIDGE
CHIMNEY STACK
125×25 FASCIA
25×6 W.I. STRAP TO SUPPORT GUTTER
16MM SOFFIT BOARDS
50×32 SOFFIT BEARER
75×50 (OUT OF) SPROCKET
BRICK-ON-END COURSE
75×75 BEDMOULD
WINDOW OPENING
FLUES
225×75 PURLIN
50×32 HANGER
75×50 RUNNER
100×50 SPARS AT 400 CENTRES
50×25 SLATE BATTENS
SPROCKET
SOFFIT BEARER
30°
100×50 TIES OR 125×50 CEILING JOISTS
INSULATION
100×75 WALL PLATE
5·5 M SPAN
SECTION
B
SCALE FOR A, B & C
SCALE FOR D

FIGURE 38

It is not necessary to have beamfilling on top of the wall plates, and this practice which is sometimes carried out cannot be too strongly condemned. Cases of dry rot in roofs have been attributed to beamfilling which has been continued for the full thickness of the walls to the backs of the spars and sprockets. Any defective slates or other roof covering at this point allow water to enter, and owing to the wood members being confined by brickwork (or masonry) they become saturated and remain so, resulting in defective timber. Adequate ventilation is just as essential for roof timbers as it is for floor members (see p. 60) if dry rot is to be prevented.

TRUSSED RAFTER ROOFS

This type of roof (Fig. 38A) consists of planed stress graded timbers fastened together in the form of trusses and placed at relatively close distances apart. It comprises rafters (spars) joined to ceiling joists and intermediate members. The trusses are prefabricated and because roofs of this type are more quickly erected and use much less timber than purlin roofs they have almost entirely replaced them for housing work.

The trusses are placed at centres not exceeding 600 mm [500 mm by 25 mm (min). tiling battens must be used] and the separate members of the truss, which must be of the same thickness, are joined by plywood gussets glued and nailed to *each* face at the joints. The adhesive used for this purpose is commonly resorcinol/formaldehyde (see Chap. 2; Vol. III); 40 mm 12 gauge galvanized nails at 100 mm centres in two rows per member are used (see C). Alternatives to plywood gussets are 18 or 20 gauge galvanized metal plates which may be either perforated for fastening with clout nails or may have integral teeth in which case a special press is needed to make the joint.

The trusses must be joined together by 75 mm by 25 mm braces nailed to the underside of the top truss member. An elevation of the side of the roof would show the braces placed diagonally in a W formation; the top of each outer leg of the W nailed under the top of the outermost trusses. Each leg of the W to pass not more than 6 trusses.

The two most popular truss shapes are the W or Fink type (see A and D) or the Fan type (B) for larger spans. Notching or birds-mouthing of the truss should not be allowed. The moisture content of the timber should be 22 per cent. or less so care should be taken to fix roof coverings quickly; trusses should be stacked flat on a level base before erection.

The following Table gives the sizes of the timbers in mm and spans in m for the two types of truss spaced at 400 mm centres.

Basic* size of truss members (mm) (*Actual size 3 mm less to allow for planing)		Pitch (degrees) 15	20	25	30	35
38 × 100	Spans (m)	7	7·7	8·1	8·3	8·6
38 × 125		8·7	9·2	9·5	9·8	10·1
44 × 75		5·5	6	6·5	6·9	7·3
44 × 100		7·5	8·2	8·7	8·9	9·2
50 × 75		5·9	6·5	6·9	7·4	7·8
50 × 100		7·9	8·7	9·2	9·5	9·8

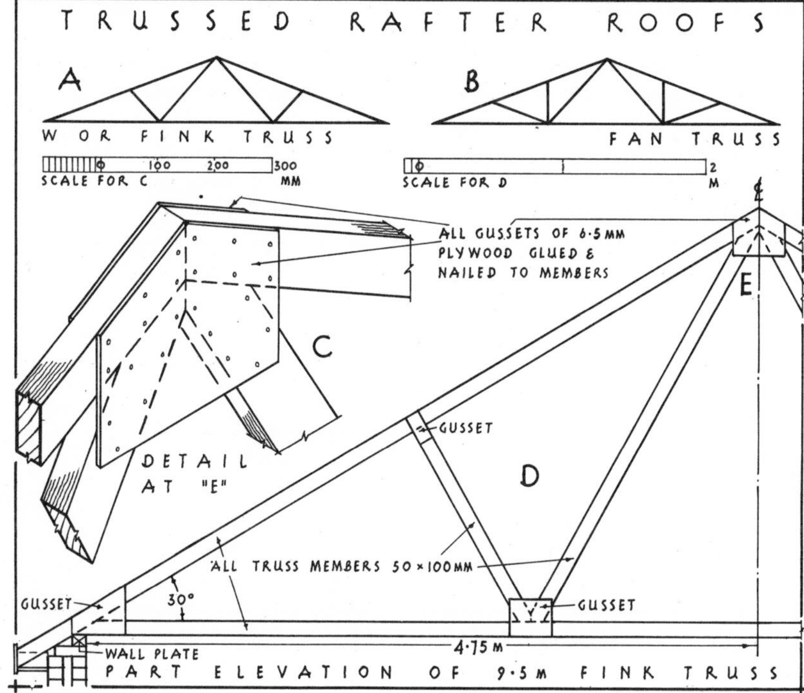

Fig. 38A

TRIPLE OR FRAMED ROOFS

The maximum unsupported length of purlins is 5 m (see p. 73) if extravagant sizes are to be avoided; if there are no cross division walls available to provide supports to limit the purlins to this span then either roof trusses (also called *principals*) are needed, or the trussed rafter arrangement used. Hence a framed roof has three sets of members, *i.e.*, spars which distribute the weight of the roof covering, snow, and wind pressure to the purlins which transmit this load to the trusses, and these transfer it to the walls. The outline of the truss must follow the roof shape, which is usually triangular. A triangle is the strongest form of framed structure for it cannot be deformed if its members are adequate and properly connected.

The student in the class in Building Science will have probably carried out the following simple experiment in connection with the solution of framed structures when loaded: A vertical load is applied at the apex of two inclined members which are hinged at the top (representing a couple of spars). They will at once spread if the feet are not restrained and the unsatisfactory couple roof (see E, Fig. 36) would act in this manner if the walls were not sufficiently strong. A horizontal member is now connected to the feet to produce a structure resembling a close couple roof (see L, Fig. 36. In a roof truss additional members are introduced to brace the structure throughly.

Built-up Roof Truss (see Fig. 39).—This is the most widely used timber truss. The example shown is for a span of 6·7m and a pitch of 30°, it is spaced at 1·8 m centres and is designed for the lightest type of traditional roof covering (*i.e.*, interlocking tiles—see description on pp. 140–141). Between the trusses spars and ceiling joists are used at 450 mm centres.

The joints are made by 12 mm dia. bolts and timber connectors. The latter are of several types, one being shown at J is a 60 mm dia. holed galvanized steel plate with twelve triangular teeth bent off at right angles to each side. The connector is placed at each interface of the timbers comprising the joint and when the central bolt is tightened the teeth become embedded in the wood to make a secure fastening.

The principal rafter or top chord consists of two 75 mm by 50 mm timbers 50 mm apart, this is supported midway by a strut of two 100 mm by 50 mm timbers 150 mm apart which are joined on each side of the top chord. Two connectors are used at the joint, one at each outer face of the chord between this and the flanking timbers of the strut. The truss takes the load from the 150 mm

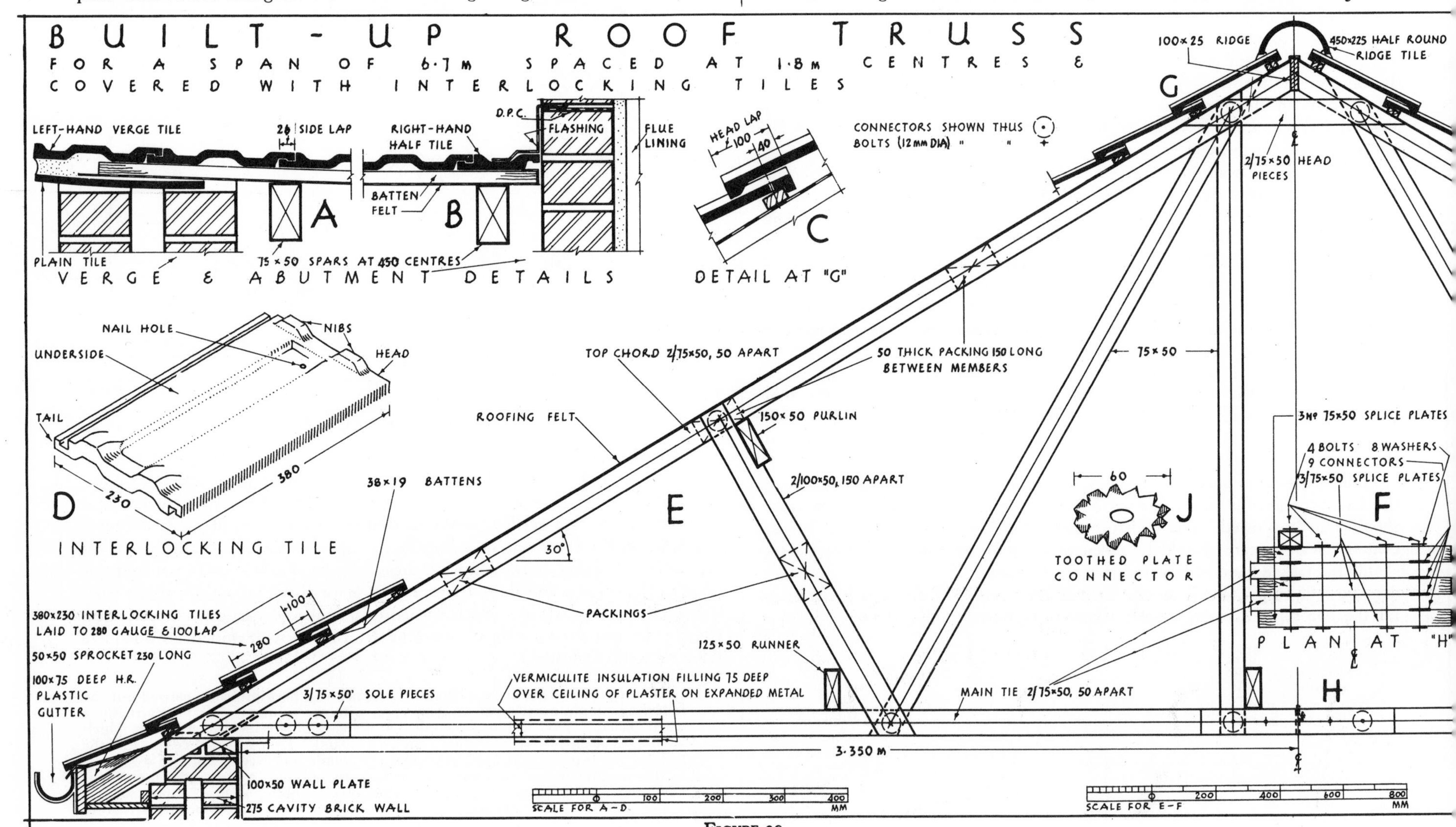

FIGURE 39

by 50 mm purlin which is notched into the strut, the purlin gives support to the intermediate 75 mm by 50 mm spars which are at 450 mm centres for this comparatively light-weight roof.

The main tie of two 75 mm by 50 mm timbers 50 mm apart is joined to the foot of the top chord by a sole piece placed centrally and one on each side. Three bolts are required each with four connectors placed at the interfaces of the members. The half of the truss is completed with two other 75 mm by 50 mm members.

The apex detail shows the use of two more bolts, the left-hand one having five, and the right four connectors. The two halves of the truss are secured by the outer 75 mm by 50 mm head pieces.

The splice detail at the centre of the main tie is shown at H and F, four bolts are used, the two central ones being without connectors; the outer left-hand bolt has five connectors and the one on the right has four. A central and two outer splice plates are required to tie the truss halves together.

Central 50 mm thick packing plates are spiked to the main members in the various positions shown.

Gutters.—Sometimes walls terminate as parapets and gutters are therefore required as shown in Fig. 73. There are two forms, *i.e.*, (*a*) *parallel* or *box gutters* and (*b*) *tapered gutters.*

(a) *Parallel Gutter.*—An application of this type is shown at A, B and C, Fig. 73. The feet of the spars are birdsmouthed to a horizontal beam, called a *pole plate*, which is notched out and spiked to the principal rafter. The gutter consists of 25 mm boarding laid to falls and supported by 75 mm by 50 mm *gutter bearers* at 400 mm centres which at one end are tongued and nailed to the pole plate and at the other end they are notched over and nailed to a *gutter plate* which is spiked to the tie beam. The section at B and plan at C, Fig. 73, should be carefully studied. Note how the bearers are fixed at varying levels to give the requisite fall to the boarding. The cross section through the gutter at A, Fig. 73, indicates the levels of the necessary roll, drip, etc. The timber details should be further considered with the subject of Plumbing (Chapter Six).

(b) *Tapered Gutter* (see J, K and N, Fig. 73).—This is so called because of its shape on plan. The boarding is supported by 50 mm by 38 mm bearers which are nailed at varying levels to the sides of the spars and 50 mm by 38 mm uprights which are half-lapped to the bearers. This construction will be better understood when the lead details in Chapter Six are studied.

TEMPORARY TIMBERING

Certain forms of timber construction are required only as temporary supports of work carried out during preliminary building operations or in the erection of permanent structures, after which they are removed. Timbering to support the sides of trenches which are to receive wall foundations, drains, etc., and that known as centering which is required to support arches during their construction are examples of this type of construction.

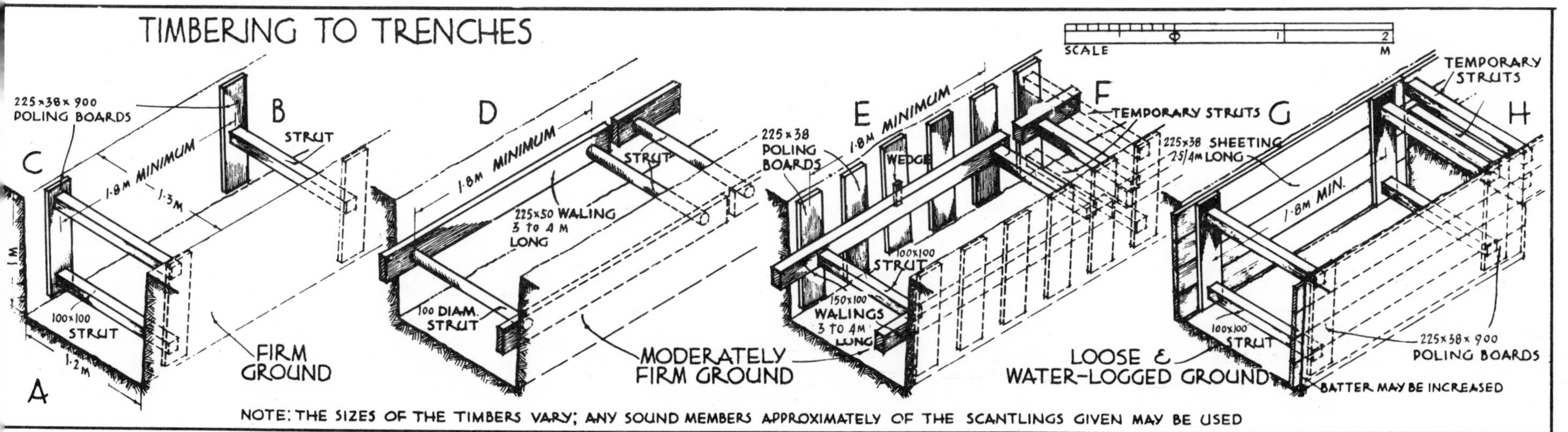

FIGURE 40

TIMBERING TO SHALLOW TRENCHES

The timbering of these excavations is done by the labourers as the work proceeds. The sizes and arrangement of the various timbers are influenced by the nature of the soil and the depth of the cutting. There are many different kinds of soil, but for convenience they may be divided into: (1) *Hard* (including rock and exceptionally hard chalk), (2) *Firm* (including hard chalk and dense gravel), (3) *Moderately Firm* (including soft chalk, loose gravel and compact clay), (4) *Loose* (including dry sand, soft clay, ordinary loamy soil and make-up ground), and (5) *Loose and Waterlogged* loamy soil and sand.[1]

Terms.—The following members are used in Fig. 40:—

Poling Boards.—Members placed vertically next to the sides of the excavation or sheeting (see below); sizes vary from 175 mm by 32 mm to 225 mm by 38 mm and are from 0·6 to 1·2 m long.

Walings, Wales, Waling Pieces or Planks.—Members placed horizontally next to the earth or poling boards; sizes vary from 100 mm by 75 mm to 225 mm by 75 mm, and from 2·4 to 4·3 m long.

Sheeting.—Members placed horizontally; of similar scantlings to poling boards and from 2·4 to 4·3 m long.

Struts.—Short lengths of 75 to 100 mm square timber driven down between poling boards or walings at a minimum distance of 1·8 m centres.

The following *typical* description may be applied to a shallow trench, excavated in various soils, to receive a foundation which is 1·2 m wide and 1 m deep. Timbering to deeper foundations is shown in Fig. 19, Vol. III.

1. *Hard Ground.*—No timbering would be required (unless there were pockets of loose soil) for the sides of the trench would be self-supporting.

2. *Firm Ground* (see A, Fig. 40).—Whilst there would be little likelihood of the sides of a shallow trench caving in if left unsupported for a short time (hard chalk will retain a vertical face, 3 m high, until weather conditions begin to disintegrate it), it is sometimes necessary to provide a light support in the form of a pair of poling boards strutted apart at a *minimum* distance of 1·8 m centres. This distance is necessary to allow sufficient working space for the men engaged in constructing the foundation. Usually it is sufficient to use one central strut to each pair of boards (as shown at B) but occasionally it is advisable to use two struts (see C).

The struts are slightly longer than the horizontal distance between the boards and they are driven down until they are tight and more or less horizontal. The sides of the trench are given a slight batter from the top inwards to facilitate this operation and to reduce the tendency for the members to become loose as the earth shrinks, as it does on the removal of moisture. Care should be taken not to over drive the struts and disturb the earth behind the boards.

[1] This division is purely arbitrary; some authorities have subdivided both sand and clay into a score or more different kinds for the purpose of assessing their bearing capacity.

3. *Moderately Firm Ground.*—Where the soil is firm, except where it is inclined to be loose in patches, the timbering may consist of the simple arrangement shown at D—otherwise the trench may require a temporary support as illustrated at E.

The wide walings at D provide a continuous support, three struts being used per 4 m length of waling.

The arrangement at E shows poling boards held in position by walings which are strutted. The poling boards are placed at a distance apart varying with circumstances; in the figure they are shown at 450 mm centres, but this distance may be reduced to 300 mm or increased to 1 m. The timbering is done in easy stages for it is not advisable in this kind of soil to defer it until a length of trench is excavated equal to that of the walings, as a section of the unsupported excavation may collapse.

The following is the procedure adopted: A short length is excavated sufficient to enable the labourer to insert and temporarily strut a pair of poling boards (thus resembling A). This is repeated until sufficient poling boards have been placed which could be spanned by the walings. A stiff waling is then placed along each side and strutted against the boards as shown, after which the temporary struts can be removed. Temporary strutting is shown by broken lines at F.

It is not necessary to drive wedges down between the waling and boards which have become loose or have been strutted a greater distance apart then usual. An example of this is shown at E.

4. *Loose Earth.*—The arrangement of the timbers is similar to that shown at G (excepting that sometimes the sheets are placed about 25 mm apart) and is described below.

5. *Loose and Waterlogged Ground* (see G).—Horizontal sheeting is necessary, for unlike the soils referred to in the first three classes, it is not possible to excavate in loose soil for several metres in depth before resorting to timbering. The sides of the trenches dug in this soil begin to fall before 300 mm depth has been reached, and hence the need for horizontal boards or sheets. The following is the sequence of operations: The excavation is made to a depth slightly in excess of the width of the sheeting to be used, when a board is placed against each side and two or more temporary struts are driven between. The excavation is continued for 225 mm depth or so and a second pair of boards is placed tight up against the bottom edge of the first set and strutted. The condition at the end of a section at this stage is shown at H. This operation is repeated until four sets of boards have been temporarily strutted or the required depth has been reached, when poling boards are placed at a minimum distance apart of 1·8 m centres and strutted as shown at G, and the temporary struts removed.

When the foundations have been completed and the walls built to a height of two or three courses above the ground level, the timbering is removed and earth is returned on both sides of the wall and rammed solid.

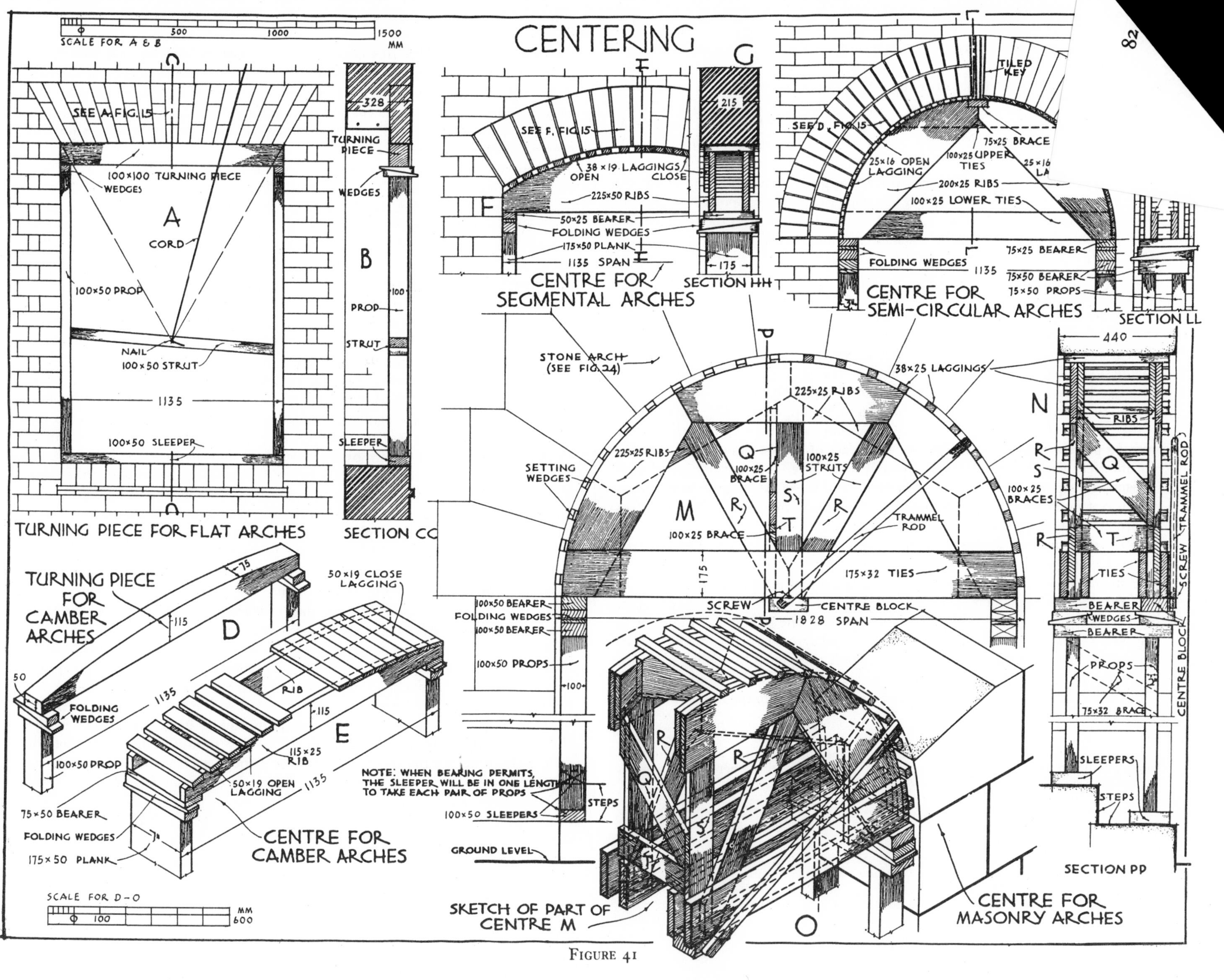
CENTERING
SCALE FOR A & B
500
1000
1500 MM
SEE A, FIG.15
100×100 TURNING PIECE
WEDGES
A
CORD
100×50 PROP
NAIL
100×50 STRUT
1135
100×50 SLEEPER
TURNING PIECE FOR FLAT ARCHES
328
TURNING PIECE
WEDGES
B
PROP
100
STRUT
SLEEPER
SECTION CC
SEE F, FIG.15
38×19 LAGGINGS
OPEN
CLOSE
225×50 RIBS
50×25 BEARER
FOLDING WEDGES
175×50 PLANK
1135 SPAN
F
G
215
175
SECTION HH
CENTRE FOR SEGMENTAL ARCHES
SEE D, FIG.15
TILED KEY
75×25 BRACE
25×16 OPEN LAGGING
100×25 UPPER TIES
200×25 RIBS
100×25 LOWER TIES
FOLDING WEDGES
1135
75×25 BEARER
75×50 BEARER
75×50 PROPS
CENTRE FOR SEMI-CIRCULAR ARCHES
SECTION LL
TURNING PIECE FOR CAMBER ARCHES
75
115
D
50
FOLDING WEDGES
1135
100×50 PROP
75×50 BEARER
FOLDING WEDGES
175×50 PLANK
50×19 CLOSE LAGGING
RIB
115
E
115×25 RIB
50×19 OPEN LAGGING
1135
CENTRE FOR CAMBER ARCHES
SCALE FOR D–O
100
600 MM
STONE ARCH (SEE FIG.24)
38×25 LAGGINGS
225×25 RIBS
225×25 RIBS
Q
100×25 BRACE
100×25 STRUTS
SETTING WEDGES
M
R
S
R
T
100×25 BRACE
TRAMMEL ROD
175
175×32 TIES
SCREW
CENTRE BLOCK
1828 SPAN
P
100×50 BEARER
FOLDING WEDGES
100×50 BEARER
100×50 PROPS
100
NOTE: WHEN BEARING PERMITS, THE SLEEPER WILL BE IN ONE LENGTH TO TAKE EACH PAIR OF PROPS
STEPS
100×50 SLEEPERS
GROUND LEVEL
SKETCH OF PART OF CENTRE M
O
CENTRE FOR MASONRY ARCHES
440
N
RIBS
R
Q
S
100×25 BRACES
R
T
TIES
BEARER
WEDGES
BEARER
PROPS
75×32 BRACE
TRAMMEL ROD
SCREW
CENTRE BLOCK
SLEEPERS
STEPS
SECTION PP

FIGURE 41

CENTERING

A *centre* is a wood member or frame used as a temporary support for an arch during its construction. The removal of this support, known as "striking," does not take place before the mortar between the voussoirs of the arch has set. A centre must of course be sufficiently rigid to support the weight of the brickwork or masonry to be constructed on it, and, in addition, provision must be made to permit of "*easing* the centre," a term which is applied to the operation of *slightly* lowering the centre before the mortar has set. A centre is supported on vertical *posts* or *props*, and the introduction of folding wedges between the heads of the posts and the centre permits of its easement and also the adjustment of the centre to the required height to receive the arch. The term *centering* includes the centre, together with the wedges, props, etc.

The shape and details of a centre depend on the type, span and width of the arch to be supported. The following illustrated examples should therefore be considered as typical:—

Turning Pieces.—The simplest form of centre is for flat arches and those having a small rise and width; it is called a turning piece, and, as shown at A, B and D, Fig. 41, it consists of a solid piece of timber having its upper surface shaped to conform with the soffit of the arch to be supported. The flat arch at A is that shown at A, Fig. 15, which has a 102 mm soffit and a 12 mm rise. The turning piece is slightly back from the front face of the wall in order that it will not interfere with the bricklayers' line and plum-rule. The turning piece rests at each end upon a pair of folding wedges,[1] and these are supported by props which rest upon a *sleeper* or *sill* placed on the brick window sill which it serves to protect. These props are strutted apart as shown.

Reference is made on p. 24 to the method which is adopted to ensure that the arch joints radiate to a common point.

A turning piece for an arch with a 65 mm camber is shown at D, Fig. 41.

Centres.—Arches which have wider soffits than 115 mm are " turned " upon centres which are constructed of *ribs* and *laggings*; one of these is shown at E, Fig. 41. The laggings or narrow battens are nailed across two 115 mm by 25 mm ribs which have a 65 mm camber. The centre is completed by nailing a 75 mm by 25 mm cross-member, called a *bearer* or *bearing piece*, to the underside of the ribs at each end. The sizes of the members vary according to the timber available, thus the thickness of the ribs is sometimes 32 mm and the laggings vary from 75 mm by 16 mm to 50 mm by 25 mm. Both open and close lagging are shown at E. The former is suitable for axed arches, and close lagging is adopted for gauged arches. The distance apart of the laggings when open varies from 20 mm to 25 mm, except when the centres are required for masonry arches, when the spacing is increased (see M, Fig. 41).

A suitable centre for a segmental arch is shown at F and G, Fig. 41. This arch is similar to that at F, Fig. 15. Both close and open laggings are shown.

A suitably designed centre for a semicircular arch (such as that at D and E, Fig. 15) is shown at J and K, Fig. 41. As it is not economical to use timber which exceeds 300 mm in width, it is necessary to construct the ribs as shown with upper and lower *ties* nailed to them. Narrow laggings should be used in order that they will conform to the curve of the arch. The 75 mm by 25 mm *brace* to which the upper ends of the ribs are notched serves as a support for the tiled key (which projects below the soffit) and also assists in stiffening the centre. Each support consists of two posts or props to which is nailed or dogged a 75 mm by 50 mm bearer at the top and a similar sleeper plate at the bottom.

A centre suitable for a semicircular arch having a span of 1·8 m, is shown at M, N and O, Fig. 41. Each of the two ribs is made of two thicknesses of 225 mm by 25 mm pieces, spiked together, which overlap and have joints normal to the curve. Such are called *built-up* ribs. Each rib has double 175 mm by 25 mm or 32 mm ties and three 100 mm by 25 mm struts, indicated by S and R, the latter being necessary to prevent the centre being deformed by the weight of the arch. The cross bracing provided by the 100 mm by 25 mm inclined brace Q and the horizontal brace T increases the rigidity. The laggings, which must be at least 25 mm thick, may be either open or close, depending upon the type of arch.

For masonry arches the laggings may be spaced to allow two per voussoir, as shown at the right half of the elevation M, or alternatively small *setting wedges* as shown on the left of the elevation may be preferred. The arch in the example is that of the main entrance shown in Fig. 24, and for each of the large voussoirs four sets of wedges would be used, two on each built-up rib. The wedges over the props are inserted between two stout bearers, and to facilitate the easing of the centre these wedges are sometimes greased. The props may be braced by an inclined member as shown by broken lines in the section PP. A trammel rod (referred to on p. 24) is cut to the net length of the radius of the arch. A block is nailed to the underside and at the centre of the ties, and the lower end of the rod is screwed sufficiently tightly at the centre of the semicircle to permit the rod to traverse the soffit of each voussoir as it is being wedged and bedded. This assures an accurately curved soffit.

[1] Students often make the mistake in examinations of showing the wedges with their length parallel to the length of the turning piece. It is obvious that when in this position the wedges cannot be adjusted because of the brick jambs.

CHAPTER FOUR

DOORS, WINDOWS, STAIRS

Syllabus.—Doors, including ledged and battened, ledged braced and battened, framed ledged and battened, framed ledged braced and battened, panelled; frames, and casings; methods of fixing frames, casings and doors; hardware. Windows, including solid frames with vertically hung sashes opening outwards, fixed sashes, boxed frame with sliding sashes, pivoted sashes, horizontal sliding sashes; hardware; metal windows. Architraves, skirting, picture rails and angle beads. Stairs. Nails, screws and fasteners. Description and uses of woodworking tools.

Joinery includes the setting out, preparation, framing and fixing of woodwork which is chiefly used as internal fittings and finishings. There are several broad differences between the crafts of the carpenter and joiner, although they are usually grouped together under " Carpentry and Joinery." These distinctions are: Carpentry is essentially structural, the timbers are left rough from the saw, the labour expended is small compared with the amount of material used, and most of the work is done on the building site. Primarily, joinery increases the habitability and appearance of a building and any stresses to which it is subjected are incidental, the wood is dressed, the labour is a large item compared with the volume of the timber employed, and most of this labour is carried out in the workshop. Joinery comprises the construction and fixing of doors and windows with their frames or linings, architraves, skirtings, stairs, panelling, etc. and floor boards. Boards have been included in Chapter Three, panelling is described in Vol. IV and the remainder below.

DOORS

External doors are secured or " hung " by metal *hinges* to solid wood *frames*, and internal doors are usually hung to wood *linings* or *casings*. A door plus frame or lining and hinges is defined as a " doorset " in BS 4787: Pt. 1.

Frames.—A door frame consists of three members, *i.e.*, two uprights or *posts* which are secured at the top to a cross-piece called a *head*. The nominal sizes of these members vary but 100 mm by 75 mm and 75 mm by 50 mm are common. The head usually projects from 50 to 100 mm beyond the posts, and these projections, called *horns*, assist in making the frame secure when it is built into the wall. These horns may be splayed (see S and the thick broken lines in the isometric detail at E, Fig. 42) and covered with splayed bricks to preserve the face appearance of the brickwork. A 13 mm to 16 mm deep recess or rebate is formed round the frame to receive the door. An alternative but less satisfactory check for the door is formed by *planting* (nailing) a 13 mm thick bead or *stop* on both posts and head, the beads being mitred at the angles (see K, Fig. 42).

Joints.—The head and posts of a frame are morticed and tenoned together, variations of the joints being: (*a*) closed mortice and tenon, (*b*) haunched mortice and tenon, (*c*) draw pinned slot mortice and tenon, and (*d*) double tenon.

(a) *Closed Mortice and Tenon Joint* (see E).—The head is morticed to receive the tenon on the post. The mortice and tenon must be correctly proportioned if failure of the joint is to be avoided, and the following are accepted rules :—

1. Thickness of tenon should equal one-third that of member.
2. Width of tenon should not exceed five times this thickness or a maximum of 125 mm, whichever is the *less*. (Thus the maximum width of a 13 mm thick tenon would be 5 by 13 mm equals 65 mm, and the maximum width of a 32 mm thick tenon would be 125 mm and *not* 5 by 32 mm equals 160 mm.)

The " thickness " and " width " of a tenon are indicated at E, and the " width " and " length " of a mortice are shown at F.

Wide tenons should be avoided as they (1) may shrink excessively, causing them to leave the wedges (see below), which thus become loose, (2) tend to bend when the joint is wedged, resulting in the splitting of the morticed members, and (3) require long mortices which tend to weaken the members.

These joints are *glued and wedged*, glue[1] being applied to the tenon and shoulders (see below) and the tenon is inserted into the mortice. Wedges, as shown, are dipped into the glue and driven in between the edges of the tenon and the mortice to secure the joint. Notice that the mortice is slightly enlarged and bevelled to receive the wedges. Oak pins or dowels, 10 mm to 20 mm diameter, are sometimes used in addition to wedges. This is called a *pinned joint*, and examples of it are shown in Fig. 44. A hole is first bored through the head and tenon, and the pin is driven in after it has been dipped in glue.

(b) *Haunched Mortice and Tenon Joint* (see F, Fig. 42).—This joint is adopted when the frame is not built in as the work proceeds. Horns are not required,

[1] There are several types of adhesive (see Chap. II, Vol. III). They may be (*a*) weatherproof, (*b*) moisture resistant or (*c*) suitable for internal use only. Some are described as close contact (CC) glues used mainly in plywood construction where heavy pressure and a thin glue line are used. Others are gap filling (GF) glues used in general joinery.

and therefore the width of the tenon is reduced, except for about 13 mm from the *shoulders* (or abutments at the bottom or *root* of the tenon), otherwise wedging would not be possible. This abbreviated portion or stump is called the *haunch* or *haunchion*, and its object is to increase the strength of the tenon at its root and prevent twisting of the post. The stub mortice made to receive the haunch is called the *haunching*. Note, the horns are not removed until the wedging has been completed, otherwise the driving in of the wedges would split the narrow portion of the head above the haunch.

(c) *Draw Pinned Slot Mortice and Tenon Joint* (see K, Fig. 42).—This joint is sometimes used for large frames. The mortice is continued to the end of the head. A hole is bored through the *cheeks* (sides) of the mortice, the tenon of the post is inserted, a point J on a 45° line from the centre of the hole is pricked on the tenon, the post is removed, with J as centre a hole is bored through the tenon, the latter is again placed in correct position between the cheeks, and finally the dowel is glued and driven into the holes to draw the shoulders of the joint together and the side of the tenon against the inner end of the mortice.

This is a good joint for external work for the following reason: Glue may soften if water gains access to it,[1] and in order to make the joints of external framing watertight and durable paint composed of a mixture of red lead, white lead and boiled linseed oil is sometimes used as a jointing material instead of glue. As wedges set in paint are apt to become loose and fall out, they are sometimes dispensed with and the draw pinned joint adopted.

(d) *Double Tenon Joint* (see K, Fig. 44).—This joint, which consists of double tenons, is usefully employed between members of large size, it being more effective than a single tenon in bringing the shoulders of the tenon tight up against the adjacent member. The combined thickness of a pair of single tenons should equal that of a single tenon.

A temporary piece of wood is nailed across the lower ends of the posts to prevent distortion of the frame before it has been finally fixed in position.

Methods of Fixing Frames.—A door frame may be fixed in position either (*a*) during the construction of the walling, or (*b*) after the walling has been completed.

(*a*) Such frames are said to be *built-in*. When the brickwork (or masonry) has been built to ground-floor level, the door is placed in position according to the plan, plumbed, and maintained temporarily in this position by an inclined strut (nailed to a joist and to the head). The brickwork is now proceeded with, the jambs being constructed close to the posts of the frame. Creosoted wood slips or *pallets* (see H and Q, Fig. 42) are built in *dry* at the bed joints of each jamb at about 300 mm intervals with one near the foot and one near the head. The weight of the brickwork makes these pallets secure. Nails are driven through the posts into the pallets after the heads (which may have splayed horns) have been bonded in and there is no likelihood of disturbing the newly built walling. Wrought iron straps (see P) are occasionally used instead of pallets; these straps are screwed to the posts in positions which will coincide with the bed joints of the brickwork, when they are well bedded in mortar.

[1] This does not apply to "weatherproof glue"—see Chap. II, Vol. III

This is a common method of fixing frames. It is not adopted in first class work as the frame is liable to be damaged during building operations and lime, etc. is apt to stain it. The arrises of the frame may be protected by lightly nailing wood strips to it. Frames are bedded in mortar as the jambs are being constructed and afterwards pointed in *mastic* (a mixture of red lead and linseed oil) to exclude rain and draughts.

External woodwork should be *primed* before being fixed. Priming is the first coat of paint to be applied. (Painting is described in Chap. IV, Vol. III.)

(*b*) The second method of fixing frames, and one which is adopted in better-class work, consists of plugging (see p. 70) the bed joints of the brick or stone jambs after the whole of the brickwork has thoroughly set. The 75 or 100 mm deep holes to receive the plugs are formed with the *plugging chisel* (see 38, Fig. 67) and hammer at 300 mm intervals (see above), the hardwood plugs (see F, Fig. 49) are driven in with their projecting edges cut off to a vertical plane (a plumb-line being used for this purpose) so that the clear distance between the plugs in opposite jambs equals the overall width of the frame. The frame is then placed in position and securely nailed to the plugs and to the lintel. The fixing of the frames is deferred until the building is nearing completion in order to minimise the risk of damage to the woodwork. They are well bedded in mortar and pointed in mastic as before described.

Additional rigidity is given to the frame if a 20 or 25 mm square or 13 mm diameter round galvanised wrought iron dowel, 50 to 75 mm long, is partly driven into the bottom end of each post before fixing. The projecting ends are inserted in mortices cut in the step and secured with red lead mastic or grouted cement (see A and R, Fig. 42). Alternatively, hollow cast iron shoes may be adopted (see L, Fig. 44 and p. 90).

Door Classification.—Doors are classified as follows: (*a*) ledged and battened, (*b*) ledged, braced and battened, (*c*) framed, ledged and battened, (*d*) framed, ledged, braced and battened, (*e*) flush and (*f*) panelled.

Sizes.—The sizes of doors vary considerably, the following standard sizes being in greatest demand: 2040 mm by 526 mm, 2040 mm by 626 mm, 2040 mm by 726 mm, 2040 mm by 826 mm. Other common sizes are 1830 mm by 610 mm, 2640 mm by 810 mm, 2080 mm by 860 mm and 2130 mm by 915 mm.

A satisfactory size of door for the modern drawing or dining room is 2040 mm by 726 mm, and that for bedrooms, box-rooms, larders, water-closets, etc., is 2040 mm. by 710 mm. External doors should be larger than internal doors in order that they may conform with the scale of the building, and those of a house may be 2080 by 900 mm.

(a) Ledged and Battened Door (see A, B and C, Fig. 42).—This consists of vertical boards or *battens* which are secured to horizontal pieces called *ledges*. The boards vary from 100 to 175 mm (nominal) wide and 20 mm to 32 mm thick. Those in "narrow widths" give a more satisfactory appearance if the door is

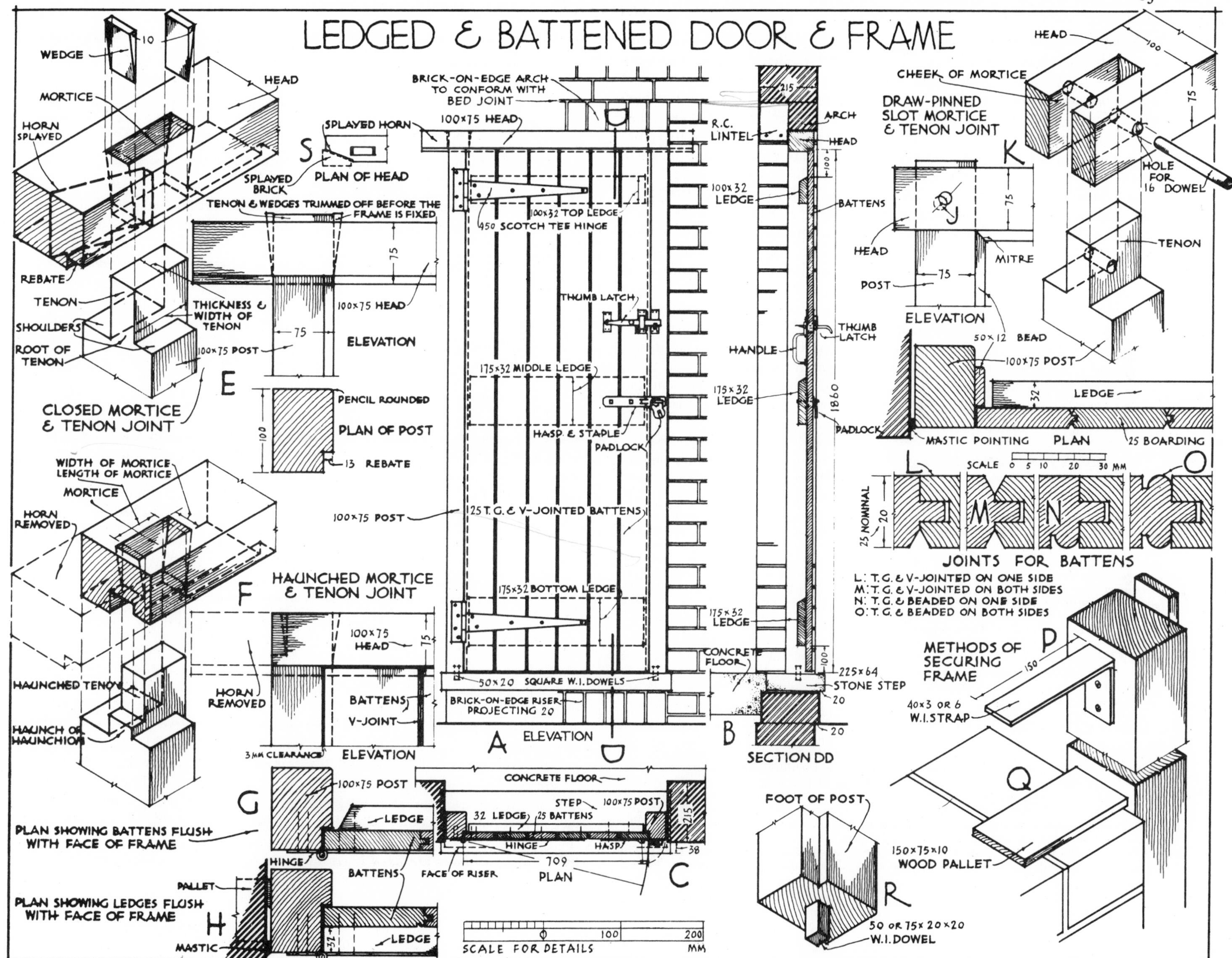
LEDGED & BATTENED DOOR & FRAME
WEDGE
10
MORTICE
HEAD
HORN SPLAYED
REBATE
TENON
SHOULDERS
ROOT OF TENON
THICKNESS & WIDTH OF TENON
100×75 POST
E
CLOSED MORTICE & TENON JOINT
SPLAYED HORN
S
PLAN OF HEAD
SPLAYED BRICK
TENON & WEDGES TRIMMED OFF BEFORE THE FRAME IS FIXED
75
100×75 HEAD
ELEVATION
PENCIL ROUNDED
PLAN OF POST
100
13 REBATE
WIDTH OF MORTICE
LENGTH OF MORTICE
MORTICE
HORN REMOVED
F
HAUNCHED MORTICE & TENON JOINT
100×75 HEAD
HORN REMOVED
BATTENS
V-JOINT
3MM CLEARANCE
ELEVATION
HAUNCHED TENON
HAUNCH OR HAUNCHION
BRICK-ON-EDGE ARCH TO CONFORM WITH BED JOINT
100×75 HEAD
100×32 TOP LEDGE
450 SCOTCH TEE HINGE
THUMB LATCH
175×32 MIDDLE LEDGE
HASP & STAPLE
PADLOCK
100×75 POST
25 T.G. & V-JOINTED BATTENS
175×32 BOTTOM LEDGE
50×20 SQUARE W.I. DOWELS
BRICK-ON-EDGE RISER PROJECTING 20
A
ELEVATION
D
R.C. LINTEL
215
ARCH
HEAD
100×32 LEDGE
BATTENS
HANDLE
THUMB LATCH
175×32 LEDGE
1860
PADLOCK
175×32 LEDGE
CONCRETE FLOOR
225×64 STONE STEP
20
B
SECTION DD
DRAW-PINNED SLOT MORTICE & TENON JOINT
CHEEK OF MORTICE
HEAD
100
75
HOLE FOR 16 DOWEL
K
J
HEAD
MITRE
POST
ELEVATION
TENON
50×12 BEAD
100×75 POST
LEDGE
32
MASTIC POINTING
PLAN
25 BOARDING
SCALE 0 5 10 20 30 MM
L
M
N
O
25 NOMINAL
20
JOINTS FOR BATTENS
L: T.G. & V-JOINTED ON ONE SIDE
M: T.G. & V-JOINTED ON BOTH SIDES
N: T.G. & BEADED ON ONE SIDE
O: T.G. & BEADED ON BOTH SIDES
METHODS OF SECURING FRAME
P
150
40×3 OR 6 W.I. STRAP
Q
150×75×10 WOOD PALLET
G
100×75 POST
LEDGE
PLAN SHOWING BATTENS FLUSH WITH FACE OF FRAME
HINGE
PALLET
BATTENS
PLAN SHOWING LEDGES FLUSH WITH FACE OF FRAME
H
MASTIC
LEDGE
CONCRETE FLOOR
STEP
100×75 POST
32 LEDGE
25 BATTENS
HINGE
HASP
38
709
FACE OF RISER
PLAN
C
SCALE FOR DETAILS
0 100 200 MM
FOOT OF POST
R
50 OR 75×20×20 W.I. DOWEL

FIGURE 42

small, and the shrinkage which occurs is correspondingly reduced. Four forms of joints between boards (known as *match-boarding*) which are adopted are shown at L, M, N and O. The " V-jointed " type is formed by chamfering both edges of each board, and the " beaded " joint shows the bead worked on the tongued edge. These joints are effective in making the appearance of the door less objectionable when shrinkage takes place and the joints open. They are sometimes only tongued and grooved, occasionally they are ploughed and tongued, and in cheap work they are butt or square jointed (see R, X and P, Fig. 34). Two other forms of beaded joints are shown at S and T, Fig. 44; the latter shows hardwood tongues or feathers which are sometimes employed when thick battens are used. The thickness of the ledges is usually 32 mm (nominal), and the middle and bottom ledges are wider than the top ledge, *i.e.*, 175 to 225 mm. When employed for external doors, the top edges should be bevelled as shown at B, to prevent water lodging on them.

This is the simplest form of door and is frequently used for narrow openings and in positions where the appearance is not material, as for temporary sheds, coal-houses, external water-closets, etc. It is relatively cheap and is apt to sag, on account of its weight, towards the bottom of the free edge. This defect may not become so pronounced if the end and central battens are screwed and not nailed to the ledges. It also has a tendency to twist, especially if the timber is not of good quality and thin ledges are used.

Preparation of Door.—The ledged and battened door is made in the following manner: The planing (on both sides), grooving, tonguing, thicknessing etc., machine operations of the tongued and grooved battens are as described on p. 61 for floor boards. The battens are fitted together on the joiners' bench and pencil lines are drawn across them to indicate the position of each ledge. A cramp (see Fig. 53) is applied near to one of the ledge positions and this ledge is lightly and temporarily nailed to the battens. The second ledge is then lightly nailed after the cramp has been applied near to it. The door is turned over on the bench, two rough pieces of wood are placed under the ledges, and oval wire nails are driven through the battens and ledges. The nails are of sufficient length to project beyond the ledges when driven in, and as they pierce the rough pieces, the ledges are not damaged by splintering as the nails protrude. The door is finally reversed and the nails *clinched* or *clenched*, *i.e.*, the points are bent over and by means of a punch (see 10, Fig. 67) and hammer and driven below the face of each ledge. The battens are cut and dressed off level at the top and bottom. The edges of the battens should be painted before cramping as this prevents water from getting into the joints and causing decay. If this is not done an unsightly appearance results when shrinkage occurs, due to the opening of the joints which exposes light unpainted margins. The backs of the ledges should also be painted prior to fixing.

Hanging and Fastening of Door.—The door is fitted between the rebates of the frame, a clearance of 1·5 mm (or " the thickness of a penny ") being allowed between the edge of the door and the frame for the thickness of the paint which is applied subsequently, and also for expansion. The width of the opening (below the head and also near the feet of the posts as the frame may not be absolutely square) is measured and transferred to the door. After allowing for the clearance, the door is placed lengthwise on edge on the floor, propped between the notch on the joiners' stool or trestle, and the uppermost edge is planed down (or " shot ") to the mark made during measurements. The bottom is also planed to allow 6 mm clearance between the door when hung and the step or floor. The door is placed in position between the frame, a wedge is inserted between the floor and the door and forced in until the door is brought square with the frame. If the door does not fit correctly, any irregularities are noted and the door taken down and planed where necessary.

The door is now ready to receive the hinges. The form of fastening usually provided for this type of door is the T-*hinge* or *cross-garnet* (see A, Figs. 42 and 43). This is a wrought iron strap pivoted to a metal plate. The *knuckle* of the hinge is a pin round which two sections of the plate and the end of the strap are bent (see X, Fig. 43). The thickness of the strap varies from 3 to 6 mm, and its length increases in multiples of 50 mm from 250 to 600 mm, measured from the centre of the pin. Two straps are secured either against the face of the battens (see A and G, Fig. 42) or screwed direct to the ledges (see H, Fig. 42). The plates of the hinges are screwed to the door posts. Those shown in the elevations in Figs, 42 and 43 are called *Scotch* T-*hinges* and are of 3 mm thick galvanised wrought iron. Thicker hinges are only used for heavy doors. Other hinges are shown at W and X, Fig. 43 and P, Fig. 44.

Hardware or Ironmongery includes hinges and fittings such as bolts and locks; it also includes door knobs and handles (sometimes referred to as *door furniture*).

All that may be necessary for the ledged and braced door is a *thumb latch*. If additional means of security is required, either a *padlock* or one or two *barrel bolts* may be used. The former is an external fitting (as for an external tool-house door) whereas the bolts would be used to secure the door from the inside. Alternatively, a *rim dead lock* may be used in lieu of a padlock or barrel bolt, or a *rim lock* may be used instead of a thumb latch and rim dead lock. The following is a brief description of this hardware :—

Thumb Latch (see O, Fig. 43).—It is sometimes called a Norfolk or Suffolk latch and consists of: (1) a *back plate* with handle and pivoted *sneck*, (2) a *keeper* through which a (3) *beam* or *fall bar* passes to engage in a (4) *stop*. The usual length of beam is 175 or 200 mm and that of the back plate is about 225 mm. Another type of thumb latch with two handles, each having a sneck which passes under the beam, is shown at A, B and C, Fig. 44. A complete fitting is usually of malleable iron, although for better-class work it is of bronze.

In fixing a thumb latch, a hole is made in the door through which the sneck is passed and the back plate is screwed to one face of the door. The keeper and plate to which the beam is pivoted are screwed to the opposite face of the door, the keeper (which limits the movement of the beam) being fixed near to the edge of the door. The plate to which the stop is attached is screwed to the inside face of the post. An alternative and less conspicuous form of keeper is shown at N, and this is fixed to the edge of the door. A similar stop fitting may be fixed to the edge of jamb of the post.

Padlock with Hasp and Staple (see A, Fig. 42, and P, Fig. 43).—The hasp and staple are usually of iron and the padlock is of galvanized iron, brass or bronze. The staple is screwed to the door post and the hasp is secured by two small bolts to the door. When the door is closed, the slotted hinged end of the hasp is passed over the staple, and the hinged ring of the padlock (after being passed through the eye of the staple) is " pressed home " to lock it.

Barrel Bolt (see A and Q, Fig. 43).—It is made of iron, brass or bronze. The length varies from 75 to 380 mm, a 150 mm bolt being sufficient for a ledged and battened door. The plate is screwed to the inside of the door and the bolt engages or " shoots " in a metal *socket* or *staple* fixed on the door frame. Sometimes two bolts are fixed horizontally as shown at A, or they may be fixed

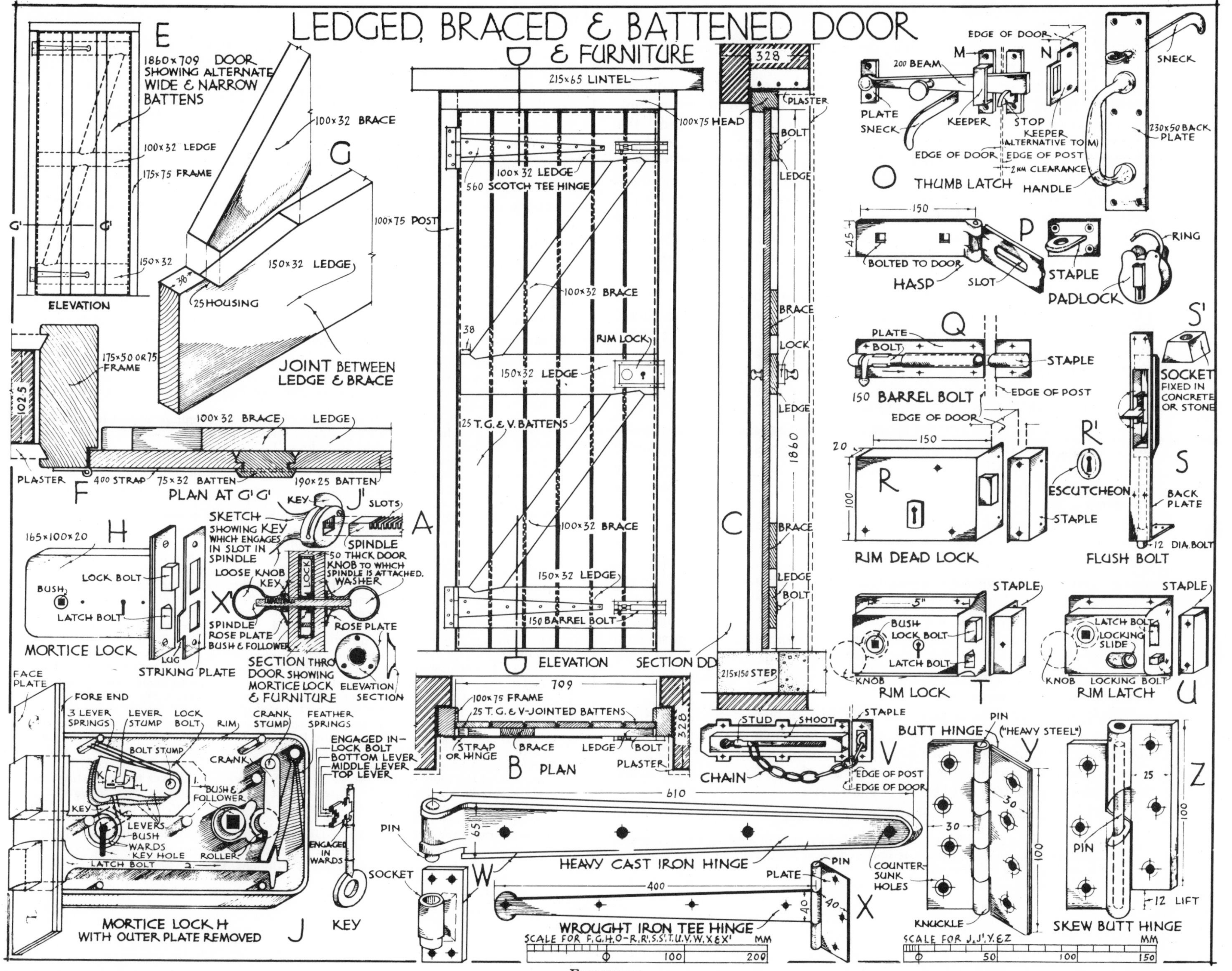
LEDGED, BRACED & BATTENED DOOR
& FURNITURE
E
1860×709 DOOR SHOWING ALTERNATE WIDE & NARROW BATTENS
100×32 BRACE
100×32 LEDGE
175×75 FRAME
150×32
ELEVATION
G
100×75 POST
150×32 LEDGE
25 HOUSING
JOINT BETWEEN LEDGE & BRACE
215×65 LINTEL
100×75 HEAD
100×32 LEDGE
560 SCOTCH TEE HINGE
100×32 BRACE
RIM LOCK
150×32 LEDGE
25 T.G.& V. BATTENS
100×32 BRACE
150×32 LEDGE
150 BARREL BOLT
ELEVATION
SECTION DD
328
PLASTER
BOLT
LEDGE
BRACE
LOCK
1860
C
215×150 STEP
175×50 OR 75 FRAME
102.5
100×32 BRACE
LEDGE
PLASTER
400 STRAP
75×32 BATTEN
190×25 BATTEN
F
PLAN AT G'G'
H
165×100×20
LOCK BOLT
BUSH
LATCH BOLT
MORTICE LOCK
STRIKING PLATE
LUG
KEY
J'
SLOTS
A
SKETCH SHOWING KEY WHICH ENGAGES IN SLOT IN SPINDLE
SPINDLE
50 THICK DOOR
KNOB TO WHICH SPINDLE IS ATTACHED.
WASHER
LOOSE KNOB
X'
SPINDLE
ROSE PLATE
BUSH & FOLLOWER
ROSE PLATE
SECTION THRO DOOR SHOWING MORTICE LOCK & FURNITURE
ELEVATION
SECTION
FACE PLATE
FORE END
3 LEVER SPRINGS
LEVER STUMP
LOCK BOLT
RIM
CRANK STUMP
FEATHER SPRINGS
BOLT STUMP
CRANK
ENGAGED IN-LOCK BOLT
BOTTOM LEVER
MIDDLE LEVER
TOP LEVER
BUSH & FOLLOWER
KEY
LEVERS
BUSH
WARDS
KEY HOLE
ROLLER
LATCH BOLT
ENGAGED IN WARDS
MORTICE LOCK H WITH OUTER PLATE REMOVED
J
KEY
709
100×75 FRAME
25 T.G.& V-JOINTED BATTENS
328
STRAP OR HINGE
BRACE
LEDGE
BOLT
PLASTER
B PLAN
EDGE OF DOOR
200 BEAM
M
N
PLATE
SNECK
KEEPER
STOP
KEEPER ALTERNATIVE TO M)
EDGE OF DOOR
EDGE OF POST
2MM CLEARANCE
O THUMB LATCH
HANDLE
SNECK
230×50 BACK PLATE
150
45
P
BOLTED TO DOOR
HASP
SLOT
STAPLE
RING
PADLOCK
S'
PLATE
BOLT
Q
STAPLE
150 BARREL BOLT
EDGE OF POST
SOCKET FIXED IN CONCRETE OR STONE
EDGE OF DOOR
R'
150
20
R
100
ESCUTCHEON
STAPLE
RIM DEAD LOCK
S
BACK PLATE
12 DIA. BOLT
FLUSH BOLT
STAPLE
5"
BUSH
LOCK BOLT
LATCH BOLT
KNOB
RIM LOCK
T
STAPLE
LATCH BOLT
LOCKING SLIDE
KNOB
LOCKING BOLT
RIM LATCH
U
STUD
SHOOT
STAPLE
CHAIN
V
EDGE OF POST
EDGE OF DOOR
610
PIN
65
HEAVY CAST IRON HINGE
SOCKET
W
400
PLATE
PIN
40
40
X
WROUGHT IRON TEE HINGE
BUTT HINGE
PIN ("HEAVY STEEL")
Y
30
30
100
COUNTER SUNK HOLES
KNUCKLE
25
Z
100
PIN
12 LIFT
SKEW BUTT HINGE
SCALE FOR F,G,H,O-R,R',S,S',T,U,V,W,X&X' MM
0 100 200
SCALE FOR J,J',Y,&Z MM
0 50 100 150

FIGURE 43

vertically when one socket is let into the head of the frame and the other (similar to S′) is let into the stone or concrete step.

Rim Dead Lock (see R, Fig. 43).—This consists of a steel case (containing a brass bolt, spring, etc.) which is screwed to the face of the door, and a staple which is screwed to the frame to receive the bolt when the door is locked. The key required to operate the bolt is comparatively long as it is needed to actuate the lock from both sides of the door. The lock may be obtained with one or two levers (see below). An *escutcheon* (see R′) or holed metal plate is sometimes fixed on the face of the door opposite to that to which the lock is attached to prevent the " keyhole " from becoming enlarged and damaged by continued action of the key. A *plate lock* or *stock lock* may be used for an external door of this type; this is similar to the above lock but the metal case is inserted in a wood block.

(b) Ledged, Braced and Battened Door (see A, B and C, Fig. 43).—This is a ledged and battened door to which inclined struts or *braces* have been added. These braces increase the rigidity of the door and prevent it drooping at the " nose," a defect which is common to the ledged and battened door. These braces must *incline upwards from the hanging edge*, otherwise they would be useless in counteracting the tendency for the door to droop out of square. The position of the middle ledge should be such as to allow the braces to have the same inclination, otherwise the appearance is not satisfactory; the appearance resulting when the braces are lined straight through is sometimes preferred (see E, Fig. 43). The width of the braces varies from 100 to 175 mm, and they are usually out of 32 mm stuff; they are housed and not tenoned into the ledges (see detail G, Fig. 43).

An alternative ledged, braced and battened door, suitable for a cottage where a simple type of door is required, is shown at E. It consists of alternate wide and narrow battens which are 25 and 32 mm thick respectively. See the detail plan at F which shows the battens tongued and grooved and V-jointed, and the T-hinges (similar to that at X) which pass through the thicker batten.

The ledged, braced and battened door is used for similar purposes as described for the ledged and battened door, but on account of its greater strength it may be selected for larger openings. It is made as described on p. 86, the battens being nailed to the ledges and the braces afterwards fitted to the ledges and clinch-nailed to the battens.

Hardware.—This door is generally hung with T-hinges; those shown at A are 560 mm Scotch T-hinges, and another form is shown at X. The furniture may consist of a thumb latch and a dead lock as already described. Alternatively, a *rim lock* or a *rim latch* may be used instead of a thumb latch and a dead lock. Barrel bolts may be used in addition, as shown at A.

There are many variations of latches and locks, the broad difference between each being :

A *rim latch* is fixed to the face of a door and consists of a casing which contains one *bevelled* bolt or latch (which is operated by a handle attached to a spindle) and a small locking bolt (see U).

A *rim dead lock* has one bolt only which is actuated by a key (see R).

A *rim lock* has two bolts, one controlled by a handle and the other by a key (see T); it is fixed to the face of the door.

A *mortice latch* has only one latch (or bevelled bolt) and the case is fitted within the thickness of the door and is only visible on the edge of the door.

A *mortice lock* is similar to the rim lock in that it has two bolts, but the case is only seen on the edge of the door as it is fixed in a mortice formed in the door (see H).

The *rim latch* shown at U is a steel case about 125 mm long which contains a brass bolt and a spring which acts upon the bolt to maintain it in the staple when the door is closed. The mechanism is similar to that of the latch bolt of the mortice lock described below. The small locking bolt is used when required to prevent the door from being opened by the knob from the outside.

A *rim lock* is obtained in standard sizes varying from 125 to 200 mm long by 75 to 100 mm deep. A typical example is shown at T, Fig. 43. It has two bolts, *i.e.*, a " dead " bolt operated by a key and a bevelled or latch bolt operated by the handle and (when the door is being closed) by the action of the bevelled end sliding over the edge of the staple.

Mechanism of Rim and Mortice Lock.—The internal construction of a rim lock is similar to that of a mortice lock. An interior of a mortice lock[1] is shown at J, and the following description refers to (1) the lock bolt mechanism and (2) the latch bolt mechanism.

(1) The lock bolt is of brass or phosphor bronze or gunmetal and has a pin or *bolt stump* attached to it to form a pivot for the three thin brass *levers* (hence this would be described as a " three lever lock ") which are fitted over it; each lever has two recesses, K and L, with a narrow connecting slot through which a small *lever stump* (connected to the bolt) passes when the bolt is operated; attached to each lever is a fine metal spring. When the door is unlocked, the lever stump occupies the upper portion of recess K. To lock the door, the key is inserted in the keyhole formed in the phosphor-bronze *bush* which has three thin raised rings called *wards*, the key (see sketch) being shaped to fit these wards. When the key is turned, it causes the bolt to move outwards and the pivoted levers to swing upwards until the slot between the recess is opposite to the lever stump. After the key (indicated by broken lines) has been rotated until it is free of the lower edge of the bolt, the lever springs shoot the bolt into the staple (in the case of the rim lock) or *striking plate* (when the lock is of the mortice type—see H), and the lever stump now occupies the upper portion of the recess L when the levers have rotated downwards. To unlock the door, the operations are reversed, the key forces the levers upwards and the bolt into the lock in the direction of arrow " 1 ", whilst the lever stump passes from recess L to the upper portion of recess K after the levers have dropped.

(2) The latch bolt is operated either by the handle or by the action of the bevelled end of the bolt upon the staple or bent " lug " of the striking plate (see H) when the door is being closed. The handles usually consist of two knobs, one of which is permanently fixed to one end of a steel *slotted spindle* and the other is loose. The spindle is passed through a *rose plate* (which is screwed to the face of the door) and through the bush and *follower* of the lock (see X′). There are various devices for securing the opposite or " loose " knob, an effective one being shown at J′ and X′ and consists of a small metal *key* which is pivoted by a countersunk screw let into the end of the loose knob; the second rose plate is passed over the projecting end of the spindle, the loose knob is fitted over it and pressed against the rose plate until the latter is brought tightly up against the face of the door, when the key is then dropped into one of the slots in the spindle; each rose plate is now screwed to the door to make the handles secure. Observe at J that one of the *feather springs* acts

[1] Manufactured by Messrs. J. Gibbons, Wolverhampton.

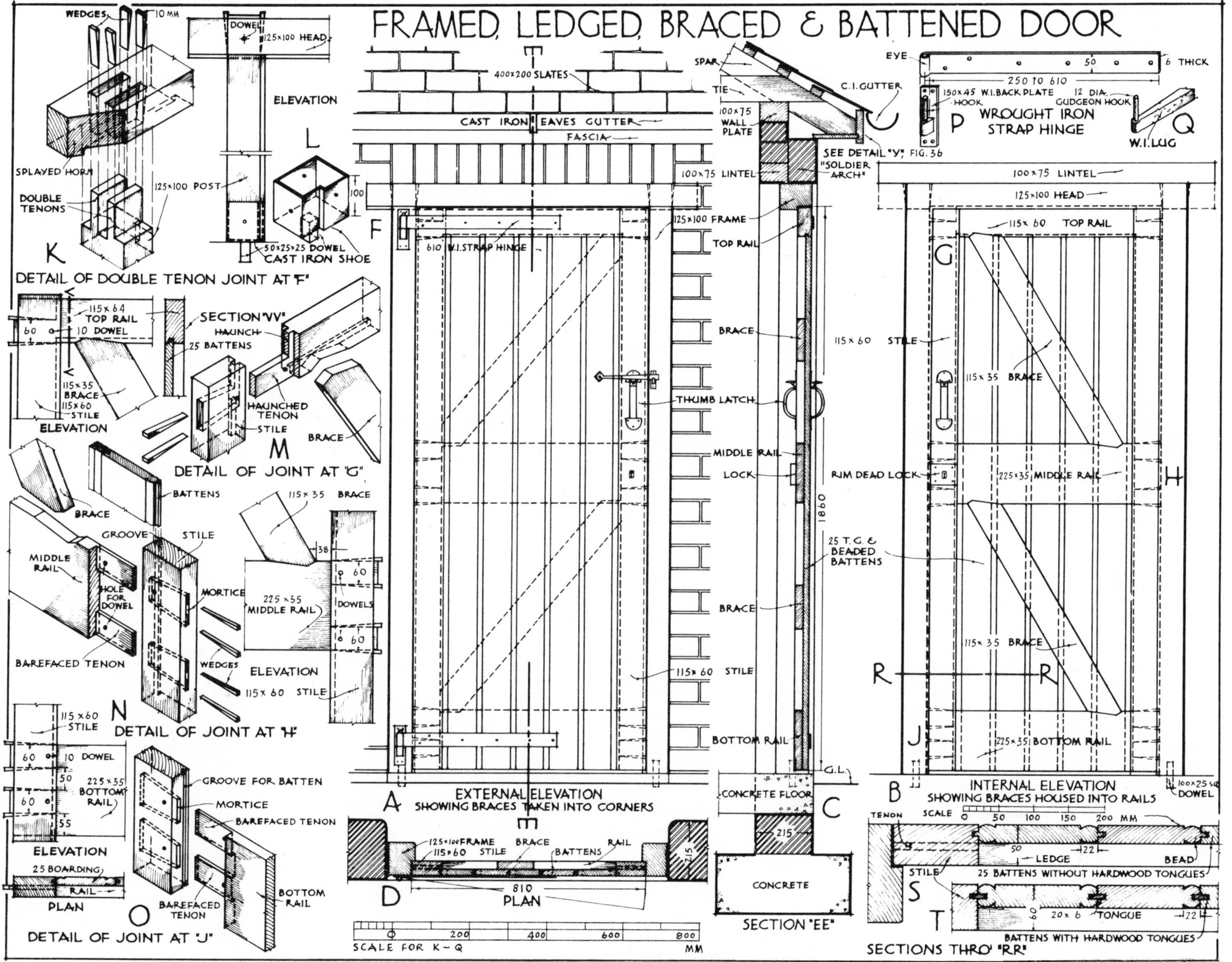
FRAMED, LEDGED, BRACED & BATTENED DOOR
WEDGES
10 MM
DOWEL
125×100 HEAD
ELEVATION
SPLAYED HORN
DOUBLE TENONS
125×100 POST
50×25×25 DOWEL
CAST IRON SHOE
K
L
F
DETAIL OF DOUBLE TENON JOINT AT "F"
115×64 TOP RAIL
10 DOWEL
SECTION "VV"
25 BATTENS
HAUNCH
HAUNCHED TENON
STILE
115×35 BRACE
115×60 STILE
ELEVATION
M
BRACE
DETAIL OF JOINT AT "G"
BATTENS
BRACE
GROOVE
STILE
MIDDLE RAIL
HOLE FOR DOWEL
MORTICE
BAREFACED TENON
WEDGES
115×35 BRACE
225×35 MIDDLE RAIL
DOWELS
ELEVATION
115×60 STILE
N
DETAIL OF JOINT AT "H"
115×60 STILE
10 DOWEL
225×35 BOTTOM RAIL
ELEVATION
25 BOARDING
RAIL
PLAN
GROOVE FOR BATTEN
MORTICE
BAREFACED TENON
BOTTOM RAIL
O
DETAIL OF JOINT AT "J"
400×200 SLATES
CAST IRON EAVES GUTTER
FASCIA
610 W.I. STRAP HINGE
125×100 FRAME
TOP RAIL
BRACE
THUMB LATCH
MIDDLE RAIL
LOCK
BRACE
115×60 STILE
BOTTOM RAIL
A
EXTERNAL ELEVATION
SHOWING BRACES TAKEN INTO CORNERS
125×100 FRAME
115×60 STILE
BRACE
BATTENS
RAIL
810
D
PLAN
SCALE FOR K–Q
0 200 400 600 800 MM
SPAR
TIE
C.I. GUTTER
100×75 WALL PLATE
SEE DETAIL "Y", FIG. 36
"SOLDIER ARCH"
100×75 LINTEL
1860
25 T.G. & BEADED BATTENS
G.L.
CONCRETE FLOOR
215
CONCRETE
C
SECTION "EE"
EYE
50
6 THICK
250 TO 610
150×45 W.I. BACK PLATE
HOOK
12 DIA. GUDGEON HOOK
P
WROUGHT IRON STRAP HINGE
W.I. LUG
Q
100×75 LINTEL
125×100 HEAD
115×60 TOP RAIL
G
115×60 STILE
115×35 BRACE
RIM DEAD LOCK
225×35 MIDDLE RAIL
H
115×35 BRACE
R
R
J
225×35 BOTTOM RAIL
100×25 SQ DOWEL
B
INTERNAL ELEVATION
SHOWING BRACES HOUSED INTO RAILS
TENON
SCALE 0 50 100 150 200 MM
LEDGE
BEAD
STILE
25 BATTENS WITHOUT HARDWOOD TONGUES
S
T
20×6 TONGUE
BATTENS WITH HARDWOOD TONGUES
SECTIONS THRO' "RR"

FIGURE 44

upon one end of the latch bolt and this causes the opposite end to protrude. The follower acts upon the *crank roller*; the latter is fitted to the *crank* which is pivoted at the *crank stump* at one end and the other end bears upon a projection on the end of the latch bolt. To open the door when the lock bolt is disengaged, the handle is turned to cause the follower to bear upon the crank roller which in turn causes the crank to rotate and operate upon the latch bolt and move it horizontally in the direction of arrow " 2 " until it is clear of the striking plate. When the knob is released the feather springs force the crank and bolt to assume their original positions.

A further reference to mortice locks is made on p. 100.

(c) Framed, Ledged and Battened Door.—This is similar to type (*d*), described below, with the exception that the braces are omitted. The door tends to become distorted because of the absence of the braces, and it is in little demand for this reason.

(d) Framed, Ledged, Braced and Battened Door (see A, B, C and D, Fig. 44). This is superior to any of the foregoing types and consists of a framing (which must not be confused with the door frame) strengthened by ledges, braces and battens. The framework consists of a *top rail* which is morticed and tenoned into two vertical members called *stiles* or *styles*. The *middle* and *bottom rails* or ledges are morticed and tenoned into the stiles and the braces are either housed into the rails at about 38 mm from the stiles (see B) or are taken into the corners and tenoned into the stiles (see A). The former is the stronger construction, although the method shown at A is often adopted because of its better appearance. *These braces must incline upwards from the hanging post* (see p. 88). The battens may be joined as explained on p. 86, where reference is made to the joints shown at S and T, Fig. 44. The upper ends of the battens are let into the top rail (see section VV at M), the side battens are tongued into the stiles (see S and T) and the lower ends of the battens *completely cover the bottom rail*[1] as shown at A, B and C.

Details of the various joints are shown in Fig. 44. That at K shows the joint between the post and head of the large (125 mm by 100 mm) frame. It is double-tenoned to ensure a tight fit at the shoulders (see p. 84). M shows the haunched tenon joint between the top rail and the stile, and the housing of the brace as indicated at G.

The middle rail has a *pair of single tenons*[2] and is notched to receive the lower end of the top brace (see N) and the top end of the lower brace. As the rail is comparatively thin, it is not advisable to form these tenons as previously described, but rather to make them flush with one face, when they are called *barefaced tenons*.

[1] The practice, sometimes adopted, of making the bottom rail the same thickness as the framing and letting the lower ends of the battens into it is unsound, for water will lodge on the rail and rot both it and the bottom of the battens.

[2] These are sometimes called " double tenons," although this description is not quite correct. A double tenon joint (as shown at K, Fig. 44) has both tenons in the *thickness* of the member, whilst a member having a pair of single tenons has both tenons formed in its *width*.

The bottom rail has also a pair of single barefaced tenons (see O). The lower tenon may be haunched like that shown at M.

The tenons are dowelled or pinned, in addition to being wedged. These dowels are of hardwood and are from 10 to 13 mm diameter (see M, N and O). One is inserted through each tenon and at a distance from the shoulders of at least twice the diameter of the dowel to prevent the wood from splitting when the pin is driven in.

The framed, ledged, braced and battened door is a very suitable type for external use and it is particularly suited for factories, warehouses, farm buildings and buildings in which the doors are subjected to rough treatment. That shown in Fig. 44 is typical of the type used for farms. The figure also includes a portion of the roof details.

Preparation of Door.—The sequence of operations in framing this door is briefly : The rails are fitted loosely into the stiles, the braces are placed in position, the battens are accurately fitted and slipped into the grooves of the stiles and top rail, the tenons are wedged and pinned (a cramp being used as described on p. 102 to tighten up the joints), and the battens are nailed to the rails and braces.

The door frame should be securely fixed as explained on p. 84. The feet are shown secured by dowels. Alternatively the door posts may be fitted with *cast iron shoes* (see L). These provide a good method of fixing and also protect the lower ends of the posts from damage such as may be caused in factories, farmsteads and similar buildings. The ends of the posts are shaped, painted and fitted tightly into the shoes which are then screwed to the posts. The frame is now fixed with the dowels let into the mortices previously formed in the step and run in with lead or cement.

Hanging and Fastening of Door.—Heavy wrought iron Scotch T-hinges are sometimes used for hanging this type of door (see p. 86). Alternatively, 6 mm thick wrought iron *strap hinges* or *bands and gudgeon hooks* are used, especially for large doors (see P, Fig. 44). One end of the strap is bent to form an eye. Two straps are required and are secured by 10 mm or 13 mm diameter bolts which are passed through the rails and battens. The door is hung by passing the eyes of the straps over the pins or gudgeons which are welded to *back plates* bolted to the frame. Sometimes doors are not provided with frames and are hung by engaging the eyes of the straps in gudgeon hooks smithed to wrought iron *lugs* (see Q). The lugs are secured to the stonework, mortices being cut to receive them. After insertion, the lugs are well caulked with lead and the reason for the dovetail shape and ragged surface is to give a greater key for the lead and increase its holding power. The heavy *cast iron hinge* (see W, Fig. 43) is another type of fastening used for very large doors. A pair of these hinges is bolted to the door and the pins on them engage in sockets fixed to the frame.

Butt hinges (see Y, Fig. 43) are often used for hanging this type of door. The flanges or *wings* of the hinges are made of either cast iron, malleable iron or steel, and they increase in 13 mm units from 25 to 150 mm long. The *knuckle* consists of a central pin which passes through alternative eyes of each wing to form five segments. The wings have countersunk holes to receive the heads of the screws used to secure the wings to the door and frame.

The door is hung by butt hinges in the following manner : It is fitted into the frame and trimmed so as to leave a uniform clearance of 1·5 mm (see p. 86). The door is removed and one wing of each hinge is screwed to the edge of the hanging stile. This is done by forming slight housings in correct position on the stile to receive a wing of each hinge which is screwed to the door. The door is again placed into the opening, wedged temporarily (p. 86), and brought to the required position. The housings for the free wings are marked on the post, the door is removed and the housings are formed. The door is placed finally in position and the wings of the hinges are screwed to the post (see K, Fig. 50). In order that the door shall swing freely, the centre of the pin of the top hinge should be 5 mm beyond the face of the door and that of the bottom hinge should be 6 mm clear.

A description of the *skew butt hinge* shown at Z, Fig. 43, and its application is given on p. 100.

Hardware.—That for this door may be as previously described. If provision is required (for purposes of ventilation, etc.) to enable the door to be kept slightly open and yet secure from unauthorized entry from the outside, then a *door chain* as shown at V, Fig. 43, may be fixed on the inside. This fitting may be either of malleable iron, brass or bronze. The plate to which the slotted shoot is attached is screwed in a horizontal position to the inside face of the door, and the staple to which the chain is fastened is screwed to the post. The free end of the chain is in the form of a stud which may be inserted in the slot at the end farthest from the staple only when the door is closed. The door may be opened to a maximum of 100 or 125 mm, when the stud is passed along the slot, and the stud cannot be removed from the outside.

(e) **Flush Door**[1] (see Fig. 45).—*This is the most popular type of door*, particularly for internal use. Two of the many varieties of flush door are shown in Fig. 45. That at A is called a *laminated flush door* and consists of a core of strips of wood glued together under great pressure and faced on each side by a sheet of three thin layers or *veneers* of wood, called *plywood* (see below), which is also glued under pressure to the core. Sheets of plywood can be obtained up to 2·5 m in width, and therefore a flush door has the appearance of a single panel. As shown at E, the core consists of 32 mm wide softwood strips or 16 mm wide hardwood strips. These strips are arranged with the grain alternating, as shown; this reduces shrinkage and distortion. A hardwood edging is fixed to cover the core and the edges of the plywood; this prevents the latter from being damaged, particularly at the striking edge. A laminated flush door is heavy and requires much material, and another type, called a *framed flush door* (see B, Fig. 45), has been evolved and is extensively used. It consists of a wood frame comprising stiles, top and bottom rails, and thin intermediate rails, and this frame is covered on both sides by sheets of plywood. The 75 mm deep top and bottom rails are tenoned to the stiles, and the thin (25 mm) intermediate rails are stub-tenoned to the stiles. The joints of the framing are glued and cramped, and the plywood sheets are glued to the framing under great pressure. Lock *blocks* are provided as shown at B for the insertion of a mortice lock. An alternative form of hardwood edging to that at E is shown in the detail F. The finished thickness of both types of door is 45 mm.

(f) **Panelled Door** (see Figs. 46, 48, 49, 50 and 52).—A panelled door consists of a framing or rim which is grooved on the inside edges to receive one or more panels.

Types of Panelled Doors.—Several designs of panelled doors are shown at A to H (inclusive), Fig. 46. The members of the frame not already mentioned include the *muntin*, which, at C, is the short vertical piece between the bottom and middle rails. Note in every case: (1) the stiles are continuous from top to bottom, (2) the top, bottom, middle and intermediate rails are joined to the stiles and (3) the muntins are joined to the rails (see later).

[1] An extended description is given in Chap. II, Vol. III.

The nominal thickness of the framing may be 38, 44 or 50 mm, depending upon (1) the size of the door, (2) the situation (external doors are usually thicker than those fixed internally), (3) the type of lock to be used (a minimum thickness

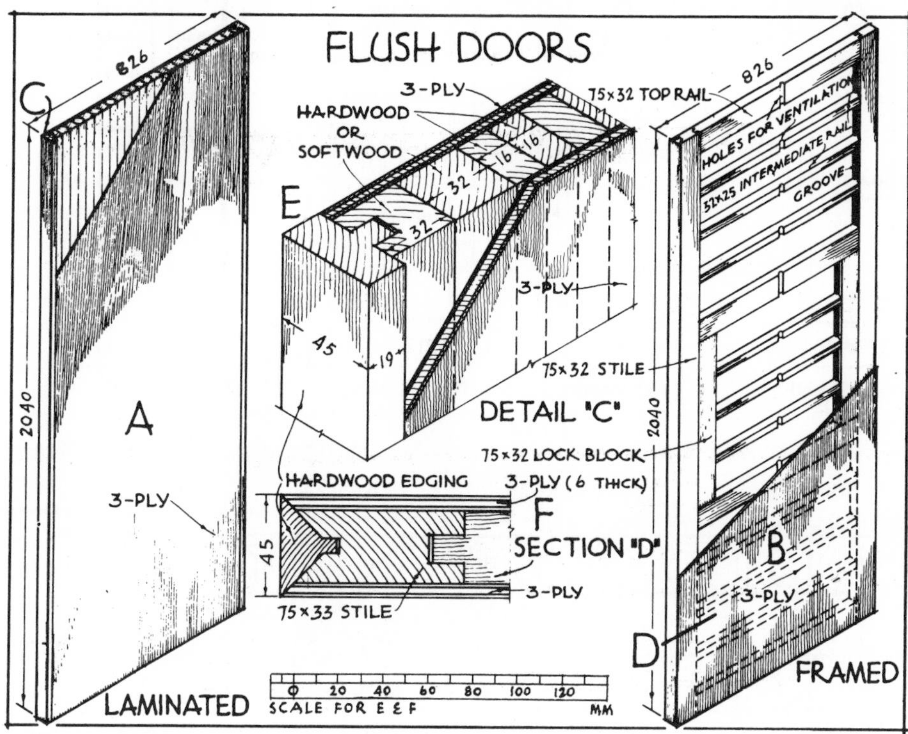

FIGURE 45

of 40 mm is necessary for mortice locks), (4) the thickness of the panels and (5) the size of the panel mouldings.

The panels may be *solid* (as shown at J, R and V, Fig. 46) or they may consist of *laminated wood*[1] such as plywood and laminboard (see N and A′, Fig. 46). The minimum thickness of solid panels is 13 mm (nominal), whereas that of plywood consisting of three veneers (termed "3-ply") is from 5 mm to 13 mm.

[1] A detailed description of the manufacture and uses of *plywood* and similar veneered products is given in Vol. III. Briefly, plywood consists of three or more thin sheets of wood which have been carefully dried, glued, pressed and trimmed off. Columbian pine, birch, oak and maple are some of the timbers used. Round logs are cut into from 1·5 to 2·5 m lengths, steamed, and subsequently each is placed horizontally into a machine called a *rotary veneer cutter* which grips it at the ends. The machine rotates the log against the edge of a long knife which extends the full width of the machine and cuts the timber into a continuous sheet.

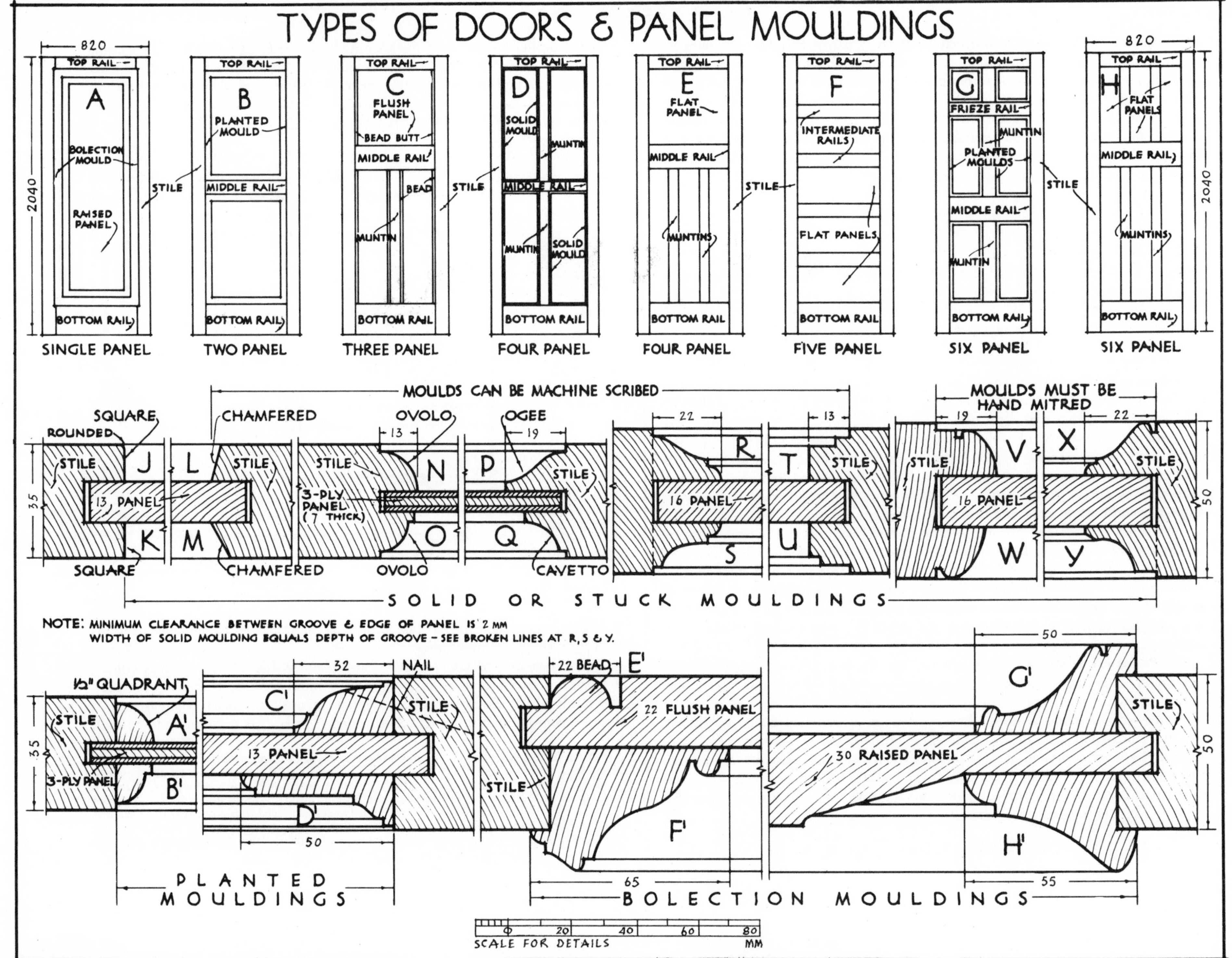
TYPES OF DOORS & PANEL MOULDINGS
820
2040
TOP RAIL
A
BOLECTION MOULD
RAISED PANEL
BOTTOM RAIL
SINGLE PANEL
B
PLANTED MOULD
STILE
MIDDLE RAIL
TWO PANEL
C
FLUSH PANEL
BEAD BUTT
MIDDLE RAIL
BEAD
MUNTIN
THREE PANEL
D
SOLID MOULD
MUNTIN
MIDDLE RAIL
FOUR PANEL
E
FLAT PANEL
FOUR PANEL
F
INTERMEDIATE RAILS
FLAT PANELS
FIVE PANEL
G
FRIEZE RAIL
PLANTED MOULDS
SIX PANEL
H
FLAT PANELS
MUNTINS
SIX PANEL
MOULDS CAN BE MACHINE SCRIBED
MOULDS MUST BE HAND MITRED
SQUARE
ROUNDED
CHAMFERED
OVOLO
OGEE
CAVETTO
13 PANEL
3-PLY PANEL (7 THICK)
16 PANEL
J K L M N O P Q R S T U V W X Y
SOLID OR STUCK MOULDINGS
NOTE: MINIMUM CLEARANCE BETWEEN GROOVE & EDGE OF PANEL IS 2 MM
WIDTH OF SOLID MOULDING EQUALS DEPTH OF GROOVE – SEE BROKEN LINES AT R, S & Y.
½" QUADRANT
A' B' C' D' E' F' G' H'
3-PLY PANEL
NAIL
22 BEAD
22 FLUSH PANEL
30 RAISED PANEL
PLANTED MOULDINGS
BOLECTION MOULDINGS
SCALE FOR DETAILS
MM

Figure 46

Treatment of Panels.—The finishes which may be applied to panels are many and varied. The panels may be finished with simple or intricate mouldings, or they may be left plain without mouldings. Elaborate mouldings may harbour dust and are difficult to keep clean. They may be expensive to produce, especially if mitred by hand (see later). As will be explained, most doors are now machine-made, and in their manufacture it is the aim to eliminate as far as possible labours performed by hand.

The following are the various panel finishes :—

Square.—No mouldings are provided, the edges of the framing next to the panels being left square (see J and K, Fig. 46, and D, Fig. 52); J shows the corner slightly rounded by sand-papering and is called " pencil-rounded." The panels are known as *square sunk* or *flat* (see E, F and H, Fig. 46). Chamfered edges, as shown at L and M, are an alternative. These finishes are much in evidence, and, provided the panels are well proportioned, such simple treatment has much to commend it.

Solid or Stuck Moulding.—The mouldings are " stuck " (meaning " worked ") on the edges of the framing. Various examples are shown at L to Y (inclusive), Fig. 46. Note that in most cases the width of each mould is equal to the depth of the groove prepared to receive the panel (see the broken lines at R, S and Y); the operations of moulding and framing by machinery are simplified when this is observed.

The joints at the angles of solid mouldings are *scribed* to give 45° mitres or intersections. Scribing is the shaping of a moulding which is required to fit against a similar but continuous moulding. This is illustrated at C and D, Fig. 47, which shows a bottom (or intermediate) rail scribed to a stile. The latter has an ovolo (or quadrant) mould worked on it for its entire length and the shoulders of the rail are hollowed out to fit accurately over the ovolo mould on the stile. This is shown clearly on the plan at C which indicates the shaped end of the rail separated from the stile; this results in a 45° mitre as shown at D and E. This mould and the solid mouldings shown at L to U (inclusive), Fig. 46, can be machine-scribed and are therefore comparatively inexpensive; whereas those at V to Y (inclusive) can only be mitred by hand and are accordingly expensive.

Planted Moulding.—These are separate mouldings which are " planted " round the panels adjacent to the framing. Examples of these are shown at A', B', C' and D', Fig. 46. The mouldings are nailed to the framing and the *nails must not pass through the panels*, otherwise the panels will crack owing to the internal stresses set up when the timber shrinks. It is important to allow for the free movement of the panels (when the wood shrinks or expands) and there should be a space of from 1·5 to 3 mm between each edge of the panel and the groove; the clearance in each of the examples shown in Fig. 46 is 1·5 mm. " Panel pins " (see F, Fig. 66) are used for fixing these moulds, as the small heads are inconspicuous and cause the minimum damage to the mouldings.

Planted moulds are formed with *mitred joints* at the angles (see A and B, Fig. 47), each adjacent end of the moulding being cut at an angle of 45°.

Planted mouldings which finish level with the face of the framing are called *flush mouldings* (see L, Fig. 49). Those which project beyond the face of the framing are called *bolection mouldings* (see F', G' and H', Fig. 46, P, Fig. 48, and K, Fig. 50); these are usually rebated over the edges of the framing to cover any shrinkage which may take place.

Occasionally the panels are made with one face flush with the framing; these are termed *flush panels* (see C, Fig. 46). A bead (see E') is usually formed on the vertical edges of the panel to render less conspicuous any openings which may occur if the panels shrink; these are called *bead butt panels* (C). If in addition a similar bead is worked on the horizontal edges of the panel, such are called *bead flush panels.*

Raised Panels.—The central portion of the panel is thicker than the edges or margin. That at H', Fig. 46, shows the panel chamfered from the edge of the moulding to leave a flat or " fielded " central portion; such is called a *raised and flat* or *raised and fielded* panel. That at P, Fig. 48, is known as a *raised, sunk and fielded* panel. Sometimes the edges of the sinking next to the central flat portion are moulded, when the panel is said to be *raised, sunk and moulded.* A *raised and chamfered* panel, when square, is chamfered from a central point down to each edge of the moulding; when the panel is oblong, the chamfered margins meet to form a ridge.

Sunk Moulding.—This is formed *below* the surface; the sinking is usually continued to form a *sunk panel* and the portion of panel enclosed by the moulding may be below or flush with the outer margin. The panel is thus formed out of the solid.

Examples of panels and mouldings are shown in the elevations in Fig. 46.

Students are advised to cultivate the habit of drawing details involving mouldings to full scale rather than make sketch details which are very frequently far too small. They should realize that it is not always necessary to show mouldings consisting of many small members and fillets, for very often the simpler the mouldings the better. In this connection it should be pointed out that whilst mouldings of hardwoods may have small members, those of softwoods should not, for they are difficult and expensive to make and disappear when two or three coats of paint are applied.

The construction of panelled doors will now be considered.

Single Panelled Door (see Fig. 48).—This is suitable for the main entrance to a house. The construction of the joints of the frame has been described on pp. 83–84. The outside edges of this frame may be pencil rounded by sand-papering them, or they may be ovolo or ogee moulded and thus rendered less liable to damage than if left square.

External doors are usually prepared with 50 mm (nominal)[1] thick framing,

[1] As previously mentioned, an allowance from the nominal sizes for dressed (finished or net or wrought) work must be made. The usual allowance for work which is given a smooth finish (as for painted work) is 1·7 mm for *each* dressed surface plus 0·8 mm for sandpapering *each* surface (see pp. 61 and 109).

especially if they are fitted with mortice locks, although there is no constructional reason why such doors of average size should exceed 38 mm in thickness if they are fitted with rim locks. In the illustrated example the door is 50 mm thick on account of the thick panel which is necessary because of its large size. Full size details must be drawn to the *finished* sizes. In accordance with the footnote stated on p. 93 the usual total allowance for painted work is equivalent to 5 mm, when both faces are dressed and sand papered. If great care is exercised in dressing expensive hardwoods, the total loss when dressing both sides may be reduced to 4 mm, and this allowance has been made in the details shown in Fig. 48.

The joints of the framing of the door may be either (*a*) morticed and tenoned or (*b*) dowelled.

(a) *Morticed and Tenoned Joints.*—These are similar to the joints of the framed, ledged, braced and battened door shown in Fig. 44, and are illustrated at H and L, Fig. 48. The width of each tenon is 58 mm. The grooves formed along the inner edges of the framing to receive the panel are shown. The depth of the grooves is usually made equal to the thickness of the panel, although it should not be less than 13 mm (see P, Fig. 48, and the details in Fig. 46). A clearance of 3 mm is shown at P to allow for the free movement of the panel (see p. 93).

(b) *Dowelled Joints.*—Typical dowelled joints are shown at J and M, Fig. 48; that at J shows two dowels used to connect the top rail to the stile, and the detail M shows the connection between the bottom rail and the stile where four dowels are used. The dowels, which are machine-made, are of hardwood. Their diameter should not be less than about one-third the thickness of the framing, and a common size is 125 mm by 16 mm (see O); they are placed at about 50 mm centres (see M). The ends of the rails are bored, glue is applied to the edges of the rails and the inside of the holes, and the glued dowels are inserted; the stiles are bored, the holes are glued, and projecting portions of the rail dowels are inserted. The dowels are grooved (see O) to increase the holding power of the glue. Only well seasoned timber should be used if the joints are to be dowelled, otherwise the shrinking and warping of unseasoned timber may cause the dowels to snap, followed by the destruction of the joints.

This method of jointing is almost universally adopted for doors made by machinery as it is a cheaper form than the mortice and tenon joint on account of the saving of timber and labour which results. Whilst there is still much prejudice against the

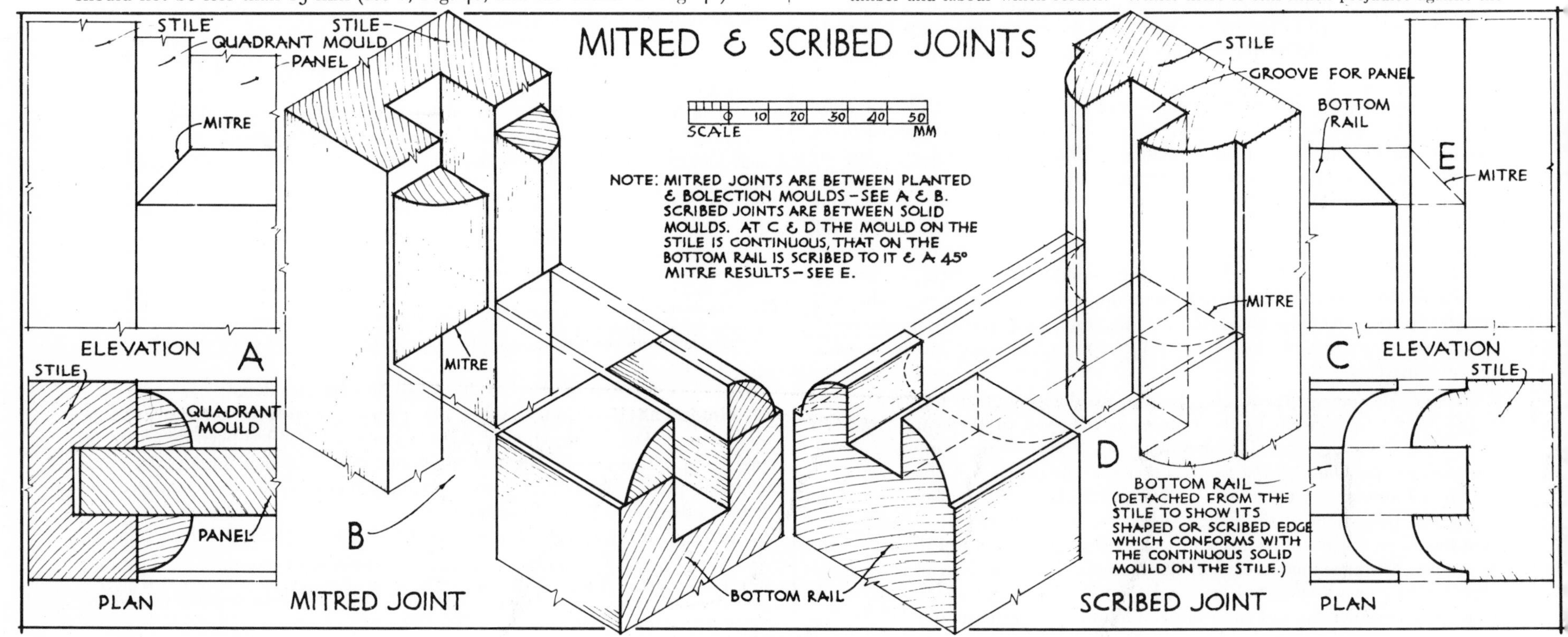

FIGURE 47

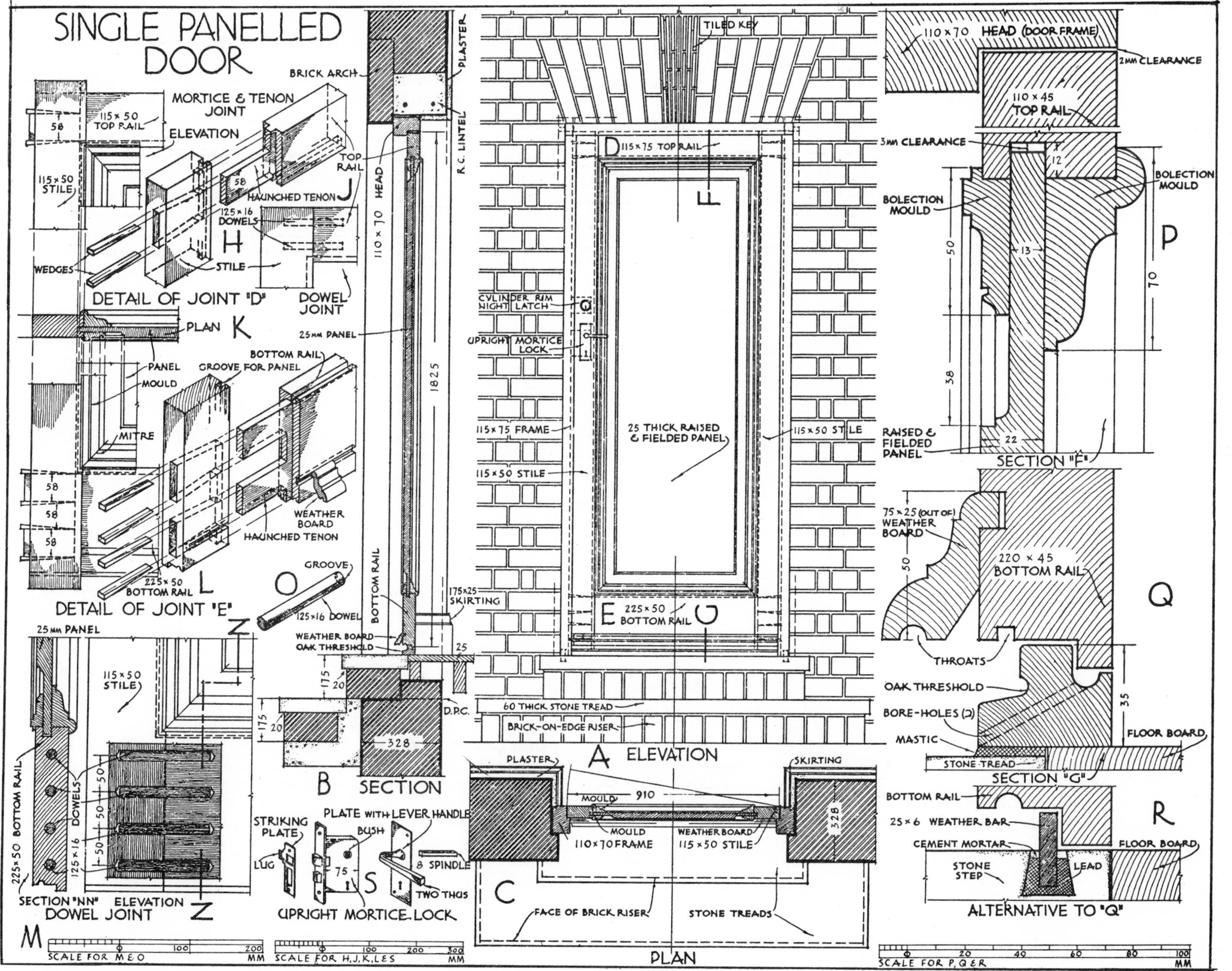
SINGLE PANELLED DOOR
MORTICE & TENON JOINT
115×50 TOP RAIL
ELEVATION
115×50 STILE
58
HAUNCHED TENON
J
125×16 DOWELS
H
WEDGES
STILE
DETAIL OF JOINT "D"
DOWEL JOINT
PLAN K
PANEL
MOULD
GROOVE FOR PANEL
BOTTOM RAIL
MITRE
WEATHER BOARD
HAUNCHED TENON
225×50 BOTTOM RAIL
L
DETAIL OF JOINT "E"
O
GROOVE
125×16 DOWEL
BRICK ARCH
PLASTER
R.C. LINTEL
TOP RAIL
HEAD
110×70 HEAD
25MM PANEL
1825
BOTTOM RAIL
175×25 SKIRTING
WEATHER BOARD
OAK THRESHOLD
25
175
20
D.P.C.
328
B SECTION
TILED KEY
D 115×75 TOP RAIL
F
CYLINDER RIM NIGHT LATCH
UPRIGHT MORTICE LOCK
115×75 FRAME
25 THICK RAISED & FIELDED PANEL
115×50 STILE
E 225×50 BOTTOM RAIL
G
60 THICK STONE TREAD
BRICK-ON-EDGE RISER
A ELEVATION
PLASTER
SKIRTING
MOULD
910
110×70 FRAME
WEATHER BOARD
115×50 STILE
C
FACE OF BRICK RISER
STONE TREADS
PLAN
110×70 HEAD (DOOR FRAME)
2MM CLEARANCE
110×45 TOP RAIL
3MM CLEARANCE
12
BOLECTION MOULD
P
50
13
70
38
22
RAISED & FIELDED PANEL
SECTION "F"
75×25 (OUT OF) WEATHER BOARD
220×45 BOTTOM RAIL
Q
THROATS
OAK THRESHOLD
BORE-HOLES (2)
MASTIC
35
FLOOR BOARD
STONE TREAD
SECTION "G"
BOTTOM RAIL
R
25×6 WEATHER BAR
CEMENT MORTAR
FLOOR BOARD
STONE STEP
LEAD
ALTERNATIVE TO "Q"
25MM PANEL
Z
115×50 STILE
225×50 BOTTOM RAIL
DOWELS
125×16
50
SECTION "NN"
ELEVATION
DOWEL JOINT
STRIKING PLATE
LUG
PLATE WITH LEVER HANDLE
BUSH
75
S
8 SPINDLE
TWO THUS
UPRIGHT MORTICE LOCK
M
SCALE FOR M & O MM
SCALE FOR H, J, K, L, E S MM
SCALE FOR P, Q & R MM

FIGURE 48

dowelled joint it is being increasingly recognized that modern methods of production have evolved a door, having dowelled joints, which is eminently satisfactory considering its relative low cost. Drastic changes have taken place in the making of doors; most imported doors and thousands of doors made daily by mass production methods in this country have dowelled and not morticed and tenoned joints.

The door shown in Fig. 48 has a 22 mm (finished) thick raised, sunk and fielded panel with bolection mouldings on both sides (see P); alternative mouldings may be selected from Fig. 46. Whilst certain timbers, such as mahogany, can be obtained of sufficient width to enable this wide panel to be formed in one piece, it may be formed in two or three pieces carefully jointed together. This jointing is done by shooting the edges of each piece to a true plane so that the adjacent edges will make a good fit throughout the length of each piece; the edges are glued, fitted together, securely cramped until the glue has set, when the panel is planed over to a smooth finish; this is called *jointing*. Any panel exceeding 280 mm in width for an average good quality internal door should be jointed in this manner.

Attention is drawn to the construction at the bottom of the door to prevent the access of water (see Q). An oak (or similar hard wearing timber) sill or threshold extends the full width of the door opening, well screwed to the floor and bedded on mastic. The large groove on the inside serves to catch any water which may have penetrated and which escapes down the two boreholes. The top of this threshold is approximately on a level with that of a door mat (assuming that a " mat well "—which is not recommended as it is difficult to keep clean—has not been provided). There is therefore little danger of anyone tripping over the threshold. Incidentally, small sills or projecting weather-bars are more dangerous in this respect than are deeper and wider sills. An alternative method of weather exclusion is shown at R, Fig. 48, the wrought-iron weather-bar being let into the dovetailed sinking and secured with molten lead, run in hot and afterwards well caulked (consolidated with a blunt chisel); this lead is covered flush with the top of the step with cement mortar so as to exclude rain-water which may otherwise cause discoloration. The moulded weather-board is tongued into the bottom rail as shown and should fit as tightly as practicable between the door posts; this throws rain clear of the threshold.

Hardware.—The door would be hung with three 100 mm butt hinges as described on p. 90. It would be fitted with a 75 mm four-lever *upright mortice lock* with *striking plate* (see S, Fig. 48). This type of lock is necessary, for, owing to the absence of a middle rail, the usual type of mortice lock (see H, Fig. 43) would be too long, and the two handles should be of the *lever* type as shown, for if knobs were used (as illustrated at X′, Fig. 43), injury to the hand may be caused owing to their close proximity to the door post. The striking plate serves a similar purpose for a mortice lock as does a staple for a rim lock, and is housed and screwed to the rebate of the post after two small mortices to receive the ends of the bolts have been cut in the post. The projecting lug on the plate is slightly bent so that, when the bevelled latch bolt strikes it as the door is being closed, the bolt will gradually be pressed in. This furniture may be obtained in bronze, brass, chromium plated or oxidized silver metal, bakelite, etc.

A Cylinder Rim Night Latch with staple (see M, N, O, P and Q, Fig. 52) would be required in addition to the above lock. This is one of many patent locks which are on the market and the complete latch consists of a bronze *cylinder* fitting N, the latch O, and the staple P; Q shows a section through the latch attached to the door. The fitting N comprises a separate circular rim with its inner edge rebated to receive the circular *face plate* which is cast on the *case* (see N and Q); the case contains the cylinder to which the spindle is attached and this cylinder is caused to rotate within the case by the action of a key. The latch bolt may be operated from the outside by the key which is inserted in the cylinder to rotate both it and the spindle for the latter to cause the bolt mechanism to function, or the bolt may be shot back from the staple by turning the knob of the latch from the inside. The *locking arm* (see O) is used when required to permanently fix the bolt so that it cannot be operated by either the key or the knob, and thus the bolt may be fixed in the staple to afford greater security or it may be fixed when it is clear of the staple.

The directions for fixing this cylinder latch are as follows: A 32 mm diameter hole is bored through the door, the centre of the hole being 60 mm from the edge of the door; the cylinder fitting N is passed through the hole from the outside, the back plate (see Q) is screwed to the back of the door; two long screws are then passed through holes in the back plate to secure the lug attached to the case; the end of the spindle is passed through the bush of the latch O, and the latter is screwed to the back of the door. The staple is screwed to the edge of the door.

One pair of antique bronze *flush bolts* may also be provided (see S, Fig. 43) These are not so conspicuous as the barrel type, as the back plate is screwed through the stile in a housing formed to bring the plate flush with the face of the stile. The end of the bottom bolt slides into a metal socket (S′) let into the floor or step, and the top bolt engages in a socket fitted into the head of the frame.

Sometimes a *letter plate*, preferably of antique bronze, is required (see K and L, Fig. 52). The flap opens inwards and is suspended on a horizontal rod round one end of which is coiled a spring which forces the flap tightly against the back of the plate. A mortice, approximately 150 mm long and 50 mm deep, is made in the door with the horizontal edges splayed downwards (see L), and the fitting, which entirely covers the hole, is secured to the door by means of two screws which are threaded to stumps.

A door chain as described on p. 91 may be fixed.

Door Casing or Linings.—Whilst external doors are hung to solid frames, it is customary to fix internal doors to casings or linings which provide a suitable finish to the openings. Casings are fixed either to (*a*) pallets, (*b*) plugs or (*c*) grounds.

(*a*) *Pallet pieces* or slips, 10 mm thick, are built into the bed joints at the jambs of the openings as shown at Q, Fig. 42, and D, Fig. 49, and at intervals as described on p. 84. This method of fixing is very general.

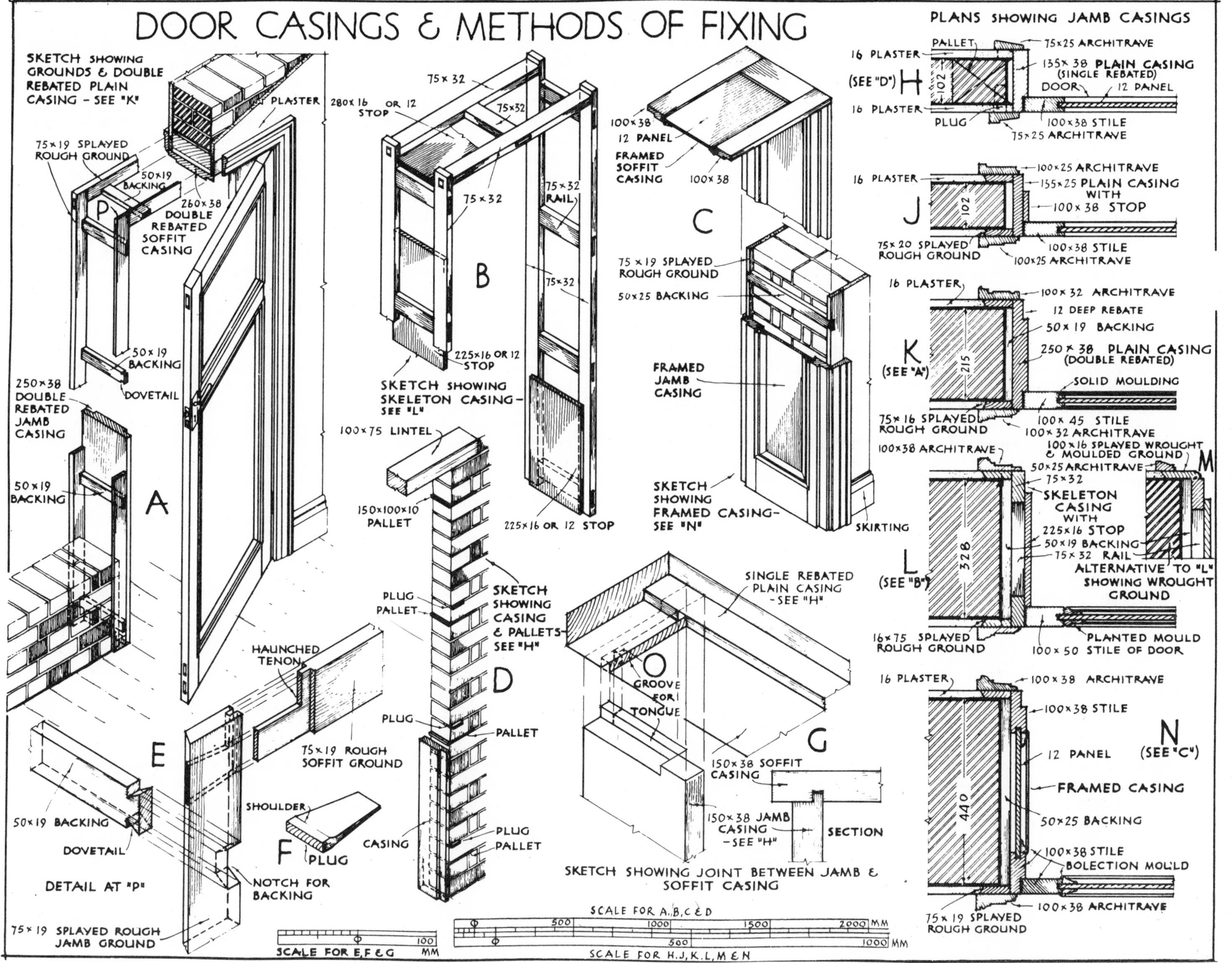
DOOR CASINGS & METHODS OF FIXING
SKETCH SHOWING GROUNDS & DOUBLE REBATED PLAIN CASING - SEE "K"
SKETCH SHOWING SKELETON CASING - SEE "L"
SKETCH SHOWING FRAMED CASING - SEE "N"
SKETCH SHOWING CASING & PALLETS - SEE "H"
SKETCH SHOWING JOINT BETWEEN JAMB & SOFFIT CASING
DETAIL AT "P"
PLANS SHOWING JAMB CASINGS
SCALE FOR A, B, C & D
SCALE FOR E, F & G
SCALE FOR H, J, K, L, M & N

FIGURE 49

(*b*) A cheaper and less satisfactory method is to plug the jambs. *Wood plugs* (which should be of hardwood but are often made from pieces of floor boards), shaped as shown at F, Fig. 49, are driven into holes formed in the mortar joints; they are driven tightly up to their shoulders and would take the place of the pallets shown at D, Fig. 49. The plugs indicated at D would be used for the fixing of architraves (see p. 120).

(*c*) *Grounds.*—As implied, the purpose of these is to provide a groundwork for the casings and architraves. This method of fixing is now only adopted in the best practice. The simplest form consists of 20 mm thick pieces of undressed timber (when they are called *rough grounds*),[1] and are usually 75 mm wide, although this depends upon the size of the architraves. They provide a continuous means of fixing for the casings such as is not afforded by plugs or pallets. One edge is sometimes splayed to afford a key for the plaster (see A, E, J, K, L and N, Fig. 49). The jamb grounds are fixed in true alignment on each face of the walls to plugs at intervals, and the head or soffit grounds are nailed to the lintel (see A). They project about 20 mm beyond the jambs, depending upon the size of the brick or stone opening and that of the door. In good work, the head grounds are haunched tenoned and wedged to the jamb grounds (see P and E). This preparation is all that is necessary for 102 mm walls; for thicker walls, however, 50 mm wide by 20 mm or 25 mm thick short horizontal *backing pieces* are fixed to the edges of the grounds (see A, C, K, L and N). These cross pieces provide extra means of fixing the wider casings and, if the ends are dovetailed and fitted into notches formed in the grounds (see A and E), they are effective in preventing the grounds from expanding and twisting when they absorb moisture from the plaster, which is applied subsequently to the walls. The backings are fixed near to the top and bottom of the jambs and at about 600 mm intervals.

There are three types of casings, *i.e.*, (1) plain, (2) skeleton and (3) framed.

(1) *Plain Casings.*—These are usually prepared from 38 mm thick boards and are suitable for openings in walls which do not exceed 215 mm thick. They may be either single rebated (see D, G and H, Fig. 49, and H and K, Fig. 50) or double rebated (see A and K, Fig. 49, and B, C and D, Fig. 52). Alternatively, in cheap work, a 13 mm or 16 mm thick stop is nailed to the casing, when the thickness of the latter may then be reduced to 25 mm (see J, Fig. 49). Double rebating a wide lining gives it a balanced appearance which is noticeable when the door is open. The soffit casing is grooved or *trenched* to receive the tongues formed on the jamb linings (see G, Fig. 49). This groove extends to the outer edge when softwood is to be used and which would be painted, but if the linings are of hardwood and subsequently polished the groove in the soffit does not extend right across but is stopped to house the abbreviated tongue as shown by thick broken lines at O, Fig. 49.

(2) *Skeleton Casings* (see B and L, Fig. 49).—This type consists of a skeleton jamb and soffit framing comprising 75 mm by 32 mm stuff to which 13 or 16 mm thick boards or stops are nailed to give the appearance of a double rebated lining. The short rails of the framing are tenoned to the long members, and the latter of the soffit framing are tenoned to the jamb framing (see B). The short rails should coincide with the backings and be nailed to them after the long members have been secured to the rough grounds; the stops are then nailed to the framing. An alternative detail is shown at M to introduce a dressed or wrought ground which requires only a small architrave. Skeleton linings for thick walls are cheap and effective, although there is a danger of the wide stops splitting if they shrink excessively, as movement is restricted when they are securely fixed at their edges.

(3) *Framed Casings* (see C and N, Fig. 49).—This is the best form of lining for openings in thick walls. It consists of panelled jamb and soffit frames, and the construction conforms to the principles of panelled door construction. The treatment of the panels should be in keeping with the design of the door. This casing is fixed to the grounds and backings as described for a skeleton lining.

Casings secured to grounds are less liable to damage during the subsequent building operations than those fixed to plugs or pallets, as they are not fixed to the grounds until after the plastering has been completed.

Although internal doors are generally fixed to casings, there are certain exceptions. Thus, heavy internal doors (such as the framed, ledged, braced and battened type), as used for warehouses, etc., are sometimes hung with straps and gudgeon hooks fixed in jamb stones (see p. 90), and the casings are then dispensed with. Another exception is shown at F, Fig. 43, where a frame and not a casing is used. Internal coal-house, etc., doors are often fixed to frames instead of casings.

Two Panelled Door (see B, Fig. 46, and Fig. 50).—The construction of the framing is similar to that described for the single panelled door with the exception that provision has to be made for the *middle* or *lock rail*, so called as the lock is usually secured to it. The height of this rail depends of course upon the design, and whilst it was the invariable practice to make it at a convenient height for the door handle (which is approximately 840 mm to the centre of the rail), this height is now often departed from. The position of the middle rail in the door shown at B, Fig. 46, is such as to give two panels of equal height, whilst the centre of the lock rail of the door in Fig. 50 is 1·4 m from the floor. It will be observed that, whilst the appearance of this latter door is satisfactory, the position of the lock is not conveniently accessible for small children. If this door is to be fitted with a rim lock, the middle rail will be formed with a single tenon at each end when the rail is only 100 mm deep as shown, and with a pair of single tenons at each end when the rail is 175 mm or wider. If, however, a mortice lock is to be used, the door is often 50 mm thick, and the ends of the lock rail will be prepared as follows: If it is a narrow rail, the end to be fitted into the " hanging " stile will be prepared with a single tenon and the opposite

[1] These are distinct from *wrought grounds* which are used in conjunction with architraves (see M, Fig. 49).

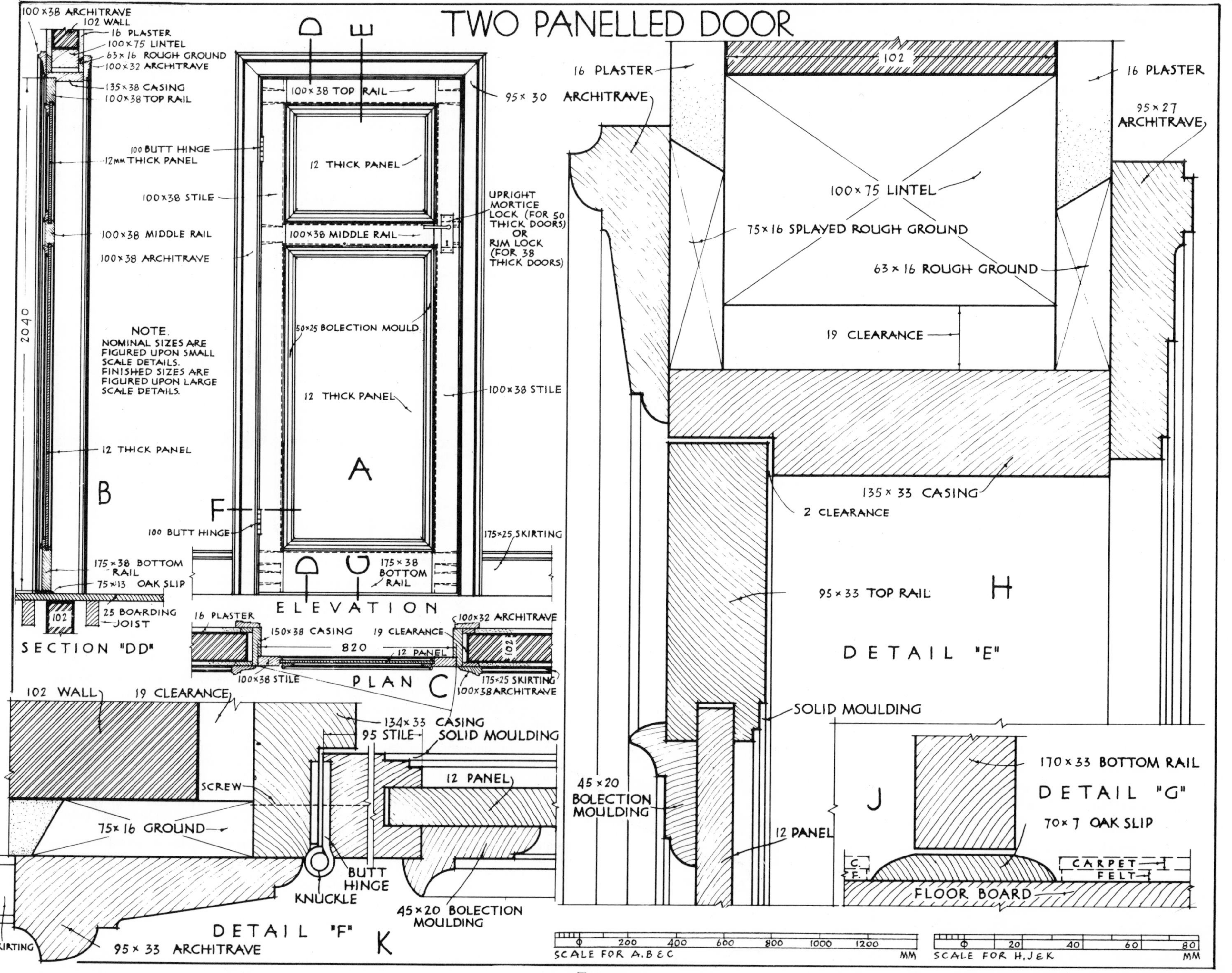
TWO PANELLED DOOR
100×38 ARCHITRAVE
102 WALL
16 PLASTER
100×75 LINTEL
63×16 ROUGH GROUND
100×32 ARCHITRAVE
135×38 CASING
100×38 TOP RAIL
100 BUTT HINGE
12MM THICK PANEL
100×38 STILE
100×38 MIDDLE RAIL
100×38 ARCHITRAVE
2040
NOTE.
NOMINAL SIZES ARE FIGURED UPON SMALL SCALE DETAILS.
FINISHED SIZES ARE FIGURED UPON LARGE SCALE DETAILS.
12 THICK PANEL
B
175×38 BOTTOM RAIL
75×13 OAK SLIP
25 BOARDING
102
JOIST
SECTION "DD"
100×38 TOP RAIL
95×30
12 THICK PANEL
UPRIGHT MORTICE LOCK (FOR 50 THICK DOORS) OR RIM LOCK (FOR 38 THICK DOORS)
100×38 MIDDLE RAIL
50×25 BOLECTION MOULD
12 THICK PANEL
100×38 STILE
A
F
100 BUTT HINGE
175×25 SKIRTING
175×38 BOTTOM RAIL
ELEVATION
16 PLASTER
150×38 CASING
19 CLEARANCE
100×32 ARCHITRAVE
820
12 PANEL
102
100×38 STILE
PLAN C
175×25 SKIRTING
100×38 ARCHITRAVE
16 PLASTER
ARCHITRAVE
102
16 PLASTER
95×27 ARCHITRAVE
100×75 LINTEL
75×16 SPLAYED ROUGH GROUND
63×16 ROUGH GROUND
19 CLEARANCE
135×33 CASING
2 CLEARANCE
95×33 TOP RAIL
H
DETAIL "E"
SOLID MOULDING
45×20 BOLECTION MOULDING
12 PANEL
J
170×33 BOTTOM RAIL
DETAIL "G"
70×7 OAK SLIP
C.
F.
CARPET
FELT
FLOOR BOARD
102 WALL
19 CLEARANCE
134×33 CASING
95 STILE
SOLID MOULDING
12 PANEL
SCREW
75×16 GROUND
BUTT HINGE
KNUCKLE
45×20 BOLECTION MOULDING
SKIRTING
95×33 ARCHITRAVE
DETAIL "F" K
0 200 400 600 800 1000 1200
SCALE FOR A.B E C MM
0 20 40 60 80
SCALE FOR H.J E K MM

FIGURE 50

end will have two tenons (to form what is called a *twin tenon*) which are equal in width to that of the rail less the depth of the panel grooves and with a space between them equal to the thickness of the lock; for a wider rail, the end secured to the hanging stile will have a pair of single tenons (as shown at A, Fig. 52) whilst the opposite or " striking " end may have four tenons, usually called a *pair of twin tenons* (see Fig. 51), in order that the preparation for the lock will not weaken the joint. This latter figure shows the mortice lock in position. Note that the combined thickness of the twin tenons equals one-third that of the rail.

Mortice locks are now available which are only 11 mm thick and they obviate the necessity for using twin tenons unless, for some special reason, a large lock is required. Another type of lock is triangular or wedge-shaped and necessitates for its accomodation the removal of only a small portion of the tenon.

A mortice lock is illustrated at H and I, Fig. 43, and its mechanism is described on p. 88. Note that the steel case is fixed to a steel *fore-end* to which is secured a brass *face plate* by two set-screws.

It is necessary to keep the bottom of the door at least 13 mm clear of the floor to enable it to pass a carpet with underfelt. It is advisable to screw to the floor a 10 mm thick hardwood slip with splayed or rounded edges in order to minimise draughts (see J, Fig. 50). Alternatively the door may be hung with a pair of 100 mm polished brass *skew butt hinges* (sometimes called *lifting* or *rising butt hinges*) instead of the ordinary butt hinges (see Z, Fig. 43). These lifting hinges cause the door to rise 13 mm (and thus clear a mat or carpet) on being opened on account of the helical knuckle joint. The top edge of the door and the rebate on the soffit of the casing must be splayed to permit of this vertical movement. These hinges are very conspicuous and are objected to for this reason, although their appearance is somewhat improved if the knuckles are provided with moulded ends.

A *door stop* is often used to prevent a door handle or projecting key from damaging the plaster or a piece of furniture situated near to a door. This stop may be entirely of rubber or a rubber pad in a bronze fitting (see R, Fig. 52), and it is screwed to the floor so as to restrict the swing of the door.

Four Panelled Door (see D, Fig. 46, and Fig. 52).—This introduces two central members of the framing called *muntins*. Note that the stiles are continuous for the full height of the door, the rails are tenoned into the stiles, and the muntins are stub tenoned into the rails for about 50 mm (see A and F, Fig. 52). The general construction follows very closely that already described. One special advantage of this door is the narrow panels which are employed. These can be obtained in one width, and therefore jointing (described on p. 96) is eliminated.

Whilst a rim lock is shown at A and B, Fig. 52, the less conspicuous mortice lock with knob or lever handle furniture may be preferred.

Finger Plates were often fixed to both sides of the stile of a panelled door just above (and sometimes below) the lock, but these are not now in much demand unless there is a likelihood of damage being caused to the paint or varnish by finger marks. These can be obtained in various sizes in bronze, oxidised silver, etc. (see J, Fig. 52).

Doors shown at C, E, F, G and H, Fig. 46.—A detailed description of these doors is not necessary for their construction will be readily understood on reference to the details shown in respect to the single, two and four panelled doors. In every case the stiles are continuous, the rails are either tenoned or dowelled to them and the muntins are similarly secured to the rails.

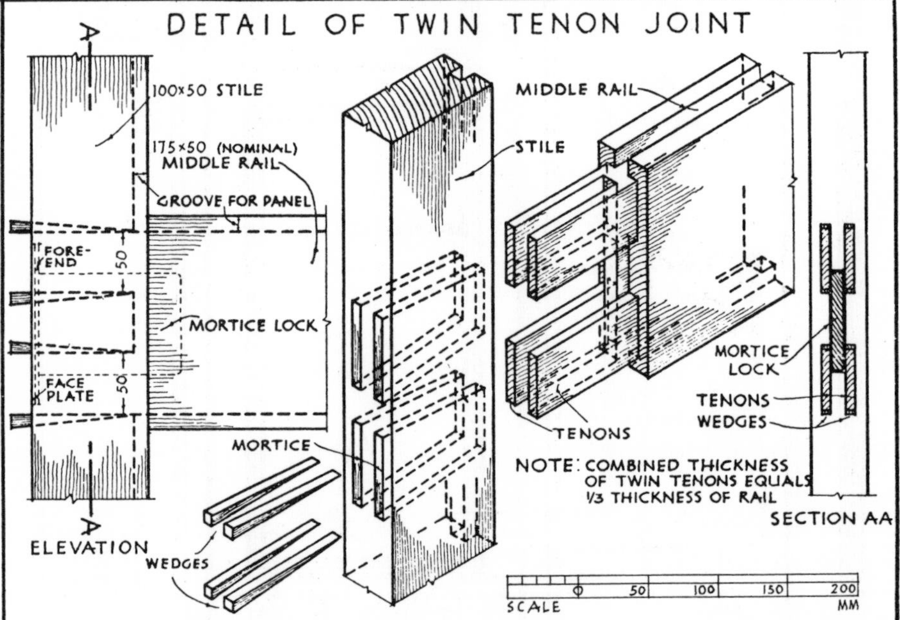

FIGURE 51

Manufacture of Panelled Doors.—Most doors are (*a*) manufactured by machinery, some are (*b*) prepared principally by hand.

(a) **Machine-made Doors.**—Reference has been made on p. 96 to the enormous number of doors which are machine made. Mass production has been responsible for a large reduction in the cost of doors and this is the chief reason for their popularity. In the manufacture of standard doors the whole of the operations of planing the timber, reducing it to the correct widths, forming the joints, gluing and finally cramping the members together are done by machinery. It is also employed to trim the door to the size of the frame, form the lock mortice and screw the hinges to the door.

Many of these doors are dowel jointed, as shown at J and M, Fig 48, and the following is a brief description of the operations involved in their manufacture: The timber is sawn to suitable scantlings, artificially seasoned, taken to the planing machine where it is surfaced on both sides and edges, sawing machines cut the door panels, stiles and rails into correct widths, rails are bored glued and dowelled by a machine in one operation, stiles are bored by a machine, glue is squirted into the dowel holes in the stiles, rails with their projecting dowels are fitted into the holes in the stiles after the panels have been slipped into the grooves and, finally, the assembled members are cramped together to complete the door.

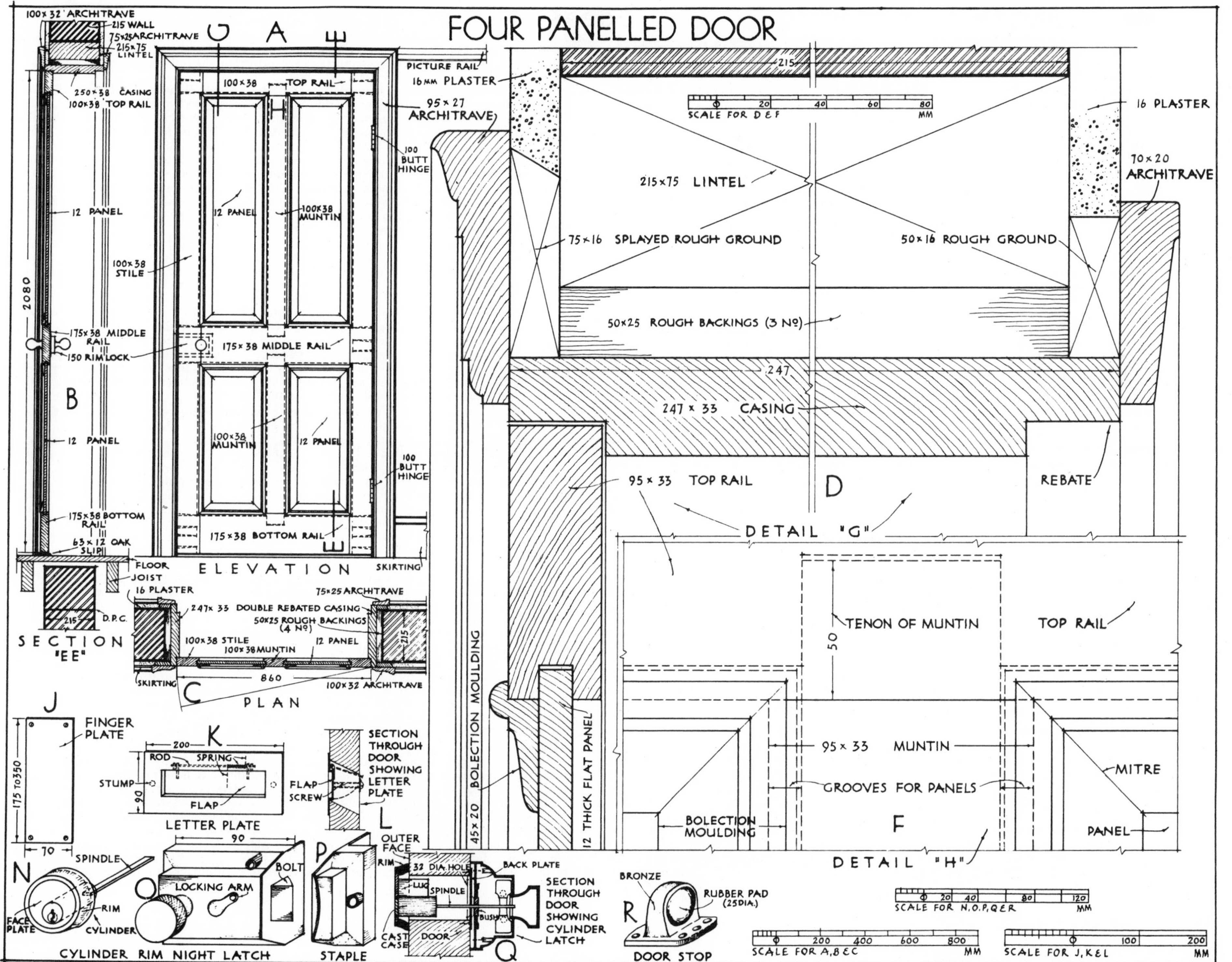
FOUR PANELLED DOOR
100×32 ARCHITRAVE
215 WALL
75×25 ARCHITRAVE
215×75 LINTEL
250×38 CASING
100×38 TOP RAIL
12 PANEL
2080
175×38 MIDDLE RAIL
150 RIM LOCK
B
12 PANEL
175×38 BOTTOM RAIL
63×12 OAK SLIP
FLOOR
JOIST
215
D.P.C.
SECTION "EE"
G A E
100×38
TOP RAIL
95×27 ARCHITRAVE
100 BUTT HINGE
12 PANEL
100×38 MUNTIN
100×38 STILE
175×38 MIDDLE RAIL
100×38 MUNTIN
12 PANEL
175×38 BOTTOM RAIL
ELEVATION
SKIRTING
PICTURE RAIL
16MM PLASTER
16 PLASTER
75×25 ARCHITRAVE
247×33 DOUBLE REBATED CASING
50×25 ROUGH BACKINGS (4 Nº)
100×38 STILE
100×38 MUNTIN
12 PANEL
860
SKIRTING
100×32 ARCHITRAVE
C PLAN
215
SCALE FOR D E F
MM
215×75 LINTEL
16 PLASTER
70×20 ARCHITRAVE
75×16 SPLAYED ROUGH GROUND
50×16 ROUGH GROUND
50×25 ROUGH BACKINGS (3 Nº)
247
247×33 CASING
95×33 TOP RAIL
D
REBATE
DETAIL "G"
TENON OF MUNTIN
50
TOP RAIL
95×33 MUNTIN
MITRE
GROOVES FOR PANELS
BOLECTION MOULDING
F
PANEL
45×20 BOLECTION MOULDING
12 THICK FLAT PANEL
DETAIL "H"
J
FINGER PLATE
175 TO 350
70
K
200
ROD
SPRING
STUMP
90
FLAP
LETTER PLATE
SECTION THROUGH DOOR SHOWING LETTER PLATE
FLAP
SCREW
L
N
SPINDLE
RIM
FACE PLATE
CYLINDER
O
LOCKING ARM
BOLT
90
CYLINDER RIM NIGHT LATCH
P
STAPLE
OUTER FACE
RIM
32 DIA. HOLE
LUG
SPINDLE
BACK PLATE
BUSH
CAST CASE
DOOR
Q
SECTION THROUGH DOOR SHOWING CYLINDER LATCH
BRONZE
R
RUBBER PAD (25DIA.)
DOOR STOP
SCALE FOR N, O, P, Q E R
MM
SCALE FOR A, B E C
MM
SCALE FOR J, K E L
MM

FIGURE 52

(b) Hand-made Doors.—Whilst machinery has eliminated most of the operations which were formerly performed by hand, there is still a demand for doors and similar framework which require a certain amount of hand preparation. This applies particularly to the highest quality framed and panelled doors and those which are not of standard size. The operations involved are: (1) setting out, (2) forming mortices and tenons, (3) gluing and wedging up and (4) cleaning off.

(1) *Setting Out.*—This is the reproduction on a board (called a *setting out rod*) of the full size details of the door.

For a framed piece, such as a door, the rod would be set out as shown at A, Fig. 53 which indicates full size vertical and horizontal sections of the four-panelled door, casing etc. illustrated in Fig. 52. Alternatively, the vertical section, called the *height rod*, is set out on one face of the board, and the horizontal section, called the *width rod*, is detailed on the reverse.

The pieces of timber to be used for the various members should be carefully selected to obviate waste during conversion. If machinery is not available, each piece is cut down by means of a rip saw (see p. 125) and across the grain by a panel saw (see p. 125). The stuff is then *trued up*. This is done by first testing for " winding " or " twist." A pair of *winding strips* (pieces of carefully dressed mahogany, 350 mm by 50 mm by 13 mm, with parallel edges) is used for this purpose, one being placed at each end on top and at right angles to the length of the timber when lying flat on the joiners' bench. If these strips are not parallel when sighting along their upper edges a jack plane (see 21, Fig. 67) is applied until the highest parts are removed and the surface is perfectly true as proved by the strips and a straight edge. A trying plane (see 26, Fig. 67) is then used to give a smooth finish. The joiner pencils his characteristic mark, called a *face side mark* (see E and G, Fig. 53), on the face and this should always point towards the best edge. This edge, called the *face edge*, is then dressed by a jack plane and subsequently by a trying plane until it is straight, smooth and at right angles to the dressed face, a try square (E, Fig. 53) being used to test for squareness. He pencils his *face edge* on this edge and this may be a single stroke as a continuation of the face side mark (see F). Both face side and face edge must be perfectly true as all subsequent gauging and setting out operations are referred to them. A marking gauge (see 4, Fig 67) is now used to mark off the width of the member, this mark being continuous from end to end and parallel to the face edge. A plane is applied to dress down to the guage mark to form the *back edge*. The piece is gauged to the required thickness and the *back face* is then planed to remove any excess of wood down to the gauge mark.

The whole of the members having been dressed in this manner are marked, the position of the rails, depth of grooves, etc., being transferred to them from the setting out rod A. Thus, commencing with the stiles, one is placed on the height rod and the postions of the rails and 13 mm depth of panel grooves are pricked on its face edge (see F, Fig. 53, which shows the lines transferred from the rod). The mortices for the rail tenons are then set out on the face edge of the stile. This and the second stile, together with the muntins, are placed as shown at E, and aided by the try square, the shoulders (see J) are squared down. The muntins are removed and squared all round for the shoulders which are to fit against the edges of the rails. The mortice lines are set out on the face edge of the second stile as shown at F, and as indicated, some joiners emphasize the mortices by drawing blue pencil lines between the mortice lines. The mortice lines are squared over to the back edge of each stile (see broken lines at F) and the positions of the 10 mm thick wedges are marked on the back edge (see G). Note that the length of the stiles exceeds slightly that shown on the rod to protect the door during transportation.

The setting of the rails from the width rod (see A) is similar to that described for stiles. The setting out for muntins, shoulders and haunches (or haunchings) on the top rail is shown at K, and the middle rail is shown set out at L—the latter indicating the names applied to the various lines.

(2) *Forming Mortices and Tenons.*—The stiles are now morticed. If a mortising machine is not available, the mortices are made with a mortise chisel (see p. 126) and mallet (see 23, Fig. 67). A mortise gauge (9, Fig. 67) is used to scribe or mark the mortices on each edge of the stile, the points of the gauge being set to the width of the chisel which should equal one-third the thickness of the stuff. These mortices are always gauged from the face side of each stile. Each mortice is cut half-way through, commencing at the centre of the back edge and removing the core by small cuts, and then the mortice is completed from the face edge in a similar manner; a paring chisel (35, Fig. 67) is used to finish off. The 50 mm deep stub mortices are formed on the rails to receive the tenons at the ends of the muntins.

The ends of the rails are gauged from the face side as shown at B, Fig. 53. The " mortice lines " are rip sawn down to the " haunch lines," the " waste " is removed, and the " gauge lines " are sawn down to the shoulder " lines " (see C). The panel groove is then formed by means of a plough (31, Fig. 67) on the face edge from end to end of each stile, the top face edge of the bottom rail, both edges of the middle rail, the bottom or face edge of the top rail and both edges of each muntin; the plough iron must be of the proper size, be set at the correct depth (13 mm in this case), and the plough must always be worked from the face side of each member. The tenon checks (outer portions) are now removed by using the tenon saw (13, Fig. 67) to carefully cut down the centre of the shoulder lines to complete the end as shown at D, Fig. 53. The tenons on the muntins are formed in a similar manner.

After the corners of the ends of the tenons have been chiselled off so that they readily engage in the mortices, the whole of the members are assembled temporarily to see if the joints fit accurately, and the framing is put aside pending the preparation of the panels.

The panels are then made. The dimensions are taken from the rod or framing, one face and edge are planed with the trying plane, and the face and edge marks are put on these. A panel gauge (see p. 125) is used to mark the required width, the panel is cut along this line, and the ends are squared and cut to the exact size. The panel is now *mulleted* or gauged; the mullet—a piece of wood grooved to the required size (see H, Fig. 53)—is slipped along the edges of the panel to indicate any excessively thick places which are eased by planing. The four panels are made in this manner, the sides are smoothed by a smoothing plane (see p. 126), glass paper is rubbed across the grain, and the panels are inserted temporarily in the framing.

(3) *Gluing and Wedging Up.*—Two pieces of scantling are placed on the bench as shown at J, Fig. 53. A cramp is necessary to ensure that the shoulders of the various members fit tightly.

One form of cramp, called a T-cramp, is shown at J. It consists of a steel bar of T-section which is from 45 to 70 mm deep, 20 to 25 mm at its flange or widest part, and from 610 to 2130 mm long; it has a series of 13 mm diameter holes along its length into which a 75 mm by 13 mm round steel taper peg is inserted; this peg is attached by a chain to a shoe, the jaws of which pass over the flange of the bar to enable the shoe to slide along it; at the other end of the bar there is a metal head which is threaded to allow the working of a screw which has a rectangular plate at one end having jaws which slide along the bar flange when the metal rod handle is rotated. An extension bar may be fitted to the cramp in order that it may be used for large framings.

The door is taken to pieces and both sides of the tenons and the insides of the mortices are glued; it is at once reassembled; the cramp is then used. Commencing at the middle rail, the cramp is fixed in the position as shown at J; the shoe is slid along to the required position, the peg is inserted in the appropriate hole, small protecting blocks of wood are placed between the stiles and the shoe and screw cheeks, and the cramp is then screwed up tightly to bring the shoulders right up. The wedges are dipped into the glue-pot and tightly driven in at each end. The cramp is moved to the bottom rail (shown by broken lines at J), tightened up and wedged as before described, the bottom wedge being driven first so as to bring the shoulders of the bottom muntin tight up against the rails. The cramp is finally moved to the third position along the top rail, glued wedges are inserted and driven home, the top wedge at each end being fixed first so as to move the top rail to close the joints between the top muntin and rails. The cramp is removed and the projecting ends of the rails are sawn off.

(4) *Cleaning Off.*—Any superfluous glue is removed from the joints. The trying plane is appled on the muntins to bring them level with the rails and the latter are levelled to the face of the stiles, any inequalities at the shoulders being removed. A smoothing plane is then used, and if necessary the surfaces are scraped before being glass papered. The outer edges of the door are not planed, nor are the horns removed, until the door is being hung in position.

If the door is moulded, the hand operations vary with the type. Thus, if the panels are to have solid mouldings, the face edges of the stiles, rails and muntins will be moulded to the required shape by means of the appropriate moulding plane (see p. 126) before they are assembled. The moulded edges of the stiles will be continuous, those on the rails will be scribed to them (see Fig. 49) and those on the muntins will be scribed to the rail mouldings. If planted mouldings are required, they are formed by planes to the required section shown on the rod. Mouldings are planted in the following manner: The ends of each piece are cut to a 45° mitre—a mitre block (see 51, Fig. 67) being used for this purpose; the two short lengths are placed in position and the two longer pieces are "sprung" into place; the mouldings are nailed to the framing and the nail heads are punched. Each panel is treated in this manner.[1]

The operation involved in framing the casing will be understood from the foregoing description.

Cutting lists are prepared which give the reference number of the job, together with the number, lengths and nominal and finished widths of the stiles, rails, etc., comprising the door. These lists are available for the workmen responsible for setting out and preparing the various members.

TIMBER WINDOWS

A window includes the frame and one or more sashes which are glazed. The frame may have solid wood members or it may be constructed of comparatively thin pieces to form what is called a *cased* or *boxed frame*. The sashes may be fixed or made to open. The latter, when associated with a solid frame, may be attached by hinges to enable the sash to open either outwards or inwards like a door, or it may be hinged at the lower edge to open inwards, or it may be hung at the top edge to open outwards. Another type of sash is pivoted at the centre to open with the upper half swinging inwards, and another form consists of one or more sashes which slide horizontally. Sashes when made to open in a cased frame slide vertically.

In order to provide sufficient ventilation the Building Regulations stipulate that the minimum area of the openable part of a window or windows shall be one-twentieth of the floor area of the room. The Regulations also require that some part of the openable area shall be not less than 1750 mm above the floor. The window area is frequently at least equal to one-quarter of the floor area and most, if not all, of the sashes are made to open.

[1] As previously mentioned, the extensive use of woodworking machinery has eliminated most of the labours formerly done by hand, and even if standard machine-made doors as described in p. 100 are not required, many of the operations detailed on pp. 102–106 would be performed by machines. Thus the stiles, rails and muntins would be cut into lengths and widths by the *circular saw*; they would be faced and edged on a *surface planer* and taken to a uniform width and thickness on a *thicknessing machine*; the tenons would be formed by a *tenoning machine* and the mortices by a *mortising machine*; if required, they would be solid moulded on the *spindle moulding machine*. Many of these operations can be done by a combined machine called a *general joiner*. The panels would be finished by a *panel planer*. Planted mouldings could be prepared on the *spindle moulder*. After being assembled and cramped, the door would be given a smooth finish by a *sand papering machine*.

Whilst some of these larger and more expensive machines are not available in the smaller shops, there are comparatively few firms who have not a circular saw and mortising and tenoning machines, and are thereby enabled to reduce some of the relatively costly hand labours.

Various woodworking machines are described in Chap. I, Vol. III.

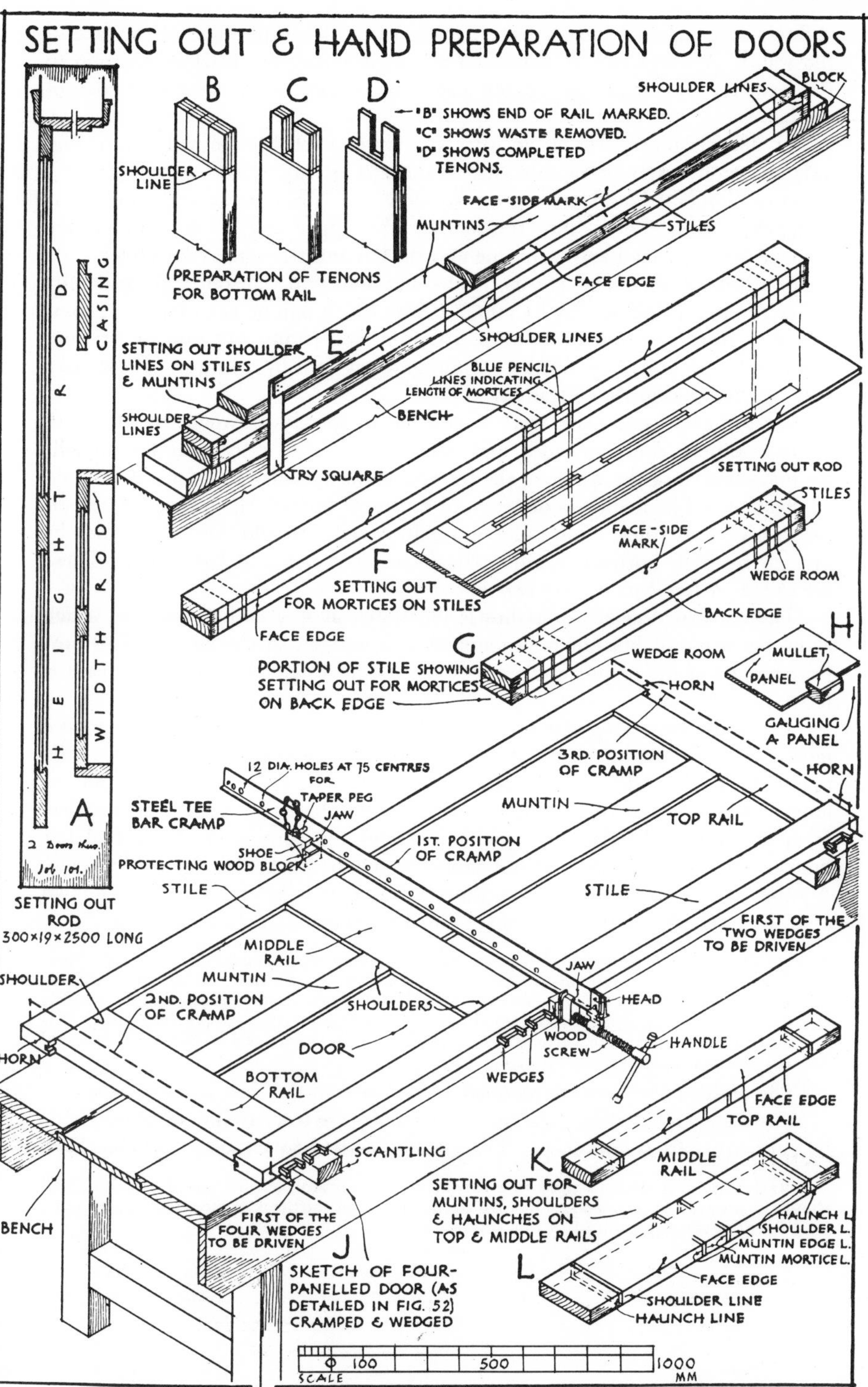

FIGURE 53

Those windows which are to receive extended treatment here are (*a*) solid frames with vertically hung sashes which open outwards, and (*b*) cased frames with vertical sliding sashes. There is also an introduction to mild steel window frames.

(a) Windows with Solid Frames and Vertically Hung Sashes Opening Outwards (see Figs. 54, 55, 56 and 57).—Sashes which are made to open like a door are called *casements*, and the window is usually specified as a *casement window*. It is adopted extensively.

Frame.—If the window has only one sash (see A, Fig. 54), the frame consists of two vertical posts, stiles or *jambs*, a head and a wood sill. If it has two sashes (see B, Fig. 54), the additional vertical member is called a *mullion*. If the frame has a horizontal dividing member (called a *transome*) in addition to mullions, the appearance resembles that shown in Fig. 22, except that the members are of wood instead of stone.

Details A, B and C, Fig. 56, show typical joints of a window frame. Note that the jamb is haunched tenoned at each end and the head and sill are morticed to receive the tenons and wedges. The outer shoulder of the lower end of the jamb is scribed to the sill (see B and section EE at C). These joints are sometimes pinned as described for door frames. The frames may be fixed as described on p. 84, the horns being removed if the frames are fixed after the walling has been completed. The bedding and pointing of the frames must receive special attention if they are not to be built in recesses. The head and jambs are rebated, 13 to 16 mm deep, to receive the sash. The inside edge of the frame may be square, pencil rounded, chamfered, ovolo-moulded, etc., as shown. The capillary grooves are referred to on p. 107.

The sill is sunk-weathered to cast off rain-water. Special attention must be paid to the bed joint between the wood sill and the stone or brick sill, as it is particularly vulnerable. Precautions taken to prevent the access of rain at this point include (*a*) the provision of a metal *water bar*, (*b*) lead tucked into a groove formed in the sill and continued as a covering to the brick sill, and (*c*) a mortar tongue formed in the groove of the sill. With reference to:

(*a*) A groove is formed in the brick sill (see Q, Fig. 58) or stone sill (see L and O, Fig. 25, and Detail T, Fig. 54) and the 25 mm by 6 mm galvanized wrought iron water (or " weather ") bar, which is the full length of the sill, is partially inserted and bedded in cement mortar. The groove in the wood sill is filled with a mixture of white lead ground in linseed oil and the frame is firmly bedded on the mortar spread to receive it with the projecting bar engaging in the groove.

(*b*) The brick sill is covered with lead (no. 4 or 5 weight) which has been *bossed* (shaped) by the plumber and the frame is carefully placed in position with the upturned portion of the lead fitting into the groove of the wood sill (see D and E, Figs. 56 and 57); the efficiency of this joint is increased if white lead mastic is spread along the edge of the lead before the frame is fitted. The lead projects 13 mm beyond the face of the wall and the outer edge is turned under to give a double thickness which adds to its appearance, increases its stiffness and makes it more effective in throwing the water clear of the face of the wall.[1] A water bar, as described above, is sometimes used in addition to the lead, the upturned edge of the lead being dressed over the upper edge of the bar.

(*c*) This is adopted in cheap work and is not a reliable method (see O, Fig. 54); the groove may be rounded (see A and B, Fig. 16).

In a mullioned and transomed window the transome is the continuous member and is tenoned into the jambs; the upper and lower mullions are tenoned into the head and transome and the sill and transome respectively.

Scantlings of Frames.—Heads, jambs, mullions and transomes are generally either 100 mm or 75 mm by 64 mm, 100 mm by 75 mm or 115 mm by 75 mm; sills vary from 100 mm by 64 mm, 100 mm by 75 mm, 115 mm by 75 mm, 115 mm by 90 mm, 125 mm by 75 mm and 175 mm by 75 mm. These sizes may be exceeded for large frames.

For ordinary good-class work it is usual to specify redwood for the head, jambs, mullions and transomes, and either oak, teak or pitch pine for the sill; for first-class work the whole of the frame may be specified to be in oak or teak.

Sashes.—The members of a sash or casement are similar to those of a door, *i.e.*, two vertical stiles, a top rail and a bottom rail. In addition, a sash may be divided by both horizontal and vertical bars or horizontal bars only. These are called *glazing bars* or *sash bars* or *astragals*.

The construction of the sashes is illustrated at H, J and K, Fig. 56, which show the top and bottom rails tenoned and wedged to the stiles. The projecting ends of the tenons and wedges are of course removed before the sash is fixed.

The joints between glazing bars are shown at M and N, Fig. 56. The *scribed joint* at M shows the horizontal bar to be continuous and morticed to receive the tenons formed on the ends of the vertical bars. The chamfered mould on the latter is scribed to the moulding on the horizontal bar. This is the commonest form of joint. The *franked joint* at N shows the continuous horizontal bar morticed to receive the halved and haunched tenons worked on the vertical bars. Another satisfactory method of jointing glazing bars is *halving* and this is shown at M, Fig. 59. All of these joints are glued immediately before assembly.

In both the scribed and franked joints the continuous bars may be either horizontal or vertical, depending upon circumstances. For casements, greater stiffness to the sash is obtained if the short horizontal bars are made continuous and the lengths of vertical member tenoned into them; for vertical sliding sashes (see later) it is customary to make the vertical bars continuous; in the halved joint both horizontal and vertical bars are continuous.

The ends of the bars are tenoned and scribed to the sash stiles or rails.

The sash is rebated for glazing; these rebates are from 16 mm to 20 mm wide by approximately 6 mm deep. The glass is secured by either putty[2] (see Figs.

[1] If the frame is set back to form a 102·5 mm outer reveal, the increased width of lead should be secured by a *lead dowel* formed in the middle of the brick or stone sill (see p. 152).

[2] Putty is whiting ground in raw linseed oil.

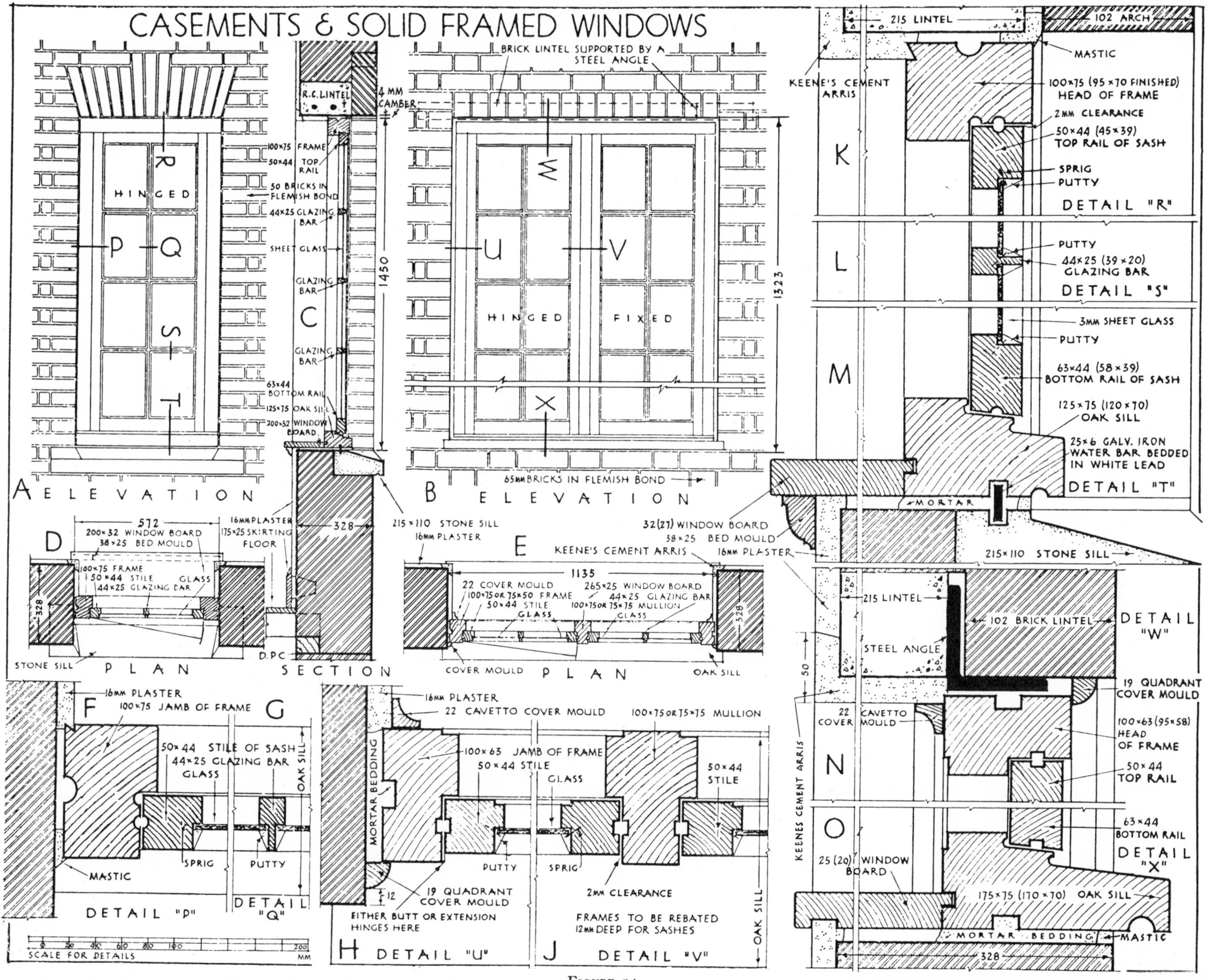
CASEMENTS & SOLID FRAMED WINDOWS
A ELEVATION
HINGED
P Q R S T
R.C. LINTEL
4 MM CAMBER
100×75 FRAME
50×44 TOP RAIL
50 BRICKS IN FLEMISH BOND
44×25 GLAZING BAR
SHEET GLASS
GLAZING BAR
C
1450
63×44 BOTTOM RAIL
125×75 OAK SILL
200×32 WINDOW BOARD
BRICK LINTEL SUPPORTED BY A STEEL ANGLE
W U V X
HINGED
FIXED
1323
65MM BRICKS IN FLEMISH BOND
B ELEVATION
215×110 STONE SILL
16MM PLASTER
328
D
572
200×32 WINDOW BOARD
38×25 BED MOULD
100×75 FRAME
50×44 STILE
44×25 GLAZING BAR
GLASS
16MM PLASTER
175×25 SKIRTING
FLOOR
STONE SILL
PLAN
D.P.C
SECTION
E
KEENE'S CEMENT ARRIS
1135
22 COVER MOULD
100×75 OR 75×50 FRAME
50×44 STILE
GLASS
265×25 WINDOW BOARD
44×25 GLAZING BAR
100×75 OR 75×75 MULLION
COVER MOULD
PLAN
OAK SILL
F
16MM PLASTER
100×75 JAMB OF FRAME
G
50×44 STILE OF SASH
44×25 GLAZING BAR
GLASS
OAK SILL
MASTIC
SPRIG
PUTTY
DETAIL "P"
DETAIL "Q"
SCALE FOR DETAILS
0 20 40 60 80 100 200 MM
16MM PLASTER
22 CAVETTO COVER MOULD
100×75 OR 75×75 MULLION
MORTAR BEDDING
100×63 JAMB OF FRAME
50×44 STILE
GLASS
50×44 STILE
PUTTY
SPRIG
12
19 QUADRANT COVER MOULD
EITHER BUTT OR EXTENSION HINGES HERE
2MM CLEARANCE
FRAMES TO BE REBATED 12MM DEEP FOR SASHES
OAK SILL
H DETAIL "U"
J DETAIL "V"
215 LINTEL
102 ARCH
MASTIC
KEENE'S CEMENT ARRIS
100×75 (95×70 FINISHED) HEAD OF FRAME
2MM CLEARANCE
50×44 (45×39) TOP RAIL OF SASH
SPRIG
PUTTY
K
DETAIL "R"
PUTTY
L
44×25 (39×20) GLAZING BAR
DETAIL "S"
3MM SHEET GLASS
PUTTY
M
63×44 (58×39) BOTTOM RAIL OF SASH
125×75 (120×70) OAK SILL
25×6 GALV. IRON WATER BAR BEDDED IN WHITE LEAD
DETAIL "T"
MORTAR
32(27) WINDOW BOARD
38×25 BED MOULD
16MM PLASTER
215×110 STONE SILL
215 LINTEL
102 BRICK LINTEL
DETAIL "W"
STEEL ANGLE
50
19 QUADRANT COVER MOULD
22 CAVETTO COVER MOULD
100×63 (95×58) HEAD OF FRAME
KEENES CEMENT ARRIS
N
50×44 TOP RAIL
O
63×44 BOTTOM RAIL
DETAIL "X"
25 (20) WINDOW BOARD
175×75 (170×70) OAK SILL
MORTAR BEDDING
MASTIC
328

FIGURE 54

54 and 55, and D and F, Fig. 56) or small fillets called *glazing beads* (see E and G, Fig. 56). Note that the rebates for the glass are on the outside when putty is used and are on the inside[1] when beads are adopted. The glass is usually *sheet glass*[2] and is specified by its thickness; *i.e.*, 2, 3, 4, 5, 5·5 and 6 mm. Glass for small panes is usually 2 or 3 mm thick. *Polished plate glass*[3] is sometimes used for glazing windows in first class work, the usual thickness is 6 mm although thicknesses up to 38 mm are also available. Small metal sprigs (which are without heads) are driven in as shown in the various details to temporarily retain the glass in position until the putty is set. Glazing heads should be secured by small screws—" cups and screws " (see J and R, Fig. 58, and O, Fig. 66)—rather than nails to allow for ready removal when broken panes have to be replaced. The glass should be well bedded in putty before the beads are fixed to prevent the entrance of water.

Scantlings of Sashes.—These vary with the size of sash. Small sashes may be 38 mm (nominal) thick, average sized sashes should be 44 mm thick and large sashes may be 50 mm thick. The stiles and top rails are generally 50 mm wide with deeper (63 to 90 mm) bottom rails to give added strength and an improved appearance. The glazing bars are equal to the thickness of the frame and are out of 25 or 32 mm thick stuff, the latter being reduced to 25 mm finished thickness unless the sheets of glass are large.

The bottom of the inside of the opening is shown finished with a 25 or 38 mm (nominal) thick *window board.* This is tongued into the wood sill (to prevent any open joint showing when the board shrinks). To prevent it casting or twisting, it is secured to plugs driven into the vertical joints of the wall or nailed to 38 mm thick bearers plugged to the top of the wall. Tiles may be used instead of a wood window board to form an internal sill; these may be white or coloured glazed tiles (about 10 mm thick) or they may be square quarry tiles (about 25 mm thick) bedded on cement (see F, Fig. 16).

The following items, not already referred to, should be considered in connection with Figs. 54 and 56. The panes of glass are comparatively small and the design is particularly suited for houses as the small sheets conform in scale. A satisfactory proportion of pane is obtained if its height approximates to the length of the hypotenuse of a right-angled triangle having both sides equal to the width (see T, Fig. 58). A reasonable size is 280 mm high by 190 to 200 mm wide and has been adopted in the elevations A and B, Fig. 54. The vertical bars may be omitted to emphasize the effect of horizontality. The windows at A and B are not built into recesses such as are shown at E, Fig. 8. This is a *weakness* for, unless great care is taken in the bedding and pointing of the

[1] Beads are placed outside when double glazing units are used (see F, Fig. 55).

[2] Briefly, sheet glass is produced by fusing a mixture of sand, silicates of soda and lime, etc. The materials are melted in a furnace where, at one end, the molted glass is drawn up a tower and cut to size (see Chap. IV, Vol. IV).

[3] Polished plate glass is formed by casting the molten material on to a metal table, rolling it to a uniform thickness, and subsequently grinding and polishing it smooth by machinery. It is also produced direct by the " float " process.

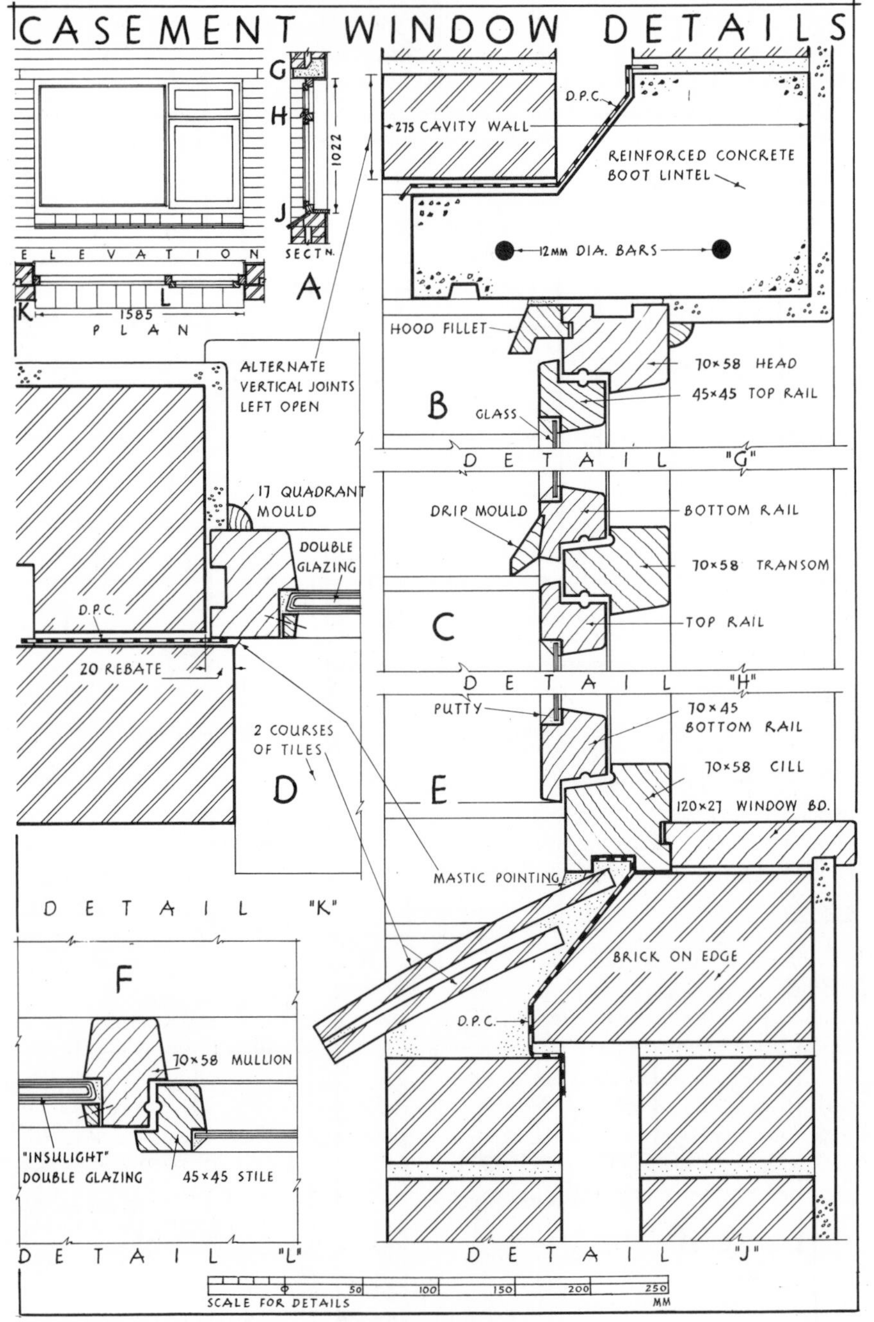

FIGURE 55

frame, water may gain entrance between it and the wall. The reason why the frame is shown in a square jamb is on account of the improved appearance which results when the maximum amount of the frame is exposed. Sounder construction is shown in Fig. 55 and also by broken lines at F, Fig. 8. The frame is checked to receive the plaster (see F, Fig. 54) or a cover mould, such as is shown at H, Fig. 54, may be provided to hide any shrinkage cracks which appear.

Notice particularly the small grooves in the rebate of the frame and in the rails and stiles. These are capable of arresting water which would otherwise proceed by capillarity between the sash and the frame to the inside.

The frame shown at D and F, Fig. 56, is wider than those shown in Fig. 54, and this makes it possible for the sash to be set farther back and the underside of the head to be throated; excepting in heavy storms, this throat is effective in causing the rain to drop clear of the top rail.

The alternative details shown at E and G, Fig. 56, have been proved to result in an excellent weather resisting window. One of the disadvantages of casement windows is the expansion of the wood which may take place to cause the sashes to "jam" or "bind." When this occurs, the sashes are "eased" (the edges being planed to remove the excess timber) and there is a likelihood of rain and wind entering the enlarged clearance when the timber shrinks subsequently. Details E and G obviate these defects; the cover fillet which is screwed to the sash overlaps the frame 13 mm and enables a 6 mm clearance to be provided which is an adequate allowance for any expansion of the timber that may occur; in addition, the fillets are effective in excluding rain and wind. The throated *hood* or *drip fillet*, tongued to the head, affords an additional protection. The sashes may be made thicker and shaped to include the fillet, and the head of the frame may be made larger so that the hood may be formed out of the solid.

The details shown in Fig. 55 are also recommended for adoption in buildings which are exposed to severe weather conditions. That at D shows a rebated jamb which gives a 20 mm cover to the frame. The window has a large fixed pane consisting of a double glazed unit (two sheets of glass separated by a 5 mm sealed air space), a side-hung opening sash and a smaller top-hung one. Double glazing reduces heat losses from the room. The sashes are lipped to give effective weather protection. The use of d.p.c.'s where the cavity is bridged should be noted at B, D and E.

Some of the window boards are shown finished with bed moulds which are returned at the ends. These moulds are usually nailed to plugs and to the window boards after the latter have been secured. Large moulds are fixed to splayed grounds which are plugged to the wall (see R, Fig. 58). The internal soffits and jambs of the openings are shown plastered. These are called *plastered linings*, and as plaster is easily damaged at the edges a satisfactory finish is provided when a comparatively hard material, such as Keene's cement, is used to form the arrises. A Keene's cement arris is at least 50 mm wide in each direction, and narrow linings may be entirely covered with this cement instead of plaster (see C, D and K, Fig. 54, and p. 32). Wood *angle beads* (see L and M, Fig. 63) or galvanized steel beads are often used instead of cement arrises (see pp. 122–123).

The brick lintel is shown at B and N, Fig. 54 supported on a mild steel angle. This is not often used for a single or double light window, where the span is relatively small and the brick head is usually built directly on the head of the frame, but such support (or the alternative forms shown in Fig. 12) complies with the principles of sound construction and must always be applied to wide windows.

The height of windows above floor level should be given consideration. That shown in section C, Fig. 54, is satisfactory for a house. Upper-floor windows of the cottage type should be as near to the eaves as possible, and a satisfactory treatment at the head is shown at A, Fig. 71.

Hardware.—This for casements consists of hinges, fasteners and stays. Fig. 57 shows the application of these.

Hinges.—Ordinary butt hinges (a pair to each sash) are used, but these are not entirely satisfactory as they are apt to be wrenched off and, when fixed to upper floor windows, difficulty is experienced in cleaning the external face of the glass from the inside. A big improvement upon the butt hinge for hanging casements is the *extension* or *cleaning hinge* which is illustrated in Fig. 57; the upper fitting is shown at A and the lower hinge is shown at B. As shown in the plan, the sash can be opened to give a clearance of from 100 to 125 mm between it and the frame, which is sufficient to enable the outside of the window to be cleaned from the inside (see also isometric sketch). The vertical edge of the free stile and the adjacent rebate on the jamb should be slightly splayed to permit of the opening of the casement. These hinges are made of steel or wrought iron which is *sherardized*, a process of rendering the metal rust proof by the application of a powdered zinc.

Casement Fasteners (see C and sketch).—The plate to which the pivoted handle is attached is screwed to the inside face of the free stile and the projecting point of the handle (when the sash is closed) engages in a slotted plate which is screwed to the frame near to the rebate. This type is also known as a *cockspur fastener* and is obtained in sherardized iron, bronze and aluminium alloy.

Casement Stay (see D, plan and sketch).—This form is called a *peg stay* and consists of a bar, holed at about 50 mm centres, which is pivoted to a small plate that is screwed to the inside face of the bottom rail; there is in addition a *peg* or *pin plate* which is screwed to the top of the wood sill. As is implied, the object of the stay is to maintain the sash when in the open position, and this it does when the peg is engaged in one of the holes. This fitting is made of sherardized iron, bronze, etc.

Fixed Sashes or Dead Lights.—One of the sashes at B, Fig. 54, is specified to be fixed. Such sashes should be well bedded in lead mastic and screwed to the frame.

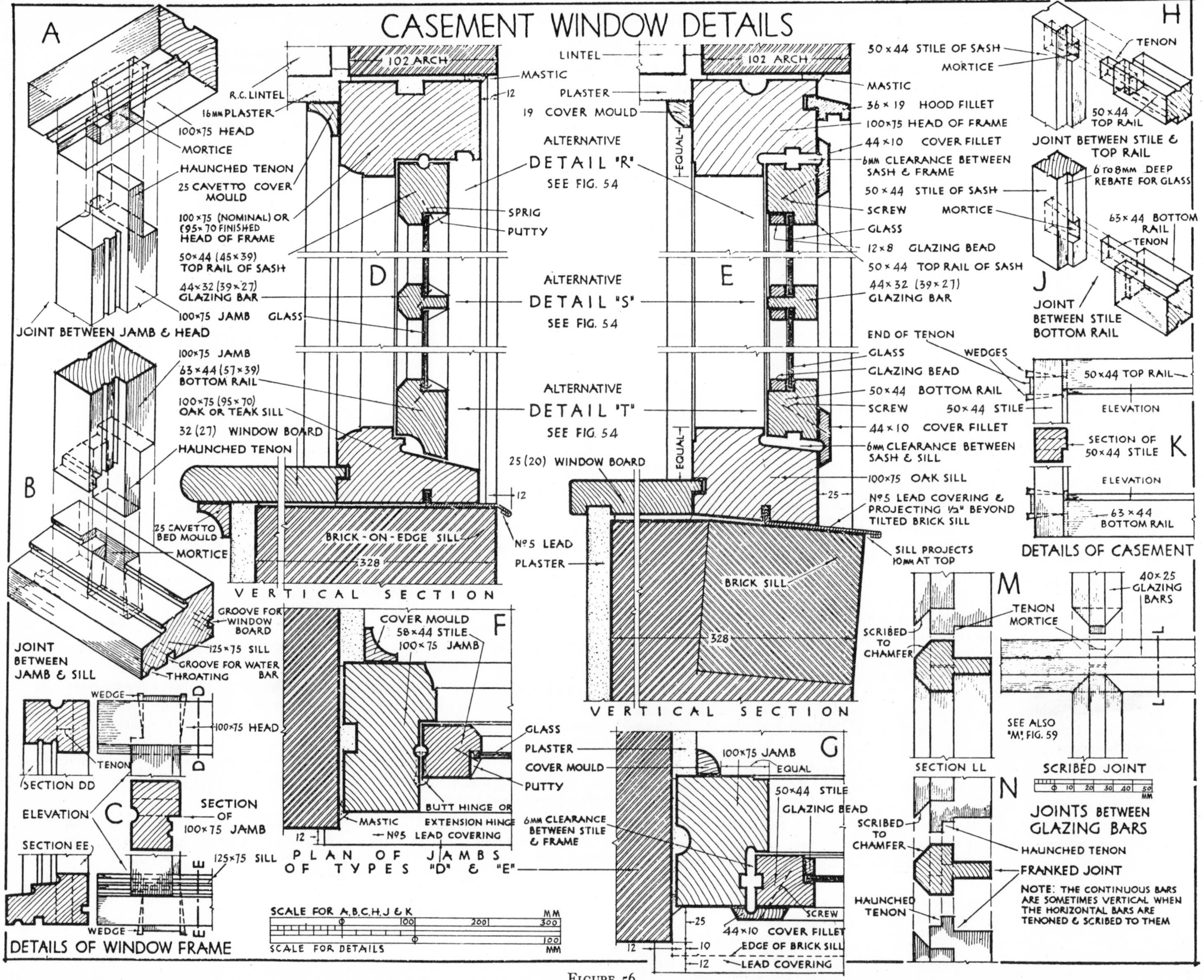

CASEMENT WINDOW DETAILS

A

R.C. LINTEL
16MM PLASTER
100×75 HEAD
MORTICE
HAUNCHED TENON
25 CAVETTO COVER MOULD
100×75 (NOMINAL) OR (95×70 FINISHED HEAD OF FRAME
50×44 (45×39) TOP RAIL OF SASH
44×32 (39×27) GLAZING BAR
100×75 JAMB
GLASS
JOINT BETWEEN JAMB & HEAD

102 ARCH
MASTIC
12
LINTEL
PLASTER
19 COVER MOULD
SPRIG
PUTTY

ALTERNATIVE DETAIL "R" SEE FIG. 54

ALTERNATIVE DETAIL "S" SEE FIG. 54

ALTERNATIVE DETAIL "T" SEE FIG. 54

D

E

EQUAL

50×44 STILE OF SASH
MORTICE
MASTIC
36×19 HOOD FILLET
100×75 HEAD OF FRAME
44×10 COVER FILLET
6MM CLEARANCE BETWEEN SASH & FRAME
50×44 STILE OF SASH
SCREW
GLASS
12×8 GLAZING BEAD
50×44 TOP RAIL OF SASH
44×32 (39×27) GLAZING BAR

H

TENON
50×44 TOP RAIL
JOINT BETWEEN STILE & TOP RAIL
6 TO 8MM DEEP REBATE FOR GLASS
MORTICE
63×44 BOTTOM RAIL
TENON
J
JOINT BETWEEN STILE BOTTOM RAIL

100×75 JAMB
63×44 (57×39) BOTTOM RAIL
100×75 (95×70) OAK OR TEAK SILL
32 (27) WINDOW BOARD
HAUNCHED TENON

B

25 CAVETTO BED MOULD
MORTICE
BRICK-ON-EDGE SILL
328
12
Nº5 LEAD
PLASTER
GROOVE FOR WINDOW BOARD
125×75 SILL
GROOVE FOR WATER BAR
THROATING
JOINT BETWEEN JAMB & SILL

VERTICAL SECTION

END OF TENON
GLASS
GLAZING BEAD
50×44 BOTTOM RAIL
SCREW
44×10 COVER FILLET
6MM CLEARANCE BETWEEN SASH & SILL
25 (20) WINDOW BOARD
100×75 OAK SILL
25
Nº5 LEAD COVERING & PROJECTING ½" BEYOND TILTED BRICK SILL
SILL PROJECTS 10MM AT TOP
BRICK SILL
328

VERTICAL SECTION

WEDGES
50×44 TOP RAIL
50×44 STILE
ELEVATION
SECTION OF 50×44 STILE
K
ELEVATION
63×44 BOTTOM RAIL
DETAILS OF CASEMENT

WEDGE
100×75 HEAD
D D
TENON
SECTION DD
C
ELEVATION
SECTION OF 100×75 JAMB
SECTION EE
125×75 SILL
E E
WEDGE
DETAILS OF WINDOW FRAME

F

COVER MOULD
58×44 STILE
100×75 JAMB
GLASS
PLASTER
COVER MOULD
PUTTY
BUTT HINGE OR EXTENSION HINGE
MASTIC
Nº5 LEAD COVERING
12

PLAN OF JAMBS OF TYPES "D" & "E"

SCALE FOR A,B,C,H,J & K — 0, 100, 200, 300 MM
SCALE FOR DETAILS — 0, 100 MM

G

100×75 JAMB
EQUAL
50×44 STILE
GLAZING BEAD
6MM CLEARANCE BETWEEN STILE & FRAME
SCREW
25
44×10 COVER FILLET
12
10
EDGE OF BRICK SILL
12
LEAD COVERING

M

TENON
MORTICE
SCRIBED TO CHAMFER
40×25 GLAZING BARS
L L
SEE ALSO "M", FIG. 59
SECTION LL
SCRIBED JOINT
0 10 20 30 40 50 MM

N

SCRIBED TO CHAMFER
HAUNCHED TENON
FRANKED JOINT
HAUNCHED TENON

JOINTS BETWEEN GLAZING BARS

NOTE: THE CONTINUOUS BARS ARE SOMETIMES VERTICAL WHEN THE HORIZONTAL BARS ARE TENONED & SCRIBED TO THEM

FIGURE 56

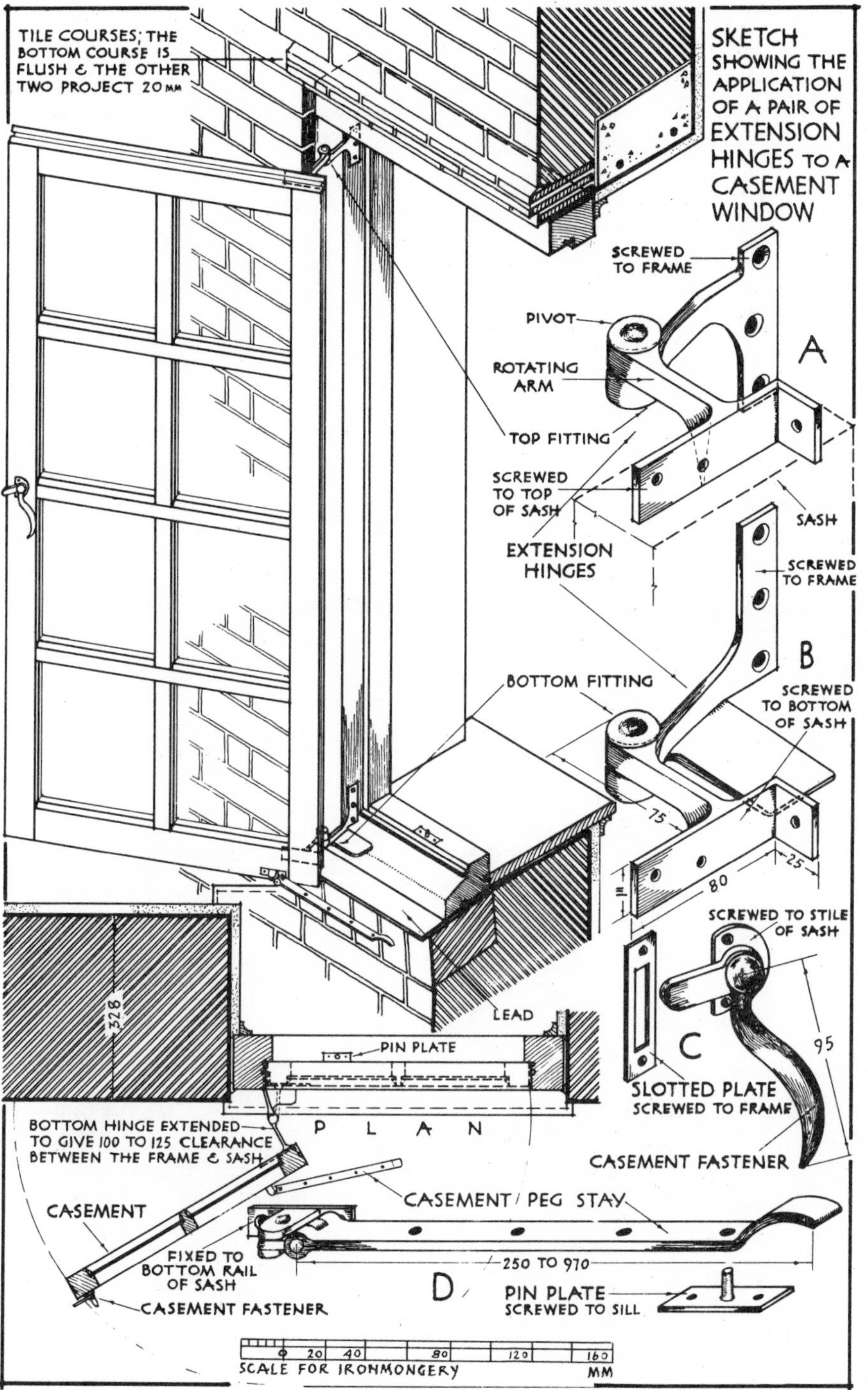

It is a common practice to dispense with a casement for a fixed light and to fix the glass directly to the frame; the mullion, jamb, head and sill being rebated for this purpose. In an elevation such as B, Fig. 54, this would spoil the appearance of the window, as the " sight lines " of the top and bottom rails of the casement would not " line through " with the top and bottom sight lines of the fixed light, the upper and lower panes of the fixed lights would be higher than the intermediates and, in addition, the sheets would be wider than those in the hinged sash.

Windows with Solid Frames and Casements Opening Inwards.—As it is almost impossible to make this window weather proof, its adoption is not recommended, and for this reason a detailed description of it is not given. The frame is rebated on the inside to receive the sashes which swing inwards. The interference with curtains, etc. caused when the sashes are open provides an additional objection.

(b) Window with Cased or Boxed Frame and Vertical Sliding Sashes (see Figs. 58[1] and 59).—This window has a pair of sashes, both of which should be made to open for the purposes of ventilation and to facilitate cleaning. The sashes slide vertically within shallow recesses formed in the frame which is built-up with comparatively thin members. A pair of metal weights contained within the frame is connected to each sash by means of cords or chains after being passed over pulleys fixed to the frame. Without the weights, the upper sash when lowered and the bottom sash when raised would of course drop to the bottom immediately the sashes were released.[2] A satisfactory appearance is obtained if the sashes are divided into panes[3] of the proportion shown at T, Fig. 58, and if the window is three or four panes wide and four panes high (see A). Both sashes are usually equal in size, although it is sometimes desirable to increase the height of the window when the upper and lower sashes may be two and three panes high respectively.

Frame.—This consists of two vertical jambs, a head and a sill.

A jamb (see N and S, Fig. 58) comprises an *inner* or *inside lining*, an *outer* or *outside lining*, a *pulley stile* (so called because the pulleys are screwed to them), and a *back lining* (often omitted in cheap work); in addition, a thin piece of wood, called a *parting* SLIP or *mid-feather*, is used to separate the two weights, a small *parting* BEAD is provided to separate the two sashes, and an *inner bead* (sometimes called a *staff bead*, *fixing bead* or *guard bead*) is fixed to complete the shallow recess for the inner or lower sash.

The head (see K and O) consists of an inner and an outer lining, a *head* or *soffit lining*, an inner bead and a parting bead, although the latter is sometimes omitted.

The solid sill, with staff bead, completes the frame.

[1] Fig. 58 is arranged to provide an example of a typical homework sheet (see p. 163). The half full size details before reproduction, were drawn to the finished sizes (see pp. 61, 94, 105 and 111).

[2] A fitting consisting of a coiled spring and called a *sash balance* may be used instead of the weights, cords and pulleys. A pair of balances would be used per sash (see p. 115).

[3] Windows in large stone buildings of the commercial or factory type especially may consist of sashes which are not divided by glazing bars into relatively small panes but each sash is glazed with a single sheet.

FIGURE 57

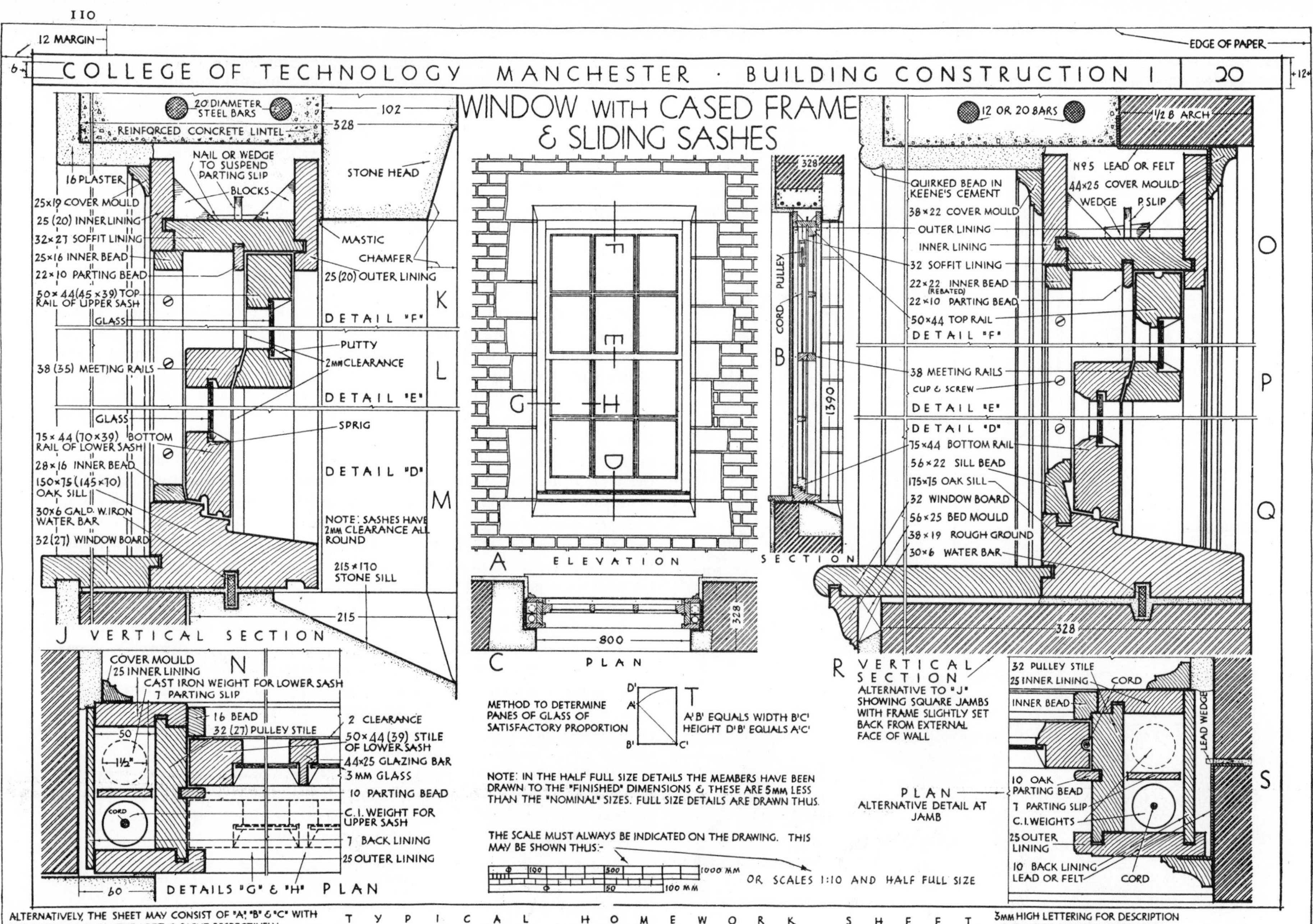
12 MARGIN
EDGE OF PAPER
COLLEGE OF TECHNOLOGY MANCHESTER · BUILDING CONSTRUCTION I
20
WINDOW WITH CASED FRAME & SLIDING SASHES
20 DIAMETER STEEL BARS
REINFORCED CONCRETE LINTEL
102
328
STONE HEAD
NAIL OR WEDGE TO SUSPEND PARTING SLIP
BLOCKS
16 PLASTER
25×19 COVER MOULD
25 (20) INNER LINING
32×27 SOFFIT LINING
25×16 INNER BEAD
22×10 PARTING BEAD
50×44 (45×39) TOP RAIL OF UPPER SASH
GLASS
MASTIC
CHAMFER
25 (20) OUTER LINING
DETAIL "F"
PUTTY
2MM CLEARANCE
38 (35) MEETING RAILS
DETAIL "E"
SPRIG
75×44 (70×39) BOTTOM RAIL OF LOWER SASH
28×16 INNER BEAD
150×75 (145×70) OAK SILL
30×6 GALD. W.IRON WATER BAR
32 (27) WINDOW BOARD
DETAIL "D"
NOTE: SASHES HAVE 2MM CLEARANCE ALL ROUND
215×170 STONE SILL
215
J VERTICAL SECTION
K
L
M
A ELEVATION
B SECTION
PULLEY
CORD
1390
C PLAN
800
12 OR 20 BARS
1/2 B ARCH
QUIRKED BEAD IN KEENE'S CEMENT
38×22 COVER MOULD
OUTER LINING
INNER LINING
32 SOFFIT LINING
22×22 INNER BEAD (REBATED)
22×10 PARTING BEAD
50×44 TOP RAIL
No 5 LEAD OR FELT
44×25 COVER MOULD
WEDGE
P. SLIP
38 MEETING RAILS
CUP & SCREW
75×44 BOTTOM RAIL
56×22 SILL BEAD
175×75 OAK SILL
32 WINDOW BOARD
56×25 BED MOULD
38×19 ROUGH GROUND
30×6 WATER BAR
O
P
Q
R VERTICAL SECTION ALTERNATIVE TO "J" SHOWING SQUARE JAMBS WITH FRAME SLIGHTLY SET BACK FROM EXTERNAL FACE OF WALL
COVER MOULD
25 INNER LINING
CAST IRON WEIGHT FOR LOWER SASH
7 PARTING SLIP
16 BEAD
32 (27) PULLEY STILE
2 CLEARANCE
50×44 (39) STILE OF LOWER SASH
44×25 GLAZING BAR
3 MM GLASS
10 PARTING BEAD
C.I. WEIGHT FOR UPPER SASH
7 BACK LINING
25 OUTER LINING
DETAILS "G" & "H" PLAN
N
METHOD TO DETERMINE PANES OF GLASS OF SATISFACTORY PROPORTION
T
A'B' EQUALS WIDTH B'C' HEIGHT D'B' EQUALS A'C'
NOTE: IN THE HALF FULL SIZE DETAILS THE MEMBERS HAVE BEEN DRAWN TO THE "FINISHED" DIMENSIONS & THESE ARE 5MM LESS THAN THE "NOMINAL" SIZES. FULL SIZE DETAILS ARE DRAWN THUS.
THE SCALE MUST ALWAYS BE INDICATED ON THE DRAWING. THIS MAY BE SHOWN THUS:-
1000 MM
100 MM
OR SCALES 1:10 AND HALF FULL SIZE
PLAN ALTERNATIVE DETAIL AT JAMB
32 PULLEY STILE
25 INNER LINING
CORD
INNER BEAD
LEAD WEDGE
10 OAK PARTING BEAD
7 PARTING SLIP
C.I. WEIGHTS
25 OUTER LINING
10 BACK LINING
LEAD OR FELT
S
ALTERNATIVELY, THE SHEET MAY CONSIST OF "A", "B" & "C" WITH DETAILS "J" & "N" ON THE LEFT & RIGHT RESPECTIVELY
TYPICAL HOMEWORK SHEET
3MM HIGH LETTERING FOR DESCRIPTION SHOULD BE BETWEEN GUIDE LINES

FIGURE 58

As shown at N and S, the inner and outer linings are each ploughed with a 10 mm square groove to receive the tongues formed on the pulley stile; the outer lining projects 13 to 16 mm beyond the face of the stile, and the edge of the inner lining is flush with the face of the stile. The upper end of the pulley stile is either housed or tongued to the soffit lining and its bottom end is housed and wedged to the wood sill (see A, B, D, E and L, Fig. 59). As shown at A and B, the lower end of the stile is about 6 mm below the outer edge of the weathering of the sill, and as indicated at L, the wedge is driven in from the inside between the stile and the vertical cut of the housing, and this wedge is securely nailed to the stile. The inner and outer jamb linings extend the full height of the frame (see B), the inner and outer head linings butt against the jamb linings at X and Y (see D), and as shown at B and E, the oak sill is cut back at each side to receive the lower ends of the inner and outer jamb linings which are nailed to the sill, pulley stile throughout its length, soffit linings along the tongued and grooved joints and at the butt joints X and Y.

The parting slip extends to within 100 mm (approximately) of the top of the sill and is suspended from the soffit lining. A slot is formed in the latter, the slip is passed through it and either a nail or wood wedge is driven through it as shown at K and O, Fig. 58, and A, B and D, Fig. 59. The centre line of the parting slip coincides with that of the parting bead.

The back lining extends from the soffit lining to the upper surface of the sill and is nailed to the jamb linings (see A and C, Fig. 59, and N, Fig. 58); occasionally one edge is housed into the jamb lining as shown at S, Fig. 58. As shown at N, Fig. 58, the clear space between the pulley stile and the back lining must be 50 mm as the diameter of the weights is usually 38 mm.

As the equivalent to a back lining is not provided at the head, the necessary stiffness is imparted by the use of 75 or 100 mm long triangular blocks spaced along the internal angles between the soffit lining and the inner and outer linings at intervals of from 75 to 150 mm, with one placed across each butt joint between the jamb and soffit linings (see K and O, Fig. 58, and A and D, Fig. 59). These blocks are glued to the linings.

The inner bead is fixed all round the frame. This bead covers the joint between the inner lining and pulley stile or soffit lining (see K and N, Fig. 58); these beads are often rebated in good work as shown at O and S; they are moulded as required and the ends of each length are mitred. A slightly wider and bevelled inner or staff bead is fixed to the sill; the bottom rail of the sash is also bevelled to ensure a reasonably tight fit which prevents the sashes from rattling (see M). Alternatively, a deeper *sill bead* (see Q) is recommended. This allows the lower sash to be raised several millimetres to permit air to enter between the meeting rails of the sashes (see later); this incoming air is deflected upwards to minimize draughts and the latter are not caused at sill level. This is sometimes called a *ventilating piece* or *draught bead.* Inner beads should be fixed with brass cups and screws (see O, Fig. 66) to permit of their ready removal when required, although they are more often just bradded (nailed).

The parting bead is fitted tightly into a 10 mm square groove ploughed in the stile and nailed. The details show a similar bead at the soffit, although this is often omitted in common work; when provided, it assists in excluding rain and draughts.

Access for Weights.—Provision must be made in each pulley stile for fixing weights; such is called a *pocket* and is situated just below the meeting rails of the sashes and extends to about 150 mm above the sill. Two forms of pockets are shown at A, B, E, F and K, Fig. 59.

Side Pocket.—The sketch at F shows this type which is indicated at A and B. The plan shows the width to extend from the back of the inner lining to the groove for the parting bead which it includes; it is about 380 mm long for average sized sashes and must be at least equal to the length of the weights; the bottom end of the pocket is bevelled at 60° and the top end is V-shaped and bevelled at 60° in both directions.[1] The *pocket-piece* is secured to the stile by a screw at the bottom end in addition to the parting bead which is fixed subsequently. The lower sash and parting bead completely cover this pocket and therefore any damage caused when the piece is removed for sash cord renewals is effectively concealed.

Central Pocket.—This is a less satisfactory form and is shown at K; it has a rebated joint at the bottom end and a rebated and bevelled joint at the top. This is not such a good type as that shown at F as the outer vertical joint and portions of the horizontal cuts are exposed and any damage caused to them on removal is conspicuous.

Sills.—The several forms of sills should be noted; that at Q, Fig. 58 is wider than the sill at M to allow the cover mould to finish on it. The water bar at Q is shown at the centre of the sill; it is often fixed with the outside of the groove in line with the back of the outer lining so that the bar will arrest any water before it has travelled more than 25 mm.

Scantlings of Frame.—As the weight of the sashes is transmitted directly to the pulley stiles, it is customary to prepare the stiles out of thicker stuff than that for the linings. The nominal thickness of pulley stiles and soffit linings is either 25 or 32 mm, and that of inner and outer linings is either 20 or 25 mm. The sizes of the various members are figured upon the drawings.

Attention is drawn to the note in Fig. 58 which states that the details have been drawn to the finished dimensions, and that these are 5 mm less than the nominal sizes. It should be noted however that the members of the frame are often only planed on their exposed faces and thus the loss in dressing is reduced to 2·5 mm; the back lining is usually just dressed along its edges.

Sashes.—It will be seen on reference to Figs. 58 and 59 that the upper sash slides in the recess formed in the frame by the pulley stile, outer lining and

[1] The cuts made to form these bevels are made by the *pocket chisel* (see p. 126); the V-shaped top end is formed by making a second cut, and the small triangular piece which is removed is glued and nailed to the back of the stile (see Section XX) to form an abutment (cleat) for the pocket-piece.

parting bead, and that the lower sash is accommodated in the recess formed by the pulley stile, inner bead and parting bead. Each sash consists of two stiles, a top rail and a bottom rail, but as the bottom rail of the upper sash meets the top rail of the lower sash when the window is closed, these two members are called *meeting rails*. A minimum clearance of 0·8 mm should be allowed all round the sashes to permit of easy movement, and this is often increased to 1·6 mm when the window is to be painted.

Joint between Stile and Top Rail of Upper Sash (see H, Fig. 56, and R, Fig. 59).—The detail at H is usually adopted. The alternative detail at R shows the top rail haunched tenoned (like a door) at each end and each stile suitably morticed to receive the tenon and wedges. Glued wedges (waterproof glue being used) and a hardwood pin or dowel complete the joint. The methods of securing the sash cord are described on pp. 113 and 115.

Joint between Stile and Meeting Rail of Upper Sash (see T, Fig. 59).—The bottom of the meeting rail of the top sash and the top of the meeting rail of the bottom sash are at least 10 mm wider (assuming that the parting bead is 10 mm thick) than the thickness of the stiles, otherwise a gap equal to the thickness of the parting bead would be left (see L and P, Fig. 58). The joint between the meeting rails are either just bevelled, or, as shown, they are *bevel rebated*; the latter joint is preferred, for it assists in preventing the sashes from rattling, effectively increases the difficulty of gaining access to the sash fastener (see O, Fig. 59) from the outside, and enables the rails to separate easily when the sashes are opened.

The stiles of the sashes may extend from 38 to 75 mm beyond the meeting rails and these projections are shaped as required to form *horns* (or *brackets* or *joggles*), but they are often omitted as they are considered to detract from the appearance. The details at T and U show both types. The horned form at T shows a mortice and tenon joint (called a *fork tenon*) with the bevelled portion passing over the inner face of the stile, which latter is dovetailed to receive it (see section and the isometric sketch); the central tongue is wedged; it is usual to leave the upper edge of the bevelled portion projecting slightly beyond the face of the stile, and this may afterwards be dressed down to the stile when the meeting rails are fitted together. In the second or hornless type at U a dovetailed joint must be adopted, otherwise the joint would readily become loosened when the sash handles (see P, Fig. 59) are pulled downwards whilst the sash is being opened. Note the shaped end in the isometric sketch and the broken lines in the alternative section which indicate the dovetailed tongue and bevelled portion. The joint is either screwed or dowelled as shown at T.

Joint between Stile and Meeting Rail of Lower Sash (see V, Fig. 59).—Like the top sash, the stiles of the bottom sash may be provided with horns, but in first class work these are omitted and a dovetailed joint between the meeting rail and each stile is adopted as shown at V, which indicates the upper end of the stile shaped to receive the dovetailed tenon and bevelled portion of the meeting rail; the latter portion passes over the outer face of the stile, and its lower edge is usually left slightly projecting beyond this face until both meeting rails are finally fitted together.[1] This joint is also pinned or screwed. A groove is formed down the edge of each stile to accommodate the sash cord; this is similar to that shown at R and S and is indicated by broken lines at V. Note the provision made on this meeting rail to receive the glass; as both meeting rails are of the same depth, it is not possible to form the usual rebate on the lower sash meeting rail and in lieu of it a groove is formed along the underside of the rail.

The ends of the bevelled portions of the meeting rails must be cut away for clearance round the projecting parting beads. The small piece so removed from the bottom sash meeting rail is indicated by broken lines at V. The groove for the cord, the clearance for the parting bead, and the dowel holes have been omitted in the sketches so as to render the details less confusing.

Joint between Stile and Bottom Rail of Lower Sash (see W, Fig. 59).—This is an ordinary pinned haunched tenoned joint. The bottom of the rail and the end of each stile are shaped as required (examples at M and Q, Fig. 58). The joint shown at J, Fig. 56 is very often adopted.

Joint between Glazing Bars.—The scribed and franked joints between sash bars are described on p. 104 and the halved joint is shown at M, Fig. 59. Glue is applied to the joints before assembling and cramping each sash.

Scantlings of Sashes.—The usual nominal thickness of a sash of average size is 45 mm, but the thickness may be increased to 50 or 60 mm for larger sashes, whilst small sashes may only be 38 mm thick. The common scantlings are: stiles and top rail, 50 mm by 45 mm thick; meeting rails, 50 mm wide by 38 mm; bottom rail, 75 to 100 mm by 45 mm thick. Glazing bars may be out of 45 mm by 25 mm stuff but a thickness of 32 mm reduced to 25 mm gives the better appearance.

Timber.—The timbers employed in the construction of windows of this type are redwood, pitch pine, teak and oak. The former is most used, although a more durable wood such as oak, teak or pitch pine is specified for the sill. Oak or teak are used throughout for first class work.

Hardware.—Although there are many patent devices on the market for use on windows of this description, the following simple fittings have been proved to be quite effective for their purpose. They include sash fasteners, sash lifts, sash handles and pulleys, together with the weights and sash cords or chains.

Sash Fastener (see O, Fig. 59).—This affords an effective security, provided it is of best quality. The fitting is of brass or bronze and comprises two castings, one being screwed to the centre of the meeting rail of the top sash, and the second (or *lug*) being screwed to the top of the meeting rail of the bottom sash; on the former casting there is a lever which is pivoted at one end and has a solid knob

[1] Students should be careful to show the joint between the meeting rails correctly. Examination scripts and homework sheets frequently show details which indicate the bevel running downwards from the inside to the outside. Movement of the sashes would not, of course, be possible if the meeting rails were constructed to such details.

at the other. When the lever is rotated, the pivoted end bears against the free end of a strong and highly tempered steel spring which is riveted to a recessed vertical portion of the casting, and the dovetailed notch on the lever engages in the solid curved lug which is riveted to the second fitting. This brings both meeting rails closely together and secures the window.

Sash Lift (see Q, Fig. 59).—This is the *hook lift* type, other forms being ring lifts, flush recessed lifts, knob lifts and hinged lifts. One pair of lifts is screwed to the inside of the bottom rail of the lower sash and at about 150 mm from each end. They are of course used to raise the bottom sash and are obtainable in brass and bronze.

Sash Handle (see P, Fig. 59).—When a sash is large (and especially when there are no glazing bars to grip when drawing down the sash) a pair of these may be fixed on the underside of the top sash meeting rail near to the stiles. They are not very convenient, as the lower sash has to be raised before the handles are accessible from the inside.

The following simple expedient is effective : A pulley is fixed to the soffit lining of the frame immediately over each stile of the upper sash, and an *eye* or ring is screwed into the inner face and near to the end of each stile of this sash; a piece of cord of a length equal to about one and a half times the height of the window is passed through each eye and over each pulley; each cord is knotted immediately above and below the eye; the ends of each double cord are equal and a handle is fixed to each. To open the top sash, one end of each cord is pulled to draw the sash downwards with the top knot bearing upon the eye. The sash is closed by pulling on the other ends of the cords which brings the lower knots against the eyes to lift the sash.

As mentioned on p. 109, in order to conveniently slide the sashes and maintain them in any desired position when open, it is necessary to fix to them sash cords which are fastened to weights situated in the casings after being passed over pulleys fixed to the frame.

Sash Axle Pulleys (see A, B, D and N, Fig. 59).—This type consists of a 60 mm diameter round grooved brass pulley (or *sheave*) having 12 mm diameter steel axles which revolve in brass or gunmetal *bushes* (6 mm thick annular bearings) mounted on a metal (iron, gunmetal or rustless steel) case which is flanged and covered with a brass or bronze plate; the pulleys may be 45, 50, 60, 65 and 75 mm in diameter. This hollow-rounded grooved type of pulley is suitable for flax cords, copper cords and metal chains of the form shown at W′. Square grooved pulleys are adopted for certain heavy chains. The cog wheel type of axle pulley (having a fixed axle with a toothed portion which bears the chain and which revolves on ball bearings) may be selected for extra heavy sashes.

The 125 mm by 28 mm face plate of the pulley is screwed flush with the outer face of a pulley stile with the top of the plate from 38 to 60 mm down from the head (see A and B); the mortice for the pulley case and the housing for the flange and face plate are shown at D. The pulleys project about 8 mm beyond the outer external face of the pulley stile (see A), and the size of the pulley must be sufficient to allow the weight to hang clear of the casing. Two pulleys per sash are required.

Weights (see N and S, Fig. 58, and A, B and C, Fig. 59).—These are cylindrical cast iron weights, 38 mm in diameter and of varying length in accordance with their weight; thus, a 2·3 kg weight is about 300 mm long. The object of these is to counterbalance the weight of the sashes. The top of each weight is holed to receive the end of the cord.

Opinions differ as to the weight required per sash, but satisfactory results are obtained if *each* of the two weights for the *top* sash is from 0·25 to 0·5 kg *heavier* than *half* the weight of the sash, and if *each* of the two *bottom* sash weights is from 0·25 to 0·5 kg *lighter* than *half* the weight of this sash. The weight of each sash is determined by means of a spring balance, and due allowance should be made for the weight of the glass to be used and that of the paint.

Sash Cords and Chains.—The weights are secured by either cords or chains which are passed over the pulleys and attached to the sashes.

Best quality stout twisted or braided cotton cord is usually specified for ordinary work. It is obtainable in sizes of " 30 m " or " 54 m " in length; its thickness varies from 5 to 10 mm, the former being suitable for weights of less than 2·3 kg, and the latter for weights up to 23 kg. The cheaper cord stretches and, therefore, each length should be well stretched before being fixed, otherwise it may elongate to such an extent as to limit the movement of the sashes, *i.e.*, the weights of the bottom sash may reach the bottom of the casing before the sash has travelled to its full height. Certain brands of the best quality are greased and are guaranteed to be stretch proof and damp proof.

The defect of flax cord is that in course of time it frays and ultimately breaks. A stronger and more durable cord is that known as *copper wire cord.* It is sold in 30 m lengths and the size is specified according to the number; thus, a " No. 3 " cord is 6·5 mm in diameter and consists of thirty-six strands of copper wire which are subdivided into six segments; the strands in each segment are intertwined and the segments in turn are intertwisted together.

One form of sash chain is shown at W′, Fig. 59. This is called the *three-and-two link copper chain*, as it comprises a series of three links or plates (each 1 mm thick) which alternate with a pair of links; the overall thickness of the five links is 6 mm. Each link has two holes and loose fitting pins or rivets pass through the five links at each connection. The chain can be used in conjunction with the ordinary axle pulley shown at N as it readily accommodates itself to the sharpest curve. Special fittings are used for connecting the chain to the weights and sashes. One form of connector to the weight consists of a hook which is simply passed through the eye of the weight. The sash fitting comprises a plate which is screwed to the edge of the sash and a pin is passed through the brackets on this plate and the holes of the chain links. The chain is an improvement upon, but is more expensive than, the flax cord, and chains have been known to last for more than thirty years before requiring attention. Chains used in conjunction with the cog wheel type of pulley used for very heavy sashes are of similar construction to the above, but the links are of rust proofed steel connected by means of phosphor-bronze rivets.

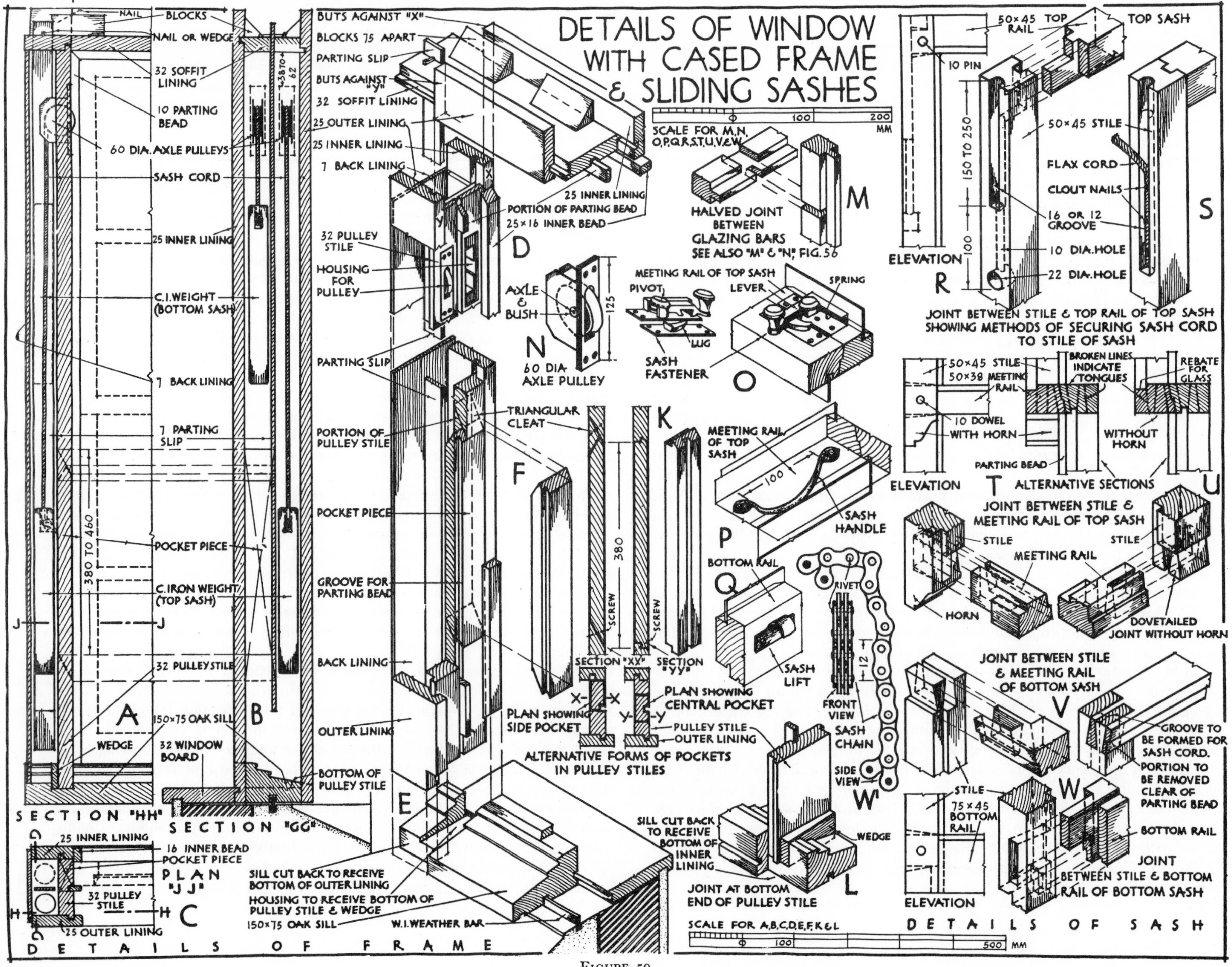

DETAILS OF WINDOW WITH CASED FRAME & SLIDING SASHES
SCALE FOR M,N, O,P,Q,R,S,T,U,V,&W
100
200
MM
NAIL
BLOCKS
NAIL OR WEDGE
32 SOFFIT LINING
10 PARTING BEAD
60 DIA. AXLE PULLEYS
SASH CORD
25 INNER LINING
C.I. WEIGHT (BOTTOM SASH)
7 BACK LINING
7 PARTING SLIP
380 TO 460
POCKET PIECE
C.IRON WEIGHT (TOP SASH)
J
J
32 PULLEY STILE
A
WEDGE
150×75 OAK SILL
B
32 WINDOW BOARD
SECTION "HH"
SECTION "GG"
38 TO 62
BUTS AGAINST "X"
BLOCKS 75 APART
PARTING SLIP
BUTS AGAINST "Y"
32 SOFFIT LINING
25 OUTER LINING
25 INNER LINING
7 BACK LINING
25 INNER LINING
PORTION OF PARTING BEAD
25×16 INNER BEAD
32 PULLEY STILE
HOUSING FOR PULLEY
D
PARTING SLIP
PORTION OF PULLEY STILE
TRIANGULAR CLEAT
POCKET PIECE
GROOVE FOR PARTING BEAD
BACK LINING
OUTER LINING
BOTTOM OF PULLEY STILE
F
K
380
SCREW
SCREW
SECTION "XX"
SECTION "YY"
PLAN SHOWING SIDE POCKET
PLAN SHOWING CENTRAL POCKET
PULLEY STILE
OUTER LINING
ALTERNATIVE FORMS OF POCKETS IN PULLEY STILES
E
SILL CUT BACK TO RECEIVE BOTTOM OF OUTER LINING
HOUSING TO RECEIVE BOTTOM OF PULLEY STILE & WEDGE
150×75 OAK SILL
W.I. WEATHER BAR
25 INNER LINING
16 INNER BEAD
POCKET PIECE
PLAN "JJ"
32 PULLEY STILE
25 OUTER LINING
H
H
C
DETAILS OF FRAME
AXLE & BUSH
125
N
60 DIA AXLE PULLEY
HALVED JOINT BETWEEN GLAZING BARS
SEE ALSO "M" & "N", FIG. 56
M
MEETING RAIL OF TOP SASH
PIVOT
LEVER
SPRING
LUG
SASH FASTENER
O
MEETING RAIL OF TOP SASH
100
SASH HANDLE
P
BOTTOM RAIL
Q
SASH LIFT
RIVET
12
FRONT VIEW
SASH CHAIN
SIDE VIEW
W'
SILL CUT BACK TO RECEIVE BOTTOM OF INNER LINING
WEDGE
JOINT AT BOTTOM END OF PULLEY STILE
L
SCALE FOR A,B,C,D,E,F,K&L
100
500 MM
50×45 TOP RAIL
TOP SASH
10 PIN
150 TO 250
100
50×45 STILE
FLAX CORD
CLOUT NAILS
16 OR 12 GROOVE
10 DIA. HOLE
22 DIA. HOLE
ELEVATION
R
S
JOINT BETWEEN STILE & TOP RAIL OF TOP SASH SHOWING METHODS OF SECURING SASH CORD TO STILE OF SASH
50×45 STILE
50×38 MEETING RAIL
BROKEN LINES INDICATE TONGUES
REBATE FOR GLASS
10 DOWEL
WITH HORN
WITHOUT HORN
PARTING BEAD
ELEVATION
T
ALTERNATIVE SECTIONS
U
JOINT BETWEEN STILE & MEETING RAIL OF TOP SASH
STILE
STILE
MEETING RAIL
HORN
DOVETAILED JOINT WITHOUT HORN
JOINT BETWEEN STILE & MEETING RAIL OF BOTTOM SASH
V
GROOVE TO BE FORMED FOR SASH CORD.
PORTION TO BE REMOVED CLEAR OF PARTING BEAD
STILE
75×45 BOTTOM RAIL
W
BOTTOM RAIL
JOINT BETWEEN STILE & BOTTOM RAIL OF BOTTOM SASH
ELEVATION
DETAILS OF SASH

FIGURE 59

Fixing Cords to Sashes and Weights.—Two methods of fixing the cords are shown at R and S, Fig. 59; that shown at S is the most common method. A better way is shown at R where a groove is ploughed to a distance of from 150 to 250 mm (depending upon the size of the sash); this is continued by a 10 mm diameter hole which is bored to a depth of about 100 mm and is terminated by a 25 mm diameter hole formed at the edge. The cord is secured by threading it through the smaller hole, the end being knotted and hammered into the bottom hole.

Sash Balances.—This fitting, referred to in the footnote to p. 109, dispenses with weights, cords and pulleys. A cased frame is not necessary, but inner, outer and parting beads must be fixed to the solid frame to form the necessary recesses for the sashes. The balance very much resembles a steel tape used for surveying purposes with a face-plate attached to the balance casing. The balances are obtainable in various sizes to suit the weights of sashes. Mortices are formed in the jambs just below the head to receive the casings of the balances; the face-plates are screwed to the jambs and the looped ends of the metal tapes (coiled springs) are screwed to the edges of the sashes. When the top sash is pulled down the tapes from the two balances are drawn out, and when the lower sash is raised the tapes in the other two balances are coiled up. Another type of balance is shown in Fig. 27, Vol. III.

Manufacture of Windows.—The preparation of the frames and sashes is done chiefly by machinery and comparatively few windows are now entirely made by hand. Standard casement windows, complete with frames and sashes, are stocked by manufacturers of mass produced windows. The various operations of setting out, preparing assembling, gluing and wedging up, and cleaning off in the making of the frame and sashes of a window are similar to the manufacture of doors detailed on pp. 100–103.

General.—The window shown in Fig. 58 is shown fixed in a building which is faced with 50 mm bricks having 10 mm mortar joints and finished at the opening with stone dressings, *i.e.*, stone head, sill and jambs. Note that the inbands and outbands of the latter course with the brickwork and that the vertical joints between the stone and brickwork are irregular. If stone dressings are not desired, the recesses may be 112 mm deep as shown in Fig. 8, when the outer face of the pulley stile conforms with the face of the outer reveal. Whilst this undoubtedly ensures a weathertight joint between the frame and brickwork, the appearance is not so satisfactory, as all but a narrow margin of the frame is concealed, hence the openings are often provided with square jambs which permit of the whole of the outer face of the frame being exposed (see R and S, Fig. 58). The defect in this construction is referred to on p. 110. One of several methods adopted to prevent water gaining access between the frame and brickwork is shown at O and S, where a narrow strip of lead (or felt) is fixed at the jambs and head.

The lead at the head is fixed between the arch and the reinforced concrete lintel when the latter is being fixed, the final dressing over the frame being done at a later stage. The lead lining at the jambs is fixed just prior to the fixing of the frame when a vertical groove is formed in each jamb, the lead is tucked into it and secured with lead wedges (see O, Fig. 74) driven in at about 300 mm intervals. After the frame has been fixed, the lead is dressed over, and as shown, this lead is covered by the wood mould.

Windows with cased frames and sliding sashes (often referred to as " double hung sashed windows ") are most effective in excluding rain and draughts and are superior to the ordinary casement windows for exposed positions.

Windows with Pivoted Sashes[1] (see Fig. 60).—This type consists of a solid frame and a sash which is pivoted to allow it to open with the top rail swinging inwards. The pivots (see later) are fixed slightly above (about 25 mm) the horizontal centre line of the sash so that the sash will tend to be self-closing. The construction of the frame is similar to that of the casement window except that it is not rebated. Both inner and outer beads are required (see details at H, J and K). As shown, the sash is in the middle of the frame with the *upper* portion of the *outer* bead and the *lower* portion of the *inner* bead fixed to the *frame*, and the *upper* half of the *inner* bead and the *lower* half of the *outer* bead nailed or screwed to the *sash*. These beads should appear to be continuous when the window is closed, and they should be cut correctly to enable the sash to be freely opened and closed when required.

A method of setting out the splay-cuts for the beads is shown at J. As indicated, a vertical section of the complete window is set up. The sash is inclined to the required maximum opening position (this varies from 10° to 20° to the horizontal) and the inner and outer beads are drawn. A line (" 3 ") is drawn through the centre of the pivot joining the points " 1 " and " 2," which are 13 mm above and below the beads, and two short lines are drawn at right angles to it and across the width of the frame beads to give the cuts. With the centre of the pivot as centre, the arcs indicated by broken lines are drawn to give the corresponding points for the splay-cuts on the sash beads. The 13 mm clearance between each of the points " 1 " and " 2 " and the sash beads permits of the removal of the sash when required.

The underside of the head of the frame is slightly splayed (about 6 mm), and the top bead and the top of the sash are made to conform to it, to allow the sash when opened to clear the frame.

Hardware.—The window fittings consist of pivots, eyelets, cleats, catches and patent ventilating gearing.

Sash Pivots or Centres.—Of the various forms, that shown at M, Fig. 60, consists of a brass, malleable iron or gunmetal pin or stub mounted on a plate, screwed to the inner face of the sash, and this engages in a metal socket the plate of which is screwed to the inner face of the frame. One pair of fittings is required per sash.

The sash pivot shown at P consists of a pin or stub plate and a slotted plate or socket. A pair of these fittings is fixed to the edges of the sash and frame. The pin plate may be fixed either to the frame or the sash. If the former, each socket plate must be screwed to the edge of the sash with the open end of the

[1] Consideration of this type of window is sometimes deferred until the second year of a Building Course.

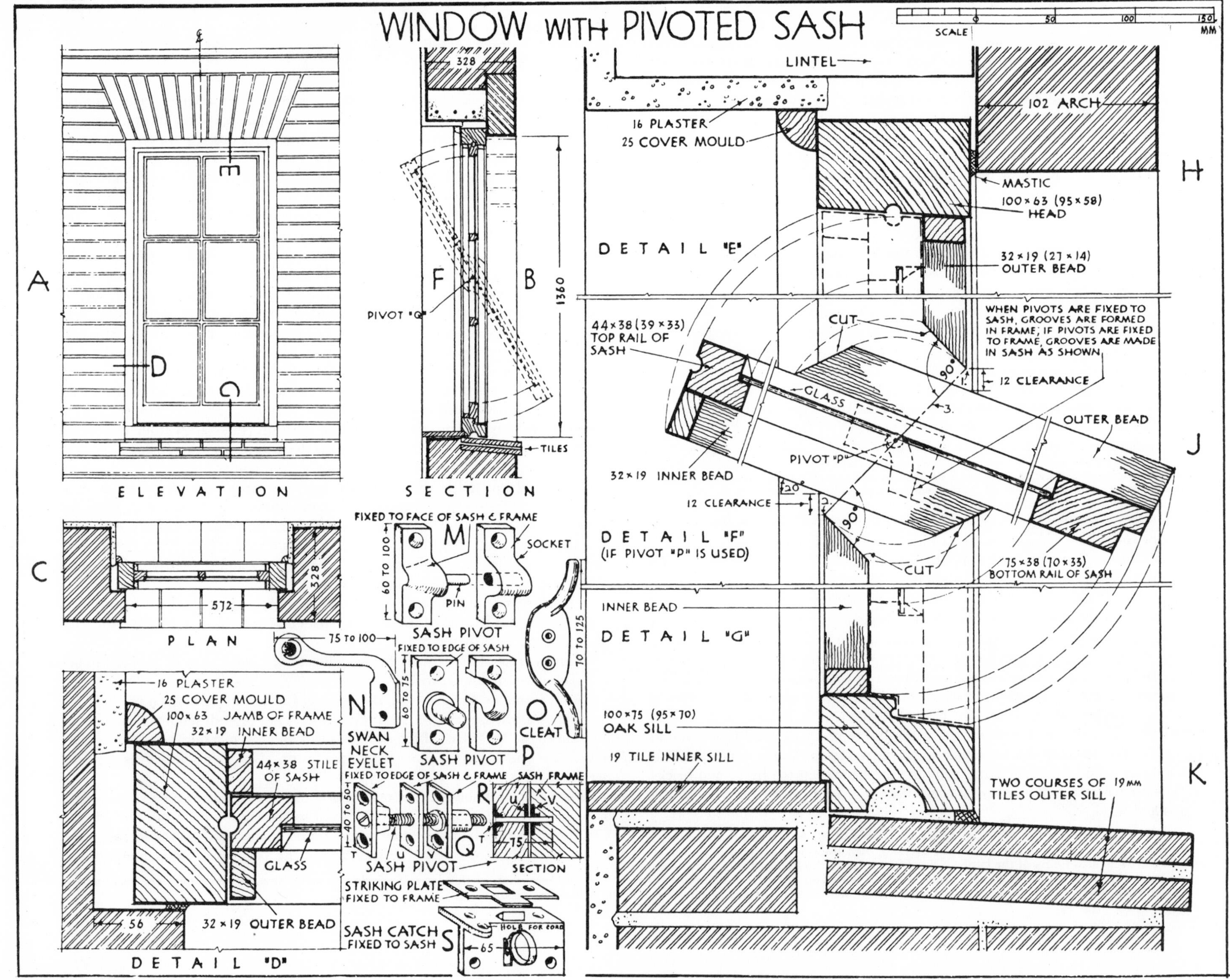
WINDOW WITH PIVOTED SASH
SCALE
0 50 100 150 MM
ELEVATION
SECTION
PLAN
DETAIL "D"
DETAIL "E"
DETAIL "F"
(IF PIVOT "P" IS USED)
DETAIL "G"
A
B
C
D
E
F
G
H
J
K
1360
328
572
PIVOT "Q"
TILES
LINTEL
102 ARCH
16 PLASTER
25 COVER MOULD
MASTIC
100 × 63 (95 × 58) HEAD
32 × 19 (27 × 14) OUTER BEAD
WHEN PIVOTS ARE FIXED TO SASH, GROOVES ARE FORMED IN FRAME; IF PIVOTS ARE FIXED TO FRAME, GROOVES ARE MADE IN SASH AS SHOWN
44 × 38 (39 × 33) TOP RAIL OF SASH
CUT
GLASS
12 CLEARANCE
OUTER BEAD
PIVOT "P"
32 × 19 INNER BEAD
75 × 38 (70 × 33) BOTTOM RAIL OF SASH
INNER BEAD
100 × 75 (95 × 70) OAK SILL
19 TILE INNER SILL
TWO COURSES OF 19 MM TILES OUTER SILL
FIXED TO FACE OF SASH & FRAME
M
SOCKET
60 TO 100
PIN
SASH PIVOT
FIXED TO EDGE OF SASH
60 TO 75
P
75 TO 100
N
SWAN NECK EYELET
O
CLEAT
70 TO 125
16 PLASTER
25 COVER MOULD
100 × 63 JAMB OF FRAME
32 × 19 INNER BEAD
44 × 38 STILE OF SASH
GLASS
56
32 × 19 OUTER BEAD
FIXED TO EDGE OF SASH & FRAME
SASH FRAME
R
Q
T U V
40 TO 50
75
SECTION
STRIKING PLATE FIXED TO FRAME
SASH CATCH FIXED TO SASH
S
65
HOLE FOR CORD

Figure 60

slot downwards (not as shown at P) and inwards; a groove for each fitting must also be formed along each inner bead attached to the sash and continued to the slot of the socket plate (see broken lines at J); when inserting the sash from the inside, the ends of the pivots are engaged in the bottom of the grooves, the sash is pushed downwards and outwards until the slots on the socket plates have been reached. Alternatively, each pin and socket plate may be screwed to the sash and frame respectively; when this is done, the socket plate is fixed with the open end of the slot uppermost (as shown at P) and the groove is formed in the frame. These pivots are not so readily fixed as the type at M, and if the sash is partially open, it can be easily removed from the outside.

The patent type shown at Q is an improvement on the above centres. This consists of a gunmetal screw bolt or pivot with three plates T, U and V. A hole is bored through the middle of the sash and frame. As shown at R, plates T and U are screwed to the edges of the stile and plate V is screwed to the frame. The pin is then inserted by screwing it through the threaded block on plate T. This is an effective fitting as it can be easily fixed, the sash can be readily removed when required, and it is a secure method of hanging the sash as it cannot be removed from the outside unless the bolts are withdrawn. The size of the bolts varies from 75 to 100 mm long and from 6 to 10 mm diameter. A pair of these fittings is required per sash.

Catches.—A simple form is shown at S, the latch fitting being fixed in the middle of the inner face of the top rail of the sash and the striking plate being screwed to the underside of the frame to receive the end of the latch; a spring retains the latch in the fixed position until the sash is required to be opened, when the latch is released by depressing the ring.

Alternatively, the sash may be secured by small barrel or flush bolts, as described for doors.

Eyelets and Cleats.—A simple arrangement which permits of the opening and closing of the sash consists of a length of cord which is attached at each end to brass or bronze eyelets screwed to the inside face of the top and bottom rails. The cord must be of sufficient length to belay it round a metal cleat fixed at a convenient point on the jamb. One form of eyelet is shown at N, and a cleat is shown at O. If the sash catch S is used, the top end of the cord is fastened through the hole provided for it and therefore only the eyelet at the bottom rail is required.

There are many patent devices for opening and closing pivoted sashes, one

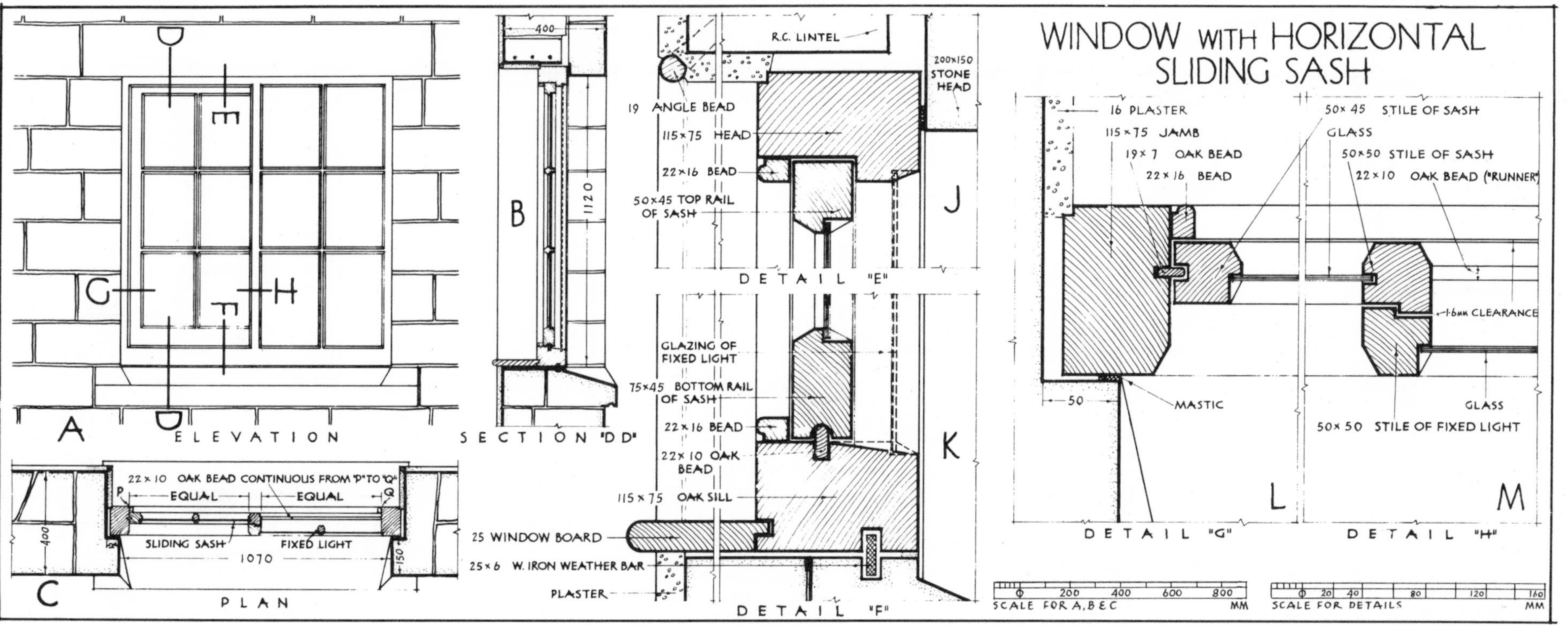

FIGURE 61

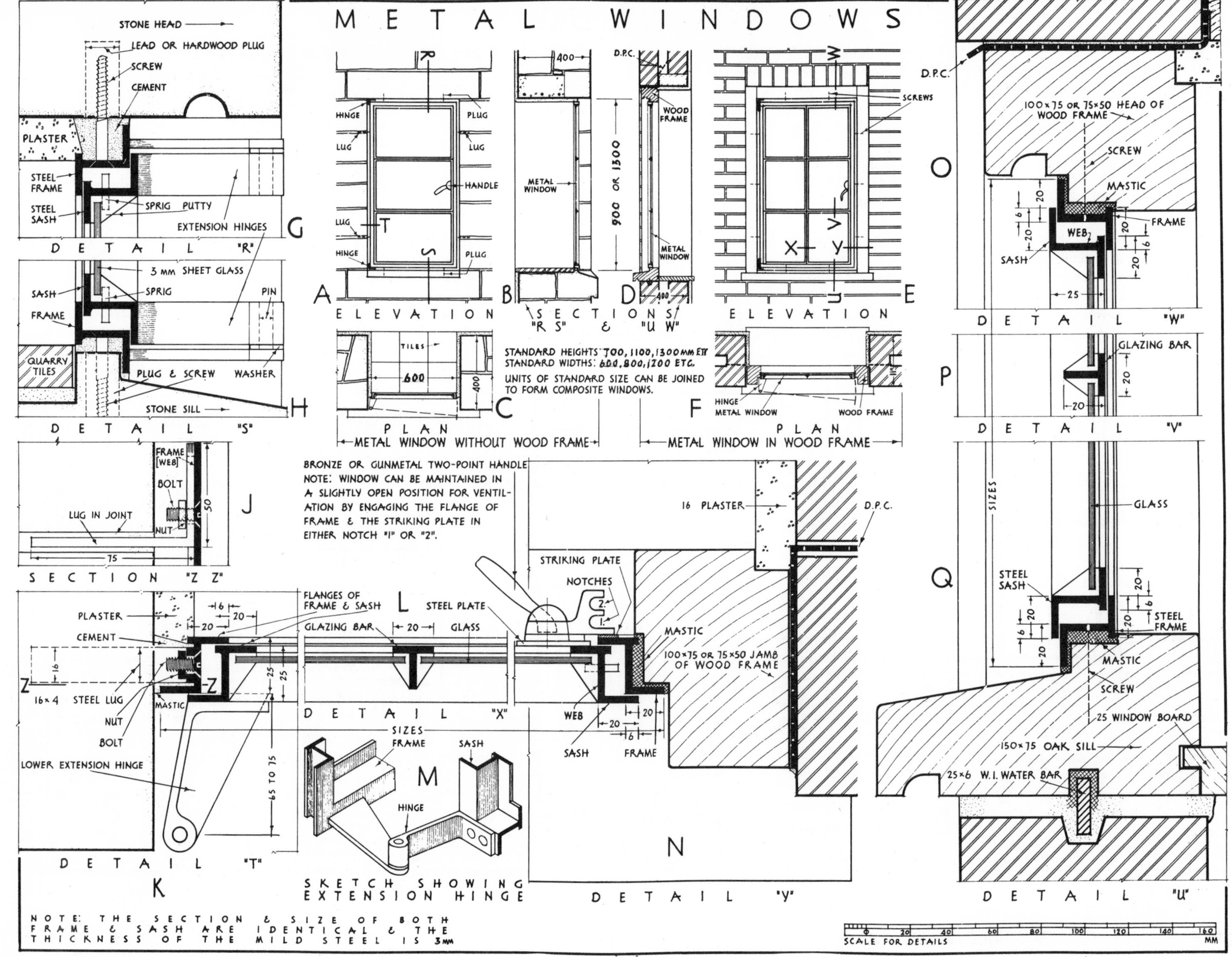
METAL WINDOWS
STONE HEAD
LEAD OR HARDWOOD PLUG
SCREW
CEMENT
PLASTER
STEEL FRAME
STEEL SASH
SPRIG PUTTY
EXTENSION HINGES
G
DETAIL "R"
3 MM SHEET GLASS
SASH
SPRIG
PIN
FRAME
QUARRY TILES
PLUG & SCREW
WASHER
STONE SILL
H
DETAIL "S"
HINGE
PLUG
LUG
HANDLE
T
A
ELEVATION
400
900 OR 1300
METAL WINDOW
B
D.P.C.
WOOD FRAME
D
SECTIONS "R S" & "U W"
SCREWS
E
TILES
600
C
PLAN
METAL WINDOW WITHOUT WOOD FRAME
STANDARD HEIGHTS: 700, 1100, 1300 MM ETC
STANDARD WIDTHS: 600, 800, 1200 ETC.
UNITS OF STANDARD SIZE CAN BE JOINED TO FORM COMPOSITE WINDOWS.
F
HINGE
WOOD FRAME
METAL WINDOW IN WOOD FRAME
D.P.C.
100×75 OR 75×50 HEAD OF WOOD FRAME
SCREW
MASTIC
O
FRAME
WEB
SASH
25
DETAIL "W"
GLAZING BAR
P
DETAIL "V"
SIZES
GLASS
Q
STEEL SASH
STEEL FRAME
MASTIC
SCREW
25 WINDOW BOARD
150×75 OAK SILL
25×6 W.I. WATER BAR
DETAIL "U"
FRAME [WEB]
BOLT
LUG IN JOINT
NUT
75
50
J
SECTION "Z Z"
BRONZE OR GUNMETAL TWO-POINT HANDLE
NOTE: WINDOW CAN BE MAINTAINED IN A SLIGHTLY OPEN POSITION FOR VENTILATION BY ENGAGING THE FLANGE OF FRAME & THE STRIKING PLATE IN EITHER NOTCH "1" OR "2".
16 PLASTER
STRIKING PLATE
NOTCHES
FLANGES OF FRAME & SASH
L
STEEL PLATE
GLAZING BAR
GLASS
CEMENT
16×4 STEEL LUG
MASTIC
NUT
BOLT
100×75 OR 75×50 JAMB OF WOOD FRAME
WEB
SASH
FRAME
DETAIL "X"
SIZES
LOWER EXTENSION HINGE
65 TO 75
M
HINGE
DETAIL "T"
K
SKETCH SHOWING EXTENSION HINGE
N
DETAIL "Y"
NOTE: THE SECTION & SIZE OF BOTH FRAME & SASH ARE IDENTICAL & THE THICKNESS OF THE MILD STEEL IS 3MM
SCALE FOR DETAILS
MM

FIGURE 62

of the simplest consisting of a vertical steel rod which has a hinged arm connected near its upper end and its lower end passing through a gunmetal winding box; the arm is secured to the bottom rail of the sash. The sash is opened and closed as required by turning the handle of the winding box.

Pivoted sash windows are convenient for lighting and ventilating high rooms, as they can be conveniently opened and closed from the floor level. They are sometimes used for factories, warehouses, laundries, staircases, etc. A pivoted sash is often used as a fanlight over a door.

Windows with Horizontal Sliding Sashes (see Fig. 61).—This type of window is fairly common, especially in certain of the northern counties. It is generally known as a *Yorkshire Light*, as such windows are a characteristic feature of many of the older stone built houses in that county. Comparatively few are now made as it has certain undesirable features, *i.e.*, an unsatisfactory appearance and a tendency for the sliding sash to jam. As shown in the elevation at A, the appearance is marred on account of the " sight lines " not being continuous, as the top and bottom rails of the sliding sash are not present in the fixed light; this causes each pair of panes in the fixed light to be of three different heights. These windows are still specified for alterations and extensions to buildings and for replacements.

The window is shown in a regular coursed rubble wall. It consists of a fixed light and a sliding sash. Detail K shows the method adopted for permitting movement of the sash. An oak bead (or *runner*), with rounded edge, is inserted in the oak sill and extends for the full width between jambs (see C and M); a corresponding but slightly wider groove is formed on the lower edge of the bottom rail of the sash. The head of the frame is rebated throughout its length to receive the top rail of the sash (see J), and the sash is retained in position by an inner bead planted on the jambs and continued round the head and sill. A 1·6 mm clearance should be provided all round the sash to permit of free movement. Rain and draughts are excluded by letting a bead into the jamb which engages in a groove in the stile (see L) and rebating the stiles of the fixed light and sliding sash (see M).

A barrel bolt is generally used to secure the sliding sash.

METAL WINDOWS[1]

These are of galvanised mild steel, bronze, and aluminium alloys; they include fixed lights, side and top hung casements opening outwards, inwards and pivoted. There are many sizes and types,[2] with or without glazing bars; simple examples are illustrated in Fig. 62. A fixed light consists of a frame only, and a casement has a sash which is attached to the frame by means of two hinges. The details show that the *frame and sash are of 3·2 mm thick metal and their sections are identical in size and shape*. They are of Z-section, 25 mm deep with 20 mm wide flanges, one of the latter having a slight projection beyond the web to allow the sash and frame to overlap 6·4 mm both internally and externally. The horizontal and vertical members of the frame and sash are welded together at the corners.

The hinges are of the extension type similar to that shown in Fig. 57; when fully extended they give a 100 to 125 mm clearance between the sash and frame enabling the outside of the glass to be cleaned from inside the room. These steel hinges are provided at the top and bottom of the sash (see A, E, G, H and K, Fig. 62), the fixed arm being riveted or welded to the frame and the moving arm (rotating on a hard wearing pin of phosphor-bronze or stainless steel) is fixed to the sash. The sketch at M shows the position of the partially extended hinge relative to the frame and sash.

The sash is fitted with a casement fastener, or *two-point handle*, and a casement stay, both are of bronze or gunmetal.

A two-point handle is shown in the two small-scale elevations at A and E and the plan at N. It is mounted on a pin attached to a back plate which is riveted or welded to the inner flange of the sash, and is so called because of the points formed at the nose by the notches (see N). As shown, a thin bronze striking plate (about 25 mm by 10 mm is secured to the inner flange of the frame. Its object is to prevent the nose of the handle contacting the flange and damaging the paint. When the position of the nose is as shown, a tight fit between the sash and the frame should result; the clearance shown is exaggerated to make the details clear. As noted, ventilation can be afforded by engaging the flange of the frame (and striking plate) in either notch " 1 " or " 2 "; an opening up to 25 mm in width can thus be maintained.

Additional ventilation can of course be obtained by applying the casement stay. This may be a peg stay (see D, Fig. 57), when a pin plate or bracket is fixed to the inner flange of the horizontal member of the frame. The objection to this stay is the damage to glass which may be caused if the sash is blown violently against the wall in the event of the window being left open without the pin engaging in one of the holes of the bar. A better form is the *sliding stay* (consisting of a horizontal arm fixed to the sash which slides through a pivoted fitting at the free end of a rotating bracket fixed to the frame), as this, whilst permitting the sash to be maintained at any angle up to 90°, always keeps it under restraint. Alternatively, friction hinges may be used which render the stay unnecessary.

Fixing.—The metal frame may be fixed direct to the wall or it may be screwed to a wood frame or surround.

The window shown at A, B and C, and detailed at G, H, J and K is fixed direct. Eight 8 mm dia. countersunk holes are provided in the web of the frame to receive the fixing screws (see A). If it is to be fixed to masonry, terra-cotta or concrete, 13 to 16 mm dia. holes are cut in the jambs, head and sill opposite those in the frame. These are preferably plugged with lead, although hardwood plugs or rawlplugs are more often used. The window is then placed in correct position and the frame screwed to the plugs. The frame is finally grouted in with cement mortar and pointed with mastic. The details G and H show these fixings. The details at J and K show an alternative method of fixing the frame by means of 100 mm by 16 mm by 7 or 5 mm lugs (provided by the manufacturers) which are bent up 50 mm and have slotted holes in the bent-up position to give fixing adjustment allowing the horizontal part of the lug to be placed in a convenient joint. If necessary, holes are cut in the jambs of the wall at the correct position, and the lugs are inserted and firmly cemented in. The frame is secured to the lugs by 7 mm dia. fixing bolts.

The above method conforms to the best practice, as windows should never

[1] See Chap. II, Vol. III for a fuller description and additional examples.
[2] E.g. Module 100 range and W20 range (Metal Window Assoc.).

be fixed in position until the roughest work has been completed. Otherwise damage may be caused, not only superficially from daubs of set mortar, etc., but sashes may become distorted and give rise to leakage.

It is, however, the usual practice in cheaper work to build the metal windows in as the construction of the walls proceeds, especially if these are of brick. Typical fixing details of a built-in frame are shown at J and K, already mentioned. The lugs are bolted to the frame and the window is placed in position. It is kept level and plumb as the wall is built, and the lugs are securely built-in with mortar. The lugs are shown bedded in the horizontal joints (see A, J and K). Lugs are also built-in at the head and sill.

A vulnerable part of a metal window whicn opens outwards is the outer flange of the top horizontal sash member where it contacts the frame. In an exposed position water may enter here even if the sash is tight fitting. It is advisable therefore to throat the underside of the head and adopt wide external jambs by fixing the windows well away from and not nearer than 50 mm to the face of the wall. The more elaborate type of window has a projecting metal strip, fixed to the top of the frame just above the sash, which serves as a protection.

Criticism is directed against metal windows fixed direct in certain types of buildings because of the mean appearance presented by the narrow frames. This is emphasized if the colour of the painted windows contrasts with that of the adjacent walling. Hence, as shown at D, E and F and detailed at L, N, O, P and Q, metal windows are often fixed in wood frames. The latter are rebated, or double rebated as shown, to receive the metal frames. *The steel frame is bedded in mastic, and this must be well done to prevent the entrance of water between the two frames.* The metal frame is then screwed to the surround, 8 mm dia. holes are provided in the former for this purpose.

Putty is used for glazing standard metal windows. Ordinary putty (whiting ground in raw linseed oil) alone is useless for this purpose, as it will " run," and gold size is added to enable it to set. Small metal 3 mm dia. sprigs are sometimes used to retain temporarily the panes of glass until the putty has hardened, these fit into holes in the web (see G, etc.). Alternatively, spring wire clips are used in lieu of the sprigs.

Steel windows, being galvanized, are very durable and compare favourably with wood casements in excluding weather. Unlike those of wood, they are not affected by atmospheric changes and consequently do not jam, a defect common to certain badly constructed wood casements due to swelling.

Metal windows can be coupled together, to form composite windows of large size, with metal mullions and transomes. Such a window may also consist of several frames and sashes fixed in a wood surround with wood mullions and, if required, wood transomes. Special types of metal windows are available for schools, hospitals, commercial buildings, etc. These, together with metal doors are described in Vol. III.

ARCHITRAVES, SKIRTINGS, PICTURE RAILS AND ANGLE BEADS

The fixing of certain joinery work can only be completed after the walls have been plastered. Architraves, skirtings and picture rails are examples of such work.

Architraves.—These are used for the concealment of the joints between the casings with their grounds and the plaster at doors and occasionally windows, and to provide an effective finish.

Casings or linings have been described on pp. 96–103 and various sections of architraves are shown at H and N, Fig. 49; architraves are also detailed in Figs. 50, 52, 63 and 64.

An architrave consists of two vertical and one horizontal members with mitred angles; they are nailed along both edges to the grounds (or plugs) and edges of the casing. Usually the feet of the architrave are continued down to the floor to which they are nailed, but in first class work they are often finished with *plinth* or *foot blocks* (see Fig. 64). These blocks are slightly thicker and wider than the architrave and higher than the skirting which is housed into them, and their shape roughly conforms with that of the architrave. A tongue is formed at the foot of the architrave and a mortice is made in the block to receive it; the tongue is glued and securely nailed or screwed to the block from the back. Plinth blocks provide a suitable finish to the architrave and skirting and serve as a protection to the moulded architrave.

The size and design of the architrave depend upon the size of the opening, the quality of the timber and the general effect desired. A 100 mm (nominal) wide architrave is usually sufficient for doors up to 915 mm wide; for large openings the width should not exceed 150 mm if in one piece as it is liable to split when shrinking. The plain architrave shown at N, Fig. 63, would be suitable if the door has square or chamfered panels (see J and L, Fig. 46), but a more elaborate architrave would be preferred if, for instance, the panel mouldings were of the section shown at F′, Fig. 46. Certain sections, such as those at L, Fig. 49, and P, Fig. 63, should be avoided unless well seasoned good quality timber (preferably hardwood) is used, otherwise unequal shrinkage will occur, resulting in the members curling or twisting on account of one-half of the section being much thinner than the other. Simplicity in design is a characteristic of modern construction (see also p. 93).

Skirtings or Plinths are provided to protect the wall plaster and to cover the joint between the floor boards and plaster. Several sections are shown in Figs. 63 and 64. The size varies, but the depth rarely exceeds 175 mm unless for very large rooms.

The best method of securing skirtings is shown at Q, Fig. 63, and B and E, Fig. 64, where horizontal rough grounds are plugged at about 645 mm intervals in the vertical joints of the brickwork. Skirtings which are 100 mm or less in depth only require one set of grounds. When two rows of grounds are fixed, the space between them is not always filled with plaster, and when it is, care should

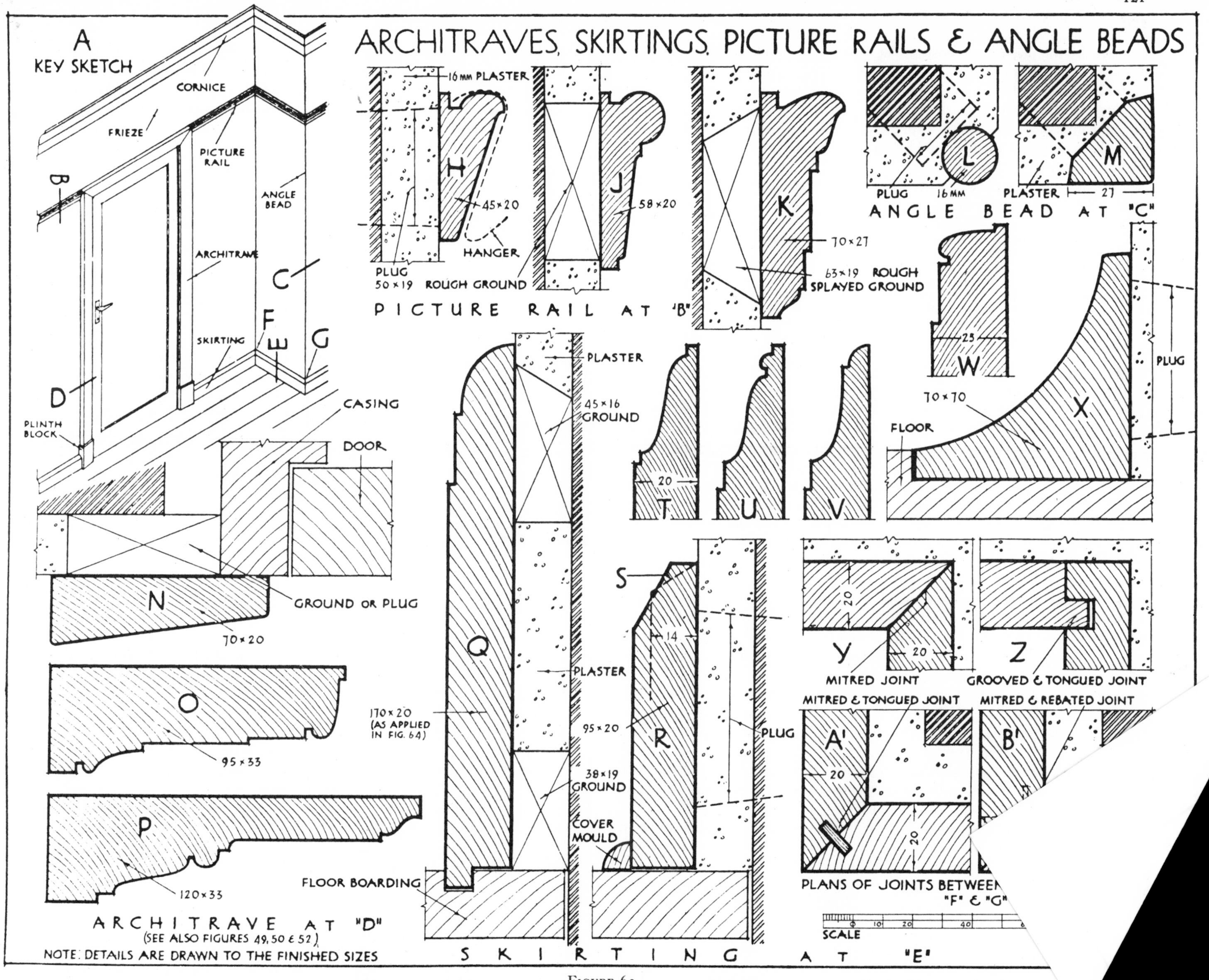
ARCHITRAVES, SKIRTINGS, PICTURE RAILS & ANGLE BEADS
A
KEY SKETCH
CORNICE
FRIEZE
PICTURE RAIL
ANGLE BEAD
ARCHITRAVE
SKIRTING
PLINTH BLOCK
B
C
D
E
F
G
16 MM PLASTER
H
45×20
HANGER
PLUG
50×19 ROUGH GROUND
J
58×20
K
70×27
63×19 ROUGH SPLAYED GROUND
PICTURE RAIL AT 'B'
L
M
PLUG
16 MM
PLASTER
27
ANGLE BEAD AT "C"
CASING
DOOR
N
GROUND OR PLUG
70×20
O
95×33
P
120×33
ARCHITRAVE AT "D"
(SEE ALSO FIGURES 49, 50 & 52)
NOTE: DETAILS ARE DRAWN TO THE FINISHED SIZES
PLASTER
45×16 GROUND
Q
170×20 (AS APPLIED IN FIG. 64)
PLASTER
38×19 GROUND
COVER MOULD
FLOOR BOARDING
S
14
95×20
R
PLUG
20
T
U
V
W
25
70×70
FLOOR
X
PLUG
20
20
Y
Z
MITRED JOINT
GROOVED & TONGUED JOINT
MITRED & TONGUED JOINT
MITRED & REBATED JOINT
A'
B'
20
20
PLANS OF JOINTS BETWEEN "F" & "G"
10 20 40
SCALE
SKIRTING AT "E"

FIGURE 63

be taken by the plasterer to ensure that the face of the plaster does not project beyond the grounds.

The cheaper and more usual method of securing skirtings is to fix them direct to plugs which have been driven into the vertical joints of the wall at about 645 mm intervals. For deep skirtings the plugs are staggered, with the plugs fixed alternately near the floor and top of the plinths. The skirting at R, Fig. 63 is shown plugged to the wall.

It is the general practice to fit or *scribe* the lower edge of the skirting to the floor, which may be uneven.

Scribing is done by placing the piece of skirting in position and packing or wedging up the lower end until the top edge is level; compasses (see 5, Fig. 67) are taken and, with the points apart equal to the height that the lowest portion of the floor is below the bottom edge of the skirting, are drawn along the face of the skirting with the points of the compass in a vertical plane; as the lower point follows the irregularities of the floor the other marks a parallel line on the plinth; the lower edge of the skirting is then sawn along this irregular line and thus a tight fit between the skirting and floor is assured when the former is fixed.

A gap invariably appears between this bottom edge of the skirting and the floor boards due to the combined shrinkage of the skirting and the floor joists. This allows both dust and currents of air to enter ground floor rooms from the space below. A small (10 to 13 mm) quadrant cover mould as shown at R, Fig. 63, may be bradded to the floor to prevent this; alternatively, the gap may be filled with a material called *plastic wood* which is pressed in whilst in a plastic condition, smoothed over with a knife and sand-papered over when set to bring it flush with the face of the skirting. A better, but more costly method, is shown at Q, Fig. 63, and E, Fig. 64; a tongue is formed on the lower edge of the skirting and this is fitted into a groove formed in the flooring.

Several joints between the ends of skirtings are shown in Fig. 63. The cheapest method is to mitre the ends at both external and internal angles as shown at Y. Another cheap internal joint consists of scribing one end to the face of the other which has been tightly and squarely fitted into the angle. A better joint for internal angles is shown at Z; one piece of the skirting is grooved from the bottom edge to the bottom of the moulding, the end of the adjacent piece is tongued and the moulded portion is scribed to that of the first piece. A joint used in very good work for both internal and external angles is shown at A′; the thin hardwood cross-tongue is glued and the joint is assembled before the pieces are fixed to the grounds. The mitred and rebated joint at B′ (also called a *lipped* joint) is a good form for external angles; cross-bradding as shown is necessary.

As indicated in Fig. 64, skirtings are housed into plinth blocks. If the latter are not provided, the ends of the skirtings should be let into architraves, otherwise cracks will show when shrinkage occurs.

The designs of skirtings, architraves and panel mouldings when associated together should conform; thus, the skirting at Q, Fig. 63 harmonizes with the architrave K, Fig. 50 and the panel mouldings N or A′, Fig. 46, and the skirting moulding W, Fig. 63, architrave O, Fig. 63 and panel mouldings V or G′, Fig. 46 form an agreeable combination; the chamfered or bevelled edge shown at R and S, Fig. 63 is preferred when a simple effect is desired. Alternative skirting mouldings are shown at T, U and V, Fig. 63; the cavetto skirting at X, Fig. 63, provides an effective sanitary finish, but the labour in forming the trenching in the floor to receive it is costly.

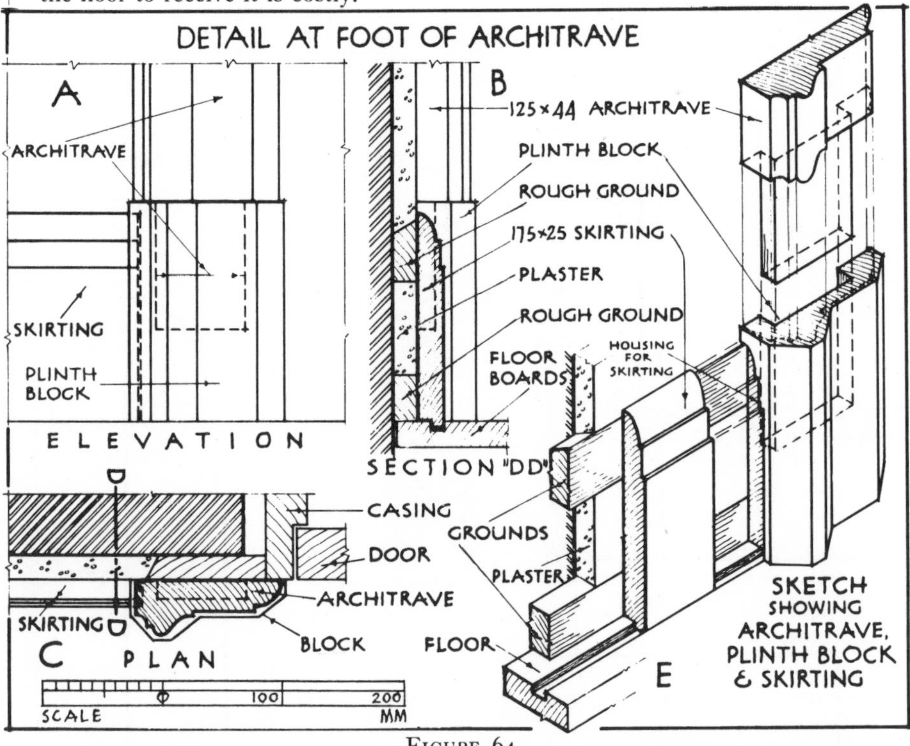

FIGURE 64

Picture Rails.—These are often omitted in the modern house, especially in rooms which may be only 2·5 m high; they have may the effect of spoiling the proportions by breaking up the wall surfaces and " lowering the ceilings."

When they are required, a satisfactory finish is obtained if they are fixed at the level of the top of the door architrave, as shown at A, Fig. 63. Alternative sections through picture rails are given at H, J and K, and the plug and rough ground (two forms) fixings are included; plugs are generally used and are driven into the vertical joints of the walling.

Angle Beads.—External angles of plastered walls have to be protected against damage to the plaster arrises. Two methods of accomplishing this are shown at L and M, Fig. 63. Plugs are driven into the joints, the projecting ends are cut off in true alignment, and 16 or 20 mm wood beads are nailed to them. The plaster should be cut or *quirked* as shown, but this is often omitted. An application of this form is shown in detail in E, Fig. 61. Another type is the galvanized steel angle bead nailed into the brick joints. The more costly Keene's or Parian cement arris has been referred to on p. 107 (see N, Fig. 54) and described on p. 32.

STAIRS

A staircase is a set of steps or *flight* leading from one floor to another. Timber and stone are two of the many materials used for constructing stairs (see Fig. 65). Each step consists of a horizontal portion or *tread* connected to a front part known as a *riser*. The *going* of a step is the horizontal distance between the faces of two consecutive risers. The *rise* of a step is the vertical distance between the tops of two consecutive treads.

It has been found that, for comfortable usage, the best proportions of a step are such that: going plus twice rise equals 584 to 610 mm. Thus at F, 305 + (2 × 152) = 609 mm. The Building Regulations require this figure to be between 550 and 700 mm.

Timber Stair.—The simple internal example shown in section at A and plan at B has a total rise of 1146 mm and there are six 191 mm risers. The risers and attached treads span between two 250 mm by 38 mm *strings* which are plugged to the side walls. The treads (see D) and the risers are housed 13 mm into the strings and glued wedges are used as shown at C to make a tight secure joint. Triangular glued blocks (six per step) are also required to stiffen the construction. The detail at C also shows how the riser is tongued, glued into the adjacent treads and screwed. The distance between the outer faces of the strings is 840 mm (to suit a space 13 mm greater between the walls); when this latter is increased to 915 mm as is common in houses, then additional support is required to the steps running centrally below the flight. This comprises a 100 mm by 75 mm raking bearer which has 150 mm by 25 mm thick timbers nailed to it to fit tightly under the treads (see Chap. II, Vol. III).

The simple handrail detailed at E is of 50 mm dia. hardwood fixed to steel brackets plugged to the wall as indicated also at A. The Building Regulations state that the handrail should be fixed at a height not less than 840 mm as shown at A.

Stone Stair.—The steps are made of hard non-slip stone such as York sandstone. The elevation at F and plan at G are of a short flight such as may be required at an entrance; it is made with solid stone steps. These have a more or less rectangular shape as detailed at H, but part of the soffit is chamfered as indicated by the broken line and shown also at J. The chamfering is not essential here but it reduces weight and gives a neater finish on the underside should the soffit be exposed to view as in open flight stairs. The steps rest on brickwork at either side as noted at G and J. The elevation at F (which is actually a section through a returned reinforced concrete landing), shows how care has

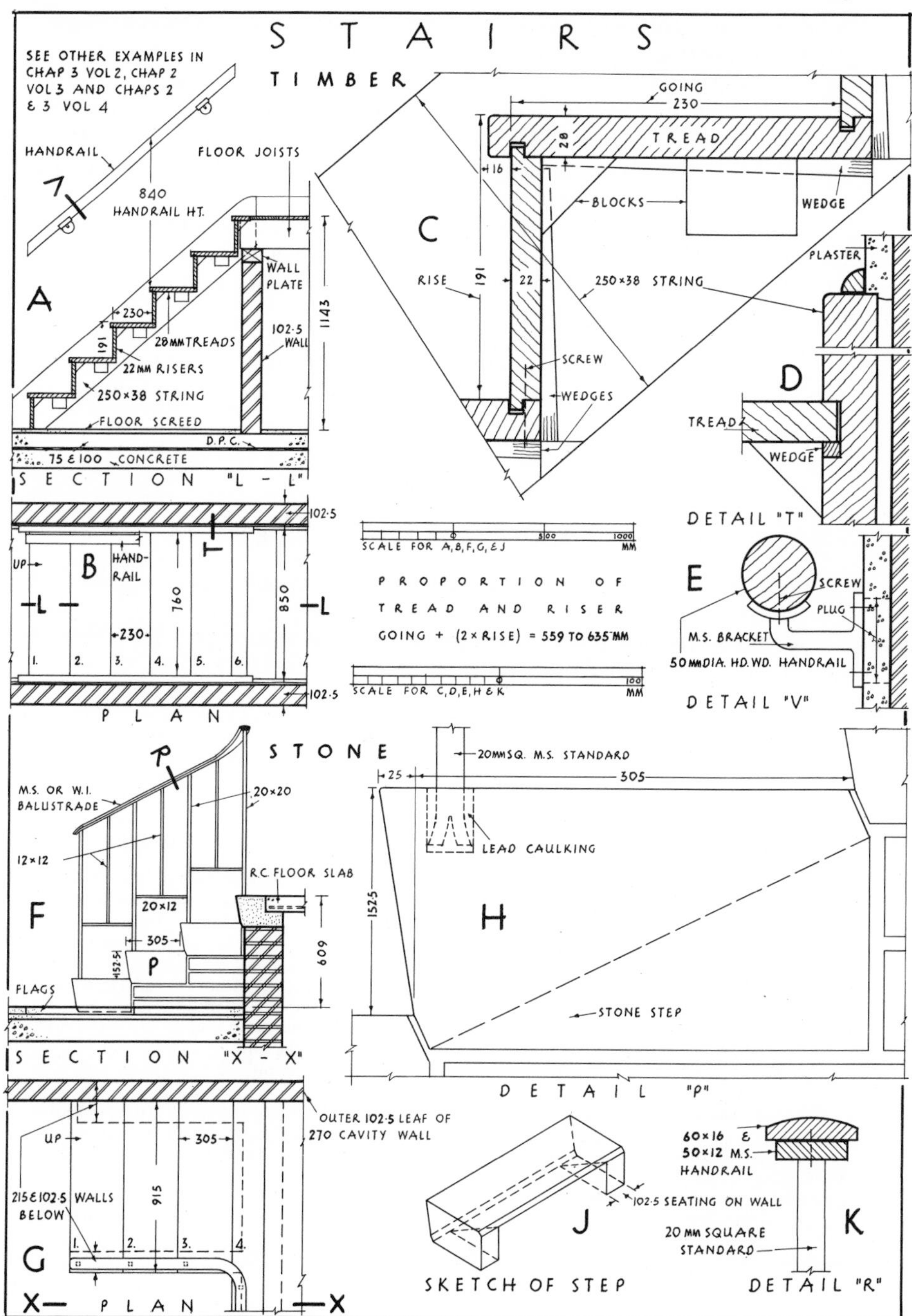

FIGURE 65

been taken to course the steps in with the brickwork so as to avoid cut bricks.

The balustrade on the open side of the flight is formed of mild steel or wrought iron members and the handrail is drawn at K. The 20 mm square *standards* or *balusters* are placed in pockets in the step as shown at H and fixed by lead which is run into the holes. Note that in accordance with the Building Regulations the height of a balustrade to a landing must be at least 900 mm for a private stairway (1100 mm for a common stairway).

Similar steps to these can be made in reinforced concrete and they can both be built 102 or 150 mm into walls to cantilever out so as to be unsupported on the outer edge. Care should be taken to provide sufficient weight of wall above the bearings to " tail " these steps down.

Further examples of stairs are given in subsequent volumes as follows: Stone and reinforced concrete in Chap. III, Vol. II. Timber in Chap. II, Vol. III. Reinforced concrete and steel (including fire escape stairs) in Chaps. II and III, Vol. IV.

NAILS, SCREWS AND FASTENERS

Steel or wrought iron fastenings used in carpentry and joinery include oval and circular wire nails, cut clasp nails, wrought nails, brads, flat and round-headed screws, coach screws, corrugated fasteners and bolts. The latter is detailed at J, Fig. 80, and other fastenings are illustrated in Fig. 66.

Wire Nails.—These are either oval (see A) or circular (see B). Oval wire nails are used for general purposes; they are tough and are not liable to split the wood when driven in; the slight shallow grooves or serrations in the stem increase the " holding power " or ability to grip the fibres of the wood into which they are driven. They are obtainable in sizes varying from 25 to 150 mm and are sold by weight. The circular nail shown at B is not so extensively used by the joiner on account of its unsightly flat circular head; it is chiefly confined to temporary or unimportant work, and in the making of boxes, packing cases, etc.

Cut Clasp Nails (see C).—These have been ousted by oval wire nails.

Wrought Nails (see D).—Tapered in both width and thickness to form a point, usefully employed for fixing thin members, as after penetrating the material the point can be readily hammered into the wood or clenched (see p. 86). The sizes vary from 25 to 100 mm.

Spikes are used for securing large wood members; wire nails which exceed 125 mm in length and wrought nails which are longer than 100 mm are classified as spikes.

Floor Brads (see E).—These were once used for securing floor boards but have now been replaced by oval nails. The length varies from 38 to 75 mm.

Joiners' Brads or Sprigs (see H).—These resemble floor brads, but the sizes are from 6 to 50 mm; they are made of steel, brass and copper.

Panel Pins (see F).—These small nails, circular in section, are generally used for fixing hardwood members (usually mouldings).

Needle Points (see G).—These are steel pins used for fixing small mouldings, veneers, etc.; they are driven in and snapped off flush with the surface; they are obtainable in six degrees of fineness.

It is difficult to drive small nails, pins, etc. into hardwood without bending unless small holes have been bored to receive them. Driving is facilitated if the points are dipped in grease.

Screws.—There are several forms of screws, but those chiefly used for fixing woodwork are the flat headed (see K) and round-headed (see L) types. These are made of wrought iron, steel and brass, and as the thread is effective in cutting into wood, they are sometimes called *wood screws*. Screws are fixed by means of the screwdriver or brace and bit (see 40 and 45, Fig. 67), and their advantages over nails are: (1) they can easily be removed when required, (2) they can be fixed in positions where jarring has to be avoided, and (3) they give a stronger job on account of their greater holding power.

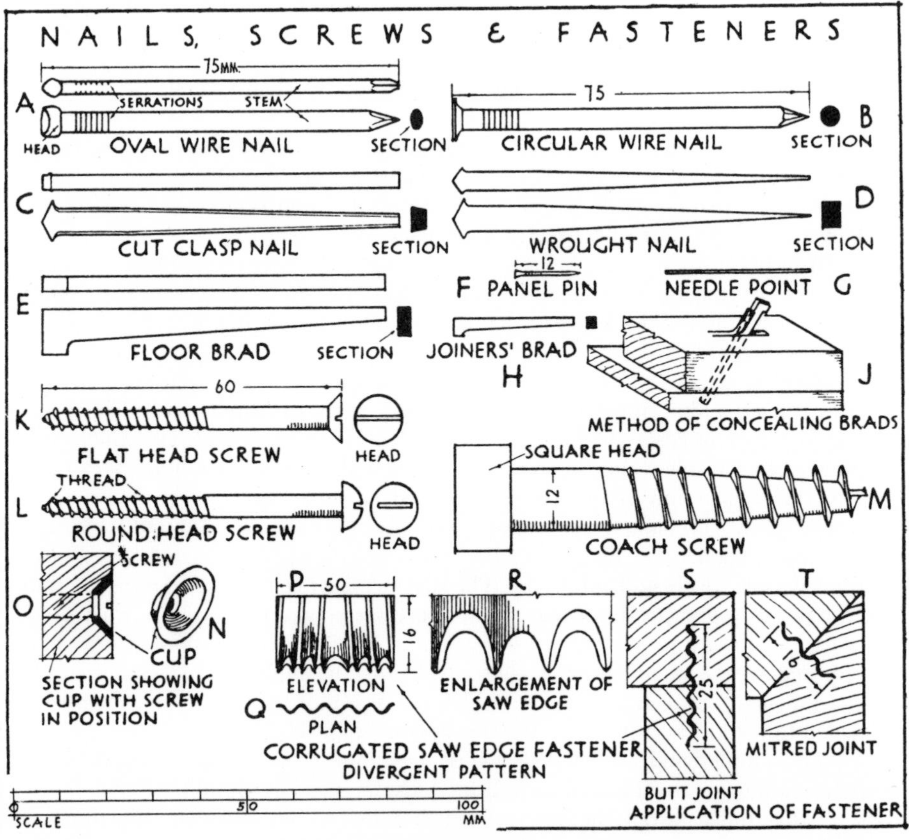

FIGURE 66

Flat-headed or Countersunk Screws.—As shown at K, the circular flat head (which is notched to receive the screwdriver) is tapered down to a point; the flat head can be brought flush with the timber; it is obtainable in sizes varying from 6 to 150 mm long and from 1·6 to 16 mm in diameter. It is desirable (and for hardwoods it is essential) to bore a hole of a smaller diameter than that of the screw by one of the several boring tools illustrated in Fig. 67 prior to inserting the screw.

Cups (see N).—These are of brass and are obtainable in various sizes to suit the head of the screws which they are to receive. They should be used wherever mouldings, beads, etc., are to be removed subsequently, otherwise the woodwork will become damaged by the removal and reinsertion of the screws. A section with a cup in position is shown at O, and examples of its use are shown at J and R, Fig. 58, in connection with the inner beads.

A hole slightly smaller than the diameter of the top of the cup, is formed by a centre bit (see 46, Fig. 67) in the required position, a little glue is placed round the hole and the cup is driven in.

Round-headed Screws (see L).—These are similar to those described above, except that the head is almost hemispherical. They are generally used for fixing metal to wood, *e.g.*, locks and similar hardware.

Concealment of Fastenings.—When nails and brads are driven into softwood their heads are driven about 3 mm below the surface by using a hammer on a steel punch (see 10, Fig. 67) and the holes are filled or " stopped " with putty before the work is painted. For hardwoods which are not to be painted, the heads are punched and the holes are stopped with material which is coloured to conform with that of the wood; this stopping, which is melted and applied with a knife as a mastic, sets hard and is then smoothed over to the surface of the wood to render the positions of the fixing inconspicuous. Another method of concealing brads is shown at J, Fig. 66; a sharp chisel is used to carefully cut and lift a small portion of the wood, the brad is punched below the surface and the chip glued down.

Pelleting is resorted to for concealing the heads of screws; this consists of sinking the head below the surface by means of a centre bit and a cylindrical plug or pellet of wood of similar grain to that of the member is glued, driven in and chiselled off flush.

Coach Screws (see M).—These are of similar construction to the wood screw, except that the heads are square or hexagonal so that they can be turned by a spanner; they are from 20 to 200 mm long and from 5 to 13 mm in diameter, and are often used for connecting metal plates, straps and angles to wood.

Corrugated Saw Edge Fasteners (see P, Q and R).—These are corrugated pieces of steel or brass which are shaped and sharpened along one edge to give what are called " tack points "; each succeeding point is sharpened on opposite sides like a saw (see R); they are made in depths varying from 6 to 25 mm. They are being extensively used for making light framings, boxes and similar temporary work, repairing cracked boards, etc. Two applications are shown at S and T, the former showing a butt joint and the latter a mitred joint. These fasteners are easily fixed by simply driving them in with a hammer, during which the wood members are drawn together.

Wrought iron bolts and rivets are described on p. 161

WOODWORKING TOOLS

Whilst machinery has very largely displaced hand labour particularly in shops where standardized units like doors and windows are made, the joiner is asked to perform many tasks necessitating the use of hand tools. The following are in general use and are essential parts of a kit :—

Classification.—Hand tools may be classified into those required for : (1) marking and setting out, (2) cutting and shaving, (3) boring, (4) impelling, (5) abrading, (6) cramping and holding, and (7) miscellaneous. Most of these are shown in Fig. 67.

(1) Marking and Setting Out Tools.—These include rules, marking knife, straight edge, try square, mitre, bevel, compasses, callipers and gauges.

Rules (see 1).—Made of boxwood : 50 cm four-fold, 1 m four-fold, etc.

Marking Awl and Cutting Knife (see 7).—Used for setting out accurate work (see p. 102), the awl (or point) being used for pricking points from the rod and the sharp edge being used to cut the shoulder, etc., lines.

Straight Edge is a 75 to 100 mm wide board 13 mm thick, 2 or 2·5 m long with one edge perfectly square and the other bevelled to distinguish it from the true edge; used for testing surfaces, marking lines, etc.

Try Square (see 2).—For setting out right angles and testing square angles during the planing up of stuff; obtainable with 115, 150, 190, 225 and 300 long metal blades.

A larger square is also required; consists of a mahogany blade which is usually 58 mm by 6 mm by 760 mm long tenoned to a 400 mm long stock.

A *Mitre Square or Fixed Bevel* has a steel blade fixed at 45° to a wood stock; this is a useful tool for setting out 45° angles.

Bevel (see 3).—The blade can be secured at any angle; used for setting out angles other than right angles; the blades are 225, 267 and 300 mm long.

Compasses (see 5).—Used for marking parallel lines to irregular surfaces such as scribing skirtings to floors (see p. 122) and mouldings to walls, and for describing circles and setting off distances; stocked in 150, 175, 200, 225 and 250 mm sizes.

A *trammel* is used for striking large areas or circles; consists of two metal heads each having a 75 to 125 mm point, which slide along a hardwood stick; the points can be fixed as desired and one of them may be replaced by a pencil socket.

Callipers are used for measuring diameters of curved surfaces; *outside* callipers, used for external dimensions, consist of a pair of hinged steel curved legs which are shaped to a fine point; *inside* callipers, for inside measurements, have two hinged and tapered legs which finish with points which turn outwards.

Gauges are tools used to mark one or more lines on the wood parallel to the edge; the varieties include the marking gauge, cutting gauge, mortise gauge and panel gauge.

Marking Gauge (see 4).—The holed adjustable beech head receives the stem, near one end of which is a steel marking tooth; after the stem has been set and the thumbscrew tightened, the face of the head (that nearest the tooth) is placed against the timber and the point is pressed down to score a line on the surface as the head traverses the edge.

Cutting Gauge.—Similar to the marking gauge except that it has a steel cutter in place of the tooth; used for cutting parallel strips from thin stuff such as veneers and for marking across the grain.

Mortise Gauge (see 9).—This has a movable pin attached to one end of a brass slide and a pin fixed to the stem, the distance between them may be adjusted from 6 to 50 mm. The gauge thus enables two parallel lines to be marked and is employed for setting out mortises and tenons; the points of the gauge are set to the width of the mortise and the head is then adjusted to the required distance from the movable pin.

Panel Gauge.—This is larger than but resembles the marking gauge; it is usually made by the joiner, the stem being about 710 mm long. The pin is fixed and the head is adjusted like the marking gauge; it is used in the construction of door panels.

(2) Cutting and Planing Tools.—These comprise saws, chisels, gouges, planes and spokeshaves.

Saws.—The many varieties include the cross-cut saw, rip saw, tenon saw, dovetail saw, compass saw, pad saw and bow saw. A saw has a spring steel blade with a wood (usually beech or apple wood) handle securely riveted to it; the lower edge or front of the blade is divided into fine teeth; this cutting edge is usually specified according to the number of *points* (not teeth) per 25 mm; thus at A, C and D, Fig. 67, the number of points per 25 mm is six, four and ten respectively. The teeth are bent alternately to the right and left of the blade; this is called *setting* (see B); in addition, the blades of the larger saws are ground thinner at the back (opposite edge to the teeth) than at the cutting edge. The setting is done by means of the *saw set* (see 20). A saw should be thin to avoid waste of material.

Cross-cut Saw (see 12).—This is essentially used for cutting across the fibres of the wood, but also with the grain, and in carpentry for general sawing; it is made in lengths of 500 to 710 mm; the number of points is 5, 5½, 6, 7 and 8 per 25 mm; the eight point saw is considered best for hardwoods, a seven-point saw for both hardwood and softwood, and a five-point saw for rough carpentry; the teeth are shaped as in the enlarged sketch at A.

Rip Saw.—This is only used if machinery is unavailable for cutting timber along the grain; it resembles the cross-cut saw, is 710 mm long, and has teeth shaped as shown at C with four points per 25 mm.

Panel Saw.—Like the cross-cut with a finer blade and teeth shaped as at A; a 680 mm blade with ten or twelve points per 25 mm is normal; it is used for accurate work and instead of the tenon saw for cutting panels and similar wide work.

Tenon Saw (see 13).—For finer work than both the cross-cut and panel saws, used for cutting tenons and where a clean cut is needed; the 350 mm blade is preferred which is stiffened by the brass or iron bar on the top edge. It has ten or twelve points per 25 mm and the teeth (called *peg* teeth) are shaped as shown at D.

Dovetail Saw (see 15).—This has a 200, 225 or 300 mm blade with fourteen points per 25 mm; used for very fine work, as for forming dovetail joints.

Compass or Turning Saw (see 16 and 17).—For cutting curves, it has interchangeable blades; the teeth are shaped as at C.

Pad or Keyhole Saw (see 18).—For forming keyholes and similar curved work; it is the smallest saw, the blade can be passed right through the handle when not in use; the teeth are similar to those of the compass saw.

Bow Saw (see 19).—Used for cutting curved work with sweeps which are too quick to be negotiated by the compass saw.

Frame Saw.—Is similar but longer and stronger than the bow saw.

Chisels have forged steel blades with ash, boxwood or beech handles; each blade is bevelled on the back and has a cutting edge. Used to remove thin layers or shavings of wood in shaping surfaces, forming mortices, etc. Various kinds include the paring, firmer and mortise chisels and gouges.

Paring Chisel (see 35).—Used for paring plane surfaces; the blade may be either square or bevelled, the latter type being useful in forming grooves; obtainable in lengths varying from 225 to 530 mm and in widths of from 6 to 50 mm.

Firmer Chisel (see 36).—A stronger type than the last one as it has to withstand the mallet used for propulsion; useful for general work and in removing wood in thin chips; the length varies from 100 mm upwards and the width from 2 to 50 mm.

Mortise Chisel.—For forming mortices, it is stronger than the firmer chisel, the one at 37 is known as a *socket mortise chisel*; the ordinary mortise chisels are 3 to 20 mm wide and the maximum width of the socket type is 38 mm.

Plugging Chisel (see 38).—Made entirely of forged steel and used for preparing holes in brickwork, etc., for wood plugs.

Pocket Chisel.—A very fine chisel, sharpened both sides, it is used for forming pockets in boxed window frames (see p. 111); obtainable in widths from 38 to 64 mm.

Gouges are curved chisels producing circular cuts. Paring, firmer, socket, etc., gouges are obtainable; that shown at 39 is an outside ground gouge for heavy work; those ground on the inside are used for paring; widths vary from 3 to 38 mm.

Planes are so called as they are chiefly used for shaving or smoothing plane surfaces after the timber has been sawn; they are of (*a*) wood (beech) and (*b*) metal (cast steel, gunmetal and malleable iron).

(a) **Wood Planes.**—Of the many types, the jack, trying and smoothing planes (known as *bench planes*) are essential items of kit; some of the others are seldom used.

Jack Plane (see 21).—This is the first plane used on a piece of wood after it has left the saw; it eliminates the saw marks and leaves the surface sufficiently smooth for the subsequent finishing with the trying and smoothing planes; it consists of a stock, double irons, wedge and handle.

The standard beechwood *stock* should be carefully selected; the handle is glued into a slot and a hole is formed to receive the irons and wedge; a 20 mm hardwood stud is fitted on top near to the *nose* of the plane to receive the blows from the hammer when the irons are being adjusted.

The irons consist of a *cutting iron* (E) and a *back* or *top iron* (F) which are made of crucible cast steel; they are made in various widths, the 60 mm size being popular. The bottom edge of the cutting iron is rounded as it is required to remove shavings which should be thickest in the centre and finer at the edge; this edge is double-bevelled (see enlarged section through the edge at G), the *grinding bevel* being slightly hollow ground and approximately 25°, the *sharpening* angle is about 32°; the thickness of the iron increases from 2 mm at the top to about 4 mm at the top of the grinding bevel; the iron is slotted to allow movement of the screw which attaches it to the back iron. The *back iron* (F) is of uniform thickness of about 3 down to about 13 mm from the bottom, when it is slightly curved and reduced to a fine edge; a brass nut is attached to the iron and receives the screw which connects both plates together (see J); the distance that the edge of the cutting iron projects beyond that of the back iron is called the *set*, and this depends upon the character of the wood to be planed and the thickness of the desired shaving; the set is approximately 3 mm for softwoods and 1·6 mm for hardwoods; the object of the back iron is to break the shaving and bend it as it proceeds through the mouth.

The irons are secured in the stock by knocking down a wood *wedge* (see 21 and H).

Trying Plane (see 26).—Used for precise work, such as removing irregularities left on the surface of the wood by the jack plane and for forming long straight edges; it is the largest bench plane (the sizes being 560, 600 and 660 mm) and resembles the jack plane; the set of irons is usually 1·6 mm for softwoods and 0·8 mm for hardwoods.

Smoothing Plane (see 29).—This is the finishing plane used to smooth the wood after the jack and trying planes have been operated; the stock is only 200 mm long and is provided with double irons set as for the trying plane.

Rebate Plane (see 28).—Used for forming rebates and has only a single cutting iron from 6 to 50 mm wide fixed by a wedge and placed on the skew.

Hollow and Round Planes (see 30).—The former is used for making convex surfaces on the timber (see enlarged section through the sole at K), the edge of the single iron conforms to the curve; concave surfaces are made by the round plane (see enlarged section L).

Bead Plane (see 33).—This moulding plane is still required, and two or three different sizes should form part of a kit; it is used for forming a half-round moulding with a *quirk* (sinking) on edges of members; the strip let into the sole of the stock is of boxwood to resist wear; a sketch showing the application is given at M.

Note.—Moulding planes, such as ogee, torus, reed, astragal, ovolo, etc., have practically fallen into disuse, as mouldings are made more cheaply by machinery.

Plough Plane (see 31) is used for forming grooves with the grain from 3 to 16 mm wide, and up to 32 mm deep; the single iron, secured by a wedge, passes down to a narrow mouth in the metal runner screwed to the stock; the depth of the groove is regulated by the metal thumb-screw which depresses or raises a metal solepiece (about 20 mm wide) which operates between the runner and wood fence; the wood nuts and screw bars are manipulated to adjust the width between the fence and the runner as required; the plough is provided with six or eight irons of different widths.

Router or Old Woman's Tooth (see 32).—Used for increasing the depth of grooves (*trenching*) formed previously by another tool; the strong iron is from 3 to 13 mm wide.

Spokeshave (see 34).—Used for planing circular work having quick curves; the iron (see O) has two tapered tongs passing through the stock; it is adjusted by tapping either the projecting ends of the tongs or the blade (see section at N).

Compass Plane.—This is a smoothing plane with a convex sole and 50 mm wide double irons for planing curved surfaces; it is not much used.

Toothing Plane.—Used for preparing surfaces of timber which are to be glued together; its 50 mm wide single iron has a serrated edge.

Tonguing and Grooving Planes (also known as *matching planes*).—Used to form tongues and grooves on the edges of boards required for match-boarding, battened doors, etc. Although most of such work is done by machinery, these planes are occasionally required, especially when preparing work during fixing.

(b) **Metal Planes.**—Most of the wood planes described above are also obtainable in metal, such as cast steel, gunmetal, malleable iron or aluminium. Some of them are an improvement upon the wood planes, but the wood jack plane especially is still considered to be the best for its purpose. The metal planes are more fragile than those of wood.

Metal Smooth Plane (see 42).—Used for smoothing the surfaces of hardwoods of best quality which have been previously dressed with the jack and trying planes. The cap secures the two irons (the *cutter*) by a screw which passes through to the frog that supports them; the cap is adjusted by lever " X "; lever " Y " adjusts the cutter sideways, the frog is adjusted either forward or backward by an adjusting screw, and the large screw or milled nut behind the frog adjusts the edge of the cutter to regulate the shaving thickness. This tool is obtainable in sizes varying from 140 to 250 mm in length of sole with cutters from 32 to 60 mm wide.

Block Plane (see 44).—This is very useful for small work which is not readily accessible and for preparing mitres of hardwood mouldings; it is well suited for planing across the grain; it has only a single 40 mm wide iron or cutter inclined at 12° to 20°; the bevel of the cutter is uppermost. To assemble the plane, the iron (which has a central slot) is placed over the small projecting lever cap screw, the cap (which has a knuckle joint) is fitted over it, and when correctly placed, pressure on the cap springs it into position; the edge of the cutter is brought parallel with the mouth (barely 6 mm wide) by lateral movement of the lever and the distance between the edge of the cutter and the front of the mouth is regulated as required by the milled screw or nut shown below the lever.

Other varieties of metal planes include the *bullnose plane* (the edge of the iron is close

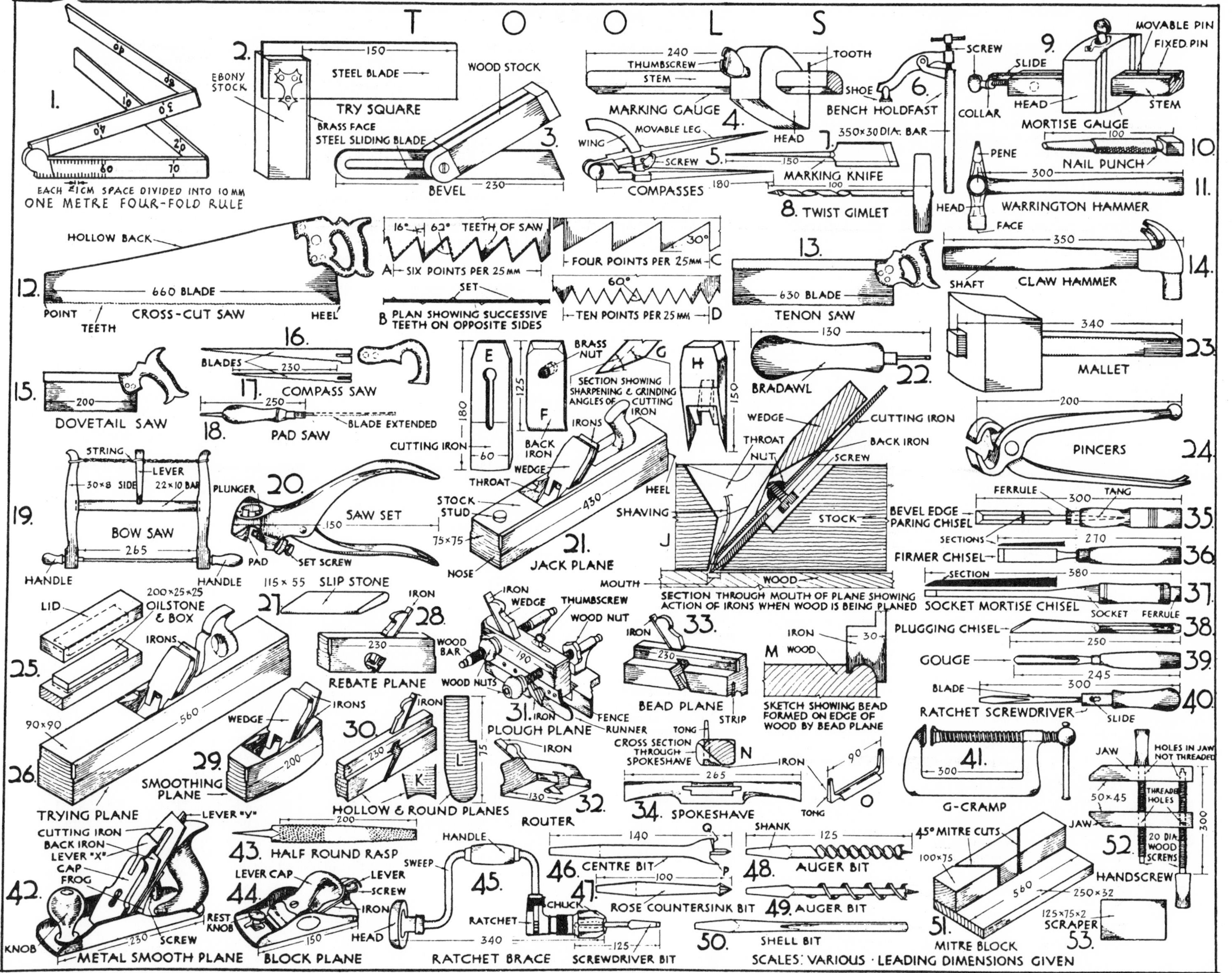
TOOLS
1.
EACH 1CM SPACE DIVIDED INTO 10 MM
ONE METRE FOUR-FOLD RULE
2.
150
EBONY STOCK
STEEL BLADE
TRY SQUARE
BRASS FACE
WOOD STOCK
STEEL SLIDING BLADE
3.
BEVEL
230
240
THUMBSCREW
STEM
TOOTH
MARKING GAUGE
4.
HEAD
WING
MOVABLE LEG
SCREW
5.
COMPASSES
180
SHOE
6.
BENCH HOLDFAST
SCREW
350×30 DIA. BAR
7.
150
MARKING KNIFE
100
8. TWIST GIMLET
9.
MOVABLE PIN
FIXED PIN
SLIDE
COLLAR
HEAD
STEM
MORTISE GAUGE
100
10.
NAIL PUNCH
PENE
300
11.
HEAD
FACE
WARRINGTON HAMMER
HOLLOW BACK
12.
660 BLADE
POINT
TEETH
CROSS-CUT SAW
HEEL
TEETH OF SAW
A
SIX POINTS PER 25MM
SET
B PLAN SHOWING SUCCESSIVE TEETH ON OPPOSITE SIDES
FOUR POINTS PER 25MM
C
TEN POINTS PER 25MM
D
13.
630 BLADE
TENON SAW
350
14.
SHAFT
CLAW HAMMER
15.
200
DOVETAIL SAW
16.
BLADES
230
17.
COMPASS SAW
250
18.
BLADE EXTENDED
PAD SAW
E
180
60
CUTTING IRON
F
125
BACK IRON
BRASS NUT
G
SECTION SHOWING SHARPENING & GRINDING ANGLES OF CUTTING IRON
H
150
130
BRADAWL
22.
340
23.
MALLET
STRING
LEVER
30×8 SIDE
22×10 BAR
19.
BOW SAW
265
HANDLE
HANDLE
PLUNGER
20.
SAW SET
150
PAD
SET SCREW
IRONS
WEDGE
THROAT
STOCK
STUD
430
75×75
NOSE
21.
JACK PLANE
HEEL
WEDGE
THROAT
NUT
CUTTING IRON
BACK IRON
SCREW
SHAVING
STOCK
J
MOUTH
WOOD
SECTION THROUGH MOUTH OF PLANE SHOWING ACTION OF IRONS WHEN WOOD IS BEING PLANED
200
PINCERS
24.
FERRULE
300
TANG
BEVEL EDGE PARING CHISEL
35.
SECTIONS
270
FIRMER CHISEL
36.
SECTION
380
37.
SOCKET MORTISE CHISEL
SOCKET
FERRULE
115×55
SLIP STONE
27.
200×25×25
LID
OILSTONE & BOX
25.
IRONS
560
90×90
26.
TRYING PLANE
IRON
28.
230
WOOD BAR
REBATE PLANE
IRON
WEDGE
THUMBSCREW
WOOD NUT
190
WOOD NUTS
31.
IRON
FENCE
RUNNER
PLOUGH PLANE
IRON
33.
230
BEAD PLANE
STRIP
IRON
30
M
WOOD
SKETCH SHOWING BEAD FORMED ON EDGE OF WOOD BY BEAD PLANE
PLUGGING CHISEL
38.
250
GOUGE
39.
245
BLADE
300
RATCHET SCREWDRIVER
SLIDE
40.
WEDGE
IRONS
29.
200
SMOOTHING PLANE
IRON
30.
230
K
L
75
HOLLOW & ROUND PLANES
IRON
130
32.
ROUTER
TONG
CROSS SECTION THROUGH SPOKESHAVE
N
IRON
265
34.
SPOKESHAVE
90
TONG
O
41.
300
G-CRAMP
JAW
HOLES IN JAW NOT THREADED
50×45
THREADED HOLES
JAW
300
52.
20 DIA. WOOD SCREWS
HANDSCREW
LEVER "Y"
CUTTING IRON
BACK IRON
LEVER "X"
CAP
FROG
42.
REST
KNOB
230
SCREW
KNOB
METAL SMOOTH PLANE
200
43. HALF ROUND RASP
LEVER CAP
LEVER
SCREW
44.
IRON
HEAD
150
BLOCK PLANE
HANDLE
SWEEP
45.
CHUCK
RATCHET
340
RATCHET BRACE
125
SCREWDRIVER BIT
140
Q
46. CENTRE BIT
P
100
47.
ROSE COUNTERSINK BIT
SHANK
125
48.
AUGER BIT
49. AUGER BIT
50.
SHELL BIT
45° MITRE CUTS
100×75
560
250×32
51.
MITRE BLOCK
125×75×2
SCRAPER
53.
SCALES: VARIOUS · LEADING DIMENSIONS GIVEN

FIGURE 67

up to the nose of the plane and is therefore useful for planing surfaces at the ends of rebates (etc.) and the *shoulder plane* (which is a form of rebate plane used for planing rebates in hardwood and particularly the ends of members such as the shoulders or rails).

(3) **Boring Tools.**—These include the brace and bits, auger, gimlet and bradawl.

Brace and Bits (see 45 to 50).—A brace holds a cutter or bit used for boring holes; hand pressure on the head of the brace assists the boring action of the bit whilst the brace (gripped by the handle) is revolved; that shown at 45 is of the *ratchet* type and is the best, for when desired the turning movement of the handle may be restricted to a small arc to allow boring in confined positions; the brace with the screwdriver bit attached is also employed to force in screws when pressure on the ordinary screwdriver would be inadequate; the chuck contains steel spring jaws into which the shank of the bit is inserted and secured; the sweep of the brace is of steel, the head and handle are of hardwood.

There are many varieties and sizes of bits. The *centre bit* (46) (3 to 38 mm dia.) is employed for boring; the edge P cuts out the circumference and the turned back edge Q removes the waste material from the hole. The *shell bit* and the *spoon bit* resemble the gouge, the *nose bit* and the *screw bit* (which has a screw thread) are used for producing holes from 3 to 13 mm dia. *Auger* or *twist bits* produce holes which are cleaner and more accurate than those formed by the above; there are many patterns, *e.g.*, Russell Jenning's (48), Gedge's and Irwin's (49); these are in two lengths, the shorter being known as dowel bits, and the diameters increase by 1·5 mm from 6 to 39 mm. The *Forstner bit* is unlike the twisted bits as the end has a circular rim instead of a point, and the larger bits have only plain and not spiral shanks; it is useful for boring in any direction. The *expansion bit* is provided with adjustable cutters of different sizes. The *screwdriver bit* (45) is an important tool and has already been referred to. *Countersink bits* are used to prepare shallow sinkings to receive heads of countersunk screws (see K, Fig. 66), etc.; the *rose* countersink bit (47) is suitable for both hardwoods and metals, the *snail* countersink bit (similar to the rose but having a sharper point and a grooved end) is used for wood only, and the *flat* countersink bit (having a flat end which is tapered to a point) is only suitable for boring through metal. *Rimers* are tapered bits which are used for either preparing tapered or conical-shaped holes or for increasing the size of holes.

Auger.—This has a steel stem, about 600 mm long (although this may be exceeded), having a round eye at one end to receive a wood cross handle; the other end is shaped like the bits of this name; is used for deep borings up to 50 mm diameter.

Gimlet.—The small tool is useful for boring holes to mark the position and facilitate the insertion of screws. The various patterns include the *twist gimlet* (8), *shell gimlet* (resembles a gouge with a screw end) and the *auger gimlet* which has an augered shank.

Bradawl (see 22).—The small steel blade is sharpened for making small holes.

(4) **Impelling Tools** include hammers, mallets, screwdrivers and nail punches.

Hammers.—That shown at 11 is called the *Warrington hammer*; the head (usually of cast steel with a tempered face and pene) is wedged to the shaped ash or hickory shaft; of the many sizes, that with the head weighing approximately 0·45 kg is most used for general purposes. The *claw hammer* (14) is made with heads weighing from 0·2 kg to 0·7 kg; the claw is useful for levering back or withdrawing nails.

Mallet (see 23).—Used for driving chisels and knocking framing together; the tapered mortice in the beech head receives the slightly tapered ash or beech shaft.

Screwdrivers.—There are two forms, *i.e.*, the fixed-blade type and the *ratchet* driver (40); the former is obtainable with the length of blade varying from 75 to 300 mm and is the firmer tool to employ for heavier framing; the ratchet screwdriver, by adjusting the slide, can be turned right or left without releasing the hand pressure; it can also be converted to the rigid type.

Nail Punches (see 10).—Used to punch nail heads below the surface of the wood.

(5) **Abrading Tools** include scrapers and rasps.

Scraper (see 53).—The two longer edges of this 1·6 mm thick steel plate are turned over to form a slight burr on each side; it is used on hardwood surfaces to remove marks left by planing.

Rasps.—Two grades of the steel half-round rasp shown at 43 are used to prepare curved surfaces; the coarse and fine files are about 250 and 200 mm long respectively; flat rasps are also obtainable.

Glass-papering, also termed *sand-papering*, is the final process applied to wood surfaces. Thus, after the surface has been planed by the jack, trying and smoothing planes and scraped, it is traversed (generally with the grain) by the *rubber*. This is a piece of cork round which is wrapped a piece of glass-paper. This is a strong paper, one side of which is coated with an abrasive; it is obtainable in various grades and usually application of two or three of them is necessary before the surface is completed. Mahogany and certain other hardwoods should be damped with a little hot water and allowed to dry before the finer grade of glass-paper is applied; this raises the grain which has been depressed by the coarser paper.

Grindstone.—Plane irons, chisels, etc., have to be ground before being sharpened on the oilstone. A hard grit stone or carborundum rotating disc is used for this purpose.

Oilstone and *Box* (see 25).—There are several natural and artificial oil-stones and these vary considerably in degree of fineness; well-known varieties are the Arkansas, Carborundum, India, Washita, and Turkey; a good quality oil should be used when sharpening the tools.

Slip Stone (see 27).—Similar to oilstones and used for sharpening gouges.

(6) **Cramping and Holding Appliances** include T-cramps, G-cramps, bench holdfasts and mitre blocks.

T-*cramp.*—This has been described on p. 102 and is shown at J, Fig. 53; it is used to cramp up framings, etc., during the gluing and wedging process.

G-*cramp* (see 41).—A metal cramp for small work; sizes vary up to 300 mm.

Bench Holdfast or Clamp (see 6).—Is of steel and its object is to grip the stuff on the joiners' bench during the process of working; the bench top is holed to receive the bar and the work is gripped by the shoe.

Handscrew (see 52).—This consists of two hornbeam, beech or metal screws with two beech jaws; it is one of the best appliances for cramping light stuff.

Mitre Block (see 51).—Made of wood to form mitres on architrave and panel mouldings, etc. The length of moulding is placed on the block with the moulded face outwards, the saw is placed in the cut, and the moulding is sawn with the mitre cuts serving as a guide.

A *mitre box* in the form of a channel with two side pieces having vertical mitre cuts and secured to a wood bed piece is sometimes used for large mouldings. The moulding is placed in the box and made rigid by wedges; the tenon saw is placed across the box and engaged in the two short cuts, and the mitre is sawn down the moulding.

A *mitre templet* used in trimming the cut mitres and *shooting and jointing boards*—used in planing mitres and edges with the trying plane—are other forms of equipment.

(7) **Miscellaneous Tools and Equipment** include the following :—

Cold Chisel.—This is a strong steel tool, about 13 mm wide, which is used for the removal of superfluous plaster, etc. prior to the fixing of architraves, skirtings, etc.

Pincers (see 24).—Used to remove nails, etc.

Axe.—This is useful for rough carpentry work.

Plumb-bob (see p. 28).—A lead, brass or iron plumb-bob, attached to a length of string, is essential for testing work that is being fixed.

Spirit Level (see 17, Fig. 19).—Used for testing levels of surfaces.

Oil Can.—The " non-leak " cone shaped type is preferred.

Portable Power Tools.—These small tools have been developed comparatively recently for use by the woodworker. They are electrically or cartridge operated and can be used on outside jobs besides in workshops. Portable electric tools are much speedier than hand tools and consequently they are capable of substantially increasing output; whilst somewhat heavier than ordinary hand tools, power tools are easily handled with much less fatigue to the operator. Each power tool is provided with a switch, usually in the handle and therefore conveniently operated. Portable power tools chiefly used for woodworking include saws, sanders, screwdrivers, hammers, planes, drills, etc. Some of them are shown in Fig. 68[1].

Portable Electric Saws.—These are provided with *circular* saw blades similar to those described in Chap. I, Vol. III; the size varies from 150 to 300 mm diameter and the corresponding cuts that can be formed are from 50 to 110 mm deep. Each saw is provided with two handles, one at the rear and one on top. The blade is provided with a guard which

[1] Those at 1 to 4 and 8 are manufactured by Wolf Electric Tools Ltd.; the electrical mechanism of these is similar to that described for drills.

covers the teeth; the safety of the operator is thus assured. Rip, cross-cut and special blades are interchangeable, and hence the tool can be used for sawing with and across the grain as desired. It is claimed that a portable electric saw can cut ten times faster than the ordinary handsaw.

The example at 1 is mounted on a sole plate which rests on the timber being cut. The blade is 180 mm in diameter, giving a maximum vertical cut of 60 mm; other blades are available, including a planer for smoothing timber and a silicon carbide abrasive disc for cutting stone, brick, cast iron, bronze and asbestos; an aluminium oxide disc is used for cutting steel. A front and rear handle, which incorporates the trigger switch, are provided for the operative to move the saw over the material being cut. The sole plate has an angle adjustment to give bevel cuts and another adjustment to regulate the cutting depth. Under load, the blade revolves at 3,000 revolutions per minute with an input of 1,050 watts. It can be fitted with a guide attached to the two screws on the sole plate for ripping long lengths of timber.

Portable Electric Sanders.—These are used to produce a smooth finish to planed surfaces. There are two classes of this sander, i.e., the *belt* sander and the *disc* sander. The belt sander, which is used for flat surfaces, has an endless belt (to which the sandpaper is attached) which passes over two pulleys at a high speed; belts from 58 to 115 mm wide are easily interchangeable; the sander is pressed down on the timber during the sanding operation; the better type of sander is provided with a vacuum dust collector or bag fixed at the rear to receive the dust during sanding. The disc sander is useful for curved or irregular surfaces; the size of disc varies from 125 to 225 mm diameter; the abrasive paper is fixed to the disc and the latter rotates at a high speed as the tool is pressed against the work. The more powerful sand-papering machines are described in Chap. I, Vol. III.

The example at 2 has a 100 mm wide belt and there is an adjustment knob to centralize this. The switch is located in the rear handle, there is also a front handle and a dust bag. The belt has a speed of 360 m per minute on light load, with an input of 775 watts on full load.

Electric Screwdrivers.—This power tool, pistol-like in appearance, has a trigger switch in the handle with an adjustable clutch at the opposite end which grips the blade. It is eminently suited for mass produced work, as it is capable of driving screws home at a very high speed. The screwing operation is facilitated and the splitting of the timber avoided if pilot holes are first made by means of an electric drill (see below) to receive the screws.

The example shown at 3 has a spindle speed on full load of 290 revolutions per minute with an input of 280 watts. It has a reversing switch for withdrawing screws and can be used for driving hexagon headed metal screws and nuts up to 10 mm dia. It has two speeds to give the correct drive for the different materials being drilled.

Electric Rotary Percussion Drill (see 4).—This is used for both normal drilling and percussive drilling, the changeover being made by an adjusting ring in the front of the machine. Four weights of percussive drive are provided to give the correct weight to suit the particular job. Where timber fixings are made to concrete the machine enables the correct action to be given for drilling through the wood, and by adjusting, straight into the concrete which requires percussive action for efficient drilling. The drill is double insulated for operator protection—this means that it does not rely entirely on earthing for its safety as the whole of the body is made of insulating material.

Portable Electric Planers.—These are metal planes, one type having a sole which is approximately 500 mm by 175 mm and a cutting iron or cutter blade of 100 mm width. It has two handles, one near the heel and the other or pressure handle near and above the nose. A trigger switch is housed in the heel handle, and the blade is readily adjusted for depth of cut by means of a thumb screw and fixed by a wing locking nut. This electric planer planes ten times as fast as the jack plane described on p. 126.

Portable Electric Drills.—These are employed for forming holes of varying diameters; like the brace and bit (p. 128) an electric drill has a chuck which tightly grips the bit of size and shape required, a secure grip being assured by rotating the chuck by means of a small key. As mentioned above, the drill is used for boring small diameter pilot holes for screws, but much larger holes can be drilled and, by fixing a special attachment, the size of hole can be up to 100 mm diameter. The smaller type is one-handed, but larger drills have

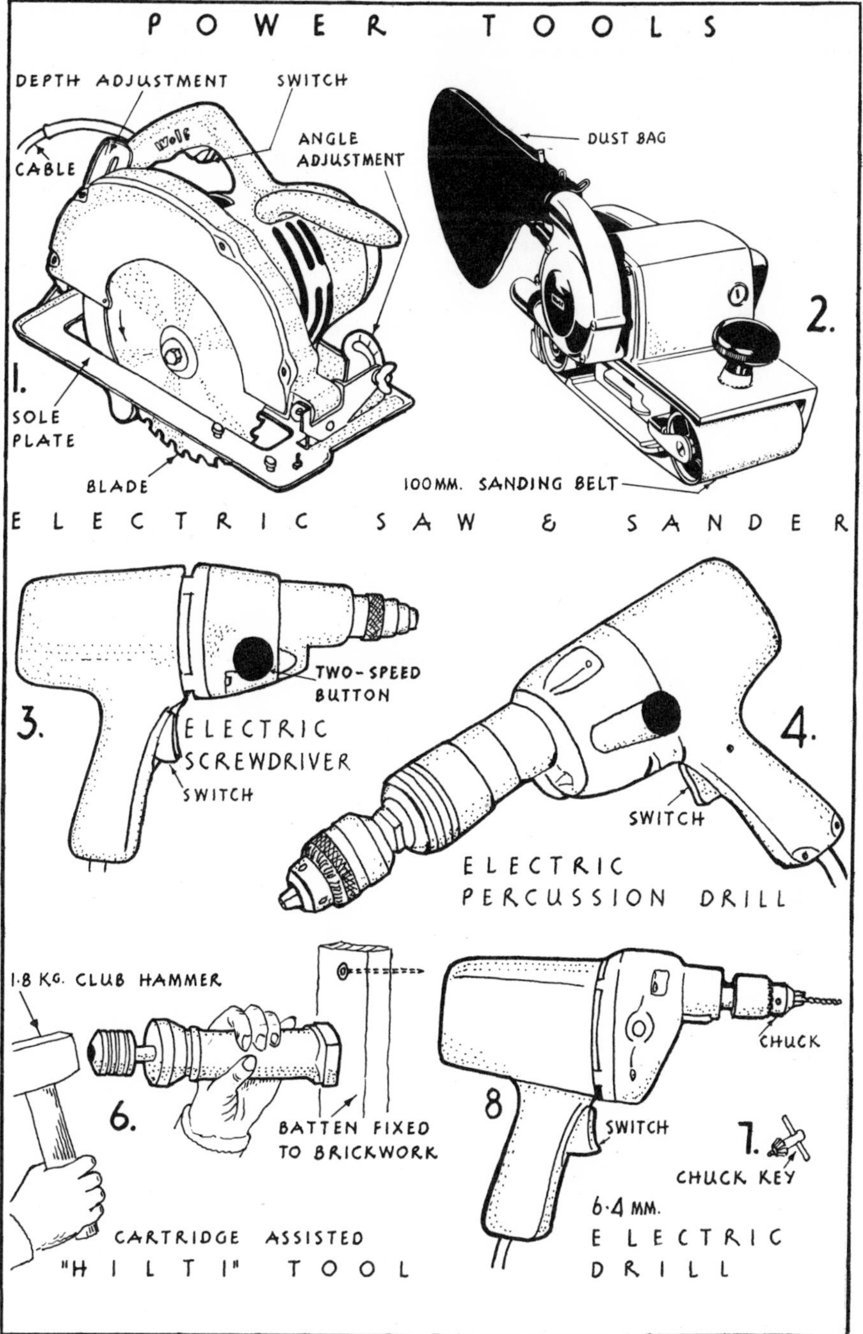

FIGURE 68

end and side (or two side) handles and, in addition, the more powerful tool is suitably dish-shaped on top to permit of breast-pressure.

The example at 8 is a small general duty drill and is the forerunner of the tools described above. It is capable of drilling 6·4 mm dia. holes in steel and 16 mm dia. holes in hardwood; on full load the bit rotates at 1,900 revolutions per minute with an input of 280 watts. When the current is switched on it flows through the coils, setting up a magnetic field causing rotation of the armature which transmits to gears; these operate a fan for cooling and also a spindle with the attached chuck. The drill is an all insulated model and, therefore, does not rely upon earthing for safety, the whole body being of insulated material to avoid operator contact with any electrical part. This complete envelope of insulation encloses a special nylon chuck spindle which isolates the metal chuck from the electrical parts. Incorporated in the chuck are three jaws for gripping the bit which can be opened or closed by fitting the key (see 7) into a hole on the outside of the chuck. Serrations on the key engage in those on the chuck, enabling the bit to be secured or released. Various attachments can be fitted to the drill to drive a disc sander, circular saw or lathe; it can also be fixed to a drill stand or press which is fastened to the bench for drilling holes vertically. The larger models (up to 25 mm dia.) can also be adapted as mortisers for cutting mortices.

" *Hilti* " *Cartridge-assisted Tool* (see 6).—This is a percussive tool[1] powered by a small cartridge explosive. It can be used for attaching door and window frames, battens, pipes, brackets and conduit clips to brick, concrete and stone. It eliminates the drilling of holes for these fixings and it can also be used to drive fastenings direct into steel. Special hardened steel nails known as *Micky pins* are used and these are forced through the item being fixed into the backing materials given above. Three main types of pin are made: with rounded head as indicated at 6, with threaded end for subsequent fixing of a nut, and with a recessed tapped end into which a bolt can be screwed. The tool comprises an outer sleeve containing a barrel wherein a cartridge plunger and a front plunger are enclosed. The outer end of the cartridge plunger has a head for receiving the hammer blow and the internal end is recessed to hold a 6·4 mm dia. cartridge. The end of the front plunger is recessed to contain the head of the pin that is being fixed. A blow from a 1·8 kg club hammer sends the cartridge plunger forward, making contact with the front plunger. This causes the cartridge to be fired, driving the front plunger forward, thus thrusting the pin into the batten and into the backing material.

[1] Manufactured by MEA-Aktiengesellschaft, Schaan, Liechtenstein, and marketed by Wordrew Ltd. in this country.

CHAPTER FIVE

ROOF COVERINGS[1]

Syllabus.—Brief description of the preparation and characteristics of slates; sizes; terms; nails; eaves, ridge, verge, hip and valley details. Plain and interlocking tiles.

SLATING

Formation.—Slate is a hard, fine-grained sedimentary argillaceous (clayey) stone. Originally, the particles of clay were deposited by water and subjected to vertical pressure to form shale (intermediate between clay and slate); this was subsequently changed into slate as a result of tremendous lateral pressure and heat. Owing to the latter action the slate is laminated, having numerous parallel *planes of cleavage*, so that large blocks are readily split into comparatively thin sheets or laminae known as slates.

The cleavage planes are oblique to the original bedding or sedimentation planes. Thus at the Honister and Yew Crag mines (Cumberland) the angle of the bedding planes is about 35°, whereas that of the cleavage planes is approximately 70° (see A, Fig. 69).

Slate is quarried in Wales (Penrhyn, Dinorwic, Bangor and Ffestiniog), Cumberland and Westmorland (Honister, Buttermere, etc.), Lancashire (Burlington) and Cornwall (Delabole), also in Scotland (Aberdeen, Argyll and Perth).

Quarrying.—Slate is obtained from either open quarries or mines. Thus the Penrhyn, Dinoric (or Velinhelli) and Delabole slate is quarried, whilst that from Ffestiniog and Honister is obtained from underground caverns approached by galleries. Gunpowder or gelignite is used to blast the rock and dislodge huge blocks of slate.

Conversion.—After the blocks have been reduced in size by the use of the mallet, chisel, etc., to permit of their convenient removal from the mine or quarry, they are transported to the sawmill for sawing, splitting and dressing.

Sawing.—A diamond or circular saw (see p. 36) is used to divide each block into sections which are from 450 to 600 mm wide and up to 360 mm thick. The saw cuts an average rate (Westmorland slate) of 3m per minute.

Splitting.—The saw blocks are now reduced to slabs which are about 15 mm thick, and each slab is divided by hand labour into thin laminae or slates. A " splitter," with the slab resting against the side of one of his legs, drives a chisel into the slab at one of the sawn ends (see C, Fig. 69). The chisel used for Welsh slates has a broad edge and is driven in with a wood mallet; that used for the tougher Westmorland slates is less broad (see B, Fig. 69) and a hammer is used instead of a mallet. In splitting a slab, it is first divided into two or three sections, each of which is carefully split to form slates of the required thickness; the chisel is driven firmly " down the grain "and prised after each successive tap on it until the split is complete.

The thickness of the slates varies according to the quality and " order " requirements. Welsh slates vary from 4 to 8 mm, and for best quality Westmorland slates " six per 30 mm " (each being 5 mm thick) is preferred.

Dressing is the final operation and may be done either by machinery or by hand.

One type of machine has a cylindrical drum with two diagonally fixed knives; a measuring gauge (resembling the size stick shown at E, Fig. 69) sticks out horizontally from one side of the machine: each slate is placed on the gauge in the notch which will give the required size; as the drum rotates, the superfluous slate is removed, leaving a straight edge which is somewhat splayed and rough on the underside.

If dressed by hand (and at the larger sheds thousands of slates are dressed in this manner) the " dresser," when in a sitting position, places each slate on the *traverse* or *brake* (see G, Fig. 69); the slate is held with an irregular edge overhanging the edge of the iron and a clean edge is formed as he makes two or three downward blows with the *whittle* (see H, Fig. 69). He then uses the *gauge* or *size stick* (see E); lengths verying from 150 to 300 mm (advancing by 25 mm) and 300 to 600 mm (advancing by 50 mm) are measured; the metal point of the stick marks a line on the slate as the stick is traversed with the required notch held against the recently dressed edge (see F); the whittle is used to remove the superfluous slate by making a cut along this line; each edge is dressed in this manner. Sometimes the two top corners are removed as shown at P; this enables the slates when fixed to lie closely on each other (especially if the beds are not perfectly flat) and reduces their weight. As a rule the holes are formed either at the slater's yard or on the building site (see p. 133). The slates are dressed to give the maximum size with the minimum waste, and they are afterwards sorted into sizes.

Sizes.—Slates are produced in a large number of sizes; some of the larger quarries supply over twenty and the Bangor slates can be obtained in no less than thirty-two standard sizes varying from 600 by 350 mm to 200 mm by 200 mm. Common sizes are 600 mm to 300 mm, 500 mm by 250 mm, 450 mm by 225 mm and 400 mm by 200 mm; larger and special sizes can be obtained at additional cost.

The Westmorland, Cumberland and North Lancashire slates are generally produced in what are termed " random sizes."

Random slates are from 300 to 600 mm long and are proportionate in width, the average width being half its length; these are " sized " after being dressed, *i.e.*, sorted into sizes 600 to 500 mm, 500 to 450 mm and 450 to 300 mm long. These slates are usually laid in regular *diminishing courses* (see p. 139) for which mixed sizes are required.

Peggies are small-sized randoms; they are 225 to 300 mm long (" best peggies ") and 150 to 250 mm long ("second peggies"), with proportionate widths.

In addition to classifying slates according to size, they are divided into three or more grades known as " qualities," *i.e.*, " firsts " (or " bests "), " seconds " and " thirds." As a rule, these terms refer to thickness only and not to value, for, in certain quarries, " best "

[1] See p. 68. Felt and lead covering for flat roofs is described on pp. 70 and 148 respectively. Pantiles, Italian and Spanish tiling, stone slating, shingles, copper and zinc coverings, asbestos sheets and thatch are described in Vol. III. Lightweight metal and asbestos sheetings and deckings are included in Vol. IV.

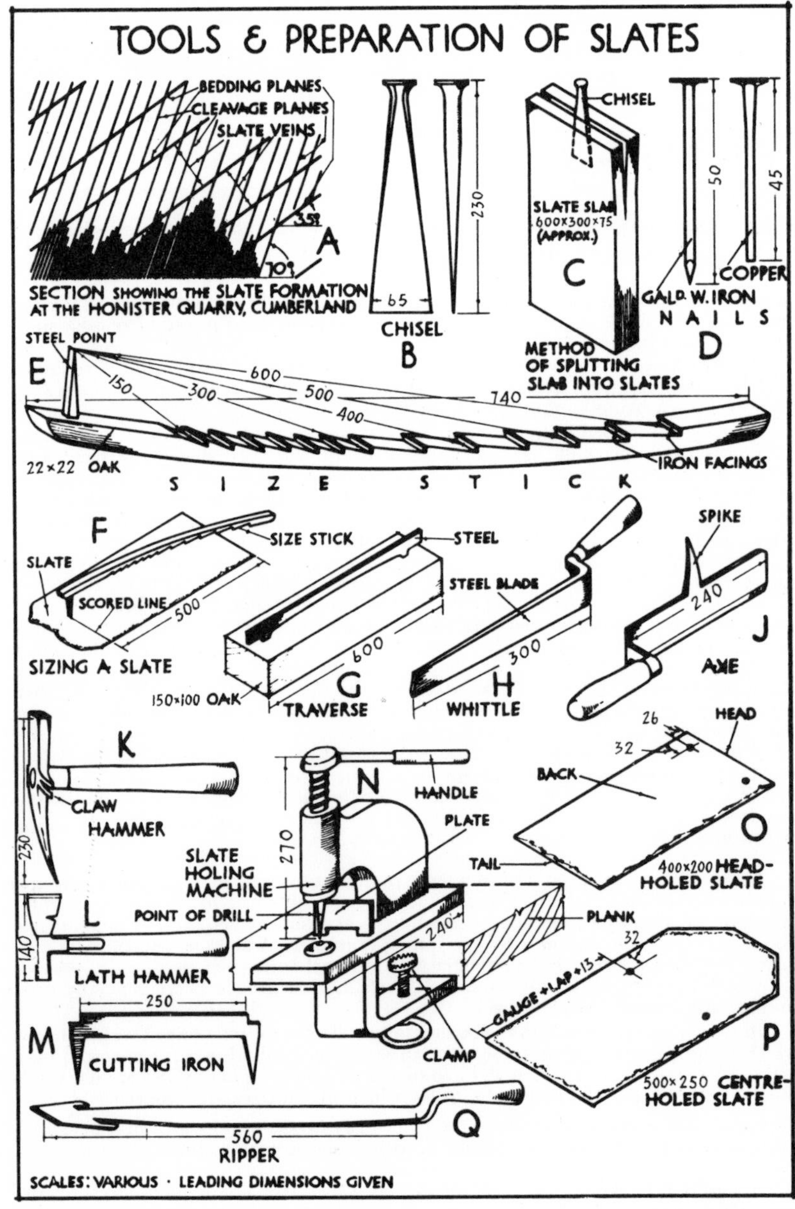

FIGURE 69

slates are cheaper than "seconds." Each of these qualities are divided into maximum and minimum thickness; "seconds" are thicker than "firsts," and "thirds" are thicker than "seconds"

Tally slates are Welsh slates which range in size from 600 mm by 360 mm to 300 mm by 200 mm and are sold by "count," *i.e.,* per thousand.

Queen slates are Welsh slates which are from 600 to 900 mm (increasing by 50 mm) long and are sold by weight.[1]

Characteristics.—A good slate should be hard, tough and durable, of rough texture, ring bell-like when struck, not split when holed or dressed, practically non-absorbent and of a satisfactory colour. Those which feel greasy are generally of inferior quality and any showing white patches or marcasite (iron pyrites) decay readily, especially if subjected to a smoky atmosphere; patches of lime also adversely affect durability.

When left immersed in water to half its height for twelve hours, the water-line on the slate should not be more than 3 mm above the level of the water in the vessel. In slates of poor quality, the water is readily absorbed and rises several inches up the slate; such slates are easily destroyed by frost action (due to the absorbed water freezing and disintegrating the slate). If a dry slate is kept in water which is kept boiling for forty-eight hours, its increase in weight should not exceed 0·3 per cent., and if a spceimen of slate is immersed for ten days in a solution of sulphuric acid it should not show any signs of flaking or softening.[2]

In general, Welsh slates are blue and Westmorland slates are green, but there are certain exceptions to this. Thus Bangor (Carnarvon) slates vary from blue, blue-purple and purple; Dinorwic or Velinhelli (Llanberis, North Wales) slates vary from red (maroon), blue-grey, green and wrinkled (purple with green markings and slightly furrowed surface) or mottled (blue-grey with rather indefinite green markings); Penrhyn (Bethesda, North Wales) slates, similar to Dinorwic; Festiniog or Portmadoc (Wales) slates, uniform blue-grey; Vronlog (North Wales) slates, various shades of green and grey; Precelly (South Wales) slates, green, grey and khaki. Westmorland slates include those quarried in Cumberland and North Lancashire as well as Westmorland; those from Buttermere, Coniston, Elterwater, Kentmere and Tilberthwaite are of various textures and many shades of green; most are light green, others are a darker green (olive) and at least one is grey-green; those from the Burlington Quarries (Kirkby-in-Furness) are dark blue in colour; Cornish (Delabole) slates are green, grey-green, green and rustic red. Some of the Welsh slates

[1] The practice of using the following terms when specifying slates SHOULD BE DISCOURAGED as, with few exceptions, they are not now used in the trade, *i.e.,* "smalls" (300 mm by 150 mm), "doubles" (330 mm by 165 mm), "ladies" (400 mm by 200 mm or 400 mm by 250 mm), "countesses" (500 mm by 250 mm), "duchesses" (600 mm by 300 mm), etc.

[2] B.S. 680 for Roofing Slates gives full details of these tests.

are very durable, whilst the best Westmorland slates are practically indestructible; the attractive colours and coarse texture (with spalled edges) increase the artistic merit of the latter slates.

Preparation of Slates on Site or in Slater's Yard.—This consists of holing and cutting the slates to various shapes and sizes. With the exception of small randoms (each of which may be secured at the head by one nail only), each slate is fixed to the roof by two nails (see p. 134). This holing is done by the slater either by (*a*) hand punching or (*b*) machine drilling.

(*a*) *Hand Punching.*—The position of the holes is marked on the slate by a *gauge stick* or *scantel*, this is a piece of lath through which two nails are driven at a distance apart equal to that between the bottom or tail of the slate and the centres of the nail holes. The *axe, zax* or *chopper* (see J, Fig. 69) is used to punch each hole by striking the slate with the spike. The smooth or bed surface of the slate is uppermost when it is being holed so that when the spike penetrates the slate small pieces are burst off round the margin and on the underside to form a rough irregular countersinking of the hole; as the slates are fixed on the roof with the surface having the rough edges uppermost the heads of the nails can be driven in flush with the surface because of this countersinking; otherwise the heads would project to cause " riding " of the slates above them and this would admit rain or snow.

(*b*) *Machine Drilling.*—This is performed by the portable *slate holding machine* shown at N, Fig. 69 which can be bolted to a bench or clamped to a plank. After the machine has been clamped a brick is fixed on the plank on each side of the machine and at the correct distance from it, the distance between the bricks being equal to the length of the slate; the slate is placed between the bricks, with the smooth surface uppermost and one edge against the plate shown in the sketch and which is 32 mm from the point of the drill; the handle is given a partial turn, the drill descends and punctures the slate, the point is withdrawn by reversing the handle, the slate is removed and replaced with the ends reversed (but with the smooth surface still uppermost) and the second hole is drilled. This is a much quicker process than hand punching and is less liable to crack the slates.

A *cutting iron, dog* or *dressing iron* (see M) is used when slates have to be cut to certain sizes or shapes on the job; it is often used on the roof, the slater driving the pointed ends into a spar or other convenient member. After being marked to the required shape, the slate is placed on the iron with the edge to be cut projecting the required amount, and a few smart blows with the axe neatly trim off the edge.

The *hammer, pick* or *peck* (see K) is used for driving the nails through the slates, the claw at the side is useful for withdrawing nails and the point is used for holing.

A *lathe hammer* (see L) is used for fixing slate laths or battens; laths are cut to length by using the sharpened blade and nails may be withdrawn by means of the notch in the blade.

The *ripper* (see Q) is used for removing defective slates from a roof; the blade is passed under the slate, and each nail is gripped and cut by the hooked end as the ripper is given a sharp pull.

Nails.—The quality of the nails used for securing slates is most important, as the cost of maintenance of a roof depends very largely upon their durability. Roofs quickly become defective if the nails corrode and heads disappear, the loose slates being easily removed by the wind.

Copper nails (see D, Fig. 69) or composition nails should always be used for good work;[1] the latter, also called " compo " or " yellow metal," are made of antimony, lead and tin or copper and zinc, and are harder than copper nails. Aluminium alloy nails are also used in good work.

Galvanized wrought iron nails (see D) and zinc nails are often used for cheaper work, but they are unsuitable for industrial and coastal districts. The former are invariably used for good work for fixing laths to the spars as the zinc covering offers a protection against corrosion.

Nails are specified according to length and weight, the size depending upon the thickness of the slates, and the length should equal twice the thickness of the slates plus 25 mm; if too small, " tight nailing " results, and this may cause damage to the holes and ultimate cracking of the slates. The following gives suitable lengths and weights of nails :—

TABLE VII

Quality of Slates (see p. 131)	Length (mm)	Copper or Zinc (per 1,000) (kg)	Composition (per 1,000) (kg)	Galvanized Wrought Iron (Gauge) thickness (mm)
Best or mediums .	38	2·27	2·95	2·9
Seconds . .	45	3·18	4·08	3·3
Randoms . .	50	4·54	5·45	3·7

Sometimes 32 mm nails weighing 1·8 kg (copper) or 2·3 kg (compo) per 1,000 are used for thin small slates.

TERMS.—Various terms used in slating are :

Back.—The upper and rough surface of a slate (see O, Fig. 69).

Bed.—The under and smooth surface.

Head.—The upper edge (see O).

Tail.—The lower edge (see O)

Course.—A row or layer of slates (see A, Fig. 70); the courses are equal when the slates are of uniform size but vary from a maximum at the eaves to a minimum at the ridge when randoms are used to form *diminishing courses* (see p. 134, and E, Fig. 71).

Bond.—The arrangement of slates whereby the edge joints between the slates in any one course are in or near to the centre of the slates immediately above and below them. When the slates are of uniform size the edge joints should run in straight lines from eaves to ridge—" keeping the perpends "—(see A, Fig. 70). This is accomplished by using a wide slate, called a *slate and a half*, or a half slate (in inferior work only) at the beginning of every alternate course. But such mechanical neatness is not always desirable, especially if Westmorland or Cornish randoms or peggies are laid with diminishing courses, when a slight deviation from straight lines results in a more pleasing appearance (see J, Fig. 70, and E, Fig. 71).

Pitch has been referred to on p. 69, and the minimum pitch for " large,"

[1] Copper, galvanized wrought iron and zinc nails should not be used for roofs which are in the vicinity of gas works or chemical works or where the slating is subjected to strong acid fumes, as the gases may destroy them. Lead nails or chrome-iron nails should be used for such roofs; the former are about 100 mm long, the stems being passed through the holes of the slates and bent round the steel purlins, etc., of the roof.

" ordinary " and " small " sizes of slates is stated. Comparatively large slates should be used on roofs of about 30° pitch. On steeply pitched roofs most of the weight of the slates is carried by the nails and therefore the slates should be small and these should be secured with stout nails. Hence the steeper the pitch the smaller the slates.

Lap is the amount which the tail of one slate covers the head of that in the course *next but one* to it; this applies to centre-nailed slates (see below). When the slates are head-nailed (see below) the lap is measured from the centre of the nail hole instead of the head. As shown in the various details in Fig. 71, there are THREE *thicknesses of slates at the lap*. The amount of lap varies with the pitch and degree of exposure of the roof; thus for roofs with 30° to 45° pitch, the lap should be 76 mm; for steeper pitches the lap may be reduced to 64 mm; for flatter pitches than 30° the lap should be increased to 90 mm to 100 mm, and in exposed positions (such as on the coast) a lap of 150 mm may be necessary.

Gauge is the distance between the nails measured up the slope of the roof (which is the same as the distance between the tails of each successive course). The gauge depends upon (1) the length of slate, (2) the amount of lap, and (3) the method of nailing, *i.e.*, centre nailing or head nailing.

Centre-nailed Slates (see A and C, Fig. 71).—The gauge equals $\frac{\text{length of slate} - \text{lap}}{2}$, thus for a roof covered with 460 mm by 230 mm slates and laid with a 76 mm lap, the gauge $= \frac{460 - 76 \text{ mm}}{2} = 192$ mm. The position of the nail holes measured from the tail of the slate is shown at P, Fig. 69, and equals the gauge, plus the lap, plus a clearance of 13 mm; the clearance is necessary to allow the nails when being driven to clear the heads of the slates in the course below.

Head-nailed Slates (see E, F and G, Fig. 71).—The holes are pierced 26 mm from the head (see O, Fig. 69) and, as mentioned above, the lap is measured from the centre of the hole. Hence the gauge equals $\frac{\text{length of slate} - (\text{lap} + 26 \text{ mm})}{2}$; thus the gauge for 460 mm by 230 mm slates with a 76 mm lap =

$$\frac{460 \text{ mm} - (76 + 26 \text{ mm})}{2} = 179 \text{ mm}.$$

In both centre and head nailing the holes are approximately 32 mm from the edges.

Comparison between Head- and Centre-Nailed Slates.—Head-nailed slates offer a better protection to the holes as there are two thicknesses of slates over each. They are not readily damaged or strained when being nailed as they have a solid bearing in the form of battens or boards. Their tails are more readily lifted by a high wind owing to their big leverage; this allows rain and snow to blow between them and the excessive movement of the slates may gradually damage and increase the size of the holes until the slates are ultimately displaced and blown off; hence large slates should not be head-nailed, especially in exposed positions. More head-nailed slates are required to cover a roof on account of the reduced gauge and therefore this method is more expensive than centre nailing.

Centre-nailed slates are less likely to be stripped because of the reduced leverage, and for the same reason, there is less likelihood of drifting snow and rain finding access. Large slates should always be centre-nailed to give greater rigidity. Less slates are required and the method is therefore more economical than head-nailing. Defective slates are more readily removed. There is greater likelihood of rain entering the nail holes if any of the slates above them are cracked and if the roof has a flat pitch, as there is only one thickness of slates over the nail holes. There is a risk of the slates being strained and sometimes cracked (which cracks may not open until later) by careless nailing owing to the space between the middle of centre-nailed slates and the battens or boarding below, and especially over the intersection between sprockets and spars (see C, Fig. 71). Centre nailing is more common than head nailing.

Diminishing Course Work.—The roof consists of randoms which are laid in diminishing courses from a maximum at the eaves to a minimum at the ridge. The slates are sorted to give carefully graded courses, those in each course being of the same size; thus a large roof may have 610 mm or longer slates at the eaves and peggies at the ridge. The gauge varies with each course or every second course, but the *lap is uniform throughout*. A very pleasing appearance results, and as shown at J, Fig. 70 the bond is irregular. The method of determining the gauge is explained on p. 139 (see also E, Fig. 71).

Margin is the exposed portion of a slate and equals the gauge multiplied by the width (see A and D, Fig. 70).

Boarding or *Close Sheeting* (see p. 69).—The usual thickness is 25 mm (nominal); it should be tongued and grooved although shot or butt jointing is used for cheap speculative work. As described below, the boarding should be covered with felt before the slates are fixed. Boarding is sometimes referred to as *sarking*, although this term is more often applied to felting.

Slating Battens or Laths.—These should be sound, sawn redwood and of the following sizes: 38 mm by 19 mm for small slates 400 mm long and downwards, 50 mm by 19 mm for light slates 460 mm long and upwards, and 50 mm by 25 mm for heavy slates 460 mm long and upwards. They are fixed to the boarding or directly to the spars, to the required gauge apart by galvanized wrought iron nails which are usually 44 mm long. They are sometimes creosoted for preservation. *Counter-battens* as shown at D, Fig. 70 and G, Fig. 71 are also used; these are generally 50 mm by 19 mm, spaced at 400 mm centres (or equal to the distance apart of the spars) and secured with 38 mm galvanized wrought iron nails.

Tilting Fillets or Springing Pieces.—These are triangular or tapered pieces of wood, from 75 to 150 mm wide and up to 75 mm thick, used at the eaves (see Fig. 71) to tilt the lower courses of slates in order to assist in excluding rain and snow by ensuring close joints at the tails. These are often omitted if fascia boards are used (see Y, Fig. 36). They are also used at chimney stacks, etc., which penetrate a roof, to cause water to fall away quickly from the vertical surfaces.

Damp Proofing.—Provision must be made to exclude rain and snow which may be blown up between the slates and to prevent the entrance of water by capillary attraction. Such includes either (*a*) covering the boarding or spars with felt or similar material, which is the most usual system, or (*b*) torching the underside of the slates.

(*a*) *Roofing Felt.*—This is similar to but thinner than the fibrous asphalt or bituminous felt described on p. 17 and is obtainable in 800 or 900 mm wide rolls. It is either laid upon the boarding with the joints running from eaves to ridge or parallel to the ridge, or, for cheaper work, the boarding is omitted and the felt (called *untearable felt*, because of its toughness, due to an extra layer of hessian cloth being embodied in the material) is laid transversely over and fixed with flat-headed 30 mm galvanized wrought iron nails ("clout nails") direct to the spars. The former is shown at D, Fig. 70, and the latter at A, Fig. 71. The joints are lapped 50 to 75 mm in each case, and it should be lapped over the ridge. The edge of the felt is clout-nailed to the boarding every 75 mm or to each spar when laid directly over them.

(*b*) *Torching or Pointing or Tiering.*—Good lime mortar, to which clean long ox-hair has been added to increase its adhesive quality, is applied to the underside of the slates along the upper edge of each cross batten; this material should be well pressed in between the slates and the mortar fillets splayed off (see D, Fig. 38).

Comparing the two methods : Felting allows air to enter and circulate under the slates and round the battens, it reduces "heat losses" (the transmission of heat and cold through the roof), it is easily fixed, but is more expensive than torching. Torching prevents ventilation, and in prolonged wet weather it retains moisture which may be transmitted to the adjacent battens and roof members and set up decay; in course of time inferior material deteriorates and drops off leaving gaps through which rain and snow may enter; if however best materials and workmanship are applied, this method ensures a "drop-dry" roof, as is evidenced by the thousands of roofs that have been dealt with in this manner and have remained watertight and in good condition for a long period of years.

Terms such as eaves, ridge, hip, valley and verge have been defined on pp. 68–69.

Special Slates.—Slates other than those of normal size and shape are required in order to maintain correct bond and conform to shapes which are more or less irregular. They include those necessary to form the bottom course at the eaves, the top course at the ridge, verges, hips and valleys.

Double Eaves Course Slates (see Fig. 71).—A double course of slates is laid at the eaves, otherwise rain would enter between the edge joints. The first layer of slates (or "doubling course") is comparatively short and equal in length to the *gauge plus lap* (when centre-nailed—see A) and *gauge plus lap plus 26 mm* (when head-nailed—see G). The practice which is sometimes adopted, of laying the normal sized slates lengthwise to form this course, is not advocated as there is a risk of some of the end joints coinciding with the edge joints of the course above.

Top Ridge Course Slates.—These are about 50 mm longer than the bottom doubling eaves course slates in order to leave a suitable margin below the wing of the ridge tile (see A, Fig. 71).

Verge Slates.—As mentioned on p. 133, either a special slate called a "slate and a half" or a half slate is used at each alternate course in order to give correct bond. A slate and a half, as is implied, is one and a half times the normal width, thus its size will be 520 mm by 390 mm if 520 mm by 260 mm slates are being used. A verge is a vulnerable part of a roof, and these wide slates, when each is secured with at least two nails, give a much stronger job than do half slates each of which may be secured with one nail only. The application of these wide slates is indicated at A and E, Fig. 70.

Hip and Valley Slates.—Extra wide slates are required for these positions and each is usually formed from a slate and a half. Hip slates are shown at G, Fig. 67, and valley slates are similar.

Open or Spaced Slating.—Roofs of temporary and certain farm buildings, etc., may be covered with slates which are laid with a space from 38 to 75 mm between the sloping edges. Whilst this method results in an economy of material, it does not give a "drop-dry" roof, and is now seldom used.

Ridges.—Slated roofs are finished at the ridges with shaped pieces made in slate, tile, stone and lead.

Slate Ridges (see E, Fig. 71) are formed in two pieces, each from 10 to 20 mm thick and up to about 460 mm long, one is a plain rectangular wing holed for screws and the other is a 175 or 150 mm wide wing with a 50 to 60 mm roll (birdsmouthed beneath) worked on the top edge. As shown, the top edge of the wood ridge is chamfered and is about 50 mm above the battens; the plain wing is bedded in mortar on the top course of slates and secured to the wood ridge by brass or copper screws; the rolled wing is bedded on the slates and over the top edge of the plain wing; in addition, the joint between each roll section is secured with a copper or small slate dowel. The joints of the ridge should "break joint" with the top course of slates. This ridge is not now much used, chiefly on account of its indifferent appearance.

Tile Ridges are made of clay, moulded to a variety of patterns, and kiln-burnt. The *half-round* ridge tile shown at A, Fig. 71, and the *hog-back* ridge illustrated at G, Fig. 71, and at B, Fig. 72 give a satisfactory finish, *provided the colour conforms with that of the slates*; they are usually in 460 mm lengths, the width varies from 230 to 280 mm and the thickness from 13 to 22 mm. A V-ridge, having a flanged or rebated joint, is shown at C, Fig. 70; this is 22 mm thick and the wings should not be less than 175 mm; the angle between the wings varies

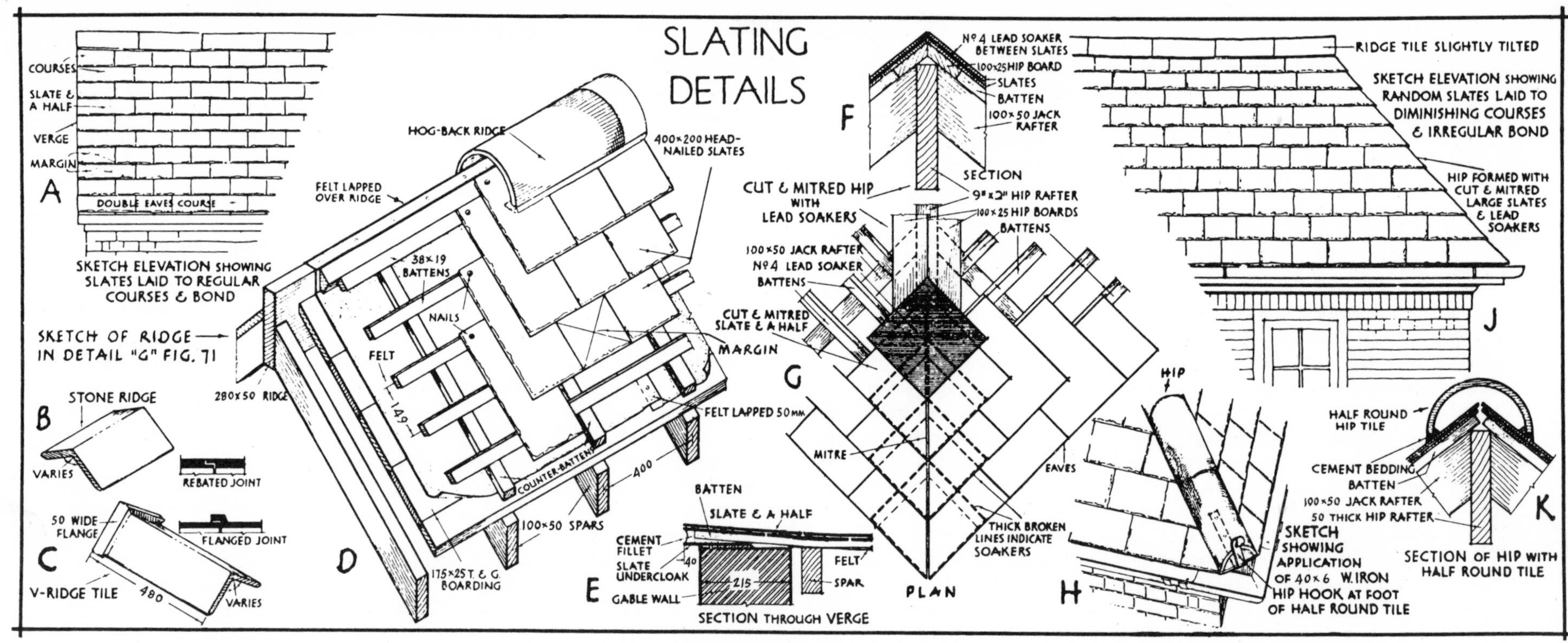

FIGURE 70

to suit the pitch of the roof. As shown, the ridges are bedded and pointed in cement mortar which is preferably waterproofed, and the transverse joints are formed of the same material.

It is not wise to bed the ridges solidly with mortar as this has been the cause of wood ridges becoming defective on account of air being excluded. Whilst the flanged joint at C is effective and is often used, ridges formed of these pieces are unsightly and the simple butt joint is preferred. The latter gives a watertight job if formed with good material and especially if a slate is inserted under each joint. Alternatively, certain makes of ridge tile are obtainable having internal flanges, and these provide a sound joint and a ridge with an uninterrupted outline. The appearance of the ridge is improved if the end one or two pieces are given a slight tilt upwards as shown at A and J, Fig. 70. These end pieces are " solid ended."

Ridge tiles can be obtained in several colours and they should therefore be carefully selected to harmonize with the slating.

Stone Ridges (see B, Fig. 70) are sawn out of the solid. They are from 230 to 150 mm wide, about 38 mm thick, and from 300 to 900 mm long. The joints are rebated in good work (see sketch) and the pieces are bedded, jointed and pointed in cement mortar. They provide an effective finish to a Westmorland slated roof, and are commonly employed in Yorkshire and the Cotswold district where comparatively thick slates from local stone form the covering material.

Lead Ridges are described on pp. 148 and 150. These form a suitable finish if Welsh slates are used, but the lead is apt to stain certain green slates.

Hips are finished with either half-round or V-shaped tiles, sawn stone, lead, or cut and mitred slates with lead soakers.

Tiled Hips (see H and K, Fig. 70) are commonly employed, and whilst they provide a sound finish, the appearance is far from pleasing, especially if the roofs are small. As shown at K, the tops of the jack rafters finish level with the top of the hip rafter, the ends of the battens are brought over it and the slates are roughly mitred. A *hip hook* should be screwed to the back and at the foot of the hip rafter to prevent the tiles from slipping (see H). Hip tiles, like those for ridges, should be of a satisfactory colour.

Sawn Stone Hips are formed of pieces of similar section to that shown at B, Fig. 70; the dihedral angle between the wings should conform with that of the roof.

Lead Hips are described on p. 150.

Cut and Mitred Hips with Lead Soakers provide the best finish to a slated roof; the method is sound, especially for pitches not less than 45°, and the appearance is effective (see J, Fig. 70). The construction is shown in the section at F and the plan at G; it is customary to provide two 100 mm wide hip boards (which are mitred over the hip rafter) to form a good bearing for the slates and a fixing for the soakers, against which the ends of the battens are butt jointed; alternatively, the top edge of the hip rafter may be bevelled and finished level with the top of the battens which mitre against the rafter. Both methods provide a true line up the hip rafter to which the edges of the slates are cut. Wide slates (slate and a half) are used and these must be carefully cut and mitred as shown. *Lead soakers* (see p. 143) are placed between the slates; as shown at G, these soakers are square, measuring from 300 to 360 mm across the diagonals (depending upon the size of the slates); each soaker is bent over the upper edges of each pair of mitred slates and twice nailed to the hip boards; the soakers lap each other at each course. The mitred slates must be securely nailed (especially in exposed positions) otherwise they are liable to be stripped by strong winds.

Valleys.—It is customary to form " open " valleys in slated roofs. These are covered with lead and their construction is described on p. 150 and shown at P, Fig. 75. An alternative and suitable finish is provided by cut and mitred slates with soakers as described above. Another very effective, but expensive, finish is the " swept valley "; the sharp angle at the valley is blocked out by means of a 250 or 300 mm by 25 mm board which is fixed above the valley rafter, and this makes it possible for each course of slates in the adjacent roof surfaces to be uninterrupted at the valley, as the slates are continued round to form a series of curved or swept courses. The slates forming the valley are cut and packed underneath as required. As swept valleys are more often formed on roofs which are covered with plain tiles, a full description of this finish is given in Chap. III, Vol. III.

Verges.—One of several methods of finishing at verges is shown at A and E, Fig. 70. For the reason stated on p. 135, a slate and a half should be used at each alternate course. The slates project as shown, and in order to direct the water from the edge and prevent it from running down the face of the gable wall, the outer slates of each course are slightly tilted upwards. This tilt is formed by bedding a course of butt-jointed slates (called an *undercloak*) on the wall in cement mortar, and the ends of the battens are laid on this course. After the slating has been completed, the open edge is well filled in with cement mortar and neatly pointed, as shown. The undercloak may consist of a double layer of slates.

Preparation of Roofs for Slating.—The groundwork may consist of either (*a*) horizontal slating battens only, (*b*) boarding and felting, (*c*) boarding, felt and slating battens or (*d*) boarding, felt, counter-battens and slating battens.

(a) *Horizontal Slating or Cross Battens* (see D, Fig. 38, A, Fig. 71, and Fig. 72).—This is the most common method as it is the cheapest. It is quite satisfactory and a drop-dry roof is assured provided either felt or torching (as described on p. 135) is applied to prevent the access of rain, snow, wind and dust.

(b) *Boarding and Felting* (see W and X, Fig. 36, and F, Fig. 71).—The boarding (described on p. 134) is nailed to the spars and then covered with felt (see p. 135). This provides a drop-dry and draught proof roof, although dampness has been caused through the penetration of water through the nail holes. Heat is less readily transmitted through this roof than that described at (*a*) and therefore rooms which are partly in such a roof are relatively warmer in winter and cooler in summer. (See also p. 141.)

(c) *Boarding, Felt and Slating Battens* (see C, Fig. 71).—The boarding is fixed, felt is nailed to it, and the cross-battens are then fixed to the required gauge to receive the slates. Although expensive it is not a satisfactory method, as any rain or snow blown up between the slates lodges on the upper edges of the cross battens causing, in some cases, a rapid decay of the battens.

(d) *Boarding, Felt, Counter-battens and Slating Battens.*—This is undoubtedly the best method and is adopted in first-class work (see D, Fig. 70 and G, Fig. 71). After the boarding and felt have been fixed, 50 mm by 19 mm counter-battens are nailed running from eaves to ridge at the same distance apart as the spars; the slating battens are nailed to them at the gauge apart and the slates are secured to them. Any driven rain and melted snow gaining access pass down between the counter-battens to the free outlet at the eaves. Besides providing a perfectly drop-dry roof, heat losses are reduced to a minimum and this construction is therefore very suitable for open roofs such as are required for churches, public halls, etc., in addition to domestic buildings where the expense is not prohibitive. (See also p. 141.)

Certain of the details in Fig. 71 not already referred to are described below.

Centre-nailed Slating.—This is illustrated at A and C, Fig. 71.

Detail A.—See p. 74 for the construction of the eaves and this page for the groundwork. An additional top batten is provided at the ridge so as to tilt the ridge course, otherwise the tails of the short slates comprising the ridge course would ride on the course below. *Note that there are* THREE *thicknesses of slates at each lap. Students in examinations frequently make the mistake of showing only two thicknesses at the lap with one thickness between laps*; this of course affords no protection at the side joints. The double eaves course projects 38 to 50 mm beyond the tilting fillet and the felt overlaps the edge of the gutter.

Detail C.—The sprocketed eaves has been referred to on p. 74 and the groundwork on this page. The distance between the slates at the junction between the sprocket and spar is rather excessive; this would be reduced if smaller slates (say 400 mm by 200 mm) were used as the sweep would then be more gradual.

Head-nailed Slating.—Examples are shown at F and G, Fig. 71.

Detail F.—The projecting ends of the spars are cut as shown and an asbestos gutter is fixed to them.

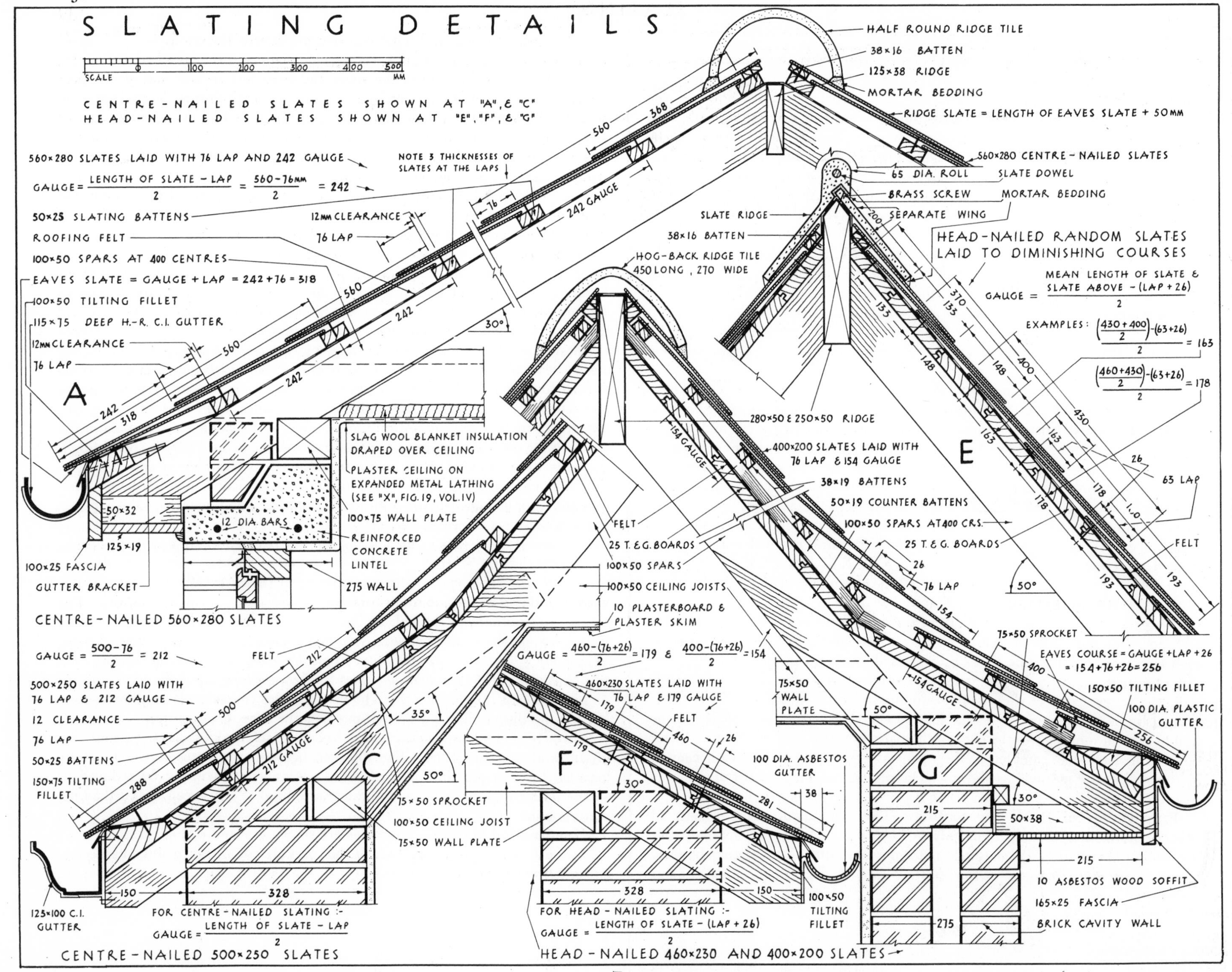
SLATING DETAILS
SCALE
0
100
200
300
400
500
MM
CENTRE-NAILED SLATES SHOWN AT "A", & "C"
HEAD-NAILED SLATES SHOWN AT "E", "F", & "G"
560×280 SLATES LAID WITH 76 LAP AND 242 GAUGE
GAUGE = LENGTH OF SLATE − LAP / 2 = 560−76MM / 2 = 242
NOTE 3 THICKNESSES OF SLATES AT THE LAPS
50×25 SLATING BATTENS
12MM CLEARANCE
ROOFING FELT
76 LAP
100×50 SPARS AT 400 CENTRES
EAVES SLATE = GAUGE + LAP = 242 + 76 = 318
100×50 TILTING FILLET
115×75 DEEP H.-R. C.I. GUTTER
12MM CLEARANCE
76 LAP
242 GAUGE
560
368
76
242
318
30°
A
50×32
125×19
100×25 FASCIA
GUTTER BRACKET
SLAG WOOL BLANKET INSULATION DRAPED OVER CEILING
PLASTER CEILING ON EXPANDED METAL LATHING (SEE "X", FIG. 19, VOL. IV)
12 DIA. BARS
100×75 WALL PLATE
REINFORCED CONCRETE LINTEL
275 WALL
CENTRE-NAILED 560×280 SLATES
HALF ROUND RIDGE TILE
38×16 BATTEN
125×38 RIDGE
MORTAR BEDDING
RIDGE SLATE = LENGTH OF EAVES SLATE + 50MM
560×280 CENTRE-NAILED SLATES
65 DIA. ROLL
SLATE DOWEL
BRASS SCREW
MORTAR BEDDING
SLATE RIDGE
SEPARATE WING
38×16 BATTEN
HOG-BACK RIDGE TILE 450 LONG, 270 WIDE
HEAD-NAILED RANDOM SLATES LAID TO DIMINISHING COURSES
GAUGE = MEAN LENGTH OF SLATE & SLATE ABOVE − (LAP + 26) / 2
EXAMPLES: ((430+400)/2) − (63+26) / 2 = 163
((460+430)/2) − (63+26) / 2 = 178
200
370
133
148
400
163
430
178
460
193
26
63 LAP
FELT
50°
E
280×50 & 250×50 RIDGE
154 GAUGE
400×200 SLATES LAID WITH 76 LAP & 154 GAUGE
38×19 BATTENS
50×19 COUNTER BATTENS
100×50 SPARS AT 400 CRS.
25 T. & G. BOARDS
FELT
25 T. & G. BOARDS
100×50 SPARS
100×50 CEILING JOISTS
10 PLASTERBOARD & PLASTER SKIM
26
76 LAP
154
75×50 SPROCKET
EAVES COURSE = GAUGE + LAP + 26 = 154 + 76 + 26 = 256
150×50 TILTING FILLET
100 DIA. PLASTIC GUTTER
75×50 WALL PLATE
50°
G
30°
215
50×38
215
10 ASBESTOS WOOD SOFFIT
165×25 FASCIA
BRICK CAVITY WALL
275
GAUGE = 500−76 / 2 = 212
500×250 SLATES LAID WITH 76 LAP & 212 GAUGE
12 CLEARANCE
76 LAP
50×25 BATTENS
150×75 TILTING FILLET
FELT
212
500
212 GAUGE
288
35°
50°
C
150
328
125×100 C.I. GUTTER
75×50 SPROCKET
100×50 CEILING JOIST
75×50 WALL PLATE
FOR CENTRE-NAILED SLATING :-
GAUGE = LENGTH OF SLATE − LAP / 2
CENTRE-NAILED 500×250 SLATES
GAUGE = 460−(76+26) / 2 = 179 & 400−(76+26) / 2 = 154
460×230 SLATES LAID WITH 76 LAP & 179 GAUGE
FELT
179
460
26
281
30°
F
100 DIA. ASBESTOS GUTTER
38
328
150
100×50 TILTING FILLET
FOR HEAD-NAILED SLATING :-
GAUGE = LENGTH OF SLATE − (LAP + 26) / 2
HEAD-NAILED 460×230 AND 400×200 SLATES

FIGURE 71

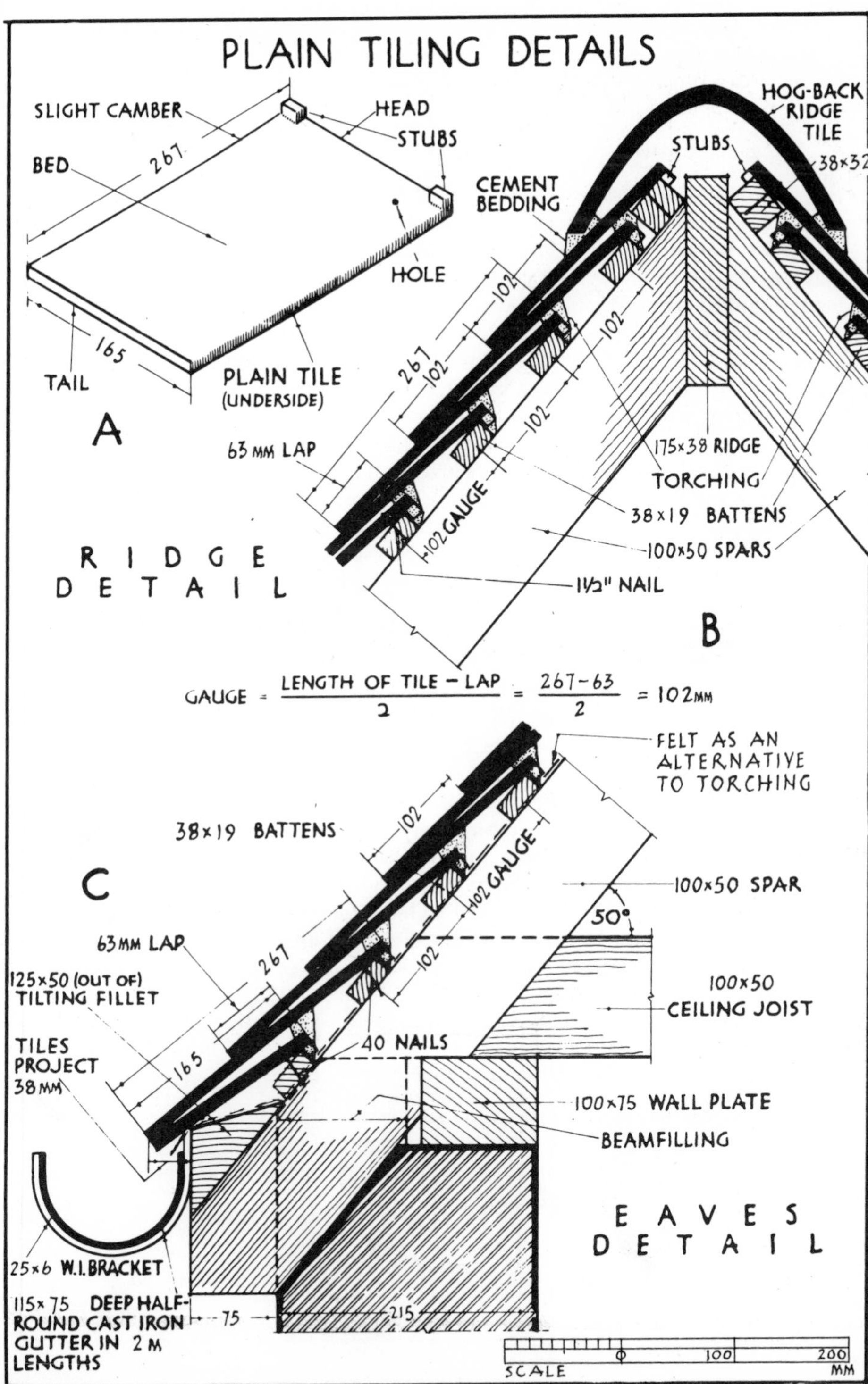

The close boarding and felt have been previously described.

Detail G.—The sprocketed eaves is similar to that described on p. 74, except that the inclination of the spars and sprockets are 50° and 30° respectively and the projection is only 230 mm; the groundwork is described on p. 137. The space between the slates over the intersection of the spars and sprockets is wide but not so serious as the defect purposely shown at C (already referred to), as the slates, being head-nailed, are not so liable to be damaged whilst being nailed; this space would be reduced if the sprockets were given a steeper pitch, and attention is drawn to the gradual sweep of the portion of the roof shown at K, Fig. 37, which is produced when the ideal and traditional pitch of the spars and sprockets of 55° and 35° respectively is adopted.

Other examples of head nailing are shown in Figs. 36, 37 and 38. The detail D in the latter figure gives a good example of the lower courses of slates having an inadequate fall due to the flat sprockets. Provided the window could be kept lower, a sounder job would result if the feet of the spars were continued and a small tilting fillet used instead of the sprockets.

Diminishing Coursed Work (see J, Fig. 70 and E, Fig. 71).—As explained on pp. 131 and 135, the random slates are sorted and laid in graded courses diminishing from a maximum at the eaves to a minimum at the ridge. Slates in each course are of the same length, but the width may vary (see J, Fig. 70). As the *lap is the same throughout*, it follows that the gauge decreases from the eaves upwards. The gauge for head-nailed slates is found by the rule stated at E, *i.e.*, $\frac{\text{mean length of slate and slate above} - (\text{lap} + 26 \text{ mm})}{2}$, where the application shows a uniform lap of 63 mm (which is adequate for a pitch of 50°) and the length of the successive upper courses to be 460, 430, 400 and 370 mm; the gauges of the 460 and 430 mm courses are 178 and 163 mm respectively as shown, and that of the 400 mm course $= \frac{\frac{400+370}{2} - (63+26)}{2} = 148$ mm. The gauge for centre-nailed slates, as in ordinary slating, is 13 mm more. Whilst the above example is a simple illustration, it should be pointed out that the reduction in length is excessive and very large slates would be required at the eaves of a large roof if a more gradual reduction was not made; sometimes the courses are diminished at every second course. Westmorland slates are usually laid with graduated courses and a very attractive appearance results. The slate ridge is described on p. 135; a sawn stone ridge or a hog-back tile ridge (provided it was of a suitable colour) would be more pleasing in appearance.

Procedure in Slating a Roof.—The following is the normal sequence of operations in slating the roof of a building which is assumed to be detached and has gabled walls :—

The metal eaves gutters are fixed immediately after the woodwork at the eaves has been completed; the battens are fixed at the gauge apart, commencing from the

FIGURE 72

eaves; stacks of slates having been placed at suitable intervals up the roof by the labourer, the slater proceeds to fix them, commencing at one end of the eaves and gradually spreading longitudinally and up the roof until the ridge is reached; the opposite slope is covered in a similar manner; the ridge tiles are bedded, jointed and pointed horizontally and in true alignment, with exception of the end pieces and those against chimney-stacks, which are given a slight tilt upwards, as previously explained. If hips are required, the specially cut hip slates will have been dressed to the correct shape and size and these are the first to be fixed in each course; if the hips are to be cut and mitred, the lead soakers (prepared by the plumber) are fixed by the slater as the slating proceeds; if hip tiles are required, these are fixed in correct alignment, commencing at the eaves and neatly mitring with the ridge tiles. If the verges are as shown at E, Fig. 70, the undercloaks are firmly bedded in cement mortar before the battens are fixed. Finally, the gutters are cleaned out and the underside of the roof is torched. Of course, if untearable felt is to be fixed in lieu of torching, this is done before the battens are fixed.

PLAIN TILING

Plain tiles are made of clay or concrete. If of clay, this is very finely ground, moulded into slabs and subsequently dried and burnt. Like bricks, both hand-made and machine-made tiles are produced in a wide range of colours. Hand-made tiles have a sand-faced surface, they have a better texture, are tougher, are less liable to lamination, and are more expensive than those which are machine-made.

The size is usually 267 mm by 165 mm by 10 to 13 mm thick (see A, Fig. 72). They have a slight camber or *set* (3 m radius) in their length which ensures that the tails will bed and not ride on the backs of those in the course below. A tile has two (sometimes three) *stubs* or *nibs* which project on the bed or underside at the head in order that it may be hung from the batten, and each tile has two holes formed at about 25 mm from the head and 38 mm from the edges. Special tiles are also made, thus : *eaves tiles* (165 mm by 165 mm) and *tile and a half* (267 mm by 248 mm or wider). The latter are used at alternate courses at verges and swept valleys.

Terms, such as bond, gauge, margin, etc., used in slating are also applied to tiling.

Plain tiles are laid in regular bond, and the preparation of a roof to receive the tiles is similar to the methods described on p. 137 with exception of "boarding and felting," as this is impracticable for tiling on account of the nibs.

The nails used are similar to those described on p. 133, and 38 mm long *copper* nails are used in most good work.

Unlike slating, every tile is not secured with nails unless for roofs in exposed positions. It is usually specified that every tile in each *fourth* course shall be twice nailed. The double eaves course tiles, ridge course tiles and all verge, hip and valley tiles must also be nailed.

[1] In some technical colleges, plain tiling is preferred to slating as a first year subject of a Building Course and hence a brief mention of it is made here. Plain tiles and other roofing materials are given more extended treatment in Chap. III, Vol. III. Industrial and light weight roof sheeting and decking are described in Chap. VI, Vol. IV.

Pitch, Lap and Gauge.—As a plain tile is a relatively small unit, a large lap is not practicable, and therefore the usual lap employed is 63 mm. This necessitates an increase in the minimum pitch to 45°. For reasons previously given, this angle should be avoided, and a pitch of 50° to 55° adopted.

The gauge equals $\frac{\text{length} - \text{lap}}{2} = \frac{267 - 63 \text{ mm}}{2} = 102$ mm. As in slating, *there must be* THREE *thicknesses of tiles at the lap.*

Typical eaves and ridge details are shown in Fig. 72.

Eaves Detail (see C).—The spars forming the simple open eaves project only 75 mm, and a tilting fillet is fixed to them to give the necessary tilt for the lower courses and the doubling eaves tiles. Felt damp proofing is shown.

Ridge Detail (see B).—The top course, like that in slating, is tilted by using a thicker batten at the ridge; the length of this course should be such as to give a 102 mm margin, and in the example it is 216 mm. Either the hog-back ridge tile as shown, or a half-round ridge tile (as shown at A, Fig. 71) provide a suitable finish, and these tiles should be bedded, jointed and pointed in cement mortar or mastic as described for slating. This pointing material may be coloured to conform with that of the tiles. The underside of the tiles is shown torched, but untearable felt (fixed as described on p. 135) may be used if preferred. Lead-covered ridges should never be used for tiled roofs on account of the colour which, as a rule, contrasts violently with that of the tiles.

Tiled verges may be constructed in a similar manner to that shown for slating at E, Fig. 70.

Hips are often finished with similar tiles to those used for ridges, but such are unsightly. The best treatment is that provided by bonnet hip tiles; these are curved and bond in with the adjacent tiling. Purpose-made V-shaped hip tiles which course in with the plaintiles are also employed.

The best form of valley for a tiled roof is the swept[1] valley where each course of tiles in the adjacent sloped surfaces is swept round to a suitable curve; this is constructed as briefly explained on p. 137. Another good form is the laced[1] valley where wide tiles are used at the intersection and each course is lifted to give a laced effect. The most common method adopted, especially for speculative work, consists of forming a lead valley as shown for slating in Fig. 75; this is not desirable on account of its unsatisfactory appearance, for in general, leadwork in a tiled roof should not be exposed to view as its colour clashes with that of most tiles.

INTERLOCKING TILES

Interlocking tiles (sometimes called single-lap tiles) are the lightest type of roof tiling—weighing 36·6 in comparison with 63·5 kg/m^2 for plain tiles. Hence the groundwork of spars and purlins can be lighter than for plain tiling

[1] See Chap. III, Vol. III.

and 75 mm by 50 mm spars at 450 mm centres are sufficient for spans up to 2 m. Interlocking tiles (see Fig. 39) are machine made of concrete in various sizes and sections, the 380 mm by 230 mm type at D is typical. The tiles are troughed as shown at A and D, have one nail hole, two nibs which engage behind the 38 mm by 19 mm battens, and the underside also has projecting lugs which fit into the troughs of the tile below. They can be laid with a straight bond or they may have a broken bond like plain tiling and slating (*e.g.* at A, Fig. 70). In the latter event, special left and right-hand tiles are used for the finish at the verge.

45 mm copper nails are used for the best work, each tile in alternate course being nailed except where the roof is exposed and steeply pitched when all the tiles are nailed. All the eaves and ridge tiles and those at the valleys, hips and verges must always be nailed.

Pitch, Lap and Gauge.—Interlocking tiles are laid with a minimum head lap of 76 mm, they also have an interlocking side lap of 26 mm as shown at A. The minimum pitch is 30° when the gauge is 280 mm and the head lap is 100 mm as shown at E. For pitches of 35° and upwards a 304 mm gauge and 76 mm head lap can be used.

Note that unlike plain tiles there are only *two* thicknesses of tile at the head lap as indicated at C.

Eaves Detail (see E).—The eaves project 215 mm and small sprockets are used to give support to the felt at this point. The truss (see pp. 77 and 78 for description) rests on a 100 mm by 50 mm wall plate to which it is spiked and the cavity wall is closed by a 215 mm brick course and one of half bricks as beam filling.

Ridge Detail (see E).—This is quite simply arranged as shown, the top batten is slightly thicker to ensure that the top course sits tightly on the course below. The ridge tile is bedded as described above for plain tiling.

Verge Detail (see A).—This shows the use of a plain tile as an under-cloak and a special left-hand verge tile to finish the edge. The treatment is similar to that already described for a slated verge.

Abutment Detail (see B).—This occurs at a chimney stack and shows the use of a simple lead cover flashing which must extend over at least one of the raised portions of the tile. (See also p. 150.)

Hips are made with third-round tiles similar to those for the ridge, the interlocking tiles being cut to the line of the hip.

Valleys are formed by using purpose-made troughed valley tiles nailed to short timbers nailed between the jack rafters and parallel to the valley rafter. The single lap tiles are laid to project over the valley tiles, and after being cut to rake to form an open valley about 100 mm wide, mortar bedding is pointed in along the cut edges.

Thermal Insulation of Roofs.—It is important to prevent the undue loss of heat through the roof and the Building Regulations include a clause to this effect. The *minimum* requirements for a pitched roof are that it should have slates or tiles plus felt with a 100 mm thick quilt of glass (or slag) wool over the ceiling (or between the ceiling joists). In the case of a flat roof having boarding not less than 16 mm thick a 75 mm thick quilt must be incorporated within it or within the ceiling to it. Insulating quilts are obtainable in 1 m wide rolls from 25 to 75 mm thick, comprising a paper covered core of slag (or glass) wool. An alternative is shown in Fig. 39, where the insulation consists of loose vermiculite (an expanded form of mica) 70 mm thick. Another insulating material is 38 mm thick expanded polystyrene insulation board fixed to the top of the ceiling joists. Thermal insulation is described in detail in Vol. 4.

CHAPTER SIX

PLUMBING

Syllabus.—Brief description of the manufacture of milled and cast sheet lead; characteristics; weights of sheet lead used for various purposes; terms; including rolls, drips, flashings and soakers. Details of leadwork at gutters, flats, chimney stacks, ridges, hips and valleys. Rain-water pipes. Domestic water services. Tools.

Lead is chiefly produced from an ore, called galena, which is a compound of lead and sulphur. The principal sources of supply are the United States of America, Spain, Australia, Canada, Germany and Mexico; comparatively little of the ore is now obtained from English mines.

Manufacture of Lead.—One of several methods of abstracting the lead is to smelt the ore in a furnace to remove certain impurities; the metal is run into pots, transferred to large copper pans, remelted to eliminate further impurities, and the soft refined metal is finally cast into bars called *pigs*. These pigs weigh from 36 to 54 kg each and are used for the manufacture of sheets, pipes, etc.

Sheet lead is used for covering roofs, gutters, ridges, etc. There are two methods of manufacturing sheet lead, *i.e.*, (*a*) milled or rolled sheet lead, and (*b*) cast sheet lead.

(a) *Milled or Rolled Sheet Lead.*—The pigs of lead are melted and cast into slabs from 1·5 to 2·2 m long, 1·2 to 1·8 m wide, and approximately 125 mm thick. Each slab is passed to the mill, the bed of which consists of a series of steel rollers, and situated in the middle and across the bed is a pair of heavy rollers; the bed rollers are caused to rotate, the slab is passed backwards and forwards between the large rollers until its thickness is reduced to a sheet which is approximately but uniformly 25 mm thick, 4·6 to 12 m long and 2 to 3m wide; the sheets are cut into suitable sizes, each piece is passed through the finishing mill to reduce it to a sheet of the required weight and thickness, and finally the sheet is rolled into a coil for dispatch to the plumber. Most of the sheet lead used at the present time is manufactured by this process.

(b) *Cast Sheet Lead.*—This is produced by melting the pigs and pouring it over a bed of sand prepared on a casting bench, which is from 3·7 to 4·6 m long and 1·2 to 1·8 m wide, and the height of the frame is about 700 mm from the floor; the sand bed is prepared, and levelled surface being slightly below the edges of the bench, depending upon the required thickness of the lead. The molten lead is poured into a trough, semicircular in section, which extends to the full width of the bench to which it is hinged at one end; the trough is rotated to tip the lead on to the sand bed and the lead is pushed forward by means of a strike or bar which runs on guides on the long edges of the frame at a height corresponding to the required thickness of the lead.

Cast lead is considered to be the best form of sheet lead—it being tougher than milled sheet—but it is relatively expensive. It is used for first class work.[1]

Ornamental leadwork, such as rain-water heads and coverings to architectural features, is produced from cast lead; the sand bed on the casting bench is levelled off and a mould of the required shape and the reverse of the surface decoration is impressed on the sand; the molten lead is poured over this prepared surface, the upper surface is levelled off by the strike, and the undersurface is ornamented with the decoration in relief; each piece of lead is trimmed, cut to the required length, shaped as required, and finally jointed by lead-burning or soldering.

[1] The roofs of the Manchester Central Reference Library and the Town Hall Extension, Manchester (completed in 1938) are covered with No. 8 *cast* sheet lead and the total weight of lead used was approximately 272 kg.

Characteristics of Lead.—This is a heavy metal, weighing approximately 1 1374 kg/m^3; soft, very malleable, tough and flexible; easily worked and readily cut; very durable (provided it is not subjected to certain acids and not in contact with certain cements); is bluish grey in colour with a bright metallic lustre when freshly cut, but this tarnishes when exposed to the air.

Lead has a *high coefficient of linear expansion* (it being 0·000029 per °C., or approximately two and a half times that of steel) and it therefore readily expands and contracts when subjected to considerable variations of temperature. It is because of this characteristic that very large sheets of lead must be avoided (especially if used to cover vertical surfaces) and ample provision made to permit of this movement. In this connection, defects such as wrinkling, bulging and cracking will be avoided if the *area of each piece of sheet lead is limited to* 2·23 *m*^{2}, *and if only two of the adjacent sides of a rectangular sheet are fixed.* Attention is drawn to the various details shown in Figs. 73, 74 and 75, which make provision for movement due to expansion and contraction.

Weights of Sheet Lead.—Despite the change to metric units, lead is specified by numbers according to its weight in lb. per square foot. Thus No. 4 lead weighs 4·19 lb. per sq. ft. The weights recommended for various purposes are :

Flats, pitched roofs and gutters	No. 6, 7 or 8 lead
Hips and ridges	No. 6 or 7 lead
Flashings	No. 5 lead
Soakers	No. 3 or 4 lead

Lighter weights than the above are often adopted in cheap work, and it is not uncommon to find that for such work No. 5 lead is employed for flats.

The thickness and colour code of the various grades are shown in brackets thus: No. 3 (1·25 mm, green), No. 4 (1·8 mm, blue), No. 5 (2·24 mm, red), No. 6 (2·5 mm, black), No. 7 (3·15 mm, white) and No. 8 (3·55 mm, orange).

Terms.—The following terms are used in plumbing :—

Bossing means " working up " and is applied to the labour in dressing lead to various shapes when forming rolls, drips, cesspools, etc., by means of the bossing stick and other tools described on pp. 156–157. Care must be taken to maintain a uniform thickness of lead when performing this operation.

Burning-in is the method which is sometimes adopted to secure the edges of lead coverings of projecting stone members. A groove or *raglet* is formed in the stonework (see A, Fig. 76), the edge of the lead is scraped clean and turned into it, and secured by molten lead which is poured into the raglet and afterwards consolidated or *caulked* by using the caulking tool shown at S, Fig. 79. The lead is poured down grooves formed in a narrow board (which rests on edge upon the cornice and is placed against the face of the parapet) and delivered into the raglet; the hot lead heats the turn-in of the covering and unites with it. This method is not now commonly employed owing to the difficulty experienced in raising the temperature of the edge of the lead covering to that required to effect complete unity between it and the molten lead, and the method adopted for fixing cover flashings to brickwork is often preferred, *i.e.*, wedges are driven in at about 300 mm intervals and the joint is afterwards pointed with mastic or cement mortar (see below and p. 148)

Solder is an alloy of lead and tin, and used by the plumber to join pieces of lead and form joints between lead pipes, etc.; this operation is called *soldering*. *Coarse or plumbing solder* is used for *wiped joints* (see p. 155) and consists of 2 parts lead and 1 part tin; *fine solder*, used for finer work, is a mixture of 1 part lead and 2 parts tin; *ordinary solder* is a mixture of lead and tin in equal parts and is used for forming *copper-bit joints* (see p. 155). Coarse solder is either heated in a melting or solder pot (U, Fig. 79) and poured on the joint by means of a ladle (M, Fig. 79), or it is cast into narrow strips which are about 300 mm by 32 mm by 0·45 kg and in this form the solder is applied to the joint by using the blow-lamp (A′, Fig. 79) to melt the strip.

Lead Burning or Welding.—This is the process of uniting by heat (fusing) pieces of lead in which gases (such as oxy-acetylene, oxy-coal gas, etc.) are utilized and special blow-lamps employed. It is a method which has been developed in recent years and used for certain purposes as a substitute for soldering.

Nails and Nailing.—The nails used for fixing leadwork to wood are of copper, 25 to 32 mm long, with clout (flat) heads. The term *close nailing* is applied when the nails are at from 25 to 75 mm intervals; in *open nailing* the nails are spaced at from 75 to 200 mm.

Soakers are thin pieces of lead (not more than No. 4 grade) which are placed between slates. The size and shape varies, thus the soakers described on p. 150 (see C and M, Fig. 75) are 175 mm wide, bent at right angles with an upturn of 75 mm and a length which varies in accordance with the length of the slates, whilst those described on p. 137 are square. They are either nailed to the boarding (at their heads) or the tops are turned over the slates. Only light lead is used for soakers to prevent the tilting or riding of the slates.

Flashings.—These are narrow pieces of lead which are required at the intersection between vertical faces of walls or framing and pitched roofs, flats, gutters, etc. They are classified into :

(1) *Horizontal Cover Flashings*, which are usually 150 mm wide strips having their upper edges turned 25 mm into the raked-out joint of the brickwork (or raglet formed in the stonework) and the lower edges lapped over and covering the *upturn* or *upstand* (vertical portion) of the lower pieces of lead (see Figs. 73 and 74, and p. 148).

(2) *Apron Flashings*, which are provided at the front of chimney-stacks, dormers, etc., and are from 200 to 300 mm wide; the lower portion is dressed over the slates and the upturn is let 25 mm into the raked-out joint or raglet (see A, B, L and O, Fig. 75, and p. 150).

(3) *Stepped Cover Flashings*, which are from 150 to 200 mm wide and have their upper edges cut into a series of steps; the horizontal edge of each step is turned 25 mm into the raked joint. They are fixed at the sides of brick chimneys, gable walls, etc. (see A, B, F, G and N, Fig. 75, and pp. 150 and 151).

(4) *Raking Cover Flashings*, which are used in lieu of (3) when the walls are of stone. The upper edge of the flashing is let 25 mm into a raglet formed parallel to the rake of the roof and this top edge is therefore not stepped (see p. 151).

Flashings are in lengths cut across the width of the roll and the maximum length therefore varies from 2·1 to 2·7 m; they are secured along their upper edges by lead wedges.

Lead Wedges are tapered pieces of lead of the size and shape as shown at O, Fig. 74. They are made either (*a*) by running molten lead into a mould and cutting the tapered strip into short pieces when cool (such are called cast lead wedges) or (*b*) by folding pieces of scrap sheet lead and beating them into shape. They are used to fix flashings and are driven in between the turn-in of the flashing and the upper edge of the joint. In the case of horizontal and raking cover flashings, the wedges are driven in at about 300 mm intervals—450 mm maximum (see B, O and Q, Fig. 73); one or two are provided at each step of a stepped flashing (see A, B and F, Fig. 75). The raked-out joint between the wedges is pointed with either cement mortar or mastic. The section at N, Fig. 74 shows a wedge in position.

If used to secure flashings in stonework in lieu of burning-in (see above), the edge of the lead is bent and turned back to completely line the raglet, and the wedges are driven into the folded edge.

Oak wedges are sometimes used in cheap work. These are apt to become loose when they shrink.

Tacks, Tingles or Clips are strips of lead used to stiffen flashings and prevent their free edges being lifted by a strong wind. They are from 50 to 75 mm wide and are placed at a distance apart not exceeding 760 mm. As shown at M, Fig. 74, each tack is fixed in the joint, and it is sufficiently long to turn over and grip the free edge of the flashing by about 25 mm. Tacks are also required to secure hollow rolls at 610 mm intervals (L, Fig. 74), and welts and ridge coverings at 610 to 1200 mm intervals (see B, R and S, Fig. 75), the fixed ends of the tacks being clout-nailed to the boarding (or ridge) as shown. Copper tacks, being stiffer than lead, are used for first-class work (see below).

Joints.—As already mentioned, provision must be made to allow lead to expand and contract, and the joints between sheets must be formed so as to permit of this movement. The various joints are: (1) laps, (2) rolls, (3) drips and (4) welts.

(1) *Lap Joints.*—These occur at a maximum of 2·1 to 2·7 m apart (depending upon the width of the roll) for flashings, upturns of gutters, ridges, hips, valleys and lead coverings of pitched roofs. They are also called *passings.* The amount of lap (distance that one piece covers the adjacent piece of lead) is usually 100 mm for cover flashings, upturns of gutters and aprons, and 150 mm for stepped and raked flashings, ridges, hips and valleys.

The side laps of lead covering pitched roofs are in the form of rolls or welts (see below) and the lower edge of each upper sheet laps the top edge of the sheet below it to form a horizontal joint. The amount of lap at such horizontal joints depends upon the pitch; it is usually 150 mm when the pitch exceeds 45°, and this may be increased to 230 mm for flatter pitches. Alternatively, horizontal welts may be used instead of wide laps, but these may detract from the appearance of the roof.

When the slope of a roof is less than 15°, the horizontal joints between the sheets of lead are usually in the form of drips (see below).

(2) *Rolls.*—This form of joint is required on lead-covered flats, pitched roofs, ridges, certain forms of hips and long gutters. They are placed at intervals varying from 460 mm to a maximum of 760 mm for flats and similar construction.

There are three kinds of rolls, *i.e.*, two forms of covering wood or solid rolls and a hollow roll.

Solid Rolls.—One form is shown at P, Fig. 73, and J, Fig. 74.[1] The wood roll is shaped as shown and is nailed or screwed to the boarding. One edge of a sheet is dressed into the angle between the roll and boarding and continued beyond the crown as shown. This is called the *undercloak* or *undersheet*. Its edge is secured with 25 mm copper nails at 25 to 150 mm apart (depending upon the quality of the work) and the edge is rasped off. The edge of the adjacent sheet is worked into the angle, passed over the undercloak and continued 25 to 50 mm on to the flat of the roof or bed of the gutter. This is known as the *overcloak* or *oversheet.*

The second form of solid roll is shown at K, Fig. 74. The undercloak is dressed and secured as above described, but the overcloak is brought over to within 7 to 25 mm of the flat on the other side. This method was generally preferred in the North of England, but now both forms of solid rolls are adopted equally there.

There is a difference of opinion as to which of the two methods shown at J and K is the best. In the former, water may gain access between the sheets by capillary attraction. Whilst this is avoided at K, this practice is not recommended for exposed positions on the free edge of the overcloak, having an inadequate grip, may be lifted by strong winds.

The treatment at the ends of solid rolls is referred to on p. 148.

Hollow Roll.—This type is adopted for best work in connection with lead-covered pitched roofs, and especially if cast lead is to be used;[1] it is also suitable for covered surfaces, such as domes, where wood rolls could not be employed economically. The roll is supported by "stout" (preferably from No. 8 lead) lead tacks or tingles which are 50 mm wide and 150 to 175 mm long; these are placed at 610 mm apart, and one end of each is secured to the boarding by two copper clout nails, the boarding having been slightly recessed to receive it. Copper tacks, being stronger than lead, are used in superior work, each end being secured by two brass screws. When turning a hollow roll, the edge of the undercloak is upturned vertically, the tacks are fixed and their free ends are turned over the undercloak, the edge of the overcloak is upturned and also turned over the undercloak, and the whole is finally dressed to the form shown in the illustration. Hollow rolls are not suitable for flat roofs as they are liable to be damaged if trodden on.

Rolls are again referred to in the following pages.

(3) *Drips* or *Steps* are formed on flats and in gutters which exceed 2·4 m in width or length, and they are placed across the fall. They are generally 50 mm and sometimes 75 mm deep.

Three forms of drips are shown at Q, Fig. 73, and R, T and U, Fig. 74. The 50 mm drips at Q and R show the upper edge of the lower sheet (called the *undersheet*) dressed into the angle, continued up the step or drip, and dressed into the 40 mm wide shallow rebate formed along the edge of the boarding to which it is close copper-nailed. The object of the rebate is to avoid a ridge in the lead. The lower edge of the upper sheet (called the *oversheet*) is dressed over it, and like the roll at J, is continued on the flat or bed for 25 to 50 mm. The 75 mm drip at T has the oversheet stopped short of the flat; water cannot thereby gain access by capillary attraction, but like the roll of similar construction, the free edge of the oversheet may be disturbed in a high gale. A second method of preventing capillary attraction is shown at U, which illustrates a "capillary groove" formed along the step and into which the undersheet is dressed; whilst this construction is excellent in theory, it is very rarely adopted in practice.

Drips are further considered later.

(4) *Welts or Seams* are often employed for jointing sheets of lead covering vertical and steeply pitched surfaces and for jointing lead and copper damp-proof courses (see p. 18). A welt is illustrated at R, S and T, Fig. 75. Like hollow rolls, the edges of the adjacent sheets are upturned with 50 mm wide lead or copper tacks between, the tacks being fixed at from 610 to 1200 mm intervals; after being folded as shown at R, the upturns are dressed down as closely as

[1] The space between the lead in these and similar details is exaggerated.

[1] Hollow rolls, 63 mm diameter, are employed on the roof of the Library referred to in the footnote on p. 142, and these are secured by 150 mm by 75 mm copper tacks at 160 mm intervals.

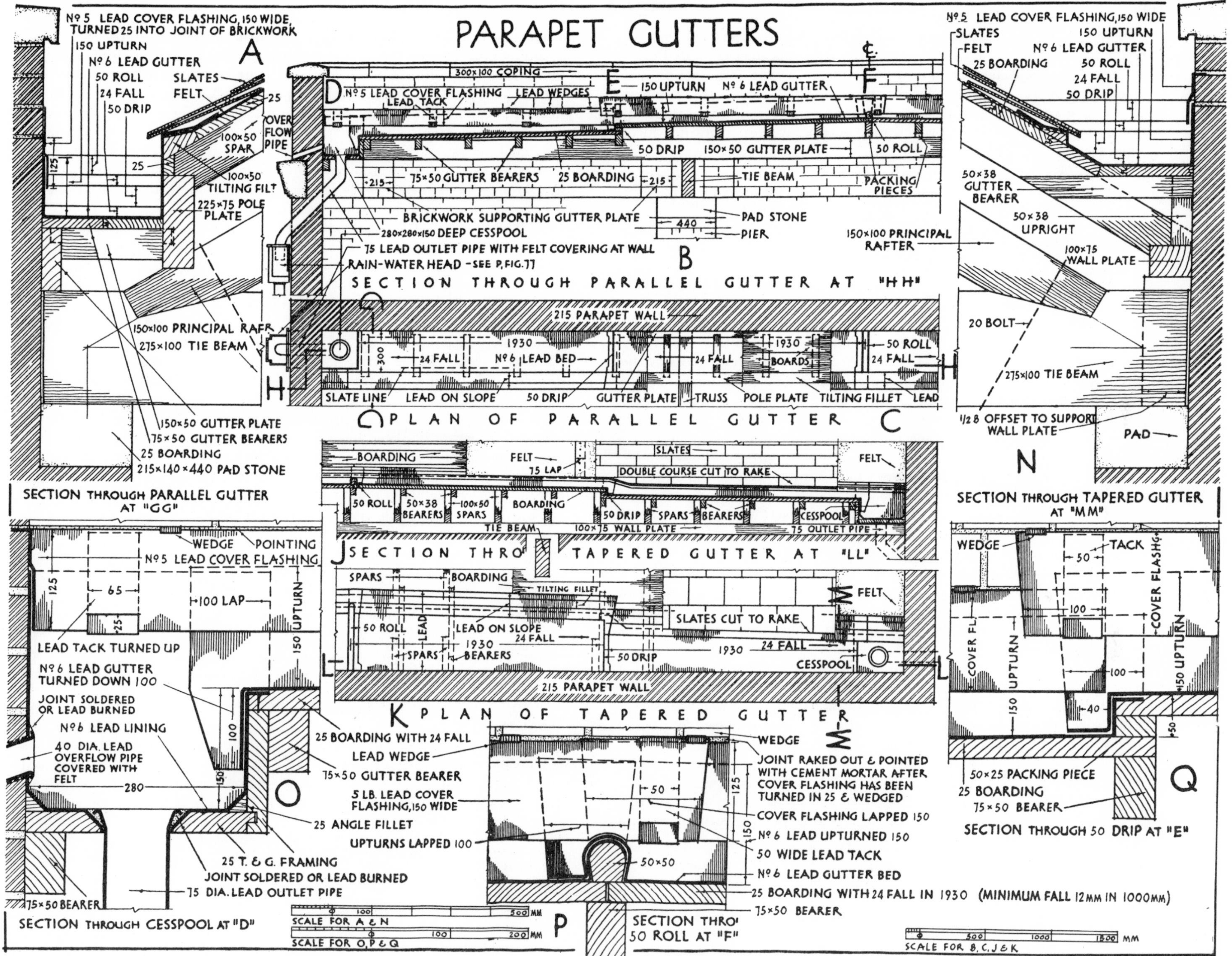
PARAPET GUTTERS
A
No 5 LEAD COVER FLASHING, 150 WIDE, TURNED 25 INTO JOINT OF BRICKWORK
150 UPTURN
No 6 LEAD GUTTER
50 ROLL
24 FALL
50 DRIP
SLATES
FELT
100×50 SPAR
OVERFLOW PIPE
100×50 TILTING FILLET
225×75 POLE PLATE
150×100 PRINCIPAL RAFTER
275×100 TIE BEAM
150×50 GUTTER PLATE
75×50 GUTTER BEARERS
25 BOARDING
215×140×440 PAD STONE
SECTION THROUGH PARALLEL GUTTER AT "GG"
300×100 COPING
No 5 LEAD COVER FLASHING
LEAD TACK
LEAD WEDGES
150 UPTURN
No 6 LEAD GUTTER
50 DRIP
150×50 GUTTER PLATE
50 ROLL
75×50 GUTTER BEARERS
25 BOARDING
TIE BEAM
PACKING PIECES
BRICKWORK SUPPORTING GUTTER PLATE
PAD STONE
PIER
280×280×150 DEEP CESSPOOL
75 LEAD OUTLET PIPE WITH FELT COVERING AT WALL
RAIN-WATER HEAD - SEE P, FIG. 77
B
SECTION THROUGH PARALLEL GUTTER AT "HH"
215 PARAPET WALL
1930
24 FALL
No 6 LEAD BED
BOARDS
50 ROLL
SLATE LINE
LEAD ON SLOPE
50 DRIP
GUTTER PLATE
TRUSS
POLE PLATE
TILTING FILLET
LEAD
PLAN OF PARALLEL GUTTER
C
No 5 LEAD COVER FLASHING, 150 WIDE
SLATES
150 UPTURN
FELT
No 6 LEAD GUTTER
25 BOARDING
50 ROLL
24 FALL
50 DRIP
50×38 GUTTER BEARER
50×38 UPRIGHT
150×100 PRINCIPAL RAFTER
100×75 WALL PLATE
20 BOLT
275×100 TIE BEAM
1/2 B OFFSET TO SUPPORT WALL PLATE
PAD
N
SECTION THROUGH TAPERED GUTTER AT "MM"
BOARDING
FELT
75 LAP
SLATES
DOUBLE COURSE CUT TO RAKE
50 ROLL
50×38 BEARERS
100×50 SPARS
BOARDING
50 DRIP
SPARS
BEARERS
CESSPOOL
TIE BEAM
100×75 WALL PLATE
75 OUTLET PIPE
J SECTION THROUGH TAPERED GUTTER AT "LL"
SPARS
BOARDING
TILTING FILLET
SLATES CUT TO RAKE
LEAD
LEAD ON SLOPE
24 FALL
1930
SPARS
BEARERS
50 DRIP
CESSPOOL
215 PARAPET WALL
K PLAN OF TAPERED GUTTER
WEDGE
POINTING
No 5 LEAD COVER FLASHING
65
100 LAP
150 UPTURN
LEAD TACK TURNED UP
No 6 LEAD GUTTER TURNED DOWN 100
JOINT SOLDERED OR LEAD BURNED
No 6 LEAD LINING
40 DIA. LEAD OVERFLOW PIPE COVERED WITH FELT
280
25 BOARDING WITH 24 FALL
75×50 GUTTER BEARER
25 ANGLE FILLET
25 T. & G. FRAMING
JOINT SOLDERED OR LEAD BURNED
75 DIA. LEAD OUTLET PIPE
75×50 BEARER
O
SECTION THROUGH CESSPOOL AT "D"
LEAD WEDGE
5 LB. LEAD COVER FLASHING, 150 WIDE
UPTURNS LAPPED 100
WEDGE
JOINT RAKED OUT & POINTED WITH CEMENT MORTAR AFTER COVER FLASHING HAS BEEN TURNED IN 25 & WEDGED
COVER FLASHING LAPPED 150
No 6 LEAD UPTURNED 150
50 WIDE LEAD TACK
No 6 LEAD GUTTER BED
50×50
25 BOARDING WITH 24 FALL IN 1930 (MINIMUM FALL 12MM IN 1000MM)
75×50 BEARER
P
SECTION THRO' 50 ROLL AT "F"
WEDGE
TACK
COVER FLASHG
UPTURN
50×25 PACKING PIECE
25 BOARDING
75×50 BEARER
Q
SECTION THROUGH 50 DRIP AT "E"
SCALE FOR A & N
SCALE FOR O, P & Q
SCALE FOR B, C, J & K

FIGURE 73

possible on to the flat. The spaces between the folds have been emphasized to show the construction more clearly, and the finished appearance of a welt more closely resembles the sketch at T. The width of the seam varies from 32 to 75 mm.

Welted joints are not suitable for flats or low-pitched roofs, but like hollow rolls, they are very effective for steep or curved surfaces. Detail D, Fig. 75, shows a section through a welt which may be employed at ridges in lieu of 150 mm laps.

The roof of the Manchester Town Hall building (see footnote on p. 142) has a 60° pitch, and the sheets of cast lead are joined at their sloping edges by welts which are 70 mm wide; the horizontal joints consist of 165 mm wide laps and the sheets are secured by turning the top edges over the boarding to which they are close copper-nailed; each board immediately above that to which the upper edge of the sheet was nailed was removed (it being left loose for this purpose) and, after nailing the sheet, this board was replaced and nailed.

Gutters.—There are three forms of lead-covered gutters, *i.e.*, (*a*) parallel parapet gutters, (*b*) tapered parapet gutters and (*c*) V-gutters.

(a) *Parallel Parapet Gutters.*—As is implied, this gutter is situated behind a parapet wall and at the bottom of a flat or sloping roof; it is also known as a *box* or *trough* gutter. The gutter is of uniform width throughout and must be at least 255 mm wide to afford adequate foot room. A long gutter is divided into sections, having a roll at the highest point, and drips at intervals not exceeding 2·4 m apart; it is given a minimum fall of 12·5 mm per metre. In Fig. 73 it receives the drainage from a sloping roof, and in Fig. 74 is associated with a lead flat.

The timber details of the gutter shown in Fig. 73 are referred to on p. 78; a part plan is shown at C and a longitudinal section is shown at B; a 50 mm roll is placed at the highest point from which the gutter falls 25 mm to a 50 mm drip and the lower portion falls 25 mm to a cesspool.

A *cesspool* or *drip-box* is a lead-lined receptacle, situated at the lowest end of a gutter, from which a lead outlet pipe, suitably bent, discharges the water into a rain-water head where it is conveyed by a rain-water pipe to a gully and drain. Rain-water heads and pipes are described on pp. 154–155. The minimum depth of a cesspool should be 150 mm. The wood framing, its support and the chamfered hole are detailed at O, Fig. 73. The lead lining is in one piece, two sides being turned up 300 mm against the walls, a third side being turned up 150 mm and dressed 38 mm into a shallow rebate formed along the lower edge of the gutter boarding to which it is nailed, and the fourth side is 510 mm long, 360 mm of which is turned vertically with the remainder dressed over the tilting fillet and roof boarding to which it is nailed. The lining is bossed to the required shape from a rectangular piece of lead before it is placed in position, and a skilled craftsman will do this without resorting to folded or " dog-eared " angles (see p. 148). It is holed and dressed over the chamfered hole formed in the wood bottom, and the outlet pipe,[1] having been formed to a swan-neck bend as described on p. 148, with its upper end enlarged by means of a tanpin or turnpin (see E, Fig. 79), is either soldered as shown or lead-burned to give a firm watertight joint. A galvanized wire or copper *balloon* or *dome* is sometimes fixed into the top of the outlet pipe to prevent it from being choked by leaves, etc. A small lead overflow or warning pipe should be provided as shown to serve as a temporary outlet for the water in the event of the pipe becoming choked. As certain mortars act chemically upon and destroy lead, it is advisable to cover the lead overflow pipe and the portion of the outlet pipe which passes through the wall with tarred felt (see B and O); alternatively, these pipes may be given a coating of bituminous paint.

[1] The size of the pipe may be determined by allowing 10 cm² of pipe area to 10·8 m² of roof surface.

The lower section of the gutter is covered with lead after the cesspool has been lined, the covering consisting of the *bed*, a 125 or 150 mm *upturn* or *upstand* against the wall, and an upturn against the pole plate which is continued over the tilting fillet to about 150 mm on the slope of the roof where it is open copper-nailed to the boarding along its edge. This lower end is dressed 100 mm down the cesspool, and the upper end forms the undersheet of the drip which has been described on p. 144.

The next section of the gutter has a similar covering; the lower end forms the oversheet of the drip and the upper end is dressed over the roll to provide the undercloak (see P).

The cover flashing is fixed, commencing at the cesspool end, after the opposite half of the gutter has been lined in a similar manner and finished with the upper end of the top section forming the overcloak of the roll. Enlarged details showing the laps, tacks and wedges are given at O, P and Q; the detail at A shows the relative heights of the roll, drip, etc.

It will be seen that each piece of lead forming a gutter (and cesspool) is fixed along two adjacent edges only, the other two edges being free to allow the lead to expand and contract.

Snow Boards should be provided to gutters in order that melted snow may have a free passage to the outlets and to protect the lead against damage by traffic; without such boards, the snow on the gutter impedes the flow of water as the snow thaws on the underside, and this may cause the water to rise above the lead covering and penetrate the roof. A snow board may consist of two 100 mm by 50 mm longitudinal bearers, extending the full length of the section, to the top of which are nailed 50 mm by 19 mm transverse laths at about 13 mm apart.

Another example of a parallel gutter is shown in Fig. 74 and a further example is shown at G, Fig. 24.

(b) *Tapered Parapet Gutter* (see J, K and N, Fig. 73).—The wood details of this gutter are described on p. 78 (see also N). This gutter, tapered on plan, is divided into sections by a roll and drips as described above. As shown on the plan K, the lower edge of the slating has to be cut parallel to the tapered side of the gutter. The section at N shows the width increases due to the fall of each " bay " of the gutter and the drip. The shape of the gutter on plan is developed by transferring to it from the section the various widths at the lower

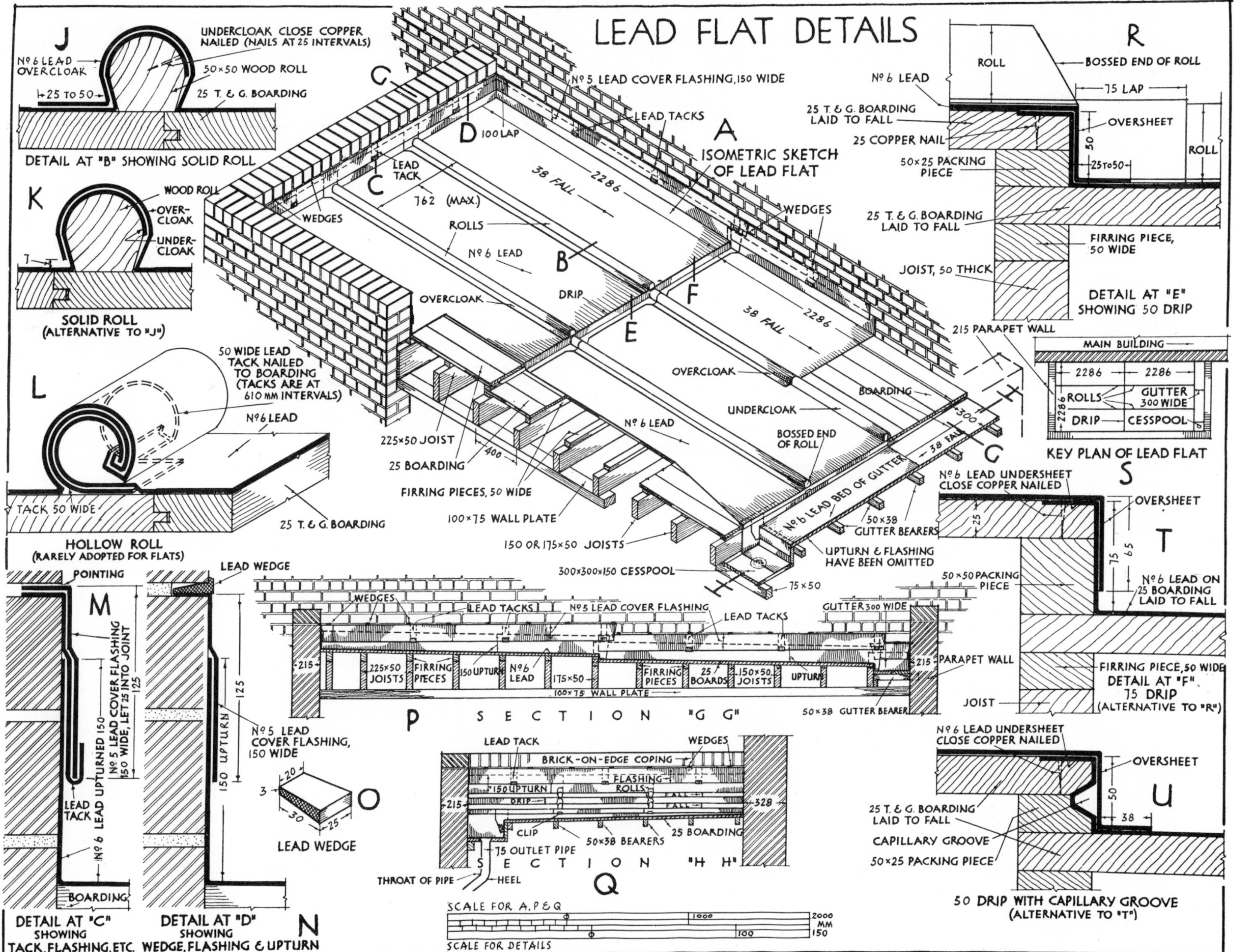
LEAD FLAT DETAILS
J
UNDERCLOAK CLOSE COPPER NAILED (NAILS AT 25 INTERVALS)
Nº 6 LEAD OVERCLOAK
50×50 WOOD ROLL
25 TO 50
25 T. & G. BOARDING
DETAIL AT "B" SHOWING SOLID ROLL
K
WOOD ROLL
OVER-CLOAK
UNDER-CLOAK
SOLID ROLL (ALTERNATIVE TO "J")
L
50 WIDE LEAD TACK NAILED TO BOARDING (TACKS ARE AT 610 MM INTERVALS)
Nº 6 LEAD
TACK 50 WIDE
25 T. & G. BOARDING
HOLLOW ROLL (RARELY ADOPTED FOR FLATS)
A
ISOMETRIC SKETCH OF LEAD FLAT
Nº 5 LEAD COVER FLASHING, 150 WIDE
LEAD TACKS
100 LAP
LEAD TACK
762 (MAX.)
38 FALL
2286
WEDGES
ROLLS
Nº 6 LEAD
DRIP
OVERCLOAK
UNDERCLOAK
BOARDING
BOSSED END OF ROLL
Nº 6 LEAD BED OF GUTTER
300
38 FALL
225×50 JOIST
25 BOARDING
400
FIRRING PIECES, 50 WIDE
100×75 WALL PLATE
150 OR 175×50 JOISTS
50×38 GUTTER BEARERS
UPTURN & FLASHING HAVE BEEN OMITTED
300×300×150 CESSPOOL
75×50
215 PARAPET WALL
R
ROLL
BOSSED END OF ROLL
Nº 6 LEAD
75 LAP
25 T. & G. BOARDING LAID TO FALL
OVERSHEET
25 COPPER NAIL
50
50×25 PACKING PIECE
25 TO 50
25 T. & G. BOARDING LAID TO FALL
FIRRING PIECE, 50 WIDE
JOIST, 50 THICK
DETAIL AT "E" SHOWING 50 DRIP
MAIN BUILDING
2286
ROLLS
GUTTER 300 WIDE
DRIP
CESSPOOL
KEY PLAN OF LEAD FLAT
S
Nº 6 LEAD UNDERSHEET CLOSE COPPER NAILED
OVERSHEET
T
25
75
65
50×50 PACKING PIECE
Nº 6 LEAD ON 25 BOARDING LAID TO FALL
FIRRING PIECE, 50 WIDE
DETAIL AT "F". 75 DRIP (ALTERNATIVE TO "R")
JOIST
M
POINTING
Nº 5 LEAD COVER FLASHING 150 WIDE, LET 25 INTO JOINT
125
Nº 6 LEAD UPTURNED 150
LEAD TACK
BOARDING
DETAIL AT "C" SHOWING TACK, FLASHING, ETC.
LEAD WEDGE
150 UPTURN
Nº 5 LEAD COVER FLASHING, 150 WIDE
DETAIL AT "D" SHOWING WEDGE, FLASHING & UPTURN
N
O
LEAD WEDGE
20
3
30
25
P
SECTION "G G"
WEDGES
LEAD TACKS
Nº 5 LEAD COVER FLASHING
GUTTER 300 WIDE
215
225×50 JOISTS
FIRRING PIECES
150 UPTURN
Nº 6 LEAD
175×50
FIRRING PIECES
25 BOARDS
150×50 JOISTS
UPTURN
PARAPET WALL
100×75 WALL PLATE
50×38 GUTTER BEARER
Q
SECTION "H H"
LEAD TACK
WEDGES
BRICK-ON-EDGE COPING
FLASHING
ROLLS
150 UPTURN
DRIP
FALL
328
CLIP
50×38 BEARERS
25 BOARDING
75 OUTLET PIPE
THROAT OF PIPE
HEEL
U
Nº 6 LEAD UNDERSHEET CLOSE COPPER NAILED
OVERSHEET
25 T. & G. BOARDING LAID TO FALL
CAPILLARY GROOVE
50×25 PACKING PIECE
38
50 DRIP WITH CAPILLARY GROOVE (ALTERNATIVE TO "T")
SCALE FOR A, P & Q
1000
2000 MM
100
150
SCALE FOR DETAILS

FIGURE 74

and upper ends of each bay. The section also shows the lead turned up 150 mm against the wall and about 230 mm up the slope. The tilting fillet is fixed with its lower edge 75 mm above and parallel to the intersection between the gutter and roof boarding. The details of the cesspool, drips, roll, flashings, etc., are similar to those already described. Another example of a tapered gutter is shown by broken lines in the elevation in Fig. 21 and the section at F, Fig. 24, the section being taken through the gutter immediately above the cesspool.

(c) V-*gutters.*—This type is formed along the lower intersection between two sloping roof surfaces. The groundwork may consist of bearers fixed to the sides of the spars (at various heights to suit the fall of the gutter) as shown at T, Fig. 36, when the construction resembles that of a tapered gutter, or the lower ends of the spars of each slope may be birdsmouthed over a pole plate as shown at A, Fig. 73, to form a parallel gutter. Long lengths of such gutters must be divided by rolls and drips as above described.

Cast iron and other eaves gutters are described on pp. 154–155.

Flats (see Fig. 74).—The wood construction has been described on p. 70. It has been mentioned that the minimum fall is 1·25 cm in 100 cm. To prevent water standing when the flat has been given such a small fall, it is necessary that precautions against warping should be taken and therefore narrow, well-seasoned boards only should be used and these should be laid with their length in the direction of the fall. The surface of the boarding should be " flogged " (*i.e.*, dressed over with a plane or machine) to remove sharp edges and irregularities which may damage the lead. Occasionally the boarding is covered with roofing felt, laid with butt joints, and this assists in ensuring a uniform surface for the lead.

The key plan at S and the sketch at A show the roof of a small building (an adjunct to a larger building) which is divided into six bays and a parallel gutter. The rolls have been shown purposely at maximum centres of 762 mm; this gives an economical roof if 2·13 m wide rolls are used which are cut up the centre to give 1·07 m widths, as the minimum waste of lead thereby results.

The construction of the rolls, drips, gutter and flashings has been already described. The detail at R shows the drip, with the oversheet turned on to the flat and over the bossed end of the roll. Note : (1) the firring piece which is nailed on to the top of the joist to give the necessary fall to the boarding, (2) the overcloak or oversheet of the drip is lapped 75 mm over the roll below and (3) the end of the roll is slightly bevelled to facilitate the bossing of the lead. In forming the bossed end, the undercloak is dressed round to partially cover the end, and the overcloak is bossed to completely cover it and the roll below. In order to minimize the risk of the overcloaks of rolls being lifted by the wind, they should be dressed with their free edges least exposed to the prevailing wind. Note that at A and Q the overcloak of the drip at the gutter is not continued on to the bed, but is dressed just clear of it at the upper end. The overcloak at the bossed end of each roll at the gutter is continued down the drip and secured by a small clip or piece of lead (which has been left on the undercloak when trimming it) which is turned over it (see Q).

Forming Lead Flats.—The following is the order in which leadwork for the flat at A would be executed : Cesspool with outlet pipe (although the fixing of the latter may be deferred), gutter, lower side bay with undercloak, lower middle bay, lower side bay with overcloak, upper side bay with undercloak, upper middle bay, and upper side bay with overcloak. The cover flashing is then fixed in the mortar joints which have been previously raked out for at least 25 mm preferably before the mortar has set; the first length of flashing to be fixed is that over the upturn of the gutter, commencing at the cesspool end, and after completing those at the sides, that along the top end is fixed; the flashings are wedged and the mortar joints are pointed with cement mortar or oil mastic.

Forming a Cesspool.[1]—A piece of lead is cut sufficiently large to form the base and sides and it is set out by chalk-marking the lines along which will be formed the angles at the base and sides. (NOTE.—*Lead must never be marked or scored with a knife or similar sharp object* as this at once weakens it). Shallow grooves are formed along the base lines by placing the setting-in stick on them and sharply striking it with the bossing mallet. The lead is turned with the bottom upwards and gently tapped parallel to and about 25 mm inside the base lines; this assists in stiffening the base and keeping it firm. The lead is turned over and the sides are bent upwards on the grooves, the corners being left. Each corner is then separately bossed up by using the mallet and bossing stick, the former being inside the " box " (cesspool) as the bossing stick is applied to work the surplus lead *gradually* from the bottom upwards. Care must be taken not to drag the lead from the corner or cause the base to lift; if a crease appears, it must be at once knocked out or the lead will pucker and split. As it is gradually bossed upwards, some of the superfluous lead at the top should be cut off to enable the remainder to boss up more easily. This process is repeated at all corners and the sides are cut off to the required height. The cesspool is holed, dressed in position as required and the outer pipe connected to it as already described.

Bending Lead Pipes.—The following describes the bending of a lead pipe such as that shown at Q, Fig. 74 : The pipe is slightly heated at the position where the bend is to be formed; it is then bent over the knee and this flattens the pipe at the *throat*; the long dummy (Y) (see Fig. 79) is now used to approximately restore the pipe to a circular section by inserting the " straight end " (head C′) and working it up and down until the throat is gradually brought out; the bending stick (C) is then applied to each side of the pipe at the bend in turn, working from the throat to the *heel* until the circular section has been roughly regained. The bobbin (F) and weight are inserted, the former being of the proper size to suit the pipe and the latter slightly less; a piece of rope is attached to the weight and passed through the bobbin and pipe; when the rope is given a series of sharp pulls, the weight gradually drives the bobbin through the bend, and as it does so the interior is brought to a uniformly circular bore. The pipe is again heated and the same operations are repeated, care being taken in working the bend with the bending stick that a uniform thickness is maintained. As the radius of the bend increases, head D′ of the dummy is used to bring the throat back. The lower bend is formed on the pipe in a similar manner. The heel hand dummy (P) is useful for shaping the heels of large pipes and the hand dummy (R) is used for small pipes. The end of the pipe is slightly enlarged by driving the tanpin (E) partly into the mouth of the pipe. Finally the pipe is prepared for soldering (or lead burning) it to the lead lining the hole formed in the base of the cesspool.

Ridges (see B, H and J, Fig. 75).—Lead-covered ridges are suitable for slated roofs, although lead is apt to discolour green slates.

The detail at H shows one method. A 50 mm wood roll is nailed to the wood

[1] See p. 156 for a description and Fig. 79 for sketches of the plumbing tools.

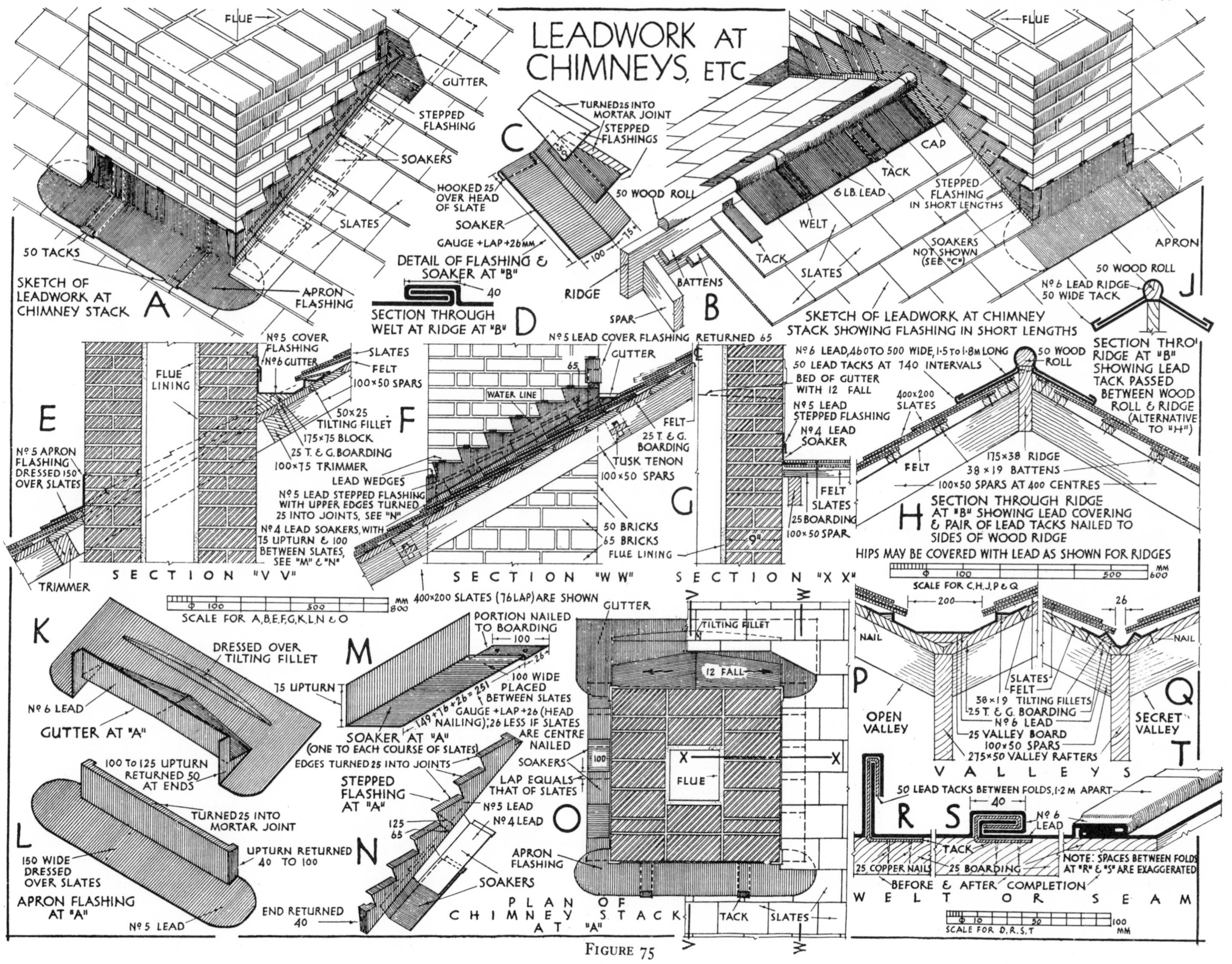
LEADWORK AT CHIMNEYS, ETC
FLUE
GUTTER
STEPPED FLASHING
SOAKERS
HOOKED 25 OVER HEAD OF SLATE
SLATES
50 TACKS
APRON FLASHING
SKETCH OF LEADWORK AT CHIMNEY STACK
A
TURNED 25 INTO MORTAR JOINT
STEPPED FLASHINGS
C
SOAKER
GAUGE + LAP + 26 MM
DETAIL OF FLASHING & SOAKER AT "B"
40
SECTION THROUGH WELT AT RIDGE AT "B"
D
CAP
TACK
50 WOOD ROLL
6 LB. LEAD
STEPPED FLASHING IN SHORT LENGTHS
WELT
SOAKERS NOT SHOWN (SEE "C")
APRON
TACK
SLATES
BATTENS
RIDGE
SPAR
B
SKETCH OF LEADWORK AT CHIMNEY STACK SHOWING FLASHING IN SHORT LENGTHS
50 WOOD ROLL
Nº 6 LEAD RIDGE
50 WIDE TACK
J
SECTION THRO' RIDGE AT "B" SHOWING LEAD TACK PASSED BETWEEN WOOD ROLL & RIDGE (ALTERNATIVE TO "H")
Nº 5 COVER FLASHING
Nº 6 GUTTER
SLATES
FELT
100×50 SPARS
FLUE LINING
50×25 TILTING FILLET
175×75 BLOCK
25 T. & G. BOARDING
100×75 TRIMMER
E
Nº 5 APRON FLASHING DRESSED 150 OVER SLATES
TRIMMER
SECTION "VV"
Nº 5 LEAD COVER FLASHING RETURNED 65
GUTTER
65
WATER LINE
F
FELT
25 T. & G. BOARDING
TUSK TENON
100×50 SPARS
LEAD WEDGES
Nº 5 LEAD STEPPED FLASHING WITH UPPER EDGES TURNED 25 INTO JOINTS, SEE "N"
Nº 4 LEAD SOAKERS, WITH 75 UPTURN & 100 BETWEEN SLATES, SEE "M" & "N"
50 BRICKS
65 BRICKS
FLUE LINING
SECTION "WW"
400×200 SLATES (76 LAP) ARE SHOWN
Nº 6 LEAD, 460 TO 500 WIDE, 1·5 TO 1·8 M LONG
50 LEAD TACKS AT 740 INTERVALS
BED OF GUTTER WITH 12 FALL
Nº 5 LEAD STEPPED FLASHING
Nº 4 LEAD SOAKER
G
FELT
SLATES
25 BOARDING
100×50 SPAR
9"
SECTION "XX"
50 WOOD ROLL
400×200 SLATES
FELT
175×38 RIDGE
38×19 BATTENS
100×50 SPARS AT 400 CENTRES
H
SECTION THROUGH RIDGE AT "B" SHOWING LEAD COVERING & PAIR OF LEAD TACKS NAILED TO SIDES OF WOOD RIDGE
HIPS MAY BE COVERED WITH LEAD AS SHOWN FOR RIDGES
100 500 600 MM
SCALE FOR C, H, J, P & Q
100 500 800 MM
SCALE FOR A, B, E, F, G, K, L, N & O
K
DRESSED OVER TILTING FILLET
Nº 6 LEAD
GUTTER AT "A"
100 TO 125 UPTURN RETURNED 50 AT ENDS
TURNED 25 INTO MORTAR JOINT
L
150 WIDE DRESSED OVER SLATES
UPTURN RETURNED 40 TO 100
APRON FLASHING AT "A"
Nº 5 LEAD
PORTION NAILED TO BOARDING
100
M
75 UPTURN
100 WIDE PLACED BETWEEN SLATES
149+76+26=251
GAUGE + LAP + 26 (HEAD NAILING); 26 LESS IF SLATES ARE CENTRE NAILED
SOAKER AT "A" (ONE TO EACH COURSE OF SLATES)
EDGES TURNED 25 INTO JOINTS
STEPPED FLASHING AT "A"
Nº 5 LEAD
Nº 4 LEAD
125
65
N
SOAKERS
END RETURNED 40
GUTTER
TILTING FILLET
12 FALL
SOAKERS
100
LAP EQUALS THAT OF SLATES
FLUE
X X
APRON FLASHING
O
TACK
SLATES
PLAN OF CHIMNEY STACK AT "A"
V V W W
200
26
NAIL
P
OPEN VALLEY
SLATES
FELT
38×19 TILTING FILLETS
25 T. & G. BOARDING
Nº 6 LEAD
25 VALLEY BOARD
100×50 SPARS
275×50 VALLEY RAFTERS
Q
SECRET VALLEY
VALLEYS
T
50 LEAD TACKS BETWEEN FOLDS, 1·2 M APART
40
Nº 6 LEAD
R
S
TACK
25 COPPER NAILS
25 BOARDING
NOTE: SPACES BETWEEN FOLDS AT "R" & "S" ARE EXAGGERATED
BEFORE & AFTER COMPLETION
WELT OR SEAM
10 50 100 MM
SCALE FOR D, R, S, T

FIGURE 75

ridge; a pair of 50 mm wide lead tacks is nailed to the side of the ridge (see B) at 610 to 1200 mm intervals; the lead covering consists of strips which are from 450 to 508 mm wide and 2·13 m long; it is passed over the roll, well worked into the angles, and dressed over the slates for 150 to 175 mm on each side; the free ends of the tacks are then turned over the edges of the lead for about 25 mm to prevent the lead from being lifted by the wind. The horizontal joints are generally lapped 150 mm (a pair of tacks being provided at each), although in best work they may be welted as shown at D.

An alternative method is shown at J where the tacks (which pass over the top of the ridge) are nailed to the wood ridge before the wood roll is fixed. The treatment at the end of the ridge abutting against the chimney stack is shown at B and described on p. 152.

Hips.—Lead may be used at the hips in the following manner: (1) wood roll with continuous lead covering as shown for ridges, (2) cut and mitred slates with lead soakers, and (3) wood roll with lead soakers.

(1) *Wood Roll with Continuous Lead Covering.*—This is similar to the ridge detail excepting that the dihedral angle is wider. The strips of lead are nailed at the heads under the laps and are also secured by the lead tacks.

(2) *Cut and Mitred Slates with Lead Soakers.*—There are two methods of using soakers, *i.e.*, (*a*) single-course soakers and (*b*) double-course soakers.

(*a*) This is the arrangement which is shown at F and G, Fig. 70, and described on p. 137. It provides an excellent finish to a slated roof and is adopted in the best work.

(*b*) In this method, the *length of the soakers is 26 mm longer than that of the slates*; the horizontal width of each wing should be slightly more than the slate below in order to cover the joint, and it tapers to about 50 mm at the head, which is nailed. A soaker is placed at every *alternate* course, and therefore at every other course the lower portion (margin) of each soaker is exposed to view. It is not often adopted.

(3) *Wood Roll with Lead Soakers.*—Soakers are provided at every course, and they are shaped to pass over the roll and between the slates at the wings. The length of soaker equals the gauge plus lap plus 26 mm for centre-nailed slates and 26 mm longer for head-nailed slates; the width is as stated at (*b*) above. They are nailed at the head. This is a sound method and one which is suitable for exposed roofs.

Valleys.—These include (1) open valley gutters, (2) secret valley gutters and (3) cut and mitred slates with soakers.

(1) *Open Valley Gutters* (see P, Fig. 75).—This is generally employed and provides a sound but unattractive looking finish. The lead is in 2·13 m lengths with 150 mm laps, and the width is about 450 mm, being dressed over the boarding and tilting fillets as shown; it is secured by close copper nailing up each side along the edge, and the ends are left free. The clear width between the edges of the slates (which are cut to the rake) should not be less than 200 mm to provide adequate foot room, as a less width often results in the slates being damaged by anyone proceeding up the valley when carrying out repairs, etc. If the roof is battened and not boarded, it is necessary to fix a 250 mm wide board (called a *lier board*) on each side of the intersection, and for the full extent of the valley, in order to receive the lead. The ends of the slating battens are cut to the edges of these boards.

(2) *Secret Valley Gutters* (see Q).—The width of the 2·13 m strips of lead are only about 254 mm as the cut edges of the slates are only about 25 mm apart. Whilst the appearance is an improvement on the open valley gutter, it is objected to for the reason that it is liable to become choked by leaves and rubbish which may accumulate and choke the valley, causing water to back up and pass over the lead.

(3) *Cut and Mitred Slates with Soakers.*—The construction somewhat resembles that for cut and mitred hips with single-course soakers (described on p. 137) in that wide slates (slate and a half) are cut and closely mitred and a soaker is placed between the slates at each course. This gives a satisfactory finish both in regard to soundness and appearance.

Leadwork at Chimneys.—Details of the requisite leadwork to two chimney stacks are shown in Fig. 75. One stack is shown intercepting one of the slopes of a roof and the other penetrates at the ridge. Sketches of these are shown at A and B in which 50 mm bricks are employed as these improve the appearance; for economy, the brickwork below the roof is constructed of 65 mm bricks (see E, F and G). The lead details at (1) the front, (2) the sides and (3) the back are explained below.

(1) *Front.*—The lead at the front is in one piece (except as stated below); this is the apron flashing (see p. 143) and is shown detached at L. It is bossed (or lead-burned) to this shape from dimensions taken from the stack. As the internal angles forming the returns of the upturn are being bossed, the lower corners of the lead gradually work upwards to an irregular curve, and it is the practice to neatly trim the ends as shown when the bossing has been completed. The apron is secured by lead wedges (see A and B). Lead tacks are provided as shown at A to secure the free edge, although these are not necessary if the apron is short and especially if the ends are tailed down by slates as indicated at B; the tacks may be continued vertically and let into the joint (as shown) or they may be short and nailed at their upper ends to the top batten.

Long lengths may consist of two pieces, *i.e.*, an apron with a 100 mm upturn and 150 mm dressed over the slates, and 150 mm wide cover flashing similar to that shown at M, Fig. 74.

(2) *Sides.*—The leadwork at each side of the stack may consist of (*a*) soakers with a continuous stepped cover flashing, (*b*) soakers with stepped cover flashing in single steps or (*c*) a single continuous stepped flashing.

(a) *Soakers with Continuous Stepped Flashing* (see A, F, G and N).—Soakers (see p. 144) are prepared by the plumber and placed in position by the slater; they have a 64 to 75 mm upturn with 90 to 100 mm width between slates. Their length equals the gauge plus lap plus 26 mm if the slates are head-nailed and 26 mm less if the slates are centre-nailed; in addition, the length (excepting the upturned portion) is increased by 26 mm for nailing to the roof boarding (see M) or for hooking over the head of the slate when secured to a batten (see C). As shown at A, F, N and O, each soaker laps that above or below it by an amount equal to that of the slates. The stepped cover flashing is formed out of a 150 or 175 mm wide strip to the shape shown at N; the 25 mm wide upper horizontal edges being let into the mortar joints and each is secured with one or two wedges; the size of the steps depends upon the thickness of the bricks and the pitch of the roof, but the distance from the " water line " (see F) to the lower edge should not be less than 50 mm (at F and N, this is shown to be 64 mm).

A raking cover flashing (see p. 143) is adopted for stone chimney-stacks as the absence of horizontal joints at from 50 to 75 mm apart preclude the use of stepped cover flashings.

The above continuous flashings are not so liable as those described below (*b*) to be dislodged by the wind.

(b) *Soakers with Stepped Flashing in Single Steps* (see B and C).—The soakers are as described above. The cover flashing is made of scrap pieces of lead to the shape shown at C to give a 50 to 75 mm lap; it is because of this lap that this method is preferred to (*a*) above, as water does not readily find access between the cut backs and the wall; each step is secured with one or two wedges and the joints which receive the turn-ins of the steps should be well pointed as before described. Sometimes the pieces are shaped with vertical front edges and not cut back as shown. These are not so attractive in appearance as those shown.

(c) *Single Continuous Stepped Flashing.*—Soakers are not used, and in lieu of them the stepped flashing is continued and dressed 150 mm over the slates. In appearance, therefore, the lower portion resembles the apron at L, whilst the upper portion is similar to the flashing at N. This method is not as sound as either (*a*) or (*b*), as water may be blown between the slates and wings of the flashing or it may enter by capillary attraction, and it does not look well. Its use is on the decrease, except where pantiles or similar interlocking tiles are used as a roof covering (see B, Fig. 39).

(3) *Back.*—The leadwork here consists of a gutter and cover flashing. As shown at E, the angle at the intersection is blocked by a triangular piece of wood which is shaped and given a slight fall in both directions from the centre (see O and the broken line at G). A tilting fillet should also be provided (although this is often omitted) and this should be tapered as indicated at O and K in order to prevent the slates immediately above the ends of the gutter from riding.

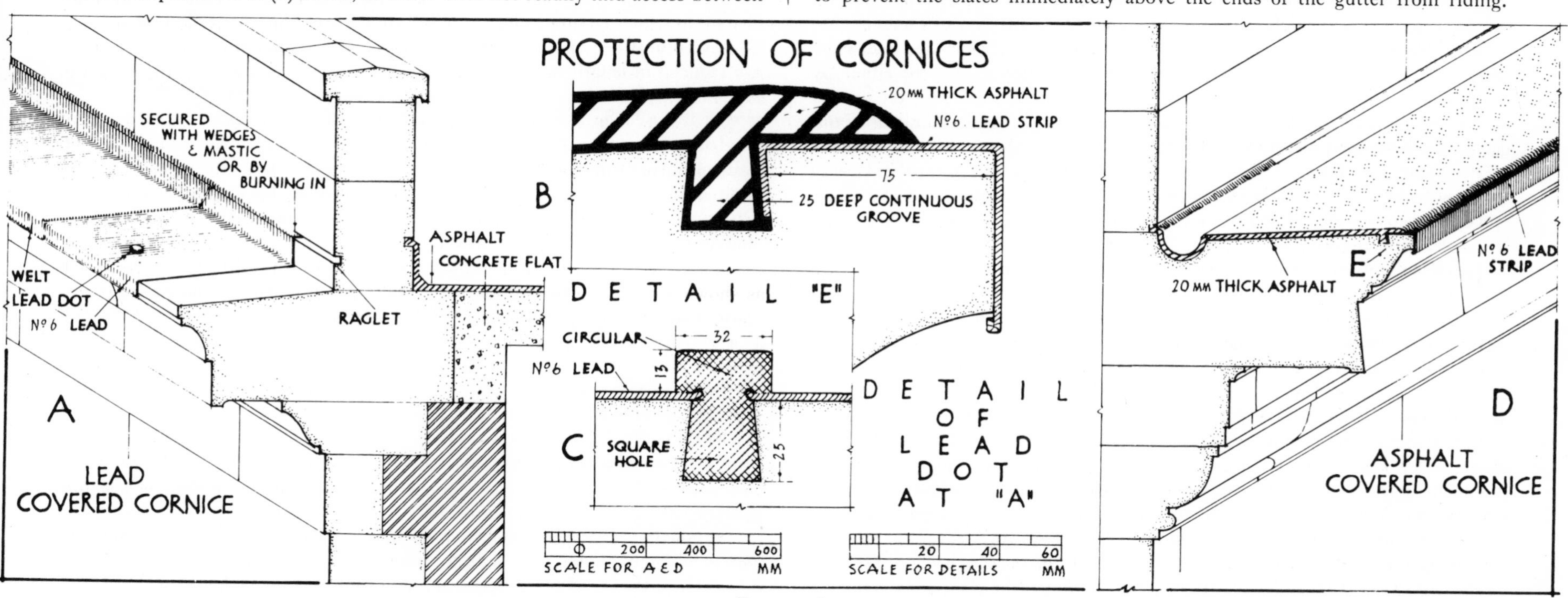

FIGURE 76

The sketch at K shows the piece of lead which has been bossed (or lead-burned) to the required shape before fixing. The 150 mm wide cover flashing is shown at E and the ends are returned (see A and F).

Finish at Ridge (see B). The end piece of lead ridge covering is turned 50 mm up the wall and the central piece of cover flashing—called a *saddle-piece*—is turned over the ridge to form a cap.

General.—A roof is made watertight at the intersection between its slope and brickwork or stonework (as at J and M, Fig. 36) by using an apron flashing with cover flashing. Similarly, any of the three types of flashings (*a*), (*b*) and (*c*) is used to exclude water at the intersection between roofs and gable walls (such as that shown in Fig. 21). In inferior work, *cement mortar fillets* are used instead of leadwork at such intersections; these are triangular fillets formed on the slates and against the brickwork or stonework; this is a very unsound substitute, as sooner or later the fillets crack (and sometimes fall away), causing the roof to leak.

Protection of Stone Cornices and String Courses.—It is especially necessary to protect the upper projecting courses of stonework against the action of rain-water which is converted to diluted acid in polluted atmospheres. The two materials generally used for this purpose are (*a*) lead and (*b*) asphalt.

(*a*) A lead-covered cornice is shown at A and C, Fig. 76, No. 5 or 6 lead being used. A raglet, about 13 mm wide and 20 mm deep, is cut along the face of the stone parapet to receive the edge of the upturn which is secured either by burning-in or wedges (see p. 143). If the parapet is of brickwork, the upturn is secured by wedges in the usual way. Exceptionally wide cornices should have free upturns which are protected by cover flashings. The lower edge of the lead is doubled and dressed over the fillet or nosing to project about 7 mm to allow water to drip clear of the moulded stonework (similar to that at B). The transverse joints between pieces of the lead (which are 2·13 to 2·74 m long) are welts similar to that shown at D, Fig. 75. *Lead dots* (also known as *dowels*, *rivets* or *buttons*) are used to secure the covering against the action of the wind; dovetailed square or circular holes are formed in the cornice at about 900 mm centres (see C); the lead after being bossed is holed, with the edge of each hole turned up slightly, and a metal dot mould (see B′, Fig. 79) is then used to form the dot by pouring molten lead through the small hole in the mould (see A and C); sometimes the " cup " of the mould is semispherical to form dots having curved tops. These dots may be formed by lead burning (see p. 143); the edge of the lead at the hole is turned down slightly and the hole in the cornice is filled with molten lead from a strip of lead held over it and reduced to a molten condition by the flame of the lead burner; the molten lead is finished flush with the covering, and the dot is made inconspicuous by lightly hammering it and cleaning it off.

(*b*) Asphalt is often used in modern construction as a covering material. In the example shown at D a small channel is formed at the back and the top surface of the cornice is given a slight fall towards it; the channel falls slightly towards one end and delivers into a rain-water pipe. A 25 mm deep dovetail groove is formed along the full length of the cornice and about 75 mm from the front edge (see B) and a 25 mm square raglet is made along the bottom of the parapet (or each stone is formed with a rebated joint before being fixed). The No. 5 or 6 lead flashing is bossed as shown at B and the hot asphalt is applied, finished smooth to a thickness of 20 mm, well tucked into both grooves and rounded off at the outer edge.

RAIN-WATER GOODS

Rain-water goods include eaves gutters (or spouts) and rain-water pipes (or down-pipes). They are made of cast iron, lead, asbestos-cement, enamelled iron, galvanized steel, aluminium or plastic materials.

Details of cast iron gutters and pipes are shown in Fig. 77 and an application is shown in the perspective sketch.

EAVES GUTTERS

Eaves gutters are provided with a *socket* (or *faucet* or *flange*) which receives the *spigot* end of the adjacent length. These are generally " outside " sockets (see A, B, D and Y), although " inside " sockets are also provided (see Y). As shown at B, the maximum length is 1·8 m, *excluding* the flange which is from 38 to 50 mm wide; shorter lengths can be obtained, and where necessary pipes are reduced in length by means of the saw. They are made of various shaped sections, *i.e.*, half-round, deep half-round, ogee, etc. A deep half-round gutter is shown in section at E and in oblique projection at A, B and D; this is a very good form, being simple and of satisfactory appearance, and it can readily be painted both inside and out and so preserved; it is sometimes provided with a bead along its outer edge similar to that shown in the middle section at H. Other moulded forms are shown at H; the disadvantage of these is the backs are inaccessible for painting if and after they have been fixed to the wood fascia boards. They are moulded in numerous stock sizes, thus the half-round gutter is obtainable in sizes varying from 100 mm by 50 mm to 300 mm by 150 mm. Note that these sizes are *external* sizes (see E and H). The thickness is 6·4 mm (" extra heavy grade "), 5·2 mm (" heavy grade "), 4·8 mm (" medium grade ") and 3·2 mm (" ordinary " or " light castings "); the latter is used for cheap work, the medium grade is used for average good work, and the two heavier castings are only specified for special work.

Special Fittings.—These include external and internal angles (see A), stop ends for sockets (C), stop ends for spigots, outlets with nozzles or drops cast on (D) and union clips (G), the latter being used to connect two spigot ends.

Supports.—Eaves gutters are supported by wrought iron brackets, generally two being required per 1·8 m length. That shown at M, Fig. 77, is twice screwed or nailed to the backs of spars (see also W and Y, Fig. 36, A and D, Fig. 38, and A, Fig. 71). The one at O, Fig. 77, is twice screwed to the sides of spars (suitable

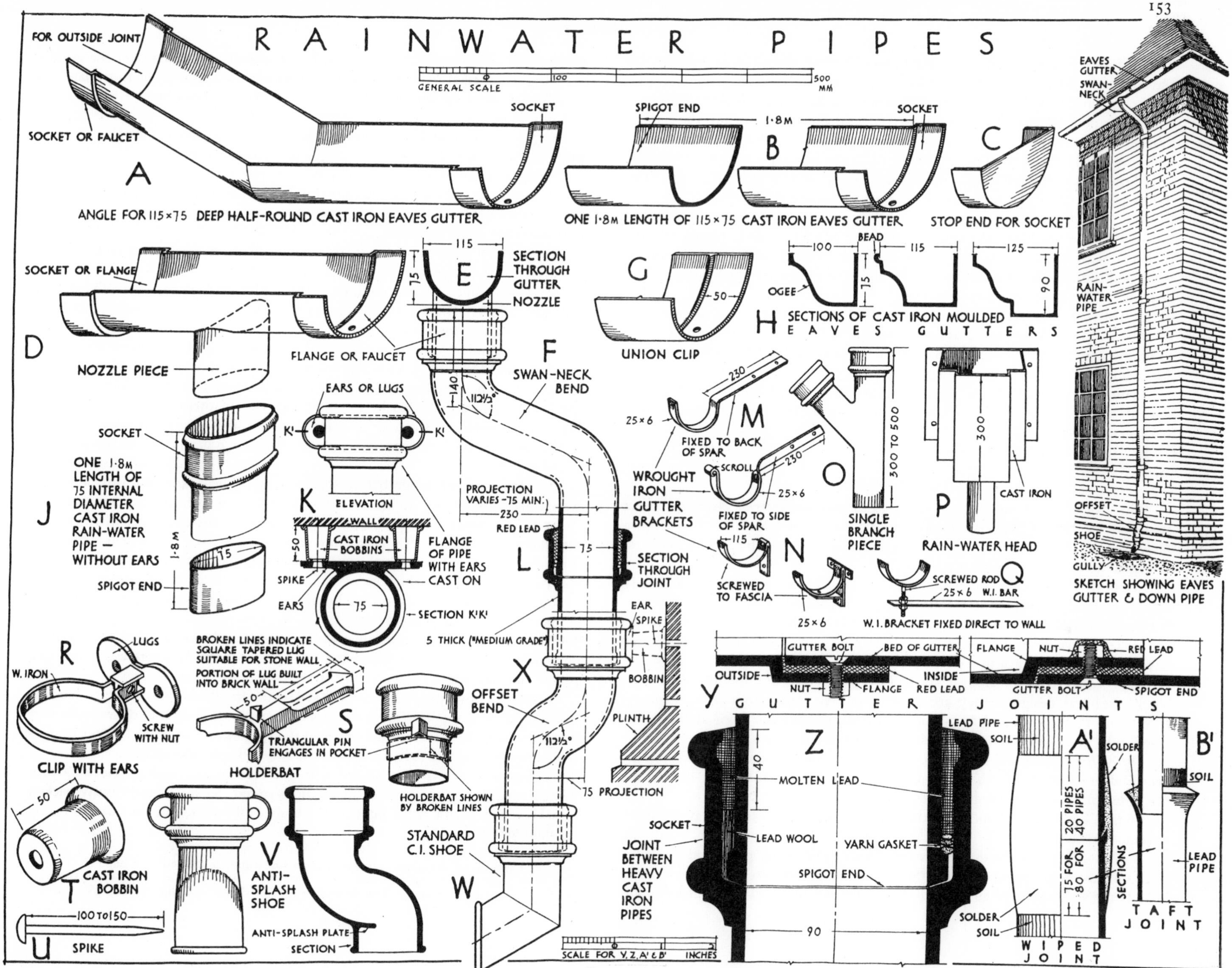

RAINWATER PIPES

GENERAL SCALE 0 100 500 MM

FOR OUTSIDE JOINT
SOCKET OR FAUCET
SOCKET
A
ANGLE FOR 115×75 DEEP HALF-ROUND CAST IRON EAVES GUTTER

SPIGOT END
1·8M
SOCKET
B
ONE 1·8M LENGTH OF 115×75 CAST IRON EAVES GUTTER

C
STOP END FOR SOCKET

EAVES GUTTER
SWAN-NECK
RAIN-WATER PIPE
OFFSET
SHOE
GULLY
SKETCH SHOWING EAVES GUTTER & DOWN PIPE

SOCKET OR FLANGE
D
NOZZLE PIECE
FLANGE OR FAUCET

115
75
E
SECTION THROUGH GUTTER
NOZZLE

G
50
UNION CLIP

100
BEAD
115
125
OGEE
75
90
H
SECTIONS OF CAST IRON MOULDED EAVES GUTTERS

F
SWAN-NECK BEND
140
112½°
PROJECTION VARIES -75 MIN.
230

SOCKET
ONE 1·8M LENGTH OF 75 INTERNAL DIAMETER CAST IRON RAIN-WATER PIPE — WITHOUT EARS
J
1·8M
75
SPIGOT END

EARS OR LUGS
K¹
K¹
ELEVATION
K
WALL
50
CAST IRON BOBBINS
FLANGE OF PIPE WITH EARS CAST ON
SPIKE
EARS
75
SECTION K¹K¹

230
M
25×6
FIXED TO BACK OF SPAR
WROUGHT IRON GUTTER BRACKETS
SCROLL
230
25×6
FIXED TO SIDE OF SPAR
115
N
SCREWED TO FASCIA
25×6
Q
SCREWED ROD
25×6 W.I. BAR
W. I. BRACKET FIXED DIRECT TO WALL

O
300 TO 500
SINGLE BRANCH PIECE

P
300
CAST IRON
RAIN-WATER HEAD

RED LEAD
75
L
SECTION THROUGH JOINT
5 THICK ("MEDIUM GRADE")

EAR
SPIKE
BOBBIN
X
OFFSET BEND
112½°
PLINTH
75 PROJECTION

R
LUGS
W. IRON
SCREW WITH NUT
CLIP WITH EARS

BROKEN LINES INDICATE SQUARE TAPERED LUG SUITABLE FOR STONE WALL
PORTION OF LUG BUILT INTO BRICK WALL
50
S
TRIANGULAR PIN ENGAGES IN POCKET
HOLDERBAT
HOLDERBAT SHOWN BY BROKEN LINES

GUTTER BOLT
BED OF GUTTER
OUTSIDE
INSIDE
NUT
FLANGE
RED LEAD
FLANGE
NUT
RED LEAD
GUTTER BOLT
SPIGOT END
Y
GUTTER JOINTS

50
T
CAST IRON BOBBIN

U
100 TO 150
SPIKE

V
ANTI-SPLASH SHOE
ANTI-SPLASH PLATE
SECTION

STANDARD C.I. SHOE
W

Z
40
MOLTEN LEAD
SOCKET
LEAD WOOL
YARN GASKET
SPIGOT END
JOINT BETWEEN HEAVY CAST IRON PIPES
90

SCALE FOR Y, Z, A¹ & B¹ INCHES

LEAD PIPE
SOIL
A¹
20 PIPES
40 PIPES
75 FOR
80 FOR
SOLDER
SOIL
WIPED JOINT
SECTIONS

SOLDER
B¹
SOIL
LEAD PIPE
TAFT JOINT

FIGURE 77

for the type of eaves shown at X, Fig. 36). The two shown at N, Fig. 77, are screwed to wood fascias and are called " fascia brackets " (see Q, Fig. 36, and G, Fig. 71), and that shown at Q, Fig. 77, is suitable for fixing direct to stone walls where the pointed end of the bar is driven into the bed joint and the curved bracket is adjusted to the required height by means of the nut and back or lock-nut which are screwed to the rod fixed to the bracket.

Joints.—A section through an outside joint is shown at Y, Fig. 77. The jointing material is red lead mastic or putty (powdered red lead mixed with linseed oil) and is applied to the inside of the socket after the gutter is placed in position on the brackets; the spigot end of the adjacent pipe is placed into the socket, the wrought iron 6 or 8 mm dia. *gutter bolt* is inserted and the nut is tightened until the head is flush with the inside of the gutter; this squeezes out any excess of mastic which is wiped off.

Whilst the above is the commonest form of joint, some gutters are specified to have inside sockets; these are necessary if the exterior of the gutter is not to be interrupted by the sockets, as is sometimes advisable for moulded gutters. An inside joint is also indicated in section at Y.

Trough Gutters.—These are large cast iron or galvanized steel gutters which are used, especially for factories, and similar buildings, instead of lead parapet and V-gutters.

DOWN PIPES

The size of down-pipes varies from 50 to 300 mm *internal* diameter, those specified for houses being generally 60 or 75 mm, and are in 1·8 m lengths *including* the sockets (see J). Short lengths are also obtainable. The thickness is similar to that of eaves gutters.

Special Fittings.—These include swan-neck bends, rain-water heads, offset bends, shoes, and single, double and Y-branches.

Swan-neck Bend (see F and perspective sketch).—This is necessary to connect the nozzle-piece or outlet (see D) of a gutter which is fixed to an overhanging eaves and the top length of a down-pipe.

Rain-water Head (or *Hopper Head*) (see P).—These are obtainable in many stock sizes and designs; they are used to receive water from parapet gutters (see B and C, Fig. 73), and as ornamental features they are fixed at the top of down-pipe stacks to receive water delivered from swan-necks.

Offset Bends (see X and sketch).—These are similar to swan-necks and are required to negotiate plinths, etc. Double offset bends, called *pass-over offsets*, are obtainable to clear string courses.

Obtuse bends, long bends, quarter-curved bends, etc., are also available for special purposes.

Shoes.—These are fixed to the lower ends of rain-water pipes and discharge over gullies—traps connected to drains (see perspective sketch). That shown at W is the standard type and is satisfactory for fall-pipes which discharge rain-water only. A nuisance may be caused by the water splashing over the gullies; such is prevented if *anti-splash shoes* (see V) are used, the projecting plate (see section) breaking up the flow. *Boots* are similar to shoes but have legs up to 300 mm long.

Single, *Double* and Y-*Branches* are used for connecting two or three branch pipes to a common down-pipe; a single branch is shown at O.

The above bends and shoes may be obtained with or without lugs cast on (see below). Cast iron pipes are also made of rectangular and square sections in sizes varying from 75 mm by 50 mm to 200 mm by 200 mm. Holderbats (see later) are made to match.

Supports.—Rain-water pipes are supported by means of (*a*) spikes which are driven through *ears* or *lugs*, or (*b*) by *holderbats*.

(*a*) Down-pipes can be obtained with or without lugs cast on. Those with lugs cast on (see K) are used for ordinary work. All cast iron pipes should be fixed at a distance of 50 mm from the face of the wall to allow the backs of the pipes to be painted, otherwise the metal will corrode and rain-water will escape through the holes or cracks which eventually form to cause disfigurement and dampness. The pipes are maintained at this distance by the use of either cast-iron bobbins (see T) or hardwood bobbins; two of these are required at each lug and the pipes are secured by driving stout spikes (see U) through the holes in the ears and bobbins into wood plugs which have been fixed in the wall (see K and X).

(*b*) One form of holderbat is shown at S. These are cast iron supports which are suitable for fixing into joints of brickwork; similar supports for fixing to stonework have dovetailed lugs (shown by broken lines) which are let into holes formed to receive them, and secured by molten lead which is caulked. The lugs project 50 mm from the wall. Each length of pipe is secured by slipping the triangular pocket which is cast on the lower bead of the socket over the triangular pin which is cast on the holderbat. This provides a neat and effective support and is used in good work.

Alternatively, rain-water pipes without ears (as shown at J) may be fixed by clips (see R); the wrought iron band or clip is secured by a screw and nut to a pair of lugs after it is passed round the socket of the pipe.

Joints.—Down-pipes are often fixed with dry joints (no jointing material being used), and the lengths of the pipes are made rigid by lead or wrought iron wedges which are driven down between the spigots and sockets. Wood wedges should *not* be used as they are apt to expand and split the sockets.

The section at L shows a joint with red lead putty; a short piece of yarn gasket (rope) is wrapped two or three times round the spigot and tightly packed to prevent any mastic from entering the body of the pipe, and the putty is neatly finished off with a fillet.

[1] The subject of drainage, which includes soil-pipes, is treated in Chap. II, Vol. II. The application of internal soil and waste pipework, one-pipe and single stack systems etc., is described in Chap. II, Vol. II and in greater detail in Chap. X, Vol. IV.

The joints between heavy cast iron pipes (such as soil-pipes[1]) may consist of (*a*) molten lead, (*b*) lead wool and (*c*) lead wool and molten lead. Two of these joints are shown at Z, Fig. 77.

(*a*) Molten pig lead is run between the spigot and socket, and then caulked to consolidate the material; a piece of yarn gasket is tightly packed before the joint is made (see right of section).

(*b*) Lead wool (fine strands of lead, twisted to form a rope) is packed into the joint and well caulked. This forms an excellent joint and the material is convenient to handle.

(*c*) The lower half of the joint is caulked with lead wool to within 38 mm from the top and the remaining space is filled with molten pig lead which is subsequently caulked (see Z).

Plastic Rain-water Goods.- These are made of polyvinyl chloride (p.v.c.) and are used widely in domestic work. The gutters are in half-round or rectangular sections and are jointed by push fit gutter brackets to leave a gap of 3 mm between lengths to allow for expansion.

Asbestos-cement Rain-water Goods.—These are strong, durable and light and need not be painted. The jointing material is a special composition provided by the manufacturers.

Enamelled Iron Rain-water Goods.—These are enamelled both inside and out and therefore painting is eliminated. These pipes are obtainable in eight standard colours (black, brown, green, etc.). A bituminous compound is the jointing material.

DOMESTIC WATER SERVICES[1]

The water for domestic services is carried in pipes of copper, lead, galvanized steel and polythene (this latter for cold services only). The use of lead pipes has diminished greatly in recent years, they are in any case unsuitable for drinking water which is soft because of the danger of lead poisoning. Lead is still sometimes used for conversion and alteration work for waste pipes where its ease of manipulation is an advantage. Galvanized steel is cheaper than copper and is used more on the larger industrial schemes, it is also adopted in some hard-water areas for it can withstand the hammering needed to remove the scale deposits which occur in such districts. Polythene is cheaper still and is being increasingly used for cold water distribution; tubes of this material have the best resistance to bursting, this can happen to pipes on thawing out after being frozen.

Most internal plumbing work is carried out with the light-gauge copper tube conforming to B.S. 659, it is a convenient material, obtainable in long lengths and having a good resistance to corrosion.

Lead Pipe.—The various joints formed between lead pipes include the wiped, taft, block and Staern joints. The following is a description of the first two :—

[1] These are considered in greater detail in Chap. X, Vol. IV.

Wiped Joint (see A′, Fig. 77).—This is generally considered to be the strongest joint for lead pipes and is therefore employed in first-class work and especially for water pipes which have to withstand high pressures. Solder (see p. 143) consisting of 2 parts by weight of pig lead and 1 part pure tin is the jointing material.

The joint is made as follows : The end of each pipe is prepared as shown in the half-section, that of the upper pipe (when it is in a vertical position) being rasped down on the outside to leave a sharp edge, and the end of the lower pipe being *slightly* filed on the outside and then opened by hammering a tan-pin (E, Fig. 79) into it. Each end is painted with *soil* (a black powder consisting of lampblack, size and whiting, well mixed with hot water) for at least 75 mm, depending upon the size of the joint. When this is dry, each end is scraped with the shave hook (G, Fig. 79) for a distance of 38 mm or more (according to the length of the joint) so as to present a clean bright surface which is essential for the thorough adhesion of the solder. The appearance of the finished joint is improved if prior to shaving, a ring is carefully chalk-marked round and at the proper distance from the end of the pipe. As solder will not adhere to soil (hence the reason for " soiling ") it follows that if the ring is carefully marked, the edge of the solder (see later) will be sharp and uniform. The inside of the lower opened end should also be shaved. Immediately after shaving, the bright ends are smeared with grease or tallow to prevent them re-tarnishing and to act as a flux (to assist fusion between the solder and lead). The pipes are now ready for soldering either by pouring or splashing it on from the ladle (M, Fig. 79) or by using the blowlamp (A′, Fig. 79) and a strip of solder (see p. 143). The former method is only adopted in certain districts for joints made on the bench and the latter for joints made on the job. When the " ladle " method is adopted, the solder is melted in the pot (U, Fig. 79) to the required temperature (denoted when the solder ignites a piece of paper), and after the pipes have been accurately adjusted the solder is poured from the ladle on to the the prepared ends until the temperature of the pipes at the ends is approximately that of the solder; the latter is then wiped round the joint with a wiping cloth (Z, Fig. 79), the surface of which has been greased to prevent the solder adhering to it; additional solder is splashed on and quickly worked with the cloth until the desired shape is obtained, when the joint is left undisturbed and allowed to cool. When the " blowlamp " method is adopted, the prepared ends of the pipes are fitted together and heated by the flame of the lamp; solder is applied by melting one end of a strip, and is gradually brought to the required shape by the use of the cloth; the joint is then left to cool. The thickness of the solder at the widest part of the joint need not exceed one and a half times the pipe *thickness*.

Taft or Copper-bit Joint (see B′, Fig. 77).—This is used where the pipes are not required to withstand much pressure, as for overflow and gas pipes.

The preparation of the ends of the pipes is similar to that for wiped joints, except that the lower pipe is opened wider, the amount of shaving is reduced and the soil is often omitted. A little powdered resin is applied to the scraped surfaces after the ends are fitted together, and this acts as a flux for the " ordinary " solder (consisting of equal parts of lead and tin) which is in the form of a thin narrow strip. The solder is melted by the heated copper-bit (N, Fig. 79) until sufficient is run to fill the space between the two pipes, as shown. Alternatively, the solder may be melted by the type of blowlamp illustrated at A′, Fig. 79.

Copper Tube.—This has been mentioned above. The two most common joints are the capillary and the compression types.

Capillary joint (see A, Fig. 78).—The application shown here is at a bend where a brass alloy elbow is used; tees, reducing pieces and straight couplings, etc., are also obtainable and they are all made on the same principle.

The fittings incorporate recessed rings containing the correct amount of solder for making the joint. After the ends of the copper tube have been cut square, they and the inside of the fittings are cleaned and brought together. A blowlamp is then applied to the outside to melt the solder which fills the annular space between the parts being joined. The joint is thus easily made resulting in a neat, compact fitting.

Compression joint.—One type of this is the *non-manipulative* fitting.

It consists of an externally threaded brass alloy coupling with internal shoulders acting as distance stops to the copper tube. A nut and an annealed brass compression ring are slid over the end of the tube which is then placed inside the coupling to fit against the shoulder. The ring seats against the mouth of the coupling, and by tightening the nut, the ring is made to grip the tube and to provide a watertight joint.

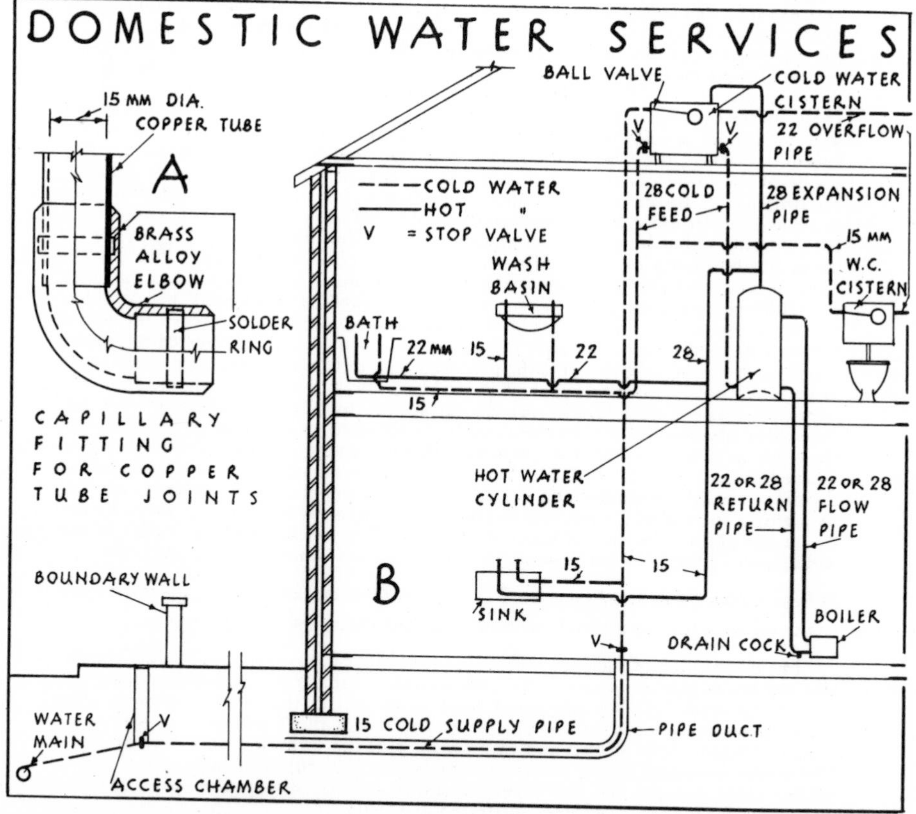

FIGURE 78

Cold and Hot Water Distribution (see Fig. 78).—For the average house a 15 mm o.d. supply pipe is adequate and this is connected to the water main and brought into the house at a depth where it will be unaffected by frost (460 to 610 mm). It must be fitted with a stop valve just outside the boundary of the premises and another one at ground floor level inside the house. The supply pipe rises preferably on an inside wall to the cold water cistern situated in the roof space or just below the first floor ceiling. *En route*, a 15 mm dia. branch is taken off it to supply the kitchen sink. The remaining 15 mm dia. cold pipes are fed from the cistern, *i.e.*, those to the bath, wash basin and W.C.

The hot water circuit shown is the *direct system*[1] which is suitable for most houses where hardness deposits do not develop in the pipes. The cylinder is warmed by water from the back boiler which is placed behind the kitchen fire. A 22 or 28 mm dia. flow pipe from the top of the boiler delivers hot water to near to the top of the cylinder. A return pipe of the same size supplies water from the base of the cylinder to the base of the boiler. These two pipes are the main circulation pipes for hot water and are known as the primary flow and return. Hot water to the various appliances is fed from a branch off the expansion pipe which rises from the top of the cylinder; this pipe acts as a vent to eliminate air locks in the system and terminates over the cold water cistern.

TOOLS

The following is a brief description of some of the tools used by the plumber, some of which have been referred to, and are illustrated in Fig. 79.

Dresser, Beater or Bat (A).—Used for dressing flat portions of lead.

Bossing Stick (B).—Used principally for working lead round rolls, etc.

Setting-in Stick (J).—Used for forming upturns of flashing, working lead into angles of rolls, etc.

Bossing Mallet (D).—Used for striking the above tools and for working lead into corners direct.

Chase Wedge (K).—Of various shapes and sizes; also called *drifts*; employed for working angles of rolls, drips, etc. in gutters where space is restricted; driven by the *wedge mallet*, a similar tool to the bossing mallet.

Drip Plate (L).—Is inserted between two sheets of lead to prevent movement of the lower sheet where the top sheet is being worked; examples, overcloaks of rolls and drips.

Bending Stick (C).—Used for bending pipes.

Bobbins.—Sizes from 25 to 115 mm; used in conjunction with the metal *weight* or *follower* for bending pipes.

Long Dummy (Y), *hand dummy* (R) and *heel dummy* (P) are used for bending pipes.

Tanpin or Turnpin (E).—Sizes from 25 to 115 mm diameter at the head; used for opening ends of pipes (see p. 155).

Mandril (T).—Used for similar purpose as bobbins for removing bulges in long pipes.

Shave Hooks or Scrapers (G and H).—Used to shave the ends of pipes prior to soldering.

Rasp (similar to that shown at 43, Fig. 67).—Used for filing ends of pipes to be soldered.

Blowlamp (A′).—This is one of many designs in which either petrol, paraffin or benzoline is used; capacity for general use varies from 0·3 to 1·2 litres; used for heating solder, etc. (see p. 155).

Soldering or Plumbing Iron (Q).—Used for heating solder (especially when jointing large pipes); largely replaced by the blowlamp.

Copper Bit (N).—Used for forming soldered joints (see p. 155). Developments of this bit are the gas heated and electric soldering irons.

Hatchet Bit (V).—Used for a similar purpose as the copper bit, and for lapped joints.

Melting or Solder Pot (U).—Sizes vary from 100 to 300 mm diameter; used to melt solder.

Ladle (M).—Used to apply the solder obtained from the melting pot (see p. 155).

Wiping Cloth (Z).—A pad of several folded layers of moleskin in various sizes and used for wiping joints (see p. 155).

Caulking Tool (S).—Used for caulking lead and is made of cast steel (see pp. 143 and 155).

[1] See Chap. X, Vol. IV for the indirect system.

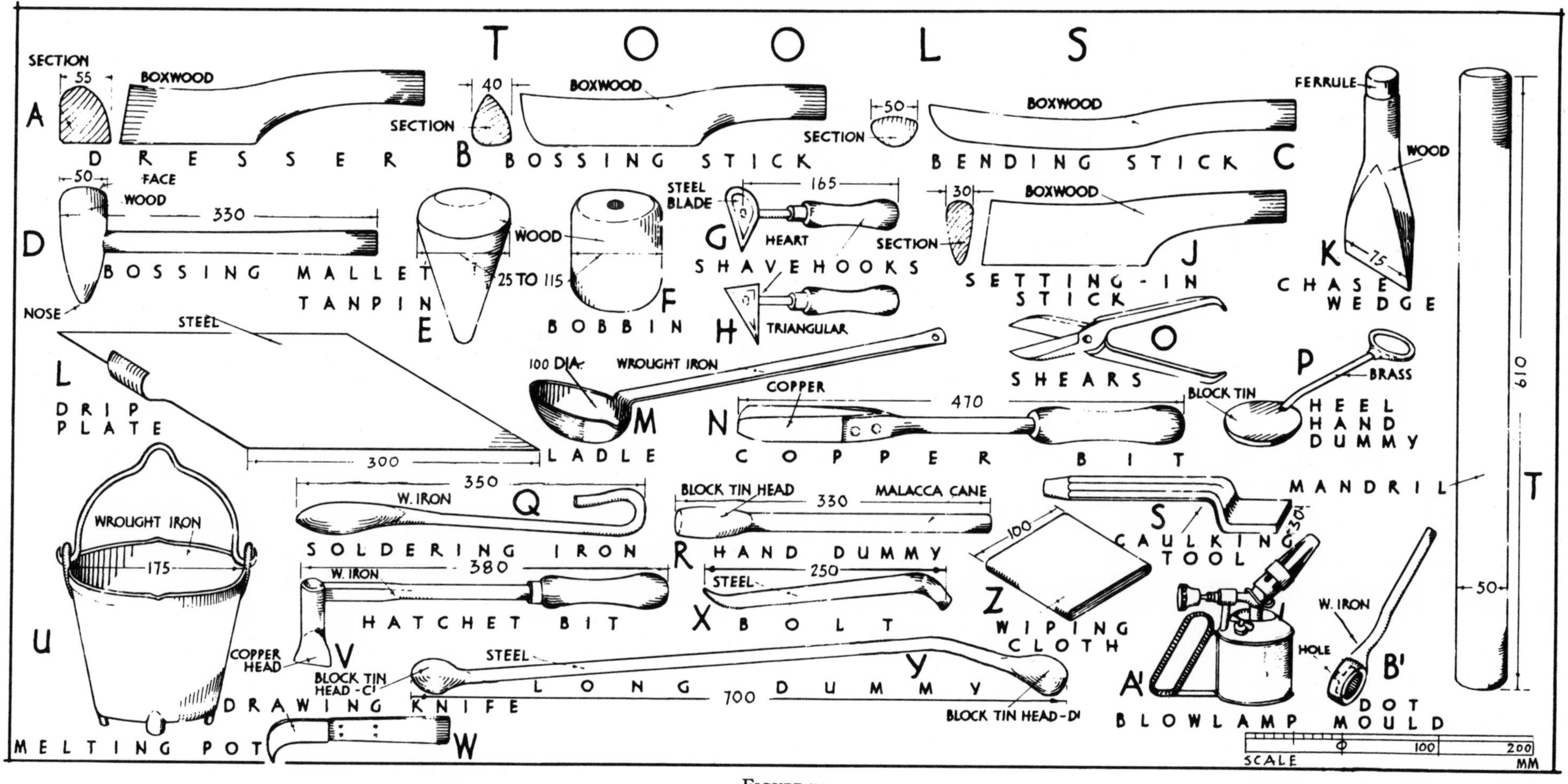

FIGURE 79

Dot Mould (B′).—Used for forming lead dots (see p. 152).

Drawing Knife (W).—Used for cutting sheet-lead; a *chipping knife*, having a stronger and parallel blade, is used for cutting lead as it is struck with the hammer.

Bolt (X).—Used for opening holes in the sides of pipes to receive branch pipes.

Other equipment includes: Hammers, pliers, screwdrivers, screw-wrench (for turning nuts, etc.), spanners, soil pot (containing soil required for wiped joints), one-metre rule, square, scribing plate (for describing circles on pipes, etc.), copper tube benders and a complete outfit for lead-burning.

CHAPTER SEVEN

MILD STEEL SECTIONS, BOLTS AND RIVETS[1]

Syllabus.—Brief characteristics of mild steel; various sections; applications.

MILD steel (complying with B.S. 4360) is a very important building material used extensively in structural engineering. Weldable structural steel to B.S. 4360 is used to a lesser extent for the same purpose. It is manufactured from iron ore (mined or quarried in certain parts of this country, Sweden, Spain, etc.) which is subjected to a very high temperature in the blast furnace to produce pig iron, this is converted into steel in the smelting furnace, re-heated and finally rolled to the required sections such as plates, angles, tees, channels, beams, etc. (see Chap. II, Vol. IV).

Structural steels are divided into two main groups according to the manufacturing process, viz. (1) hot rolled sections and (2) those obtained by cold rolling. The former comprise the heavier sections. Steel components are used in five ways :—(*a*) as beams and lintels for members which suffer bending stresses, (*b*) as columns which resist compression and bending stresses, (*c*) as ties where the stresses are tensile, (*d*) in roof trusses and lattice girders where the forces are compressive and tensile, and (*e*) for the reinforcement in reinforced concrete.

Characteristics of Steel.—It is elastic, ductile (capable of being drawn into wire), malleable (can be beaten out), weldable and can be tempered to different degrees of hardness. The maximum carbon content of mild steel is 0·25 per cent., and its breaking strength in compression and tension is 430 to 510 N/mm^2.

Some of the various standard sections into which mild steel are rolled are illustrated in Figs. 80 and 81.

HOT ROLLED SECTIONS

Flat Bars (A, Fig. 80).—Obtainable in sizes varying from 3 mm by 12 mm to 2 m by 25 mm or more, the wider sections being known as *plates* (see E′, Fig. 81); purposes for which flats are used have been indicated in previous chapters (such as bars supporting lintels, floor joists, straps, etc.), and they are still used (but not so extensively as formerly) for tension members in steel roof trusses. Plates are used for connections in steel roofs, base plates and caps of steel pillars, etc.

[1] This is sometimes included in a first-year course in Building Construction to familiarize students with the principal members used in structural details which are included in subsequent years of the course. Steel and reinforced concrete structures are described in Vol. IV.

Square Bars (B, Fig. 80).—Sizes vary from 5 to 305 mm length of side; not much used for building purposes.

Round or *Circular Bars* or *Rods* (C, Fig. 80).—Diameters vary from 6 mm to 300 mm; the smaller ones are used in the construction of reinforced concrete floors, pillars, foundations, lintels, etc., and the larger (X, Fig. 81) for columns.

Angles (D and E, Fig. 80 and A to C, Fig. 81).—Those with equal arms, are called *equal angles*, and the others are known as *unequal angles*. They are specified according to the overall dimensions, thickness and weight per metre: thus in Fig. 80, D is a 50 mm by 50 mm by 6 mm by 4·47 kg/m British Standard Equal Angle (abbreviated to " B.S.E.A."), and E is a 75 mm by 50 mm by 6 mm by 5·65 kg/m British Standard Unequal Angle (abbreviated to " B.S.U.A."); the sizes of the equal angles vary from 20 mm by 20 mm by 3 mm by 0·88 kg/m to 200 mm by 200 mm by 24 mm by 71·1 kg/m and unequal angles from 30 mm by 20 mm by 3 mm by 1·12 kg/m to 200 mm by 150 mm by 18 mm by 47·1 kg/m. Angles are widely used in structural engineering, including all members of a steel roof truss.

Tee Bars or Tees.—These consist of a *web* and a *flange* and are of four kinds: tees cut from Universal Beams and Universal Columns (see below), rolled tee bars with short stalks (webs) and rolled tee bars with long stalks. Tees are commonly used in steel roof trusses.

Tees cut from Universal Beams.—In these the web is parallel and the flange may be parallel or have a 2° 52′ taper. They range in size from 102 mm deep by 133 mm wide by 13 kg/m to 459 mm by 305 mm by 126 kg.

Tees cut from Universal Columns have both web and flange parallel. They vary in size from 76 mm deep by 152 mm wide by 12 kg/m to 191 mm by 395 mm by 118 kg.

Rolled steel tee bars with short stalks have flange and web with a ½° taper. They range in size from 38·1 mm by 38·1 mm by 4 kg to 152·4 mm by 152·4 mm by 36 kg. (An example of one is given at F, Fig. 80.)

Rolled steel tee bars with long stalks have a parallel web with a ½° tapered flange. They vary from 76·2 mm deep by 25·4 mm wide by 3·65 kg to 254 mm by 127 mm by 35·42 kg.

Channels (G, Fig. 80 and E, Fig. 81).—The flanges are thicker than the web; the sizes vary from 76 mm by 38 mm by 6·69 kg to 432 mm by 102 mm by

65·48 kg B.S.C. (British Standard Channel); the web is of uniform thickness and the flanges are tapered from the root to the toe. They may be used as girders, pillars, roof purlins, etc. These can be built up for heavier loads as at K, Fig. 81.

Beams.—There are six main kinds of beam: British Standard Universal Beams (B.S.U.B's), rolled steel joists (R.S.J.'s) known also as British Standard Beams (B.S.B.'s), beams with flange plates, castellated beams, plate girders and lattice girders.

The *British Standard Universal Beam* is the most widely used type of beam. It is available in many sizes from 203 mm deep by 133 mm wide by 25 kg/m to 920 mm by 420 mm by 387 kg. An example of the former is drawn at H, Fig. 80; see also I, Fig. 81. The web is of uniform thickness and the flanges may be parallel or have a 2° 52′ taper as shown at H, Fig. 80. The web joins the flanges with a small radius curve at the roots;[1] the toes of the flanges are square to facilitate welding. These beams are extensively used in the construction of floors, lintels, etc. and have largely replaced the next type of beam mentioned which was once the most popular type.

Rolled Steel Joist, six sizes of this are made from 76 mm deep by 51 mm wide by 6·7 kg/m to 203 mm by 102 mm by 25·3 kg. The web is of uniform thickness and the flanges have a 5° taper; the web joins the flanges with a small radius curve and the extremities of the flanges have a small radius at the toe. An example is shown at H, Fig. 81.

Plated beams are made by riveting or welding flange plates to the flanges of the above two types of beam, see L, Fig. 81. They may also be made by similarly attaching flange plates to channels as at K, Fig. 81. Plated beams are used for heavy loads or where thick walls have to be supported.

Castellated beams (see O, Fig. 81) are formed by cutting a steel beam in a zig-zag line along the web and welding the two parts together to increase the depth. This is used for long lightly loaded beams where the stresses are greater in the flanges than in the web. Hence the web area is reduced and the resistance to deflection is increased.

Plate Girders are used to carry loads beyond the capacity of Universal Beams. They are of two kinds. The one at P, Fig. 81 has flange plates riveted to a

[1] Many students at examinations show carelessly drawn sections of beams, common errors being: webs thicker than flanges and the latter either tapering to a point or provided with bulbous toes.

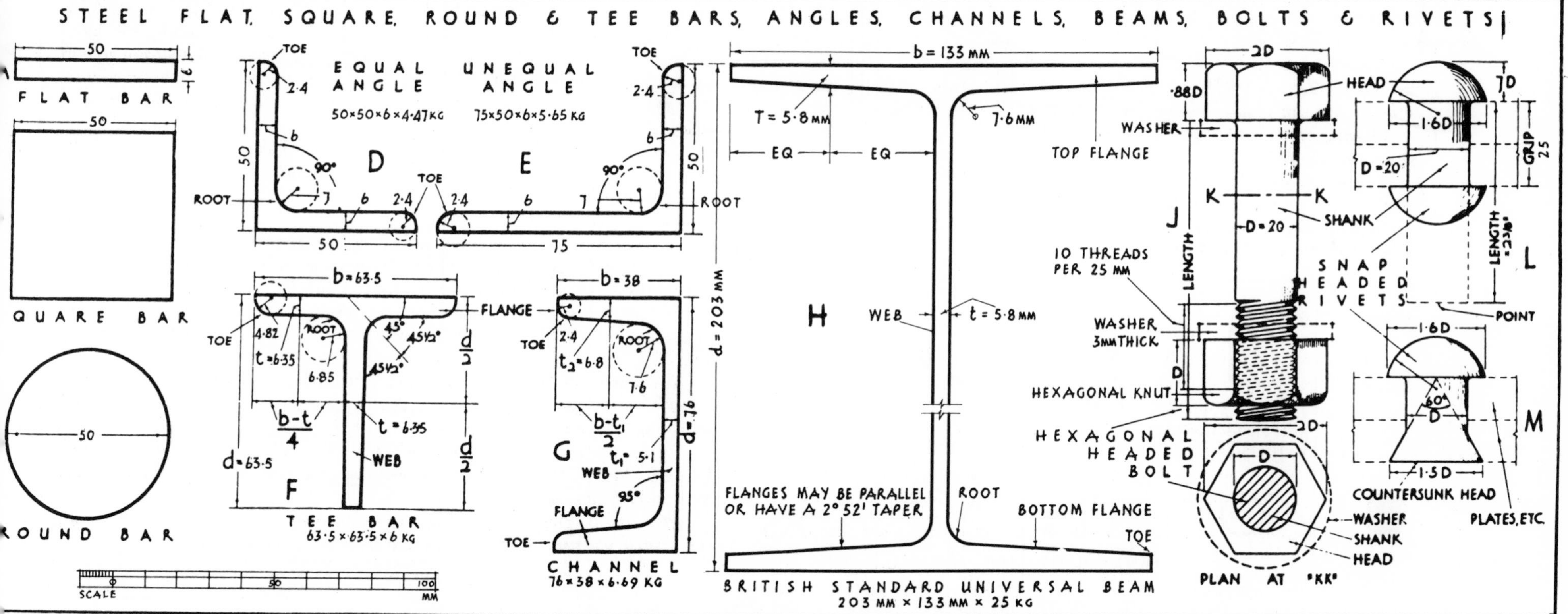

FIGURE 80

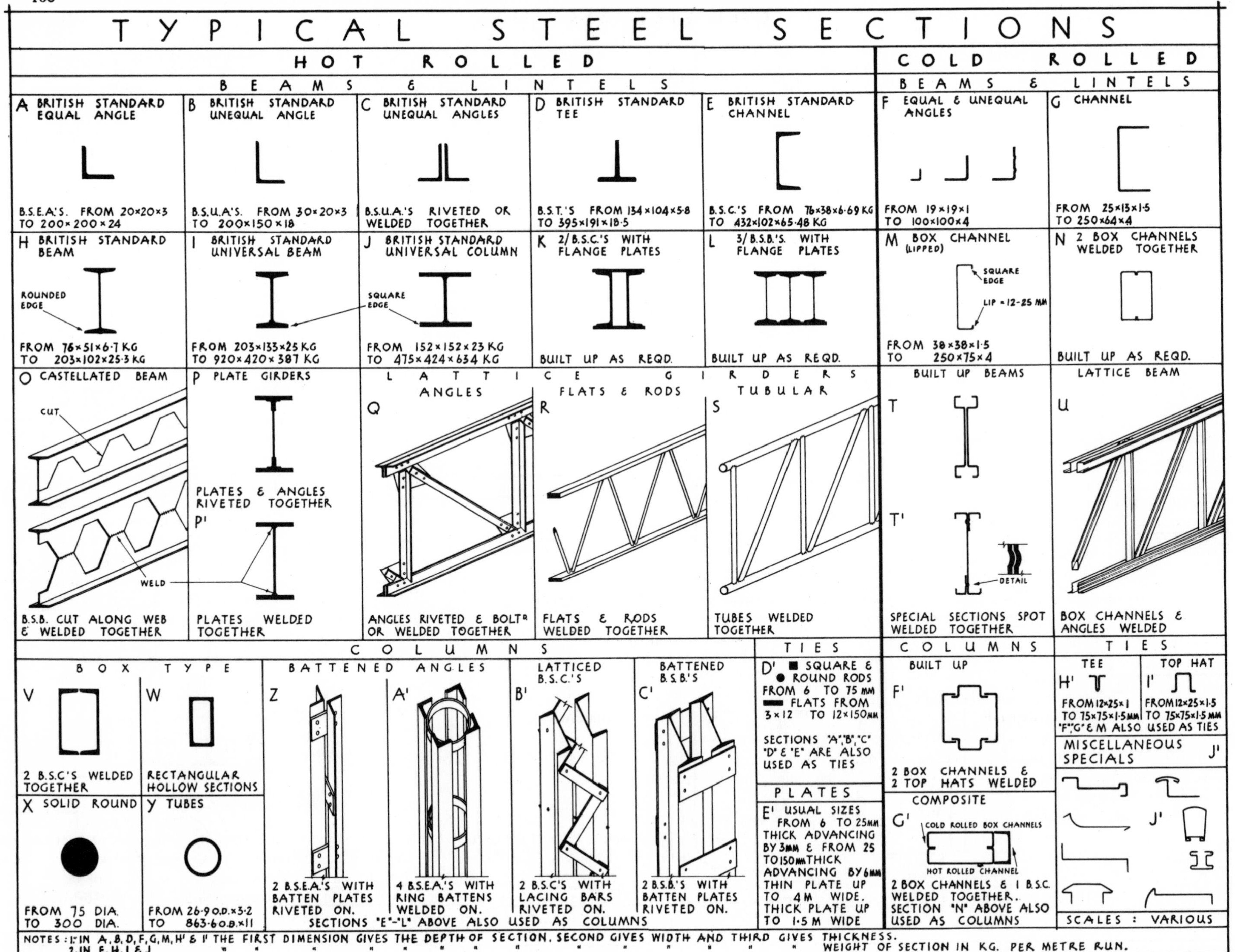

TYPICAL STEEL SECTIONS
HOT ROLLED
COLD ROLLED
BEAMS & LINTELS
BEAMS & LINTELS
A BRITISH STANDARD EQUAL ANGLE
B.S.E.A.'S. FROM 20×20×3 TO 200×200×24
B BRITISH STANDARD UNEQUAL ANGLE
B.S.U.A.'S. FROM 30×20×3 TO 200×150×18
C BRITISH STANDARD UNEQUAL ANGLES
B.S.U.A.'S RIVETED OR WELDED TOGETHER
D BRITISH STANDARD TEE
B.S.T.'S FROM 134×104×5·8 TO 395×191×18·5
E BRITISH STANDARD CHANNEL
B.S.C.'S FROM 76×38×6·69 KG TO 432×102×65·48 KG
F EQUAL & UNEQUAL ANGLES
FROM 19×19×1 TO 100×100×4
G CHANNEL
FROM 25×13×1·5 TO 250×64×4
H BRITISH STANDARD BEAM
ROUNDED EDGE
FROM 76×51×6·7 KG TO 203×102×25·3 KG
I BRITISH STANDARD UNIVERSAL BEAM
FROM 203×133×25 KG TO 920×420×387 KG
J BRITISH STANDARD UNIVERSAL COLUMN
SQUARE EDGE
FROM 152×152×23 KG TO 475×424×634 KG
K 2/B.S.C.'S WITH FLANGE PLATES
BUILT UP AS REQD.
L 3/B.S.B.'S. WITH FLANGE PLATES
BUILT UP AS REQD.
M BOX CHANNEL (LIPPED)
SQUARE EDGE
LIP = 12-25 MM
FROM 38×38×1·5 TO 250×75×4
N 2 BOX CHANNELS WELDED TOGETHER
BUILT UP AS REQD.
O CASTELLATED BEAM
CUT
WELD
B.S.B. CUT ALONG WEB & WELDED TOGETHER
P PLATE GIRDERS
PLATES & ANGLES RIVETED TOGETHER
P'
PLATES WELDED TOGETHER
LATTICE GIRDERS
ANGLES
Q
ANGLES RIVETED & BOLTD OR WELDED TOGETHER
FLATS & RODS
R
FLATS & RODS WELDED TOGETHER
TUBULAR
S
TUBES WELDED TOGETHER
BUILT UP BEAMS
T
T'
DETAIL
SPECIAL SECTIONS SPOT WELDED TOGETHER
LATTICE BEAM
U
BOX CHANNELS & ANGLES WELDED
COLUMNS
BOX TYPE
V
2 B.S.C'S WELDED TOGETHER
W
RECTANGULAR HOLLOW SECTIONS
X SOLID ROUND
FROM 75 DIA. TO 300 DIA.
Y TUBES
FROM 26·9 O.D.×3·2 TO 863·6 O.D.×11
BATTENED ANGLES
Z
2 B.S.E.A.'S WITH BATTEN PLATES RIVETED ON.
A'
4 B.S.E.A.'S WITH RING BATTENS WELDED ON.
LATTICED B.S.C.'S
B'
2 B.S.C'S WITH LACING BARS RIVETED ON.
BATTENED B.S.B.'S
C'
2 B.S.B.'S WITH BATTEN PLATES RIVETED ON.
SECTIONS "E"-"L" ABOVE ALSO USED AS COLUMNS
TIES
D' ■ SQUARE & ● ROUND RODS FROM 6 TO 75 MM ▬ FLATS FROM 3×12 TO 12×150 MM
SECTIONS "A","B","C" "D" & "E" ARE ALSO USED AS TIES
PLATES
E' USUAL SIZES FROM 6 TO 25 MM THICK ADVANCING BY 3 MM & FROM 25 TO 150 MM THICK ADVANCING BY 6 MM THIN PLATE UP TO 4 M WIDE. THICK PLATE UP TO 1·5 M WIDE
COLUMNS
BUILT UP
F'
2 BOX CHANNELS & 2 TOP HATS WELDED
COMPOSITE
G'
COLD ROLLED BOX CHANNELS
HOT ROLLED CHANNEL
2 BOX CHANNELS & 1 B.S.C. WELDED TOGETHER. SECTION "N" ABOVE ALSO USED AS COLUMNS
TIES
TEE
H'
FROM 12×25×1 TO 75×75×1·5 MM
TOP HAT
I'
FROM 12×25×1·5 TO 75×75×1·5 MM
"F","G" & M ALSO USED AS TIES
MISCELLANEOUS SPECIALS
J'
J'
SCALES : VARIOUS
NOTES : 1. IN A, B, D, F, G, M, H' & I' THE FIRST DIMENSION GIVES THE DEPTH OF SECTION, SECOND GIVES WIDTH AND THIRD GIVES THICKNESS.
2. IN E, H, I & J " " " " " " " " " " " WEIGHT OF SECTION IN KG. PER METRE RUN.

FIGURE 81

web plate by angles; this is not now so common as the one at P′ where the plates are welded together to form a more economical section. One type of this beam is the *Autofab beam* produced in standard sizes up to 2 m deep by 560 mm wide and 24 m long. This is available in mild steel or high yield stress steel and is formed by automatic machine welding together of the three plates.

Lattice Girders.—Details at Q, R and S, Fig. 81, are of different types of lattice girder, these are used where plate girders would become excessively heavy over large spans. They are often associated with North-light roof trusses for covering large floor areas (see Fig. 15, Vol. IV). The example at Q requires gusset plates at the connections, but these can be omitted when welding is adopted. The girder at R would be suitable for light loads. The welded tubular one at S makes a neat pleasing design; the tube is a sound, economical load carrying member, for it has good stiffness in relation to the small amount of metal. Prior to the use of welding,[1] the jointing[2] of tubes was a clumsy business; the practice of welding and the employment of tubes is increasing.

Columns.—The most widely used columns are the Universal Columns which range from 152 mm by 152 mm by 23 kg to 475 mm by 424 mm by 634 kg. They have parallel flanges. The beam members at E to L, Fig. 81, can also be used as columns, as can the sections at the bottom left-hand side of the same Figure. The one at V is a box-section made of two channels welded together, angles can be similarly used. That at W is a rectangular hollow section (R.H.S.), this is obtainable in sizes from 50·8 by 25·4 by 2·64 mm thick by 2·8 kg to 304·8 by 203·2 mm by 12·5 mm thick by 12·5 kg. The R.H.S. has a greater resistance to bending than the tube over which it also has the advantage of having flat sides to simplify welding. Square hollow sections (S.H.S.) are also made in a similar range.

When stanchion sizes have to be kept to a minimum, the solid round section at X can be used. Beams are connected to this by a cap plate which is shrunk or welded on. The use of tubes at Y has already been mentioned, they can be adopted for columns, or girders (S, Fig. 81) and vary in size from 26·9 mm overall dia. by 3·2 mm thick to 863·6 mm o.d. by 11 mm thick.

The other columns at Z to C′ are built up from the sections given to form stiff columns. The one at A′ has four angles to which internal ring battens are welded, the angle size depends, of course, on the load. For example, four 50·8 mm by 50·8 mm by 6·4 mm angles made into a 152 mm square will carry single-storey domestic span roof loadings. The ones at B′ and C′ will carry heavy loads, the former shows single lacing but double lacing in a criss-cross pattern is also used.

Bolts, Nuts and Washers (J, Fig. 80).—These are used for securing members comprising wood and steel roof trusses and similar framed structures, built-up wood lintels, steel beams, etc. When the bolts are used to fasten wood members (as in trusses—see F, Fig. 39), washers must be introduced between the timber and the heads and nuts to prevent the latter from being forced into the timber as the nuts are being tightened by a spanner. A bolt consists of a *shank* and *head*, and, as shown, the proportions of the head and nut are related to the diameter of the shank. The end of the shank is in the form of a screw having a *pitch* (distance between *threads*) which varies according to the diameter of the bolt (which is that of the shank); thus a 6 mm diameter bolt has 16 threads per 20 mm, 24 mm bolts have 6, and a 20 mm bolt as shown has 8 threads per 20 mm. The depth of the thread varies; in the example it is approximately 1·6 mm. Bolts vary in size from 6 mm to 150 mm diameter, but rarely is 38 mm exceeded in building construction, and 20 mm bolts are often employed for fixing steel-work; the length (which is that of the shank) also varies. The thickness and diameter of a washer depend upon the size of the bolt; that shown at J is 3·2 mm thick and the external diameter is either 41·3 or 70 mm. Bolts, nuts and washers are made of mild steel, wrought iron and brass, the former being used for steel-work. The head and nut shown at J are hexagonal on plan, and this is the type in general use; square-headed bolts (see T, Fig. 33) and nuts are also made but these are now rarely used in building and structural engineering.

Rivets are made of steel and are used at the connections of steel beams, pillars, roof members, etc.; the 20 mm dia. size is the most common.

The *snap-headed rivet* shown at L is the usual type employed; it is also known as a *cup-headed rivet*. Note the proportion of the head in relation to the shank; the shanks (which are slightly tapered) vary in diameter from 9 mm to 45 mm. The shank before fixing (" riveting ") extends to the length indicated by broken lines and this length depends upon the diameter of the rivet, the method of riveting (machine or hand) and the amount of *grip* (the overall thickness of the plates, angles, etc. which are connected together). The second head is formed during riveting, the heated end of the shank being forced into a cup shape.

Countersunk Rivets (M) are employed when the bottom head is required to finish flush with the underside of the lower member being riveted, *e.g.*, at the connection between the foot of a principal rafter of a steel roof truss and the plate which is supported by the wall and which should have a level bearing.

Note that rivets are seldom used now in steel building frames having been replaced by welding—see Vol. 4.

COLD ROLLED SECTIONS

These have been increasingly used since the 1939 war; because of their lighter weight, the load carrying capacity is not so great as the hot rolled sections. Even so, they are a useful adjunct to the builder's range of materials and have successfully been adopted for school and house construction. They are ideally

[1] See Chap. II, Vol. IV.

[2] The methods of jointing tubular work are three in number. In the example shown, the tube ends are machined to fit together and then welded. Secondly, the tube ends are flattened, cut to shape and welded. Where five or more tubes are connected at one point, they are cut and welded to a steel ball or ring in which a diaphragm plate is welded.

suited for prefabricated structures where the light weight leads to rapid site erection. The thickness of metal varies according to requirements, a common thickness being 4 mm. The shapes into which the metal can be pressed or rolled are almost unlimited and the sections have a wide range of uses from beams and columns to skirtings, door frames, gutters, etc. Jointing is best done by shop welding, bolts being needed for site connections. Cold rolled sections should be well protected from corrosion by galvanizing or similar effective process. Some typical sections are shown in Fig. 81.

Beams.—Details F, G and M are self-explanatory and the range of sizes is given, the stronger type of channel is provided with lips, this is known as the *lipped* or *box channel*. There is also the *outward lipped channel* (or top-hat, see F′) made in sizes from 38 mm by 38 mm by 1·2 mm to 100 mm by 100 mm by 4 mm.

The built-up beam at T is of two sections spot-welded together, it is used in lieu of and at the same centres as timber floor joists. The hollow flanges allow for the insertion of wood fillets for nailing the floor boards. The one at T′ is used for the same purpose, it comprises a Z-section and two angles. The kinks in the web trap the nails used for fastening down the boarding and so timber fillets are not needed.

The lattice girder at U has a top boom of two lipped channels 75 mm apart and a bottom boom of two angles. The intermediate members are lipped channels welded into the spaces. A similar example to this is shown in Fig. 17, Vol. IV.

Columns.—These are shown at F′ and G′, the former being made of two plain and two outward lipped channels welded together, diaphragm plates may be welded inside the cavity at intervals. The one at G′ is made with two cold rolled and one hot rolled channels welded together. Stanchions of this sort at 2·5 m centres have been used to carry floor beams 6 m long which support a precast beam floor and a similar roof load above. The box channels extend two storeys to the roof and the B.S.C. is stopped off beneath the first-floor beam.

Cold rolled sections can be formed into practically any shape for special purposes, some examples are given at J′ where there is a skirting, a panelling trim, a mullion cover pressing, etc.

HOMEWORK PROGRAMME

THE nature and amount of homework in Building Construction set each week are influenced by a number of considerations, such as the character of the course, length of each class period, number of periods per session, type and special requirements of students, treatment of subject in class, etc.

The following homework schedule is based upon the author's experience in teaching the subject to architectural students preparing for degrees in Building, R.I.B.A. examinations and those attending National Diploma and Certificate courses, and whilst it is clear that the programme cannot have general application, it is hoped that it will serve as a useful guide. It is assumed that each sheet will be commenced in class and completed as homework.

Whilst it may be considered that the programme unduly emphasizes the section devoted to Brickwork, it should be pointed out that there is now a general tendency to concentrate upon bonding, etc., in the first year in order that subsequent years of a course may be free for the greater development of other sections including those concerned with new materials and forms of construction. The programme may with advantage be modified, especially for architectural students, to include less brick bonding and more details of the units of construction.

It is likely that the drawing sheets will be of A2 size. Care should be taken to ensure a well-balanced set of drawings, and a suggested lay-out of a sheet is given in Fig. 58. As indicated, each sheet should be given a suitable title, the printing of which by the student affords practice in plain lettering. The details should be drawn to a large scale, and *wherever possible these should be to full size*; this applies particularly to joinery details.

As the length of session varies in different colleges, the homework programme provides for the maximum number of sheets, numbering from twenty-four to twenty-eight, which may be produced per session.

Sheet Number				Subject of Drawing
Number of Lectures per Session				
24	25	26	27	
1	1	1	1	Draw, to a scale of 1 : 10, alternate plans of stopped ends H, J, K and L, and part elevations at G, Fig. 3.
2	2	2	2	Draw, to a scale of 1 : 10, alternate plans of stopped ends E, F, G and J, and part elevation D, Fig. 4.
3	3	3	3	Draw, to a scale of 1 : 10, alternate plans of right-angled junctions, A, B, C, D and F, Fig. 5.
4	4	4	4	Draw, to a scale of 1 : 10, alternate plans of right-angled quoins A, B, D and E, and sketch G, Fig. 6.
5	5	5	5	Draw (*a*) to a scale of 1 : 10, elevation and plan of window A, Fig. 55; and (*b*) full size details G, J and K of cavity walling and joinery.
	6	6		Draw, to a scale of 1 : 10—(*a*) plans and elevations of piers F, L, O and Q, Fig. 7, and (*b*) alternate plans of rebated jambs E, H, L and O, Fig. 8.
			6	Draw, to a scale of 1 : 10, complete details of piers in Fig. 7.
			7	Draw, to a scale of 1 : 10, complete details of rebated jambs in Fig. 8.
6	7	7	8	(*a*) Draw, to a scale of 1 : 10, sections through foundations A to D, Fig. 10, and sections through foundations similar to A suitable for 215 mm and 440 mm walls; (*b*) sketch, approximately to 1 : 20 scale, timbering to trenches in Fig. 40.

Sheet Number				
Number of Lectures per Session				Subject of Drawing
24	25	26	27	
7	8	8	9	Sketch: (*a*) offset A, corbels L, M and cap Q, R, Fig. 11; (*b*) lintels A, B and C, Fig. 12; (*c*) threshold D, Fig. 16; (*d*) copings B, J and plinths N, R, Fig. 17.
8	9	9	10	Draw, to 1 : 10 scale, the arches in Fig. 15; thickness of joints between voussoirs need not be shown. (Leave space for sections G and K, Fig. 41); see Sheet No. 16 (or 17 or 18 or 19).
9	10	10	11	Draw, to 1 : 20 scale, portions of rubble work A and B, Fig. 20, and F, G and H, Fig. 22. Include quoins, jambs, part plan AB and section CD, Fig. 22; the mullions and transome need not be shown.
10	11			Draw: (*a*) 1 : 20 elevation of arch N with portion of walling and section at F including cornice, parapet and coping, Fig. 24; (*b*) 1 : 5 scale sections of cornice A, Fig. 26, string course D, Fig. 26, window sill L, Fig. 25, and copings A and C, Fig. 27.
		11	12	Draw, to 1 : 20 scale, plan, sections and part elevation of façade shown in Fig. 24.
		12	13	Draw to 1 : 5 scale, sections through cornice A and string course D, Fig. 26, window sill L and plinths Q and U, Fig. 25, copings A and C, Fig. 27 and cornice D, Fig. 78.
11	12	13	14	Draw: (*a*) 1 : 20 scale half of plan A and sections B and C of floor, Fig. 32; (*b*) 1 : 10 scale sections J and U, Fig. 32, with alternative sleeper wall detail at C, Fig. 10; (*c*) sketches of joints G, M and P, Fig. 32; (*d*) full-size section through joint R, Fig. 34.
12	13	14	15	Draw: (*a*) 1 : 20 scale part plans of floors P, Fig. 33, and A, Fig. 34, showing trimming of hearths; (*b*) 1 : 10 scale section F, Fig. 34, including adjacent bridging joist with elevation of strutting and section similar to KK; (*c*) quarter full-size details of tusk tenon L and housed joints M and N, Fig. 34.
13	14	15	16	Draw: (*a*) 1 : 20 scale elevations of flat roof A, lean-to roof H and close couple roof L, Fig. 36; (*b*) 1 : 10 scale details Q, R, S, G, P, X and Z. Omit slating details.
14	15	16	17	Draw: (*a*) 1 : 20 scale elevation of collar roof E, Fig. 37, omitting hips, angle ties and jack rafters; (*b*) 1 : 10 scale eaves details Y, Fig. 36, and L, Fig. 37, showing boarding in lieu of battens.
15	16	17	18	Draw 1 : 20 scale part elevation E and plan F of built-up truss, Fig. 39, and 1 : 20 scale isometric eaves detail.
16	17	18	19	To 1 : 10 scale, add centering for arches A, B, F, G, J and K, Fig. 41, to Sheet No. 8 (or 9 or 10—see adjacent), and sketch M and N, Fig. 41.
17	18	19	20	Draw: (*a*) 1 : 10 scale A, B, C and D of framed, ledged, braced and battened door, Fig. 44; (*b*) one-fifth full-size details L, M (elevation and section), N (elevation) and O (elevation and plan).
18	19	20	21	Draw: (*a*) 1 : 10 scale A, B and C of two-panelled door, Fig. 50; (*b*) full-size details H, J and K, Fig. 50—architrave and panel mouldings to be selected from Figs. 46, 48, 50, 52 and 63.
19	20	21	22	Draw: (*a*) 1 : 10 scale A, B and C (or D, E and F) of steel window, Fig. 62; (*b*) full-size details G, H, K, L and O, Q and N.
20	21	22	23	Draw: (*a*) 1 : 10 scale A, B and C of cased frame window, Fig. 58; (*b*) half full-size details K, L, M and N.
21	22	23	24	Draw 1 : 5 scale wood and slating eaves and ridge details A and eaves details F and G, Fig. 71. Cast-iron gutter to be shown in each case; incorporate a swan-neck bend F, Fig. 77. Alternatively, draw one-fifth full-size plain tiling details, Fig. 72, and interlocking tile details, Fig. 39.
22	23	24	25	Draw: (*a*) full-size details J, R, M and N, Fig. 74; (*b*) one-fifth full-size details A and O, Fig. 73.
23	24	25	26	Draw: (*a*) 1 : 5 scale sections E, F and G, Fig. 75; (*b*) sketch, approximately to 1 : 10 scale, K, L, M and N; (*c*) draw 1 : 10 scale details H, P and Q, Fig. 75.
24	25	26	27	Draw full-size steel sections D, F, G and H, Fig. 80, sketches O and A′, Fig. 81.

If twenty-eight lectures per session, include either (*a*) sheet upon domestic water services, Fig. 78, or (*b*) one on stairs, Fig. 65.

INDEX

D

E

F

INDEX